INTRODUCTION TO
EDUCATIONAL MEASUREMENT

INTRODUCTION TO
EDUCATIONAL MEASUREMENT

Fourth Edition

VICTOR H. NOLL
Emeritus, Michigan State University

DALE P. SCANNELL
University of Kansas

ROBERT C. CRAIG
Michigan State University

HOUGHTON MIFFLIN COMPANY

Boston
Dallas   Geneva, Illinois   Hopewell, New Jersey
Palo Alto   London

CONTENTS

Nine

THE MEASUREMENT OF CAPACITY:
GENERAL INTELLIGENCE 271

Ten

THE MEASUREMENT OF CAPACITY:
SPECIAL APTITUDES 314

Eleven

THE MEASUREMENT
OF PERSONALITY AND AFFECT:
SELF-REPORT TECHNIQUES 338

Twelve

THE MEASUREMENT
OF PERSONALITY AND AFFECT:
OBSERVATIONAL TECHNIQUES 373

LIST OF FIGURES

LIST OF TABLES

PREFACE

Introduction to Educational Measurement is intended to assist potential or practicing classroom teachers, guidance personnel, and school administrators in developing better tests of their own, in making more effective use of standardized tests, and, in general, in encouraging and assisting in the best possible use of measurement in the schools. To these ends, the text offers an orientation to the field of educational measurement and evaluation, a foundation in measurement theory and elementary statistical methods, an acquaintance with published standardized tests and sources of information about them, basic understanding and skill in constructing tests and evaluative devices for local use, and instruction in the interpretation and application of the results of measurement in the schools.

The text is designed for use in an introductory course. No previous study or experience in educational measurement or statistical methods on the part of the student is assumed. For most students in education, this assumption has proved, in our experience, to be sound.

The year 1979 marks the twenty-second anniversary of the publication of the first edition of *Introduction to Educational Measurement*. During the intervening years hundreds of instructors and thousands of students of educational measurement have used the book as a text or as a reference. That the work has had wide acceptance and continued use is naturally a source of satisfaction. It is hoped that the fourth edition will be received as well as earlier editions have been.

Any fourth edition has a long past but also must look to the present. Many changes in the field of educational measurement have taken place over the years. Many new tests have been published; older tests have been revised and norms updated; further computerized techniques have been developed and used in the analysis of test data; and legal issues regarding the use of test results in selection and promotion have been raised. In this new edition we have attempted to take note of such changes and trends.

Those familiar with previous editions will find substantial changes in this one. Historical material has been reduced, and in recognition of the controversial atmosphere surrounding the use of standardized tests today, treatment of current issues has been expanded. Some of these issues have been with us for many years; others have come to the fore more recently. Most readers are probably aware of these issues and hold opinions of them. We have attempted to present and discuss the issues objectively, and early in the book, but we do not continue to invoke them in our presentation of other aspects of educational measurement.

Users of earlier editions will find the following chapters completely rewritten: Educational Measurement: An Overview; The Development of Educational Measurement; Finding and Selecting Good Measuring Instruments; Measuring Achievement in the Elementary Grades; Measuring Achievement in the Secondary Grades; The Measurement of Personality and Adjustment: Self-Report Techniques; and The Measurement of Personality and Adjustment: Observational Techniques. In the process of rewriting, the first two chapters listed above were combined into one, as were the two dealing with measurement of achievement. All other chapters have been revised and updated. Also, in order to simplify the presentation of statistical concepts, we have included fewer computations in the body of the text. However, an appendix, Further Statistical Computations, which was included in the first two editions, has been reinstated to accommodate the needs of students with different educational backgrounds.

It is a pleasure to acknowledge our indebtedness to the many persons and organizations that have contributed to the production and development of the fourth edition. They include Leo M. Harvill of the University of South Dakota, Samuel T. Mayo of Loyola University, Charles W. Smith of Northern Illinois University, and William M. Stallings of Georgia State University. In particular, our gratitude is conveyed to Dr. Clarence H. Nelson, Professor Emeritus in Evaluation Services, Michigan State University, for his services in preparing the Instructor's Manual to accompany this new edition. We also express our thanks to the many authors and publishers who granted us permission to reproduce materials from their works. An inquiry to faculty members who used the third edition as a text in their classes provided useful suggestions for improvement. Finally, we are most appreciative of the valuable assistance rendered by the editorial staff of the College Division of Houghton Mifflin Company throughout the process of revision and final production of the book.

V.H.N.
D.P.S.
R.C.C.

One

EDUCATIONAL MEASUREMENT:
AN OVERVIEW

Accurate, dependable measurement is a fact of life in our modern, technical society. It is essential to efficient production in agriculture and industry. It is indispensable in many professions such as medicine, nursing, and engineering and in all scientific work. Measurement is a valuable tool in making personnel decisions in business, government, and the armed forces. What is true of these areas is equally true of education. Most important educational decisions, whether by or for individuals or in general matters such as promotion, counseling, accreditation, and methods of teaching, depend, at least in part, on the results of measurement. This book is about educational measurement—its nature, purposes, procedures or methods, and uses. In this introductory chapter, we present, first, a brief account of the development and importance of measurement in education and its present status and problems and, second, an overview of its nature and characteristics.

After reading this chapter you should be able to answer the following questions:

1. How has the development of measurement in education been influenced by measurement in the sciences?
2. What are the basic principles of effective measurement in education?
3. What is meant by *standardized tests* in education? What are some uses of such tests? What are some of their limitations?
4. Are the terms *measurement* and *evaluation* synonymous? If not, what are their differences? their similarities?
5. What is the difference between norm-referenced and criterion-referenced tests?

6. What are some major issues and problems facing the practice of measurement in education at the present time?
7. What do you expect to gain from a study of this book?

MEASUREMENT: HISTORICAL DEVELOPMENT AND CURRENT STATUS

Earliest records indicate that by the dawn of recorded history people had developed systems of measurement. The ancient Egyptians used accurate methods of measurement in building the pyramids. The Book of Genesis states that Noah built his ark three hundred cubits long, fifty cubits in breadth, and thirty cubits high.[1] There is also reference in the same source to the weighing of gold and silver.

The ancient Greeks and Romans had well-developed systems of measurement and performed very exact work in constructing roads, bridges, buildings, arches, and monuments. Before modern times units were developed and adopted that have come down to this day, in name at least. The foot was based on the length of the human foot, the pennyweight (weight of a penny) was equal to thirty-two wheat-corns in the midst of the ear, and the ounce was twenty pennyweights.[2]

Some early attempts at standardization were necessary. For example, the foot unit came to be the length of not just any man's foot but of one particular foot—that of the king. Naturally, if the king died or was deposed and a new one came to the throne, the length of the foot might change also. The sheer inconvenience of having variable units and, of course, the development of scientific methods made constant units and exact measurement necessary. Since natural units tend to vary, it became the usual practice to fix unit measures arbitrarily by law or royal decree. Ultimately this process reached its present level in the development and general acceptance in most countries of the world and in scientific work everywhere of the metric system of weights and measures. In this system natural but stable measures form the basis for units that have been adopted and made permanent standards by international agreement.[3]

It is unlikely that measurement in education will ever reach the precision characteristic of measurement in the so-called hard sciences. Some

[1]A cubit was the distance from a man's elbow to the tip of his outstretched middle finger, a distance of about eighteen inches.
[2]William Hallock and Herbert T. Wade, *The Evolution of Weights and Measures and the Metric System* (New York: Macmillan, 1906), chap. 1.
[3]For example, the meter, the unit of length in the metric system, equals one ten-millionth part of the distance measured on a meridian of the earth from the equator to the pole. For ordinary purposes, the meter is 39.37 inches.

of the reasons for this are obvious. The chemist and physicist measure, as a rule, inert, inanimate materials that can be manipulated as desired. By contrast, educators and psychologists generally administer tests to people—living, growing, changing individuals who are not as subject to manipulation or control.

Nevertheless, it is undeniable that great improvement has been made in educational tests and evaluative procedures during the past fifty years. Widely accepted standards for constructing, evaluating, and using tests have been developed.[4] Compared to the methods of testing and examining commonly used in schools and colleges before World War I, present-day techniques and procedures are more objective, more carefully planned and constructed, and more thoroughly evaluated than their predecessors. In producing a standardized test, it is now generally routine to determine the probable amount of error in a score on that test. The user thus has a measure of the accuracy of scores obtained. It is also part of recommended practice to make allowance for error in the interpretation of scores, particularly with reference to individuals.

Many standardized tests of proven quality are available today. They contribute substantially to the resources of people qualified to use them properly—teachers, counselors, school psychologists, administrators—in judging and improving the quality of education. Much of what follows in this book discusses established methods of building good tests and criteria for appraising tests' quality; the book also provides detailed descriptions of standardized tests and critical evaluations of their worth.

Measurement in the Schools

In order to judge the attainment of pupils accurately and fairly, a teacher must have access to the best measurement techniques and instruments available and must know how to use them properly and how to interpret results obtained by their use. For example, in order to make satisfactory judgments of a child's achievement, one must know as accurately as possible both past achievement and probable ability to achieve. A child whose achievement is low may be doing all that he or she is capable of doing, while actually achieving less than others who may not be using nearly all their ability. A pupil may have special abilities or aptitudes that result in great irregularity in day-to-day attainment. The pupil may do good work in language, history, and literature while performing distinctly below average in arithmetic and science. Appropriate and systematic measurement is indispensable in such situations. And, of course, teachers must make daily, or at least frequent, appraisals of the work of

[4]See American Psychological Association, *Standards for Educational and Psychological Tests* (Washington, D.C.: American Psychological Association, 1974), and *Standards for Providers of Psychological Services* (Washington, D.C.: American Psychological Association, 1974).

every pupil in terms of instructional objectives to determine the progress each pupil is making in light of his or her abilities. To do this a teacher should be familiar with and have access to the widest possible range of appropriate measuring instruments and techniques.

It is also important that every teacher, counselor, and school psychologist have a thorough knowledge of available measuring devices and techniques applicable in their respective areas of competence. Moreover, there are many situations in which it is desirable for individual teachers to devise tests and examinations of their own, especially where none is available that meets the needs of a particular situation. To meet such particular needs, the teacher must know how to construct and use appropriate measurement devices. Measurement devices or techniques prepared by the teacher are often the best—and sometimes the only—means of determining how well classes or individual pupils are progressing toward the objectives of instruction. For example, teachers must often devise their own methods of evaluating how well a child is learning to work and play with others or what changes have taken place in attitudes toward other children.

Today measurement touches upon and influences every phase of education. Whether it is in marking, promoting, guiding and counseling, developing curriculum, instructing, or some other aspect of the work, measurement usually plays an important role. However, while recognizing the pervasiveness and usefulness of measurement in education, the student and teacher must keep in mind that measurement is a tool, a means to an end, not an end in itself. We do not generally measure anything just for the sake of knowing how long or how heavy it is. We have a use for the knowledge or some reason for acquiring it. We measure the dimensions or weight of an object to see whether it fits, whether we can carry it, or how much it will cost. Perhaps more importantly, we measure the object to determine whether it will serve a specific purpose. In education we attempt to measure the capacity of an individual so that we can help evaluate strengths and weaknesses in skills and knowledge, or we measure to determine the extent of a learner's progress toward the goals or objectives of education. Measurement in education should always serve to help do a better job of educating people.

LEARNING EXERCISES

1. What characteristics of measurement in the sciences are applicable to measurement in education? Use as an example the determination of whether or not a pupil is achieving up to capacity.

2. Name and describe some techniques of measurement in the sciences or in industry that have applications in educational measurement.

At the turn of the century, standardized tests as commonly used today were unknown.[5] The first such test in a school subject to be published and made generally available was one in arithmetic by Stone.[6] By 1920 the first standardized tests of intelligence and of personality, a number of tests in school subjects, some aptitude tests, and some general survey tests of school achievement had appeared. Also, the first books on educational measurement and on statistical methods as applied to educational measurement were published during this period.

Standardized Tests: Widespread Use

By the early 1920s, standardized intelligence tests were used in many schools and colleges of the United States. In 1930 Odell cited data collected several years earlier (perhaps in 1925–1926) indicating that somewhere between thirty and forty million standardized tests had been sold in the United States during one of these years.[7] A more recent survey estimated that "each of the fifty million or more school children in the United States takes, on the average, three standardized tests each year."[8] In addition, pupils take many tests and examinations prepared by their teachers. A conservative estimate of the number of standardized tests administered to school children in the United States today would easily exceed 250 million. This would not include such tests given to students in postsecondary institutions or to people in the armed forces, business, industry, and civil service.

Another kind of evidence for the increasing use of tests is the number of organizations engaged in developing, standardizing, and distributing them. Buros lists more than 150 organizations in this country that publish tests; for some twenty of these, the development and publication of tests constitutes the major or at least a significant part of their business.[9]

---

[5]A *standardized* test is one that has been carefully constructed by experts in the light of acceptable objectives or purposes; procedures for administering, scoring, and interpreting scores are specified in detail so that no matter who gives the test or where it may be given, the results should be comparable; norms or averages for different age or grade levels have been predetermined. Certain types of standardized tests may also be designed to measure the degree of success on specified tasks.

[6]C. W. Stone, *Arithmetical Abilities and Some Factors Determining Them*, Contributions to Education 19 (New York: Teachers College, Columbia University, 1908).

[7]C. W. Odell, *Educational Measurement in High School* (New York: Appleton-Century-Crofts, 1930).

[8]David A. Goslin, *The Search for Ability* (New York: Russell Sage Foundation, 1963), p. 54. See also, O. G. Brim, Jr., et al., *American Beliefs and Attitudes About Intelligence* (New York: Russell Sage Foundation, 1969).

[9]O. K. Buros, *The Seventh Mental Measurements Yearbook* (Highland Park, N.J.: Gryphon Press, 1972).

Standardized tests of ability, aptitude, achievement, and personality also find wide use in business, industry, and the military. Scarcely any large business organization or industrial concern could function today without a personnel manager or director and a staff of trained personnel technicians or psychologists. Much use is made of standardized and special tests in selecting persons for employment, determining what type of work they are fitted for, and measuring their efficiency. In addition to educational, business, and industrial use of measurement materials, the armed forces use large quantities of tests, rating scales, and other measuring instruments. Men and women are tested at pre-induction centers and during recruit training for selection, special training, fitness for unusual kinds of duty, adjustment to the military, and countless other purposes. The first military group tests of intelligence, Army Alpha and Army Beta, were devised especially for use in World War I, and the development and use of all kinds of measuring devices were greatly expanded during and after World War II.

State and National Testing Programs

In addition to the uses already mentioned, tests have an important function in external testing, such as in the College Entrance Examination Board, National Merit Scholarship, and National Teacher Examination programs. Most states now maintain one or more statewide testing programs, the oldest and best known of which is the New York State Regents' examinations. Colleges and universities also widely use tests that they devise or choose for admission to graduate and professional schools such as law, medicine, and nursing as well as for admission to undergraduate programs.

As examples of outstanding national testing programs of recent years, two may be mentioned. Project Talent, begun in 1960, seeks to determine the value of a wide variety of tests and inventories as predictors of success and satisfaction in careers chosen by American youth. A battery of twenty-eight aptitude and achievement tests and inventories was administered to a carefully drawn sample of some 440,000 students in grades 9 through 12 in 1,353 public, private, and parochial schools in all parts of the country. Each class tested is followed up one, five, ten, and twenty years after graduation from high school to obtain information on success and satisfaction in chosen careers and to determine the relationship of this success and satisfaction to test scores and background information. The program has already yielded a rich store of data on the capabilities and potentialities of American youth and on the worth of tests as predictors.

Another nationwide testing program is National Assessment of Educational Progress. Its purpose is to determine what our children are learning in school and the progress they are making. Tests in literature, science, social studies, writing, citizenship, music, mathematics, reading, art, and vocational education are being given to between 120,000 and 140,000 individuals in four age groups (9, 13, 17, and 26 to 35) in a sample carefully chosen to represent different geographical regions, types of schools, types of communities, races, and socioeconomic levels. Plans called for testing in three subject areas in 1969, three or four in 1970, and the remainder in 1971, after which the cycle is repeated. The test exercises are unique in that they are designed to measure instructional objectives such as "believes in the role of law and can justify this belief" at three levels of attainment: what practically all are able to do, what an average number can do, and what only the ablest can do. No individual takes more than a few tests, and no comparisons are made between individual regions, schools, communities, races, or levels. The emphasis throughout is on *criterion-referenced testing*—that is, on measuring the proficiency of defined groups on specified tasks and not on comparing one group's performance with that of others or with norms. Reports are made in terms of what such groups as boys of high socioeconomic status in large cities in the Northwest, 26 percent of nine-year-olds, and 45 percent of thirteen-year-olds knew or could do.

Role of the Federal Government

In 1958 Congress passed the National Defense Education Act, which provides federal funds to establish programs of testing, counseling, and guidance in secondary schools. The purpose of the testing programs, as stated in the act, is to identify students with outstanding aptitudes and abilities. Obviously, this requires wide-scale testing. There can be no doubt that this law has encouraged and stimulated many schools to inaugurate testing programs where none at all or perhaps haphazard and unsystematic ones existed before. In addition, money is provided for programs of guidance and counseling in the schools and for grants to institutions of higher education to establish institutes for training guidance and counseling personnel. Since the work of such personnel requires the use of tests, these provisions have also certainly stimulated their use in the schools.

In 1965 Congress passed the Elementary and Secondary Education Act, which provides federal funds for a variety of innovative and experimental programs. It also requires objective measurement of educational achievement at least annually to evaluate the effectiveness of programs for educationally deprived children. These objective measurements of educational achievement have, in many instances, included standardized tests.

Current Issues

More testing by schools, industry, and government has meant that more decisions affecting the life of each person may be based, at least in part, on test results. It is not surprising, therefore, that criticism of testing has also increased and that issues about testing are more hotly debated than ever before.[10]

Test critics and their motives vary greatly. Some who take issue with tests and testing programs speak for social and political groups that are seriously concerned about potential threats to the rights of citizens generally or to the rights of members of their groups in particular. Others are journalists who have found actual or alleged test abuses a fertile field for headlines and exposés. The measurement professionals—psychologists and educators who are active in developing and using tests—are also critical of poor tests and of errors in the use of tests. They combat test abuse by educating and by monitoring the observance of the principles and practices set forth in such publications as *Standards for Educational and Psychological Tests* and *Standards for Providers of Psychological Services.*[11]

Some tests and test uses should certainly be challenged. Almost everyone agrees that test scores should not be used mechanically or uncritically and that additional pertinent information about people who are tested should also be used whenever possible. Much of this book is about how to improve tests and use them appropriately.

Other criticisms of testing probably are not justified. Some critics are uninformed, misinformed, or self-serving. Any criticism may be beneficial, however, if it does nothing more than cause people who make, advocate, or use tests to become more competent and as sure as they can be that what they do is defensible. This book and courses in tests and testing can help.

In the remainder of this section, we introduce several social and political issues in testing. The issues are complex, and we do not attempt a complete evaluation of differing views or conflicting evidence. Later chapters will prepare the reader to inquire further into the merits of the criticisms and to see how tests may be used to benefit individuals and society while minimizing errors and hazards.

---

[10]See, for example, Banesh Hoffman, *The Tyranny of Testing* (New York: Crowell-Collier, 1962); two issues of *National Elementary Principal,* "The Myth of Measurability" (March–April 1975) and "The Scoring of Children: Standardized Testing in America" (July–August 1975); Arlene Silberman, "The Tests That Cheat Our Children," *McCall's Magazine,* April 1977, pp. 214–222, and *Testing and the Public Interest,* Proceedings of the 1976 Educational Testing Service Invitational Conference (Princeton, N.J.: Educational Testing Service, 1977); Herbert C. Rudman, "The Standardized Test Flap," *Phi Delta Kappan,* 59, No. 3 (1977), 179–185; Robert L. Ebel, "The Paradox of Educational Testing." *NCME Measurement in Education,* 7, No. 4 (1976), 5–6.

[11]American Psychological Association, *Standards for Educational and Psychological Tests* and *Standards for Providers of Psychological Services* (footnote 4).

ACCOUNTABILITY In the past few years, the term *accountability* has come into vogue in educational literature. The general concept that school personnel who have been given the task of educating students should be responsible for the results is not new, but more attention is being given to the costs of achieving the results. The cost effectiveness of school programs—that is, how well they use tax dollars—is often questioned, and requests for more funds are frequently defeated at the polls. During the 1970s many states established accountability programs to assess student achievement of minimal objectives or basic skills. In some there were proposals to use the results for allocating funds to schools.[12]

There is no single approach to being accountable. Suggestions to teachers and schools generally include statements of (1) objectives for student outcomes, (2) programs specifically designed to achieve the objectives, (3) measurement of the expected outcomes, and (4) systematic reporting of results with explanations of costs and apparent strengths or weaknesses. In any case, school personnel are considered accountable for producing measurable progress toward desired instructional goals.

In the abstract, the concepts of demonstrating educational results to justify costs and assigning responsibility for failures appear logical. But many teachers and administrators feel they are not practical, because many factors that affect achievement—in the individual, the home, and the community—are beyond the school's control. The education of the parents, the socioeconomic level of the community, and the achievement of friends are some of the variables that have been shown to be positively related to a student's achievement. It may not be possible to untangle diverse relationships to determine who is responsible for what. Spokesmen for national teachers' organizations think that it is not, and they fear the consequences to teachers of attempts to do so.[13]

Determining the causes of measured differences is a major problem for educational researchers and evaluators, and no generally applicable or practical solution has been found. A full explanation of approaches to a solution is beyond the scope of this book. Other measurement problems associated with measuring gains or growth in student achievement for which we may seek to assign responsibility are explained in later chapters.

Determining who is responsible is only part of the issue. For what should schools be responsible? Four possibilities have been described by

---

[12]Allan C. Ornstein and Harriet Talmage, "The Rhetoric and the Realities of Accountability," *Today's Education*, 66 (1973), 70–80.
[13]*Ibid.*; R. E. Campbell, "Accountability and Stone Soup," *Phi Delta Kappan*, 53, No. 3 (1971), 176–178; E. L. Lindman, "The Means and Ends of Accountability," *Proceedings of the Conference on Accountability* (Princeton, N.J.: Educational Testing Service, 1971).

Downs.[14] Schools can be asked (1) to bring all students to a minimum level of competence, (2) to bring all students to the maximum of their potential, (3) to give every student equal opportunity for achievement, or (4) to concentrate efforts on the students who learn most easily in order to maximize the output of the entire system. The choice is clearly not one of measurement but of philosophical or political values.

For what educational objectives should schools be held responsible? While consensus is high among educators and laymen with respect to the importance of basic skills in the traditional three R's, there is somewhat less agreement with respect to history, geography, citizenship, science, music, art, and physical education. Many respondents to a Gallup Poll of public attitudes thought basic skills also include such things as respect for teacher, good manners, obedience, and respect for elders.[15] Some people doubtless think that such outcomes and attitudes as a healthy self-concept are equal to or greater in importance than the three R's. Others consider them relatively unimportant. Later chapters will show that development of such attitudes is difficult to measure and therefore likely to be neglected in accountability programs.

We expect the concept of accountability to continue as a matter of major professional and public concern. Positive effects on measurement practices may be seen in the serious attention being given to educational objectives and the assessment of related outcomes, although many problems with respect to the meaningful and equitable use of measurement data remain.

INVASION OF PRIVACY   The issue of invasion of individual privacy by testing has been lively and, at times, hot in a number of areas, especially in government and education. Congress has investigated the use of psychological tests, especially personality tests, with applicants for government employment. In education the clamor has been loudest when children have been asked to respond to inventories containing questions on such matters as home conditions, family relationships, sexual attitudes and practices, and religious beliefs. The concern revolves around several questions. Is the gathering of such types of information a violation of an individual's privacy and, indeed, of constitutional rights? Perhaps equally serious is the confidentiality of such information. What guarantee is there that, since all individuals have a social security number by which they can always be identified, information that should

---

[14]A. Downs, "Competition and Community Schools," paper prepared for the Conference on the Community School, the Brookings Institution Economic Studies Program, Washington, D.C., December 1968.
[15]George H. Gallup, "Ninth Annual Gallup Poll of the Public's Attitudes Toward the Public Schools," *Phi Delta Kappan,* 59, No. 1 (September 1977), 33–48.

be held in the strictest confidence will not be used by others than those to whom it was originally confided?

Concern about the privacy and confidentiality of test information is not limited to personality tests. In recent years an individual's rights with respect to all types of information have received political and legal attention. The Buckley amendment to the General Education Provisions Act of 1974 prohibits the use of federal funds to aid schools that furnish information to any third party without the written permission of the student's parents, or of the student if older than 18. Another provision is that parents, and students older than 18, have the right to inspect and challenge the records. This right of review can be an important safeguard against test scores that may be in error because of weaknesses in the tests or the conditions under which the tests were given. The individual has the opportunity to ask that test information be verified, perhaps by the administration of additional tests.

Many federally supported research and service testing activities now require the informed consent of the respondent or the respondent's parents. "Informed consent" means that persons agree to release the test information after knowing and understanding what will be asked, what purpose it will serve, and how it will be used and that they have the right to refuse.

In some circumstances, however, such as when one needs a job or wishes to be admitted to a hospital for treatment, it is difficult to refuse. Informed consent also causes problems for testers when refusals mean that some important research or service cannot be completed or when knowledge of how the information will be used causes respondents to falsify their answers, thus destroying their usefulness.

When informed consent is explicitly given without pressure, it significantly lessens apprehension about privacy. In other situations, so does assurance of anonymity. This can be given when the attitudes, opinions, or behavior of a group rather than of any particular individual are of interest. This might be true, for example, if we wanted to evaluate changes in the attitudes of a fifth-grade class toward smoking after viewing a filmstrip demonstrating a relationship between smoking and cancer.

Resistance is least and requests for personal data are most defensible when the information is needed to help the individual who gives it. This is generally true when a person seeks help from a counselor or clinic. Most classroom tests for instructional purposes are in the same category. When one is asked to take tests or give information for the good of society, the degree of cooperation varies with the perceived value of the social goal. If the data are to be used to screen airline pilots or surgeons for emotional stability or to plan the allocation of educational funds to school systems on the basis of need, there will be fewer objections than if they are needed to help a business increase profits or a university student obtain an advanced degree. We are not suggesting, however, that test data on emotional stability or other individual characteristics be used without supporting information.

School personnel generally have been inclined to take informed consent for granted in most testing situations. A student's presence in a class or in the counseling center has been assumed to imply consent to the tests or questionnaires a teacher, counselor, or visiting researcher wants to use. The appropriate limits of this practice are being scrutinized more carefully than ever before. There is certainly reason to doubt that the assumption of implied consent should extend to personality tests.

A helpful discussion of this issue is in the report of a symposium called "Invasion of Privacy in Research and Testing."[16] The members of the symposium included a test publisher, officials of the federal government and an educational foundation, a director of educational research, and university professors of psychology and education. The issue often appears to boil down to a conflict between methods and values. On the one hand, there is the behavioral scientist seeking new knowledge and developing instruments and methods to obtain it. On the other hand, there is the public who are jealous of their rights as individuals. Between the scientist and the public some accommodation must be found or progress toward the goal of helping children and adults as much as possible will be increasingly difficult. The social scientist and the educator must find a very fine, sometimes seemingly invisible, line beyond which they may be permitted to proceed with their work only with the willing support and cooperation of the people whom, in the last analysis, they intend to serve.

PSYCHOLOGICAL HAZARDS   Some anecdotal evidence appears to support the charge that testing harms some children psychologically. They have been observed to be anxious before and during a test; a few break into tears. Poor performance on a test is said to damage self-esteem, block future achievement, and divert students from more education and many careers. Tests are somewhat anxiety-provoking for many persons, perhaps the majority, and poor performance on tests can be a blow to the ego. For some these effects are probably serious, and some authors believe that testing is a very serious threat.[17]

[16]Warren W. Willingham (ed.), "Invasion of Privacy in Research and Testing," Supplement to the *Journal of Educational Measurement*, 4, No. 1 (Spring 1967), 1–31.
[17]Sherwood Davidson Kohn, "The Numbers Game: How the Testing Industry Operates," *National Elementary Principal*, July–August 1975, p. 14.

Dyer, who describes himself as an optimistic critic of tests and test users, takes a more moderate view. He recognizes that it can be tough on self-esteem to score consistently low on tests, to know that so many others are out in front, and to see that one may be barred from some opportunities. When this happens, some individuals quit trying. But Dyer believes that others try harder or change their plans to accommodate measured competence. He urges getting students accustomed to testing as a necessary part of teaching-learning strategies and an aid to self-understanding and growth.[18]

Ebel also recognizes the possible hazard to some individuals. He finds, however, that no substantial data refute the commonsense conclusion that most people are not harmed by testing. He finds it "normal and biologically helpful" to be anxious in many situations and suggests that the child who breaks down when faced with a test has other, more basic adjustment problems that testing did not cause. Ebel also suggests that something is wrong with the educational program, not the testing, if a pupil who tries consistently gets low scores.[19] Many teachers would say the problem is in the trying rather than either the testing or the teaching.

Concern about the hazards to which we have referred is greatest when tests are used to classify or label individuals. Children who have been labeled mentally retarded, learning disabled, or delinquent may find themselves placed in special groups. In addition to experiencing threat to self-esteem and motivation, children so labeled may be stigmatized by the school and the social system, and this has implications for their future.

It may be argued that individuals who have special needs have a better chance of obtaining special resources and appropriate educational programs when their needs have been identified. However, special educational programs frequently have more limited educational goals than regular classrooms, and the individuals in special education classes may be rejected by their peers. In 1975 Samuel Kirk, author of a test used widely to test individuals with learning problems, examined the pros and cons of labeling and categorization.[20] He found much evidence of mislabeling, especially among racial and cultural minorities. He saw this evidence, the racially segregated nature of many special classes, and the evidence that special classes are not beneficial as factors lending support to a movement away from special classes toward *mainstreaming*, or returning special students to regular classrooms as much as possible.

---

[18]Henry S. Dyer, "The Menace of Testing Reconsidered." *Educational Horizons*, 43, No. 1 (1964), 3–8.

[19]Ebel (footnote 10), pp. 5–6.

[20]Samuel A. Kirk, "Labelling, Categorizing and Mainstreaming" (Paper delivered at the International Conference of Special Education, University of Kent, Canterbury, Eng., July 30, 1975).

Although mainstreaming has its opponents and although providing for the needs of some children with special problems is sometimes difficult in regular classrooms, Wendel reported that mainstreaming was increasing significantly in the school systems of most states by 1977. His survey of state department officials also indicated that the civil rights of handicapped individuals and the weight of related court decisions were thought to be the most significant factors in the movement. "Emphasis on humaneness" and "improvements in psychological testing" were among the items least often chosen as important factors.[21]

All who make and use tests need to be on guard against contributing to the human tendency to label others and to think of labels as explanations. A test score should be recognized as one descriptive fact that may be used, in conjunction with other available facts, to help us understand people.

FAIRNESS TO CULTURAL MINORITIES When test scores of members of ethnic, racial, or poverty groups are lower on the average than the scores of others, the tests may be accused of bias against the lower-scoring groups. The probability that critics will say tests are biased and the significance of this charge vary with the type and use of tests.

Achievement tests, used to reveal differences in the ability to perform tasks that are the intended outcomes of instructional programs, are least often thought unfair, although they are criticized when the results are used to highlight group differences rather than to help individual students. The adequacy of the instructional program is the more frequent target. When members of one group appear to have learned less of what is being tested than members of another group, teachers and the system are often held accountable. Critics may cite test results as evidence of a school's weakness in providing for minorities.

Tests used to assess potential for further learning or to predict future job success are more often thought unfair. Tests measure present learning. For individuals for whom past opportunities to learn have been seriously limited, measures of present learning are not good predictors. Whether some students have experienced serious inequities in learning opportunities is not always easy to decide. Furthermore, the causes of differences in test scores between groups is also controversial. We discuss in Chapter 9 the relative influence of heredity and environment as well as attempts to develop measures of aptitude that are culture fair—that is, relatively uninfluenced by environmental differences, including differences in opportunities to learn.

[21]Frederick C. Wendel, "Progress in Mainstreaming" *Phi Delta Kappan*, 59, No. 1 (1977), 58.

Tests are called unfair when their scores are used mechanically to select individuals and when their use diminishes the access of individuals in some groups to educational or vocational opportunities. Although some people point out that unfairness is in the use of tests as predictors rather than in their measurement of achievement, the practical result is the same: Members of some groups are disproportionately barred from some opportunities. There is no simple answer to the charge that this is inequitable.

The Supreme Court has ruled against the use of tests and other standards in employment unless those standards are "significantly" related to successful job performance (*Griggs* v. *Duke Power Co.*, 1971). Although the use of tests was not completely ruled out, the Court did not give much guidance with respect to their just and equitable use. Any relationship other than one of chance is *statistically* significant, but just what relationships are *practically* significant has not been clearly defined. Measurement specialists look for evidence that decisions made with the use of test scores are better than those made without tests. But some critics appear to expect nearly perfect decisions, a standard that probably will never be met.

What use of tests for classification or selection is fair to minorities? Flaugher discusses several different answers that have been suggested by measurement experts.[22] One would equalize errors in the prediction of success for each group tested. Another would equalize the probability of selection of the members of different groups who would be successful *if selected*. Neither approach offers assurance that equal proportions of each different group (for example, an ethnic minority and a majority group) can be chosen, although this result is sometimes asked for in the name of fairness.

Darlington provides for the application of a correction to the scores of a lower-scoring group when the selector places a greater value on balancing opportunities or correcting inequities among different groups than on selecting individuals who appear to have the greatest probability of success.[23] There is a precedent for this in the bonus points that have been added to the Civil Service examination scores of military veterans. Something similar may be done in admitting athletes and musicians to colleges and universities.

Reluctance to define success narrowly in terms of grade-point average or economic productivity has increased. Evidence of the usefulness of

[22]Ronald L. Flaugher, "The New Definitions to Test Fairness in Selection: Developments and Implications," *Educational Researcher*, 3 (1974), 13–16.
[23]Richard D. Darlington, "Another Look at 'Cultural Fairness,'" *Journal of Educational Measurement*, 8, No. 2 (1971), 71–82

tests in predicting these criteria is often challenged. An adequate physician in an urban ghetto or the rural South, for example, may achieve more in terms of social utility than a brilliant physician who competes for fees in the surburbs.[24] To prepare adequate rather than brilliant professionals thus may be a better investment of public funds. The issue involves philosophical and political values that have little to do with tests.

Questions of values and of definitions of test fairness are equally applicable in education and employment. But because test tasks are more like the tasks one performs in school than in most jobs, test scores are frequently more closely related to success in learning what one needs to know to enter an occupation than to success in a job after one has been hired.

In education as in employment, the fairness of tests to cultural minorities has been challenged most often because of their use as screening devices. Such challenges go beyond what is usually meant by access to future opportunities, however. They emphasize that members of cultural minorities may be more exposed to psychological risk and that benefits for individuals and minorities should be considered while accountability in relation to school objectives is being assessed. The probability and relative importance of risks and benefits will continue in debate as both local and general issues.

In spite of criticisms, and certainly to some degree because of them, great advances and improvements in measurement and evaluation have come about. This can and must and will continue. Reputable publishers, specialists in measurement, and writers in the field have consistently stressed that tests are fallible and must always be used with full regard for their limitations. The common goal is constantly to work toward the improvement of the instruments and their proper implementation. Critics have the responsibility to inform themselves fully and accurately before expressing seriously critical views; they should also make certain that their criticisms are based on fact and that they bear on major issues.

With this discussion of issues, we conclude our brief presentation of the development of educational measurement from its beginnings early in the present century to the somewhat stormy present. In the remainder of this chapter, we consider the essential characteristics of measurement in general and the nature, place, and function of measurement in education in particular.

---

[24]Robert L. Thorndike, "Where Ignorance Is Bliss—'Tis Folly To Be Testing," *Testing and the Public Interest*, Proceedings of the 1976 Educational Testing Service Invitational Conference (Princeton, N.J.: Educational Testing Service, 1977), p.68

LEARNING EXERCISES

3. Compare Project Talent and National Assessment of Educational Progress regarding purposes, procedures, anticipated outcomes, and usefulness.
4. What are some current criticisms of the use of standardized tests of intelligence? of achievement? of personality? How would you respond to each of these criticisms?
5. Read one of the technical reports of the investigations sponsored by the Russell Sage Foundation on the social consequences of testing. Prepare a ten-minute report to be either written and handed in or presented to the class, as your instructor directs.
6. Compare the article by Kohn with the report of the Russell Sage Foundation that you read for Exercise 5. What are your impressions?
7. Do you agree that fairness of tests to minorities is more a question of values than of measurement? If so, why? If not, why not?

THE NATURE
OF EDUCATIONAL MEASUREMENT

According to *Webster's Third New International Dictionary*, to measure is "to ascertain the quantity, mass, extent, or degree of a standard unit."[25] All these terms imply a result expressed in numbers rather than descriptive phrases. When we measure something, we express our findings in units of length, weight, or the like. To say merely that an object is flat or round or green or heavy does not satisfy the quantitative aspect of the definition. Since measurement is a quantitative process, the results of measurement are always expressed in numbers—so many feet long, so many degrees of temperature, so many quarts or pounds.

Essential Characteristics of All Measurement

Moreover, measurement is expressed, insofar as possible, in constant units. When the yard was the distance between a person's nose and outstretched finger tips, it was not a constant unit. Some people have longer arms or noses than others. The English stone might be a large stone or a

[25]*Webster's Third New International Dictionary* (Springfield, Mass.: G. & C. Merriam Co., 1966). For another definition of measurement, see S. S. Stevens, "On The Theory of Measurement," *Science*, 103 (1946), 677–680.

small one. People in time came to realize that such variation in measuring units leads to endless trouble and confusion, and they eventually reached agreement on certain units. In the Western world, two systems of measurement came into existence: the English system, with which we are all familiar, and the metric system, used today in most European countries and now gradually being adopted in the U.S. The metric system is common in scientific work the world over. Units are constant in both systems. An inch is an inch everywhere and a gram is the same in Paris and Chicago.

Standards such as the standard meter bar in Paris are used to calibrate or check other measuring instruments. It must be noted, however, that varying conditions sometimes affect the constancy of the unit measure. An object weighing a pound at sea level weighs less on top of a mountain, and a steel rule is longer at 100°C than it is at 20°C. Therefore, in order to have strictly constant units we must have constant or, at least, specified conditions. For all except the most exact scientific work, however, fine distinctions are not necessary; ordinary measurement requires that the units be only relatively constant.

The idea of constant units also implies that the unit of measurement is exactly the same at all points on a scale. The difference between 95° and 96° must be the same as the difference between 10° and 11°; a centimeter should be the same at all places on a single meter stick and on all meter sticks.

These two characteristics, quantitativeness and constancy of units, are fundamental to all measurement. It must be recognized, of course, that the degree to which they are attained varies from one field to another. They can be obtained in physical measurements, for example, to a higher degree than in the measurement of mental or emotional traits, at least at the present stage of development of measuring techniques. It is also important to keep in mind that the degree of constancy of units is governed in large part by the situation. *Constancy*, as used here, is a relative term. There is less need for exact equivalence of units on a carpenter's rule or a household thermometer than on the extremely fine instruments used in scientific laboratory research.

LEARNING EXERCISES

8. Define the terms *quantitative* and *qualitative*, as used, for example, in chemistry. Apply the distinctions thus expressed to educational measurement.

9. What is implied by the concept *constant unit* as it applies to educational measurement?

Error in Measurement

Occasionally everybody makes mistakes in arithmetic or in reading a scale or measuring the dimensions of a room. But error in measurement has a somewhat different connotation. Suppose you were conducting an experiment that required you to record temperatures. You might read the thermometer as accurately as possible and follow all directions closely and yet still find some degree of error in the results. Why? To answer this question, let us consider the nature and sources of error in measurement. They are chiefly of three types.

One is the error of observation, sometimes referred to as the human equation. This type of error has not always been recognized. It is said that one observer in a world-famous astronomical observatory in the late 1700s was discharged because his observations consistently differed from those of his co-workers. It was not commonly believed then that such differences, though possibly the result of carelessness on an observer's part, are often the result of differences in how independent observers actually see the instrument readings. It is now a well-known fact that even highly trained observers may observe the same phenomenon at the same time and yet differ in their reading of a scale or in their description of what took place. Moreover, a single observer's own readings commonly vary from one observation to the next, even though the actual conditions are essentially unchanged.

A second source of error is inherent in the measuring device or instrument. Variations from one instrument to another—slight and perhaps imperceptible variations in units of the scale and similar mechanical variations—result in instruments of measurement that are something less than infallible. The more carefully a device is made and the better the materials used are, the smaller the amount of error is likely to be. But in spite of all the painstaking care with which scientific measuring tools are made and calibrated, none is perfect. This source of error is especially significant in educational testing devices for reasons that we will discuss later.

A third source of error in measurement stems from lack of uniformity in what is being measured. Whether one is measuring the strength of a piece of twine or the performance of a child in arithmetic, some degree of uniformity is vital to accurate measurement. The strength of the twine varies in different segments of the samples and according to age, moisture, and so on; the behavior of the child varies somewhat according to motivation, environment, and health and mood. For practical reasons it is generally impossible to measure all of a material such as a carload of ore or all of an individual's behavior or knowledge under all conditions. Therefore, an attempt is always made to measure a representative or typical sample of the material or behavior.

Knowing and understanding the possible sources of error are essential to an intelligent use of measuring instruments in any field, and by knowing and understanding we improve our methods of measuring. We can also make more intelligent use of the results of measurement, for knowing the limits of accuracy is very helpful in making interpretations.

LEARNING EXERCISES

10. Bring a thermometer to class and hang it on the wall for ten or fifteen minutes. (If the classroom has a thermometer already installed, use it.) Have the temperature read by a dozen members of the class, each one estimating as accurately as possible to the nearest tenth of a degree. Have each person write down each reading as it is made. When all have finished, list the readings on the board. How do you explain the results?

11. Compare the readings of two thermometers, two yardsticks, two balances, or some other pair of measuring instruments. Do they agree? How closely?

Characteristics of Educational Measurement

Let us apply the concepts of quantitativeness and constancy to educational measurement. First, we may say that *were measurement in education not quantitative, it could not properly be called measurement.* By using educational measurement we get scores, norms, IQ's, averages, all of which are numerical expressions. Not all methods of appraisal or evaluation in education are quantitative, but most—even pass-fail grading and either-or and true-false responses—can be quantified by assigning numbers to qualities according to arbitrary rules (as when we establish a binary system—for example, 0 and 1—or when we say $A = 4$, $B = 3$, and so on).

Second, *in the development of educational measuring devices, substantial progress has been made toward creating constancy of units.* This aspect of measurement cannot be discussed without getting into technical matters, but we may say that the development of certain types of derived scores represents at least an approach to the establishment of constant units of educational measurement. We should remember, however, that "constancy" is relative and that there are few absolutely constant units of measurement in any field.

Third, *error is present in educational measurement* as it is in all fields. Yet no sensible person would advocate discontinuing measurement in astronomy, physics, or even in biology or psychology. Instead, the scientist determines the causes of error and tries to eliminate them; knowing that this cannot be done entirely, the scientist tries to determine amount of error or degree of accuracy and then proceeds to measure to the best advantage, fully recognizing the limits of accuracy in the results.

As we gain knowledge and experience in a field, measurement techniques improve, margin of error decreases, and results become more exact. As workers in any subject area learn more about measurement, they learn to suspend judgment and use caution, which helps them to avoid making rash statements and conclusions not justified by the data or the degree of accuracy of their measurements. Moreover, knowing the probable limits of the error of their measurements makes it possible to specify the degree of accuracy quite closely. Instead of saying that a child's IQ is 115, for example, one learns that it is more accurate and just as useful to say that it is highly probable that the IQ is between 105 and 125 or that there is a 50-50 probability that the IQ is between 110 and 120. This may seem like rather rough or only approximate measurement; compared with results in some other fields, it is. Nonetheless, even with that degree of possible error in IQ measurement, for example, the results are still much more accurate than in any other known methods of estimating the intelligence of children; perhaps equally important is that the degree of accuracy and the probable limits of error are known.

Fourth, *educational measurement is generally indirect rather than direct.* The weight of an object can be determined directly in pounds and ounces or kilograms and grams by use of a balance or scale. But educational measurement is indirect. We measure such traits as intelligence or mechanical aptitude not directly but by inference. As an individual becomes able to perform designated tasks, we are able to draw from the results of the performance certain conclusions about the performer's intelligence or aptitude. The same is true with measurements of school achievement or personality or interests. Here the pupil's knowledge, adjustment, or motivation is measured indirectly, by inference based on behavior and, especially, performance on tests.

Fifth, *educational measurements are often relative though they are not necessarily so.* Scores on many educational tests, especially standardized tests, are interpreted by comparative methods. Thus, when a teacher gives an informal classroom test, the scores of individual pupils are usually interpreted by comparing each one's score with those of other members of the class or with some more general measure such as the class average. Performance on educational tests, especially standardized tests of achievement, is interpreted by comparison with age or grade norms based on average or typical groups. A student's score on a reading test may be 40, a number that by itself has no clear meaning. But if we know the age and grade of the student and that the average score on the test for students of the same age and grade is 35, then the score of 40 takes on some meaning. Furthermore, if we find that 15 percent of student scores on this test are above 40, the score takes on added meaning. The test in this instance is said to be "norm-referenced"; interpretation of its scores is relative. We may say that the degree of excellence or deficiency with respect to human abilities or traits is a relative matter that cannot be defined in absolute terms. There is no "absolute zero" of human intelligence measurement comparable to that concept in physics.

Relative scores do not tell us in a direct, meaningful way what a student can or cannot do, however. If we wish to evaluate some specific performance, not how that performance compares with other performances, then we must compare it with a predetermined goal or standard. For example, if our objective is to have a student spell all the words in a given list correctly or swim the length of a pool unaided or name all the presidents of the United States in chronological order, the issue is whether or not the student can perform as specified. How well others perform is not the question. This type of measurement, generally called "criterion-referenced" or "objectives-referenced," is of great interest among test specialists and researchers as well as educators at the present time. (We will discuss it more fully in a later chapter.) It emphasizes mastery of predetermined goals or objectives, and the learner is encouraged to keep working until the desired criterion of mastery has been attained.

Criterion-referenced measurement and testing for mastery have had, on the whole, a substantial impact on educational measurement. It seems safe to say, however, that both norm-referenced and criterion-referenced tests will continue to be needed and used in the foreseeable future. It is probably also appropriate to mention that neither criterion-referenced measurement nor the mastery concept in education is entirely new. Before modern standardized achievement tests, with their carefully established procedures and norms, emerged, much of the testing that went on in classrooms might have been regarded as criterion-referenced.

Did the student correctly solve a set of problems involving multiplication of two-place numbers by two-place numbers? Was the symbol for each of the common chemical elements given from memory? Did the student recite the Bill of Rights without error? The concept of mastery has also been with us for many years.[26] The mastery concept in its practical application in the classroom requires that much if not all instruction be individualized. Obviously, not all students can attain a desired degree of mastery in the same amount of time; some will perhaps not attain it at all. While some will have long since achieved mastery as defined, others will still be struggling. Adjustment to individual differences in learning ability, motivation, and perseverance—a logical alternative to mastery—requires a great deal of flexibility from the teacher and the instructional program.

The foregoing discussion should suggest that measurement in education is faced with many of the same difficulties as measurement in other fields, but those difficulties seem greater in education than in the more exact fields. One of the main reasons for this is that the materials being measured—human beings—are constantly changing and difficult to control. Chemists are able to handle most of their samples in any way they choose; most chemical samples remain fairly constant and uniform and can be divided or mixed. With children, uniformity of sample and control of conditions is extremely difficult to attain. In a somewhat comparable field, it may be noted that biologists are able to control and measure organisms that grow and change. No one would say that measurement in biological science is impractical or useless. Biologists lean heavily on quantitative methods for research and for practical work, yet they measure living, growing, changing organisms—a guinea pig or a cow or a tomato plant—that differ from people, as far as measurement is concerned, only in degree of complexity and susceptibility to control.

Measurement is only a tool. It is a means to an end. Yet it is valuable to the extent that it helps teachers, counselors, administrators, and others connected with the schools to do a better job of educating children and adults. Few would question that measurement has done much to help appraise what we do in education, to move education out of the realm of opinion and into the realm of valuable facts, and to point out ways in which the job can be done better.

LEARNING EXERCISES

12. A pupil's permanent record card shows an IQ of 115 on test X and 125 on test Y given one year later. How would you explain this?

[26] See, for example, Henry C. Morrison, *The Practice of Teaching in the Secondary Schools* (Chicago: University of Chicago Press, 1926).

13. For what educational situations or decisions would comparing a student's test performance with the performances of other students be most useful? When would it be most useful to compare a student's performance with specific standards? Justify your answer.
14. Which of the five characteristics of educational measurement—quantitativeness, constancy, error, indirectness, relativity—do you consider most important? Least important? Why?

Testing,
Measurement,
Evaluation

These terms *testing, measurement,* and *evaluation* are often used interchangeably with some confusion. *Testing,* as seems obvious, means using tests. It may mean testing the strength of materials, such as textiles; it may mean testing a class in arithmetic; it may mean testing an individual's intelligence. It usually involves the use of some specific instrument or set of instruments to determine a certain quality or trait or a series of qualities or traits. For example, we may use a test battery to measure achievement in a variety of school subjects. As generally used in education, the term *testing* has come to have a rather specific and somewhat limited connotation and, in some instances, a slightly unfavorable one. A tester is regarded by some persons (whether rightly or wrongly) as a technician who is more interested in the scores and statistics of the results of tests than in what the results mean in relation to the children or adults who made the scores. There is probably some justification for this attitude on the part of teachers if, for example, the tests are given to their pupils by administrative order and they have no voice in the matter.

We have defined *measurement* as a process in terms of the ideal attributes of quantitativeness and constancy of units. As the term is used in education, it is generally conceived of somewhat more broadly than testing, and it considers such matters as purposes, interpretation, and use of results. It is thought of as including the use of types of instruments other than tests, such as rating scales, check lists, score cards, and any tools that yield or can be made to yield quantitative results, though these may not meet the ideal criteria of a measuring instrument.

Evaluation is the broadest of the three terms. In measurement we generally strive to be as objective as possible and to minimize the role of judgment; in evaluation we tend to emphasize the role of judgment in considering a variety of relevant information when we determine progress toward a goal, describe the worth of a program, or reach a decision. In educational evaluation all available types of data, qualitative as well as quantitative, may be brought to bear. A few illustrations may help make this clear. A teacher who wants to evaluate progress toward an instructional goal may use test scores, written work, classroom recitations, and personal observations in judging how much progress each pupil has made toward the goal. In this illustration, evaluation includes identifying and formulating the goal, selecting or devising tools for measuring progress toward the goal, using the tools, and forming judgments based on the results obtained from their use. A counselor who wants to assist a student in deciding what course to follow in college (business administration, engineering, medicine, the humanities, whatever) may together with the student collect a variety of relevant data. They might include the student's interests, the student's overall grades in high school as well as grades in particular areas, scores on college aptitude and other standardized tests, and descriptions of the number of years required to complete each course, the cost per year, and the family's financial status. All these as well as other types of information that the counselor and the student's parents and teachers may be able to supply can be used in making a decision. In this illustration, evaluation is directed toward making a sound choice from various alternatives.

Testing, measurement, and evaluation have much in common. The differences are not as great as is sometimes implied. They designate separate but overlapping processes. No matter which term is appropriate, however, certain important principles should never be overlooked. The instruments or techniques should be chosen or designed to fit the objectives. Whether a process is called testing, measurement, or evaluation is not nearly as important as whether the progress or status of the learner with respect to the desired goal can be determined. Another principle of equal importance is that no technique is worth using unless the results it yields can be depended on. An evaluation procedure, like any test, is useful only to the extent that it yields accurate data that mean what they seem or are believed to mean. Unless results are gathered by procedures that yield accurate, dependable data, they are useless and even misleading. Finally, it is essential in the evaluation process that interpretations of data and judgments be as objective and as free of personal bias as possible. Otherwise, they have little or no value.

As the number and variety of tests, scales, and other instruments have increased, the importance of using different kinds of instruments and relating data from one to another has become more and more evident. The broad concept of evaluation has contributed materially to the development of this point of view. It has emphasized the need for a large variety of measures or samples of an individual's behavior, and it has stressed the interrelatedness of such information in understanding and helping the individual. Evaluation has also served to emphasize the importance of traits or qualities or conditions not easily measured by objective tests.

We use the term *measurement* throughout to express the field with which this book is concerned. We consider and discuss all the instruments commonly used in education today—tests, inventories, rating scales. We give major consideration to tests, since they greatly exceed in number, variety and extent of use all other types of instruments. We also discuss evaluation procedures in formulating instructional objectives and devising tests to measure them, interpreting scores on a variety of tests, marking, and using tests and other tools to improve instruction in the schools.

LEARNING EXERCISES

15. As a curriculum specialist, you wish to evaluate the program in your high school for training stenographers. How would you proceed?
16. Some comparisons use the expression that "differences are of 'degree' rather than 'kind.' " What does this mean? Does it have any application to the question of distinctions between testing, measurement, and evaluation? The distinction between quantitative and qualitative?

PURPOSES OF THIS BOOK

The purpose of this book is basically orientation. We presume that most students in a first course in educational measurement have had little or no systematic presentation of the principles and practices of the field. Consequently, we assume no background other than the usual introductory education courses required of people who are preparing to teach.

Another important purpose of this book is to assist teachers and others who devise their own tests and evaluative devices. Almost all teachers make tests and examinations for classroom use. This is a necessary and important part of the job of teaching. It is essential that it be done as well as possible, if only to insure that the least possible injustice is done to individual pupils. More positively, adequate measurement skills are important because without them it is impossible to determine whether we are making progress toward our educational goals. If we are making progress, we must know how much progress is being made, not only by groups but also by individuals. Therefore, one of the major purposes of this book is to provide principles and "know-how" so that people who have the responsibility of making examinations and other measuring instruments will be able to do this better.

A further purpose of the book is to present the tools and techniques for the intelligent use and interpretation of the results of standardized tests and other measurements. Moreover, it is the particular aim of this book to show how such results can be put to practical use in the school for the benefit of the students and for the improvement of the educational process. Too often testing programs are undertaken with great enthusiasm; considerable time and money are spent in selecting, administering, and scoring the tests; and the tests are filed away or neatly tied up in bundles, scarcely to be looked at again. Unless the results of tests are put to use, the testing process becomes wasteful and pointless.

In order to use tests and measurements effectively, it is necessary to know what materials are available. We do not pretend to make an exhaustive survey of all available educational measuring instruments; such a survey would be quite impractical. However, we do include descriptions and discussions of methods and devices in major areas such as achievement, intelligence, and personality. We make no attempt to describe or even list all available tests in such subjects or areas. Our purpose is simply to describe prototypes or typical examples so that the beginner will be able to gain some knowledge and understanding of the kinds of instruments that have been developed and found useful.

SUGGESTED READING

COMMITTEE ON ASSESSING THE PROGRESS OF EDUCATION. *Progress Toward a National Assessment of Education.* Ann Arbor, Mich.: Committee on Assessing the Progress of Education, 1968. A brief review of the genesis of National Assessment and its purposes, procedures, and expected outcomes.

FLANAGAN, JOHN C., et al. *Design for a Study of American Youth.* Boston: Houghton Mifflin, 1962. The background, purposes, and design of Project Talent. Sampling procedures, planning, construction, and content of tests and inventories. Includes details of procedures for giving the tests and analyzing the data.

———. "Changes in School Levels of Achievement: Project Talent Ten and Fifteen Year Retests." *Educational Researcher,* 5 (September 1976), 9–12. A report of the results from retesting about eighteen hundred students in grades 9, 10, and 11 in seventeen schools that participated in Project Talent in 1960. The students took the same tests in 1975 that had been given in 1960.

GARRETT, HENRY E. *Great Experiments in Psychology.* New York: Appleton-Century-Crofts, 1930. Chap. 1, 2, 8, 9. Outstanding contributions in psychological method, including accounts of the work of Binet, Galton, Thorndike, and Cattell in measurement and in developing Army Alpha.

GOSLIN, DAVID A. *The Search for Ability.* New York: Russell Sage Foundation, 1963. Chap. 2. Discoveries in the nineteenth century that helped lay the foundation of modern measurement. Events and developments in the twentieth century. Brief comparison of educational testing in Russia, Great Britain, and the United States.

———. *Teachers and Testing.* New York: Russell Sage Foundation, 1967. The role of the teacher in testing. The use of tests in elementary and secondary schools; the competence of teachers in this aspect of their work and their attitudes toward it; the issue of coaching for tests. The potential impact of tests on school curricula.

GRONLUND, NORMAN E. *Measurement and Evaluation in Teaching.* 3d ed. New York: Macmillan, 1976. Chap. 1. Evaluation in education presented as an inclusive process. Discusses the development of instructional objectives and the selection or construction of evaluation procedures for those objectives.

JOHNSON, S. S. *Update on Education.* Denver, Colo.: Education Commission of the States, 1975. A digest of what the National Assessment of Educational Progress has revealed about the achievement of young Americans in science, social studies, music, literature, reading, writing, and citizenship.

JONES, LYLE V. "The Nature of Measurement." In *Educational Measurement.* 2d ed. Edited by Robert L. Thorndike. Washington, D.C.: American Council on Education, 1971. Chap. 12. An excellent discussion of the fundamental characteristics of measurement and its methods. Not written primarily for beginners in this field but well worth their study.

KLEIN, STEPHEN P., and JACQUELINE KOSEKOFF. *Issues and Procedures in the Development of Criterion-Referenced Tests.* ERIC TM Report 26. Princeton, N.J.: Educational Testing Service, 1973. An excellent overview of major issues and steps in developing criterion-referenced tests: purposes, item construction and selection, validity. Includes a survey of present efforts to develop such tests and a bibliography.

NATIONAL SOCIETY FOR THE STUDY OF EDUCATION. *The Impact and Improvement of School Testing Programs.* Sixty-second Yearbook. Part 2. Chicago: University of Chicago Press, 1963. Chap. 9. The impact of external testing programs. Definition of an external testing program, discussion of problems of such programs as seen by school administrators, and suggestions for solutions.

———. *The Scientific Movement in Education.* Thirty-seventh Yearbook. Part 2. Chicago: University of Chicago Press, 1938. Chap. 29, 30, 31. Factors influencing the development of achievement testing during the first thirty years of the twentieth century. Tests of intelligence, aptitude, and personality. Observation, questionnaires, and rating scales are discussed in historical perspective.

ORNSTEIN, ALLEN C., and HARRIET TALMAGE. "The Rhetoric and the Realities of Accountability." *Today's Education*, 66 (1973), 70–80. Discusses claims that are made for this controversial educational development and emphasizes the difficulties of fixing responsibility for the success or failure of learning.

PAYNE, D. A., and R. F. MC MORRIS, ed. *Educational and Psychological Measurement: Contributions to Theory and Practice.* 2d ed. Morristown, N.J.: General Learning Press, 1974. Articles from a variety of sources on a number of current issues to help the reader achieve a broad perspective on educational measurement.

PETERSON, JOSEPH. *Early Conceptions and Tests of Intelligence.* New York: Harcourt Brace Jovanovich, 1925. Historical account of the background and development of modern concepts of intelligence and methods of measuring it, up to and including the work of Binet.

WRIGHTSTONE, J. WAYNE, THOMAS P. HOGAN, and MURIEL M. ABBOTT. *Accountability in Education and Associated Measurement Problems.* Test Service Notebook 33. New York: Harcourt Brace Jovanovich, n.d. An excellent discussion of the concept of accountability in education. Includes measurement and evaluation with emphasis on the methods and problems of measuring growth.

Two

STATISTICS
IN EDUCATIONAL MEASUREMENT

Although most of us probably make no claim to extensive statistical knowledge or training, we all have at least an elementary understanding of statistics. For example, baseball fans are familiar with batting and fielding averages as a measure of the skill of the professional baseball player. Most people who work for a living follow the newspaper reports of changes in cost of living. Most of us understand weather reports on the average rainfall, temperature, and barometric pressure. Statistics about birth and death rates have some meaning for us all.

As students and teachers or prospective teachers, we know well the significance of the class average in planning instruction and assigning marks. Few of us are totally unfamiliar with the meaning of such terms as *rank in class, percentile, median, quartile,* and *correlation.* So, while we may not be statisticians in any formal or learned sense, most of us use statistics in our work and in our recreation.

The primary purpose of this chapter is to round out the understanding of basic statistical ideas and techniques most students already have and to show how statistical analysis of a relatively simple nature can be applied by teachers and counselors to make scores on tests more meaningful and therefore more useful. For people who are interested in a more extensive treatment of simple statistical analysis, Appendix A includes an expansion of the techniques with examples and guides.

After studying this chapter, you should be able to answer questions and apply processes such as the following:

1. What statistical concepts are helpful in describing how well a student performed on a given test?

2. What statistical concepts are useful for comparing student performance on different tests?
3. Given a set of scores, compute the mean, median, semi-interquartile range, and standard deviation.
4. Describe ways in which measures of average and variability can be used by teachers in planning instruction.
5. Describe the meaning of correlation coefficients of different values.

THE NEED FOR STATISTICS IN ASSESSMENT

The value of a measurement program is largely determined by the thoroughness and appropriateness with which the results are analyzed. Some type of systematic treatment of scores is necessary if the scores are to be useful for pupils and teachers. This does not mean that every set of scores must be exhaustively analyzed, but it does mean that test scores in themselves have little significance and that statistical analysis enhances the value of a measurement program. For example, to know that a pupil's score on a mathematics test is 36 tells us very little about the pupil's level of achievement in mathematics. Before we can interpret such a figure, we need more information. Taken by itself it is merely a number. Likewise, if we wish to use the results of a test to make comparisons between classes or groups or to do a better job of teaching or counseling, we must make some analysis of the test scores. Such analysis can be performed only by statistical methods, however elementary these may be. Statistical methods are simply tools to help us acquire understanding of pupils from scores or numbers that in themselves are of little or no value to the teacher.

The results of a school testing program are generally available to teachers for use in planning instruction. For the data to be optimally useful, a teacher must know how to use norms, how to interpret a class average score, and how to relate individual pupil scores to both norms and the class average. The teacher should additionally know how to interpret measures that describe the relative homogeneity or heterogeneity of pupils in the class and relate this information to the need for individualizing instruction. With classroom tests the teacher should know how to report test results to individual pupils and to the total class so that individuals will be able to assess their performance and the achievement it represents. The techniques you will need for the purposes noted here are described in this chapter and in Chapter 3.

1. What uses does the average consumer make of statistics? What use does the government make of them? the classroom teacher?
2. Make a list of statistical terms or concepts that you know. How many can you define?
3. Examine a daily newspaper for articles using or quoting statistics. How many do you find?

ORGANIZING SCORES
TO FACILITATE INTERPRETATION

An unordered set of test scores such as can be obtained from an alphabetical listing of pupils is not convenient to interpret. Some of the common questions that teachers ask about the results on a test include: What is the highest and what is the lowest score in the class? What is the average or typical score made by the pupils in the class? How does one student's score compare with the scores made by classmates—is it high, low, or near the middle of the set? After a test has been scored, a useful first step in interpreting the results is to organize the scores in such a way that the teacher can easily answer questions similar to these. One simple but effective way of accomplishing this is to order the scores from highest to lowest.

Ordering Scores

Let us suppose that a pupil's score of 36 was earned on a mathematics test and that the scores for the class are as shown in Table 2.1. When the scores have been rearranged from highest to lowest, the arrangement shown in Table 2.2 is obtained.

Now most of the questions posed earlier can be answered at a glance. The highest score is 52 and the lowest score is 14. The score for J, 36, is above the middle of the set but is not among the highest scores. The few minutes required to organize the scores for a typical class are soon saved as the teacher interprets the performance of students in the class. Even when the teacher intends to calculate some statistics for the set of scores, a simple ordering may be useful in discussing the results with the class.

Hypothetical Test Scores *Table 2.1*

Pupil	Score	Pupil	Score
A	44	N	38
B	21	O	33
C	14	P	33
D	18	Q	29
E	46	R	38
F	45	S	32
G	52	T	29
H	30	U	42
I	39	V	28
J	36	W	26
K	31	X	33
L	22	Y	25
M	23		

Ordered Test Scores *Table 2.2*

Pupil	Score	Pupil	Score
G	52	K	31
E	46	H	30
F	45	Q	29
A	44	T	29
U	42	V	28
I	39	W	26
N	38	Y	25
R	38	M	23
J	36	L	22
O	33	B	21
P	33	D	18
X	33	C	14
S	32		

Simple Ranking

The interpretation of a score of 36 given above is not entirely satisfactory because of its inexactness. When scores have been ordered, a simple additional step can improve the precision with which they can be described. A fairly common method is to assign a rank to them in terms of the position that they occupy within a group. Usually the highest score is assigned a rank of 1, the second highest a rank of 2, and so on. When this is done for the set of mathematics test scores above, we obtain the results shown in Table 2.3. J, with a score of 36 in this class, ranks 9th or, to put it another way, eight pupils have scores higher and sixteen have scores lower than 36. This gives a more definite meaning to the score than it had before ranks were assigned.

Table 2.3

Ranked Test Scores

Pupil	Score	Rank	Pupil	Score	Rank
G	52	1	K	31	14
E	46	2	H	30	15
F	45	3	Q	29	16.5
A	44	4	T	29	16.5
U	42	5	V	28	18
I	39	6	W	26	19
N	38	7.5	Y	25	20
R	38	7.5	M	23	21
J	36	9	L	22	22
O	33	11	B	21	23
P	33	11	D	18	24
X	33	11	C	14	25
S	32	13			

Notice that where two or more scores are the same, the places that they would otherwise hold have been averaged and the average thus obtained has been given as the rank to every pupil with the same score. For example, students N and R each have a score of 38. Student I, with the next higher score of 39, ranks 6th, and J, with the next lower score of 36, ranks 9th; thus N and R occupy the 7th and 8th places. By averaging these ranks—that is, by adding 7 and 8 and dividing by 2—each score receives a rank of 7.5. Similarly, the positions of O, P, and X have been averaged to obtain the rank of 11 for each of them, and the positions of Q and T have been averaged to obtain the rank of 16.5.

Percentile Rank

The method of ranking just described has certain disadvantages that sometimes are rather troublesome. The most important of these arises from the fact that the procedure takes no account of differences in the size of groups. For example, a rank of 15 in a group of fifteen is quite different from a rank of 15 in a group of one hundred. In the group of fifteen, the rank is the lowest in the group, whereas in the larger group it is one of the highest. As long as comparisons of individual ranks are based on groups of the same size, this is no problem. Where the groups are quite different in size, however, we must use some other procedure if a person's standing in one group is to be compared with the standing in another group.

One such method uses percentile ranks. *Percentile ranks* differ from simple ranks in that they express the position of any score in a group in terms of the percentage of the group that stands below that score. In our example of simple ranking, we said J's score of 36 gave a rank of 9 in the class of twenty-five, higher than sixteen other scores. Putting this in another way, we can say that 16 / 25 × 100, or 64 percent of the class, made a score lower than J did on the mathematics test. This is the percentile rank. When we use percentages, we make comparable the ranks of individuals in groups of unequal numbers.[1]

Now J might take a history test with the whole grade of several hundred pupils. If the rank J achieved on this test were 44, we would find it meaningless to compare this with the rank of 9 in mathematics. Even if we knew that J's rank of 44 on the history test had been based on a group of two hundred pupils, it would still be difficult to compare it with the rank of 9 in a group of twenty-five. However, we know that the percentile rank in mathematics is 64. In order to calculate the percentile rank on the history test, we find the number of pupils who made lower scores than J. We find 200 − 44 = 156. Then we can calculate 156 / 200 × 100 = 78, giving J a percentile rank of 78. In other words, 78 percent of the class made lower scores on the history test. Thus, we can compare J's standing on the two tests directly and say that J's achievement on the mathematics test is apparently not as good as achievement on the history test.

LEARNING EXERCISES

4. Rank the following scores, made on a test of word meaning by twenty-four ninth-grade pupils: 45, 50, 41, 39, 45, 33, 42, 44, 38, 44, 25, 44, 50, 32, 42, 40, 49, 60, 29, 50, 37, 24, 47, 55.
5. Find the percentile ranks for pupils with scores 33, 42, and 60 in Exercise 4. Can a pupil have a percentile rank of 100? Justify your answer.

MEASURES OF CENTRAL TENDENCY

A very useful descriptive measure for a set of scores is an *average*, or measure of *central tendency*. An *average* is a number, not always an

---

[1]For such comparison to be useful, the two groups, though different in number of pupils, should be comparable on some relevant trait, such as that all the pupils are at the same grade level.

actual score, that is taken as the most likely or typical value for a group of numbers or scores. There are several kinds of averages, but the kinds used most often in educational work are the arithmetic mean[2] and the median.

The Mean

The *arithmetic mean* is the sum of a group of scores divided by the number of scores. Thus, the arithmetic mean for the twenty-five mathematics test scores in the case we have been describing can be found by finding the sum of the scores and then dividing the sum by 25. In this case, the sum is 807, which when divided by 25 gives an arithmetic mean of 32.28. In a similar manner, we could determine the mean height of a group of 10-year-old boys, the mean cost of a pound of butter, and the mean annual rainfall in a particular locality. In the first instance, we would measure each boy, add all the heights, and divide by the number of boys; in the second, we would determine the variation in the cost of a pound of butter over a period of days or weeks or in different markets, and proceed to find the mean cost in the same way (dividing by the number of dates or by the number of markets); in the third instance, we would find the total rainfall in inches by adding individual measures of rainfall over many years, divide by the number of years, and thus arrive at the mean amount of rain per year.

The Median

Another common measure of central tendency is the *median*. This is simply the middle score or the point in a series that has 50 percent of the scores above it, or higher than it is, and 50 percent below it, or lower than it is.

Where data are arranged in rank order, the position of the middle score can be determined by using the formula $(N + 1)/2$, where N is the number of scores. For example, if we had five papers that had been scored 80, 70, 60, 50, and 40, then $(N + 1)/2 = (5 + 1)/2 = 3$, identifying the middle score as the third in the set. Here the third score is 60. If one score were added to the series, say 90, then $(N + 1)/2 = (6 + 1)/2 = 3.5$. The score at position 3.5 is halfway between the third (60) and fourth (70) scores; thus the middle score is 65. It should be noticed again that to use this procedure, we must arrange scores in order of magnitude.

When the number of cases is odd, the median is the score that stands exactly in the middle. When the number of cases is even, the median is midway between the lowest score of the upper half and the highest score of the lower half.

---

[2]Although we use the term *average* in the generic sense, it is frequently used for the term *arithmetic mean*.

6. Find the mean of the scores in Exercise 4. Find the median.

We should mention one other measure of central tendency. It is a crude, *The Mode*
inspectional average called the *mode,* defined as the score that occurrs
with the greatest frequency. The mode is of little importance, statistically speaking. Its chief use is to show the point of the greatest concentration of scores.

Although both the mean and the median are satisfactory measures of *Comparison*
central tendency for most purposes, some important differences should *of Mean*
be noticed. The mean is a *weighted average* in that it is affected by the *and Median*
actual amount or size of every score in the distribution. The median,
however, is a *counting average,* or an average of position.

One of the the chief differences between the arithmetic mean and the
median can be shown by the following example. Suppose we want to find
the average salary of a group of workers whose annual salaries were
$50,000, $20,000, $15,000, $13,000, and $12,000. The arithmetic mean
would be calculated thus:

$$\begin{array}{r} \$\ 50{,}000 \\ 20{,}000 \\ 15{,}000 \\ 13{,}000 \\ 12{,}000 \\ \hline 5\,\overline{)\$110{,}000} \\ 22{,}000 \end{array}$$

The median or middle salary is $15,000. Which of these would be the
more representative or more typical average? It requires no technical
knowledge to answer this question since it is obvious that the median—
$15,000—is more representative of the five salaries than the arithmetic
mean, which is $22,000. The median is not influenced by the size of ex-
treme scores as much as the mean is. However, in a situation in which it
is important from a statistical standpoint to give every score or measure
its full weight according to its magnitude, the arithmetic mean is the

average to use. In nearly all ordinary situations encountered in school-work, the median serves as well as the mean and has the advantage of being easier to calculate and understand.

In summary, we may say that we should use the mean when every score should be given its full weight and when further statistical calculations are to be made, since many of them proceed from the mean. The median is preferable, however, when a few scores deviate markedly (as in the example above) and when it is advantageous to use a measure of central tendency that is easily calculated and understood.

LEARNING EXERCISES

7. Would you use the mean or median in each of the following? Give your reasons.

   a. the cost of homes in a community with a population of 5,000

   b. the average of test scores 70, 42, 80, and 58, if the score 70 is to be given three times as much weight as the others

   c. a set of test scores that includes several for students who did not finish the test

8. Why is the mean different from the median in Exercise 6?

MEASURES OF VARIABILITY

Although central tendencies or averages provide a meaningful reference point for interpretation of individual scores in a series, such as the scores of a specified class, grade, or age, they are limited in what they reveal about the group as a whole. They do not tell us anything about the form of the distribution of scores. In other words, it is quite possible to have two or more groups whose averages are the same but that are quite unalike in their range or spread.

Let us look at an example. In the accompanying table we have four sets of scores whose central tendencies are identical but that are quite different in their composition or spread. (Of course, this type of comparison can be made only when the same or equivalent tests have been taken by all groups being compared.)

Group A	Group B	Group C	Group D
100	80	70	60
80	70	65	60
60	60	60	60
40	50	55	60
20	40	50	60
Mean = 60	60	60	60

To make the point even clearer, let us suppose that a teacher has two classes in general science and has given both of them a test. The teacher has calculated the median scores of class 1 and class 2 and they are exactly the same—namely, 47. To make the illustration very simple, let us assume that there are nine pupils in each class and that the scores on the test in the two classes are as shown in Table 2.4. For convenience, we present the scores in rank order.

An inspection of these scores shows that the median of the two groups is 47, as we have stated; the arithmetic mean of the two is also the same for both—namely, 46. A teacher or counselor who made no further analysis of these scores might easily conclude that the two classes are comparable in all respects as measured by the test. A closer study shows a marked difference between the groups, not in central tendency but in spread or variability. No informed teacher would handle these two classes in the same way. Whereas class 1 has a score range of 51 points, from a low of 19 to a high of 70, class 2 has a range of only 30 points, from 31 to 61. In other words, we can say that, on this test, class 2 is more homogeneous than class 1, or class 1 is more heterogeneous than class 2. This difference would have considerable bearing on the methods used in handling the two classes.

Two Groups Having Same Average and Different Spread or Range of Scores   *Table 2.4*

Pupil	Class 1	Pupil	Class 2
A	70	L	61
B	64	M	55
C	59	N	53
D	51	O	50
E	47 (median)	P	47 (median)
F	44	Q	40
G	32	R	39
H	28	S	38
I	19	T	31
	9)414		9)414

Mean = 46
Range = 70 − 19 = 51

Mean = 46
Range = 61 − 31 = 30

The Range	The *range* is a very crude or rough measure of variability since it is based on only two measures, the highest and lowest scores. For this reason it is not a very stable measure and is used little in statistical work. Our reason for considering range here is that the concept of variability in describing distributions and interpreting results is important. In comparing groups or classes, it is sometimes more important to know something about their respective spreads or variabilities than to know what their averages are. Generally speaking, knowledge of both types of measures is necessary for adequate comparison of groups of test scores.
The Semi-interquartile Range, Q	Whereas the range is based on the difference between the two most extreme scores in the set, the *semi-interquartile range* (Q) is based on the spread of the middle half of the distribution. The point below which 75 percent of the distribution is located is called the 75th percentile, the third quartile, or Q_3. The point below which the lowest 25 percent of the distribution stands is called the 25th percentile, the first quartile, or Q_1. The middle half of the distribution lies between Q_3 and Q_1 and the formula for finding the semi-interquartile range is

$$Q = \frac{Q_3 - Q_1}{2}$$

The procedure for finding Q_1 and Q_3 is similar to that for finding the median. In finding Q_1 we use $N/4$ to locate the point below which 25 percent of the scores stand; we use $3N/4$ to find the point below which 75 percent of the scores stand. Between these points are the middle 50 percent of the scores. Then $Q = (Q_3 - Q_1)/2$.

For the set of twenty-five mathematics scores we looked at in Tables 2.1–2.3, $N/4$ is 25/4, or 6.25, and $3N/4$ is $3 \times 25/4$, or 18.75. Thus, to locate Q_1 and Q_3, we can round off these values and count up 6 and 19 scores, respectively. The 6th score from the bottom of the set is 25, and the 19th is 38. Then, $Q = (Q_3 - Q_1)/2 = (38 - 25)/2 = 13/2 = 6.5$.

If we compare the semi-interquartile range of two groups or classes on the same test and find Q to be larger in one group than in the other, we know that the one with the larger Q is more varied or heterogeneous than the other on the trait measured by the test. The semi-interquartile range is a refinement of the crude range. It eliminates the highest and the lowest 25 percent of the scores, which are likely to be scattered and unreliable, and expresses variation in terms of the more stable and concentrated middle 50 percent of the scores. Whereas the range can be affected by one score at the top or bottom of the distribution, the Q is not affected at all by a single extreme score or, in most instances, by several such extreme scores.

LEARNING EXERCISE

9. After a test has been scored, the teacher finds an error in the key so that every pupil's score is 2 points too high. How does this affect the range? The semi-interquartile range? Explain. Would the correction affect the mean? How?

From a statistical standpoint, the best measure of variability is the standard deviation. Usually designated S, the *standard deviation* is a measure of variability based on the deviations of scores from a measure of central tendency, in this case the arithmetic mean, and it is the most reliable one because it takes into account the actual variation of each score from the mean of the series.[3]

The Standard Deviation, S

To illustrate how the standard deviation is calculated, we reconstitute in Table 2.5 the two sets of scores from Table 2.4. The formula for the standard deviation is

$$S = \sqrt{\frac{\Sigma d^2}{N}}$$

In this formula, Σ stands for sum, d stands for deviation from the mean, and N stands for the number of scores or cases. Substituting in this formula the values shown in Table 2.5, we get:

$$\text{class 1} \qquad S = \sqrt{\frac{2{,}348}{9}} = \sqrt{260.89} = 16.2$$

$$\text{class 2} \qquad S = \sqrt{\frac{746}{9}} = \sqrt{82.89} = 9.1$$

To recapitulate, what we have done can be described thus:

1. We have determined the difference (or deviation) between each score and the mean, giving scores below the mean a negative sign.
2. We have squared each deviation, to get rid of negative signs.

[3]The standard deviation is represented by various symbols (S, S.D., σ). We use S here to designate the standard deviation of actual scores. Sigma (σ) is widely used to represent the standard deviation in more theoretical work.

Table 2.5   Calculation of a Standard Deviation

		Class 1					Class 2	
Pupil	Score	d (score − mean)	d²	Pupil	Score	d (score − mean)	d²
A	70	24	576	L	61	15	225
B	64	18	324	M	55	9	81
C	59	13	169	N	53	7	49
D	51	5	25	O	50	4	16
E	47	1	1	P	47	1	1
F	44	−2	4	Q	40	−6	36
G	32	−14	196	R	39	−7	49
H	28	−18	324	S	38	−8	64
I	19	−27	729	T	31	−15	225
	414	0	2,348		414	0	746

Mean = 46

N = 9

$$S = \sqrt{\frac{2,348}{9}} = \sqrt{260.89} = 16.2$$

Mean = 46

N = 9

$$S = \sqrt{\frac{746}{9}} = \sqrt{82.89} = 9.1$$

3. We have found the sum of the squared deviations.
4. We have divided the Σd^2 by N, the number of scores in each class (in this case, $N = 9$).
5. Finally, we have extracted the square root of the quotient obtained in step 4 (because we squared the deviations in step 2, and extracting the square root restores the measure to the original units).[4]

The obtained values for S, 16.2 and 9.1, tell us that class 1 is substantially more variable or heterogeneous than class 2.

    Although the meaning of a standard deviation and the way to compute the index should be known by educators, teachers seldom need to obtain an exact measure of a standard deviation. For most classroom purposes, a good estimate is sufficient, and a simple and reasonably accurate shortcut procedure has been developed. The following formula can be used:

$$\text{estimated } S = \frac{\text{sum of upper } ⅙ \text{ of scores} - \text{sum of lower } ⅙ \text{ of scores}}{\text{half of } (N - 1)}$$

This procedure is illustrated in Table 2.6, using the twenty-five mathematics scores from Tables 2.1–2.3.

[4]For method of extracting square root, see Appendix B.

Table 2.6

Shortcut Method for Estimating the Standard Deviation of a Distribution of Twenty-Five Scores

Step 1.	Find the number of scores equal to one-sixth of the total: $25/6 = 4.17$ (use the four largest and four smallest scores).
Step 2.	Add the four largest scores: $52 + 46 + 45 + 44 = 187$.
Step 3.	Add the four smallest scores: $14 + 18 + 21 + 22 = 75$.
Step 4.	Find the difference (step 2 minus step 3): $187 - 75 = 112$.
Step 5.	Find one-half of $(N - 1)$: $(25 - 1)/2 = 12$.
Step 6.	Divide the result in step 4 by the result in step 5: $112/12 = 9.33$.

The estimated standard deviation obtained in Table 2.6 is 9.33. Were we to compute the actual value of the standard deviation for the twenty-five scores by using the formula $S = \sqrt{\Sigma d^2/N}$, the value would be 9.15. (This could be verified by using the data on page 33.) The estimate found here is slightly larger than the actual value, but the size of the difference is not so large as to introduce serious discrepancies in the uses of a standard deviation most often made in the classroom.

A standard deviation can be thought of as a distance along a score scale of a distribution. Many distributions of scores on educational and psychological tests have the majority of scores near the average score, with progressively fewer scores in both directions toward the ends of the distribution. In such situations, approximately two-thirds of all scores are within a distance of one standard deviation from the mean score. For example, the scores in the mathematics example have a mean of 32.28 and S of 9.15. Adding 9.15 to 32.28 gives 41.43; subtracting 9.15 from 32.28 gives 23.13. In this set of scores, there are fifteen scores between 41.43 and 23.13. Since there are twenty-five scores in the set, 15/25, or 60 percent, are within one S of the mean.

LEARNING EXERCISES

10. Order the thirty scores given below, and compute the mean and standard deviation.

31	22	31	34	34	36
29	30	30	33	26	24
43	31	25	30	39	31
24	32	30	27	37	34
28	28	40	30	21	33

11. Estimate the standard deviation by using the method shown in Table 2.6. How does the value thus obtained compare with the value found by using the longer method?
12. Find Q for the distribution. How do Q and S compare?

In our discussion of measures of central tendency, we interpreted test scores by describing their location with reference to an average. The lack of precision in this type of interpretation results from the use of different score units; we could improve the precision by reporting the distance between a score and the mean in units of the standard deviation. For example, we could note that J's score of 36 is approximately four-tenths of a standard deviation above the mean. This approach illustrates one of the most important uses of the standard deviation for classroom teachers—namely, the establishment of a scale based on standard deviation units. We will consider the topic in detail in the next chapter in the section on standard scores.

Comparison of Q and S

The semi-interquartile range and the standard deviation are useful measures of the spread or dispersion of a set of scores. Q is easier to find, being based on only two points, Q_3 and Q_1, in a distribution. The standard deviation requires more computational effort, but it is the most widely used measure of dispersion. Because the computation is based on all scores in a distribution, S is usually more dependable and provides a more reliable index for comparing the spread of two or more distributions.

For a satisfactory description of a set of scores, a measure of central tendency and a measure of dispersion are required. The measure of average describes the typical level of performance or the typical score; the measure of dispersion describes the extent to which the scores are clustered (homogeneous) or spread out (heterogeneous). Together, a measure of average and a measure of spread provide an adequate basis for the most common uses of classroom test data.

The median and Q are similar in that they are based on counting measures—that is, points in a distribution found by counting up some fraction of the scores from the lowest score. The mean and S are similar in that they are based on the arithmetic treatment of all scores in a set. When the median is used as the average score, it is common to use Q as the measure of dispersion. When the mean is used as the average, S is typically the measure of dispersion used. It would be unusual to use Q and the mean or S and the median together as descriptive measures. The mean and S have desirable mathematical properties and are most widely used in statistical work. However, as we noted previously, the median and Q are easier to find and are satisfactory for many classroom purposes.

MEASURES OF
CORRELATION OR RELATIONSHIP

We often hear the term *correlation* or see it in educational and psychological discussions and literature. Reference is made to a *high correlation* or a *low correlation* or *no correlation*. If such phrases are to have meaning, it is necessary that the term *correlation*, and the use of *high*, *low*, and *no* with reference to this term, be given some meaning.

Correlation is a method of expressing the degree of relationship between two traits or quantities that can change or vary in amount. For example, people vary in height, weight, intelligence, industry, and countless other ways. Each of these quantities is a variable. If two of the variables, height and weight, are selected for study, it is possible to say from observation that there seems to be a degree of correspondence between them. That is, tall persons tend to be heavier, and short persons tend to weigh less. The correspondence is not perfect because there are many combinations of heights and weights, but generally it can be said that there appears to be a definite relationship between height and weight. The index used for expressing quantitatively the degree of the relationship between two variables is called the *coefficient of correlation*. It ranges from a *maximum* of $+1.00$ through zero to a *maximum of* -1.00. If the two measured variables tend to vary together, as in the case of height and weight, the relationship is direct and positive and approaches $+1.00$ as a maximum. If the relationship is negative—that is, if an increase in one variable tends to be accompanied by a decrease in the second—the coefficient is negative, approaching -1.00 as a maximum. If there is no tendency for the traits or qualities to vary simultaneously, either directly or inversely, the correlation is zero, or we say that there is no correlation or that there is absence of relationship.

Meaning of Correlation

A correlation of $+1.00$ denotes a perfect positive relationship. This exists when a change in one trait is *always* accompanied by a *commensurate* change in the *same direction* in the other trait. Likewise, a correlation of -1.00 denotes a perfect negative correlation, which means that a change in one trait is *always* accompanied by a *commensurate* change in the *opposite* direction in the other trait. Perfect correlations, either positive or negative, are rarely found in educational measurements, and negative correlations of any size are quite uncommon.

An illustration of a positive correlation has already been given. The correlation between age of automobiles and their cash value is generally negative, since value decreases as age increases. The correlation between ages of school children and intelligence quotients would be zero since the proportions of bright, average, and below-average children are approximately the same at all age levels.

One of the most useful and easily understood devices for showing relationship between two variables is called a *scatter diagram,* in which the individuals or objects being measured are located or plotted with respect to both variables at the same time. This kind of chart may also be used as the basis for one of the best methods of determining relationship, the *product-moment correlation,* or r.

To make clearer the nature of correlation and different values of the coefficient, we will present several scatter diagrams. In each, two variables are involved. In the first and second case, the results are based on measurements of university students; the third is based on measurements of weather conditions and fuel.

In Figure 2.1, the scatter diagram shows what would be called a moderate positive correlation. There is a distinct tendency for high scores on one test to be accompanied by high scores on the other and vice

Figure 2.1   Scatter Diagram Showing Positive Correlation. Each tally represents a person located according to the scores earned on a factual test and on a reasoning test in educational measurement. $r = .51$.

Scores on reasoning test	30–31	32–33	34–35	36–37	38–39	40–41	42–43	44–45	46–47
65–69					///	//	///	//	
60–64			/	/	////	//	LHT	///	
55–59		/	//	///	///	LHT	//	/	/
50–54	/			LHT	////	///	/	//	/
45–49	/	/	/	//		/			
40–44	/		/	/	/				
35–39	/								

Scores on factual test

STATISTICS IN EDUCATIONAL MEASUREMENT

versa. Some individuals who make high scores on the reasoning test make average or even low scores on the factual test, however, and the opposite is also true in some instances. If such exceptions did not occur, the correlation would be +1.00. This moderate positive correlation is quite typical of what is found when mental measurements are correlated. The correlations between scores on tests in various school subjects, and between IQ and achievement test results, tend to be in the general vicinity of .30 to .50.

Figure 2.2 shows the relationship between two other variables—scores on a test of manual dexterity and scores on a vocabulary test. The correlation is almost zero, indicating that there is no evident relationship. In other words, knowing an individual's score on either test would provide no basis for estimating or predicting the score on the other test.

Scatter Diagram Showing Negligible Correlation. Each tally represents a person located according to the scores earned on a test of manual dexterity and on a vocabulary test. $r = .06$. *Figure 2.2*

Scores on manual dexterity test

	50–59	60–69	70–79	80–89	90–99	100–109	110–119	120–129	130–139	140–149
40–44				/	/					
35–39					/	//	///	//		/
30–34	/		//	///	////	////	//	LHT		/
25–29				/	////	//	////	//		/
20–24	/			////	//		LHT	/	/	/
15–19				/	//	////		/		
10–14		/		/	/	/	///	//		
5–9			/	//		//				
0–4						/			/	

Scores on vocabulary test

Figure 2.3   Scatter Diagram Showing Negative Correlation. Each tally represents one day located according to average temperature and tons of coal burned in a community during a twenty-four-hour period. $r = -.74$.

Average daily temperature	0–99	100–199	200–299	300–399	400–499	500–599	600–699	700–799
80–89	//	///						
70–79	LHT	LHT LHT	LHT LHT	/// LHT				
60–69	//	// LHT LHT	LHT LHT LHT	/// LHT LHT	LHT			
50–59		// LHT	LHT LHT	LHT LHT	// LHT	///		
40–49			////	/// LHT LHT LHT	LHT LHT LHT	LHT		
30–39				// LHT LHT	LHT LHT	/// LHT	////	
20–29					/ LHT	/ LHT	// LHT	//

Tons of coal burned per day

Figure 2.3 shows a negative correlation of −.74 between average daily temperature and tons of coal burned per day, a fairly high degree of inverse relationship. The data are hypothetical and serve only to illustrate a negative or inverse relationship. Such a relationship is obvious in this case, since the higher the mean temperature for any given day is, the lower will be the amount of coal burned for heat. What the true correlation would be is not determined. It would, of course, be affected by other atmospheric conditions such as wind, humidity, and sunshine.

The scatter diagram for a perfect correlation would show that all points fall on a straight line; there would be no scatter. For a −1.00 correlation the line would extend from upper left to lower right, and for a +1.00 correlation the line would extend from lower left to upper right.

It should be clear that theoretically one may have high negative or even perfect negative correlations, just as high or perfect positive correlations are possible. In actuality, however, as we mentioned previously, perfect correlations are rarely found in educational measurement. It should also be noticed that a negative correlation designates just as close a relationship as its positive counterpart. A correlation of $-.70$ is just as high for predictive purposes as one of $+.70$ is. It is the size of the correlation, not its direction, that determines how close the relationship is. The calculation of correlation coefficients is somewhat complex. One method is described and illustrated in Appendix A.

LEARNING EXERCISES

13. Cite three illustrations each of positive correlation, approximately zero correlation, and negative correlation.
14. Would you expect positive, negative, or no correlation in each of the following comparisons?
    a. IQ and marks in algebra
    b. speed and accuracy in addition
    c. scores on two equivalent forms of an achievement test
    d. age and IQ within one school grade
    e. age and IQ over a range of grades
    f. cost of a product and supply available.
15. Ask your instructor for two sets of scores made by the same pupils on two different tests. Make a scatter diagram based on them. Suggestion: Write down the pupils' letter designations and then, in parallel columns, each one's scores on the two tests. From this arrangement make a plot locating each pupil with respect to both scores simultaneously. Comparing the result with the three diagrams given, what do you estimate the correlation to be?

The coefficient of correlation is an index or number that gives a measure of the degree of relationship between variables. Most commonly, only two traits or quantities are considered at one time, though there are methods of determining correlation between more than two. The correlation coefficient is *not* a percent. A correlation of .60 does not mean 60 percent of perfect correlation. As we have said, it is simply a number or index that can vary from $+1.00$ through zero to -1.00. We repeat for emphasis that the amount or size of the correlation coefficient expresses the degree to which two traits tend to vary simultaneously, or the extent to

Further Ideas About Correlation

which increases (or decreases) in one tend to be accompanied by increases (or decreases) in the other.

It may be appropriate to mention one or two additional cautions about correlation. Remember that a relationship between two variables does not prove them to be *causally* related. They may vary together or tend to do so because of a third factor that affects both. Age is frequently such a factor. For example, a substantial positive correlation might be found between height or weight and mental maturity among school children. Such a correlation would be the result of the effect of age on physical growth and mental growth, not evidence that increase in height or weight causes mental growth. When the factor of age is eliminated or held constant, the correlation between height or weight and mental age is approximately zero.

It should also be clear that correlation can be determined only where there is some basis for relationship, as in a case when the same group is tested twice. There is no basis for correlation between two different groups of persons being tested even with the same test. This fact seems self-evident, yet there is a common misconception that a coefficient of correlation may be determined between test scores of two different classes or groups. The computation of *r* requires pairs of scores for the same individuals.[5] There are many kinds of correlation coefficients, each with particular and specific uses, but the simplest and most common is the one we have discussed here, known as a *linear correlation between two variables.*

*Size of
Correlation
Coefficients*

A question of concern to everyone using correlations has to do with the size of the coefficient. Since the coefficient can vary in either direction from zero to 1.00, it is important that we try to determine what is a *high* correlation, a *moderate* one, and a *low* one. No simple and rigid rules for answers to such questions can be given. The same correlation may be high in one situation and only moderate or even low in another. Correlations between two equivalent forms of a test of achievement or intelligence may be .90 or higher, sometimes as high as .98. On the other hand, correlations between measures of mental ability and school marks ordinarily are not higher than .50. Correlations between measurements of physical traits or abilities such as rate of tapping or strength of grip and scores on mental tests are usually not far from zero. The interpretation of a coefficient of correlation depends on the situation.

A more useful method of interpreting the size of the correlation coefficient involves forecasting or predictive value. For example, if we know a

---

[5]The only common exceptions are in the study of the resemblance between twins or other relatives in specific traits, and in educational experiments in which individuals in one group are paired or matched with individuals in another group on some basis such as intelligence.

pupil's level of intelligence, how accurately can we predict that pupil's achievement in algebra? Knowing a given pupil's IQ score will never tell us exactly what the score will be on an algebra test. But if both tests have been previously administered to the same group of pupils, then the size of the correlation coefficient between the scores on the two tests will give us some idea of how confident we can be later in predicting an algebra score from the score on the intelligence test. If the two tests prove to have a correlation of .90 or higher, then we would be fairly safe in predicting that a given individual will have roughly the same relative score on the algebra test as on the intelligence test. For *individual prediction* to be sufficiently accurate to be useful, the correlation must be very high—at least as high as .90.[6]

One way in which the size of a correlation coefficient is related to predictive accuracy is shown in Table 2.7. It can be seen that the higher the correlation is between two measures, the greater is the consistency with which students' scores appear on the same side of the median of the two measures. Assume that we wish to predict which students will be above average in an algebra class. Table 2.7 shows that, if the other measure, called a *predictor*, correlates .90 with grades in algebra, then 85 percent of the students who are above average on the predictor will also be above average on grades in algebra. It should be noted that, when the coefficient is zero, there is a chance relationship between the two measures and only half of the group above the median on one measure will be above the median on the second measure. Table 2.7 is based on only one type of distribution, but it is the most common type for educational and psychological tests. The table should suggest that low correlations improve predictive accuracy very little, but the improvement increases rapidly for coefficients above .50.

Percent of a Group Above and Below Median of Two Measures   *Table 2.7*

r	Percent
1.00	100
.90	85
.70	75
.50	67
.30	60
.10	53
.00	50

[6]Procedures can be found in statistics books for predicting the most probable score for a person. The techniques require knowing a person's score on one test and the correlation between that test and the one for which the prediction is made. The standard deviation of errors in such predictions is called a *standard error of estimate* and is discussed in Appendix A.

If we wish simply to have some assurance of being right more often than wrong in *group prediction*, then correlations of .50 or even less are often quite useful. In such cases it is also possible to say with considerable assurance that one group will do better or worse than another.

Another problem in correlation is this: If we measure a group of children on a test today, how closely will the results agree with those obtained from the same test given to the same children several days later? Here, where we are interested in knowing how consistent the results of a test are, usually correlations of .80 or better are considered necessary to assure acceptable stability or consistency. We will consider these matters further in the discussion of reliability and validity in Chapter 4.

LEARNING EXERCISE

16. Think of some variables that might show a relationship (correlation) because of a third factor. How would you explain the relationship to a teacher who has not studied statistics?

SUGGESTED READING

CRONBACH, LEE J. *Essentials of Psychological Testing.* 3d ed. New York: Harper & Row, 1970. Chap. 4. A rather condensed presentation emphasizing theoretical aspects of statistical methods. The computing guides are practical and helpful, though not easy for a beginner to follow.

DOWNIE, N. M., and HEATH, R. W. *Basic Statistical Methods.* 4th ed. New York: Harper & Row, 1974. A thorough coverage of basic statistical concepts commonly used with classroom tests. One chapter reviews basic arithmetic fundamentals.

DUROST, WALTER N., and PRESCOTT, GEORGE A. *Essentials of Measurement for Teachers.* New York: Harcourt Brace Jovanovich, 1962. Chap. 11 and Appendixes A–E. A practical discussion of basic statistical techniques applicable to test scores. Appendixes contain tables of squares, square roots, reciprocals, and formulas useful in calculations.

KATZ, MARTIN, ed. *Short-Cut Statistics for Teacher-Made Tests.* Evaluation and Advisory Service Series 5. Princeton, N.J.: Educational Testing Service, 1964. Presents short-cut procedures for the statistics

STATISTICS IN EDUCATIONAL MEASUREMENT

most widely used in a classroom for test-score interpretation. A useful guide for teachers.

MCCALL, ROBERT B. *Fundamental Statistics for Psychology.* 2d ed. New York: Harcourt Brace Jovanovich, 1975. Relates statistics to measurement, covering some basic assumptions. The coverage of measures of central tendency and variability, percentiles, and correlation is quite complete.

SMITH, G. MILTON. *A Simplified Guide to Statistics for Psychology and Education.* 3d ed. New York: Holt, Rinehart and Winston, 1962. In less than one hundred pages all the statistics that most teachers, counselors, and beginners in research will need. Lucid and practical. Includes a table of squares and square roots.

STAHL, SIDNEY M., and HENNES, JAMES D. *Reading and Understanding Applied Statistics.* St. Louis: C. V. Mosby Co., 1975. A programmed textbook with chapters covering graphs and tables, measures of central tendency, and measures of dispersion. The self-testing approach may be helpful to some students.

TATE, MERLE W. *Statistics in Education and Psychology.* 2d ed. New York: Macmillan, 1965. A textbook for a first course in statistics assuming no mathematical prerequisites beyond high school algebra. Written primarily for teachers; the first eight chapters are particularly appropriate for students using this textbook.

Three

DERIVED SCORES AND NORMS

The point was made in Chapter 2 that a single score on a test, expressed as the number of correct answers, does not by itself provide a meaningful indication of the quality of the performance of the pupil who achieved the score. It was suggested that performance can be interpreted with more meaning when the score is compared with other scores earned on the same test. The first type of score, the number right, is commonly referred to as a *raw score*, and a score obtained by comparing raw scores or relating a raw score to some other factor or test characteristic is referred to as a *derived score*.

Two quite common methods for computing derived scores from raw scores were suggested in Chapter 2. We first considered how a pupil's score can be described in terms of its location within a group; ranks and percentile ranks for ungrouped data were used for this purpose. Second, we noted that a score can be described in terms of the linear distance between it and the mean, expressed in units of the standard deviation.

In this chapter we will examine more thoroughly techniques that are based on the characteristics of a single set of scores. We will also consider an approach that uses the average scores of consecutive groups (for example, grade or age groups) as reference points for deriving meaningful score *scales*. The scores that we will consider are those that are widely used with standardized tests and those that are useful and practicable for classroom teachers. In addition, we will consider the meaning and limitation of norms that are provided with commercially standardized tests to assist users in interpreting scores on the tests.

At the completion of this chapter you should be able to answer questions and solve problems such as the following:

1. What derived scores for classroom tests can be used to assist pupils in following their progress?
2. Given a set of scores, find z-scores and sigma scores for each class member.
3. Compare the uses and limitations of various types of norms.
4. Conduct a profile analysis, for individual pupils and classes, noting the conclusions that seem warranted and those that seem questionable.
5. Describe the meaning of percentile ranks, standard scores, stanines, and age and grade scores in such a way that a parent, on hearing your descriptions, could draw useful conclusions from the results of tests used in the school.

ABSOLUTE AND RELATIVE SCORES

The ideal measurement scale is comprised of absolute units, but, as we have noted, education tests seldom yield such a score scale. A unit has absolute meaning when it always refers to the same amount of a specified trait; for this to be possible, a universally accepted standard must exist. The metric unit of distance, the meter, is an absolute measure because a standard exists against which all meter sticks can be calibrated. All measures of distance recorded in terms of a meter are meaningful to people who are familiar with this unit. If the height of an overpass were listed as 4.7 meters, a truck driver familiar with the metric system would know immediately whether a given truck could be driven beneath the overpass; the driver would not have to ask about the nature of the instrument that was used to measure the height of the overpass, how the measurement was obtained, or anything else about the measurement process. The meter as a unit represents the same distance on all meter sticks and in all locations, and therefore measures reported in this unit have an absolute meaning.

In contrast to the situation described above, absolute units are not available to describe the pupil traits that are of greatest interest to teachers. To know that a pupil can spell correctly thirty-five words on a test means very little by itself. Before this score can be useful in a descriptive way, one needs to know something about the test and about the distribution of scores on the test. For example, a score has more meaning if we know the number and difficulty of words that were included on the test, the average score made by the pupils at a given grade level, or other information about the nature of the test and the distribution of pupils' scores on the test.

DERIVED SCORES

As a means of reporting test performance more meaningfully than can be done with a raw score alone, users of tests frequently convert raw scores by relating them to relevant and commonly understood measures. As we have said, scores obtained in this way are often called *derived scores*. Even though derived scores do not provide absolute units, they are more meaningful than raw scores and they do make possible some types of interpretation that cannot be made with raw scores. In particular, they permit the construction of *norms* tables, tables of statistics that describe the test performance of a defined group of examinees. For example, a table showing the performance of pupils in grade 3 on a punctuation test would be a norms table. Frequently the average score for a group is referred to as a norm. That is, the average score of pupils in grade 3 might be referred to as the norm for that grade. It is important to note that norms reflect a situation in terms of what it is, not in terms of what might be desirable. In the pages that follow, we will consider various types of derived scores that can be used to establish norms tables.

LEARNING EXERCISES

1. Describe a test on which 100 percent would represent complete mastery of some skill or area of content. What distinguishes the test from one not satisfying this condition?
2. A sample of one hundred words is selected at random from a collegiate dictionary and used as a spelling test. If a student spelled sixty words correctly, would it be safe to predict that the same student could, without the use of a reference book, spell about 60 percent of the words she or he would use in writing a theme? Explain.

Percentiles and Percentile Ranks

In Chapter 2 we briefly considered how to obtain percentile ranks. A *percentile rank* (abbreviated PR) is a type of derived score that reports a pupil's performance in terms of the percentage of the class earning scores lower than the one in question. Thus, through a percentile rank, the quality of performance of a pupil earning a certain raw score is indicated as the percentage of the group that the pupil has outperformed.

Percentile rank and *percentile* are complementary terms. Whereas percentile ranks are used to describe the relative performance of pupils, percentiles refer to score points in a distribution. In general terms, if a student's score yields a *percentile rank of x,* that score point is the *xth percentile.* It will be recalled that in Chapter 2, J's score of 36 on a mathematics test equated to a percentile rank of 64; therefore, J's score, 36, is the 64th percentile. To describe the quality of J's performance on the test, we could say that J *earned* or *has* a percentile rank of 64 or that the raw score is *at* the 64th percentile.

Whereas percentile ranks report the percentage of a group with lower scores than a given student, percent-correct scores are found from the fraction of possible items that is answered correctly. Sometimes these two types of scores are confused with each other. A few years ago percent-correct scores were extremely popular with teachers, and, in spite of the weakness of such scores, many teachers continued to use them. The preference for this practice was based on the belief that percent correct is more meaningful than number correct. The recent trend toward mastery learning models and the use of criterion-referenced, or domain-referenced, tests has added to the resurgence of percent-correct scores. We discuss criterion-referenced testing in detail in Chapter 4, but several features should be noted here in as much as they relate to score-reporting practices.

Percent-Correct Scores

Many inherent limitations in educational measurement affect the usefulness of percent-correct scores. For a percent-correct score to be meaningful, a perfect score, 100 percent correct, should represent a known and fixed quantity. A score of 72 percent tells little more than does a score of 36 on a test of fifty items, unless something is known about the nature of the fifty items. For example, 72 percent correct on a test of adding two-digit numbers would mean something quite different from 72 percent on a test involving mathematical reasoning.

In addition to the question of test difficulty and content covered, another limitation arises from the fact that almost all educational tests include only a sample of the important skills or knowledge that legitimately could have been covered by the test. A spelling test does not include all words that pupils at a given grade level could be expected to know, the problems on a mathematics test do not cover all the situations in which mathematics principles could be used, and an intelligence test does not include all the possible ways in which intelligent behavior can be demonstrated.

Percent-correct scores must therefore be interpreted with great care, taking into consideration the level and breadth of knowledge represented by the test. For mastery learning models and criterion-referenced tests, percent-correct scores are useful only to the extent that the tests sample quite thoroughly the domain of skills or knowledge of the instructional unit and to the extent that 100 percent on the test guarantees mastery of essential material.

LEARNING EXERCISES

3. In what ways are percentile ranks and percent-correct scores different? Can a student's PR be estimated from just the percent-right score? Explain.
4. Does the quality represented by a PR depend more on the difficulty of the test or the nature of the group taking the test? Explain.

Interpretation of Percentile Ranks

On standardized tests, percentile ranks are probably the most widely used type of derived score. Publishers frequently report several types of scores, and, regardless of which are used, percentile ranks are nearly always included. The reason for this widespread use is probably the simplicity and the apparent ease of interpretation of the percentile rank. A score that reports the percentage of a group scoring lower than a given student has a directness of meaning that students, teachers, and parents seem to appreciate.

A few simple cautions for the interpretation of percentile ranks should be emphasized. First, PRs are not the same as percent-correct scores. Second, the interval represented by a PR is not constant across the scale. In the center of a distribution or at points on a scale where relatively large frequencies occur, a change of one point on the raw-score scale will result in a relatively large change in PR. Thus, the difference in level of performance between students who earn PRs of 45 and 55 might be relatively small, perhaps only one or two raw-score points. At the extemes of a distribution or where the frequencies are small, however, PRs for consecutive raw scores do not differ greatly. The third caution relates to the second: The extent to which the highest scores differ from each other may be concealed somewhat in a PR scale (and the same is true for the lowest scores). For example, consider a distribution of twenty-five mathematics scores in which the second highest score is 46 and the corresponding PR is 92, while the highest score is 52 and the PR is 96; if the highest score had been 47, one point more than the second highest score, then the PR for it still would be 96. PRs do not allow us to draw valid conclusions about the extent to which extreme scores differ from each other.

If the limitations of percentile ranks are recognized, this system of derived scores can be quite useful for reporting results on classroom tests. And, as we noticed earlier, percentile ranks are widely used for reporting level of performance on standardized tests.

LEARNING EXERCISES

5. After computing PRs for a class, a teacher discovers an error on the scoring key so that all pupils have scores one point higher than originally determined. How will this error affect the PRs that were found?
6. The PRs for two pupils on a classroom test are found to be 40 and 85, but scoring the test again shows that each should have a score one point higher. The PRs are recomputed and found to be 55 and 87. Explain the sizable difference in the change in PR that occurred.

An extremely useful way of describing performance on a test is to locate a pupil's score with reference to the average for the group and to describe the distance between the pupil's score and the average score in terms of the standard deviation of the distribution. For example, we noticed in Chapter 2 that J's score of 36 on the mathematics test was approximately four-tenths of a standard deviation above the mean for that test. To illustrate further the advantages of this approach, the means and standard deviations for two tests and J's scores are shown in Table 3.1. The mathematics test is the one referred to in Chapter 2; we will assume that J's class also took a reading test, with results as shown in the table.

Standard Scores

Even though the two sets of numbers are quite different, comparisons are possible because the scores were earned by the same group of pupils. The mean scores are comparable since they represent average achievement of the same pupils, and, similarly, the standard deviations are comparable; thus, scores can be compared in terms of these values. The point that is one standard deviation below the mean on the mathematics test would be 32.3 − 9.2, or 23.1. The comparable point on the reading test would be 75.5 − 15.4, or 60.1. These two points represent the same levels of achievement on the two tests, since they represent the same relative

Table 3.1

Comparison of Results of Mathematics and Reading Tests

	Mathematics	Reading
Class mean	32.3	75.5
Standard deviation	9.2	15.4
J's scores	36	80

position in their distributions. Similar points can be worked out all along the scale, both below and above the mean, in standard-deviation units.

Thus, J's mathematics score is 3.7 points above the mean (36 − 32.3 = 3.7). Dividing 3.7 by the standard deviation for that test yields a value of .40 (that is, 3.7 / 9.2 = .40). This indicates that on the mathematics test J's score is .40 of a standard deviation above the mean of the class. On the reading test, J's score is 4.5 points above the mean (80 − 75.5 = 4.5). The standard deviation for this test is 15.4, so we can divide 4.5 by 15.4, which yields a value of .29 (4.5 / 15.4 = .29). Since both these values, .40 and .29, are expressed in the same units—namely, in terms of the means and standard deviations of the two distributions—they may be compared directly. Therefore, we can say that J's score on the mathematics test is slightly better than the score on the reading test, even though the reading score is numerically greater and even though it exceeds the mean by more raw-score points than the score on mathematics does.

Scores expressed in terms of their linear distance from the mean in units of the standard deviation are called *standard scores;* those just described are expressed on a standardized scale with a mean of zero and a standard deviation of 1. In this instance, if a pupil's raw score is equal to the class raw-score mean, the standard score will be at the mean derived score, zero. Similarly, if a pupil's raw score is one standard deviation above the raw score mean, the standard score will be +1. This type of standard score is called the *z-score.*

z-SCORES   The calculation of z-scores can be generalized in a formula:

$$z\text{-score} = \frac{X - M}{S}$$

where X = the actual score
M = the mean
S = the standard deviation

It will be readily seen that a score below the mean will yield a negative z-score. For example, in the reading test, for a score of 69 we get a z-score of (69 − 75.5)/15.4 = −6.5/15.4 = −.42. This value indicates that the raw score is .42 of a standard deviation *below* the mean.

Although z-scores are easily found and have a standard meaning, they are not widely used because of the inconvenience of decimals and negative values. The method of finding z-scores is basic to several other types of more widely used standard scores, however, and therefore the process is important.

LEARNING EXERCISES

7. Using the data for the mathematics and reading tests in Table 3.1, find the z-scores for raw scores 40 and 20 in mathematics and 90 and 45 in reading.
8. Using the same data, find the average raw scores in mathematics corresponding to z-scores of +1.5 and −.7.

SIGMA SCORES   The inconvenient features of z-scores can be eliminated easily by converting the z-score to another scale with arbitrarily selected and more convenient values for the mean and the standard deviation. The generalized formula for accomplishing this is:

$$\text{standard score} = (S' \times \text{z-score}) + M'$$

where S' represents the desired standard deviation and M' represents the desired mean. We refer to scores derived from this formula as *sigma scores* to distinguish them from z-scores. A convenient—and perhaps the most widely used—scale has a mean of 50 and a standard deviation of 10. In this case, the formula for finding sigma scores would be:

$$\text{sigma score} = 10z + 50$$

Thus, J's z-score .40 in mathematics can be changed to a sigma score by multiplying $.40 \times 10 = 4$ and by adding 50, which gives 54. Similarly, the z-score of $-.42$ that we found earlier can be changed to a sigma score by multiplying $-.42 \times 10 = -4.2$ and by adding this to 50; the result is 45.8, which is rounded to 46.

These values, 54 and 46, show essentially the same information that z-scores of $+.40$ and $-.42$ do. That is, the score of 54 is four units above the average on a scale with a standard deviation of 10; therefore, the score is .4 of a standard deviation above the mean. Similarly, 46 is four units below the average and thus is interpreted as .4 of the standard deviation below the mean. Even though this is essentially what we said before, the values 54 and 46 are positive whole numbers and therefore easier to record and use.

LEARNING EXERCISES

9. Change the z-scores found in Exercise 7 into sigma scores.
10. How low must a z-score be for the corresponding sigma score to be negative? Describe this same score in terms of raw scores in relation to the raw-score mean and standard deviation.

A FEW COMMENTS ABOUT z-SCORES AND SIGMA SCORES   The standard scores that we have considered are based upon linearly derived scales because the relationships among raw scores are unchanged on the standard-score scale, even though different numbers are used to report the scores. Consider, for example, a test that has a raw-score mean of 26 and a raw-score standard deviation of 5. A raw score of 30 would give a z-score of $+.8$ and a sigma score of 58. A raw score of 25, similarly, would yield a z-score of $-.2$ and a sigma score of 48. Now it can be seen that the two raw scores, 25 and 30, are one standard deviation—that is, 5 points—apart on the raw-score scale. However, it can also be seen that the z-scores of $-.2$ and $+.8$ are one standard deviation apart on the z-score scale and that sigma scores of 48 and 58 are separated by 10 points on the scale, which has a standard deviation of 10 points. In this case, transforming the raw scores on a single test into z-scores and sigma scores has done nothing more than substitute in a systematic way arbitrary but convenient values for the original raw scores.

As we noticed earlier, standard scores are most useful in comparing scores on different tests, since the means and standard deviations are comparable; two conditions must be met, however. First, the scores must be those of the same students on the different tests or of two groups of students on the same test. Second, the form of the distributions on the two tests or for the two groups on the same test must be similar. Generally speaking, the form of distributions of human measurements is bell-shaped or close enough to bell-shaped that no serious error is introduced.

Many teachers find standard scores a convenient way of recording test scores in their grade books. When scores are recorded by using the same scale, the relative quality of performance on different tests is immediately evident. Another advantage of this approach is realized when scores must be combined to obtain a total or composite score, as when obtaining a semester composite from the unit tests given during the semester. Adding standard scores gives equal weight to each test. If one or more of the tests should be given more importance, the standard score for that test can be multiplied by an appropriate factor before the scores are added. For example, if two unit tests are equally important and the final examination should be twice as important as a unit test, the composite could be found thus:

$$\text{composite} = SS_1 + SS_2 + \left(2 \times SS_{\text{final}}\right)$$

It could be recommended that teachers in junior and senior high schools take the time to explain to students the meaning of standard scores. If this were done, scores on different tests could be compared easily by both students and teachers, and changes in performance level would be meaningful to both.

NORMALLY DISTRIBUTED STANDARD SCORES   We have noticed that z-scores and sigma scores have the same shape of distribution as the raw scores from which they are derived and that this characteristic affects the comparability of the standard scores when two raw-score distributions differ markedly in shape. Although z-scores and sigma scores are quite useful within a classroom, raw scores on standardized tests are more often transformed by a procedure that yields not only a prescribed mean and standard deviation but also a distribution with a known shape or form. The most common model is a normal curve, a graph that accurately represents many distributions of scores on educational and psychological tests. A graph of a normal curve is shown in Figure 3.1. Methods that change the shape of the distribution are called *area transformations*. Some area transformations yield other than a normal distribution, but the normal curve provides the most popular model.[1]

T-SCORES   One of the most widely used normalized standard-score systems, called the *T-score*, is based on a method recommended by McCall in 1939.[2] T-scores, like sigma scores, have a mean of 50 and a standard deviation of 10. The difference between the two systems lies in the fact that T-scores are always normally distributed whereas sigma scores may

---

[1]Normal distributions are described in more detail in Appendix A.
[2]William A. McCall, *Measurement* (New York: Macmillan, 1939), pp. 497–518.

Figure 3.1

Graph of a Normal Curve. The arrows indicate the direction of increasing frequencies and higher scores.

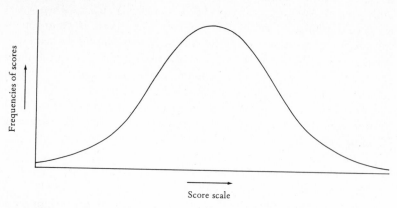

not be. Regardless of the type of raw-score distribution for a test, the *T*-scores derived from it will always be normally distributed.

We will not discuss the procedures for deriving *T*-scores from raw scores in detail. Most introductory statistics books present a complete description of the process. Here we give only a brief explanation.

The first step in deriving *T*-scores is to find the percentile rank for each raw score. Then a table for the area of a normal distribution is consulted to locate the *z*-scores in the normal distribution that have the same PRs as the raw scores.[3] Each *z* is then multiplied by 10 and the product is added to 50.

Most of the standard scores reported with standardized tests are obtained by some type of area transformation. The primary advantage of such score scales is, of course, the fact that scores on different tests are directly comparable regardless of differences in the distributions of raw scores on which they are based. For example, a *T*-score of 60 will always have a percentile rank of 84, a *T*-score of 70 will always have a percentile rank of 98, and similarly with other points or scale values.

A normalized set of standard scores need not have a mean of 50 and a standard deviation of 10; some of the more widely used normalized scales employ other constants. For example, one widely used test has a scale with a mean of 500 and a standard deviation of 100; another scale uses a mean of 100 and a standard deviation of 20. Later in this chapter we will refer to deviation IQs, which are in effect normalized standard scores with a mean of 100 and a standard deviation of 15 on some and 16 on other widely used tests.

[3] A particularly useful table for obtaining *T*-scores is given in Paul Blommers and E. F. Lindquist, *Elementary Statistical Methods* (Boston: Houghton Mifflin, 1960), pp. 510–511.

LEARNING EXERCISES

11. Explain how it would be possible for a given raw score to convert to a sigma score of 67 and a T-score of 60.
12. Why would it be important on a standardized test covering different curricular areas to report scores on a scale with a common type of distribution?

STANINES   Another type of standard score with a prescribed scale unit is called a *stanine*. The name is a condensation of the expression, "standard nine." Stanines are standard scores with nine units in the scale ranging from a low of 1 to a high of 9, with a mean of 5.

The stanine scale is based on the proportions of a normal distribution that fall into nine units, each one-half of a standard deviation in width. The middle category, numbered 5, represents the segment one-fourth of a standard deviation on each side of the mean and contains approximately 19 percent of the total distribution. On either side of this are four stanines, each one-half of a standard deviation in width. The percentages of the total distribution in each of the nine intervals are shown in Table 3.2.

Percentage of Total Group Falling in Each Stanine   *Table 3.2*

Stanine	Percentage of group
9	4
8	7
7	12
6	17
5	19
4	17
3	12
2	7
1	4

The process of determining stanines for raw scores is quite simple. The highest 4 percent of a set are assigned the value 9; the next highest 7 percent are assigned 8; and the process is continued until the lowest 4 percent are assigned the value 1.

Stanines have certain virtues for describing performance on tests that have led to their expanding acceptance. They are convenient to work with since they are only single-digit scores. They are easily recorded and easily manipulated statistically. In addition, because each stanine represents a relatively broad range of achievement, the possibility that small and questionably significant differences on tests will be over-interpreted is reduced. This last point should be examined in more detail. As an example, students with percentile ranks of 55 and 45 on a test would both receive stanines of 5. Whereas the difference of 10 between the percentile ranks appears to be relatively large and might be regarded by some teachers as highly significant, a difference of this size in the middle of a distribution could be associated with a difference of only one or two raw-score points. As a result, the educational significance of the difference might be slight and perhaps teachers would be well advised to regard the pupils who earned these two scores as about the same in the subject covered by the test. This similarity is reflected in the stanine scale, since the pupils would both receive scores of 5. However, this characteristic is also a weakness of the system when scores at the extremes of the distribution are involved. Let us assume two scores with percentile ranks of 88 and 78. As we approach the extremes of a normal distribution, similar differences between percentile ranks represent much larger raw-score differences than they do at the middle of the distribution. In this case PR 88 and PR 78 would both fall in stanine 7, even though the difference between the two raw scores might be large and significant.

It should also be noticed that the coarseness of the intervals on the stanine scale is a weakness of the system. Since each stanine category represents a relatively broad range of achievement, small differences occurring at some points on the raw-score and percentile-rank scales are magnified when the scores are transformed into stanines. For example, a pupil with a percentile rank of 89 would be assigned stanine 8 and a pupil with a percentile rank of 88 would be assigned stanine 7. Most teachers would regard the difference of 1 in percentile rank as insignificant, but because of the broad width of each stanine interval, the difference between an 8 and a 7 would probably be regarded as educationally important. This type of problem is present on all scales and cannot be avoided; there are always borderline cases. When the number of intervals in the scale is small and each is broad, it is possible that differences between borderline cases will be magnified. For these and other reasons, a scale such as percentile ranks with 99 units may be preferred.

Norms in the form of stanines are now provided with many standardized tests, and their popularity has been increasing rapidly during recent years. Almost all classroom teachers encounter stanines at one time or another. In addition, stanines may be used for recording scores on classroom tests and activities. Even if a teacher is reluctant to convert scores on major tests to stanines, less formal instruments (quizzes, laboratory exercises, homework) seldom justify the use of more than nine categories, and stanines provide a convenient system.

LEARNING EXERCISES

13. On three unit tests, two students receive the following stanines: student A, stanines 4, 5, and 6; student B, stanines 6, 5, and 4. How would you interpret their relative performance on each test, overall and in terms of trends?
14. How dissimilar in performance, as measured by standard scores, could the students be who earn the lowest and highest scores that convert to a stanine of 9? Explain.

INTELLIGENCE QUOTIENTS   The *intelligence quotient*, or IQ, has become a familiar term to the layman as well as to professional educators and psychologists. Although it is doubtful that the average person could give a precise definition of IQ, most people know that it is supposed to be some indication of degree of intelligence. Until quite recently the intelligence quotient was defined as the ratio of mental age to chronological age, multiplied by 100 to eliminate decimals. The theory on which this definition was based assumed that individuals grow or develop mentally at a fairly steady rate from birth to a few years before maturity and that any two different individuals may develop mentally at the same or at different rates.

Essentially a *ratio IQ* was intended to represent the rate at which an individual develops mentally. If a child was found to be able to perform the tasks generally performed by an average child of age 12, that child was said to have a mental age of 12. IQ was then found by dividing 12 by the chronological age and multiplying by 100. For example, if the child was 10 years old chronologically, the IQ would be $12/10 \times 100 = 120$. This was interpreted to mean that the child was developing 1.2 years mentally for each year of chronological age. An IQ of 100 was established as the average for each age group, since the average score on an intelligence test for each age group was taken as a measure of mental age for that group. In other words, if a representative sample of 10-year-old children make an average score of 65 on an IQ test, that score represents a mental age of 10 and any child making that score is said to have a mental age of 10 regardless of chronological age.

The concept of the ratio IQ has been very commonly useful in mental measurement for many years. However, for a number of reasons, mostly technical and statistical in nature, it has now been largely replaced by what is known as the *deviation IQ*, a standard score with an arbitrarily assigned mean and standard deviation for all age levels. The generally assigned values are mean = 100 and standard deviation = 16. These are the values that have been determined for the *Stanford-Binet Intelligence Scale*, a test widely used for many years. By converting distributions of IQ obtained from applying another test to this scale, we equate it to the Stanford-Binet. We present details of this procedure and discuss other considerations relating to the measurement of intelligence or general mental ability in Chapter 9.

Theoretically, the range of IQ is from 0 to 200 or more. Since the norm or standard is the level of development of the average child of a given age, it follows that the average IQ must always be 100 so long as these norms or standards are kept up to date. IQs in the range between 90 and 110 are generally designated as average. This includes, in a normal distribution, approximately one-half the population.

LEARNING EXERCISE

15. Should deviation IQs be thought of as representing rate of mental growth? Explain.

Relationships Among Certain Derived Scores

The relationship of the types of scores we have discussed is shown very clearly in Figure 3.2. The graph is for a normal curve that has been divided into units that are one standard deviation in width. The scales given below the graph indicate the percentile ranks for the points in the graph and also show the relationship among some common derived scores that are reported with standardized tests. Figure 3.2 is worth careful study because it shows clearly the relationship of various types of derived scores to each other and to the normal curve.

Figure 3.2

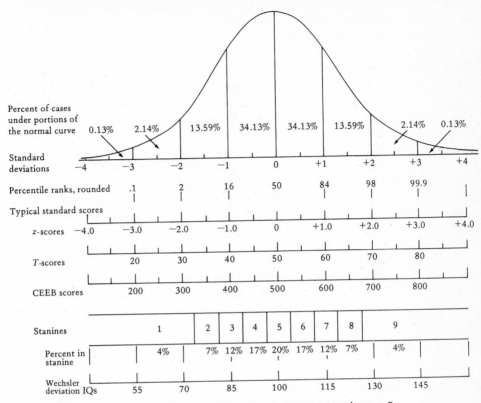

NOTE: This chart cannot be used to equate scores on one test to scores on another test. For example, both 600 on the College Entrance Examination Board (CEEB) and a *T*-score of 60 on a classroom test are one standard deviation above their respective means, but they do not represent "equal" standings because the scores were obtained from different groups.

SOURCE: Adapted from *Test Service Bulletin*, No. 48, p. 8. Reproduced by permission. The Psychological Corporation, New York, N.Y.

NORMS FOR AGES AND GRADES

Earlier in this chapter, we defined *norms* as statistics that describe the test performance of a defined group of pupils. We saw that frequently the average score for a group is referred to as a norm. The average score of fourth-graders on a test of reading comprehension is a norm; so is the average score of ten-year-olds on a spelling test. In this section we will look particularly at norms for ages and grades.

We considered briefly the principle underlying the determination of such norms in the section on intelligence quotients, where we noted that mental age scores are defined in terms of the chronological age of pupils for whom a given raw score is the average. It can be seen that this process is one of identifying the norm for a defined group of people. When the reference group is determined on the basis of age, the norm is called an *age score*; when the group is determined on the basis of grade in school, the norm is called a *grade score*, or *grade equivalent* (GE).

A conversion table for an achievement test that provides both age and grade scores is shown in Table 3.3. In this instance—the *Gates Basic Reading Test*, Type GS—both age and grade equivalents are given for each score in terms of the number of paragraphs correct. Both age and grade scores are classified in units of one month. In age scores the divisions include the entire twelve months of the year, while in grade scores the range is usually from the exact year, such as 9.0, to 9.9, representing the last month of the school year. Thus, in tables of age scores we find values such as 7-10 or 9-11; these represent 7 years, 10 months, and 9 years, 11 months, respectively. In tables of grade scores, we might find 5.4 and 7.7 representing the fourth month of the fifth grade and the seventh month of the seventh grade, respectively. Some publishers report grade equivalents as two-digit scores without a decimal point. Instead of 3.3, for example, they report 33. Regardless of whether a decimal point is included, the first digit refers to the school year and the second digit refers to the month of the school year.

The apparent simplicity and directness of meaning for age and grade scores are largely responsible for the popularity of these scales for use

Table 3.3   A Table of Norms: Grade and Age Scores for Type GS (Reading to Appreciate General Significance)—Time, 10 Minutes

Raw score	Reading grade	Reading age	Raw score	Reading grade	Reading age
0	2.5	7-8	13	5.4	10-6
1	2.6	7-10	14	5.6	10-8
2	2.7	7-11	15	6.0	11-2
3	2.9	8-1	16	6.4	11-8
4	3.2	8-5	17	6.8	12-1
5	3.4	8-7	18	7.2	12-6
6	3.6	8-9	19	7.4	12-8
7	3.8	9-0	20	7.6	12-11
8	4.0	9-2	21	8.1	13-5
9	4.3	9-6	22	8.7	13-11
10	4.6	9-9	23	9.2	14-5
11	5.0	10-2	24	9.8	15-1
12	5.2	10-4			

Reading grades are in years and tenths; readings ages in years and months.

SOURCE: from *Gates Basic Reading Tests*. (New York: Teachers College Press, Teachers College, Columbia University, © 1958 by Arthur I. Gates.) Reproduced by permission of the publisher.

with tests at the elementary school level. It seems quite straightforward to report that a student's achievement in arithmetic is similar to that of the average pupil in the third month of grade 4. There is a problem, however, if one accepts the literal meaning of age and grade scores. Developmental rates are not the same in all curricular areas, and therefore the differences between average scores at successive grade levels vary across subject matter areas. Scores in reading, vocabulary, and other language skills generally have larger yearly differences than do scores in such subjects as arithmetic and the work-study skills. Because of this, student achievement in different subjects should not be compared in terms of age and grade scores. For example, it is quite possible that for grade 5 pupils a grade score in arithmetic of 6.5 could represent achievement just as outstanding as that in reading represented by a grade score of 7.5 or even 8.0. We will discuss a more appropriate approach for cross-subject comparisons later in this chapter.

All pupils earning the same grade or age score do not possess identical skills. An outstanding pupil in grade 3 and a low-achieving pupil in grade 7 could both receive grade equivalent scores of 5.0 on the same test, but these scores, though equal, could have been earned in different ways. The grade 3 pupil might have done extremely well on the items covering material that had been studied; on the other hand, the low-achieving older pupil might have answered questions on a wider range of topics but have done so less well than the grade 3 pupil. Although grade and age scores provide convenient scales for following pupil progress at the elementary school level, teachers must take care not to make unwarranted assumptions about the meaning of the scores.

LEARNING EXERCISES

16. Refer to the table of norms for the *Gates Basic Reading Test*.
    a. What reading grades and reading ages would correspond to scores 9, 16, and 23?
    b. Reading grade 5.6 corresponds to reading age 10-8; reading grade 7.6 corresponds to reading age 12-11. How do you explain this apparent discrepancy?
17. Plot the age and grade scores in Table 3.3 on a graph with the age scores on the vertical axis and grade scores on the horizontal axis. Do the points form a straight line? What does the shape of the line suggest?

Profiles

One practical use of standardized test results is called *profile analysis.* This is a comparison of an individual pupil's performance on a variety of tests. A standardized achievement battery is usually comprised of separate subtests in the major curricular areas, and it is useful to a teacher to know how well a pupil does in each area. Percentile ranks provide a convenient basis for this type of comparison, and many test publishers encourage profile analysis through percentile ranks by providing forms for plotting each pupil's profile.

Figure 3.3 shows a report intended for distribution to parents. The re-

Figure 3.3   Profile Chart for a High School Achievement Battery

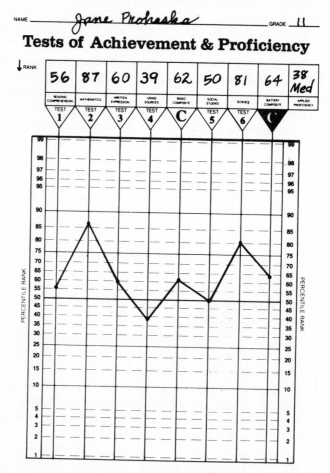

port is for a pupil in grade 11. The pupil's percentile ranks are written in the blanks at the top of each column, and the points are plotted on the corresponding lines. The profile is constructed by connecting these points. In this example, the pupil is at or above the national median (50th percentile) for grade 11 pupils on all tests except Using Sources. The Battery Composite reflects overall achievement as measured by Tests 1–6, and the Basic Composite reflects performance on Tests 1–4; both are slightly above the norm. The Applied Proficiency score is not plotted, but "Med" indicates medium performance. The pattern or profile with peaks and valleys is typical of what is found among high school pupils.

It should be noted that the graph includes, in addition to the median or 50th percentile, solid lines for the 90th, 75th, 25th, and 10th percentiles. These are convenient reference points for interpreting a pupil's standing in comparison with national norms.

It is also possible to construct a profile for a class or group of pupils based on the average scores on each of the subtests of the battery, and the profile thus prepared shows the strengths and weaknesses of the class or group. It should be noted, however, that class or group averages should not be interpreted on the basis of pupil norms. For example, if the average percentile rank in a class were 75, the class probably would not be at the 75th percentile as compared with other *classes*. Some publishers provide norms for school averages to facilitate the interpretation of school performance; such norms vary markedly from norms for individual pupils, particularly in the high and low parts of the distributions.

A further word of caution is that a difference between scores on two tests is subject to influence from the errors associated with each of the tests and therefore is less reliable than a score on a single test. Since profiles reflect differences between scores on different subtests, caution should be exercised in order not to attribute undue significance to variations among the subtests included in the profile. The need for caution is increased, of course, if the subtest scores are based on a small number of items and therefore not highly reliable. As a general rule, scores from subtests with reliability coefficients less than .90 should be interpreted conservatively and regarded merely as a general indication of the achievement in a particular area, and profiles of such scores should be interpreted in only the most general terms.

The need to exercise caution in interpreting stanines, profiles, age scores, and grade scores applies with equal force in interpreting percentile ranks. In this instance, the small size of the unit may lead to attaching unwarranted significance to very small differences in the trait or characteristic reflected by the scale. To minimize this error, some publishers report norms in what are called *percentile bands*. A conversion table using percentile bands is shown in Table 3.4. These bands represent a range of values between which the theoretical true value for an actual

Table 3.4

Converted Score (Standard Score) and Percentile Band Norms for 1960 *Cooperative English Tests*—Total English

Converted score	Percentile band					
	Grade 9	Grade 10	Grade 11	Grade 12	Grade 13	Grade 14
182–183					99.7–99.9	99–99.9
180–181				99.7–99.9	99.1–99.9	98–99.7
178–179				99.4–99.9	98–99.7	96–99.2
176–177				99–99.7	96–99.1	93–98
174–175		99.6–99.9	99.5–99.9	98–99.4	93–98	88–96
172–173	99.8–99.9	99.2–99.9	99–99.8	96–99	89–96	84–93
170–171	99.4–99.9	98–99.6	97–99.5	95–98	83–93	78–88
168–169	99–99.8	97–99.2	95–99	92–96	77–89	70–84
166–167	98–99.4	96–98	92–97	89–95	71–83	61–78
164–165	97–99	93–97	88–95	85–92	63–77	53–70
162–163	94–98	90–96	83–92	79–89	56–71	44–61
160–161	92–97	86–93	78–88	74–85	48–63	35–53
158–159	88–94	81–90	72–83	68–79	39–56	27–44
156–157	84–92	76–86	65–78	61–74	32–48	21–35
154–155	79–88	69–81	58–72	54–68	26–39	16–27
152–153	73–84	62–76	51–65	47–61	21–32	11–21
150–151	66–79	55–69	44–58	40–54	16–26	7–16
...						
138–139	20–36	14–26	9–18	6–14	1–4	0.5–1
136–137	14–28	10–19	6–13	3–10	0.8–2	0.5–0.8
134–135	8–20	6–14	3–9	2–6	0.4–1	0.4–0.5
132–133	4–14	3–10	2–6	1–3	0.2–0.8	0.3–0.5
130–131	2–8	2–6	0.7–3	0.5–2	0.1–0.4	0.2–0.4
128–129	0.9–4	0.6–3	0.4–2	0.2–1	0.1–0.2	0.1–0.3
126–127	0.3–2	0.2–2	0.1–0.7	0.1–0.5		0.1–0.2
124–125	0.1–0.9	0.1–0.6	0.1–0.4	0.1–0.2		
122–123	0.1–0.3	0.1–0.2				
120–121						
Median	144	147.2	150.2	151.3	159.1	161.8
Lower quartile	137.7	140.3	143.1	144.0	152.1	155.7
Upper quartile	151.3	154.3	157.7	158.9	165.8	167.8

SOURCE: From Manual for Interpreting Scores, *Cooperative English Tests.* Copyright © 1960 by Educational Testing Service. All rights reserved. Adapted and reprinted by permission.

score is likely to fall. Thus, if the converted score of a student in grade 10 is 160, we can say with some confidence that the true score would lie between percentile ranks 86 and 93. The authors and producers of the *Cooperative English Tests* believe that percentile bands are more realistic and useful in interpreting individual scores on a test than percentile ranks because the latter give a false, or at least questionable, impression of accuracy. In other words, the percentile band is a more cautiously conservative interpretation. Although percentile bands have not been universally accepted, they are used widely enough now that classroom teachers should be able to interpret them.

Further study of Table 3.4 reveals that there are two types of derived scores shown there. Besides the percentile bands just referred to, the converted scores in the first column represent a type of standard score. If we look, for example, at the column for grade 12 and find the percentile band of 40–54, we see that this corresponds to a converted score of 150–151. In the same column, the percentile band of 74–85 corresponds to a converted score of 160–161. This suggests that the standard scale used here for grade 12 has a mean of 150 and a standard deviation of 10. Similar values can be determined for each grade column.

LEARNING EXERCISES

18. By referring to Table 3.4, answer the following questions.
    a. What is the percentile band of a converted score of 153 for ninth-grade students? for eleventh-grade students? for first-year college students?
    b. What converted score does a student in the tenth grade have to make in order to be in percentile band 69–81? What converted score is required in the twelfth grade to achieve approximately the same standing?
    c. Between what two grades does the greatest average improvement on this test occur? How do you account for this?
19. What is the basis for the statement that the converted score scale for grade 12 has a mean of 150 and a standard deviation of 10? Can you support these statistics by reference to another part of the grade 12 scale? By reference to figures for another grade? Prove it.

The term *norm* has been defined as the average performance on a test by a defined group. In this chapter we have considered various ways in which norms can be described. Age and grade scores are norms; the average standard score earned by a carefully defined group is a norm, and the 50th percentile would be the norm for a group in which percentile ranks had been determined. It should be emphasized, however, that norms are

Norms as a Basis for Comparisons: Cautions

not standards for performance by every member of a class or group. That is, in almost any group there will be some below, some at, and some above the norm. It would be unrealistic and undesirable to expect all students to achieve the norm. Gifted children should obviously be expected to earn scores substantially above the norm, and pupils with learning disabilities or disadvantages have achieved exceptionally well if they earn scores as high as the norm. An important aspect of individualized instruction is the establishment of individual goals for all pupils.

Norms for tests are developed to assist teachers and others interpret test scores. Careful and expensive programs are conducted to establish norms for standardized tests. Great care is taken to select samples for the norming program that will be representative of the groups for which the test is intended. Factors such as sex, socioeconomic status, size and type of community, geographic location, and other individual and group factors that may affect test performance are carefully controlled in the selection of the sample. In spite of the care that is taken, however, truly representative national samples are very difficult to obtain. Some schools that are drawn at random by the test publisher are unable to participate in a standardization program for a variety of legitimate reasons. This fact, and the difficulty of controlling all relevant factors, limits the representativeness of any sample. In spite of these limitations, national norms provide the best basis, all things considered, for interpreting results obtained by use of standardized tests.

To avoid some of the difficulties encountered in establishing national norms, and to provide norms appropriate in a particular situation or for a particular purpose, sectional, regional, or perhaps more broadly differentiated norms are sometimes established. This means simply that norms are based on a defined group from a particular geographical region, a defined type of community, a particular ethnic or racial group, or the like. This does not eliminate all the problems encountered in trying to establish national norms, but it does reduce their number, so that for any defined group fewer factors need be taken into account. Such a procedure implies the establishment of norms for many different groups or purposes. Therefore, larger communities or school systems may set up local norms based on their own school population by means of locally constructed tests or standardized tests. Local norms are restricted by definition to a particular community or area. Where the school population is small and perhaps atypical, they probably are of quite limited value and may even be misleading. Local norms, of course, do not permit comparisons with schools or populations outside the local community, which is one of the chief advantages of norms based on a broader sampling.

Different types of norms can be useful for different purposes, and local and national norms can be used in a complementary fashion. If one wishes to compare progress of different pupils who have been exposed to the same educational opportunities, local norms may be quite useful. In addition to this type of comparison, there is usually an interest in comparing local performance with the performance of students across the country. For this purpose, national norms are necessary.

SUGGESTED READING

BAUERNFEIND, ROBERT H. *Building a School Testing Program.* Boston: Houghton Mifflin, 1969. Chaps. 3 and 4. A good discussion of the development and use of local stanine norms. Tables are given for the number of students who should receive each stanine in groups of different size. Chapter 4 has a thorough discussion of the meaning of correlation.

ENGELHART, MAX D. *Using Stanines in Interpreting Test Scores.* Test Service Notebook 28. New York: Harcourt Brace Jovanovich, 1963. A discussion of strengths and weaknesses of grade scores, percentile ranks, and standard scores, followed by presentation of the various uses of stanines in interpreting scores on tests. Concludes with summary of advantages of stanines and some cautions regarding their limitations.

GRUNLUND, NORMAN E. *Measurement and Evaluation in Teaching.* 3d ed. New York: Macmillan, 1976. Chap. 15. A thorough presentation of the types of norms used with standardized tests, in which profile analysis, local norms, and cautions in interpreting test scores are particularly good.

HILLS, JOHN R. *Measurement and Evaluation in the Classroom.* Columbus, Ohio: Charles E. Merrill Pub. Co., 1976. Chap. 11. A discussion of derived scores and methods to assist in the interpretation of test performance. Includes discussion of common errors made in test score interpretation.

LYMAN, HOWARD B. *Test Scores and What They Mean,* 2d ed. Englewood Cliffs, N.J.: Prentice-Hall, 1971. Chap. 5. A simple and practical consideration of the use of norms, including directions for reading tables of norms of different types. Chapter 6 describes derived scores and a scheme for classifying types of derived scores. Chapter 8 illustrates profiles from several tests.

LEMKE, ELMER, and WILLIAM WIERSMA. *Principles of Psychological Measurement.* Chicago: Rand McNally, 1976. Chap. 3. Considers z-scores and T-scores with examples of computational procedures. Also includes a discussion of percentile norms and age and grade scores.

MARTUZA, VICTOR R. *Applying Norm-Referenced and Criterion-Referenced Measurement in Education.* Boston: Allyn and Bacon,

1977. Chapter 3 covers percentage scores and interrelationships of various types of scores. Chapter 11 covers norms and norms tables for standardized tests.

MEHRENS, WILLIAM A., and IRVIN J. LEHMANN. *Standardized Tests in Education*, 2d ed. New York: Holt, Rinehart and Winston, 1975. Brief but good on the interpretation of scores in standardized tests. Chapter 6 covers the broader aspects of evaluation, including the interpretation of test scores to the community. Some important issues are covered fairly.

STANLEY, JULIAN C., and KENNETH D. HOPKINS. *Educational and Psychological Measurement and Evaluation*. Englewood Cliffs, N.J.: Prentice-Hall, 1972. Chap. 3. A different and interesting description of norms, how they are established, and how they can be used. The presentation complements very well the material in this book.

THORNDIKE, ROBERT L., and ELIZABETH HAGEN. *Measurement and Evaluation in Psychology and Education*, 4th ed. New York: John Wiley & Sons, 1977. Chap. 4. A thorough and rigorous treatment of many important topics related to norms. Especially useful to students using this textbook are comparisons among types of norms and use of norms for group and individual student interpretations.

Four

FINDING AND SELECTING
GOOD MEASURING INSTRUMENTS

In this chapter we discuss a problem of concern to all who want to use a test for a specific purpose or in a specific situation. In deciding which test to use, one should not rely on hearsay or the opinions of individuals who have little actual knowledge of measurement. A test should not, for example, be chosen, purchased, and used simply because it is recommended by another teacher, principal, or counselor. When a test is selected in this manner, there is at least a fair chance that it will not be entirely appropriate or satisfactory. In most cases, if the testing is not successful, there is a danger that the test itself may be condemned when actually its failure may result from the fact that it was not intended for the purpose or situation for which it was used.[1]

This chapter has been planned to enable you intelligently to answer measurement questions such as the following:

1. How do I go about locating tests to help answer specific questions such as these:

    a. Is there a reliable test for measuring the interests of high school seniors?

    b. What is a good test to use for estimating the chances that a student will succeed in college?

    c. How can I locate tests that will identify the specific reading skills in which my students are deficient?

---

[1]Although the discussion in this chapter is largely about published standardized tests, the principles presented also apply, to a considerable extent, to measuring instruments and devices of all types.

d. Is there a test that will identify the students who have already mastered the objectives of our fifth-grade mathematics curriculum?

e. How does the science achievement of students in our schools compare with that of students in other schools?

2. What do I need to know about the tests available for a particular purpose in order to select one for use? Where is this information to be found?

3. How are correlation coefficients used to estimate the validity and reliability of tests? How large must these coefficients be to be acceptable?

4. What evidence of test validity would be most important in selecting a test to answer each of the different questions posed in question 1?

5. What are the steps in building a standardized test?

PRELIMINARY CONSIDERATIONS

An all-important first step in selecting a test for a particular purpose is to specify in detail what information is needed. A general statement of a problem or a question about tests, such as the questions posed in the preceding paragraph, will usually suggest the general type of test needed. Knowing that an aptitude test, an achievement test, or an interest inventory is needed does not, however, give us much direction in choosing a particular test. Suppose that an elementary teacher has questions about the achievement of a class of students. Just what should the results of an achievement test reveal about the students' achievement? A basic question is whether the teacher is primarily interested in finding out how the achievement of students in this class compares with that of other students or whether, by contrast, the teacher mainly wants to find out how well students have mastered the specific objectives of instruction.

Norm-Referenced and Criterion-Referenced Measurement

Comparing the achievement of particular students with that of other students requires a test that provides information about the scores of a reference group of students. In earlier chapters we noted that such a reference group is called a norm group, and when we use norms to interpret test scores we use what is called norm-referenced measurement. Most published tests are norm-referenced, but as more and more instructional programs are being designed to help students master sets of specific objectives, publishers have begun to provide for a different interpretation of achievement test results.

When students' achievement with respect to their mastery of each of a set of specific objectives is to be evaluated, the test must identify each of the objectives tested in terms of a set of instructionally relevant tasks that the students are expected to perform. Then it must give results that tell which students have achieved some minimum level of performance (the criterion level) on tasks for each different objective. The test items for an objective are a sample of these tasks. A suitable test measures the ability of a certain group of students to perform the particular tasks specified in the objectives that have been set for these students. This is the approach to testing and test interpretation that is called criterion-referenced or objectives-referenced measurement. The students' performance is evaluated by comparing their achievement not to that of a reference or norm group but to a specified criterion—such as four out of five correct solutions to relevant tasks or items—for a specific performance objective—such as letter discrimination, letter blending, or following written directions.

In the considerable debate in recent years over the relative merits of norm-referenced and criterion-referenced measurement, the important consideration is whether a chosen test will give the information that is needed to answer the questions that have been asked. One's purposes may, for example, require comparisons like those used with both norm-referenced and criterion-referenced instruments. A teacher may wish to compare the students of a class with the students of other schools on the number and type of objectives that have been mastered. This would require comparing student test performances with criteria for the mastery of objectives (a criterion-referenced interpretation). The same teacher may also wish to compare the number of objectives mastered by the students of this class, individually and as a group, to norms that give the average number of objectives mastered by a large, representative group of students (a norm-referenced interpretation). The percentage of students in the class group who have mastered each different objective might also be compared with the percentage of students in the norm group who have mastered the same objective.

A teacher may recognize the need for a norm-referenced achievement test or a criterion-referenced test or both, but this does not completely specify what is needed. The teacher still needs to outline or otherwise define the particular items of content and skill that the test must measure if it is to allow a valid evaluation of what students have achieved. If, in addition, one wishes to be able to diagnose student difficulties or plan future instructional changes, it will be necessary to specify the number and type of reliable subscores that the test should yield.[2] A teacher

The Importance of Specificity

---

[2]Tests designed to yield a single overall estimate of a student's achievement in a given subject or content area are called *survey tests*. Tests designed to isolate specific strengths and weaknesses in a student's achievement are called *diagnostic tests* (Chapter 8). Either type may be norm-referenced or criterion-referenced, depending on whether scores are interpreted with respect to norms or to performance criteria.

cannot be too specific about what information is needed from a test and we cannot overemphasize the importance of this analysis as a prerequisite of test selection.

How a
Standardized
Test Is
Produced

Assuming that the purpose of testing and the specific information that tests should yield are known, how does one proceed to select a particular test? In the remainder of the chapter we will consider this question in two major divisions: (1) the sources of information about available measuring instruments and (2) the characteristics of good measuring instruments. A brief description of the stages in the production of a standardized test should provide a useful focus for the discussions in these major divisions.

In Chapter 1 we briefly defined the term *standardized test*. Here we will describe the development of standardized achievement tests. The steps in preparing and producing high-quality tests are generally similar for both norm-referenced and criterion-referenced instruments, but there are some differences in the way each step is actually taken. We will give more information on developing other published measuring instruments —aptitude tests, personality tests, interest inventories—in later chapters.

The first step in developing a standardized achievement test is to draw up a plan or set of specifications for the proposed test. This is usually done by the authors of the test alone or in consultation with a committee that may include experts in test construction, specialists in subject matter, classroom teachers, and school supervisors. The personnel of such committees varies, of course, with the nature and purposes of each test. In any case, for a norm-referenced test, typical specifications include statements of the purposes of the test, the content or constructs to be measured, the grade or age levels for which the test is intended, tentative decisions regarding the length of time for administration of the test, the number of parallel forms to be built, and the types of items to be used.

The plan of specifications for a criterion-referenced test additionally includes an inventory of objectives that describes what the student is expected to do and the number of item tasks for each objective. A systematic plan for constructing or selecting item tasks to insure a representative sample is made, and the standards of performance that must be attained on the items if the objective is to be considered mastered (for example, that 80 percent of the questions must be answered correctly or that some portion of the test must be completed in less than two minutes) are stated.

Developing specifications for a standardized test of achievement in any school subject is particularly important if the test is to be maximally useful. To this end, a careful and systematic analysis of textbooks, courses of study, and other widely used instructional materials is made to determine the common learning on which the test is to be based. Since the test is based essentially on the elements of content or behavior that are widely taught in a given subject, it can be used in many different schools and localities.

Once the specifications have been formulated, the next step is to prepare test items. Item preparation is usually the responsibility of the authors of the test, although it is becoming increasingly common to involve experts, usually provided by the prospective publisher of the test. It is customary to prepare nearly twice as many items as one expects to use in the final forms, to insure that a sufficient number of useful items will survive tryout and item analysis. It is important that a sufficient variety of items remain if the required content, constructs, or (for criterion-referenced tests) objectives are to be measured adequately by each form.

After items have been prepared and carefully edited, they are allocated to what are called preliminary or trial forms. An attempt is made to distribute the items to achieve balance between forms with respect to content and estimated overall difficulty. These preliminary forms are duplicated or printed with detailed instructions for administering and scoring.

The preliminary forms are then administered to a sample of pupils in the age or grade range for which the test is intended. Since this tryout is not to establish norms, the population need not be as widely representative nor as large as that used later for norming purposes. Usually the trial forms are given to a sample of several hundred pupils or subjects per grade or year of age in perhaps a half-dozen schools in different localities.

After the preliminary forms have been given to the population sample, they are scored, generally by the prospective publisher through a scoring service. When these preliminary forms have been scored, the items are analyzed for difficulty and discrimination. The first of these tells what percentage of students answered each item correctly. The second indicates how well the item differentiates between the more able and the less able persons who took the preliminary forms. Further statistical analyses also reveal how well-balanced the preliminary forms are with respect to content, range of scores, central tendency or averages, and correlations.

Efforts to improve the item quality of criterion-referenced tests also give attention to an item's sensitivity to instruction—that is, its ability to discriminate among students who have received differing amounts of instruction relevant to the objective. Student performance on a "good" item will be better after instruction than before. One approach to measuring an item's sensitivity to instruction is to give the same or equivalent items repeatedly during the course of instruction until students demonstrate mastery of an objective. A record is kept of the number of times each student passes and fails an item. A desired pattern of passing (P) and failing (F) an item by an individual student as instruction progresses would be Fail, Fail, Pass, Pass (FFPP); an undesirable pattern would be PFFP. This approach to measuring item sensitivity can be used only if carryover effects from one testing to the next can be minimized or corrected.

From these analyses and careful scrutiny of individual items, two or more parallel forms are constructed. If a sufficient number of items have been written for three preliminary forms, these may now be reduced to two final forms by using only the best items. Instructions for administering are carefully revised to fit the final forms; new scoring keys are devised; and all the materials are printed, except for the manual, which comes last.

The next major step, constructing the norms, is essential in interpreting scores for norm-referenced but not criterion-referenced tests. For norming purposes, a sample population has to be carefully drawn, taking into account geographical location, type of community, ethnic and socioeconomic characteristics. The sample should be as broadly representative as possible within reasonable and practical limits. Once the sample has been drawn, letters to the schools or groups chosen request their cooperation in giving the test for the purpose of establishing norms. It is customary, in inducing cooperation, to offer the tests and scoring at minimal or no cost. Responses are generally affirmative, although it is by no means rare for schools or other groups to decline. Since the test is usually given for norming purposes near the end of the school year, schools occasionally decline because of the press of other activities. It is customary to approach prospective collaborators early in the fall so that they can plan for testing well in advance.

After the test has been given and scored, the results are collated, usually by the publisher, to develop tables of norms and to determine other statistics such as reliability coefficients, standard errors of measurement, and correlations between forms and with other measures such as IQ scores. Publishers commonly furnish an intelligence test along with the test being standardized, both as an additional inducement to cooperate and as a useful adjunct to the new test.

The final step in standardizing is the preparation of the manual. This includes statements of the rationale of the test, its purposes, and the procedures used in developing it; an analysis of the content in relation to instructional objectives; detailed instructions for administering, scoring, and interpreting; tables of norms; statistics on reliability, validity, and other matters as deemed necessary; and suggestions for using the results.

Criterion-referenced tests are frequently packaged in new ways to facilitate their use in individualizing instruction. The tests may, for example, be published on duplicating machine masters so that each teacher can make only as many copies of parts that measure a given objective as are needed. Objectives or even items are sometimes cross-referenced to curriculum materials so that the teacher may direct students who fail to master an objective to relevant materials for additional instruction.

Standardization programs are complex, and this account should give some notion of the time and effort required to produce a standardized test. People who are not involved in such programs may be surprised to learn that the time required to produce a standardized test is usually between three and five years, and the cost of producing such a test may run into thousands of dollars. For these reasons it is obvious that revision of a standardized test, requiring almost as much time and money as production of the original, is not undertaken lightly or more frequently than is deemed absolutely necessary to keep a test current.

SOURCES OF INFORMATION

For a preliminary survey of the tests available for any purpose, publishers' catalogues are invaluable.[3] Most catalogues supply enough information to give the prospective purchaser a fairly complete overview of each test without going into great detail. These catalogues are free upon request. All the publishers listed in Appendix C are reputable firms that gladly send catalogues or lists of tests upon request. When corresponding with publishers about tests or test literature, one should write on school stationery, stating one's official connection or position, because publishing firms do not usually send such materials to unauthorized persons.

Publishers' Catalogues

The catalogues and other advertising material distributed by the test publishers generally contain fairly objective and reliable information about each test. Usually included are brief statements concerning such matters as the purpose for which the test is intended, cost, number of equivalent forms, grade level for which the test is appropriate, and types of norms available. Most test publishers are restrained from making false or exaggerated claims for a test by the very keen competition in this field and by the certainty that a test must prove to be good during a period of

---

[3]Another way to begin a survey is with a list of tests of the desired type that have been reviewed favorably in Oscar K. Buros, *Mental Measurements Yearbook,* which is described later in this section.

Figure 4.1

A Typical Test Description from a Publisher's Catalogue

NELSON-DENNY READING TEST

James I. Brown, M. J. Nelson, E. C. Denny

COPYRIGHT: 1973

FORMS: C and D

GRADES: 9-12; college; adult

TIME: 30 minutes.

- ■ Results of this widely used test help to diagnose reading problems, to determine potential for general academic success, and to classify incoming high school or college students or prospective employees

- ■ **Both vocabulary and reading comprehension** plus **reading rate** are measured

- ■ The test is easily administered in a single class period

- ■ Special **cut-time administration** (22½ minutes) is possible for use with superior students and with adults in speed reading classes

- ■ Comparable Forms C and D, contemporary in content, make retesting convenient

- ■ Score conversions provided are percentile ranks and grade equivalents

- ■ **Examiner's Manual** contains all technical information, including special norms for adults and for cut-time administration

- ■ For regular administration, student report folders are available

- ■ **Self-interpreting reading profiles** are available for use with cut-time adult norms

- ■ When used with the Nelson Reading Test, continuous measurement of reading ability from Grade 3 through the adult level is provided

- ■ **Houghton Mifflin Scoring Service,** which electronically scores *MRC answer cards,* provides a variety of useful reports

ITEM AND PACKAGING	CODE NO.	SCHOOL PRICE
Test Booklets (pkg. 35)		
No other materials included. Answer cards or answer sheets and Examiner's Manual must be ordered separately.		
Form C	9-72676	9.81
Form D	9-72678	9.81
MRC Answer Cards, Forms C and D (box of 100)		
Includes 1 Order Form for Scoring Service, 10 ID Cards	9-72867	6.18
Self-Marking Answer Sheets, Forms C and D (pkg. 35)		
Includes 1 Manual, 1 Class Record Sheet, 35 Student Report Folders ("Your Personal Record").	9-72680	10.26
Self-Marking Answer Sheets, Forms C and D (pkg. 250)		
No other materials included.	9-72681	35.76
IBM 1230 Answer Sheets, Forms C and D (pkg. 500)		
No other materials included.	9-72686	45.78
IBM 1230 Scoring Masks (single copy)		
Form C	9-72687	1.17
Form D	9-72688	1.17
Digitek Answer Sheets, Forms C and D, not pre-coded (pkg. 500)		
No other materials included.	9-72690	60.51
Digitek Scoring Masks (single copy)		
Form C	9-72691	1.17
Form D	9-72692	1.17
Class Record Sheets (pkg. 35)	9-72695	2.64
Examiner's Manual	9-72693	1.80
Student Report Folders, "Your Personal Record" (pkg. 35) — for use in grades 9-16	9-72699	2.64
Self-Interpreting Reading Profiles (pkg. 35) — for use with cut-time adult norms	9-72697	2.64
Examination Kit	9-72700	2.64

From description of *Nelson-Denny Reading Test,* Forms C & D, by James I. Brown, M. J. Nelson, and E. C. Denny, published by Houghton Mifflin Company, © 1973. In *1978 Catalog of Tests and Scoring Services,* Houghton Mifflin Company, pp. 45–46.

several years if it is to show a profit. Critical reviews by test specialists who are often in a position to recommend tests also lead publishers to be conservative in advancing claims for the quality of their tests. The sample entry shown in Figure 4.1 was taken verbatim from the catalogue of a publisher to illustrate the types of statements usually found in test publishers' catalogues.

Specimen Sets

Although test publishers' catalogues provide valuable information about their tests, they do not make possible a thorough and adequate comparison when a choice must be made between several tests presumably equally suitable for a given purpose. For example, let us suppose that a search of several catalogues for available reading tests for intermediate grades has revealed at least three on the market. It would not be possible to make an intelligent choice without more information than is provided in the respective publishers' catalogues. The best way to obtain more information is to ask the publisher of each of the three tests for a specimen set. Such a set, usually costing a dollar or two, will include a copy of the test, the manual, a scoring key, and perhaps other accessory material such as a class record sheet. Now it is possible to examine the test for content, length, and appropriateness for local conditions. The prospective user may even want to take each test to become thoroughly familiar with it.

Although the test itself is perhaps the most interesting item in a specimen set, it is the manual that provides the data for a critical evaluation. A good manual will contain information about purposes, procedures of development, plan of organization, directions for administering and scoring, validity and reliability, norms and scales, interpretation of scores, and use of results. All these are useful criteria in comparing standardized tests and making a selection. Lack of information regarding the meeting of these criteria or evident failure to meet any of them may be sufficient reason for eliminating a test from consideration.

With specimen sets one can make a careful appraisal and comparison of each test under consideration. There is no better way to do this short of actual experience in using a test over a period of time.

Several test publishers periodically issue, free to users, series of short articles about practical problems of testing. Several others who formerly did so have recently discontinued the practice for reasons of economy. Examples of currently available titles that are particularly useful to school personnel are:

Free Materials

Making the Classroom Test: A Guide for Teachers, rev. ed. (Princeton, N.J.: Educational Testing Service, 1973)

Martin Katz, *Selecting an Achievement Test*, rev. ed. (Princeton, N.J.: Educational Testing Service, 1973)

Paul B. Diederich, *Short-Cut Statistics for Teacher-Made Tests*, rev. ed. (Princeton, N.J.: Educational Testing Service, 1973)

Blythe C. Mitchell, *A Glossary of Measurement Terms*, rev. ed., Test Service Notebook 13 (New York: Harcourt Brace Jovanovich, 1971)

Roger T. Lennon, *Testing: Bond or Barrier Between Pupil and Teacher?* Test Service Notebook 82 (New York: Harcourt Brace Jovanovich, n.d.)

Lois E. Burrill, *How a Standardized Test Is Built*, Test Service Notebook 125 (New York: Harcourt Brace Jovanovich, n.d.)

Jerome E. Doppelt, *How Accurate Is a Test Score?* Test Service Bulletin 50 (New York: Psychological Corp., 1956)

James H. Ricks, Jr., *On Telling Parents About Test Results*, Test Service Bulletin 54 (New York: Psychological Corp., 1959)

Harold G. Seashore, *The Identification of the Gifted*, Test Service Bulletin 55 (New York: Psychological Corp., 1963)

James H. Ricks, Jr., *Local Norms—When and Why*, Test Service Bulletin 58 (New York: Psychological Corp., 1971)

Such articles apply the results of test research to the problems of teacher, counselor, or administrator. Copies of the articles listed are free and, although intended to help the sales of the respective publishing houses, they are worth the thoughtful consideration of every person interested in problems of measurement.

University Research and Service Bureaus

Most universities have an office or bureau to which prospective users of tests may turn for advice and help. The members of the staff of such an organization are frequently able to lend copies of available tests from their files and give advice on the strengths and weaknesses of various tests. They are usually willing to meet with and help committees of school personnel authorized to choose tests for particular purposes. Such bureaus nearly always have files of test publishers' catalogues and specimen sets or copies of many published standardized tests. The persons in charge of these organizations are often experienced test technicians and supervisors who can help inexperienced school people avoid mistakes and save time and money.

However, one should not rely too much on the help of such individuals, expert though they may be. Ideally, every teacher and counselor should be qualified to appraise and select tests objectively in the light of her or his own situation.

The persons connected with test and research bureaus, the instructors in courses in measurement, and even representatives of test publishers whose job it is to help people select the best tests for the purpose at hand seldom try to force a particular test on anyone. These specialists usually follow the more ethical procedure of making available several different tests with information about each, permitting the prospective user to choose the one best suited to the needs of the situation.

Mental Measurements Yearbooks

The meticulous user of tests often wants even more information than that obtainable from the sources already mentioned. Having examined catalogues and specimen sets of tests and talked with colleagues and perhaps even with an expert, one may still be undecided and want more facts. The best and most complete source of evaluative data on tests is the *Mental Measurements Yearbook*, new editions of which are published at frequent invervals.[4] The Yearbooks have earned a unique position in measurement literature. Each edition contains impartial, critical reviews of the majority of available standardized tests. Moreover, the more widely used tests are reviewed in successive editions of the Yearbook to show how the tests compare over a period of years. No equally objective, reliable, and comprehensive source of information and expert opinion concerning published tests is available.

Certain journals, such as *Educational and Psychological Measurement*, the *Journal of Educational Measurement*, and the *Journal of Counseling Psychology*, publish test reviews that are generally more useful to a test specialist or research worker than to a classroom teacher or guidance counselor. However, when the prospective user of a test is undecided, the reviews in such periodicals and in the *Mental Measurements Yearbooks* may help materially in reaching a decision. It is much easier to find commentary on a particular test in the Yearbooks, since the reviews are contained in one volume. In the periodicals, of course, the reviews appear in various issues.

Other Periodical Reviews

Having consulted all or most of the sources of information about tests, one should be in a position to make a choice. The prospective user has first found out what is available to meet the needs and has gathered information about the tests that seem to be possibilities. When this information has been related to the situation in which the test is to function and the purposes for which it is to be used and when a test has been selected, the prospective user will have done everything possible to insure success and efficiency, short of actually using the test. What we should consider when selecting from the tests that appear to be good possibilities will be discussed in more detail in the section that follows.

LEARNING EXERCISES

1. Examine catalogues of several test publishers. How complete are the entries for each test? How do they compare in different catalogues?

---

[4]Oscar K. Buros (ed), *The Eighth Mental Measurements Yearbook* (Highland Park, N.J.: Gryphon Press, 1978).

2. Examine an entry for a test in Buros's *Tests in Print*. What information is provided? How is it organized? How does it differ from that provided by the *Mental Measurements Yearbook*?
3. Ask your instructor for a specimen set of a standardized test. Examine it for information about the criteria on page 87. Do you consider it adequate? In what respects, if any, do you consider it inadequate?
4. Read the reviews of a particular standardized test (perhaps the one used in Exercise 2) in the latest edition of the *Mental Measurements Yearbook*. Write a short evaluation of the test, basing it upon the Yearbook reviews.

CHARACTERISTICS OF A GOOD MEASURING INSTRUMENT

After studying the information available from the sources described above, how does one select one of the several tests available from reputable publishers? We shall assume that the tests under consideration appear to be equally suited to local conditions and that the strengths and weaknesses of the tests are fairly well balanced in their obvious and non-technical features. What, then, are the basic criteria of a more technical nature that may be used as guides in selecting a test or other measuring device?

All good measuring instruments have certain primary qualities in common. These are the universals—the qualities that differentiate good tests from inferior ones—whether they are to be used by the educator, the psychologist, the medical technician, the physicist, or people in other fields. A test that lacks a known and substantial degree of these primary qualities is not a measuring instrument in any true sense, and little or no dependence can be placed on results obtained by its use. The two generally accepted universals are *validity* and *reliability*.

Besides these two universal requirements for a good test, whatever the field, certain secondary characteristics are desirable in all good educational and psychological tests: *objectivity, ease of administering, ease of scoring,* and *ease of interpreting*. These characteristics are far less crucial than validity and reliability, but they affect validity and reliability to some extent, and in any event they make the use of a test much simpler.

In addition to these secondary characteristics, valuable in all educational and psychological tests, certain other attributes present in good standardized tests distinguish such tests from the informal, unstandardized, or teacher-made tests. These attributes are *adequate norms, equivalent forms,* and *economy*. They are important for any good standardized test, although they are seldom applicable to unstandardized tests. Norms are not essential for criterion-referenced tests—that is, tests that are to be used only to assess the mastery of clearly specified minimum objectives.

Of the two primary requisites of good measurement—those we have referred to as universals—validity is generally regarded as the more important. Validity has traditionally been defined as the degree to which a test measures what it is intended to measure. In this statement, *intended* may refer to the purposes for which tests are used as well as those for which they were designed. Both must be considered. For this reason the following definition may be more generally satisfactory: *Validity* is the effectiveness of a test for the purposes for which it is used. The meaning of validity in a testing situation may be elucidated by such questions as these: What does this test actually measure? To what extent does it measure a particular ability, quality, or trait? In what situation or under what condition does it have this degree of validity? In short, the question is essentially: To what degree does the test do the job it is intended to do?

Validity

In constructing achievement tests, for example, an attempt is usually made to measure important outcomes of instruction, such as computation ability in arithmetic. To the extent that a test does measure the degree of attainment of this objective, it is considered to have validity. To the extent that it measures something else, perhaps reading ability, its validity as a measure of computational ability is lessened.

A test used to predict success in college or university work is valid to the extent that the people who make higher scores on it get better marks, stay in school longer, and are more likely to graduate than those who get lower scores. A test used to measure musical aptitude is valid to the extent that it distinguishes between persons who will succeed in varying degrees in musical careers.

From the foregoing it is clear that validity is specific to both the purpose and situation for which a test is used. A test might be a highly valid measure of intelligence for third-grade children and decreasingly valid for this purpose for fifth-graders, ninth-graders, high-school graduates, and college seniors. A test of manual dexterity might be a highly valid measure of probable success in assembling parts of small electric motors but decreasingly valid for predicting success in farming, selling automobiles, managing a publishing establishment, or teaching mathematics. A test that measures the thinking ability of seventh-grade pupils might well be almost a pure memory test for older persons who have been out of school for a long time. Thus, a test may be highly valid for one purpose and almost wholly lacking in validity for another. In the same way that a thermometer is used to measure temperature only and a barometer is used to measure atmospheric pressure only, each valid testing instrument provides measurement for its intended use.

Validity for any use is always a matter of degree. We do not ordinarily speak of a test as being completely valid or entirely invalid for any given use. Our concern is, rather, *how* valid is it, or how well does it serve the purpose it is intended to serve? Does it do so extremely well, to a reasonable degree, or very little? To answer this question, in educational and psychological measurement we often employ the correlation techniques described in Chapter 2.

With these preliminary and basic considerations, we may discuss different concepts of validity and methods of determining the degree of validity of a particular technique of measurement or test. A national committee has described three types of validity information that it has named *content validity, criterion-related validity,* and *construct validity.*[5] This terminology has been widely adopted. We will now define and illustrate each type of validity and discuss appropriate methods for determining it.

CONTENT VALIDITY   When a teacher gives a test that measures appropriately the content and behavior that are the objectives of instruction in a particular class, the test is said to have *content validity.* If a test has content validity, we are justified in making inferences from a person's test score about that person's probable performance in other situations like those represented by the test items.

Let us suppose that some of the rules for writing formulas of chemical compounds have been taught and illustrated with a variety of actual formulas showing how each one is written in accordance with the system of chemical symbols, the valence of the elements, and so on. After perhaps a week of such instruction, the instructor makes a test the questions of which are based on the same rules and on the same or similar formulas that have been taught. Under such circumstances the content validity of the test is assured.

The degree of content validity of a standardized test for general use is proportional to the extent to which it measures the goals of instruction and content that are common to courses of study and textbooks on the subject. Validity for general use does not guarantee, however, that a test will be valid in every situation. The validity of a test for measuring the

[5]Joint Committee of the American Psychological Association, American Educational Research Association, and National Council on Measurement in Education, *Standards for Educational and Psychological Tests* (Washington, D.C.: American Psychological Association, 1974).

achievement of students of a particular school with respect to the curriculum of that school depends on the extent that it measures what that school includes and emphasizes in its curriculum.[6]

A test must nearly always measure only a sampling of the universe of content available. An achievement test in American history, for example, could not possibly include items on every fact, concept, or task in the course of study or textbook or even those in which the student has had some instruction. It must, for obvious reasons, be restricted to a sampling of such content or objectives. The validity of the test therefore depends, in part at least, on the care exercised in sampling the universe of content available. When one is selecting a test, attention should be given to the description of how sampling was accomplished and the evidence of how well it was done.

Efforts to develop educational programs that teach understanding, interpretation, and application rather than mere memorization have focused attention on problems of verbalism, concerning which much has been said and written. Tests that measure only the ability to verbalize—that is, to repeat or identify what has been memorized—have little validity as tests of understanding or usage. The items of more valid tests will also include tasks that require students to demonstrate what they can do with what they have been taught.

The content validity of a standardized test for use in a particular class or school is best determined by a thorough inspection of the items of the test in relation to what has been taught. There is no numerical expression of this type of validity. It is a matter of judgment, and classroom teachers are often the best people qualified to make this judgment for their respective situations. Tests developed for use throughout the country always have some items not directly relevant to the curriculum in a given school, but in the authors' experience a test can usually be found that has at least 75 to 80 percent relevant items.

Content validity is extremely important in the selection of a criterion-referenced test, a test to assist the attainment of some specific criteria, standard of achievement, or objective. Statistical measures of the extent to which test performance is related to nontest criteria such as grades are not generally sought because test scores are not used to predict success in other situations. The items of a useful criterion-referenced test must be keyed to specific performance objectives, and there must be an adequate sample of items for each different objective. The test is expected to be a direct measure of the behavior we wish to evaluate.

[6]When achievement tests are to be judged by how well their content corresponds to the curriculum, as in these examples, content validity is often referred to as *curricular* validity.

CRITERION-RELATED VALIDITY *Criterion-related validity* is generally based on agreement between the *scores* on a test and some outside measure, called a *criterion*, such as graduation from college.[7] Criterion-related validity applies when we wish to infer from an individual test score the person's probable standing on another measure. Correlation between test scores and some other measure (marks, another test, ratings) *taken at or about the same time* may be referred to as *concurrent* validity. Correlation between test scores and some measure of performance or success *later* (graduation, success on the job) may be referred to as *predictive* validity. Criterion-related validity is a more general concept that applies to both. Because determining either depends on the observation and collection of data, another term for criterion-related validity is *empirical validity*.

Criterion-related validity requires some other acceptable measure or criterion of the same quality, ability, or trait as that which the test being validated purports to measure. It is widely used with tests of achievement, intelligence, and aptitude, since many other criteria of what these tests are designed to measure are readily available. The basic procedure is to determine the correlation between scores on the test and some criterion judged to be a valid measure of the same quality, ability, or trait. In the case of an achievement test in arithmetic, for example, a comparison of marks given in arithmetic with scores made by the pupils who took the test would be evidence of validity. It would be possible to work out a coefficient of correlation between the teacher's marks and the actual test scores as one measure of the validity of the test.

With intelligence tests, correlations between IQs and various measures of scholastic success are frequently cited as evidence of the validity of the tests. Similarly, correlations between test scores and ratings by teachers, between test scores and job success, and between test scores and results of other tests or measures judged to have validity are all commonly used as evidence of the degree of validity of tests.

Techniques other than correlation are also used in assessing criterion-related or empirical validity. For example, scores on a test of mechanical aptitude can be compared with performance in a particular line of work, such as auto mechanics. Criteria in this case might be success as measured by supervisors' ratings and advancement or permanence in the occupation. A personality inventory might be validated by comparing scores on it with clinical diagnoses or psychiatrists' judgments. In

[7]Criterion-related validity is estimated by relating test scores to another measure statistically. It should not be confused with *criterion-referenced tests*, which we have discussed earlier; that term refers not to evidence of validity but to an approach to testing and test interpretation that we have contrasted to norm-referenced tests. (See pp. 80–81.)

such instances it is customary to compare average test scores of people in widely spaced groups such as successful versus unsuccessful or well-adjusted versus poorly adjusted. In the case of a personality test, scores of people rated well-adjusted would be compared with scores of others judged to be poorly adjusted. If the average scores of these widely spaced groups differed significantly, this would be regarded as evidence of the validity of the test as a measure of adjustment.

The appropriateness of the criterion to which a test-maker relates test scores is centrally important when evaluating evidence of validity. If a test is intended to predict possible success in a profession such as teaching, for example, a test-developer may choose as the criterion of success such measures as grades in education courses, ratings by practice-teaching supervisors, principals' ratings of classroom performance, the achievement of students taught, or self-ratings of job satisfaction. None of these is entirely satisfactory, but some are clearly preferable to others, and a combination of several is probably better than any one alone.

Whatever the criteria for test validity, these should be described completely and accurately. Evidence should be presented to justify their use. The number and characteristics of the persons for whom validity data were obtained should be described fully so that potential users may judge whether the demonstrated validity is likely to hold for another situation. Ideally, we hope for evidence of the validity of a test when it is used with persons of the same age and educational situation as those we plan to test.

CONSTRUCT VALIDITY   The third type of validity is employed when a test author wishes to be able to use test scores to make inferences about the degree to which different individuals possess a hypothesized trait or quality. For example, performance on a test of sociability might be used to make inferences about the degree to which the person tested possesses a theoretically defined trait called sociability.

Basically, *construct validity* is concerned with the question of how well differences in test scores conform to predictions about individual characteristics that are based on an underlying theory or construct. This may sometimes be tested by empirical methods, but in the absence of criteria to which scores on the test can be related, it is necessary to resort to logic. Judgments of construct validity are in fact most often based on a combination of logical analyses and an accumulation of empirical studies designed to show that individuals with different test scores also differ in other ways that the theory predicts. A few examples may help to make this clear.

The well-known *Seashore Measures of Musical Talents* is a series of records presenting tasks of pitch discrimination, judgment of time intervals, identification of rhythm patterns, and other basic musical abilities. These are not generally the subject matter of instruction in music classes, yet the test author by logical analysis has resolved musical aptitude into a few fundamental traits or abilities. These constitute theoretical constructs of musical talent. The test represents the attempt to measure these abilities. Its validity may be thought of in two ways: first, as a measure of ability in pitch discrimination and the like and, second, as a measure for predicting success in a musical career. In both cases validity depends on the degree to which the test author's constructs account for musical talent and success. Similar examples can be drawn from mechanical aptitude and clerical aptitude. In each case the test is based on a theory about the qualities, abilities, or traits that enter into successful performance. The validity of the tests is proportional to the degree to which the tests reproduce and measure the actual skills involved.[8]

In intelligence tests, construct validity is attained to the extent that the tests contain tasks that actually require intelligence for successful performance. The nature of the tasks is usually arrived at by introspective, logical analysis. Alfred Binet, the originator of our present-day approach to the measurement of intelligence, was the first person to arrive at a logical analysis of what an intelligent act involves psychologically. He came to the conclusion that judgment, comprehension, and reasoning are the essentials of intelligence. Binet and his co-worker, Theodore Simon, devised tests that seemed to them to measure these abilities. Other authors have analyzed intelligence somewhat differently and chosen different tasks to fit their own concepts of intelligence. Also, the specific content of the Binet-Simon tests, the terms and problem situations, were chosen for the children to be tested, and authors of tests for other age and cultural groups have sought to use words and situations more suited to their populations. Nevertheless, the basic approach Binet and Simon used to ensure construct validity has scarcely been improved on.

In an intelligence test, a logical theory (a construct) of intelligence is that scores on such a test should increase as age increases, at least to the point of maturity. Thus, we would expect the average score of ten-year-olds on an intelligence test to be higher than that of nine-year-olds. This idea is consistent with all our theories of intelligence and our knowledge and observation of child growth and development. Therefore, such a progression would be evidence of construct validity.

---

[8]The term *logical validity* is also used to describe this method, in order to contrast it with more statistical approaches.

It can been seen from the examples we have given that while a theory can be the basis for planning and building a test, the validity of the theory must still be verified by empirical means. Thus, the test of musical talent is validated by determining how well it differentiates between those whom competent judges identify as having little musical talent and those having much, or by predicting musical accomplishment. The theory of intelligence is checked against actual scores of groups of children differing in age and the test is validated by determining how well it correlates with other measures of success such as school marks, tests of subject matter achievement, and the like. If the relationships predicted by the author's theoretical constructs are not found, either the theory or the test may be at fault.

VALIDITY COEFFICIENTS   In concluding the discussion of validity, we should consider the interpretation of validity data. What is an acceptable coefficient of validity? The answer to this question depends on the situation in which it is determined. For example, correlations between scores or IQs on an intelligence test and teachers' marks usually range from the .30s to the .50s. This is numerically not very high, and one might ask why. The reason is not difficult to find. For one thing, teachers' marks are influenced by many factors other than intelligence. The attitudes of the teacher toward students and their industry, interest, and previous preparation all influence marks, and the attitudes are not measured by the intelligence test at all. Furthermore, since validity is influenced or determined in part by reliability (as we shall see shortly) and since the intelligence test is not perfect with respect to reliability, and teachers' marks are notably unreliable, no matter how well a test actually measures intelligence the correlation between it and marks is always less than perfect.

Correlations between standardized tests of achievement and teachers' marks in the same subject are generally somewhat higher, and the correlation between a standardized achievement battery and grade-point average or rank in class is generally in the .60s or even .70s. In either instance the correlation will be higher because of greater similarity between what the test measures and teachers' marks; in the first instance the grade-point average will be a more reliable measure of a student's scholarship than a mark in a single subject.

Correlations between two tests of intelligence or two standardized tests of achievement generally range from the .60s to the .80s. Similarly, correlations between good intelligence tests and standardized achievement tests are often in the same range.

In interpreting validity coefficients it is necessary, therefore, to take into account the situation in which the correlation has been determined.

The less similar the measures and the less reliable, the lower such coefficients will be. One of .35 may be all that can reasonably be expected in one case, whereas in another, a coefficient of .65 or .70 may be quite likely.

LEARNING EXERCISES

5. Classify each of the following as evidence of content, criterion-related, or construct validity:

   a. the correlation between scores on a standardized test in arithmetic and success in first-year algebra

   b. a teacher-made test based on a detailed outline of the work assigned and covered over a six-week period in class

   c. on a test of musical aptitude, a mean score of 85 for music majors and a mean score of 40 for an unselected group of freshmen

   d. a table showing the chances of success in a particular curriculum for different levels of performance on a test

6. Approximately what would you expect the correlation to be between the following?

   a. scores on an intelligence test and freshman grade-point average

   b. job ratings of machinists by their foreman and a test of manual dexterity

   c. scores on an achievement battery for ninth-graders and their IQs

   d. rank in class of high-school graduates and marks in first-year college work

7. Answer question 4 in the group of questions near the beginning of this chapter. Compare your answer with the answers of other members of the class. Discuss the differences and choose a best answer.

Reliability In discussing the two universal criteria of a good test, it is customary to think of validity as the most important quality and to discuss it first, as we have done. However, it is worth noting that reliability is essential to validity but that the opposite is not so. A test may be reliable without being valid, whereas the validity of a test depends in part on its reliability; therefore, the validity of a test is limited by its reliability. Reliability refs to the consistency of measurement. The meaning of consistency may be best clarified in a few illustrations. It was observed long ago that an individual who measures the diameter of a very accurately turned steel ball several times with an exceedingly accurate pair of calipers does not get exactly the same result every time. Even with the most accurate instruments available and the best possible control of conditions, the successive measurements of the diameter of the steel ball always vary somewhat. The extent of such variations is a measure of the consistency, or the lack of it, in this measuring situation.

The relation between reliability and validity may be simply illustrated with an analogy from archery. When shooting is reliable, the arrows are closely grouped, as in either the left or the middle of the accompanying sketch. When it is valid, the arrows are grouped in the bullseye, as in the portion of the sketch at the left only. Thus, we see that validity requires accuracy as well as consistency; reliability requires consistency only.

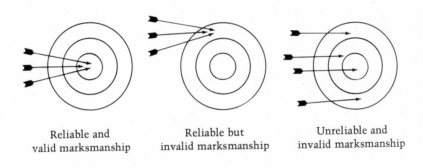

| Reliable and valid marksmanship | Reliable but invalid marksmanship | Unreliable and invalid marksmanship |

In educational and psychological measurement we have another way of expressing and gauging consistency. In measuring the qualities of human beings it is seldom possible or even appropriate to determine the consistency of measurement by many repeated measurements of the same thing, as in the illustration of the steel ball. Since we are all living, changing organisms, we cannot expect numerous repeated measurements to show nearly such close agreement. Therefore, when measuring attributes of people, we determine consistency by measuring a number of individuals—only twice as a rule—and comparing the relative standings of the individuals on the two sets of measurements or scores. Two successive measurements are usually not more than a few days apart.

To illustrate with a simple example, let us suppose we have given a group of seven children a test of clerical aptitude and ranked them according to their scores. A day or two later we repeat the test *on the same*

Table 4.1

Comparison of Scores Made by Seven Children on the Same Test Administered Twice

	First testing		Second testing	
Pupil	*Score*	*Rank*	*Score*	*Rank*
A	52	4	55	4
B	60	2	65	2
C	45	5	48	5
D	68	1	69	1
E	57	3	60	3
F	29	7	40	6
G	31	6	35	7

group of seven children and rank them again. The results might be as shown in Table 4.1.

The degree of consistency of measurement can be judged here by the extent to which the pupils tend to hold the same relative positions in their group. We can see that this tendency is high in this case since all pupils except F and G hold the same rank in both applications of the test, and even F and G shift only slightly.

All the children in this example show a gain in score between the first and the second testing, but their relative standings or ranks change in only two cases. If all individuals made the same score both times, or made lower scores the second time, the test would still show a high degree of consistency provided that the ranks of the individuals did not change. This, then, is what we mean by consistency. Conversely, a lack of consistency is shown by the degree to which individuals do not hold the same or similar relative positions in a group when measured twice with the same test.

In determining the reliability or consistency of measurement of a standardized test, the number of individuals tested is usually much larger, probably several hundred in all, but the principle is the same. While there are various methods of estimating the reliability of educational or psychological tests, those most commonly used are based on two measurements (or what is considered an equivalent procedure) of the same individuals.

Although we generally speak of reliability with reference to tests, this quality is equally important in other measuring and evaluating techniques. Rating scales, personality tests, interest inventories, and even questionnaires are of little value unless we can be sure that the results obtained by their use are reasonably reliable.

Unreliability or inconsistency in a measuring instrument stems from two sources. These are, first, the situation in which it is used, including the physical and psychological state of the individuals tested, and, second, the test itself. Such variable factors as conditions of testing, time limits, and directions can be fairly closely controlled provided that the persons using the test are willing to study directions carefully and follow them exactly. Conditions of the individual such as fatigue, low motivation, illness, and similar temporary factors, though not always as serious as sometimes imagined, are harder to control. There is no doubt that these conditions tend to reduce the reliability of measurement, but it is also a fact that most of our good standardized tests show remarkably high reliability in spite of their operation.

The principal factors in the measuring instrument itself that may affect its reliability are the quality of the individual questions or items and the length of the test. The quality of the questions can affect reliability many ways. For example, a question may be ambiguous; that is, it may be subject to more than one interpretation, or it may be so worded that its meaning is simply not clear.

Avoiding ambiguity in test items contributes materially to the attainment of reliability, although even the most skillful test-makers cannot always avoid this fault. In preparing a test one should guard against vagueness and eliminate items that prove on tryout to be ambiguous. Practice and experience in making tests and a thorough knowledge of the subject matter are the best preventives against ambiguity in test items.

The other factor, inherent in the test itself, that affects the consistency of measurement is the number of questions or the length of the test. Other things being equal, the reliability of a test is proportional to its length; that is, the longer a test is, the more reliable it tends to be. If we consider the implications of this statement, we see that it seems perfectly logical. It means simply that the more samples we take of a given area of knowledge, behavior, or material, the more reliable our appraisal of that knowledge, behavior, or material will be. A chemist would not think of basing an analysis of a carload of iron ore on a half-dozen samples taken at one end or at one or two levels as the car is unloaded. Instead, the chemist systematically samples the iron ore at all locations and depths, and then, by a system of "coning and quartering," reduces the many samples to one of a few ounces that can be taken into the laboratory. Here, the ore is sampled once more, and the chemist makes a final judgment, based not on the analysis of one sample but on duplicate or even triplicate samples, which are carefully checked against each other for agreement.

If we represent the areas of knowledge, behavior, or material to be sampled or tested by circles, as in the accompanying diagram, the effect of more adequate sampling (or more items or questions) is evident. In A we have a sampling of the area by ten items and in B by nineteen. Unless

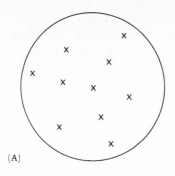 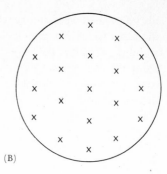

(A)   (B)

the area sampled is the same everywhere, and other things being equal, the sampling in B will yield more consistent and reliable results than that obtained in A.

Eventually we may reach a point of diminishing returns, where sampling is so thorough and reliability so high that additional sampling or testing does not improve reliability enough to justify the extra time and effort required. There is a formula for determining the relation between the increased length of a test and its consequent increased reliability. Known as the *Spearman-Brown Prophecy Formula,* it is very useful in showing how much the length of a test must be increased to attain a desired reliability or, conversely, how much the reliability of a test will be increased if its length is doubled, tripled, or increased by other multiples of itself. The formula is

$$r_{nn} = \frac{nr}{1 + (n-1)r}$$

where r_{nn} = estimated reliability when the length of the test is increased
n times
r = the reliability of the test in question

Thus, if a test of one hundred items was found to have a reliability of .80 and one wished to know what its reliability would be if the number of items were doubled, then $n = 2$ and $r = .80$ and

$$r_{nn} = \frac{2 \times .80}{1 + (2-1).80} = \frac{1.60}{1.80} = .888$$

This tells us that if the number of items were increased from one hundred to two hundred, the reliability of the test would be increased from .80 to .888 (or .89). The formula can also be used to determine how much a test's length would have to be increased to attain a desired reliability. In this case one simply substitutes in the formula the desired reliability (r_{nn}) and the obtained reliability (r) and solves for n. The usefulness of the Spearman-Brown formula rests on the assumption that the items added to increase the length, and therefore the reliability, of a test are of equal quality with the original items.

LEARNING EXERCISES

8. Suppose you have determined that the reliability of a fifty-item test is .75. How would increasing the number of items to 150 affect its reliability?
9. A test has a reliability of .80, but you desire a reliability of .90. How much longer would this test have to be to have the desired reliability?

SELF-CORRELATION (STABILITY) Reliability of measuring instruments is usually determined by one of three methods. All employ correlation techniques as discussed in Chapter 2. These three methods are *self-correlation, correlation of equivalent forms,* and *split-halves* or *interitem correlation.* The values obtained by these methods are often referred to as coefficients of *stability, equivalence,* and *internal consistency,* respectively, for reasons that will be explained.

The example we gave on page 100 of a test was given twice to the same children with a day or so between testings illustrates the *self-correlation* (or *test-retest*) approach to determining reliability. By calculating the coefficient of correlation between the two sets of scores, we can obtain an estimate of the stability of measurement over time. This test-retest method has the disadvantage of repeating exactly the same questions to the same individuals, a procedure that may operate differently in individual cases. After the first administration of a test, some pupils may remember many items and look up the answers they did not know, while others may forget the whole thing at once. In this method of determining reliability, practice effect is also generally at a maximum. By *practice effect* we mean the improvement of scores that results when the same pupils take the same test a second time. If this effect were uniform for all persons taking the test, it would not influence reliability. On some tests, though, all or nearly all students remember and repeat the answers they gave previously; then the correlation between the two sets of scores is higher than if the students had been tested on two equivalent but different forms of the test.

Although it is an accepted method of estimating reliability when other approaches are not possible, self-correlation does not take into account variation of test scores that might occur if another sample of items were chosen. It is an estimate of the stability of scores on the same items over an interval of time.

Whenever a self-correlation method is used, precautions should be taken to prevent examinees from remembering the answers they marked first and repeating these on the second administration of the test. When this happens, the correlation between the two sets of scores will be spuriously high. Both the length of the test and the interval between test administrations should be long enough to discourage this possibility.

CORRELATION OF EQUIVALENT FORMS If two or more equivalent forms of a test are available, reliability is measured by giving both forms to the same individuals and then calculating the coefficient of correlation from the two sets of scores. The two forms may be administered at one or two sittings, depending on the time required, the age and maturity of the persons tested, the nature of the test materials, and so on. Estimates based on two forms administered at the same time provide a coefficient of *equivalence* for the two forms of the test. In most cases it is customary to let several days intervene between testings. This helps insure that the estimate of reliability takes into account changes that occur with time as well as changes related to the sampling of test items. This procedure then yields a coefficient of *equivalence and stability.*

The stability of the test, thus determined, is for a period of several days. A longer period between two administrations of a test of achievement might permit factors such as additional amounts learned to reduce the correlation, thus suggesting a lower reliability than the test deserves as a measure of achievement at a given point in time.

The interval of time between test administrations for either the self-correlation or the equivalent-forms method should be planned with consideration of the interval of time for which the scores will be expected to be stable. For the initial assignment of students to reading groups by measurement of their present skills, an interval of a day may be adequate, if it is expected that students will be reassessed and reassigned in the course of reading instruction. At the other extreme, if scores on a test of general aptitude are to be used in decisions about individuals over a period of several years, evidence of the stability of scores over a period of a year or more would be needed.[9]

[9]*Standards for Educational and Psychological Tests* (footnote 5), p. 54.

When we employ two forms of a test, we are virtually using two equal halves of the same instrument. Equivalent forms are constructed to be alike in degree and range of difficulty. They cover the same areas of knowledge and skill with different items or questions. Using equivalent forms eliminates or reduces to a minimum the practice effect that is present when the same test is given twice.

SPLIT-HALVES CORRELATION (INTERNAL CONSISTENCY) It is often impossible to employ either of the methods described above to determine test reliability. It may not be feasible to test twice, equivalent forms may not be available, or there may be other valid reasons for not using either the self-correlation or the equivalent-forms correlation methods. In such cases a split-halves technique may be used to provide an estimate of the degree to which different subgroups of the test items yield consistent scores. In this procedure, a test is given in the ordinary manner, the papers are scored as usual, and then two scores for each individual are obtained by scoring alternate halves of the test separately.

Such scoring can be done in several ways. Probably the most commonly used method of obtaining two scores for each person is to base one score on only the odd-numbered items of the test and the other on only the even-numbered items. In a test of 100 items, one set of scores would be based on 50 items numbered 1, 3, 5, 7, . . . , 99, and one set would be based on the 50 items numbered 2, 4, 6, 8, . . . , 100. Therefore, if a pupil missed 10 of the 50 odd-numbered items and 12 of the 50 even-numbered items, the two scores would be 40 and 38. The total score would be 78, the sum of 40 and 38, or $100 - (10 + 12)$.

Sometimes the test is split by selecting pairs of items thought to be equivalent and allocating one of each pair to each half of the test. The test may be divided in the middle with the scores based on the first and second halves. Finally, tests may be split by allocating groups of items to alternate halves. Each procedure has its own advantages and disadvantages, and the choice of which to follow must be made on the basis of which procedure will give *the most nearly equivalent halves of the test.*

Having obtained two scores for each person tested, we can then calculate the coefficient of correlation between the two sets of scores. This is, in effect, the correlation between the two equivalent halves of the test administered at one sitting. If the two halves are truly equivalent and if other necessary conditions as described above are met, the correlation thus achieved is likely to be fairly high. One more step is necessary to enable us to determine the reliability of the entire test, in this example a test consisting of 100 items. The correlation coefficient obtained in our example is based on scores that represent only halves of the test—that is, scores on only 50 items. Since we wish to know the reliability of the

100-item test, we apply the Spearman-Brown Prophecy Formula and calculate the estimated reliability coefficient for 100 items—that is, for the whole test.

The split-halves method of determining reliability does not take into account changes in testing conditions or in individuals that may occur from one time to another. Because it is unaffected by these sources of unreliability, it usually gives results higher than those obtained by separately timed equivalent-forms methods. For this reason, reliability coefficients thus determined are generally regarded as approaching the maximum value that could be reached under ideal conditions. The method gives spuriously high reliability coefficients whenever test scores depend largely on speed, and so it should not be used in such cases.

If these limitations are kept in mind, the split-halves method may be used in obtaining estimates of reliability in a wide variety of situations, often where no other method is available. Test publishers often have difficulty, for example, in getting cooperation from school systems to obtain the time for even one administration of a test that is under development; two administrations may be impossible. Under these conditions, particularly for measures of achievement at a given point in time, estimates of reliability based on a single test administration, such as split-halves, may be used.

KUDER-RICHARDSON ESTIMATE OF RELIABILITY   As we have indicated in our discussion of split-halves reliability, there are various ways of splitting a test, though odd-even halves are by far the most commonly used. It is possible to avoid splitting a test altogether by using a Kuder-Richardson formula that provides an estimate of split-halves reliability.[10] The formula known as KR_{20} is

$$r = \frac{n}{n-1} \left(1 - \frac{\Sigma pq}{S^2} \right)$$

where n = number of items in the test

p = proportion of persons responding correctly to each individual item

q = proportion of persons responding incorrectly to each individual item—that is, $1 - p$

Σpq = sum of pq products for the n individual items

S^2 = square of the standard deviation of the test, called the variance

[10] G. F. Kuder and M. W. Richardson, "The Theory of the Estimation of Test Reliability," *Psychometrika*, 2 (September 1937), 151–160.

Calculation of p and q for every item in the test can be time-consuming if the test has many items. As an approximation of the sum of the pq products, the mean (M) may be used. This assumes either that the items are all of equal difficulty or that the average difficulty of the items is 50 percent, in which case the mean is at the middle of the distribution of scores. The formula, known as KR_{21}, then becomes

$$r = \frac{n}{n-1} \left(1 - \frac{M(1 - M/n)}{S^2} \right)$$

Collecting terms, we get

$$r = \frac{nS^2 - M(n - M)}{S^2(n - 1)}$$

Since the assumptions underlying the use of KR_{21} are usually imperfectly met, it can generally be assumed to yield an underestimate of split-halves reliability for unspeeded tests. On the other hand, like other procedures based on a single administration, this formula provides an overestimate of the reliability of speeded tests.

STANDARD ERROR OF MEASUREMENT Reliability coefficients are useful for comparing tests, but they have limited value in interpreting test scores. Once a coefficient of reliability has been determined by one of the four methods described, it may be used to determine a statistic useful in the interpretation of test scores that is called the *standard error of measurement*. This statistic gives us an estimate of the accuracy of a single score on a test whose reliability coefficient and standard deviation are known. Put in another way, the standard error of measurement provides answers to such questions as: Knowing an individual's actual score on a test, what is the probability that the true score does not differ markedly from the obtained score? This is a method for answering the question of how reliable a single score on a test is. For this purpose we employ a formula

$$S_{meas} = S\sqrt{1 - r}$$

where S_{meas} = the standard error of measurement
$\quad\quad S$ = the standard deviation of the test
$\quad\quad r$ = the reliability of the test

To illustrate the use of this formula, let us assume that the reliability of a certain reading test has been determined by the split-halves technique to be .91 and its standard deviation is 10. Substituting, we have

$$S_{meas} = 10\sqrt{1 - .91}$$
$$= 10\sqrt{.09}$$
$$= 10 \times .3$$
$$= 3.0$$

This result indicates that the chances are about 2 to 1 that any obtained score on this test will not vary from the true score by more than 3 points. More specifically, the chances are about 2 to 1 that the true score of an individual who makes an actual score of 72 on this test will be somewhere between 69 and 75. Furthermore, we can say with much greater assurance (chances about 19 to 1) that the true score lies between 66 and 78 (that is, it does not differ from the obtained score by more than 6 points); and we can be practically certain that it lies between 63 and 81.

The usefulness of the S_{meas} can be seen in Table 3.4. There it was applied in the concept of *percentile bands*. These bands are based on the standard error of measurement for a single score on the *Cooperative English Tests*. They provide a measure of the confidence levels for interpretation of individual scores on these tests. Thus, a converted score of 150–151 for grade 10 is equivalent to a percentile rank between 55 and 69, which represents a range of 1 standard error of measurement above and below the specified score of 150–151. This gives an estimate of the confidence or limits of accuracy within which a score may be interpreted.

LEARNING EXERCISE

10. Reference to Table 3.4 shows that the width of the percentile bands decreases markedly for scores at the upper and lower extremes of the distributions. Explain why this is so.

INTERPRETING RELIABILITY INFORMATION   A very natural and important question concerns the desirable magnitude of reliability coefficients. Of course, it is advantageous to have tests with the highest possible reliability. As we have pointed out earlier, the degree of reliability is influenced by a number of factors such as the condition of the subjects being tested, the length of the tests, and the nature of the items. Nevertheless, the best standardized tests of achievement quite consistently show reliability coefficients as high as .90 or even higher. Standardized tests of intelligence commonly have reliabilities almost as good—generally .85 or higher. The reliability coefficients for instruments such as personality tests and interest inventories are usually lower, the average being most often in the .70s and .80s, although some have not attained a correlation as high as .70.

Another consideration in interpreting a reliability coefficient is the range or variability of the test scores for the group tested. Tests have a substantially lower reliability coefficient when they are given to a group of children in a single grade than when administered to a group ranging over several grades. For practical purposes this means that the reliability of a test should be judged in terms of the circumstances under which its reliability was determined. A test whose reliability is suitable for a range of several grades or several years in chronological age may be unsuitable for use in discriminating among children in the same grade or of the same age. For such purposes a test with proven reliability in the narrower range should be sought. If this is impossible, greater reliance might be placed on the standard error of measurement, because it, unlike the reliability coefficient, is relatively independent of the range of test scores. For this reason it is more useful as an index of the accuracy of test scores to be expected when testing groups more or less variable than the group for whom reliability coefficients are reported.

The desirable minimum level of reliability for tests differs according to purpose. When a test is intended only for use in studying groups, a lower reliability coefficient (around .75) may be sufficient to make fairly accurate comparisons. When individual differentiation is the goal, reliabilities of .95 or higher are very desirable.

If the purpose is to compare the scores of two individuals or two different scores for the same individual, it is important to realize that the differences between scores are notoriously unreliable. The standard error of a difference between two scores is larger than that of either score used to compute it. If one uses the band-score interpretation recommended earlier, test publishers suggest that two scores not be considered significantly different unless they are far enough apart so that the bands around them do not overlap. This means that they must be further apart than the sum of their separate standard errors of measurement. If the standard error of one test score is 3.0, as it was in the reading test illustration of the preceding section, the scores of two students would not be considered reliably different unless they were at least 2 × 3.0 or 6 points apart. The student who scored 42 on this test before instruction would have to score higher than 48 (42 + 6) before the gain would be significant. Thus, the standard error of a difference between two test scores is about twice the standard error of a test score.

The manual of a published test should report both the reliability of the test and the standard error of measurement. The procedures and the test populations used to obtain these statistics should be described and the reader should be advised of the effects on test reliability of such factors as group variability and the time interval between test administrations.

LEARNING EXERCISES

11. A teacher gives a 100-item objective final test to students in high-school biology (120 students in 5 sections). The test cannot be repeated for the purpose of reliability determination. Describe how one could proceed to determine the test's reliability in this situation.

12. The correlation between two equivalent forms of a standardized test given to the same students is .90. What is its reliability coefficient?

13. A test is given on two successive days to the same 50 students. On comparing the scores, it is found that all improve their scores somewhat the second time but the ranks on the two testings remain the same. What would be the coefficient of stability?

14. The standard error of measurement of an IQ obtained from a well-known intelligence test is 5 points. Apply this fact in the case of a student whose score gives an IQ of 110 and tell what it means. What can we conclude about the difference in the IQ of this student and one whose score obtains an IQ of 115?

15. Why are validity coefficients of standardized tests consistently lower than their reliability coefficients?

16. Assume the following data: (1) correlation between IQ and marks in algebra = .64; (2) reliability of test of intelligence = .91; of teacher's marks in algebra = .51; (3) standard deviation of scores on intelligence test = 16; of teacher's marks (4 for A, 3 for B, 2 for C, 1 for D, O for F) = 1.0. Using these data, calculate the standard error of measurement of the intelligence test and of the teacher's marks in algebra.

Aside from the two universally applicable criteria discussed to this point, certain secondary attributes, important in all good tests in education and psychology, have already been mentioned and will be discussed briefly. These are *objectivity, ease of administering, ease of scoring,* and *ease of interpreting.*

A test is objective to the extent that competent persons agree on the scoring of answers. In other words, a test may be said to be objective to the extent that the opinion or judgment of the scorer is eliminated from the scoring process. Objectivity is usually attained by (1) stating the questions specifically and precisely, (2) requiring specific, precise, short answers, and (3) scoring the test by the use of a previously determined scoring key. This key may be printed, in which case most of the scoring can be done by clerical workers, or, if properly prepared answer sheets are used, the test can be scored by a machine in a matter of a few seconds. In extensive testing that involves thousands of cases, the test-scoring machine saves much time and money.

Objectivity

Objectivity is a matter of degree; few if any tests are either wholly objective or wholly subjective. The conventional essay test, which consists of a few questions asking the student to "discuss," "describe," "give reasons for," is relatively lacking in objectivity. Essay tests emphasize such matters as judgment, opinion, and interpretation on the part of both the student and the person who evaluates the answers. It is inevitable that different persons, all judged competent in the subject, will evaluate the same examination paper differently. Yet much can be done to make this type of examination more objective by careful phrasing of the questions, preparing of ideal answers, agreement among readers or judges on rules for evaluating answers, and other such precautions. The maximum change in the direction of objectivity is achieved by using objective questions designed to eliminate ambiguity in their answering and by using mechanical scoring with previously prepared scoring keys.

A questionable reliability is the most serious weakness of subjective tests, since, as we have said, reliability is directly affected by the degree to which the judgments, biases, and emotions of the scorer enter into the evaluation of the answers. It is only fair to the individual whose test is being evaluated that these personal factors be kept to a minimum.

Objectivity is essential to published standardized tests if the tests are to achieve maximum effectiveness. It would be very difficult, perhaps useless, to attempt any comparative interpretations of test results not arrived at objectively. Comparisons with norms, comparisons between individuals, classes, schools, sexes, regions, or grades, would be largely meaningless if different users of the test scored it according to their own independent ideas of the quality of the responses. One of the chief values of the standardized test is that personal judgments and biases are largely eliminated in the scoring.

*Ease of
Administering*

It seems reasonable to assume that the simpler a test is to administer, the less probability there is of making mistakes that will affect the results. Contrast, for example, two well-known older group intelligence tests, the Army Alpha and the Otis Self-Administering. Both tests were at one time among the most widely used tests of intelligence.

The Army Alpha consists of eight parts or subtests, each precisely timed. The time limits are short, varying from one and a half minutes to four minutes. Since each part has to be timed exactly with a stopwatch and all participants are supposed to begin and stop work on each part of the examination at the same time, administering the test places a great burden on the examiner, especially one not highly trained in the administration of group tests. The test is subject to frequent errors in timing, misunderstanding of directions by examinees, and failure of individuals to begin and stop working at the right times.

The Otis Self-Administering test series, published about the same time as Army Alpha, presented a notable improvement over Army Alpha in ease of administration. The Otis tests are not subdivided; all questions are together in a single set or part. The preliminary directions explain thoroughly each type of item the examinees encounter in the test and provide an opportunity for them to receive further explanations when needed. When all examinees are ready, the signal to begin is given and work proceeds uninterrupted until the time allowed for the entire test has elapsed. These tests are properly called *self-administering*. Any intelligent, conscientious person can administer them correctly with a little preliminary study of the directions. No additional equipment, not even a stopwatch, is needed.

In the half-century since the Otis Self-Administering tests were first published, many improvements have been made in group tests, but it is doubtful that any of these tests have surpassed the Otis Self-Administering in ease of administration. This criterion, while not of supreme importance, is nonetheless of considerable concern to users of standardized tests, and producers of such tests are generally well aware of it. Also, as we noted above, ease and simplicity of administration contribute to accuracy of results since there is less probability of error in directions, timing, and so on.

A recent development in test administration is the use of records or tapes. In some instances only directions are recorded; in others the entire test, including directions to students, is on record or tape; *Seashore Mea-*

sures of Musical Talents is one of the earliest examples of the latter type. Use of records or tapes seems to be increasing. This has the obvious advantage of completely standardizing administration of a test. It is necessary for the person in charge only to distribute the test materials, start the recording, do whatever supervising is required, and collect materials after the recording ends.

Much of what we have said about ease of administering applies with equal force to ease of scoring. In fact, the test that is simple and easy to administer may also be easy to score, though this is not necessarily so. Sometimes administering and scoring are complicated because the test is designed to yield subscores or part-scores for diagnostic purposes. In such cases ease of administering and scoring must be sacrificed in order to achieve some other more important aim.

Ease of Scoring

An important factor affecting ease of scoring is objectivity. If the test items do not call for specific objective answers, scoring is more or less subjective, requiring judgment on the part of the scorer as to the correctness or acceptability of responses. Most standardized tests require only the selection of the correct answer and use of symbols such as T or F or numbers or letters of choices on an answer sheet. Such answer sheets are now generally scored mechanically by machines.

In some situations—for example, in tests for pupils below fourth grade—use of separate answer sheets is not recommended.[11] Here, pupils write their answers in spaces provided or indicate them by encircling or by drawing lines. Hand scoring is therefore commonly employed. However, test publishers and authors have recognized the problems young children have in using separate answer sheets, and recently techniques have been developed for machine scoring booklets in which students write their answers. This avoids some of the problems associated with separate answer sheets and retains many of the values of machine scoring.

The use of properly prepared stencils, scoring keys, and so on also does much to simplify test scoring. Test publishers have developed various schemes for simplifying the scoring of standardized tests. For example, the *Clapp-Young Self-Marking Tests*[12] were the pioneers in the use of a double sheet. The pupil marked the answers on the front and back of the closed double answer sheet or booklet. Parts of the inside surfaces of the double sheet were printed with a carbon ink strip facing printed squares or other symbols that designated the correct answers. Thus, when the student penciled the markings on the front and back of the closed double sheet, the

[11]V. J. Cashen and G. C. Ramseyer, "The Use of Separate Answer Sheets by Primary Age Children," *Journal of Educational Measurement*, 6 (Fall 1969),155–158.
[12]*Clapp-Young Self-Marking Tests* (Boston: Houghton Mifflin, 1929).

carbon strip inside carried the impression of the mark to the area of the printed symbols indicating the correct answers. Upon completion of the test, the scorer separated the double sheet and quickly tallied the correct answers by counting the number of carbon impressions that coincided with the printed ones. Similar systems have been used by other test publishers.

Where the new type of answer sheets are used, publishers generally provide with the test a perforated scoring stencil for hand or machine scoring. This stencil fits over the answer sheet and has holes so placed that the pencil marks of correctly answered items are visible. Scoring can be done quite rapidly by fitting the stencil over the filled-out answer sheet and simply counting the number of marks that appear in the holes of the stencil. The same or similar stencils are also used for machine scoring. When scoring tests in this way it is necessary to check each answer sheet to see that no one has marked more than one space in answering any item. Teachers often make their own scoring stencils, which greatly facilitates the task of scoring examinations.

In recent years a number of different systems for the rapid and accurate scoring of standardized tests by mechanical or electronic devices have been developed. These systems have made possible the scoring of thousands of answer sheets or cards in a few hours. Many test publishers provide such a scoring service to users of their tests for an additional fee. The user of a test can purchase the scoring service with the tests and answer media. At additional cost an analysis of the results, including distributions, means, standard deviations, percentile ranks, correlations—almost anything one wants and is willing to pay for—can be obtained. All this can be provided in a comparatively short time. For users of large quantities of standardized tests such services are not only very helpful but also economical both in the time saved and in the actual cost of doing the work.

A few other considerations have bearing on this point. The more complicated the scoring, the greater the chance for errors and the more time-consuming the job of correcting the work. Also, if scoring becomes too burdensome and time-consuming it may never be finished. Tests may even be enthusiastically purchased and administered, only to be placed on shelves somewhere, the scoring never completed. Certainly there may be other causes contributing to such a state of affairs, but lack of time and energy for the burdensome job of scoring must be reckoned with.

Finally, the success of the scoring process depends to some extent on having simple, accurate, and clear directions for scoring. There is some variation among manuals for standardized tests with respect to this point. Directions for scoring some tests are so clear that the scorer seldom goes wrong; at the other extreme are directions that are a veritable puzzle, even for experienced testers. However, the aim of test authors and publishers is to make their directions as simple and intelligible as possible. It is not to be expected that this goal will be uniformly attained in all tests, mainly because of the variation in complexity and scope of different tests.

A test may meet all the criteria so far mentioned and yet present great difficulties when it comes to interpreting the results. Ease of interpretation generally depends on two factors: first, the mechanics of interpretation and, second, the aids provided for giving meaning and significance to the scores. *Ease of Interpreting*

The first point largely concerns the transmutation of the raw score on a test to some derived score. For norm-referenced tests this is generally done through tables of norms, which can be read easily and accurately. It often helps to present norms in the form of both tables and graphs. A graph, such as a percentile curve, may make the transition from raw scores to percentile equivalents easier, faster, and more accurate than a table can, especially in cases that require interpolation. Where profiles, either individual or group, are used, sample profiles should be given to assist inexperienced test users in constructing some for their own cases.[13]

For the sake of easy interpretation it is also desirable not to crowd too much into one chart or table. In their desire to have everything in one convenient place, test authors and publishers sometimes crowd so much into a small space and use such small type that the ordinary user of the tests will become confused and lost in the maze of different types of scores, percentiles, mental ages, chronological ages, deciles, grade norms, and diagnostic devices presented on one page or in one chart.

The second point concerns what is probably one of the most common and serious faults in the entire process of using standardized tests. After the tests are given and scored, the inevitable question is, What do the results mean? It is sad but true that too often the test experts themselves, although proficient in their knowledge and advice about tests and how to administer and score them, are less skillful in providing practical aids for interpreting and applying the results. This is not wholly the fault of the so-called experts. It is extremely difficult to establish general rules that will apply in all or even most situations for interpreting and using test results. What may be right for one test may be entirely inappropriate for

[13]Refer back to sample profile, Figure 3.3.

another. The test manual usually suggests a variety of ways in which the test scores may be interpreted and used, and from the manual accompanying each test or group of tests the prospective user of any given test will gain some suggestions that are appropriate and useful. This is the function of the test manual. Some of our best tests now have manuals that in themselves are small textbooks on testing. These are usually written clearly and without unnecessarily technical language so as to appeal to teachers and other prospective users of the tests. Usually the manuals contain a profusion of aids for simplifying the use and interpretation of the tests and many suggestions of ways in which the results can be used for better learning by, and counseling of, pupils. When considering the criterion of ease of interpretation in relation to a particular test, the prospective user should examine the manual carefully to find evidence of how well the criterion is met.

LEARNING EXERCISES

17. Discuss several considerations in making measuring instruments more objective.
18. Why should standardized tests be as objective as possible?
19. Some tests are very difficult and time-consuming to administer. Are there any situations in which this would be justifiable?
20. If a test-scoring machine is available in your vicinity, try to see the machine in operation. What are the limitations on the use of such equipment?
21. Examine a specimen set of a standardized test for its objectivity, ease of administering, scoring, and interpreting. Is it satisfactory in every respect? If not, in what ways could it be improved?

We shall next discuss a group of characteristics that apply as a rule only to standardized tests. In fact, they apply so rarely to unstandardized, informal, classroom, and teacher-made tests that they may be considered as representing perhaps the chief differences between the two groups. These characteristics are *adequate norms, equivalent forms,* and *economy.* An informal, locally made test seldom has norms in any general sense; it rarely has two or more equivalent forms, and the question of cost is not usually as crucial a factor. In the case of norm-referenced standardized tests, these factors are all important.

One of the main purposes of standardization is to establish norms. These *Adequate* may be of many types, depending on the type of test and the uses for *Norms* which it is intended. The common types of norms have been illustrated and discussed in Chapter 3, so they need not be repeated here. Adequate usable norms are essential to a good norm-referenced standardized test. If scores are to be interpreted by reference to the average score of other students, reputable test publishers will seldom put a test on the market before norms have been established on a controlled sample of the population with which the test is intended to be used. Reviewers are very critical of tests published with norms deemed to be inadequate in any respect. The prospective user of a test should be satisfied that the norms are based on a population sample that is representative from the standpoints of geographic areas, rural and urban populations, grade level, sex, socioeconomic status, and types of schools. At this point the considerations regarding norms discussed in Chapter 3 find application. Careful reading of the test manual, particularly the parts describing how the normative population was chosen, generally reveals whether the norms are representative, dependable, and useful.

It might be well to emphasize that the fact that a test is printed does not mean it is standardized and that all tests which claim to be standardized do not invariably have adequate or useful norms. Furthermore, a test with adequate norms for a certain group will not be usable with people to whom these norms do not apply. For example, norms for a test that has been standardized mostly on children from superior environments would probably have limited use with culturally disadvantaged children.

We have already pointed out that the way the norms are presented and the adequacy of instructions for their use are important in the ease of interpreting test results for many purposes. It should be mentioned again, however, that the prospective user of a test can usually determine these qualities by carefully examining and studying the test and the accompanying manual.

As a rule, a standardized test should have two or more equivalent forms. *Equivalent* Equivalent forms are needed when students are to be tested at different *Forms* times because of security problems, when students are to be retested for the measurement of achievement gains, and for the determination of reliability. This is one of the common differences between standardized and unstandardized tests. However, the fact that a test has two or more forms is not always to be taken as satisfactory evidence that the forms are really equivalent, for it will sometimes be found upon careful scrutiny of the test and manual that they are not. Alternate forms may cover quite different areas of subject matter so that they are not at all comparable in this respect. They may also be unequal in difficulty—in either range of difficulty, or average difficulty or both. Or they may be equivalent at some levels and not at others. For example, in a test of achievement for use in several successive grades the two forms may show equivalent difficulty at one grade level but not at the next higher or lower level. Such situations are probably the exception rather than the rule, but it is well for the test buyers to know that these possibilities exist and to keep them in mind when examining tests for possible use. By studying the test and the manual it should be possible to determine whether or not the different forms of the test are really equivalent.

Economy   The factor of cost, which we have already discussed at several points, is a real consideration, and we should emphasize here, first, that it must be reckoned in broad rather than narrow terms and, second, that—as far as possible—economy should be a determining factor in selecting tests only if all other criteria are equally well satisfied.

In elaboration of the first point, we may point out that, as with automobiles for example, the important consideration is not so much the initial cost as the upkeep. The price per copy of the test booklet and answer sheet may well turn out to be one of the minor items in the total cost of testing, and it is a good idea to try to make accurate estimates of the total cost per pupil before embarking on any testing program. This estimate should include, in addition to the cost of the test materials themselves, the expense of scoring the tests, analysis of the results, and follow-up. Sometimes a test that costs less initially will cost more in the long run. It may be made of cheaper materials and have to be replaced sooner; or it might not be set up for use with answer sheets, in which case it can be used only once; it may require more scoring time; or it might even be inadequate for its intended purpose.

The cost per pupil of testing with a battery such as the *Stanford Achievement Test*, reviewed in Chapter 8, may be estimated at anywhere from fifty cents to one dollar per pupil, depending on the initial cost of the test and answer sheets, if used, plus the cost of scoring. If the scoring is done by teachers and no allowance is made for the time required to do so, the cost will be increased very little. On the other hand, if scoring is done by clerks or by mechanical means, this will add to the total cost per pupil. Costs must always be calculated on the basis of more factors than the price of the tests and answer sheets alone. It is also important in estimating costs to remember that where separate answer sheets are used test booklets may be used over and over again. In this case, the initial cost of the tests is spread over multiple testings and their repeated use requires the purchase of additional answer sheets only. These usually cost from five to fifteen cents per copy.

The second point relating to the criterion of economy is that no test is a bargain if it is inferior in other important respects. Only if two tests are equally good for the purpose at hand should cost be the deciding factor. The prospective purchaser must be satisfied by all the information available that two (or more) tests will do a job equally well before making a cost comparison. This is not to say that one should disdain a test merely because it is cheap. In the days when all tests were consumable—that is, when pupils marked their answers on the test itself rather than on separate answer sheets—some test publishers used cheaper, smaller print and a less expensive format with no evident harm to the usefulness of the test. If a test is not to be used over and over again with separate answer sheets, a test in the cheaper format may answer the purpose just as well as a more expensive one.

To summarize, economy in testing goes far beyond the list price of the test in the publisher's catalogue. For most users of tests in small quantities a difference of a few dollars per year may not be of great importance. Those who use large quantities of standardized tests year after year, however, should calculate carefully, taking many factors into account. Where large numbers of tests are used, small differences in cost per pupil will become very considerable in the aggregate and over long periods.

LEARNING EXERCISES

22. What are the advantages of equivalent forms? How would equivalent forms of a standardized test be made?
23. Discuss several factors—besides the cost of tests or other instruments used—that affect the economy of measurement programs.

SUGGESTED READING

ANASTASI, ANNE. *Psychological Testing.* 4th ed. New York: Macmillan, 1976. Chaps. 5, 6, 7. A clear, practical discussion of reliability and methods for determining and utilizing validity data. The applications and illustrations are taken primarily from psychological testing, but the principles are applicable to all types of measurement of human abilities.

————, "Some Current Developments in the Measurement and Interpretation of Test Validity," and ROBERT L. THORNDIKE, "Reliability." In *Testing Problems in Perspective.* Edited by Anne Anastasi. Washington, D.C.: American Council on Education, 1966. Excellent discussions of the theoretical aspects of the topics as presented in the form of papers read at the Invitational Conference on Testing Problems in 1963.

BUROS, OSCAR K., ed. *The Eighth Mental Measurements Yearbook.* Highland Park, N.J.: Gryphon Press, 1978. See also the earlier volumes dating from 1938 to 1972. Each yearbook contains critical reviews of all obtainable published tests and books on measurement written in English. Most publications are reviewed independently by two or more specialists. Reviews in earlier editions are cross-referenced in later ones. This is one of the most useful publications in educational and psychological literature for the user and student of measuring instruments.

————, ed. *Tests in Print II.* Highland Park, N.J.: Gryphon Press, 1974. A guide to nearly 2,500 tests in print and an index to references on tests. Also contains a directory of publishers and a reprint of *Standards for Educational and Psychological Tests.*

CRONBACH, LEE J, "*Test Validation,*" and JULIAN C. STANLEY, "Reliability." In *Educational Measurement.* 2d ed. Edited by Robert L. Thorndike. Washington, D.C.: American Council on Education, 1971. Somewhat technical but a thorough and authoritative treatment of validity and reliability.

EBEL, ROBERT L. *Measuring Educational Achievement.* 2d ed. Englewood Cliffs, N.J.: Prentice-Hall, 1972. Chapter 15 is on reliability; Chapter 16 is on validity. Contains many useful suggestions for estimating and improving reliability and validity.

————, ed. *Encyclopedia of Educational Research.* 4th ed. New York: Macmillan, 1969. Excellent discussions of all the recognized criteria of a good test by leading authorities in the field.

GLASER, ROBERT, and A. J. NITKO. "Measurement in Learning and Instruction." In R. L. Thorndike, ed. *Educational Measurement.* 2d ed. Washington, D.C.: American Council on Education, 1971. Pages 652–656 give a clear, concise description of criterion-referenced tests and their development. Pages 656–661 contain a more technical description of the generation of test items, reliability estimates, and standards of mastery.

GRECO, THOMAS H., JR. "Is There Really a Difference Between Criterion-Referenced and Norm-Referenced Measurements?" *Educational Technology,* 14, No. 12 (December 1974), 22–25. Argues that the desirable qualities of the two types of measurement are the same and that they differ primarily in the specificity or narrowness of the domain of achievement tested.

GRONLUND, NORMAN E. *Preparing Criterion-Referenced Tests for Classroom Instruction.* New York: Macmillan, 1973. A brief, practical guide for preparing criterion-referenced tests with emphasis on classroom use.

JOINT COMMITTEE OF THE AMERICAN PSYCHOLOGICAL ASSOCIATION, AMERICAN EDUCATIONAL RESEARCH ASSOCIATION, AND NATIONAL COUNCIL ON MEASUREMENT IN EDUCATION. *Standards for Educational and Psychological Tests.* Washington, D.C.: American Psychological Association, 1974.

KLEIN, S. P., and J. KOSECOFF. *Issues and Procedures in the Development of Criterion-Referenced Tests.* Report 26. Princeton, N.J.: ERIC Clearinghouse on Tests, Measurement, and Evaluation, 1973. A summary of the basic steps and problems in the development of criterion-referenced tests. In addition, representative test systems and published tests are reviewed.

MEHRENS, WILLIAM A., and IRVIN J. LEHMANN. *Standardized Tests in Education.* 2d ed. New York: Holt, Rinehart and Winston, 1975. Chaps. 1 and 2. A discussion of the nature and functions of standardized tests and their selection and use. Includes a practical consideration of basic statistical concepts and a thorough treatment of reliability and validity for criterion- as well as norm-referenced tests.

TENBRINK, TERRY D. *Evaluation: A Practical Guide for Teachers.* New York: McGraw-Hill, 1974. Chap. 14. Contains a useful summary of how the desirable characteristics of standardized tests are related to the purposes for which they are selected.

Five

OBJECTIVES AS THE BASIS
OF ALL GOOD MEASUREMENT

Teaching involves five essential processes—defining goals or objectives, choosing content, deciding on methods of instruction, delivering the instruction itself, and measuring results. The order of these processes is not absolutely fixed, but the definition of goals comes first if teaching is to have direction and purpose. Trying to teach and evaluate without defining objectives is like starting on a journey without knowing where you want to go. It may be pleasant to wander around for a while, but you are likely to conclude after some wandering that you have made no progress.

After studying this chapter you should be able to answer questions and develop materials such as these:

1. How can statements of objectives prepared by national committees or professional associations be most useful to a classroom teacher?
2. How can a teacher use statements of objectives for a course to improve teaching and raise pupil achievement?
3. Construct behavioral and criterion-referenced objectives for a class you may teach.
4. Develop a table of specifications for a unit test in a course you may teach.
5. Outline a plan for developing a rating scale or questionnaire to measure outcomes implied by a statement of objectives.

THE IMPORTANCE
OF DEFINING OBJECTIVES

To a large extent the activities of a classroom are determined by the objectives chosen or formulated by the teacher. Materials and methods are selected in accordance with the objectives, instruction guides pupils to accomplish the objectives, and measurement is used to determine how well or to what degree the objectives have been attained by pupils in the class. Although it has been traditional to think of most courses or subjects in terms of the body of content to be covered, many educators believe that greater direction could be given and more learning would occur if the emphasis were on the objectives rather than the content. In some areas such as basic mathematics, the content to be learned virtually dictates the objectives. However, in many areas—for example, grammar and map reading—skill development is clearly more important than the particular content studied. In such subjects the teacher must select from a wide array of content and materials those that he or she judges are most appropriate and effective for enhancing pupil development toward the objectives.

Objectives may be stated in different ways, some of which will be discussed and illustrated later in this chapter. Some teachers may not consciously formulate any objectives at all, but there is growing evidence that class progress is enhanced when learners know the objectives toward which they are working. Whatever the objectives and no matter how they are formulated or thought of, they constitute an essential element in the teaching process. Every teacher necessarily has some objectives that give direction and purpose to a class, and it is highly important that these objectives be stated clearly and explicitly so that their meaning and implications are clear and well understood, particularly by pupils in the class.

What has been said about defining objectives for teaching applies with equal force to measurement and evaluation. In order to measure the results and effectiveness of instruction, it is essential to know what the members of the class are expected to accomplish. When objectives are poorly defined or perhaps not defined at all, it is impossible to do an effective job of evaluation.

In the five-step description of the teaching process mentioned at the beginning of this chapter, measurement is shown as the fifth or final step. Measurement is usually involved at several stages of the instructional process, however. Sometimes pretesting is used to determine the appropriate level for beginning instruction. During instruction many teachers monitor pupil progress continually, sometimes using tests or quizzes and sometimes in less formal ways, and this type of measurement, referred to as formative, is used to adjust instruction or activities for individual pupils so as to enhance progress toward objectives. At the close of a unit of instruction, measurement is used in a summative sense to determine the extent to which the objectives of instruction have been attained. Unless there is systematic and effective appraisal, the extent to which progress is attained in the classroom will remain a matter of subjective opinion or conjecture.

Certainly teachers' opinions are valuable in determining the status and growth of pupils with respect to educational goals. However, they are only one element in the total process, and it is important to supplement them with systematic and more objective measures. The teacher should employ the widest possible variety of measuring and evaluative tools and techniques that are practical and appropriate for the given situation. The use of a wide range of measurement tools is essential, not only from the standpoint of making appraisal more reliable but also because different objectives or goals require different techniques of appraisal. If we want to know how well students have learned some of the facts about the early history of their country, we use one kind of instrument, possibly an objective test; if we wish to know how well pupils can handle rulers, read thermometers, or weigh objects, we employ another approach to measurement. Still other techniques are needed to determine the extent to which some of the precepts of good citizenship carry over into out-of-school behavior.

To summarize what has been presented so far, it might be said that objectives and measurement complement each other and are integral parts of a whole. Unless objectives are defined, we do not know what to try to measure, and unless we can measure, it is impossible to tell whether, and to what degree, objectives have been realized.

ARRIVING AT
USEFUL STATEMENTS OF OBJECTIVES

Objectives or goals may be stated in various ways. For example, there are immediate objectives and ultimate objectives. Immediate objectives are often stated in terms of something specific to be learned, some skill, knowledge, or understanding to be mastered. Ultimate objectives are more often stated in terms of some long-term goal and are likely to be focused more on the learner than on what is learned. They tend to emphasize the *function* of what is learned rather than the knowledge itself. In civics, for example, immediate objectives may be to learn about the organization of government, the responsibilities and functions of its different branches, and the duties and responsibilities of citizens in a democracy. Ultimate goals in civics might be to establish a continuing interest in improving our government and a willingness to perform conscientiously and consistently the duties of citizenship—such duties as examining and comparing political platforms, candidates, and issues and exercising the right to vote.

Teaching and measurement are all too often concerned with immediate objectives rather than ultimate goals—testing for recall of instructional materials rather than for the ability and willingness to apply the knowledge and skills learned. There are several reasons for this. One is that teaching and testing for immediate objectives are more practical. Of course, every teacher hopes that what is taught today may be remembered and, more important, carried over into action tomorrow and the next day and a year or two or ten years from now. Also, every teacher hopes that what is learned in the classroom will function on the playground, at home, and elsewhere. But it is often not practical—or even possible—to measure accurately the achievement of these long-range goals. Testing for immediate objectives is easier. It is simpler to measure present comprehension than to measure ability and disposition to apply knowledge. It is much easier in the classroom or even in the shop or laboratory to measure a pupil's knowledge of the parts and structure of a gasoline engine than to measure ability to repair such an engine; it is easier to measure knowledge of traffic regulations than to measure respect for and adherence to them. Basically, for reasons of economy of time and effort, most measurement in schools is limited to various types of paper-and-pencil tests. And since immediate learning is often subject-matter oriented, teachers' efforts have been largely directed toward the measurement of knowledge acquisition, to the neglect of learning concerned with action and actual performance, which often cannot be measured at all by paper-and-pencil devices.

Yet schooling has accomplished little if it produces only verbalization of knowledge. Such verbalization is comparatively easy to measure, but it demonstrates little more than that learners can recite what has been taught or read. Formulations of objectives can be very useful in instruction and evaluation *if* they emphasize the functions of knowledge as well as knowledge itself and *if* the objectives are expressed in terms of learners' performance and behavior as well as in terms of the facts learned.

Illustrative of much of what we have been saying about instructional objectives is the *Taxonomy of Educational Objectives*.[1] In the analyses
that make up the Taxonomy, the authors present a general outline of
major categories of instructional objectives. In the cognitive domain
these categories are (1) knowledge, (2) comprehension, (3) application, (4)
analysis, (5) synthesis, and (6) evaluation. Each such major category is
further subdivided. For example, some subdivisions under *knowledge* are
knowledge of *specifics,* such as recall of dates, atomic weights, multiplication tables, and technical terms; knowledge of *criteria,* such as the
criteria for setting up or judging the worth of a testing program; and
knowledge of *principles and generalizations,* such as Mendel's Law in
genetics. *Synthesis* includes production of a unique communication—
that is, communication in writing or speaking of ideas, feelings, or experiences; production of a plan, or proposed set of operations—as, for
example, a lesson plan by a teacher; and derivation of a set of abstract
relations, such as the formulation of an hypothesis to explain observed
phenomena or behavior of experimental animals under controlled laboratory conditions or to derive a principle from a set of data as in a national
educational survey.

In the Taxonomy of the affective domain, the major categories are (1)
receiving (attending), (2) responding, (3) valuing, (4) organization, and (5)
characterization by a value or value complex. Again, each major category
is subdivided. For example, *receiving (attending)* includes *awareness*
("almost a cognitive behavior"), which includes consciousness of aesthetic factors in dress, furnishings, color, form, and the like; *willingness
to receive* (a step above awareness), including careful attentiveness to
what others are saying, appreciation and tolerance of different cultural
patterns, and sensitivity to human need and pressing social problems;
and *controlled or selected attention,* including apparent ability to listen
to music with some discrimination as to mood and meaning, and alertness to human values and judgments on life as recorded in literature.

The Taxonomy for the psychomotor domain includes six major classification levels: (1) reflex movement, (2) basic-fundamental movements,
(3) perceptual abilities, (4) physical abilities, (5) skilled movements, and
(6) nondiscursive communication. The *reflex movement* category is not
related to educational objectives, but proper reflex movements form the
foundation of the more complex movements. Examples of the *basic-*

---

[1] Benjamin S. Bloom et al. (eds.), *Taxonomy of Educational Objectives: The Classification of
Educational Goals,* Handbook 1, *Cognitive Domain* (New York: David McKay, 1954); David
R. Krathwohl, et al., *Taxonomy of Educational Objectives: The Classification of Educational
Goals,* Handbook 2, *Affective Domain* (New York: David McKay, 1964); and Anita J. Harrow,
A Taxonomy of the Psychomotor Domain: A Guide for Developing Behavioral Objectives
(New York: David McKay, 1972).

fundamental movements are walking, finger manipulation, and gripping. *Perceptual abilities* include interpretations of various stimuli and the adjustment of movement to the environment, such as following instructions, jumping a rope, and catching a ball. *Physical abilities* include the physical strength and stamina required for sustained effort, agility, and a wide variety of other activities. The *skilled movements* category refers to efficiency, grace, and skill in performing complex tasks involving movement and physical abilities. *Nondiscursive communication* refers to nonverbal communication such as gestures, choreographic movements, and facial expressions.

The Taxonomy represents one of the most thoughtful analyses of the structure and nature of educational objectives in behavioral terms now available. It provides useful tools, particularly in the cognitive domain, for the teacher or curriculum worker, both as a source of ideas for potential instructional goals and as a comprehensive outline against which to check objectives chosen for a certain class.

The material described above from the Taxonomy represents only a limited outline. The original sources must be consulted for more adequate information and understanding.

What has been said so far suggests that formulating objectives for a field like science or social studies, or even for a single subject, is a rather intricate procedure. Because of the inevitable complexities involved, statements of objectives are usually the work of local, state, or national committees or groups. Such groups are chosen carefully to assure representation of different viewpoints and localities, and the resulting formulations generally represent the best, most forward-looking ideas that the group can produce at that time. Such statements usually represent in some degree a compromise between various viewpoints and may not, therefore, wholly satisfy either the very progressive or the very conservative members of the group. *Sample Statements of Objectives*

Statements of objectives formulated by state or national committees may also not always be acceptable or appropriate in their entirety to local schools or individual teachers. Moreover, curriculum guides of particular school systems and local conditions may suggest objectives differing from some included in state or national pronouncements. We do not mean to imply that the individual classroom teacher should accept such statements uncritically or in total as blueprints for instruction; they will generally be more comprehensive and more precisely formulated, however, than any individual teacher or colleagues are likely to produce. They will be especially useful in suggesting goals of instruction and evaluation, as will be illustrated later in this chapter.

Several illustrative statements of instructional objectives are reproduced below. The first group deals with instruction in science in grade 6. The objectives were abstracted from the teacher's guides that are published as a supplement to the science textbooks.

Models: Electric and Magnetic Interactions[2]

PART I REVIEW

To understand and use certain scientific terms: interaction, system, subsystem, evidence of interaction, interaction-at-a-distance, energy source, variable, circuit, closed circuit, and open circuit

To assemble closed circuits

To identify and investigate conditions under which objects interact

PART II MODELS

To propose models for explaining observation of simple mechanical and electrical systems

To evaluate models by interpreting evidence, making predictions, and performing experiments

PART III A MAGNETIC FIELD MODEL

To predict that magnets will attract or repel other magnets under specified conditions

To identify permanent and temporary magnets

To investigate the field of a magnet system by using a compass or iron filings

To identify variables that affect the operation of a coil-rivet system in a closed circuit

PART IV AN ELECTRICITY MODEL

To draw and interpret diagrams of simple circuits

To use an electricity model for predicting and explaining energy transfer in electric circuits

To identify variables of an electric circuit

PART V PROJECTS (Optional)

To plan and carry out independent investigations of variables in electric interactions

To raise questions about electric interaction and energy transfer

To use graphs for displaying data obtained in experiments

Ecosystems[3]

PART I CLASSROOM ECOSYSTEMS

To use terms introduced in previous life-science units to explain changes that occur in aquarium-terrarium systems

[2]Science Curriculum Improvement Study, teacher's guide for *Models: Electric and Magnetic Interactions,* pp. 22, 45, 60, 82, and 102. Reprinted with permission from the *SCIS Models Teacher's Guide,* published by Rand McNally and Co. Copyright © 1971 by The Regents of the University of California.
[3]Science Curriculum Improvement Study, teacher's guide for *Ecosystems,* pp. 22, 42, 58, 78, and 82. Reprinted with permission from the *SCIS Ecosystems Teacher's Guide,* published by Rand McNally and Co. Copyright © 1971 by The Regents of the University of California.

To use the term *ecosystem* to refer to a community interacting with its physical environment

PART II THE WATER CYCLE
To describe conditions that are necessary for the evaporation and condensation of a liquid

To use the term *water cycle* to refer to the evaporation and condensation of water

To compare the experimental water cycle to the water cycle in nature

PART III THE OXYGEN–CARBON DIOXIDE CYCLE
To use data to verify hypotheses about gases that plants and animals produce and use

To use the term *oxygen–carbon dioxide cycle* to refer to the exchange of gases between organisms and their environment

PART IV CYCLES IN AN ECOSYSTEM
To describe ecosystems in terms of materials cycling through organisms in the environment

PART V POLLUTION
To use the term *pollutant* to refer to a substance that is added to an ecosystem in a quantity harmful to organisms

To describe the effect of pollution on the structure of a biotic community

To identify sources of pollution in an ecosystem

The example below for reading at the grade 9 level illustrates a set of objectives prepared by a state department of education.[4]

III. Reading comprehension
   A. Main ideas
      11. Given a paragraph with the main idea stated, the learner identifies the main idea of the paragraph.
      12. Given a selection from which a main idea can be inferred, the learner identifies the best main idea for the selection.
      13. Given a selection, the learner identifies the best summary of the major ideas in the selection.
   B. Details
      14. Given a selection that specifies a setting, the learner identifies the setting of the selection.
   C. Cause-effect
      15. Given a selection which includes a description of a cause-and-effect relationship between two or more items, the learner identifies the cause and effect of a given situation.
      16. Given a selection with a stated cause, the learner identifies the effect that can be inferred from the selection.

[4]Florida Department of Education, "1974–75 Priority Objectives for Communication Skills (Reading and Writing) and Mathematics in Florida, Grade 9," mimeographed (1974), p. 5.

D. Outcomes and conclusions
    17. Given a selection that compares and contrasts two or more items, the learner identifies the comparison stated in the selection.
    18. Given a selection in which the author draws a conclusion, the learner identifies the author's conclusion.
    19. Given information from which a conclusion can be drawn, the learner identifies the most logical conclusion.
E. Author's intent
    20. Given a selection from which the author's purpose may be inferred, the learner identifies the best inference about the personality or actions of the character.

The social studies objectives listed below are intended to represent terminal objectives at the secondary school level and are written in behavioral terms.[5]

Demonstrate your ability to perceive the relevance of social science data to the topic being considered, to the authority of its source and its freedom from bias.

Demonstrate your ability to use information sources as required in social studies.

Demonstrate your ability to present and support a hypothesis regarding an area of social studies. Your presentation may be written or oral and may take the form of a plan or a simulation model.

Demonstrate your ability to combine concepts, principles, and generalizations by using varied resource materials to develop a library research paper in which you present a hypothesis related to a social studies problem.

Demonstrate your ability to make judgments regarding personal decisions based on reliable data.

Demonstrate your ability to use maps and globes as needed in social studies.

It is obvious that few teachers have the breadth of view or knowledge represented by committees, local or national, or the time that has been available for the committees that have formulated statements of objectives. Yet each teacher has personal ideas as to what objectives are important and useful for a particular class of pupils. Statements of objectives such as those given above can be studied, modified, and adapted for a local purpose. In this process the teacher will learn and grow, and the statements will serve their ultimate purpose, the improvement of instruction. And, of course, students in the classroom will be the ultimate beneficiaries.

[5]Reprinted by permission of the publishers from *Social Studies Behavioral Objectives: A Guide to Individualizing Learning,* by John C. Flanagan, William H. Shanner, and Robert E. Mager. Copyright © 1971 by Westinghouse Learning Corporation, Sunnyvale, California.

Statements of objectives that may be directly useful or that might be modified for local use can be obtained from several sources. Catalogues can be obtained by writing to the following addresses:

Instructional Objectives Exchange, Box 24095, Los Angeles, California 90024
Russell Sage Foundation, 230 Park Avenue, New York, New York 10017
Westinghouse Learning Corporation, P.O. Box 30, Iowa City, Iowa 52240
Objectives and Items CO-OP, School of Education, University of Massachusetts, Amherst, Massachusetts 01002

Many teachers find it useful to take specific portions or items from such statements and relate them to methods, content, and evaluation techniques. This practice may be illustrated as follows:

Objective or goal	Method-content	Evaluation
Ability to take part in group discussion	Committee appointed to plan for a field trip to local city hall	Check-list rating scale
Understanding of time in the geological sense	Study of table of geological eras; field trip to study rocks and fossils	Paper-and-pencil test: identification of rocks and fossils, pictures of animals and plants of prehistoric times

The value of any statement of objectives is determined by the extent to which the statement is accepted and incorporated into the thinking and practice of teachers and to the extent that the statement provides useful guidance for pupils. It is the responsibility of the alert, professionally minded teacher to read and ponder such formulations, to select objectives that best apply in a particular situation, and, as far as possible, to relate teaching and measurement practices to the objectives chosen.

Nothing that has been said above should be taken to mean that classroom teachers should not attempt to formulate statements of objectives for their classes. One of the most useful and thought-provoking activities in which teachers can engage is formulating a statement of objectives for each subject they teach. Clearly perceived objectives can vitalize teaching and make a teacher intelligently critical of the procedures he or she uses. However, teachers should not be condemned if they adopt as their own the objectives expressed either explicitly or implicitly in good textbooks. Whatever the nature and source of their objectives, it is important that teachers think about those objectives, adopt whichever objectives seem good to them (or possibly to their local curriculum committee), and incorporate them into their teaching.

No single test, examination, or procedure can measure all objectives, nor can one teacher do an adequate job of weighing all the many possible objectives in a given field. Each teacher must choose from a list of good objectives those that will be attempted at any given time and then formulate a teaching and measurement program on the basis of the objectives selected; another time the teacher will decide upon another goal or set of goals to be measured and may well use quite different teaching and measuring procedures. By constantly re-examining and reappraising objectives, the teacher will gain a broader outlook on teaching and will develop breadth and skill in measuring a variety of outcomes. This will inevitably result in a fairer and more adequate evaluation of the pupil's status, growth, and progress.

LEARNING EXERCISES

1. Select some element of a subject such as fractions in fifth-grade arithmetic, customs of a people like the Eskimos, rules of punctuation in language arts, the writing of simple formulas for chemical compounds, or some other with which you are thoroughly familiar. State some of the objectives you would attempt to achieve or have your pupils achieve if you were teaching.

2. Criticize constructively one of the sample statements of objectives given above. Does the statement seem to you to be appropriate for the grade level or levels indicated? Clear and precise? Important within the specified area of the curriculum? Of practical value to a classroom teacher?

3. Relate the statement of objectives for science (p. 128), reading (p. 129), or social studies (p. 130) to the *Taxonomy of Educational Objectives*, both cognitive and affective domains. Key the objectives in the statement you choose to the Taxonomy by coding them, using letters for the domains (C or A) and numbers for the categories, thus: C-2, A-1. How comprehensive are the statements of objectives? Do they neglect major categories in the Taxonomy? If so, which ones? How would you remedy such omissions? Do any of the objectives relate to the psychomotor domain?

Most objectives developed or selected for a particular class refer to the knowledge to be gained or the understanding to be developed as a result of instruction. To be most useful, objectives should be stated in terms of changes that should occur in pupils if the anticipated achievement is realized. This approach puts the focus of the objective on student behavior, indicating the knowledge, skill, or understanding to be possessed at the close of instruction. One way to insure the focus on student characteristics is to use behavioral verbs in objectives. Objectives written in this way are commonly referred to as *behavioral objectives.*

Many objectives are stated in general terms such as "to know the parts of the human eye." This objective could be converted to a behavioral form such as "Given a diagram of a human eye, the pupil can label each part correctly." This objective converts the "to know" into a specific illustration of what "to know" means.

Another objective in rather general form might be "to use punctuation correctly." A number of different behavioral objectives could be derived from this general objective, such as "Given sentences containing punctuation errors, the pupil rewrites the sentences using correct punctuation."

Many of the statements of objectives prepared by national committees now use the behavioral approach. Because of the widespread acceptance of this approach, lists of behavioral verbs have been collected and published. The set given below is an example of such lists.[6]

add	define	identify	prove
analyze	describe	interpret	record
assemble	diagram	itemize	rewrite
bisect	disassemble	list	sing
build	dissect	locate	solve
calculate	divide	make	subtract
choose	draw	measure	summarize
compare	explain	multiply	support
construct	extract	outline	tell
contrast	extrapolate	play	translate
correct	factor	predict	weigh
criticize	graph	produce	write

Although behavioral objectives are rather specific with regard to the nature of the achievement that is expected, they do not specify the

[6]From Dale P. Scannell and D. B. Tracy, *Testing and Measurement in the Classroom* (Boston: Houghton Mifflin, 1975), p. 44.

quality of the performance that will be minimally acceptable. Behavioral objectives can be modified to indicate the level of performance expected, and such objectives may be referred to as criterion-referenced objectives. The criterion-referenced approach to the two behavioral objectives given above might be:

> Given the drawing of a human eye, the pupil can correctly label the parts with no more than one error.
> Given sentences containing punctuation errors, the pupil will rewrite these sentences using appropriate punctuation in at least 80 percent of the sentences.

Criterion-referenced objectives are most useful when used within a mastery model of teaching. Such a model normally includes sequenced objectives and activities and involves frequent testing to determine the level of pupil achievement. Within such a model pupils must demonstrate minimal competence in one instructional unit before moving to the next instructional activity; pupils who fail to meet the criterion specified are presented remedial or supplementary instruction and are required to repeat the mastery test for that unit of instruction.

The concept of teaching for mastery is not new to education. Promotions from one grade to the next or from one course to the second in a sequence (such as from French 1 to French 2) are based on the notion that a certain amount of learning is required at one level before a pupil can profit from the next level of instruction. Traditionally decisions such as these have occurred at the end of a semester or a year's work, and the new aspect to the mastery learning model is the frequency with which decisions about progress are made by teachers. Instructional units in a mastery model may require less than one class period for a pupil or may extend over several days, but in all cases demonstrations of mastery would be required frequently during each quarter or semester of the school year.

Mastery models are most useful within an individualized system of instruction. In theory, all pupils are expected to reach at least a minimal level of achievement or mastery, and the time allowed for learning varies with individual pupils. There is some question about the extent to which such individualization of instruction can occur in the typical class or school as presently organized. Even so, the use of criterion-referenced objectives and mastery tests has gained increased acceptance in recent years and may continue to influence educational practice for a number of years to come.

4. Select five objectives from the examples presented on pages 125–131 and, if they are not in behavior terms, convert them to behavioral objectives. Then convert the behavioral objectives into criterion-referenced objectives, using standards that you feel would be appropriate at some specified level of instruction.

HOW OBJECTIVES FUNCTION IN GOOD MEASUREMENT

So far we have emphasized the importance of objectives in measuring the results of instruction and have given some sample statements of educational objectives in subject-matter areas and some suggestions regarding how teachers may adapt these to their own purposes or develop some objectives of their own. In the remainder of the chapter we shall see how objectives may actually function in the process of devising measuring instruments or techniques.

Once we have selected the objective to be measured, our chief task is to decide on the method of measurement and then construct suitable tests or other instruments. Of course, as has already been noted, the measurement of different kinds of goals presents problems of a widely varying nature. Objectives such as the ability to solve certain problems in addition, subtraction, multiplication, and division are easier to measure than the ability or inclination to keep accurate financial accounts in the home. Indeed, little of our measurement in the schools gets at these more remote, yet very important, outcomes. It is easier to measure knowledge objectives than to measure attitudes or appreciations. It is possible to determine quite satisfactorily how well an individual has learned the principles of good sportsmanship, but it is quite a different matter to measure disposition to follow these principles and adhere to them in athletic competition. However, great progress has been made in the development of a wide variety of measuring and evaluative techniques. Teachers and others responsible for the evaluation of educational products should keep these difficult-to-measure goals always in mind and continually experiment with ways of measuring them accurately.

One of the steps in measurement that often presents difficulties is the relating of content or subject matter to educational goals. For example, just what is the purpose from the pupil's standpoint of learning this or that specific thing? In the case of subjects like homemaking or auto mechanics, the answers to such questions are fairly clear. However, in the case of the more academic subjects like algebra or Latin, the answers are not so obvious, though they may be inferred from such statements of objectives as have been cited above. In making tests of certain educational goals it is essential to relate course content to objectives. One device helpful in doing this is a two-way chart or table of specifications; an example for high-school biology is shown in Table 5.1.

The major areas of course content are outlined at the left, while the educational objectives in terms of pupil behavior are listed across the top. The figures in the main body of the table represent the points of intersection of these two aspects of the work being tested. These figures represent the test-maker's judgment as to the amount of emphasis that each area should receive in the total examination, in terms of the proportion of questions or items to be included in the test. This is a subjective process, and these proportions should be determined on the basis of relative emphasis placed on different topics as gauged by the time spent in class and number and scope of assignments on them, not on the ease with which such topics lend themselves to construction of objective test items.

For example, the proportion of content on characteristics, structure, classification, and grouping of living things is 30 percent. This means that 30 percent of the items in the test should be based on this content. Now, under the major category of objectives, *knowledge* is given a weight of 25 percent. If we multiply .30 × .25, the product is .075. This tells us that 7.5 percent of the items in the test should be based on the content area *living things* and should be designed to measure knowledge about their characteristics and structure, as listed in the chart. The area *methodology and research* represents 10 percent of the total content and the objective *application*, 35 percent. Therefore, we find that .10 × .35, or 3.5 percent, of the test items should be about this matter.

Although the totals in the columns and the rows agree with the theoretical or desired percentages, those in the cells or boxes do not always do so. For one thing, we could obviously not have a fraction of an item in a cell. For another, the test-maker will find in writing items that certain content does not lend itself to the measurement of certain objectives whereas other content may serve the purpose particularly well. Therefore, it should not be regarded as necessary to adhere rigidly to the theoretical values in each cell of such a chart, though much of its value in test construction is lost if it does not function as a rather specific guide to the work. It is highly important to construct such a chart and build a

Distribution and Relationship of Content and Objectives for a Test in High-School Biology. Unlabeled numbers in table body represent percentages of items. *Table 5.1*

	Objectives			
Content	Knowledge (25% weight)	Understanding (40% weight)	Application (35% weight)	Total 100%
Living things (30% of items) Characteristics, cellular and molecular structure, classification and grouping	8	12	10	30%
Life processes (50% of items) Human health and functions Plant and animal life Life cycles, reproduction, heredity, and biological history	12	21	17	50%
Ecological relationships (10% of items) World biome, natural resources, and conservation	3	4	3	10%
Methodology and research (10% of items) Experimental reasoning, procedures, and terminology	2	3	5	10%
Total	25%	40%	35%	100%

SOURCE: Adapted by permission of Clarence H. Nelson, Michigan State University.

test *from* it rather than to construct a test and then analyze what has been produced. This is "putting the cart before the horse" and negates entirely the purpose of the chart.

The development of such a chart by a teacher or prospective teacher is a most useful and rewarding activity. It requires facing up to and answering several of the following questions: What content shall I teach or attempt to cover? How shall our time and effort be apportioned? Why am I teaching this and why should my students study it? Specifically, what are our mutually understood goals of instruction? And, eventually, how will I measure the degree to which my students, individually and as a group, have attained these objectives? These are searching questions—questions everyone who wishes to be a good teacher should and must face and answer.

One of the major problems in developing a highly valid achievement test is that of sampling pupil achievement thoroughly and with appropriate emphasis on the various facets of the instructional objectives. The use of a chart helps minimize the problem, as will serious attention to the questions such charts raise. Even so, there is another aspect of the sampling process that all teachers should consider while planning a test.

Most objectives can be measured by a large number of different items, each reflecting the objective but based on different content. In addition, item format must be selected from the various approaches that could be used. As a result, even though a cell in a table of specifications identifies an objective with some phase of subject matter, the teacher still must select the content and format for the items that will represent the cell on the test.

One example will be given to illustrate these points. Suppose that a cell in a chart is concerned with the appropriate use of end punctuation in expository writing. This segment of the achievement domain could be measured by items based on a virtually infinite number of sentences that could be constructed or selected. The content could include questions, declarations, exclamations, and simple and compound sentences and could include the use of quotation marks. The possible formats include written and oral questions, completion items with a blank where the punctuation is to be indicated, multiple-choice items that present a sentence and give five possible ways to punctuate the ending, a multiple-choice item with five different sentences, one of which is incorrectly (or correctly) punctuated; or pupils could be asked to write themes or sentences on an assigned topic.

One approach that teachers can use to facilitate this phase of planning is to prepare separate two-way charts for each cell of a test chart. One side lists the major categories of content that can be used; the other shows the formats that are feasible. Using the previous example, a teacher might have a chart such as the following:

Content category		*Item format*		
	Completion	*Multiple-choice*	*Assigned writing*	*Dictated sentences*
Simple sentences				
Compound sentences				
Questions				
Exclamations				

OBJECTIVES AS THE BASIS OF ALL GOOD MEASUREMENT

Then the teacher must decide which combinations of content and format are essential or extremely important and must decide how to allocate the previously determined number of items across these combinations. The use of this approach will enhance the contribution that systematic planning makes to improving the quality of classroom measurement by further refining the definition of achievement that pupils are expected to make.

LEARNING EXERCISE

5. Using Table 5.1 as a model, construct a chart showing objectives and content for a unit of work or a subject you feel competent to teach. Indicate the subject, grade level, and scope of the content. You need not fill in the numbers in the cells but you should make a judgment as to the percentage emphasis for each objective and each area of content. (It is usually helpful if two people construct such a chart together.)

An excellent illustration showing how test items may be keyed to specific objectives is to be found in the *Iowa Tests of Basic Skills*, Multi-Level Edition, for grades 3–9, Form 5.[7] Figure 5.1 shows a page from the test of Work-Study Skills. Also reproduced here is a page from the *Teacher's Manual* corresponding to the map-reading section of the Work-Study Skills test (see Figure 5.2). Notice the statements of the various skills involved in map reading and the table showing the relationship of each test item to a specific skill-objective.

Altogether, the test includes eighty-nine map-reading items for grades 3–9. Items 79–84, as shown in Figure 5.1, are for grades 8 and 9. After the test has been given and scored, the items answered correctly and those missed can be checked against the analysis of skills and the key. Thus, a teacher is able to determine which map-reading skills have been attained and which have not. This can be done for individual pupils as well as for the class as a whole.

A teacher may wish to construct a test or some other device for measuring the results of instruction on a single objective such as

[7]E.F. Lindquist and A. N. Hieronymus, *Iowa Tests of Basic Skills* (Boston: Houghton Mifflin, 1971).

Page 60

The map shown below is a part of a road map. To help you find quickly any city or town shown on the map, the names of the cities and towns have been arranged in alphabetical order, beginning near the top. The key to the map is given below it.

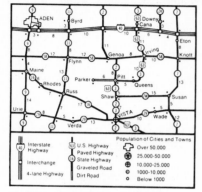

79. Which of these highways begins at U.S. Interstate Highway 40?

1) ⑦   2) ⑪   3) ㉔   4) ⑥③

80. What might be the population of Pitt?
   1) 983   2) 3241   3) 18,364   4) 12,716

81. Which of these highways would one take to travel by the shortest route from Wade to Downy?
   1) ㉙ , ⑦ , ⑳ , ㉔
   2) ㉙ , ⑥③ , ⑳
   3) ㉙ , ⑥③ , ⑳ , ㉔
   4) ㉙ , ⑦ , ㉞ , ⑥③ , ⑳ , ㉔

82. How many miles closer is it from Vista to Susan by way of Wade instead of through Shaw?
   1) 2   2) 7   3) 8   4) 20

83. Where might one see this highway sign?

   1) Three miles south of Byrd
   2) At Interstate 40 interchange, 10 miles west of Cana
   3) At Flynn
   4) At the junction of ⑦ and ㊞

84. Mr. Forbes is traveling east on Interstate Highway 40, going to Knott. To make the best time, at which of these state highways would he probably leave Highway 40?
   1) ⑦   2) ⑦   3) ⑨   4) ⑪

From *Iowa Tests of Basic Skills*, Form 5, by A. N. Hieronymus & E. F. Lindquist, published by Houghton Mifflin Company, © 1971. Reprinted by permission.

problem-solving ability. This task likewise involves a breakdown of the objective into behavioral elements that can be observed or tested and recorded as evidence of the learner's progress toward the desired goal.

Several examples are given below to show how test items can be related to the more functional objectives in various areas of common learning. The first three are in the area of study skills.[8]

Objective: Ability to differentiate between fact and opinion.
Directions: In the list below, some of the sentences are statements of *fact*, and others are statements of *opinion*. Indicate to which class you think each statement belongs by placing the proper letter in the space provided for it. *Do not* try to decide if each statement is true or false, but only whether it should be classified as a statement of *fact* or of *opinion*.

F—Fact
O—Opinion

(O) 1. The Democratic party has done more for this country than the Republican party has.
(F) 2. In 1939 there were two World's Fairs held in the United States.
(F) 3. Alaska is northwest of Oregon.

[8]Horace T. Morse and George H. McCune, *Selected Items for the Testing of Study Skills and Critical Thinking*, 4th ed., Bulletin No. 15, National Council for the Social Studies (Washington, D.C.: National Education Association, 1964), pp. 36, 43, 80–81. Reprinted with permission of the National Council for the Social Studies and George H. McCune.

A Page from the *Teacher's Manual* Corresponding to the Map-Reading Section of   *Figure 5.2*
the Test of Work-Study Skills

TEST W-1 MAP READING

Skills Classification

1. Ability to orient map and determine direction
   a) To determine direction from orientation
   b) To determine direction from parallels or meridians
   c) To determine direction of river flow or slope of land

2. Ability to locate and/or describe places on maps and globes
   a) Through the use of standard map symbols
   b) Through the use of a key
   c) Through the use of distance and/or direction
   d) Through the use of latitude or longitude

3. Ability to determine distances

a) Determining distance on a road map
b) Determining distance by using a scale of miles
c) Determining distance on a globe
d) Comparing distances

4. Ability to determine or trace routes of travel

5. Ability to understand seasonal variations, sun patterns, and time differences

6. Ability to read and compare facts from one or more pattern maps

7. Ability to visualize landscape features

8. Ability to infer man's activities or way of living
   a) From outline maps
   b) From pattern maps

TEST W-1 MAP READING

Item No.	Form 5	Form 6	Item No.	Form 5	Form 6	Item No.	Form 5	Form 6
1	4	3d	31	6	8b	61	6	3b
2	3d	1a	32	8b	3b	62	6	6
3	2b	4	33	2a	8b	63	6	8b
4	4	3d	34	3b	7	64	8b	7
5	7	2c	35	8b	3d	65	6	6
6	3a	3d	36	6	5	66	8b	6
7	2b	2a	37	6	8a	67	6	8b
8	2b	2c	38	3d	2b	68	6	7
9	4	1a	39	2b	4	69	8b	6
10	2c	3d	40	2b	4	70	8b	8b
11	3d	4	41	8a	2b	71	6	6
12	8a	4	42	4	3a	72	6	6
13	4	2a	43	2c	4	73	6	6
14	2a	2c	44	2b	3d	74	6	6
15	2a	2a	45	3d	2c	75	8b	8b
16	2a	2a	46	4	3d	76	7	8b
17	1a	2a	47	3a	2a	77	6	7
18	8a	4	48	2d	2d	78	6	2d
19	2c	8a	49	5	2d	79	4	4
20	1c	3d	50	2d	5	80	2b	3a
21	2a	1a	51	1b	1b	81	3d	4
22	7	7	52	8a	1b	82	3d	3d
23	8a	2b	53	5	5	83	2c	2b
24	1c	3b	54	5	8a	84	4	3a
25	2b	7	55	5	5	85	1b	1b
26	3d	3d	56	2d	5	86	5	4
27	3b	1c	57	1c	2d	87	2d	2d
28	2b	5	58	3c	1b	88	4	5
29	8b	7	59	1c	1c	89	1b	1b
30	7	8b	60	3b	8b			

From E. F. Lindquist & A. N. Hieronymus, *Teacher's Manual* for the *Iowa Tests of Basic Skills* (Boston: Houghton Mifflin Company, 1971). Reprinted by permission.

(F) 4. Scientific research often results in the production of new products.
(O) 5. No war has ever accomplished any good for the world.
(O) 6. A high tariff increases the prosperity of the country.
(O) 7. Only his defeat at the battle of Waterloo prevented Napoleon from making himself master of Europe.

Objective: Understanding of use of common references.
Directions: The degree to which a social-studies library is useful to students is determined partly by the ability of students to obtain needed information. Below are two lists. One contains those books which could compose a Social Studies Reference Shelf. The other contains a list of questions which you might wish to have answered. Do *not* try to answer the questions. Indicate whether you could find the answers, by placing beside the *number* of the

question the *letter* of the reference work in which you would be likely to find the answer most satisfactorily.

Example:

(F) 0. How many students are enrolled in American colleges and universities?

The answer *F* refers to the *World Almanac,* a handbook of current information.

Reference Shelf

A. *Dictionary of American History*
B. An Atlas
C. *A Guide to the Study of the United States of America*
D. *Historical Statistics of the United States*
E. *Who's Who in America*
F. *The World Almanac*

G. *Readers' Guide to Periodical Literature*
H. Official State Government Handbook
I. *Dictionary of American Biography*
J. *Harvard Guide to American History*

Questions

(B) 1. How does North America compare in size with Africa?
(H) 2. Who is the chief justice of your state supreme court?
(F) 3. How many persons were killed by autos last year?
(A) 4. When was the Cumberland Road built?
(H) 5. Who is the official custodian of state law?
(G) 6. What was the political significance of the last Congressional election?
(F) 7. How much cotton was exported from the United States from 1950–1960?

Objective: Recognizing statements which support generalizations.

Directions: After each of the main headings or generalizations lettered A, B, C, and D, there are numbered statements. Consider each generalization and its statements as a unit. Study each unit carefully and if in your judgment any statement below each generalization could be used as a base to support the generalization, indicate the same by placing the letter Y (for "yes") opposite the number of the statement. If the statement does not uphold the general statement, indicate the same by placing the letter N (for "no") opposite the number of the statement.

A. Milton said: "Liberty to know, to utter and to argue freely according to our own conscience, is the highest form of liberty."

(Y) 16. The facts of history suggest that radical doctrines are never dangerous so long as they may be freely discussed.
(N) 17. A common saying is, "Let your conscience be your guide."
(Y) 18. The denial of free speech is a poor way to combat dangerous ideas.
(Y) 19. Free expression of opinion is essential to political liberty.

The examples above illustrate the design of paper-and-pencil tests that go beyond the measurement of mere knowledge and get at understanding such as the ability to interpret and the ability to apply knowledge. In most subjects, particularly academic ones, measurement is largely confined to paper-and-pencil devices. It is possible, however, to use other kinds of tests in some areas like shop, business, homemaking, and agriculture. Here, actual performance can be observed and rated. For example, when a pupil is given a recipe for a cake and access to the necessary ingredients and equipment and is permitted to prepare the cake according to directions, it is possible to observe the pupil's behavior and appraise it by means of a checklist and to judge the product by the use of some kind of a rating device. A series of rating scales for different products of food preparation has been worked out by Clara M. Brown.[9] A sample scale for evaluating a cake will illustrate the nature of these rating devices:

Cake (Angel or Sponge)

		1	2	3	Score
Appearance	1.	Sunken or very rounded top	Flat or slightly rounded top		1. _____
	2.	Sugary surface or deep crevices	Slightly rough surface like macaroons		2. _____
Color	3.	Dark brown or pale	Even, delicate brown		3. _____
Moisture content	4.	Dry or insufficiently baked	Slightly moist		4. _____
Texture	5.	Coarse	Small holes, uniformly distributed		5. _____
Lightness	6.	Heavy	Very light		6. _____
Tenderness	7.	Tough	Very tender		7. _____
Taste and flavor	8.	Flat, too sweet, eggy, or too highly flavored	Pleasing, delicate flavor		8. _____

A good performance test of achievement should be based on the following elements:

1. Development of a statement of instructional objectives
2. Detailed analysis of the task to be performed in the light of instructional goals
3. A set of specific directions for performance of the steps or parts of the task and the sequence or order in which they are to be carried out
4. A list of the tools, equipment, and materials that will be needed
5. A detailed description of the procedure for evaluating performance. This probably will include:
   a. time deemed necessary for each step
   b. efficiency rating in handling tools, equipment, and materials
   c. quality rating of the product

[9]Clara M. Brown, *Food Score Cards* (Minneapolis, Minn.: University of Minnesota Press, 1940).

The evaluation is usually carried out by means of checklists providing for ratings by the observer of each aspect of the work and quality of the product (if any) such as the example given above.

In most vocational subjects it is possible to measure behavior in situations that closely resemble actual working conditions, though it is not easy to do so in the more academic subjects like science or mathematics or history. In such areas the ultimate and more remote goals such as scientific attitudes, problem-solving skills, and good citizenship can usually be measured only in a verbalized form. It is generally possible to determine what a pupil *says* the appropriate behavior would be under a given set of circumstances, but it is much more difficult—if not impossible—to subject the student to realistic circumstances for measurement purposes. Yet, as the illustrations that we have given demonstrate, considerable progress has been made and more will certainly come. Teachers and others responsible for measurement and evaluation in the schools should always keep before them the ideal of making their practices in this area functional; that is, measurement should be concerned with the appraisal of behavior as far as possible rather than with verbalization.

At the same time, teachers and prospective teachers should use or experiment with all current methods of measurement, though, as was pointed out in the beginning of this chapter, paper-and-pencil tests will continue to be the mainstay of the measurement program. Moreover, behavior should not be conceived of in too narrow a sense. When a child solves an arithmetic problem, reads a story with understanding, or interprets a map or a chart, behavior is exhibited that can be adequately measured by paper-and-pencil tests. The teacher's goal should be to make tests as adequate as possible and to supplement them whenever possible with a wide variety of other types of measurement and evaluation. The broader and more comprehensive the approach, the better the chances of encompassing in the measurement program all of the important objectives of instruction.

LEARNING EXERCISE

6. In Exercise 1 you were asked to select some defined and limited phase of a subject and to state some of the objectives you would consider important if you were teaching. Considering these same objectives, describe in detail with examples the kind of measurement techniques you would use to determine how well your goals had been achieved.

OBJECTIVES AS THE BASIS OF ALL GOOD MEASUREMENT

SUGGESTED READING

BAKER, EVA L., and POPHAM, JAMES W. *Expanding Dimensions of Instructional Objectives*. Englewood Cliffs, N.J.: Prentice-Hall, 1973. A programmed paperback on humanizing objectives, affective objectives, defining content, and developing tests to measure objectives.

BLOOM, BENJAMIN S., et al., eds. *Taxonomy of Educational Objectives*. Handbook 1. *Cognitive Domain*. New York: David McKay, 1956. A discussion of the problem of classifying educational objectives in a systematic way. Somewhat advanced for the beginner in test construction but contains many useful ideas.

EBEL, ROBERT L. *Essentials of Educational Measurement*. 2d ed. Englewood Cliffs, N.J.: Prentice-Hall, 1972. Chap. 2. An excellent discussion of basic questions on the formulation of educational objectives and the problems of developing effective procedures for measuring them. Use and limitations of objectives in test development on pages 57–61.

GRONLUND, NORMAN E. *Stating Behavioral Objectives for Classroom Instruction*. New York: Macmillan, 1970. A how-to-do-it booklet on preparing objectives for teaching and testing. Emphasizes stating of objectives as learning outcomes and in terms of specific types of behavior to be demonstrated as evidence of learning.

KRATHWOHL, DAVID R., et al. *Taxonomy of Educational Objectives*. Handbook 2. *Affective Domain*. New York: David McKay Co., 1964. A companion volume to Bloom, discussing the classification of educational goals in the noncognitive domain.

KRYSPIN, WILLIAM J., and JOHN F. FELDHUSEN. *Writing Behavioral Objectives*. Minneapolis: Burgess Pub. Co., 1974. A programmed paperback covering techniques for developing behavioral objectives and objectives at higher cognitive levels. Some useful examples of preparing tables of specification and relating behavioral objectives to the Taxonomy.

LINDQUIST, E. F., ed. *Educational Measurement*. Washington, D.C.: American Council on Education, 1951. Chap. 5, "Preliminary Considerations in Objective Test Construction," by E. F. Lindquist. Chap. 6, "Planning the Objective Test," by K. W. Vaughn. Both chapters, though somewhat advanced in concept for ordinary measurement activities in the classroom, present many good ideas and useful suggestions on objectives and construction of tests.

NATIONAL SOCIETY FOR THE STUDY OF EDUCATION. *The Measurement of Understanding*. Forty-fifth Yearbook. Part I. Chicago: University of Chicago Press, 1946. Emphasizes the importance of trying to teach and test for understanding. The main body of the report consists of twelve chapters, each on a major area of instruction and presenting a discussion and examples of the measurement of objectives in that area. A wealth of ideas on the improvement of objective measures of achievement.

NELSON, CLARENCE H. *Measurement and Evaluation in the Classroom.* New York: Macmillan, 1970. Chap. 3 and 5. A practical discussion of the role of instructional objectives in classroom measurement and evaluation. Includes suggestions for drawing up a table of specifications for a test.

THORNDIKE, ROBERT L., ed. *Educational Measurement.* 2d ed. Washington, D.C.: American Council on Education, 1971. Chap. 2, "Defining and Assessing Educational Objectives." A broad and sometimes philosophical overview of the role of objectives in instruction and measurement.

TUCKMAN, BRUCE W. *Measuring Educational Outcomes.* New York: Harcourt Brace Jovanovich, 1975. Chapter 2 includes discussion of constructing objectives and taxonomies. Chapter 3 discusses ways of relating objectives to test planning and development. A thorough treatment.

Six

PLANNING AND CONSTRUCTING
THE TEACHER-MADE TEST

Most schools in the United States today use standardized tests of one kind or another. Most tests of intelligence, aptitude, personality, and interests are standardized, made by specialists for a test publisher, and sold by the publisher throughout the country. Few schools or school systems, except in the very large city organizations, attempt to develop such tests for their own use.

The situation with respect to achievement tests is somewhat different. There are, of course, many standardized achievement tests on the market, and literally millions are used every year, including tests in separate subjects as well as achievement batteries. Teachers usually feel that these tests do not adequately measure their own or the local objectives of instruction, however. Standardized tests are very useful in some ways, but they are not usually the principal method of measuring achievement. In general, the classroom teacher formulates achievement tests. It is important, therefore, that the teacher's professional training include some instruction on effective ways of planning, constructing, and evaluating various measuring instruments.

After studying this chapter, you should be able to perform the following tasks related to planning and developing tests for classroom use:

1. Distinguish between appropriate uses of standardized and locally constructed tests of achievement. Describe how standardized and locally developed tests can be used to complement each other.
2. Describe the preliminary steps and the purpose of each step a teacher should take in developing a classroom test.

3. Use textbook materials, courses of study, statements of learned societies, and other relevant materials to select or develop objectives for the courses or grade levels you will teach. Identify each objective as one most appropriately or efficiently measured by essay questions or by one of the following types of objective items: short-answer, completion, true-false, matching, multiple-choice, key-list, and situational and interpretive exercises using true-false or multiple-choice items.
4. Develop essay questions and scoring procedures and objective items to measure the objectives you have selected or developed.
5. Discuss the effect that various technical errors in essay and objective items have on the efficiency and effectiveness of testing.

STANDARDIZED VERSUS TEACHER-MADE TESTS

Clearly, no standardized achievement test can completely serve the needs and purposes of every local situation. The requirements for a standardized test are such that the test must be largely confined to the elements of instruction common in a large number of schools. A test cannot, if it is to be widely useful, include all the elements peculiar to any one or even a limited number of schools. The most desirable and probably the most common practice is to use both standardized and teacher-made measuring instruments. Both serve useful though somewhat different purposes, and both are important parts of a well-rounded measurement program.

Since teacher-made tests play an important part in the evaluation practices of schools, it is well to give some attention to accepted principles of *planning, constructing, using,* and *evaluating* such instruments. These are the four main stages in the process of testing. We will consider the stages of planning and constructing in this chapter, and we will examine the use and evaluation of teacher-made tests in Chapter 7.

We have already seen that in developing a standardized test—as, for example, for first-year algebra—the planning is generally quite extensive and detailed (Chapter 4). Textbooks, courses of study, and committee reports are analyzed for common objectives and content; the tests are carefully planned with regard to length, administration, and scoring.

When a committee of teachers plans a test for local use, some of the same steps are carried out, though in a less elaborate and formal way. Similarly, a teacher constructing a test or measuring device for classroom use does not usually need to go through such a formal procedure. For one thing, the teacher has some degree of choice regarding objectives and methods. For another, the teacher knows fairly clearly what the test should cover or measure, when the test will be used, and how much time can be given to it. Finally, the teacher knows what has been taught and what testing has already been done so that the proposed test can be fitted into the situation appropriately. In other words, much of what constitutes planning in making a standardized test is taken care of more or less incidentally and automatically when teachers devise tests for local classroom use.

We have already discussed some aspects of planning in Chapter 5. Examples were given there of test questions designed to measure different kinds of instructional objectives. Those examples illustrated different types of test questions. In the rest of this chapter, we will give additional consideration to planning tests and the problems and principles of constructing good questions or items for locally made tests.

LEARNING EXERCISES

1. Examine a standardized achievement test in a subject and grade level that you expect to teach. What objectives does it seem to measure adequately? What objectives are omitted or covered insufficiently?
2. What are the advantages and disadvantages of having teacher committees develop major examinations for use throughout a school district in a particular grade level or subject? How would a committee's process differ from a teacher's process in developing tests independently?

BASIC QUALIFICATIONS OF THE TEST-MAKER

To make an appropriate and effective achievement test requires three somewhat different abilities. In the first place, one must have adequate knowledge of the subject matter. It is not possible to construct a good examination without adequate knowledge of the field, whether it is reading, civics, driver-training, or some other specialty. The person who attempts to construct examinations without such a foundation quickly reveals deficiencies both to associates and, sooner or later, to pupils.

A second requirement for making good test items is some degree of knowledge and skill in the techniques of test construction. This, contrary to what some students suppose, is not something that comes naturally. The techniques of making acceptable test items have been developed by the experience of test experts and teachers over a period of many years, and much of value has thus been learned. Even in the preparation of an essay examination, considerable thought and effort have been spent in finding ways to eliminate some of the shortcomings without sacrificing the good qualities.

The third requisite for the successful test-maker is a knack of putting ideas accurately, concisely, and unambiguously into words. The ability to apply subject matter knowledge and test-construction skill to the formulation of items that are brief and clear and measure accurately what the maker of the instrument intends is almost an art. This ability can be developed to some extent by most teachers who possess the first two qualifications and who have a good command of the language and a desire to learn.

In the kinds of courses for which this book is intended, little or nothing can be done about the first and third requirements. Adequate knowledge of subject matter and the ability to put ideas into good, clear English are not the objectives of a course in measurement. However, it is an objective of such a course and of this book to provide some understanding of the basic principles of making good classroom tests and, as far as possible, to give some practice in doing this.

LEARNING EXERCISE

3. Rate yourself on the following scale by indicating where you think you stand with respect to each of the characteristics listed.

    a. Command of my subject or major in comparison with my classmates: superior _____; better than average _____; average _____; distinctly below average _____; weak _____.

    b. Experience in making test items or questions: a great deal _____; substantial _____; a fair amount _____; little _____; none _____.

    c. Command of English: one of my strongest assets _____; rather good _____; just average _____; not too strong _____; poor _____.

    Rank yourself on the three characteristics listed above: best _____; next best _____; least _____.

PRELIMINARY STEPS

As we have emphasized in Chapter 5, the first step in planning a test or measuring instrument is to decide what goals or objectives to measure. Since goals are reached primarily through course content and class activities, we recommended and illustrated the development of a two-way chart, or test plan, in Chapter 5 as an effective way of relating goals to content and activities. Using a test plan increases the likelihood that the test will reflect with appropriate emphasis all important aspects of instruction and will thus be valid. In addition, teachers find that a test plan serves a guidance function for developing and selecting ideas to include on the test.

Once the teacher has identified the objectives to be covered on a test, the next step is to decide what type of test will best accomplish the purposes. Perhaps an essay test will be best, or perhaps the teacher will decide to use an objective test. If an objective test is chosen, the teacher must decide whether to use true-false, multiple-choice, matching, or short-answer questions or some modifications or combinations of these. This decision is usually influenced by the types of items the teacher has had the most success with and the nature of the content, processes, or skills to be measured. Often it is better not to make a firm decision on this matter in advance but to construct the kinds of items that seem most suited to the particular objectives and content as one progresses with the construction of the test.

In practice, it is customary to begin with a canvass of the instructional materials and activities that have been used in attaining the educational objectives to be measured by the test. These include reading assignments, problems, experiments, film showings, discussions, and field trips. As the teacher reviews the materials and activities, their relationship to important outcomes will be re-emphasized and will probably suggest approaches to evaluation. The test-maker who decides to use objective techniques may find that one phase of the work lends itself to one type of item, whereas another purpose may be best served by a different type. In such cases the test-maker should generally follow natural inclination and not attempt to make all the true-false items at once, then all the multiple-choice items, and so on. The nature of the knowledge, skill, or outcome to be tested usually suggests and may even determine the kind of item that is most appropriate. When it seems possible to accomplish one's purposes equally well with either of two different types of items, other considerations will help settle the choice of which type to use.

As the items are devised, each might be written on an index card. If a test plan has been developed, it is useful to code each card in terms of the cell of the plan that the item covers. When all the items have been written, the cards may be stored and arranged in any way or on any basis desired—type of item, content, length, estimated difficulty, source. Information obtained on the effectiveness of items by trying them out can be entered on the cards, as well as dates of construction and use and cross-references. Cards provide a high degree of flexibility, which is of great value. They are easily filed and grouped. Also, single cards can be easily eliminated without disturbing the rest of the file if any of the items prove ineffective. The teacher who builds up a file of test items will be able to select different samples of questions for various tests and purposes.

TYPES OF TEST ITEMS

In this discussion we will be making a distinction between the more *subjective* types of questions, such as the essay and short-answer, and the more *objective* types of items,[1] such as true-false, multiple-choice, and matching. This is actually a distinction of degree rather than of kind. Objectivity is a continuous and variable quality; that is, test items are neither wholly objective nor wholly subjective. For example, the short-answer question may be thought of as a variation of the essay question, but it is somewhat more objective than typical essay forms that ask the student to "discuss," "explain," or "analyze."

Usually the objectivity of an examination question is judged by the complexity of the pupil's answer and the resulting degree of difficulty in scoring. If the scoring requires judgment and evaluation of the response, the question or item is said to be subjective; to the extent that judgment and evaluation are reduced or eliminated from the scoring process, the item is objective. Most standardized tests, except those for young children, can be scored by clerical workers using a scoring key or by a test-scoring machine. The process in either case is mechanical. Questions of the essay or short-answer variety, on the other hand, cannot be so scored. But questions of this type can be more or less objective, as we will show later; they are not all equally or wholly subjective.

The nature of scoring and the judgment it requires depend also on the nature of the responses the pupil is required to make. If a response consists of a number, a "plus" or a "minus" sign, a letter, or a black mark between two printed lines, the scoring can be done mechanically. When the student is asked to write out answers in words, draw a figure, make

---

[1]The term *item* will be used consistently except in reference to essay, short-answer, and completion questions.

an outline, or do something else of this nature, the scoring becomes more complex and subjective.

Sometimes a distinction between test types depends on whether *recognition* or *recall* is required. Perhaps a more realistic classification can be made in terms of whether the student *selects* or *supplies* the answer to a question. Selection items include multiple-choice, matching, and true-false items; supply questions include essay, completion, and short answers. Even though bases for distinguishing among item types are less than clear, they may be helpful when we think about objectivity.

With these few preliminary observations in mind, we may proceed to the various commonly used kinds of examination items, beginning with the most subjective and going on to the more objective.

LEARNING EXERCISES

4. Classifying test items as *objective* or *subjective* is something like trying to classify all people into two groups—tall or short, bright or dull. Is such classification defensible? Justify your answer.

5. Even when a teacher uses nothing but the most objective tests, there are still some subjective elements in the job of evaluating and marking. Name some of them.

Although the more objective tests have been widely accepted in the last fifty years, the essay question is still used extensively. In a survey of measurement practices of some 2,303 high school teachers in thirty-five states, 13.7 percent of the teachers questioned said they used no essay tests at all.[2] It seems reasonable to conclude that most of the other 86.3 percent *do* use them, at least occasionally. Also, 81.2 percent reported using short-answer or completion items "very often" or "fairly often."

Essay Questions

The essay question is probably so well known that it requires no definition here; nevertheless, a few words of explanation may serve to clarify or supplement what the student already knows. The essay test usually consists of questions beginning with or including such directions as "discuss," "explain," "outline," "evaluate," "define," "compare,"

[2]Victor H. Noll and Walter N. Durost, *Measurement Practices and Preferences of High School Teachers,* Test Service Notebook 8 (New York: Harcourt Brace Jovanovich, n.d.).

"contrast," "describe." The pupil is allowed comparative freedom with respect to what the answer shall include as well as its wording, length, and organization. Here are three examples from typical teacher-made tests:

> Compare simple ranks and percentile ranks in terms of their advantages and disadvantages for use by teachers on classroom tests.

> Discuss the techniques of character development used by Dickens in *A Tale of Two Cities*.

> Describe the steps in processing milk from dairy farm to consumer.

Although the essay question has continued in favor among teachers for a long time and is stoutly defended by its many advocates, it has also been the object of much criticism. Much experimentation designed largely to show its weaknesses and to prove its unreliability has been reported in educational literature. The pioneer study of the essay question in the United States was reported by Starch and Elliott in 1912.[3] These investigators had a typical examination paper written by a pupil in English graded independently by a large number of teachers of English; the same was done with a geometry paper and a history paper. The results found in the different studies were quite similar: the same paper received marks ranging all the way from nearly perfect to very low failure. Similar results were reported during the next decade by other investigators.

This weakness in the scoring of essay questions has been demonstrated in still another way. One investigator had teachers score the same set of papers twice, with an interval of several months between.[4] The findings pointed to the conclusion that these teachers were not consistent judges of the quality of the same set of papers.

A second principal weakness of the essay examination is that it allows only limited sampling. The typical essay test consists of from five to twelve questions. An objective test that allows the same amount of time for answering questions as the essay test might well include one hundred or more items. Although the essay questions cover larger units, they do not usually constitute as adequate and representative a sample of the field being tested as the one hundred objective items. Therefore, in the case of the essay test, the teacher must base the evaluation of a pupil's accomplishments on a fragmentary, limited, and sometimes biased sam-

---

[3]Daniel Starch and Edward C. Elliott, "Reliability of Grading High School Work in English," *School Review*, 20 (September 1912), 442–457. Subsequent articles on mathematics and history appear in *School Review*, 21 (April and December 1913), 254–259 and 676–681.
[4]Walter C. Eells, "Reliability of Repeated Grading of Essay Type Questions," *Journal of Educational Psychology*, 31 (January 1930), 48–52.

pling. In a one-hundred-item test, a pupil's achievement is sampled one hundred times because the student makes that number of separate responses or judgments. In an examination consisting of ten essay questions, the person reading the paper has a much smaller sampling of the student's accomplishments upon which to make a judgment; also, a student who happens to be weak or deficient in one or two essay questions is apt to be penalized far more heavily than would be true for equivalent deficiencies on the objective test. Limited sampling affects the reliability of the essay test and also its empirical validity, since such a test is likely to give lower correlations with other measures of the same abilities than results obtained from measures that sample more adequately.

A third disadvantage of the essay question is the time required to read the answers. While this kind of examination is rather easily and quickly made, judging and scoring the answers is very time-consuming and often tiresome. This, of course, makes the essay test expensive, since it must be read either by the teacher or by equally competent scorers. Usually such a test cannot be evaluated by clerical workers or by mechanical methods.

The chief advantages claimed for the essay examination may be stated as follows: (1) it is easier to construct than a comparable objective test; (2) it can be used to measure the ability to think and to organize and apply knowledge and it can therefore measure learning of a different kind from that measured by the objective test; (3) it provides exercise in expressing written thoughts clearly, concisely, and correctly—a skill the objective test does not measure; and (4) it requires a more useful and rewarding kind of study and preparation than that required by the objective test.

On the first advantage, there is probably no serious difference of opinion. It is easier and much less time-consuming to prepare ten essay questions and write them on the board or have them duplicated than to prepare a one-hundred-item objective test. In practice, the essay examination is often prepared at the last minute, whereas such hurried preparation is not possible for an objective test. It should be recognized, however, that one does not prepare good essay questions in this manner. It is possible to dash off a few essay questions on the way to class, but such questions are almost certain to be poor in quality unless this expedient has been preceded by a good deal of thought. Even then, as we will see shortly, much can be done after essay questions have been written to improve their quality and usefulness.

Of the second advantage, we can say only that it is hard to find evidence that the essay examination actually measures mental processes different from those measured by the objective test. This is not to deny that such advantage may exist but simply to point out that no one has apparently been able or taken the trouble to find and present evidence to support this assumed advantage of the essay examination. Implicit in the claim is the idea that the objective test does not or cannot measure the higher mental processes. Here again, evidence to support this implication seems to be lacking. Some work has been done to develop objective tests that measure mental abilities of a higher order, such as the ability to interpret data and draw conclusions, and this research suggests that it may be possible to measure such abilities by means of objective tests. We have described some work along these lines in Chapter 5. Until further research produces some evidence on the question, this claimed advantage of the essay examination must be taken largely on faith.

With regard to the third advantage, it seems questionable whether writing answers to essay questions can substantially improve a student's writing ability. For one thing, the proportion of total instructional time spent in taking examinations is too small to make very much impact. For another, it seems highly unlikely that the pressure of an examination is conducive to skillful and careful writing, particularly when the student is concentrating on the substance of the answer. A more logical and probably more effective procedure for the teacher would be to emphasize good oral and written expression consistently, correcting all mistakes made by students in these areas. Perhaps most important of all, the correct and effective use of our language should be the concern of every teacher, whether of English or shop or mathematics. When students learn that high standards in composition and oral expression are expected, their writing and speech probably will improve. Too often only the English teacher is concerned with the quality of a student's expression, and, as a result, students may practice good English in those classes but be careless or indifferent about it elsewhere.

The fourth advantage—that preparation for essay tests is more rewarding than preparation for more objective tests—seems not to be unequivocally supported by evidence. Some studies have been reported showing that when students expect an objective test they study for details, while in preparing for an essay test they focus attention on relationships, trends, and organization.[5] However, studies by Vallance and Hakstian failed to confirm these findings.[6] Even so, students should be told in advance what type of examination they will be given so that they have an opportunity to study differently if they wish to do so.

[5]See, for example, Paul W. Terry, "How Students Review for Objective and Essay Tests," *Elementary School Journal*, 33 (1933), 592–603. Also, Harl R. Douglass and Margaret Tallmadge, "How University Students Prepare for New Types of Examinations," *School and Society*, 39 (1934), 318–320.
[6]Theodore R. Vallance, "Comparison of Essay and Objective Examinations as Learning Experiences," *Journal of Educational Research*, 41 (1947), 279–288; A. Ralph Hakstian, "The Effects of Type of Examination Anticipated on Student Test Preparation and Performance," Paper Abstracts of the 1969 Annual Meeting of the American Educational Research Association (Washington, D.C.: AERA, 1969), p. 82.

LEARNING EXERCISE

6. What are some other important advantages or serious shortcomings of essay tests? Consult some of the references at the end of this chapter for evidence.

IMPROVING ESSAY QUESTIONS Having reviewed the main lines of discussion and criticism of the essay question, we might ask what can be done about it. Is the essay question a type that can be recommended for general use? Perhaps a sensible point of view for the student of measurement might be expressed as follows. The essay question is believed by its advocates to have a number of unique advantages over the more objective types; apparently these advantages have been neither fully proved nor disproved, though some of the basic weaknesses have been clearly demonstrated; nevertheless, since the essay question is used regularly by many teachers, we should try to improve its use in every way possible.

Suggestions for improvement of the essay question are usually directed at the preparation of the questions and directions and at the scoring and evaluation of the answers. A good deal of helpful material has been written on these two points. Although a complete review of such material is not appropriate or necessary here, a summary of the most useful ideas should be helpful. With respect to planning, constructing, and using essay questions, the following recommendations are often used as guides.

1. *Define and restrict the field or area to be covered by the question.* For example, in high school chemistry one might say

> Describe the contact process for making sulfuric acid.

whereas it would be better to say

> Write the equations for the contact process for making sulfuric acid.
> Name all the substances used and the products.
> Draw a labeled diagram showing where each step of the process takes place.
> What are the by-products of the process and how are they used?

2. *The teacher should give more time and thought to the preparation of essay questions.* It is logical and obvious that if essay questions are to

measure higher thought processes adequately, there must be some forethought in the planning of the questions. As we have already mentioned, it may seem easy to write a few questions on the board on the spur of the moment, but it is almost impossible to produce really good questions without fairly extensive preparation.

Furthermore, after essay questions have been written out well in advance, careful study and editing are necessary. The teacher must ask and answer such questions as: What am I really trying to measure with this question? Will my students understand exactly what I am trying to get at? Is this something they can reasonably be expected to know or do? Such criteria of careful preparation and editing must be met before the teacher can be satisfied that an essay question is as good as it can be.

3. *The value or weight of each question on an essay examination should be indicated.* This is true regardless of whether all questions have the same weight or different weights. The student is entitled to know what the basis is for earning a score or mark.

4. *The quality of handwriting, spelling, grammar, and punctuation and clarity of thought should be checked and should carry weight in the evaluation of every essay or composition assigned by English or foreign-language teachers.* This is one of the reasons for requiring writing; students will not learn correct usage if their mistakes are not pointed out.

5. *Errors in spelling, grammar, and usage should be checked in a student's written work by every teacher but should not affect the mark or grade except in language classes.* Consistent with the viewpoint espoused above, one of the claimed advantages of essay tests over objective tests is that they provide practice in writing. Such practice loses most if not all its value if the students' errors are not corrected. However, if a student's work in mathematics, science, or any subject other than language is accurate and correct, pointing out such errors should be sufficient.

6. *Prepare enough questions to sample the learning of the students adequately.* Do not use an essay examination consisting of only one or two questions. When this is done, either the questions must be so broad and general as to cause difficulties in interpretation and delimitation by the student or the sampling of outcomes to be measured must be extremely limited.

7. *Optional questions that give pupils a choice should not be provided. Such process reduces the comparability of the sampling of learning and therefore of the basis for scoring.* When pupils have a choice of questions, the lessened comparability of the individual papers affects the accuracy of grading and makes it much more difficult to evaluate the papers on a common basis.

IMPROVING THE GRADING OF ESSAY QUESTIONS Suggestions for improving the scoring of essay questions are rather generally agreed upon by those who have studied the matter. The following represent some of the more frequently mentioned suggestions.

1. *Determine in advance the methods to be used in scoring the answers on the examination.* Basically there are two approaches that can be taken—*relative* and *analytical.* In the *relative* method, the basis for assigning marks is a comparison of the different students' answers to the question, with the best answers receiving the highest marks and the poorest answers receiving the lowest marks. Before using this method to score a test, the teacher should decide what scale will be used for each question (0–3, 0–5, and so on) and what mark will be assigned to answers of average quality in the class. The range of the scale should be adequate for the number of different levels of quality that are important and can be identified with sufficient reliability. An unnecessarily large range (for example, 0–20) permits, and may even encourage, the reader to make distinctions among answers that are virtually equal in most important aspects. The score selected to represent the average answer generally should be the middle score of the scale. With most essay questions, relative marking requires at least two readings of each paper in order to ensure that marks are sufficiently reliable. The purpose of the first reading should be to divide the papers tentatively into different groups, such as the average answers and the above- and below-average answers. The second reading provides an opportunity for the teacher to check the accuracy of the initial assessment and to assign specific marks to each paper.

In contrast to the relative method in which marks are assigned on the basis of an overall, global assessment of the answer, the *analytical* procedure requires the use of a scoring key that rather precisely outlines the different features of a perfect answer and the point value for each aspect that will be considered. A student answer is then assigned points for each of the features judged as having been covered satisfactorily. Whenever the teacher can prepare a check list itemizing the features of a perfect answer, the analytical method can be used. An example of a question for which this can be done is given below. A physics class is presented the diagram for an electrical circuit that includes a source of voltage and some appliances with stated resistance, and the question is:

In items (a) to (d) below, possible changes in the circuit are described. In each case you should indicate how the change will affect the voltage, resistance, and current in the circuit. Describe in a short statement how Ohm's Law allows the changes to be predicted. You will receive one point for each change correctly identified and a maximum of two points for describing the application of Ohm's Law.

In this case, the teacher can identify in advance and with relatively high precision every aspect of a complete answer. Although in a sense relative scoring might be used to decide which papers are to receive two points, one point, or zero on the last part of the question, separate aspects of the answer can be identified in advance and can be scored separately.

The analytical method focuses the reader's attention on a smaller and more easily defined aspect of the answer than the relative method does, and therefore agreement among independent readers is usually higher when the analytical method is used. However, some types of essay questions do not easily admit of the development of an analytical scoring key. For example, questions that ask the examinee to develop an argument for or against some topic may not require the use of one particular approach or set of facts, and perhaps the most important part of the answer in the opinion of the teacher is the organization of the answer and the skill with which the argument is presented. With such questions it would be difficult or impossible to develop an itemized key and, thus, quality must be judged comparatively.

2. *Write answers to each question before administering the test.* There are two main reasons for doing this. First, in writing an answer the teacher has an opportunity to think about the implications of the question and to discover faults, which will suggest improvements in or elimination of the question. Second, the availability of a model answer will help the teacher maintain a common frame of reference while reading student papers. Although this latter advantage is less important when an analytical key can be developed, the former is sufficiently important to justify the preparation of model answers, regardless of which scoring procedure is used.

3. *Remove or cover all pupil-identifying data on the papers to be read.* It is not always easy for the teacher or scorer to avoid being influenced by irrelevant matters when the identity of the pupil who wrote a paper is known. The evaluation should be based, as far as possible, only on what the pupil has written, and other factors should not be permitted to influence the scorer's judgments. Pupils may be instructed to fasten sheets together and write identifying data only on the back of one page.

4. *Read all papers for one question at a time instead of reading each paper in its entirety.* In other words, if there are five essay questions in the test, the scorer should read the answers to the same question across all papers, apply the scoring technique, and arrive at a mark on that question for each student. Then the scorer should proceed to another question, reading all the answers to that question and arriving at a mark for each paper. When all questions on the test have been marked for all students, the total score for each student can be obtained by adding together the scores for individual questions.

Related to this point are two other suggestions to help a reader maintain common standards. One is to record item scores on a separate record sheet or at some place on the paper where it cannot be seen when the next item is scored. This will avoid the possibility that the reader will be influenced by student success on the previous item. Also it is a good practice to shuffle papers after an item has been scored across all papers. This will minimize the possibility that a given student's responses will be consistently read after a good or poor response and scored higher or lower than they should be.

When the relative marking system is used, and marks are determined comparatively, the need for grading tests one question at a time is most important. When analytical marking is used, this method helps to ensure the comparability of minimum standards for assigning credit to each aspect of the answer.

5. *If a number of different factors—accuracy, methods used, possible correctness, ease of expression—are to be taken into account, evaluate each separately.* Reliability of grading will be increased if one factor is considered at a time. Lumping two or more together in evaluating responses almost certainly encourages fuzziness and inaccuracy in judgment.

6. *After a set of papers has been graded, lay them aside for several hours or a day and then look them over again.* This often reveals small but possibly important points that may have been overlooked during the first grading. This suggests not a complete re-scoring—few teachers have time for that—but merely a second "once-over" to catch obvious slips or inaccuracies.

LEARNING EXERCISES

7. Criticize the following as an essay question: Discuss the historical background of present-day intelligence tests.
8. Revise the question in Exercise 7 in the light of your criticisms, retaining its good features as an essay question.
9. Write a model answer for your revised question. Compare the answer with some of the source material given in the references at the end of Chapter 1.
10. Develop an essay question that would be suitable for analytical scoring and prepare the scoring key.

Short-Answer Questions As the term suggests, the short-answer item consists of a question that can be answered with a word or short phrase. It may be in the form of a direct question, as

What city is the capital of Switzerland? _____

or it may be in the form of an incomplete statement, as

The capital city of Switzerland is _____.

In general, high school teachers seem to favor the short-answer question, probably because they think it has some of the claimed advantages of both essay and objective test questions. It is relatively easy to construct; it requires the pupil to supply the answer; it is not difficult to score or mark (certainly much easier than the essay question); and time and space requirements will usually permit the use of a large number of such questions in a test, thus obtaining for the teacher an improved sampling without making the test too laborious for the student.

While short-answer questions have these advantages to a greater or lesser degree, they have certain disadvantages as well. One of the foremost is the concentration upon specific, often unrelated, facts. In testing for such bits and pieces of knowledge as the capital of Switzerland, the number of ounces in a pound, the opposite of "big," or the discoverer of the Pacific Ocean, the teacher may lose sight of and fail to measure more important objectives. Furthermore, it is often difficult to phrase the short-answer question so that only one or even a few answers will fit. Unless the teacher succeeds fairly well in this, it will be impossible to anticipate the variety of answers that pupils will think of and that will have to be judged as acceptable or unacceptable.

Since the short-answer question has some advantages and is favored by many teachers, let us look briefly at ways of planning and improving its construction.

1. *Select and state the questions in such a way that they can be answered with a word or a short phrase.* Avoid such questions as

What is the best method of making angel food cake?

Although it might be possible to answer such a question by one word (a name for a method), there is nothing to prevent the willing pupil from writing a paragraph or two describing the best method. It would be better to say

List the five chief ingredients of an angel food cake.

2. *Select and phrase short-answer questions so that only one or a very small number of answers will be correct.* Do not say

Name the major cause of high prices of consumer goods.

To such a question a dozen or more answers could probably be given, each supported with cogent arguments. It is better to say

At what level is the price support of wheat fixed by present law?

This question calls for a definite, specific, and probably undebatable answer. If the teacher wishes to ask a question relating to the cause or causes of high prices, the short-answer form probably should not be used. It would be preferable in such an instance to use the essay form or perhaps the multiple-choice form, in which the pupil is required to choose the best of a limited number of alternatives.

On the whole, short-answer items are easy to construct, though one should not expect to make good short-answer items by taking statements verbatim from the text and merely omitting a word or two. The item should rephrase the idea or point being tested or make an entirely original statement of it. Short-answer questions are useful primarily in testing knowledge of facts and quite specific information. However, because of the shortcomings mentioned earlier, this type of item is not frequently used in standardized tests.

LEARNING EXERCISE

11. Construct five short-answer questions about a subject you are likely to teach. Try these out, if possible, on one of your fellow students. Do the results bring out any weaknesses and suggestions for improvement?

What we have said about the short-answer question applies also to the completion form. In the short-answer type the blank is nearly always at the end, whereas in the true completion type the blank or blanks may

Completion Questions

occur anywhere in the statement. It is particularly important in this case to phrase the statement in such a way that only a single answer will be correct. Indefiniteness of the statement or other conditions that permit a variety of defensible answers will multiply the difficulties of the scoring process. Here are a few suggestions for the construction of good completion questions.

1. *Omit only significant words from the statement.* Do not omit articles, prepositions, conjunctions, or similar words unless the purpose is to test the usage of such words (as in the case of a grammar test). If the statement to be used is

> Democracy is that form of government in which all the people or some numerous portion of them exercise the governing power through deputies periodically elected by themselves.

one might devise two questions as follows:

> Democracy is that _____ of government in which all the people or _____ numerous portion of _____ exercise the governing power _____ deputies periodically elected _____.

or

> Democracy is that form of _____ in which all the _____ or some numerous portion of them exercise the governing _____ through _____ periodically elected by _____.

In the first case, inconsequential words like *form, some, them, through,* and *by themselves* are required, and it is quite apparent that such words have no significant relation to the important ideas the statement conveys. The second case tests the essential and important ideas that the completed statement makes about government, the people, power, deputies, and self-representation in periodical elections.

2. *In omitting significant words, leave enough clues to enable the competent person to answer correctly.* If this principle is not adhered to, filling in the blanks becomes impossible, just a guessing game, or the demonstration that a statement has been memorized. To illustrate, do not use

> The _____ Canal connects _____ and _____.

This item cannot be answered with assurance because there are many canals and, of course, they connect different cities or bodies of water. However, if the statement said

The Erie Canal connects _____ and _____.

it would be more definite and could be answered by most students who had prepared for the test. The effect of excessive omissions is even more marked with statements that are more complex.

3. *In scoring short-answer and completion items, it is generally most satisfactory to allow one point credit for each blank, unless the item requires several words or a phrase.* For example,

In many large manufacturing plants, items are moved from one worker to

another on a ___*conveyer*___ ___*belt*___.

Here, although two words are needed to complete the statement, only one point should be allowed in scoring, and no partial credit should be allowed for either word alone. Neither is correct by itself, and both are necessary to convey the essential idea.

In the following example, however, seven points would be given, one for each correct response:

The seven continents are _____, _____, _____,
_____, _____, _____, and _____.

This system simplifies scoring and avoids many difficulties arising from methods in which partial credits are given.

LEARNING EXERCISES

12. In what ways are completion items objective and in what ways are they subjective? What can be done to increase objectivity without affecting desirable features of this item format?
13. Try to convert the short-answer items from Learning Exercise 11 to good completion items. Do you consistently favor one form over the other?

In the early days of objective-test development, the true-false item was very popular. Some of the first published tests consisted entirely of this type of item. In recent years its popularity has declined to such an extent   *True-False Items* that one finds it used only rarely in standardized tests. There are at least two reasons for this: the type has some inherent weaknesses, especially in the effect that chance or guessing may have on scores; and the misuse of the type by people who are deceived into believing that good true-false items are easy to develop. The true-false item usually consists of a declarative sentence to which the examinee responds by marking it "true" or "false," thus:

( ) Edgar Allan Poe was the author of "The Raven."

or

( ) The first manned space flight to orbit the moon was in 1967.

A variety of modifications of the true-false item have been tried, nearly always in an attempt to lessen the effect of its chief weakness—the element of chance success through guessing. One modification is to have the pupil correct the false item by crossing out the word or part that makes it false and writing in the word or phrase that will make the statement correct. For example, an item appears on the tests as follows:

( ) A pair of scissors is an example of a lever of the second class.

The pupil marks it "false" and corrects it, thus:

first
(F) A pair of scissors is an example of a lever of the ~~second~~ class.

The statement is false because scissors are first-class levers. The item is correctly marked, as shown above, by crossing out the word *second* and writing above it the word *first*. Or one might draw a line through the phrase *pair of scissors* and write in an example of a second-class lever, thus:

nutcracker
(F) A ~~pair of scissors~~ is an example of a lever of the second class.

This arrangement might be a little less satisfactory than the preceding one, in which only one word, *first*, would be an acceptable answer, whereas in the variation a large number of examples of second-class levers would have to be accepted. In both instances, true statements are simply marked "true" with the designated symbol; nothing further need be done.

If a teacher wants to ensure that students focus on only one aspect of the statement, such as the class of the lever in the example above, the critical part can be underlined. When this is done, students can be told to judge whether the underlined portion is true or false and, if it is false, to correct the statement. For example,

( ) A pair of scissors is an example of a lever of the <u>second</u> class.

Every true-false question calls for a choice between alternatives. A statement is either right or wrong, true or false. Hence, the possibility of guessing the right choice, mathematically speaking, is one in two, or 50 percent. Therefore, with one hundred such items, a student would be expected to get half of them right on the basis of pure chance alone. The pupil who has answered half of the one hundred items right and half wrong can thus be assumed to have done no better than a pupil who has guessed through the entire test. To discourage students from guessing and, it is believed by some, to eliminate the effect of guessing on test scores, scores on true-false tests are sometimes obtained by the formula $S = R - W$, where S = score, R = number of true-false items answered correctly, and W = number of true-false items missed.[7]

In the case of a student answering half correctly in a test of one hundred items, $S = 50 - 50 = 0$. For a student who gets seventy right and thirty wrong, the score would be $70 - 30$, or 40. Items not attempted are usually disregarded in the scoring. For example, if another student omits twelve of one hundred items, and gets sixty right and twenty-eight wrong of the remaining eighty-eight, the score would be $60 - 28$, or 32, the twelve omitted being disregarded in arriving at the score.

The assumption is that people guess right as often as they guess wrong. If 30 items are incorrect, an equal number are assumed to be correct only as a result of chance. Consequently, a corrected score of the student with 70 correct is obtained by the formula $S = R - W$, or $S = 70 - 30 = 40$.

In this connection, it should be noted that if all students attempt, or answer, every item, the correction for chance success makes no difference in the ranking of scores on the test. For example:

				Rank	
Student	R	W	R − W score	R	R − W
J	70	30	40	3	3
M	60	40	20	4	4
T	88	12	76	1	1
Z	76	24	52	2	2

[7] To eliminate the expected effect of chance success in objective tests, the general formula for correction is $S = R - [W/(n-1)]$. Here, n equals the number of choices. In a true-false item, $n = 2$, so the formula becomes $S = R - W$.

However, suppose students are instructed not to guess but to omit items they are uncertain about. In this circumstance, the results might be as follows:

Student	R	W	O	R − W score	Rank R	Rank R − W
J	65	25	10	40	3	4
M	56	14	30	42	4	3
T	80	12	8	68	1	1
Z	70	24	6	46	2	2

We can see that the $R - W$ system of scoring works to the advantage of the cautious, conservative student, in this case student M. By attempting only the seventy items of which the student is relatively certain and omitting the thirty uncertain answers, M achieves a higher rank by the $R - W$ formula than on the basis of R alone.

Such a lengthy discussion of the scoring of true-false items may seem unnecessary as far as the practice of the typical classroom teacher is concerned. True-false items are generally scored on the basis of right answers alone. Very few students are happy when papers are returned with true-false items scored $R - W$. Nevertheless, this does happen, especially in college classes, and what we have done here is to present in brief form the rationale for the correction for chance.

The tendency of inexperienced and relatively untrained persons to fall into the error of assuming that good true-false questions are easy to construct has also reduced the prestige and use of this type of item. Inexperienced teachers often lift sentences verbatim from the textbook, insert a negative or introduce some other slight modification, and expect thereby to produce a good true-false item. It should be emphasized that superior items are almost never formulated in this manner. The true-false question requires very careful planning and construction. The suggestions below will materially help the student avoid many of the common weaknesses of true-false tests.

1. *Do not include more than a single idea in one true-false item, particularly if one idea is true and the other is false.* Except in special situations where the testing may be directed toward unusual objectives, it is better to make each true-false item contain one idea and to use a statement that is either wholly true or wholly false. Otherwise, the item will surely be ambiguous. For example,

( ) The climate of England is colder than the climate of most other countries at the same latitude because of the influence of the Atlantic Gulf Stream.

This statement is ambiguous because it contains correct and also incorrect information. It would be better to make two items, thus:

( ) The climate of England is colder than the climate of most other countries at the same latitude.
( ) The climate of England is influenced by the Atlantic Gulf Stream.

This makes both items acceptable since the first is clearly false while the second is clearly true, and neither sentence is ambiguous.

2. *Avoid negative statements wherever possible.* If negative statements are used, the word or phrase that makes them negative should be emphasized by italics or underlining. A false negative statement results in a double negative—or a positive—and such statements are nearly always confusing. Since our primary purpose is to test learning, not to confuse students or test their ability to solve puzzles, there seems little justification for the use of ambiguous statements. The statement

( ) A true-false question should *not* be negatively stated.

is true and the word that makes it a negative is italicized. Consider, however, the following item, a perfectly straightforward, positive statement:

( ) Washington is the capital of the United States.

Nearly everyone would mark this correctly as a true statement. In the form given, it poses no special problems. If, on the other hand, the statement is changed to read,

( ) Washington is not the capital of the United States.

confusion may result because of the negative introduced.[8]

3. *Use approximately equal numbers of true and false items.* The probability of guessing an item correctly may increase if a student correctly notes the existence of a trend.

4. *Avoid long and involved statements, especially statements containing dependent clauses, many qualifications, and complex ideas.* These tend to cause the items to test reading comprehension rather than achievement in a subject. It is better to break up long statements into

---

[8] The instructor may easily demonstrate this confusion. First, write on the board a positive statement—for example, "There are three feet in a yard,"—and ask the class to say aloud whether it is true or false. Erase the positive statement and write the negative one in its place ("There are *not* three feet in a yard"). Now ask for a true-or-false response. Usually some will say "False," some will say "True," and the majority will say nothing.

two or more separate items that will be more easily understood and that will yield more exact and specific information about the student's attainments.

5. *Use the true-false form only with statements or ideas that are clearly and unequivocally true or false as stated.* It should be obvious that a test item, the correct response to which is uncertain or debatable, is not suitable for use as a true-false item, simply because no scoring key can be devised. A teacher may wish to use arguable matters for purposes of class discussion, but these topics have no place in an objective test. Consider, for example, the following:

( ) The greatest woman in history was Marie Curie, the chemist.

Immediately we hear: How about Cleopatra? Elizabeth the First? Jane Addams? Florence Nightingale? Catherine the Great? The answer would never be agreed upon.

LEARNING EXERCISES

14. Some authorities have suggested that true-false questions are better stated in the form of a question, such as "Is a cow a biped?" Rather than in the assertive form, such as "A cow is a biped." Can you see any measurement reason for doing this? Do you think there are other reasons for this point of view?

15. Construct ten true-false items about a subject of your choice. Check these against the suggestions given in the preceding section. How good a job have you done? Ask a colleague or classmate to judge the quality of your items.

Matching
Items

Matching items are used widely in situations in which relationships of more or less similar ideas, facts, or principles are to be examined or judged. For example:

Directions: In the space at the left of the nutrient in the first column, write the letter of the substance in the second column that is an example of the nutrient.

( ) carbohydrate		a. butter
( ) fat		b. lean meat
( ) protein		c. salt
		d. sugar
		e. water

The correct answers are *d*, *a*, and *b*, respectively. The pupil indicates the correct choice in each case by writing the letter of the correct choice in the parentheses preceding the name of the nutrient the substance represents. In practice, the lists are usually longer than in this brief illustration.

A modification of the matching question is the classification item, which may also be used to advantage in some cases. For example, in the illustrative matching set below, a list of terms is given together with a key to be used in identifying or classifying the terms:

Directions: In the parentheses before each of the examples listed, write the letter of the correct classification. Classifications may be used more than once.

( ) eagle	( ) cow	a. bird
( ) mouse	( ) whale	b. mammal
( ) alligator	( ) pike	c. fish
( ) bat	( ) frog	d. amphibian

The matching type of item lends itself well to testing knowledge of words, dates, events, persons, formulas, tools, and many other such matters involving simple relationships or categories. However, matching questions are less well suited to the testing of broader concepts such as the ability to organize and apply knowledge. The suggestions that follow have been found helpful in improving the quality and usefulness of matching items.

1. *A matching exercise usually should not contain more than ten or twelve items.* That is, the number of terms, names, and so on to be identified or matched should not exceed ten or twelve, because longer lists become quite burdensome and tiring to the person taking the test. Where more than a dozen items are to be tested, it is usually better to construct two or more separate matching exercises.

2. *Avoid one-to-one matching by allowing the response terms to be used more than once or by having a greater number of response terms than items in the primary column or list.* In other words, there should be a number of optional choices or alternatives from which to choose items for matching. For example, instead of

(c) fast	a. forte
(a) loud	b. pianissimo
(b) very softly	c. presto

use this:

(e) fast	a. forte
(a) loud	b. legato
(c) very softly	c. pianissimo
	d. poco
	e. presto

In this way, the possibility of chance success is decreased because it is not easy to arrive at choices by the process of elimination. In the first example, the pupil who knew two of the three terms would get the third one right automatically; in the second example, the pupil would still have to choose from among three remaining terms.

3. *The same response may be used more than once, but there should not be more than one correct choice for any term.* This is a better arrangement, for example,

(c) adjective	a. and
(b) noun	b. run
(b) verb	c. rare
	d. to
	e. when

than this one is, which should be avoided:

(d) adjective	a. and
(b or c) noun	b. boy
(c or d) verb	c. run
	d. slow
	e. to

4. *There should be a high degree of homogeneity in every set of matching items.* All the items or terms in each exercise should belong to the same category; those that do not will be much easier to match than the rest. To illustrate:

(f) capitals	a. is used at end of direct query
(b) apostrophe	b. is used to show possession
(c) period	c. appears at end of declarative sentence
(a) question mark	d. is used after expression of strong feeling
(e) semicolon	e. shows balance between coordinate sentence elements
	f. begin all proper nouns
	g. sets off nonrestrictive clauses

In this example, the category *capitals* is different from the others because it is not a punctuation mark. By looking at the list of options, alert pupils can easily determine which one fits. They will quickly reason that *f* is the only choice that could possibly fit *capitals*, since all other options have to do with punctuation. Moreover, they will observe that *capitals* is the only plural form in the first column and that *begin* is the only verb in the second column that requires a plural subject. Irrelevant clues such as these are easily overlooked, and matching items should be carefully scrutinized for them.

Using titles or headings for the columns of premises and responses will help ensure that the lists are homogeneous. In the preceding example, if the teacher had called the first column "types of punctuation marks," the inappropriateness of *capitals* in the list would have been apparent. In the same example, the second column could have been called "use of punctuation marks."

5. *Wherever possible, the terms in both lists or columns of a matching exercise should be arranged alphabetically or in any other logical or systematic order.* Ordered arrangement facilitates finding items in the lists and reduces the reading and searching task. When items consist of phrases, clauses, or sentences or material of a nonverbal character such as chemical formulas, numbers, and algebraic terms, alphabetizing is out of the question. However, whenever some systematic arrangement that does not furnish clues to correct choices is possible, it should be followed.

6. *The classification type of matching item may be appropriately used as a variation of the standard form, particularly in testing such objectives as the ability to apply or interpret.* For example:

    a. adjective
    b. adverb
    c. conjunction
    d. interjection
    e. noun
    f. preposition
    g. pronoun
    h. verb

(f) We went *over* the river on the bridge.
(b) Turn your paper *over.*
(h) We have been *over* that once before.
(e) John scored a *run.*
(h) Mary said she would *run* fast.
(e) *Running* is hard work.

Here, various situations are provided in which the pupil may apply what has been learned about parts of speech.

7. *Pictorial items can often be used advantageously as a variation in the matching type of item.*

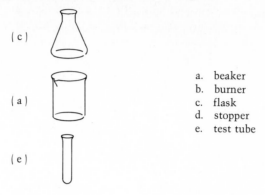

(c)

(a)

(e)

a. beaker
b. burner
c. flask
d. stopper
e. test tube

Such items may be used for subjects in which apparatus, equipment, or tools are used. Pictures of objects may be matched with their names, uses, or other characteristics.

8. *Directions for matching items should indicate (a) the basis of the matches or relationships, (b) the method of indicating answers, and (c) the number of times the same choice or term may be used.* Clear, explicit directions for matching items are among the most difficult to write. The test-maker should prepare them carefully and review them to make certain that the directions are clear.

The sample directions given below for a matching exercise in American literature illustrate these points.

Directions: Below are two columns; the first contains titles of short stories and the second contains names of authors. For each title in the first column, you are to select the name of the short story's author in the second column. Write the letter that precedes the author's name in the space before the title. There are more authors' names than titles, so you will have some names left over after you have filled in all blanks. Note that an author's name may be used with more than one short story.

Although matching items are used quite frequently in informal and locally made tests, their use in published, standardized tests seems to be declining. The reasons for their lack of popularity among professional test-makers are not altogether clear. One reason may be limitations on the types of achievement that can be measured with the matching item; another reason may be the lack of research data on its value as a measurement device; and a third reason may be that key-list items, to be discussed later in this chapter, can measure the same achievements, are more similar in format to multiple-choice items, and thus are more easily included on a test with which separate answer sheets are used. Nevertheless, for informal tests made locally, matching items furnish a useful variation and will probably continue to be used by many teachers and other persons who are interested in broadening and improving their own measurement techniques.

LEARNING EXERCISES

16. Make a list of some learning outcomes in your subject that you believe could be measured efficiently by matching questions. Are there goals for which you could not use matching items? If so, list some.
17. Prepare a set of matching exercises for one of the outcomes you identified above. Try them out on a classmate.

Multiple-Choice Items

The percentages of high school teachers reporting the use of multiple-choice items "fairly often" or "very often" in the survey previously cited are 50.6 and 16.4, respectively, or a total of 67 percent.[9] The multiple-choice item apparently is the most popular of the objective types. (Corresponding percentages for the matching type of item are 45.1 and 16.0, a total of 61.1; for true-false the percentages are 37.4 and 11.3, or 48.7 percent.)

The multiple-choice item usually consists of an incomplete declarative sentence or a question followed by a number of possible responses, one of which is clearly correct or best. For example:

The Prime Minister of England at the close of World War II was
a. Harold Macmillan.
b. Neville Chamberlain.
c. Winston Churchill.
d. Harold Wilson.
e. Lloyd George.

An example in the form of a question is:

[9] Noll and Durost (footnote 2).

Who was the author of *Advise and Consent?*
a. Charles Hailey
b. Helen MacInnes
c. John Steinbeck
d. Allen Drury
e. Vance Packard

These two examples represent items in which the response to be chosen is clearly in the category of "correct." In the first, only Winston Churchill was the Prime Minister at the close of World War II; the others named were not. In the second, only Allen Drury was the author of the book.

Multiple-choice items may be devised in which the student is asked to compare the quality of various choices and make a judgment as to which is best. Consider, for example, the following:

Which of the following best describes the intent of the phrase "return to normalcy" as used in the United States in the early 1920s?
a. Seek world peace through joining the League of Nations.
b. Reinstate trade with all world powers.
c. Avoid world politics and emphasize domestic improvements.
d. Return the economy to normal peacetime production.
e. Outlaw narcotics, alcohol, and civil disturbances.

Here no single answer can be proved correct, yet the item provides an opportunity for the student to weigh various factors and arrive at the *best* answer in terms of what had been learned in reading, class discussions, and consideration of all relevant knowledge. When such items are used, the best answer must be one on which competent authorities or judges would agree.

Still another variation of the multiple-choice item is one in which the instructions ask the student to choose the answer that does not belong with the others. For example:

Which one of the following tools differs from the others in a fundamental characteristic?
a. axe
b. chisel
c. hatchet
d. knife
e. saw

Here the obvious answer is "saw," since a saw has a serrated edge, unlike the others. In using this type of item, however, great care must be taken to make certain that only one basis of comparison or relationship is possible. Consider the following example:

Which one of the following does not belong with the rest?
a. glass
b. salt
c. soda
d. sugar
e. water

The author of this hypothetical item might have in mind *a* as the correct answer, since the others are chemical compounds and glass is a mixture. In another dimension, however, *e* could be supported as the correct answer since the others are solids and water is a liquid. Still another possibility might be *d* since sugar is the only organic compound in the list. We will describe other variations of the multiple-choice form later in this chapter.

The multiple-choice item is probably the most versatile of the objective choice types. It lends itself to a wide variety of situations, objectives, and content. It can be quite objective in its scoring, it provides opportunity for wide coverage in the choice of alternatives, and it is less conducive to chance success than true-false items are. It is so generally regarded as the best and most widely applicable type that it has become the stock-in-trade, the basic type, for most standardized tests today.

Here we give a number of suggestions and some examples of good techniques for multiple-choice items.

1. *The item should cover an important achievement, and the stem should clearly and distinctly identify the task posed by the item.* An item can be outstanding in a mechanical sense and still be unacceptable if it is not based on a significant achievement and phrased so that the nature of the problem is evident to students who have the necessary ability and background to grasp its import. The item stem can be either a question or an incomplete statement, but in either case a complete idea must be presented. In most items the stem can and should be made sufficiently precise so that capable students can attempt to recall the relevant information, weigh and if necessary relate the appropriate facts, and formulate a tentative answer before reading the responses. Consider the following stem:

Rail freight as compared with air freight:

The knowledge to be covered or the understanding to be demonstrated is not made clear by this stem. It is conceivable that the item asks for knowledge of cost, time delay in delivery, maximum size of parcels, or any number of other topics. In actual practice the responses for stems of this type frequently relate to markedly different factors or characteristics, and in one sense the item becomes a collection of statements, each of which is to be judged true or false. Consider:

Rail freight as compared with air freight is
a. faster.
b. less expensive.
c. more closely regulated by the ICC.
d. less widely available in the U.S.
e. increasing in popularity among large businesses.

If the intent in this item is to measure students' knowledge of the comparative cost of the two types of freight, the stem should be addressed to that factor and all of the responses should be concerned with cost. For example, the item could be:

How does the cost of air freight compare with that of rail freight?
a. more expensive under all conditions
b. more expensive for parcels under five pounds; about the same for heavier shipments
c. more expensive for distances under a hundred miles; less expensive for longer distances
d. less expensive for parcels under five pounds; more expensive for heavier shipments
e. less expensive under all conditions

Generally, if an item is to measure some form of understanding, all parts of it—the stem and each response—must be related to one central problem.
2. *The alternatives or choices should be stated with the same clarity and preciseness as the stem. They should be relevant to the question or problem, and all should appear plausible to the uninformed or poorly prepared student.* One of the most important skills in developing good multiple-choice items is the ability to create a set of four or five tenable responses, one of which experts would agree is correct or clearly better than the other choices. To illustrate:

The city in the United States with the largest population is
a. Chicago
b. Los Angeles
c. New York
d. St. Louis
e. Washington

Each of these choices could probably be chosen as the answer by pupils at different levels living in different parts of the country. As it stands, this might be a good question for grade 4. But if we change the alternatives, we might have this:

The city in the United States with the largest population is
a. Atlantic City
b. Milwaukee
c. New York
d. Reno
e. San Antonio

The item is now easier because the four wrong choices are somewhat more obvious than the choices in the first example. If we went still further in this direction, the item might become:

The city in the United States with the largest population is
a. London
b. New York
c. Paris
d. Rome
e. Tokyo

This item is probably even easier than the others, because most children in school who have studied any social science, whether they know that New York is the answer or not, could probably arrive at it by the process of elimination. The item can also be made absurdly easy:

The city in the United States with the largest population is
a. air
b. birds
c. China
d. New York
e. wheat

It is worth noting at this point that the function of choices as plausible distractors depends on the ability or knowledge of the students as well as the skill of the test-maker. To some people certain choices in the preceding items would seem ridiculous, for example, but the same choices would probably function satisfactorily with younger or less able students and even better if the items were used in a test of the English reading ability of foreign-born immigrants.

The illustrations above show how the selection of alternatives affects the difficulty of a multiple-choice item and the functioning of the choices themselves. A choice that does not seem plausible or that appeals to no one serves no purpose. If there is one such alternative in a five-response multiple-choice item, the item becomes, in effect, a four-response item. If there are two such alternatives, it becomes a three-response item, and so on. The successful author of multiple-choice items must have skill in formulating alternatives that are functional—alternatives that, even though incorrect, are plausible enough to be chosen.

3. *A multiple-choice item should not have more than one acceptable answer.* In a multiple-choice item with more than one possible correct choice, we have in effect a set of true-false statements equal in number to the number of choices. The truth of each must be considered and responded to, and each response must be scored as a separate true-false item. For example:

> What pronoun could be used in the blank?
>> Lynn has never liked _____ kind of story.
> a. this
> b. them
> c. that
> d. those
> e. these

Both *a* and *c* are acceptable choices, but how should the item be scored in the following instances, assuming that pupils have been instructed that one or more than one choice is acceptable?

J chooses *a* and *b*—one right, one wrong
M chooses *a* and *c*—two right
T chooses *d* and *e*—two wrong
Z chooses *a, b, c,* and *d*—two right, two wrong

Pupils	R	R − W
J	1	0
M	2	2
T	0	−2
Z	2	0

If scoring is based only on the number of right answers, M and Z get the same score, although M makes no errors while Z makes two; also, Z gets a higher score than J, who makes fewer errors.

If scoring is based on right answers minus wrong answers, T gets a negative score, though this is undesirable; if no score lower than zero is given, T scores the same as J and Z, who get one and two right, respectively. It is generally far more satisfactory to make two items—in this case, one with *this* as the acceptable choice and the other with *that:*

1. Lynn has never liked ＿＿＿＿＿ kind of story.
   a. this
   b. them
   c. those
   d. these
2. Lynn has never liked ＿＿＿＿＿ kind of story.
   a. that
   b. them
   c. those
   d. these

It is unlikely that a teacher would include both these items in the same test. We should notice, however, that since three choices are the same in both items, it would be quite easy to deduce that the correct choice must be "this" in the first and "that" in the second. Clues like this that lead to a correct answer but are irrelevant to the real purpose of the item reduce the effectiveness of the test.

4. *The choices in an item should come at or near the end of the statement.* When the item is presented as a question, the choices usually occur near the end naturally. For example, an item could be presented as:

What city is the capital of Kentucky?
a. Corbin
b. Frankfort
c. Lexington
d. Louisville
e. Memphis

The most natural way of presenting the alternatives seems to be as indicated. However, one could state the item thus:

a. Corbin
b. Frankfort
c. Lexington
d. Louisville
e. Memphis
＿＿＿＿＿ is the capital city of Kentucky.

Or the item could be presented in this form:

The city of ＿＿＿＿＿ is the capital of Kentucky.
a. Corbin
b. Frankfort
c. Lexington
d. Louisville
e. Memphis

It is usually preferable to place the alternatives at the end of the item, however, because it is a more natural sequence to seek the suggested answers after the problem has been stated, and this arrangement is likely to cause little confusion for the person taking the test.

5. *In multiple-choice items the best or correct answer should be placed equally often in each possible position.* That is, if there are five choices in each item and a considerable number of items in the test, the best answer as *a* should occur with approximately the same frequency as *b, c, d,* and *e.* If the best answer appears much more often in one position than in the others, its position might serve as an irrelevant clue. It is also essential to randomize the best-answer position. That is, the first 20 percent of the items should *not* all be *a,* the next 20 percent should *not* all be *b,* and so on. If, as multiple-choice items are constructed, the best answer of the first one is placed in the *a* position, the best answer of the next in the *b* position, and so on, there will result an equal distribution. When the items are finally arranged, usually according to difficulty, the order of correct choices will automatically be randomized.

There is an exception to the preceding recommendation, however. Some writers recommend that when responses are single words or short terms, alphabetical order should be used. The suggestion has merit, and this method should not cause a serious deviation from an attempt to balance the location of the keyed response. The items in suggestion 2 above illustrate alphabetical listing of short responses.

6. *Choices should be parallel in form wherever possible.* For example:

> The first activity on a cold wintry morning was
> a. to gather wood and build a fire.
> b. eating a hearty breakfast.
> c. fishing for mackerel.
> d. go for fresh water.
> e. a dash around the yard.

This item is improved if the wording is changed to

> The first activity on a cold wintry morning was
> a. gathering wood and building a fire.
> b. eating a hearty breakfast.
> c. fishing for mackerel.
> d. going for fresh water.
> e. dashing around the yard.

7. *Do not use responses that can be eliminated on some basis other than the achievement being measured.* The most frequent violations of this recommendation come from grammatical or logical clues. For example,

A chain of islands is called an
a. archipelago.
b. isthmus.
c. bay.
d. peninsula.
e. portage.

In this item, only responses *a* and *b* would be appropriate grammatically with the article *an*. The problem sometimes can be avoided by using "(a, an)" in the stem or by making the stem a question, as:

What is a chain of islands called?
a. an archipelago
b. an isthmus
c. a bay
d. a peninsula
e. a portage

Sometimes clues arise from responses that are not logically consistent with the stem. For example:

What legislative action was most influential in the increase of U.S. territorial expansion during the last half of the nineteenth century?
a. The Indian tribes did not assert their rights so violently.
b. Additional troops were stationed in the Plains states.
c. Free land in the territories was made available for white settlers.
d. Eastern cities had become overly crowded.
e. Rail transportation had become readily accessible.

Since the stem asks for "legislative action," responses *a* and *d* could be eliminated readily and responses *b* and *e* would be only questionably appropriate.
8. *The length of the item and the length of the choices should be determined by the purpose of the item.* For example, in a test for knowledge and understanding of words, an item might read:

A word that means the same as "vanished" is
a. broadened
b. disappeared
c. decreased
d. changed
e. narrowed

Understanding the theme or main idea of a story might be tested as follows:

The lesson the speaker learned from his friend was that
a. old age can be the happiest, most useful time of life.
b. it is not desirable for old people to wish to become young again or to be-
    have in the carefree manner of youth.
c. seeking the fountain of youth is well worth the effort.
d. it is impossible to make a magic potion that will make people perma-
    nently young.
e. you are as young as you feel and act.

9. *The number of choices in multiple-choice items should be at least
four; the generally preferred number is five.* It can be assumed that as the
number of choices is reduced, the chance factor increases. With four
choices there is, theoretically, one chance in four of guessing the answer;
with three choices, the chance becomes one in three; and with two alternatives the chance is mathematically the same as in a true-false item.
Common practice in standardized tests has been to use five choices or
responses, although more recently there appears to be some tendency to
use only four. The basis for this is seemingly not well established. It is, of
course, more difficult to devise five choices than four, and there is some
feeling that the difference in chance success between four and five
choices is not great enough to warrant the additional effort required to
devise a fifth choice. There is no question, however, that four is the
minimum acceptable number. It is also a generally accepted procedure to
provide the same number of choices for each item in a given test or set.
10. *Words that would be repeated in each response should be part of
the stem.* For example:

In national elections in the United States, the president
a. is chosen by the people directly.
b. is chosen by the members of the Senate.
c. is chosen by the members of the cabinet.
d. is chosen by the members of the House of Representatives.
e. is chosen by the electoral college.

In this illustration, the words "is chosen by the" should be made part of
the stem so that it would read:

In national elections in the United States, the president is chosen by the
a. people directly.
b. members of the Senate.
c. members of the cabinet.
d. members of the House of Representatives.
e. electoral college.

11. *Use "none of the above" and "all of the above" as choices only occasionally and as variations from the usual pattern.* Use them sparingly,
however. Where "none of the above" is the correct choice, there should
be no possible doubt that the other choices are all clearly incorrect. For
example:

> The area of a rectangle is equal to
> a. the sum of its sides.
> b. the square of its shorter side.
> c. the square of its longer side.
> d. one-half the product of its shorter and longer sides.
> e. none of the above.

"All of the above" is probably less desirable than "none of the above."
It is difficult to devise items of this type that stand up under critical
analysis. The choices are so obvious that either the item becomes too
easy or it is used simply as a filler to avoid the effort required to find
another good choice. Where either of these two choices is used, care
should be taken to see that it is the correct answer in a few items but not
all.

Moreover, we emphasize that these responses should be used only
when the choices are clearly right or wrong, not when items call for best
answers.

The suggestions and examples of the multiple-choice item we have
presented should serve to orient the beginning classroom teacher, counselor, or supervisor to the construction and evaluation of this most
widely used and versatile type of objective test item. When carefully and
thoughtfully constructed, it provides the best means so far devised of
measuring outcomes of instruction. Its use is by no means confined to
achievement testing; it is used in measuring intelligence, aptitude, interests, and other qualities or traits, and that this is so attests to its wide
usefulness. The test-maker will generally find practice in constructing
and using multiple-choice items rewarding and satisfying.

LEARNING EXERCISE

18. Construct a multiple-choice item to measure each of the following:
    a. knowledge of the capital city of your state

b. understanding of a rule of punctuation—for example, use of the comma

c. ability to interpret a graph of a table showing the relationship between children's height and their weight

d. skill in defining a problem in general science—for example, determining a safe reducing program for a high school student who is overweight

---

Key-List Items

An extremely useful choice-type item is one that contains some features of both multiple-choice and matching exercises. Called a key-list item, it includes a list of terms or descriptions that are to be used as the choices for a series of questions, statements, or some other type of stem. For example:

Directions: For items 1, 2, and 3 you are to use the following key. For each item, select from the key the one letter that indicates the sport in which the activity could occur.

Key:
a. ice hockey
b. tennis
c. American football
d. basketball
e. golf

( ) 1. The official calls for a jump ball.
( ) 2. A server commits a double fault.
( ) 3. A player is sent to the penalty box for 5 minutes on a major penalty.

The number of questions may vary from two to perhaps fifteen, but usually there are six or seven. This format is quite efficient for measuring achievements that extend from simple verbal associations, such as labels and terms, to the interpretation or application of related principles, concepts, or definitions. We give some suggestions for the development of key-list items below.

1. *Key-list items should be used only when the categories in the key are related.* The values of this item are reduced markedly if the key contains elements that are not tenable as responses for each question or term in the series. In the example above, if *d* and *e* had been "chess" and "checkers," the number of reasonably attractive responses to the statements would have been reduced to three. Moreover, statements appropriate for chess and checkers would not be associated by many students

with the more active sports listed. This recommendation and the reasons for it are similar to those we gave in the fourth suggestion for matching exercises.

2. *Categories in the key should not overlap logically, temporally, or in any other way.* Overlapping categories may make an unnecessary source of frustration for students and may introduce the possibility of more than one satisfactory answer to certain questions. An example of overlapping is the use of "post–World War I" and "the Roaring Twenties" in the same exercise concerning the time when certain social legislation was enacted in the United States.

3. *The number of categories in the key list should not be long.* The longer the list is, the more difficult it is for students to keep in mind the task and to locate answers, and the more likely it is that categories will not be closely related. If the list is much longer than five, generally it would be desirable to divide the exercise into two different exercises, adding categories as necessary to each part.

4. *When a logical sequence exists among the elements in a key, it should be followed.* A series of dates or numbers should be ordered from earliest to latest (or latest to earliest) or from least to most (or most to least). When one-word answers form the list, alphabetical listing is appropriate.

LEARNING EXERCISE

19. Develop a key-list exercise for a topic in a subject you will teach. Ask some friends majoring in the area covered by the exercise to take the test and criticize the items.

A type of item that has found considerable favor among test-makers is one that presents a reading selection, describes a situation, or provides a chart, table, map, or sketch to fit the subject matter and the objectives and then follows this with several items based on the material presented. Such items are generally in multiple-choice form, though true-false may also be used. Examples of the situational type may be seen in Figure 5.1—a part of a road map on which are based a number of multiple-choice items that can be answered by referring to the map. Other examples appear in Chapter 5 but use different situational material.

Situational or Interpretive Items

Although the situational test is not a type of item in the same sense as matching or true-false, it represents certain distinct characteristics and assumed advantages. Among these are, first, that it attempts measurement in what might be called a more global or inclusive fashion than isolated objective test items. Second, it reduces differences between individuals in background knowledge and information, since these are supplied to all. Third, it purports to measure complex outcomes of instruction such as the ability to interpret information, to draw valid conclusions, and to make applications. An example of a situation item is given below.

Directions. Use the passage below to answer items 1, 2, and 3.

A student dissolves a white, powdery solid in distilled water. When dilute H_2SO_4 is added, a colorless gas is given off. The gas is found to be heavier than air, will not burn, and will not support combustion, but is soluble in water.

1. What gas could have been released when the acid was added?
   a. CH_4
   b. CO_2
   c. CO
   d. Cl_2
   e. H_2

2. How could the gas have been collected?
   a. water displacement from an inverted bottle
   b. water displacement from an upright bottle
   c. air displacement from an inverted bottle
   d. air displacement from an upright bottle
   e. none of the above methods

3. When a glowing splint is introduced into a bottle of the gas, it
   a. bursts into flame.
   b. ceases to glow.
   c. continues to glow.
   d. slowly burns away.
   e. causes an explosion.

Although situational or interpretive exercises require a higher order of skill to prepare than most other types of objective test items, they have great potential value in measuring some of the most valued goals of instruction. Some suggestions for developing interpretive passages are given below.

1. *The passage (or chart or graph or whatever) should permit a reasonable number of items to be based on it.* It is not always possible to find a selection (except perhaps in literature) or a table that lends itself satisfactorily to the intended outcome to be measured. The test author who cannot find one must either create the material or revise existing material.

Since the interpretive item requires students to read and study material, the number of items must justify the time required. Some passages can be edited by adding a small amount of new material to provide the basis for additional questions or by deleting material not required for the items presented. In either case the result is a reduction in average student time required per item. Although there are no precise rules for the relation between the length of the passage and the number of items, the limiting feature, of course, is the goal of obtaining a sufficiently reliable test within the time available for testing.

2.   *If the entire test is made of interpretive items, the number of selections should be sufficient to guarantee adequate sampling of content and goals.* Interpretive items obviously are more interrelated than items on ordinary multiple-choice and true-false tests. Thus, to obtain valid tests, and in fairness to students, a test must contain sufficient passages to sample adequately from the goals and different elements of content the test is intended to cover. In other words, for a test of given length it is generally preferable to use short selections and more of them than would be possible with longer passages.

3.   *Items must be carefully developed so that they cannot be answered from a mere searching of the material or from general information.* The quality of a situational test exercise rests largely on the teacher's skill in writing items based on the passage that require students to apply skills developed during instruction. If the questions are too general, bright and well-read students might be able to answer them regardless of level of achievement. On the other hand, if items are too specific to the material presented, they may measure reading or deductive skills rather than achievement. The teacher must strive for some point between these extremes.

4.   *The recommendations concerning the construction of true-false and multiple-choice items should be followed in developing situational items.* Most if not all of the suggestions we gave earlier apply with equal force here.

LEARNING EXERCISE

20.   Develop an interpretive passage and items for the same area of content you used in Learning Exercise 19. Ask your instructor to read and criticize it.

OBJECTIVE TEST ITEMS:
GENERAL SUGGESTIONS

We have offered many suggestions in the preceding pages for planning and constructing different types of test questions or items, from the essay to the most objective. An attempt has been made in this presentation to include suggestions primarily relevant to the type of item under consideration. Some basic principles or ideas apply to all types, however. We now present and discuss these briefly in concluding this chapter. Some of the statements have already been touched on in the discussion of particular types of items, but they bear repetition here since they are very important.

1. *Avoid ambiguity, a common fault of tests.* One of the most common weaknesses of test items of all types is ambiguity. This means that the meaning of the item is not clear or that it may be interpreted in more than one way. This fault is easy to commit but often difficult to detect, and so it may be evident only once the item has actually been used. Nevertheless, there are some suggestions which, if conscientiously adhered to, will help avoid ambiguous and unclear items.

First, strive for clear-cut, concise, exact statements. Long and complicated statements are more difficult to comprehend. Qualifying statements may make an item less ambiguous, but they can also have the opposite effect.

Second, avoid negative statements, particularly in true-false items, where a false negative statement results in a double negative, which can be very confusing. Some ideas and objectives being tested seem to lend themselves best to the negative form; in those cases, emphasize the word that makes the negative as much as possible, by capitalizing or underlining it.

Third, have another teacher or counselor look over your test items critically. Teachers are often reluctant to show their tests to colleagues, but having a friendly critic check them can be very helpful. The viewpoints of others are often valuable in detecting faults the maker of the test has overlooked.

Finally, the surest way to detect ambiguity in test items is to try them out in actual practice. Of course, it may then be too late to do anything about it, but if the test is to be used again some repairs may be possible. An ambiguous item will nearly always show up when the results of the test are analyzed (as we explain in the next chapter). An item that is missed more often by the best students than by the poor students is probably ambiguous.

2. *Statements to be used in test items ordinarily should not be taken verbatim from the textbook or other instructional material.* Sometimes there may be a need to test for knowledge and understanding of the exact wording of a text, but this will probably not occur often. If one wishes to measure the extent to which pupils know, understand, and use what has been taught, it is desirable to test by rephrasing, reorganizing, and restating the content so that the exact wording of the original is not reproduced. Instead of using the key sentence of a paragraph as a test item, the teacher who is testing for the understanding of a central thought or principle should use a form or words different from those used in the textbook. In so doing, the teacher will discourage memorization of the words of a textbook and will be able to determine more adequately whether or not a pupil really understands and can apply what has been read.

3. *Restrict the number of types of items used in any given test.* Although it was stated earlier in this chapter that the type of item one uses is determined in part by the purpose of the test or the objective being measured, it is generally desirable to restrict to two or three the kinds of items used in the same test. The purposes of the test can usually be achieved with a few types of items, and the use of too many different ones may confuse and disturb some pupils.

4. *Avoid giving irrelevant clues.* Unless it is carefully constructed, a test item may in itself furnish an indication of the correct or expected answer. For example, the following item is subject to criticism because of the similarity of the word *parallel* in the item and *parallelogram* in the answer:

> A four-sided figure whose opposite sides are parallel is called
> a.   a trapezoid.
> b.   a triangle.
> c.   a parallelogram.
> d.   an octagon.
> e.   a hexagon.

In preparing test items, the teacher must always be on guard against inadvertently providing such clues. Listed below are several other ways in which irrelevant clues are commonly, though unintentionally, provided in the test item.

   a.   There is a tendency for longer statements or choices to be true or correct more often than not.

   b.   True-false items containing universals such as *always, never, all,* and *none* are likely to be false, while those containing *generally, usually, some, many,* and *sometimes* are more apt to be true. If such terms are used, the correct response should not be in line with the specific deter-miner; that is, more often than not the statements containing *always, never,* and the like should be true and those containing *some, usually,* and so on should at least occasionally be false.

c. The correct (or incorrect) answer to one item should not be given by another item. To illustrate from a teacher-made true-false test in U.S. history, two items were stated as follows:

( ) The Eighteenth Amendment gave women the right to vote.
( ) Repeal of the Eighteenth Amendment occurred during the administration of Franklin D. Roosevelt.

Here, the correct answer to the first item may be deduced from the second item, for the student who knows that the second item is true also knows that the first must be false.

5. *Do not make an item difficult by requiring unnecessarily exact or difficult operations.* In mathematics, for example, if the understanding of a principle is the objective being tested, the calculations in solving a problem should be made as simple as possible without being obvious. The student should not miss the item because of mistakes in calculation if the point is to test whether the principle is known. A similar caution is pertinent in science. To illustrate:

The molecular weight of H_2SO_4 is
a. 32
b. 64
c. 96
d. 98
e. 196

This item could be made needlessly subject to errors in calculation if the answers provided were based on exact atomic weights and therefore in-cluded decimals, when all that presumably is being tested is whether the student knows how to determine the molecular weight of a compound.

6. *The difficulty of an item should be appropriate to the level of the students being tested.* Beginners in test construction are apt to overesti-mate what their students can do. They often construct tests that are too long or tests in which the individual items are too difficult to read or an-swer. Any teacher can construct a test for which most if not all the stu-dents will answer correctly a low percentage of the questions, but this helps neither students nor teacher. The purpose of a test is to find out what the students have learned or can do as well as what they have not learned or cannot do. In a test of appropriate difficulty, all students should find some items they can answer correctly and the best students

should be challenged to the limit of their ability. Furthermore, a test of achievement should not be above the reading level of the group for whom it is intended. To make it so introduces an extraneous factor in the evaluation of the results, since, for example, one cannot know whether a student has done poorly because of lack of ability in the subject or because of reading difficulty.

SUGGESTED READING

EBEL, ROBERT L. *Essentials of Educational Measurement.* 2d ed. Englewood Cliffs, N.J.: Prentice-Hall, 1972. Chap. 6–8. An excellent and thorough discussion of topics related to development of essay, true-false, and multiple-choice tests. Many examples of both good and poor items.

FURST, EDWARD J. *Constructing Evaluation Instruments.* New York: David McKay Co., 1958. Part 1 discusses the objectives of testing. Among the considerations are determining what to evaluate, defining behavior, selecting situations in which to observe or measure, and establishing criteria for sound measurement. Part 2 discusses in detail how to plan and construct a test, how to reproduce and use it, and how to analyze the results. The treatment is probably more extensive than necessary for beginners, but the book constitutes a sound reference on the subject.

GERBERICH, J. RAYMOND. *Specimen Objective Test Items.* New York: David McKay Co., 1956. The nature of test items and their applicability in measuring various objectives in different subject-matter areas, illustrated by thousands of objective test items of different types. Excellent as a source of ideas but not recommended as a source of items for the teacher's own tests.

GRONLUND, NORMAN E. *Measurement and Evaluation in Teaching.* 3d ed. New York: Macmillan, 1976. Chap. 6–10. Principles of classroom testing and of choice and supply tests. A good and thorough treatment of the topics, supplementing material in this chapter.

HILLS, JOHN R. *Measurement and Evaluation in the Classroom.* Columbus, Ohio: Charles E. Merrill Pub. Co., 1976. Chaps. 1–3 cover the planning of a test and developing test items. Chap. 6 covers criterion-referenced testing. Suggests the advantages and disadvantages of different item types.

REMMERS, H. H., N.L. GAGE, and J.F. RUMMEL. *A Practical Introduction to Measurement and Evaluation.* New York: Harper and Row, 1965. Chap. 8. A good comparison of essay and short-answer testing. Also includes suggestions for constructing many of the types of tests used in the classroom. The suggestions for grading essay examinations and the illustration of analytical scoring are particularly useful.

STANLEY, JULIAN C., and KENNETH D. HOPKINS. *Educational and Psychological Measurement and Evaluation.* Englewood Cliffs, N.J.: Prentice-Hall, 1972. Chaps. 8–10. These chapters give general principles of developing tests to measure cognitive achievement and of developing and using objective and essay tests. The topics and suggestions complement those presented in this book.

THORNDIKE, ROBERT L., ed. *Educational Measurement,* 2d ed. Washington, D.C.: American Council on Education, 1971. Chap. 4 covers the research literature pertaining to item characteristics and the development of various types of items. Chap. 10 considers the same topics as they pertain to essay tests. Discussions may be more detailed and complex than necessary for students of this course but the presentations are excellent.

TUCKMAN, BRUCE W. *Measuring Educational Outcomes.* New York: Harcourt Brace Jovanovich, 1975. Chaps. 4–5 consider the development of choice-type, short-answer, and essay tests. Variations of format are presented, and examples are given of attempts to measure the use of knowledge.

Seven

TRYING OUT AND EVALUATING
THE TEACHER-MADE TEST

After the teacher or test-maker has prepared the test items as described in Chapter 6, he or she is ready to assemble, reproduce, and score the test using the principles and procedures that will now be presented. This chapter will also include a discussion of ways to use data from students' responses to the test to evaluate and improve it.

After studying this chapter, you should be able to answer questions and use processes such as these:

1. Describe the factors that should be considered as items are arranged on a test.
2. Describe the advantages and disadvantages of a separate answer sheet for tests you will use in your teaching.
3. Prepare scoring keys for true-false, completion, matching, and multiple-choice tests.
4. Describe how to establish curricular validity for a classroom test constructed for use in your teaching field.
5. Given data for a test, compute the discrimination and difficulty indexes for individual items.
6. Given data for a test, compute the reliability coefficient for the test.
7. Describe the statistical characteristics of a "good" test item and explain why these characteristics are desirable.
8. Compare the analysis of a criterion-referenced test with that of other classroom tests.

ASSEMBLING THE TEST

When the test items have been constructed and recorded, either on cards, as suggested in the preceding chapter, or in some other manner, the next step is to arrange them preparatory to having the test reproduced. For an essay test, the sequence of questions presents no problem, since such a test usually involves writing the questions on the board at the time of the examination, although it is probably preferable to duplicate the set of essay questions and give each pupil a copy. For tests employing items of a more objective nature, however, the requirements are different. In the following section we shall discuss some of the problems relating to the organization of an objective test.

Arranging the Items

A number of factors have a bearing on the arrangement of items in an objective test. Among these are (1) difficulty, (2) type of item, (3) content, and (4) anticipated use of the scores. Ordinarily, in a standardized test the items are arranged in accordance with most or all of these criteria at the same time. For example, in nearly all such tests the items are arranged in order of difficulty, from the easiest to the most difficult. This system has two advantages. First, it encourages the person taking the test by starting with items that can be easily answered. Second, it tends to avoid the possibility of the student's getting stuck on a difficult item, which might not leave time enough to answer many easier ones that follow. Of course, the difficulty of individual test items is determined on the basis of responses by groups and does not necessarily coincide with the item-difficulty pattern of any particular individual. The assumption that must be made is that the average difficulty based on responses of the group is the best available difficulty index for the individuals in the group.

It is customary to group items according to type—that is, to place true-false items in one group, multiple-choice in another, and so on—and then to arrange the items within each category according to difficulty, as just described. If there are a great many items of one kind, they may, of course, be divided into two or more groups according to some other criterion such as content. For example, if there are fifty multiple-choice items and fifty true-false items to be arranged, each type might be subdivided into two groups of twenty-five each, particularly if there is some obvious and logical basis for such a division. If, in an arithmetic test, half of the true-false items deal with fractions and half with decimals, the items might be divided on that basis, and similarly the multiple-choice questions. In instances in which part scores on these aspects of arithmetic are desired, such an arrangement will make it easier to obtain them.

Basically, then, in most objective tests items are arranged according to type and within the type groups, according to difficulty. The classroom teacher, as distinguished from the professional test author, usually has no basis for determining the difficulty of individual test items except personal judgment. Whereas the producer of standardized tests tries out the items in preliminary forms to determine difficulty, the classroom teacher almost never has the opportunity to do this. Therefore, the items are arranged according to the best estimate of their difficulty. Parenthetically, a word might be added here concerning the grouping of items according to type. This practice is now almost universal and the reasons are fairly obvious. In the first place, it facilitates scoring, since items all of the same type are easier to score than a mixture of various types. In the second place, a test in which items are grouped according to types of items is usually more agreeable to the examinee.

Arranging items within the type groups according to estimated difficulty cannot be a very exact process, and the test-maker will usually have to rely upon personal experience and judgment in this matter. It is sometimes quite satisfactory to arrange items according to length, placing the shortest first. Length is never a valid basis for judging difficulty, but an arrangement of this sort may encourage the examinee to assume that the hardest items will come at the end of the test.

Items may be arranged according to content, as in the example of the arithmetic test given above. In every field of concern, the teacher has certain ideas or plans for organization of the subject matter. Usually, subject matter is organized by units and by areas within the units. For example, a unit on transportation may be organized according to historical periods or according to kinds of transportation—land, sea, and air, or mechanical and animal. Items in such divisions as these may in turn be arranged according to type, difficulty, and content simultaneously, provided, of course, that there are enough items. For short tests of twenty-five items or less, the grouping of the items on any basis except type is not often practical or useful.

There is one other situation in which the grouping of items is important—namely, when diagnosis is the purpose of the test. Let us assume that in arithmetic, English, or reading, the examiner wishes to identify specific strengths and weaknesses in the pupils' grasp of fundamentals. The first step in constructing a test for diagnostic purposes is to make a careful analysis of the rules and skills that are basic to progress in the subject. The next step is to construct an adequate number of items on each rule or skill and then arrange them in the test so that each group constitutes a measure of understanding of one of these. Thus, when the test results are available the responses of each pupil, as well as of the entire class, to items testing a particular rule or skill will be easily determined. Advance arrangement of items for such purposes will facilitate diagnosis and remedial instruction. This will be discussed and illustrated in more detail in Chapter 14.

LEARNING EXERCISES

1. The term *mental set* is used to describe the student's orientation or approach to a particular task or type of problem. How should consideration of mental set affect the organization of a test?
2. What are the advantages of grouping items according to type? Are there any advantages to an omnibus or spiral arrangement of items? (Note: In this arrangement items occur in cycles. For example, a series of simple items on a set of topics is followed by another series of more difficult items on the same topics, followed by a series of still more difficult items; or if there are several different types of items in a test, each type appears once in each cycle as, for example, TF, MC, analogies, TF, MC, analogies, and so on.)

Preparing Directions

When the arrangement and grouping of the test items have been determined, the next step is to prepare directions. Before the test is duplicated, directions should be prepared for the test as a whole, as well as for the subtests or parts. If the test is to be used as a semester-end or year-end final examination, a title page may be used. This gives the test a more finished appearance; also, if pupils are not to start work on it until preliminary directions have been given, a title page serves to cover the test proper until the directions have been read and the pupils told to begin. If there is to be a title page, it may be set up in a form similar to Figure 7.1.

If the examination is a cooperative effort and is given to classes under the supervision of several different teachers, there should be space for the pupil to indicate the section and the teacher's name, so that the papers can be readily sorted.

If a title page is not used, the essential information can be put at the top of the first page of the test.

Directions for each part should come at the beginning of the part, as follows:

```
          Score                    Name _____

    Part 1 _____           Date _____

    Part 2 _____        Section _____

    Total _____    Teacher's Name _____




                     FINAL EXAMINATION

                       English 10A

    DIRECTIONS: Do not turn the page until you are told to
    do so. The examination consists of two parts. Part 1
    is True-False and Part 2 is Multiple-Choice. Directions
    are given in the test for each part. Please read them
    carefully and follow them exactly. You will have forty
    minutes to work on the test. Try to answer every ques-
    tion, but if you do not know the answer to a question
    go on to the next ones and come back to it later. Do
    not "skip around." Begin at the beginning and work
    straight through. Your score on the test will be
    the number answered correctly.
```

Directions: The statements in this part are either True or False. Read each one carefully. If you think it is *true,* place a + in the parentheses in front of the statement; if you think it is *false,* place a 0 in the parentheses.

If the scoring is to be on the basis of right answers minus wrong answers, the following should be added:

If you are not sure of the correct answer but can make an intelligent guess, mark the statement; if not, omit it. Your score on this part of the test will be the number of right answers minus the number of wrong answers.

If the scoring is to be based on the number of right answers only, the following should be added:

Mark every statement. Your score will be the number right.

If locally duplicated answer sheets are used (see page 203), the directions given first above should be modified in part as follows:

If you think it is *true,* place a + on the answer sheet opposite the number that corresponds to the number of the statement. If you think it is *false,* place a 0 on the answer sheet.

If machine-scored or printed answer sheets are used, the directions should be:

If you think it is *true,* make a heavy black mark between the dotted lines in Column 1 opposite the number that corresponds to the number of the statement. If you think it is *false,* blacken the space between the pair of lines in Column 2. You should use only pencils provided or, if directed to do so, a soft lead pencil (No. 2 or No. 2½) to mark the answer sheet. Do *not* use a pen or colored pencil.

In similar fashion, directions for multiple-choice, matching, or short-answer items should be worked out and reproduced on the test paper so that the directions will precede the part to which they apply.

With younger pupils especially, and in any case where pupils are not accustomed to objective tests, it is well to include a sample item with the directions. For example, the following could be used after the directions for matching items:

Example:

	Name of animal	Type of animal
(b)	1. cow	a. bird
(a)	2. robin	b. mammal
		c. reptile

A cow is a mammal, so the letter *b* has been placed in the parentheses before *cow;* a robin is a bird, so the letter *a* has been placed in the parentheses before *robin.* Mark the items below in the same way. Notice that there are more items in the right-hand column than in the left, so that after all blanks have been filled you will have some on the right that you have not used. Some of the items in the right-hand column may be used more than once.

Directions for the test and the subtests or parts should be carefully worked out in advance and incorporated into the test. The ideal to strive for is to make the test as nearly self-administering as possible, so that the pupil understands the task with a minimum of supplementary explanations. This is especially desirable if the test is to be used by more than one teacher, and it is advantageous in any case because a test that is nearly self-administering makes for uniformity and objectivity of administration. Otherwise, there is a danger that supplementary instructions will not be identical when given to various pupils or groups at different times.

LEARNING EXERCISES

3. Write a set of directions for multiple-choice items for a test for a fifth grade. Include an example.
4. Prepare directions for a set of matching items including an example like the one above. The directions should be clear without the example, however. Submit the directions to the class for criticism. In your directions specify the basis for the matching, the method of indicating answers, and whether the same choice may be used more than once.

Preparing the Test Sheets

In most cases, teacher-made tests are duplicated in the school office. Copy is prepared by the teacher, often in handwritten form. It is important to make clear to the typist such matters as capitalization, punctuation, spacing, and provisions for marking answers. Capitalization and punctuation generally do not cause any difficulty, provided the test-maker knows and indicates clearly what is wanted. Words to be emphasized should be written in capitals or underlined or both.

The matter of spacing is important in setting up objective tests. All material on the page should be arranged and spaced in a manner that will make it as clear and legible as possible for the pupil. This procedure should be followed at all grade levels and especially when preparing tests for younger children. If answers are to be written or marked on the test itself, sufficient space should be provided and it should be clear that the space left is for this purpose. For example, when answers are to be marked within parentheses, they should be spaced thus (   ), not thus (). If words or phrases are to be written, ample space for writing them should be provided. This is usually accomplished by leaving a ruled space, thus, _____, as in short-answer or completion items. The teacher can give a clue to the length of the word by the amount of space provided. This is not generally recommended, however, since it provides what might be considered an irrelevant clue. If the size of the space is not intended to provide a clue, the directions should indicate this fact.

There should always be a double space between successive test items. It is poor economy to crowd them together; however, the statement of each item itself may be single-spaced. In the case of multiple-choice items, general practice favors setting them up in this manner:

( ) The study of living things is called
   a. physics.
   b. chemistry.
   c. biology.
   d. geology.
   e. astronomy.

The "ladder" method is generally preferred to the plan of listing choices thus:

( ) The study of living things is called (a) physics, (b) chemistry, (c) biology, (d) geology, (e) astronomy.

Items should be numbered consecutively through the entire test rather than consecutively within each part. The latter procedure results in having two or more items with the same number, as two number *1*'s, two number *2*'s, and so on. If there are several parts, there will, of course, be an item numbered *1* in each, and so on. This leads to confusion, particularly if locally made answer sheets are used. Most teacher-made answer sheets are set up with numbered spaces in columns, as shown in Figure 7.2.

Pupils will become confused if the numbers on the items do not correspond with the numbers on the answer sheet. When the numbering of items in different parts of the test begins in each case with number *1*, no standard answer sheet can be used; instead, each test must have its own answer sheet with numbers coinciding with those on the test. The consecutive arrangement shown in Figure 7.2 is nearly always followed with answer sheets accompanying standardized tests.

Any study or analysis of individual test items is also facilitated by a consecutive numbering system, since each number quickly identifies a particular question and its corresponding answer and distinguishes that question and answer from all others on the test.

Tests may be reproduced by a number of different processes, each of which has some advantages. If more than one method is available, the choice will be determined by local needs and circumstances. Objective

Sample of a Teacher-made Answer Sheet   *Figure 7.2*

```
┌─────────────────────────────────────────────────────────────────┐
│                                                                   │
│    Subject_____      Score     Name_____     │
│                                 ____                              │
│                                                                   │
│    Instructor_____                Date_____     │
│                                                                   │
│                                                                   │
│                                                                   │
│     1._____    26._____    51._____    76._____   │
│     2._____    27._____    52._____    77._____   │
│     3._____    28._____    53._____    78._____   │
│     4._____    29._____    54._____    79._____   │
│     5._____    30._____    55._____    80._____   │
│     6._____    31._____    56._____    81._____   │
│     7._____    32._____    57._____    82._____   │
│     8._____    33._____    58._____    83._____   │
│     9._____    34._____    59._____    84._____   │
│    10._____    35._____    60._____    85._____   │
│    11._____    36._____    61._____    86._____   │
│    12._____    37._____    62._____    87._____   │
│    13._____    38._____    63._____    88._____   │
│    14._____    39._____    64._____    89._____   │
│    15._____    40._____    65._____    90._____   │
│    16._____    41._____    66._____    91._____   │
│    17._____    42._____    67._____    92._____   │
│    18._____    43._____    68._____    93._____   │
│    19._____    44._____    69._____    94._____   │
│    20._____    45._____    70._____    95._____   │
│    21._____    46._____    71._____    96._____   │
│    22._____    47._____    72._____    97._____   │
│    23._____    48._____    73._____    98._____   │
│    24._____    49._____    74._____    99._____   │
│    25._____    50._____    75._____   100._____   │
│                                                                   │
└───────────────────────────────────────────────────────────────────┘
```

tests should *always* be duplicated. Although some attempts have been made to administer objective tests orally by reading the questions aloud, this method is not recommended. The pupil is entitled to have a separate test and should not be expected to keep the questions in mind or make snap decisions at the moment the questions are read aloud.

Tests reproduced by processes available in most schools should be duplicated on one side of the sheet only. It is generally not satisfactory to use both sides because unless extra-heavy paper—and extreme care— are used, some of the print will show through and the material will be difficult to read. Also, when a test consists of several pages **fastened** together, it is easier for the pupil to handle if print appears on only one side of each page. This is especially true when tablet-arm chairs are used and when answers are marked on the test itself rather than on a separate answer sheet.

For ease in scoring, the test should be set up and duplicated so that answer spaces appear in a straight line, all at the same margin. This is easily arranged for true-false, multiple-choice, and matching items by placing parentheses before the number of each item. With short-answer and completion questions a plan similar to the example below may be used:

15. The surrender of ____(a)____ took place at   a. _____

Yorktown in the year ___(b)___.   b. _____

Here all answers are written in the lettered spaces at the right-hand margin. Also, since all the answer spaces are of the same length, there is no irrelevant clue to the length of the correct answer.

If answers are written on the test itself, enough copies of the test must be made so that there will be a new one for each examinee every time the test is administered. If separate answer sheets are used, the tests themselves can be used repeatedly. When the same test is used with several groups, it is important to collect all copies each time it is used, for if copies get into circulation the examination will obviously lose its usefulness as a testing or measuring instrument. It is helpful to number all copies and require each pupil to write the number of the copy being used on the answer sheet, provided separate answer sheets are used. In this way, missing copies of the test can be traced and usually recovered. It is also necessary, if tests are used more than once, to scan them after each use and erase all marks made on them by the previous users.

In arranging objective tests for duplication it is not desirable to have a question continue from one page to the next; starting a question on a new page is preferable to dividing it. *This is particularly important with matching questions,* for the examinee would become justifiably annoyed if it were necessary to turn a page back and forth to consult the two parts of each list on two separate pages.

Making the Scoring Key

When answers are to be marked on the test proper and the blanks are spaced in the manner suggested above, the preparation of a scoring key is simple. The scoring key usually consists of a strip of heavy paper or cardboard about an inch and a half wide and as long as the answer column on the test page. The correct answers are entered on this strip, spaced to match exactly the spacing of the items on the test page. Then the strip is laid alongside the column of answers and the scorer checks the wrong or the right answers, whichever method is being used in scoring. The answers on the key should be typed or printed near the edge of the strip so that when it is laid on the test the correct answers will be close to the answer spaces on the test.

When locally made answer sheets are used, the same type of scoring key is usable, since the spaces on these answer sheets are usually arranged in columns—usually four to the page—about an inch to an inch and a half wide. One hundred such spaces can easily be typed, double spaced, on an ordinary sheet of paper, with twenty-five items in each of the four columns, as shown in Figure 7.2.

When the machine-scorable type of answer sheet is scored by hand, the most convenient key is one made of a sheet of cardboard the same size as the answer sheet. At each place where a correct answer mark should appear on the answer sheet, a small hole is punched in the cardboard. This makes a stencil that can be laid over the answer sheet. Scoring is then done by simply counting the number of marks that appear through the holes in the stencil. This type of scoring stencil is usually provided by publishers of standardized tests. It may be used for hand scoring as well as for machine scoring. When using such a scoring stencil, it is necessary to scan the answer sheet before covering it with the stencil to see that only one space is marked for each item. Where more than one space is marked, such items should be counted wrong unless, of course, there is more than one correct answer to the items in question.

Another type of locally produced answer sheet, shown in Figure 7.3, incorporates some features of the machine-scorable sheet. Rather than providing spaces in which short answers can be written, this sheet provides spaces corresponding to the answer alternatives only. Pupils indicate their answers by either blackening or crossing out the intended

A Locally Prepared Answer Sheet with Response Positions   *Figure 7.3*

```
Subject_____    Score    Name_____
Instructor_____    _____    Date_____


        1 2 3 4 5      1 2 3 4 5      1 2 3 4 5      1 2 3 4 5
    1.○○○○○  26.○○○○○  51.○○○○○  76.○○○○○
    2.○○○○○  27.○○○○○  52.○○○○○  77.○○○○○
    3.○○○○○  28.○○○○○  53.○○○○○  78.○○○○○
```

Figure 7.4   A Key for a Locally Prepared Answer Sheet

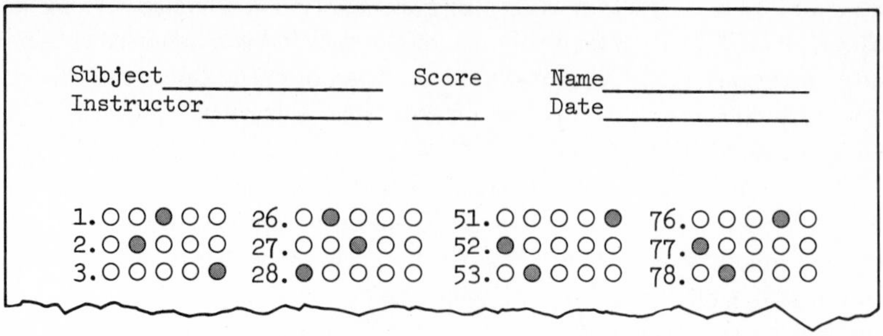

Subject_____	Score	Name_____
Instructor_____	_____	Date_____

```
1.○○●○○   26.○●○○○   51.○○○○●   76.○○○●○
2.○●○○○   27.○○●○○   52.●○○○○   77.●○○○○
3.○○○○●   28.●○○○○   53.○●○○○   78.○●○○○
```

space. If the sheets are reproduced by multilith or duplicating equipment, some copies can be run on heavy paper or cardboard for use in preparing keys. The example of a key in Figure 7.4 shows that spaces are punched to correspond to the correct answers.

If answers are marked on the test itself, spaces for recording scores should be provided either on the title page as shown in Figure 7.1 or at the top of page 1 of the test. If part-scores are determined, they should be recorded separately and added to obtain the total score. If derived scores of some type such as ranks or standard scores are calculated, they should also be recorded in additional spaces provided for the purpose. The same principles apply if separate answer sheets are used, but the scores are recorded on the answer sheets, not on the tests.

ANALYZING TEST RESULTS

After a test has been tried out and scored, the results may be analyzed in two ways. One is from the standpoint of what the results reveal about the pupils' learning or how successful instruction has been. This means far more than simply tabulating total scores on the test, since high scores may result from an easy test as well as from good teaching and, conversely, low scores may be caused by a difficult test or by inferior teaching. Thorough analysis of test results involves some attempt at diagnosis, even though the test may not have been set up with this purpose clearly in mind. It is always desirable to formulate some kind of analysis showing the degree of success with specific items and parts of the test in order to appraise the efficacy of teaching and learning. Unless an attempt at such analysis is made, the results of the test cannot be put to maximum use.

A simple analysis of the results of a test for diagnostic purposes can be performed in two ways: (1) the teacher can tabulate the responses to each item, which will show how often each item was missed, or (2) the scored tests or answer sheets can be returned to the students, who are asked for a show of hands on each item by those who missed it. (In either case, the scoring should be done by checking *wrong answers.*) In this way it is possible to analyze the performance of the students on the test and to identify individual points and areas of content or objectives that have not been well learned. The results of such analysis may provide a basis for reteaching or remedial work with individual students.

Another type of analysis has for its purpose the evaluation of the test as a measuring instrument. How effective is the test and how well does it function? Although careful analytical appraisal is an essential part of the process of producing a standardized test, this is not generally practiced by classroom teachers in test-making. Yet some evaluation of this sort might well be a part of every teacher's measurement program. Unless teachers are willing to "test the test," the effectiveness of their measurement techniques cannot be satisfactorily determined.

The rest of this chapter will be devoted to an explanation of a few simple techniques that any test-maker can use with a locally constructed test to appraise its worth as a measuring instrument.

It will be remembered that validity refers to the degree to which a test measures what it is intended to measure. How can a teacher appraise the validity of classroom tests? Obviously, content or curricular validity is one measure. If the teacher has constructed the test on the basis of instructional objectives, and if the test covers or measures what has been taught, the test may be said to have a degree of curricular validity; that is, it is valid because it tests what the teacher has been teaching. *Validity and Item Discrimination*

If the teacher wishes to go beyond curricular validity, the test scores can be compared with scores on other tests that have been given, with marks based on class and laboratory work, and with other measures of achievement such as standardized tests in the same subject. Correlation is the usual method of determining the extent of such relationships, as has been explained in Chapter 4.

The discrimination power of individual items on a test is a valuable index for evaluating their quality. It has been regarded by some authorities as an indicator of validity or lack of it. The argument runs something like this: One must assume, first, that scores on the whole test have some validity and, second, that scores on a particular valid item should agree with scores on the whole test. Let us examine these assumptions. The first usually implies that the test has curricular validity. There may be other evidence of validity, but generally when item-discrimination is used as a means of establishing validity, the test, which is in this case the criterion of validity, is assumed to have curricular validity because it measures what has been taught. The second assumption is tested by comparing results on a given test item with scores on the whole test. Since the test is assumed to have some validity, an item that agrees with the scores on the test also has some validity. That is, an item answered correctly by a higher proportion of those who make high scores on the test than of those who make low scores is functioning in a manner consistent with the scores on the whole test. Whether or not we accept this line of reasoning as justification for regarding the discrimination power of items as evidence of validity, the technique is a widely used and generally accepted method of identifying "good" items and culling out "poor" ones.

To consider how this is done, let us assume that a test has been given and scored and that the papers have been arranged in order of score, from highest to lowest. We may call the highest one-fourth of these the *high group* and the lowest one-fourth the *low group*. In a class of forty, the highest ten on the test would constitute the high group, the lowest ten the low group.

Now let us consider that the results of a hypothetical test item are as follows:

Item No. 15

Answered correctly by

High group	7 (of the top 10)
Low group	3 (of the lowest 10)

We may conclude that this item discriminates as it should; that is, 70 percent of the pupils in the high group get it right, while only 30 percent in the low group do so. Such an item is said to have a positive discrimination value, or to discriminate positively. On the other hand, not every test item will discriminate positively. For example:

Item No. 16

Answered correctly by

High group	4 (of the top 10)
Low group	7 (of the lowest 10)

This item is said to discriminate negatively because a higher proportion of the low group get it right than of the high group. Items showing negative discrimination are not common, but it should be the aim of the good test technician to identify and eliminate them whenever they are found.

The following item is one that actually discriminated negatively in a national tryout:

2. Temporary teeth in children do *not* include
   a. incisors.
   b. bicuspids.
   c. canines.
   d. molars.

In trying out this item with about 1,500 students in grades 7, 8, and 9, it was found that "*b.* bicuspids," the correct answer, was chosen by 11 percent of the lowest fourth and by only 8 percent of the highest fourth. Moreover, for some reason, 67 percent of the top fourth and 42 percent of the bottom chose "*d.* molars" as the right answer. Of all the students tested, only about 10 percent answered the item correctly. There is no factor here of ambiguity, since *b* is unquestionably the right choice. It is simply a matter of difficulty. The item was not included in the final forms of the test because of its negative discrimination.

The usual explanation for negatively discriminating items is ambiguity in the statement of the item itself. In such items the abler, more thoughtful pupil may see some implications that the maker of the test has overlooked and may thus be led to choose an answer that has not been labeled as the correct one. The less able pupil, on the other hand, considering the item on a more superficial basis, arrives at the answer which has been keyed as correct.

Sometimes the maker of a test feels that a question missed by a substantial proportion of a class is a bad item or that it reflects inadequate teaching. Consider the following typical results:

Item No. 37
Answered correctly by

High group	30 (percent)
Low group	10 (percent)

This item has been answered correctly by less than one-third of the high-scoring pupils and by 10 percent of the low scorers. Of the class as a whole, probably about one-fifth would get it right. However, the item appears to be a good one since it discriminates clearly between the high and low groups in a positive direction. Some items of this difficulty level can justifiably be included on a test, but a test containing a large proportion of such items will not be maximally efficient in discriminating among various levels of achievement.

It should be kept in mind that most item-discrimination techniques start with all the members of the group who have taken the test. Suppose, for example, that a teacher has given a test to four classes in first-year algebra. There are 120 students in the four classes. After scoring the test, the teacher arranges the test papers in order from highest score to lowest score. Then, starting at the top, the first thirty (top 25 percent) are taken off; and starting with the paper having the lowest score, thirty (another 25 percent) are counted from the bottom. These are, respectively, the high and low fourths of all 120 students who took the test. Now, beginning with item 1, the teacher counts the number in the high group who answered it correctly and the number in the low group who answered it correctly. These two numbers are the basis for determining the discriminating power for that item.

A simple formula for determining the discriminating power of a test item is

$$d = \frac{n_H - n_L}{N}$$

where d = the discrimination index
n_H = the number in the high group answering the item correctly
n_L = the number in the low group answering the item correctly
N = the total number in either high or low group (N = 25 percent of all who took the test)

For example, if $n_H = 20$, $n_L = 10$, and $N = 30$, $d = (20 - 10)/30 = 10/30 = .33$. The discrimination index has a possible range from +1 to −1. An item answered correctly by all the highs and missed by all the lows would have an index of +1. Conversely, an item answered correctly by all the lows and missed by all the highs would have an index of −1. An item answered correctly by equal numbers of highs and lows has an index of 0. A reasonable criterion in using this index would be a value of .25. An item having an index lower than this would be considered a poorly discriminating item.

Functioning of Choices

Professional test-makers apply another type of analysis to multiple-choice items—namely, the determination of how the choices in each such item function. As we mentioned in Chapter 6, a choice that no examinee chooses as the correct answer is simply filler or deadwood. In determining the quality of multiple-choice items, it is customary to determine how often each choice is marked as the correct answer. In the case of a positively discriminating item, the *correct* answer must be chosen more often by the high group than by the low group; but each of the wrong choices, or distractors, should be chosen by some.

Thus, a complete analysis for a multiple-choice item might look like this:

Item No. 10

Choices (percent)

	1	2	3*	4	5
Highs	10	12	50	7	21
Lows	13	17	31	11	28

*Correct answer.

Here it can be seen that 50 percent of the "highs" answered the item correctly as compared with 31 percent of the "lows." All choices function—all were marked correct by some examinees. Consider, however, the following example:

Item No. 11

Choices (percent)

	1	2*	3	4	5
Highs	5	84	0	11	0
Lows	14	70	4	12	0

*Correct answer.

This item is also a "good" item in that it discriminates positively. However, choice 3 was marked correct by only 4 percent of the lows and none of the highs, and choice 5 was chosen by none of either group. This item would probably be carefully studied, and the third and fifth choices would be revised or replaced, since they are so obviously wrong that they are contributing little or nothing to the usefulness of the item.

The teacher who makes a test for repeated use can carry out a simple item analysis, as explained here, and enter the results on the item card. Items that do not discriminate positively—that is, that are not answered correctly by a larger proportion of the best pupils than of the less able ones—should be studied for clues to the reason for the negative discrimination. Unless negatively discriminating items can be shown to have other important values, or can be made positively discriminating, there is little reason to retain them, for they detract from the quality of the test as a whole.

LEARNING EXERCISES

5. An item on a test in general science, given to 80 students, is answered correctly by 10 students in the high one-fourth and by 5 in the

low one-fourth. Using the formula above, find the discrimination index of the item. Another item on the same test is missed by 12 of the top fourth and 8 of the bottom fourth. What is its discrimination index?

6. If you can obtain copies of a test that has been given either to your class in measurement or elsewhere and that has been scored, it will be interesting to make an analysis of some of the items. You should have at least ten papers in the highest fourth of the class and ten in the lowest fourth. Set up a table such as the following one and enter the data:

Item	Highest fourth, number right	Lowest fourth, number right	Discrimination index
1.			
2.			
3.			
4.			
5.			
etc.			

Using the formula given, find the discrimination indexes of the first ten items. Would you retain all of them? If not, which ones would you discard? Justify your answer.

Difficulty

Closely related to considerations of the discrimination values of test items is the question of difficulty. Except for special and unusual reasons, items answered correctly or missed by all pupils are not considered good, for such items make no discrimination whatever in the class or group being tested. A test made up entirely of such items would result in everyone's getting the same score, either perfect or zero. Obviously, such a result tells nothing about differences in achievement among members of the class. Rather, it demonstrates that the test was either entirely too easy or too difficult and thus reflects unfavorably on the test-maker's ability.

The simplest way to determine whether a test is appropriate in difficulty for the group tested is to study the distribution of scores on the test. If the mean is at or near the middle of the range and if there are no perfect or zero scores, the teacher may be fairly certain that the test is suitable for that group. For example, on a test containing 80 questions it is found that the mean score is 42 and the range of scores is from 11 to 75. Such facts indicate that the test was suitable in range and difficulty for this class. Let us suppose, however, that with another class or grade the same test shows an average score of 69 and a range from 50 to 80; obviously the test was too easy for this group. If, on the other hand, the mean is 15 and the range from 0 to 40, the test would have been too difficult.

Thus it may be inferred that difficulty has a bearing on the discrimination value of a test—that a test that is too hard or too easy will not discriminate between individuals of different levels of achievement as well as one that is more appropriate for the range of abilities in the group.

Though absolutely fixed points for acceptable averages or range can rarely be established, the following general principles may serve as a useful guide:

1. Items missed or answered correctly by every pupil are not discriminating in that group.
2. On a test appropriate in difficulty for a given group, the mean should be near the middle of the range of possible scores.
3. On a test suitable for a group of the usual variability, the range of scores should be as wide as possible, short of zero or perfect scores.
4. If the number of pupils tested is fairly large (about 30 or more) and fairly heterogeneous, and the foregoing principles are met, the scores on a test should be distributed symmetrically around the average.
5. Tests that give zero scores or perfect scores are not discriminating for the individuals who make such scores.

LEARNING EXERCISES

7. In Exercise 6 you found discrimination values for certain test items. Find the difficulty values for these items by averaging the percent right in the top fourth and the percent right in the bottom fourth. Do you find that the items have difficulty values in the satisfactory range, not too easy nor too difficult?
8. Find the mean and the range of scores on the test. Do they indicate that the test was suitable for the group, too easy, or too difficult?

Table 7.1   Summary Analysis of Essay Test Items

High group			Low group		
Item score	f	f × score	Item score	f	f × score
5	4	20	5	0	0
4	3	12	4	1	4
3	2	6	3	1	3
2	1	2	2	3	6
1	0	0	1	4	4
0	0	0	0	1	1
	10	40		10	18

Analysis of Essay Test Items

The procedures given on the preceding pages must be modified for use with essay tests.[1] The first steps are the same—identifying the high and low 25 percent of the group tested. Then a summary table for each item is prepared for each group, as shown in Table 7.1. In this example, the highest possible score on the item is 5 points, and the number of points earned is tabulated separately for pupils in the high and low groups.

The index of discrimination is found from the formula

$$d = \frac{S_H - S_L}{N(\text{Score}_{max} - \text{Score}_{min})}$$

where d = the index of discrimination
S_H = the sum of scores for "highs"
S_L = the sum of scores for "lows"
N = 25 percent of the number tested
Score_{max} = the highest *possible* score on the item
Score_{min} = the lowest *possible* score on the item

Substituting the data from the table gives

$$d = \frac{40 - 18}{10(5 - 0)}$$
$$= \frac{22}{50}$$
$$= .44$$

[1] The procedures given here are based on an article by D. R. Whitney and D. L. Sabers, "Improving Essay Examinations III. Use of Item Analysis," Technical Bulletin 11, mimeographed. (Iowa City: University Evaluation and Examination Service, 1970).

This item has a discrimination index of .44, showing that it does a good job of distinguishing between the high and low scorers on the test.

To find the difficulty index for essay questions, the formula used is:

$$\text{diff} = \frac{S_H + S_L - (2N \times \text{Score}_{min})}{2N(\text{Score}_{max} - \text{Score}_{min})}$$

where the symbols have the same meaning as above. Substituting data from the table gives

$$\text{diff} = \frac{40 + 18 - (20 \times 0)}{20(5 - 0)}$$

$$= \frac{58 - 0}{100}$$

$$= .58$$

and the difficulty index is .58. The groups analyzed received 58 percent of the possible points on this item.

The analysis of essay test items will take only slightly more time than for objective tests, and the time and effort required could lead to the development of better essay tests, a goal to be desired.

Criterion-referenced tests are generally used within a mastery model of learning and differ in terms of basic purpose from achievement tests that are designed to show differences in accomplishment across the entire achievement continuum in a class. The most pervasive use of criterion-referenced tests is to aid in a decision about whether a student has mastered a topic or unit sufficiently well to proceed to the next topic or unit within a learning sequence.

Analysis of Criterion-Referenced Test Items

The key feature of a criterion-referenced test is the existence of a predetermined score for deciding which pupils have passed and which have failed the test. Usually this score is above 80 percent of the possible score, with scores of 85 and 90 percent the most common ones reported in journals and curriculum projects. As a result, analyses based on high and low groups of 25 percent of the class are inappropriate and of little use.

One way to view the discrimination quality of an item is to compare the success on the item by those who pass the test with those who fail the test. A discrimination index could be defined as the difference between the proportion of passing students who answer the item correctly and the proportion of failing students who answer the item correctly:

$$d = P_{passing} - P_{failing}$$

For example, if 20 of 30 pupils passed a criterion-referenced test, and if on a given item 15 from the "pass" group and 5 from the "fail" group answered the item correctly, then

$$d = \frac{15}{20} - \frac{5}{10}$$
$$= .75 - .50$$
$$= .25$$

and it would be noted that the discrimination index is .25. Since difficulty level influences the size of a discrimination index and since most items on a criterion-referenced test are designed to be answered correctly by most pupils, the size of discrimination indexes can be expected to be lower than on discriminatory achievement tests. An index of .25 might well be regarded as adequate for an item on a criterion-referenced test.

Another way to view the discrimination quality of items on criterion-referenced tests is to compare the success of students on an item before and after they attain mastery, as judged by their scores on the total test. A simple nonmathematical way of doing this was described in Chapter 4. A record is kept of each student's passing (P) or failing (F) an item on a pretest given before instruction and on a posttest given to check mastery after instruction. The quality of the item is judged by the typical pattern of success and failure of the students on the two administrations of the test. When most students achieve mastery, an item that measures achievement of mastery should have the pattern FP for most students. On the other hand, an item that is too easy would show PP; one that is too difficult would show FF. Items that do not show the same progress for students on the test as a whole would have a pattern PF.

If mastery tests are given more than twice, as they often are following successive periods of instruction, desirable patterns of item performance, such as FPPP, FFPP, or FFFP, and less desirable ones, such as PPFF, PFPF and FFFF, may be recorded.

A simple way to quantify this approach to describing the quality of an item is to find what proportion of the students who achieve mastery on the test passed the item as a result of instruction. One index that can be used is

$$d = P_{post} - P_{pre}$$

For example, if we assume that 20 of 30 students in a class achieve mastery and that 15 answered the item correctly after instruction and that 5 had answered it correctly before instruction, the d value is

$$d = \frac{15}{20} - \frac{5}{20}$$
$$= .75 - .25$$
$$= .50$$

The higher the value of d, the more sensitive the item is to the effect of instruction. Items with low values are either so general that many students can answer them before instruction or so difficult that even students who achieve mastery have difficulty in answering them after instruction.

Difficulty levels for items on criterion-referenced tests can be obtained as described earlier in this chapter, but the interpretation must differ. In theory it would be desirable to have items that are answered correctly by the same proportion of pupils as the proportion used as the cutting score on the test. If 90 percent is the cutting score, item difficulty levels would ideally be approximately 90—that is, individual items answered correctly by 90 percent of the class.

Since all students are expected eventually to master the material on a criterion-referenced test, the percentage of a class answering an item may reflect more on the quality of teaching than on the quality of the item. In any case, item-analysis data for criterion-referenced tests must be interpreted in terms of the purpose of the test.

Another characteristic of importance to the test-maker is reliability. *Reliability* This is a measure of the consistency with which a test measures whatever it is intended to measure. Various methods for determining reliability—the test-retest, equivalent-forms, and split-halves methods —are described in Chapter 4. However, the shorter of the Kuder-Richardson estimates described there (p. 107) is accurate enough for classroom tests and other ordinary situations. It requires the calculation of only two measures, the mean and the standard deviation of the distribution of scores on the test. The formula follows:[2]

$$r_t = \frac{nS_t{}^2 - M(n - M)}{S_t{}^2(n - 1)}$$

where r_t = reliability of the test

$\quad n$ = number of items in the test

$\quad S_t$ = standard deviation of the scores on the test

$\quad M$ = mean of scores on the test

---

[2] G. Frederic Kuder and M. W. Richardson, "The Theory of the Estimation of Test Reliability," *Psychometrika*, 2 (September 1937), 151–160.

An example will help clarify the use of this formula. Suppose that a teacher has given a test of 50 items and has found the mean to be 30 and the standard deviation 6. Though circumstances make it inconvenient to use any of the usual methods of determining test reliability, the teacher wants to estimate the reliability of this test. To do so, she uses the formula given above, substituting these values: $n = 50$, $M = 30$, and $S_t = 6$:

$$r_t = \frac{[50 \times (6)^2] - [30(50 - 30)]}{(6)^2(50 - 1)}$$
$$= \frac{(50 \times 36) - (30 \times 20)}{36 \times 49}$$
$$= \frac{1800 - 600}{1764}$$
$$= \frac{1200}{1764}$$
$$= .68$$

Thus the teacher finds that this test has a reliability of .68, which is not very high. However, some comfort can be taken from the knowledge that this formula nearly always gives a lower estimate of reliability than most other approaches give and that this test therefore probably has a reliability at least as high as .68. Knowing the reliability of a test enables the teacher to determine how much reliance can be placed on the scores obtained from it.

Generally acceptable and convenient methods of determining reliability coefficients for criterion-referenced classroom tests have not been developed. For such tests the question of accuracy or consistency should be concerned with the identification of pupils who have "passed" the test. One way to assess this quality is to divide a test into two parts that are roughly equivalent. On most tests this can be accomplished by designating the odd-numbered items as one test and the even-numbered items as the second. Reliability, then, could be viewed as the proportion of students who are above the cutting score—for example, 85 percent of the items answered correctly—on both of the two equivalent tests. The weakness of the procedure is the fact that the coefficient is based on tests one-half as long as the actual test, and no convenient method is available for estimating the coefficient for the full test.

LEARNING EXERCISE

9. Obtain the results of a standardized test given to a class or group of pupils and calculate the reliability coefficient by the method shown

above. In the manual that accompanies the test you should find a reliability coefficient given. How does the value you obtained compare with that given in the manual? Is the difference significant? How do you account for any difference found?

There are many refinements and technical details of test analysis which, because they are beyond the scope of the usual first course in educational measurement, are not mentioned here. The average teacher or counselor, however, should be able to follow the suggestions and procedures presented here; use of such procedures will contribute to the steady improvement in the construction of tests and in the whole measurement program, and thus the teacher will experience a sense of genuine satisfaction in this important part of guiding pupil growth.

SUGGESTED READING

DIEDERICH, PAUL B. *Short-Cut Statistics for Teacher-Made Tests.* 3d ed. Princeton, N.J.: Educational Testing Service, 1973. Describes some simple and practical procedures that teachers can use to obtain data for item analysis and suggests standards for appraising the quality of test items. Also includes discussions of reliability, standard error, and correlation. A useful and easily read pamphlet.

EBEL, ROBERT L. *Essentials of Educational Measurement.* 2d ed. Englewood Cliffs, N.J.: Prentice-Hall, 1972. Chapter 9 gives suggestions for administering and scoring tests. Chapters 13–16 provide a thorough consideration of both subjective and statistical methods of determining the quality of a test and test items. Topics include item analysis, reliability, and validity.

HILLS, JOHN R. *Measurement and Evaluation in the Classroom.* Columbus, Ohio: Charles E. Merrill Pub. Co., 1976. Chapter 4 covers administration and scoring of classroom tests. Chapter 5 includes a discussion of analyzing test data for the purpose of improving testing techniques. Chapter 6 provides an overview of the issues and techniques as they pertain to criterion-referenced tests.

PAYNE, DAVID A. *The Specification and Measurement of Learning Outcomes.* Waltham, Mass.: Blaisdell Pub. Co., 1968. Chap. 8. A practical discussion of item analysis procedures with classroom tests. Relates item characteristics to test validity and reliability.

THORNDIKE, R. L., and ELIZABETH HAGEN. *Measurement and Evaluation in Psychology and Education.* 4th ed. New York: John Wiley & Sons, 1977. Chap. 7. The major portion of the chapter deals with planning, constructing, and using locally made tests.

THORNDIKE, ROBERT L., ed. *Educational Measurement.* 2d ed. Washington, D.C.: American Council on Education, 1971. Chapters 5, 7, 8. The presentation is slanted toward standardized tests but has a bearing on classroom procedures and provides an interesting view of the painstaking procedures used. Chapter 5 describes tryout and selection of items. Chapter 7 covers test administration. Chapter 8 describes methods of scoring, reporting results, and analysis of data.

TUCKMAN, BRUCE W. *Measuring Educational Outcomes.* New York: Harcourt Brace Jovanovich, 1975. Chapters 8–10 are concerned with the evaluation of a test, including ways of assessing test appropriateness, validity, and reliability. Chapter 10 includes a consideration of item-analysis procedures.

Eight

STANDARDIZED
ACHIEVEMENT TESTS

This chapter discusses the measurement of achievement in the elementary and secondary grades and describes the types of standardized achievement tests most commonly used. Since hundreds of achievement tests are published, it is beyond the scope of this book to attempt to describe all or even a substantial number of them. The examples chosen for description constitute a reasonably representative sample of the better achievement tests available today, but no claim is made that they are the best available. Unquestionably, other tests of equal overall quality might have been chosen as examples. The differences among the recent offerings of competing publishers are most frequently in terms of special features or usefulness in particular settings. The catalogues of publishers listed in Appendix C, Buros's *Mental Measurements Yearbooks*, and the procedures of Chapter 4 should be used when selecting tests of each type for actual use.

After studying this chapter, you should be able to answer questions such as these:

1. Why are achievement test batteries used more widely in elementary schools than in secondary schools?
2. For what subjects are separate tests published?
3. What is the justification for using a separate mathematics test when a school uses a battery with a subtest in mathematics?
4. How are all diagnostic tests in reading alike? How do they differ?
5. How are the items and procedures of standardized tests adapted to the reading abilities of young children?
6. What approaches have test-makers used to choose the appropriate content for high-school tests?

7. How have publishers of norm-referenced tests sought to help users make criterion- or objectives-referenced interpretations of the results?
8. How may published criterion-referenced tests be used to diagnose pupil difficulties and plan remedial instruction?

TESTS FOR THE ELEMENTARY GRADES

The general procedures for the construction and use of standardized achievement tests are much the same at any grade level. The makers of tests for the elementary schools have some unique advantages and some special problems, however, and so do those who make tests for secondary schools.

At the elementary school level, there is a well-established core of objectives and content in fundamental areas. Finding time for testing is seldom a problem because elementary schools have flexible schedules. One elementary teacher usually has one class and one room, and it is not difficult to arrange a time to give tests.

The makers of tests for the elementary schools do have the problem of adapting traditional test forms and procedures to the experience and abilities of younger pupils. At the lower or primary levels pupils have difficulty attending to the same task for more than a few minutes at a time. They have little or no previous experience with objective tests or answer sheets, and they are often unable to read either instructions or test items. Consequently, each part of elementary school tests must be relatively brief. Practice tests should be given before regular testing begins. For pupils of primary grades nearly all instructions and many test items must be read aloud by the teacher. How tests are adapted for use with younger pupils is illustrated later in the chapter with items from the *Stanford Achievement Test*.

TESTS FOR HIGH SCHOOLS

Unlike the elementary schools, high schools have no well-established common core of studies. The most common areas of study in high school are English, social studies, science, and mathematics, and the content and emphases of courses vary widely even in these areas. For instance, social studies courses may be anything from participation in local politics to the study of ancient history. Courses may be for part of the school year or extend over a period of three or four years. An English course may review the grammar lessons of elementary school, encourage creative writing, or evaluate Chaucer and Shakespeare. Science and mathematics courses are somewhat less diverse, but the choice of courses also varies from school to school, and within schools different students may choose different courses.

Although the subject areas just mentioned are the most common in high school, a great variety of others are also offered; and, as we have noted, the diversity in the tests that are needed does not end with the names of subjects and courses. It extends to the objectives and contents of courses with similar titles. An extreme example of such diversity might be found in literature, where it would be practically impossible to construct one test whose content would satisfy all or even a majority of English teachers. In varying degrees, this same difficulty is found in other subject areas.

Time also complicates the situation for the maker and user of standardized tests in high schools. Generally speaking, there are few fixed periods and rigid schedules in the elementary grades. The high-school program, on the other hand, is nearly always on a fixed schedule of class periods, averaging perhaps 45 minutes in length. To detain a group or class for more than one period for testing on any given day nearly always requires consultation with others, adjustments in schedules, and approval of arrangements by several persons. As a result, high-school tests sometimes seem to be constructed to fit a time schedule rather than to adequately measure important instructional goals. Batteries have been designed, however, to be given in several sittings that adhere to the school schedule and yet provide reasonably adequate measurement in each subject.

Finally, since there is such a wide variety of individual study patterns and subjects in any area of the high-school curriculum, standardized achievement tests for this level must include items covering a wide range of difficulty and content in order to satisfy a majority of users. To formulate a test that is inclusive and that samples an area adequately poses difficult problems for those who construct standardized tests at the secondary level. The situation is reflected by high-school teachers in a frequently voiced criticism of standardized tests—namely, that "they don't measure what I teach."[1]

SELECTING TEST CONTENT

In their attempt to select appropriate content for school tests, most makers have generally followed the conventional practice of basing subject-matter tests on a comprehensive survey of leading textbooks and courses

[1]Victor H. Noll and Walter N. Durost, *Measurement Practices and Preferences of High School Teachers,* Test Service Notebook 8 (New York: Harcourt Brace Jovanovich, n.d.).

of study, putting into the tests only such content and skills as are found in all or nearly all curricular material.[2] As the number and variety of courses in a curricular area increased, so did the problems of obtaining a comprehensive or representative sample of content for that area. More and more makers of achievement tests for the secondary school have chosen what may be called a *functional* approach. They plan a test that measures the development of skills and abilities generally needed in education or life rather than in end-of-course outcomes. The product is sometimes called a test of *developed abilities.* Tests of this sort emphasize measures of a wide variety of objectives that cut across subject-matter areas, objectives such as study skills, ability to write effectively, or ability to apply or generalize knowledge to unfamiliar problems.

No sharp line of demarcation can be drawn to identify all current standardized tests for secondary schools with one approach or the other. Although most modern tests for high schools lean in the functional direction, many have a definite content orientation as well. This combination certainly has its place in schools, for it is difficult to conceive of persons interpreting and applying knowledge which they do not have, unless it is always to be given to them. Both types of achievement are valuable, and an ideal evaluation program should attempt to measure both.

LEARNING EXERCISES

1. Is the content of fifth-grade arithmetic more standardized than the content of ninth-grade algebra? If one did not know, how could one find out?
2. What role do you think standardized tests play in increasing or reducing diversity in the objectives of schools? Summarize your conclusions.

SURVEY BATTERIES

When an overall measure of achievement in the common branches or subjects of instruction is needed for purposes of grade placement, promo-

[2]This approach has been most successful when the curriculum materials and courses were further restricted to those of academic or college preparatory programs.

tion, or grouping, the survey battery is most often used. A battery is useful for comparisons among individual pupils, classes, schools, or school systems or for comparisons of the individual pupil with norms for the appropriate age or grade.

The survey battery is also a convenient instrument for revealing the general strengths and deficiencies of each pupil. For example, a pupil may be at or above the grade norms in certain areas, such as reading or social studies, but below the norms in certain others, such as arithmetic. The survey test results may then be followed up with diagnostic tests in the deficient areas to identify specific weaknesses. Survey batteries are well adapted for comparing a pupil's achievements in different areas because the norms for the area subtests of the battery are based on the same population sample and are therefore directly comparable. Generally speaking, the norms are not comparable when separately published tests are used in different subjects.

It is important to keep in mind, however, that comparisons of a student's relative performance on the different tests of a battery must always be made and interpreted with caution for another reason. The subtests of a battery are often quite short, which means that the reliability of the scores on them may be quite low. Consequently, differences between scores on these tests may be very unreliable and have no significance. As we explained in Chapter 4, publishers of test batteries have the obligation to provide information on the reliability of scores for each subtest and to furnish data and illustrations to enable teachers to determine the reliability of the differences among a pupil's scores for different areas.

Because there is much more uniformity of objectives and content in the elementary grades than at the high-school and college levels, batteries that attempt to survey common content and skill outcomes have found widest use in elementary schools. There have been survey batteries for other educational levels for years, however, and in the past few years, since about 1970, elementary and secondary batteries have been coordinated to facilitate continuous measurement of student progress from kindergarten through high school and community or junior college.

The extensive use of survey batteries by the schools over a long period of time indicates that they have met the needs of many teachers and administrators. The example to be described, the *Stanford Achievement Test* series, has been widely used for over fifty years. It is an example of a series that includes batteries for elementary and secondary grades. The Stanford batteries will be reviewed in some detail, to show readers who have not had the opportunity to examine specimen sets what modern standardized tests are like. The examples for areas such as reading or social studies illustrate more than the nature of battery tests, however. Separately published single-subject tests for the same area and grade levels are similar in most respects. Some of the area tests of the Stanford and other batteries are themselves available for purchase as separate tests. Of course, tests planned as single-subject tests also have some advantages compared to battery tests. Some of these have already been suggested; others will be presented in a later section.

The Stanford Achievement Batteries: A Modern Standardized Test

The *Stanford Achievement Test* was the first survey battery for the elementary grades. It first appeared in 1923; revised editions appeared in 1929, 1940, 1953, and 1964; the sixth edition was issued in 1973.[3] With the publication of two related batteries, the *Stanford Early School Achievement Test* (1969, 1970)[4] for kindergarten through grade 1.8 and the *Stanford Test of Academic Skills* (1973),[5] the Stanford series provided for the testing of knowledge and skills on the same continuous scale of scores from early childhood to the junior or community college level.

Nature and Purpose According to the test manual, the elementary school batteries of the *Stanford Achievement Test* (SAT) are survey tests "designed to measure the important understandings, skills, and abilities that are the desirable outcomes of the elementary . . . curriculums. The tests are intended to provide dependable measures of these outcomes, comparable from subject to subject and from grade to grade, for use in connection with improvement of instruction, pupil guidance, and evaluation of progress."[6]

The *Stanford Early School Achievement Test* (SESAT) assists, say the directions for administering the test, "in the assessment of the background of pupils upon entrance to school and helps to establish the baseline where instructional experiences in school may best begin."[7] It also measures progress during kindergarten and grade 1.

The *Test of Academic Skills* (TASK) surveys basic skills of reading, English, and mathematics at the high-school and junior college levels, after instruction in "three R's" is relatively complete. It is an example of a battery that emphasizes knowledge and skills prerequisite to success in

[3]*Stanford Achievement Test* (1973), *Stanford Early School Achievement Test* (1969, 1970), and *Stanford Test of Academic Skills* (1972), all published in New York by Harcourt Brace Jovanovich. Authors of the *Stanford Achievement Test*, 1973 edition, are Richard Madden, California State College, San Diego; Eric F. Gardner, Syracuse University; Herbert C. Rudman, Michigan State University; Bjorn Karlsen, California State College, Sonoma; and Jack C. Merwin, University of Minnesota.
[4]Madden and Gardner are co-authors.
[5]Madden, Gardner, Merwin, and Robert Callis of the University of Missouri are the authors.
[6]Excerpts from SAT are quoted throughout this section. Quotations in test descriptions reproduced from *Stanford Achievement Tests*. Copyright © 1973 by Harcourt Brace Jovanovich, Inc. Reproduced by special permission of the publisher.
[7]Excerpts from the SESAT are quoted throughout this section. Quotations in test descriptions reproduced from *Stanford Early School Achievement Tests*. Copyright © 1969, 1970 by Harcourt Brace Jovanovich, Inc. Reproduced by special permission of publisher.

Figure 8.1

List of Stanford Achievement Tests by Battery Level and Number of Items and Administration Time per Test[a]

COMPLETE BATTERY[b] TESTS by LEVEL	Primary Level I Gr. 1.5-2.4 16 pages		Primary Level II Gr. 2.5-3.4 24 pages		Primary Level III Gr. 3.5-4.4 32 pages		Intermediate Level I Gr. 4.5-5.4 32 pages		Intermediate Level II Gr. 5.5-6.9 32 pages		Advanced Level Gr. 7-9.5 32 pages		TASK Level I Gr. 9-10 16 pages		TASK Level II Gr. 11-13 16 pages	
	Items	Time	Items	Time	Items	Time	Items	Time	Items	Time	Items	Time	Items	Time	Items	Time
Vocabulary	37	20	37	20	45	25	50	25	50	25	50	20	—	—	—	—
Reading Comprehension[c]	87	45	93	45	70	35	72	35	71	35	74	35	78	40	78	40
Word Study Skills	60	25	65	25	55	25	55	25	50	20	—	—	—	—	—	—
Mathematics Concepts	32	25	35	20	32	20	32	20	35	20	35	20	48	40	48	40
Mathematics Computation[d]	32	30	37	30	36	30	40	35	45	35	45	35	—	—	—	—
Mathematics Applications	—	—	28	20	28	25	40	35	40	35	40	35	—	—	—	—
Spelling	30	20	43	25	47	15	50	15	60	20	60	20	—	—	—	—
Language	—	—	—	—	55	35	79	35	80	35	79	35	69	40	69	40
Social Science	—	—	27	20	44	25	60	30	54	30	60	30	—	—	—	—
Science	—	—	27	20	42	25	60	30	60	30	60	30	—	—	—	—
Listening Comprehension	26	25	50	35	50	35	50	35	50	35	—	—	—	—	—	—
Stanford Total	304	190	442	260	504	295	588	320	595	320	503	260	195	120	195	120

[a]In minutes of testing time. Does not include time for distributing materials or rests between tests administered at the same sitting.
[b]Basic Battery Primary Level II through Advanced excludes Social Science, Science, and Listening Comprehension tests.
[c]Reading at Primary Levels I and II is in two parts which may be administered separately.
[d]Mathematics Computation and Applications is a combined test at Primary Level I.

SOURCE: From *Stanford Achievement Test,* Copyright © 1973, & *Stanford Test of Academic Skills,* Copyright © 1972, by The Psychological Corporation. Reprinted by special permission of the publisher.

high-school courses. It may be used to identify students needing remedial instruction in basic skills.[8]

Grade Levels and Equivalent Forms   The grade-level ranges of the six SAT batteries and the two TASK batteries are shown in Figure 8.1. Two levels of the SESAT (grades K.1–1.1 and grades 1.1–1.8) extend the range of the batteries downward to the beginning of kindergarten.

Although the SAT batteries were primarily designed for the grade levels shown in Figure 8.1, the norming makes it possible to use any level of the test at a higher grade level. "Extended" norms are provided to make it possible to use the same level for both pre- and post-testing in the same grade—for example, Primary Level III may be used at the end of grade 4 as well as at the beginning and middle of grade 4. This feature is especially useful for testing slower or low-achieving pupils. It permits matching the difficulty of the test to the level of the student. No useful purpose is served by tests that are too easy or too difficult.

[8]Excerpts from TASK are quoted throughout this section. Quotations in test descriptions reproduced from *Stanford Test of Academic Skills.* Copyright © 1972 by Harcourt Brace Jovanovich, Inc. Reproduced by special permission of the publisher.

There are two forms, A and B, of each complete SAT and TASK battery, and a special abbreviated Form C containing only reading and mathematics tests is planned. There is one form of each SESAT battery.

Content The tests of each SAT and TASK battery are listed in Figure 8.1. With few exceptions, the same content and skill areas are tested from the Primary through the Advanced levels of the SAT. Note that a "basic battery" over the three R's is also available at each level.

A brief description of each of the tests of the SAT Intermediate Level I battery (grades 4.5–5.4) will illustrate the nature of the eleven tests listed in Figure 8.1. The general objectives of a given test are similar at every grade level. The specific objectives differ, of course, to reflect differences in the content and skills generally taught at each level. The items at different grade levels vary also in difficulty and complexity, and the methods of presenting test items are adapted to the reading level of the students.

1. *Vocabulary.* Knowledge of word meanings independent of reading abilities. Incomplete sentences and answer choices are dictated. The student selects the correct meaning of words. Words taught in school and words used in out-of-school activities are both sampled.
2. *Reading Comprehension.* Ability to comprehend implicit and explicit meanings, make inferences from context, and gain information from connected discourse. Students read a selection and choose the word or phrase that best completes a sentence about the selection or that best answers a question about it.
3. *Word Study Skills.* One subtest of "phonetic analysis" items measures students' ability to recognize sounds of letters and letter combinations that appear in their most common spelling words. A second set of "structural analysis" items assesses students' ability to blend word parts such as prefixes, suffixes, and syllables into meaningful words. Students are asked to choose the one part of four they are given that is *not* needed to form a word.
4. *Mathematics Concepts.* Ability to read and interpret mathematical terms, symbols, number operations, mathematical sets, geometric relations, and measurement
5. *Mathematics Computation.* Ability to perform a wide variety of calculations with numbers and symbols. Items are presented entirely in numerical terms.
6. *Mathematics Applications.* Verbal statements of problems that occur in everyday life. Measurement and interpretation of graphs and scales are included.
7. *Spelling.* Ability to identify misspelled printed words among groups of words chosen from those frequently used in students' reading
8. *Language.* Understanding and ability to use conventions of capitali-

zation, punctuation, and usage (for example, agreement of subject and verb); language sensitivity (for example, choice of words and recognition of complete and incomplete sentences); and dictionary skills, including alphabetizing, use of guide words, and choice of appropriate meanings for a given context

9. *Social Science.* Factual information and reasoning skills with the subject matter of the various social science disciplines, geography, history, economics, political science, anthropology, sociology

10. *Science.* Items from physical and biological sciences test basic concepts, basic processes (predicting, classifying, inferring), basic measurement skills, and the use of the scientific method (controlling variables in an experiment).

11. *Listening Comprehension.* This test, new to the 1973 revision of the SAT, measures ability to comprehend and extract meaning from spoken communications, just as the Reading Comprehension tests do for written communications.

The TASK high-school and junior college batteries yield one score for each of three skill areas: reading, English, and mathematics. The component skills of these areas are not tested separately, as they are in the longer SAT batteries. Brief descriptions of the three TASK area tests follow.

1. *Reading.* Several subtests are used to obtain a single reading score. Multiple-choice items covering reading passages measure objectives such as comprehension of implicit and explicit details and the ability to logically analyze and draw conclusions from content. Word usage is measured by items that require students to select among several alternatives for omitted words in paragraphs. Vocabulary is tested by matching items that require the matching of words in one column with those in a second column on the basis of similarity.

2. *English.* A total score derived from five groups of items reflects knowledge of the English language. These five groups are: (a) use dictionary and reference materials; (b) identify errors in punctuation, grammar, and capitalization; (c) identify incorrectly spelled words; (d) select the sentence that best expresses an idea; and (e) order sentence parts to express an idea properly.

3. *Mathematics.* Concepts, computation, and applications are measured by a single omnibus test. The knowledge and skills tested are considered part of general education and basic preparation for further study in mathematics.

The two levels of the SESAT have tests on the environment (social studies and science), mathematics, letters and sounds, and aural comprehension (listening comprehension). Level II also has word-reading and sentence-reading tests. Examples of SESAT items are included in the next section.

Item Types With few exceptions the tests of the Stanford batteries use multiple-choice items.[9] The items were prepared by experts to measure the content and skills generally taught in a representative national sample of schools. Methods of presentation and provisions for student responses were adapted to the abilities of the students at each different grade level. Several innovative modifications of the basic multiple-choice format were employed to make the test tasks more realistic or efficient. Nevertheless, the items of the Stanford, and those of other standardized tests, are generally similar to the multiple-choice items described for use in the teacher's own tests (Chapter 6).

Adaptation to Reading Levels All items of Level I of the SESAT (grades K–1.1) are read aloud by the teacher because students have not yet learned to read. Students see only pictured answers, and they record their responses by placing a mark under a picture. Examples for three tests follow (the teacher reads all words):

1. Environment

Mark under the map of a city.

2. Letters and Sounds

Move your marker under the . . . box . . . that starts with a picture of a star. Mark under the letter B.

[9]An optional spelling test for the Primary Level I battery of the SAT requires the students to write words dictated by the teacher, and the Reading test of TASK batteries uses matching items to test vocabulary.

3. Aural Comprehension

Doris, Sandy, and Ann are sisters. Ann is taller than Sandy, and Sandy is taller than Doris. Mark under the picture of Doris.

The items for Level II of the SESAT (grades 1.1–1.8) are given the same way except that Word Reading and Sentence Reading, introduced at this level, require students to read answer choices expressed in words. In the following example the teacher's instructions are "Which sentence tells about the picture? Mark the circle in front of the sentence that tells you about the picture."

At the Primary I and II levels of the SAT (grades 1.5–3.4) the examiner reads all instructions and items for all tests except Reading tests. Answer choices may be presented to students in pictures, numbers, or words. If in words, the teacher reads the words aloud while students read them silently and mark their choices. Reading tests are an exception; students read both the material to be comprehended and the answer choices for Reading Comprehension.

From Primary Level III through the Intermediate levels of the SAT (grades 3.5–6.9), the teacher reads both items and answer choices for Vocabulary and Listening Comprehension tests. For other tests at these levels of the SAT and for all tests of Advanced SAT and TASK, the teacher reads only general instructions. Individual items and response options are read by the students.

Multiple-Choice Modifications Modifications of the basic multiple-choice format in the Reading Comprehension tests for all Primary levels and in the Language test for Primary Level III through Advanced of the SAT are intended to make the tasks performed by students more realistic and, hence, easier and more readily acceptable. The following is an example of the items used:

We saw a happy boy and a sad girl.
The girl was

A. crying   flying   purple   asleep,
    ○   ○   ○   ○

but the boy was

B. sick   laughing   hurt   angry.
    ○   ○   ○   ○

Language-test items on punctuation, capitalization, and usage are also based on a continuous discourse or story form rather than the presentation of isolated items. An example for the lower levels of the SAT is:

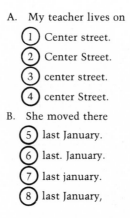

A. My teacher lives on
    ① Center street.
    ② Center Street.
    ③ center street.
    ④ center Street.
B. She moved there
    ⑤ last January.
    ⑥ last. January.
    ⑦ last january.
    ⑧ last January,

Mathematics Computation tests for the Primary II through the Advanced levels of the SAT present groups of items in a format that is especially efficient, in that a maximum of information can be obtained in a relatively short testing time. The items used have three options, as follows:

> "is greater than"
< "is less than"
= " is equal to

2+4 ● 3+3   > < =
                ○ ○ ○

The general instructions and a sample item of the TASK English test are reproduced here to show how punctuation, grammar, and capitalization skills are tested on the high-school level.

TEST 2: English   Part B

STEPS TO FOLLOW

I. Read each selection.
II. Determine if there is an error in each underlined group of words. Some underlined groups have no error, but there is never more than one error in any underlined part.
III. Find Test 2, Part B, on your answer sheet and mark the space that corresponds to the type of error you have found.

MARK:

G for GRAMMAR ERROR
P for PUNCTUATION ERROR
C for CAPITALIZATION ERROR
NE for NO ERROR

IV. Look at the sample and see how it has been marked on your answer sheet.

SAMPLE

S   Our dog barked when <u>the doorbell rang.</u>
                            S

Validity   In Chapter 4 reliability and validity were described as the two most important characteristics of good measuring instruments. The test manuals for the SAT and TASK batteries provide complete information on these qualities.

Of the several types of validity described in Chapter 4, content validity has special relevance for achievement tests. Care was taken to insure that SAT and TASK measured a representative sample of outcomes that are goals of today's schools. Widely used texts were reviewed for each content area, studies of children's abilities at each age level were analyzed, and specialists were consulted. The final selection of items followed extensive tryouts of a larger number of items, approximately twice the number in the published tests.

Teachers and administrators may judge the content validity of the SAT for their use by referring to an accompanying index of instructional objectives. The objectives and the difficulty level of each item of each test are given. Teachers may use this reference to analyze student performance in terms of specific objectives of knowledge, understanding, and skill, in line with criterion-referenced emphases. TASK manuals present similar information for item subgroups within each test of each battery. SESAT manuals present content outlines that may be used to judge how well these tests sample early school learnings; however, procedures for the selection of these samples are not described.

Although content validity received major emphasis in the construction of the Stanford batteries, and appropriately so, evidence of construct validity is also found in statements of the rationale for the tests and in studies relating student success on the tests to grade-level progress and to achievement on other tests. One of the criteria for final selection of the items for the SAT was that the proportion of students passing an item increase from one grade level to the next higher grade level, as would be expected; and SAT tests are shown to be positively related to other tests with similar objectives. Grade-to-grade increases in average TASK scores are positive but small, perhaps because direct instruction in the basic skills is minimal in high school.

Reliability Split-halves and Kuder-Richardson estimates of reliability and standard errors of measurement are given for all tests of all SAT batteries. Separate coefficients and standard errors are reported for each grade. The reliabilities of test scores are consistently high, ranging from about .70 to .95 with all but a few higher than .85. Standard errors of measurement range from 2.0 to 4.0 score points.

Reliability coefficients for the three tests of each TASK battery are all above .92, and the standard errors of measurement range from 2.5 to 3.4. Split-halves reliabilities and standard errors for SESAT tests are given for the beginning of kindergarten and grade 1, and also for the middle and end of grade 1. Separate test reliabilities range from .61 to .95 with about half above .85. Total battery score reliabilities are above .95. Standard errors for the separate tests range from 2.10 to 3.56; the total test score has a standard error of about 7.

On the whole, the reliabilities of the Stanford batteries are appropriately high for separate test scores and total scores and compare well with similar statistics for other popular batteries. The reliabilities for item groups measuring a specific instructional objective will be considerably lower, however, and more satisfactory for class averages than for individual scores. The reliabilities for individual performance on individual items of any test will be too low to suggest using these data for more than indications of strengths or weaknesses that may merit further study.

Administration Directions for administration are clear and complete, for both general procedures and specific directions for each different test. They are designed for use by the teacher. No special training or experience is required. However, the user should become thoroughly familiar with the tests and all directions and follow the directions exactly.

A practice test is available for each level of the SAT. The authors of the tests recommend that this be given a day or two before the battery itself in order to familiarize students with the testing procedures and the types of test tasks. A practice page of the SESAT is used for the same purpose. In addition, all batteries have sample or practice items preceding each different test.

Scores and Scoring Both machine-scorable and hand-scorable booklets are published for the three Primary levels and for SESAT batteries. Any of several different separate answer sheets may be used with Intermediate or Advanced SAT booklets or TASK booklets. Answers may also be marked in these booklets for hand scoring. If a separate answer sheet is used, the choice will depend on the scoring service that will be used and the type of report of results desired.

A number right or raw score on each test is obtained by counting the number of items answered correctly. Four types of derived scores may be obtained for SAT tests by referring raw scores to tables of equivalents in the manual. The derived scores are percentile ranks, grade equivalents, scaled scores, and stanines. Machine-scoring methods report these types of scores also.

Stanines, percentile ranks, and scaled scores are obtained for TASK batteries. Grade equivalents are not provided in the manual because they are less meaningful at high-school and junior college levels. Only stanines and percentile ranks are reported in the manuals for the two levels of the SESAT, but grade equivalents and scaled scores are available from the test publisher.

The scaled scores developed for the Stanford batteries provide a common score scale for the measurement of achievement from kindergarten to junior college. To measure student progress, comparisons of scaled scores within a subject area such as reading may be made from grade to grade, from battery to battery, or from year to year.

Scaled scores are not comparable from one subject-area test to another, however. Stanines, percentile ranks, or grade equivalents should be used to compare students' achievement in one subject area with their achievement in other areas. Chapters 3 and 14 describe the use of profiles of students' scores for this purpose.

A variety of useful scoring reports for these several types of scores may be ordered from the publisher's scoring service. Separate reports for individual students, class lists with each student's scores, and class averages for the use of administrators are available. Interpretive aids such as these will be illustrated in the last chapter of this book, "Using the Results of Measurement."

For criterion-referenced interpretation, the publisher provides the objective and the difficulty value (p) for each test item. No claim is made, however, that a correct response to an item designed to measure an objective is sufficient evidence of the mastery of that objective, although it indicates some degree of competence with respect to it. Item p-values are the percentages of different reference groups that answer an item correctly. The publisher can provide local p-values for each classroom, each building, the entire school system, and the national norm sample. Mean p-values are provided for groups of related items, such as all the items for a particular objective or for one domain of achievement such as reading. With this information, teachers and administrators can compare the performance of local groups of students with each other and with the national sample to identify objectives that may need special attention. They can also compare the performance of the same group of students at the beginning of a particular grade and the end of that grade to evaluate instructional efforts, or at the end of one grade and the beginning of the next, after a summer's vacation, to check the retention of learning.

Norms and Norming   The norms of the 1973 SAT are for a national standardization sample of over 275,000 students in grades 1 to 9. This norm or standardization group was selected so that each major geographic, economic, educational, and ethnic or cultural subgroup of the population would be represented in the proportion found for that subgroup in the 1970 census. Major characteristics of the schools attended by students were similarly controlled.

Norm groups were tested in October and May to reflect performance at the beginning and end of the year. In addition, the SAT Primary I and II batteries were also given in February to obtain midyear norms. As explained in the section on grade levels and forms, "extended" norms are also provided at a half-grade above the grade range for which each battery is primarily intended.

A separate norms booklet for each SAT level has tables for each type of score. In addition, stanine norm tables for school groups are given in an administrator's guide. These group norms permit comparison of the mean score for a school group with the means of the national sample of school groups. A given school group's relative achievement in different subject areas can also be compared by using these norms. However, schools within a system should not be compared unless they can be shown to be comparable in terms of ability and other factors controlled in the national sample. The Stanford tests do not provide separate norms for boys and girls or for different community types or geographical regions. Some competing batteries do.

Finally, all forms of the SAT were administered simultaneously with the *Otis-Lennon Mental Ability Test* (OLMAT) to enable the publisher to insure that the norms at each grade level and form are for a sample of students similarly and typically distributed with respect to a measure of intelligence. At each grade level the norms are for a normally distributed group with a mean OLMAT IQ of 100 and a standard deviation of 16.

The standardization samples for TASK and SESAT batteries were selected by procedures generally similar to those described for SAT. Much smaller groups were used, however, and fewer characteristics of the sample could be controlled. The manuals of TASK and SESAT provide much less information about standardization than the manuals of the SAT.

TASK norms are for fall semester testing only. Stanines and percentiles are given in the manuals for each grade from 8 through 13. For SESAT, percentile and stanine norms are given for the beginning and end of kindergarten and the beginning, middle, and end of grade 1.

The Manual The manual of the SAT is published in five parts and is clear and comprehensive. It rates high in the characteristics described in Chapter 4. Part I, "Teacher's Directions for Administering," Part II, "Norms Booklet," and Part III, "Teacher's Guide for Interpreting," are different for each of the six SAT batteries. There is but one Part IV, "Administrator's Guide," which addresses the use of results for classes, groups, or schools at all levels. Part V, "Technical Data Report," provides information on all levels of the tests for use in research.

The much briefer manuals for TASK and SESAT are generally satisfactory but not comparable to the SAT manual in comprehensiveness or technical excellence. One SESAT booklet, titled "Directions for Administering," describes the development of the tests, gives technical data, norms, answers, and examples of the ways results may be interpreted.

A single TASK manual for grades 8–12 contains descriptive information on test development, technical data, and suggestions for the use of test results. A manual for junior and community colleges provides similar information for use with grades 11–13.

Other Testing Accessories and Test Format Accessories for use with the SAT include the practice tests and indexes of instructional objectives, both described previously, and a related brochure titled "Objectives-Referenced Interpretation." A class record and a class analysis chart are provided with test booklets for use in studying the results of the testing for a class as a whole. Answer keys are also sent with booklets.

SESAT test packages include a class record sheet, but scoring keys must be ordered separately. TASK test packages include a manual only. Answer keys are ordered separately.

A series of *Stanford Research Reports*, each several pages long, are published at irregular intervals to provide more detailed data on standardization, additional norms, and equivalent scores for the 1973 and other tests such as the 1964 SAT and the *Metropolitan Achievement Tests*. Eleven were available when the technical handbook was published and more were being prepared.[10]

The publishers of the Stanford have also prepared four sound filmstrips, called "Stanford Strategies," for use by schools to explain reasons for testing, administration procedures, score interpretations, and the use of test results.

The paper, print, and general organization of the Stanford tests, manuals, and other acccessories are well planned and good examples of what one may expect to find in recently published batteries. The use of distinctive coordinated colors for the materials of each different battery is convenient and attractive.

Cost When this was written the cost per package of thirty-five test booklets was as follows: SESAT I, $11.95; SESAT II, $16.00; Primary I, $11.95; Primary II, $14.50; Primary III, $15.50; Intermediate I or II, $17.50; Advanced, $17.50; TASK I, II, or III, $10.25.[11] SAT test packages include teacher's directions for administering, norms booklet, class record, class analysis, and scoring keys. SESAT packages include only tests, directions for administering, and a class record sheet. TASK packages include only tests and manual.

Summary The Stanford series of test batteries have been presented as an example of good practice in achievement test construction. They are norm-referenced batteries that provide for objectives-referenced interpretations also. Other useful features of the Stanford that are also found in some other recent batteries are: (1) related subject-area tests with a common score scale from kindergarten through junior college, (2) content that samples both traditional and modern curricula, (3) items that have been carefully edited to eliminate cultural bias, (4) norms for school groups as well as individuals, and (5) a wealth of suggestions for use by teachers, counselors, and administrators.

No test is perfect, of course. The content of the Stanford batteries is not as valid for some class uses as other readily available tests, and the norms are not the most appropriate standards for judging every student's achievement. The Stanford tests may be criticized also for not giving more emphasis to some newer curricular innovations, for having occasional items with more than one correct answer, for requiring students to

---

[10]See R. Madden, E. F. Gardner, H. C. Rudman, B. Karlsen, and J. C. Merwin, *Stanford Achievement Test Technical Data Report* (New York: Harcourt Brace Jovanovich, 1975), p. 41.

[11]Cost is obviously not the most important factor to be considered in choosing a test, although it is generally of interest to test users. The prices listed for this test are fairly representative of prices for other achievement batteries. Test prices change rapidly, however, and do not, as a rule, include the cost of separate answer sheets or accessories other than those stated. They do not include the cost of shipment from publisher to purchaser. The reader who desires more information on cost should consult the latest catalogues of the test publishers.

remember too much in listening comprehension tests, and for failing to standardize the rate at which teachers read items aloud. These weaknesses may be considered minor for most uses, however, and they should be relatively easy for the publishers to correct.

LEARNING EXERCISES

3. Select another elementary or a secondary survey battery for further study. Read reviews of it in one of the *Mental Measurements Yearbooks*, and examine a specimen set, if one is available. Write a one-page appraisal of it.
4. Use the *Education Index* to locate a journal article reviewing a standardized achievement test, reporting on the use of tests, or discussing an issue in the use of tests. Write a one-page report summarizing the article and evaluating its contribution to your understanding of standardized tests for the schools.

Several other batteries for the primary and elementary grade levels are widely used. The Stanford and the first three of those listed here are the most up-to-date batteries. The last two batteries have long been popular but they are not as current. *Other Elementary Batteries*

Comprehensive Tests of Basic Skills (CTBS) (Monterey, Calif.: California Test Bureau/McGraw-Hill, 1971–1973).
Iowa Tests of Basic Skills (ITBS), Forms 5 and 6 (Boston: Houghton Mifflin, 1971–1973).
SRA Assessment Survey: Achievement Series (SRA-AS), Forms E and F (Chicago: Science Research Associates, 1954–1973).
Metropolitan Achievement Tests (MAT) (New York: Harcourt Brace Jovanovich, 1931–1971).
California Achievement Tests (CAT) (Monterey, Calif.: California Test Bureau/McGraw-Hill, 1934–1970).

Some schools have continued to use the Metropolitan or the California batteries in order to have a more direct comparison of the achievement scores of present and former students and of the present scores of students with their scores at lower grade levels. At this writing the content and norms of the MAT and CAT do not appear as current or representative of present schools as those of other batteries, but they may be revised and updated again as they have been several times in the past.

The more recent batteries have many of the desirable features we have described for the Stanford series. They are carefully constructed, technically adequate, and attractively presented. They emphasize the *use* of knowledge and skills as well as the knowledge and skills themselves, and stress modern as well as traditional objectives. They publish specifications and report results in ways that aid either norm- or objectives-referenced interpretations. Items are carefully edited to reduce racial, sexual, and cultural bias.

All these batteries for the elementary grades test the fundamental areas of reading, mathematics, and language. The CAT tests these areas only; the ITBS adds a test of study skills, such as using references, interpreting graphs, and reading maps. All the other batteries referred to here also test the content areas of science and social science at higher grade levels.[12] All the batteries provide for a separate score on the three fundamental areas; and those with other tests also provide for a partial battery that does not include test materials for science, social studies, or special-feature tests, such as the Listening Comprehension test of the SAT.

The major subareas within a common area are also somewhat similar from one battery to another. Reading usually includes vocabulary and comprehension; mathematics or arithmetic includes concepts, computation, and problem-solving; and language has spelling, capitalization, and usage. The Work-Study Skills test of the ITBS is well-known for its emphasis on map-reading skills, which may or may not be relevant to the curriculum of a particular school. Study skills are included in the tests for other areas on the SAT and MAT but are tested separately in other batteries. The ITBS offers a separate modern mathematics supplement that may be substituted for the arithmetic test of the battery.

ITBS tests for grades 3–8 are published in a single multilevel booklet, although separate booklets for each grade level are available. The multilevel arrangement is advantageous in that the same materials may be used with all students; the less able can begin with easier items, while there is no ceiling on the level of achievement of more able students. Stopping and starting at different places in the booklet may be confusing to some students, however, and adds to administrative problems. SRA-AS uses three overlapping booklets for grades 4–9, and CTBS uses three booklets for grades 2.5–8.9.

---

[12]Science and social studies tests begin at grade 2.5 in CTBS and SAT at grade 4 in SRA-AS, and at grade 5 in MAT.

Scores on these batteries are expressed as grade equivalents and standard scores. The standard score scales of more recent batteries are coordinated with those of secondary school batteries, and a test of general aptitude is administered with the achievement battery so that achievement norms will be for groups of known ability.

Several batteries report norms for the beginning, middle, and end of the school year to more nearly match the time tests are given in the schools. All provide separate norms for several of the following subgroups: male, female, regional, Catholic, large city, and rural–small town. Publishers may prepare special local norms as well.

The CTBS, the CAT, and earlier editions of the MAT, like the SAT, have batteries for secondary grades as well as elementary grades. Publishers of other elementary school batteries have provided for coordinated measures of achievement for elementary and secondary grades by standardizing their elementary and secondary batteries together. *Batteries for Secondary Schools*

Thus, ITBS for grades 1.7–8 has been coordinated with the same publisher's *Tests of Academic Progress* (TAP) for grades 9–12. The *SRA Assessment Survey* now includes the *SRA Achievement Series* for grades 1–9 and the *Iowa Tests of Educational Development* (ITED) for grades 9–12. A revision of a highly respected achievement series for the upper elementary grades and secondary schools, the *Sequential Test of Educational Progress* (STEP II), has been coordinated with the *Cooperative Primary Test* to provide continuous measurement from primary grades through grade 14.[13]

Two approaches to the design of tests for secondary schools have been described as the *conventional* (or *comprehensive sampling*) *approach* and the *functional* (or *generalizable skills*) *approach*. Test batteries emphasizing the latter may be further subdivided into those focusing on measurement of the continued development of the basic skills of the "three R's" of elementary schools and those that attempt to measure more complex skills that are expected outcomes of secondary instruction.

BASIC SKILLS BATTERIES The TASK battery of the *Stanford Achievement Test* is an example of a secondary battery constructed to measure skills in the three R's after formal instruction in those skills is essentially complete. Of course, these skills continue to be important during high school and college. In fact, they may be considered prerequisites to

---

[13]D. P. Scannell et al., *Tests of Academic Progress*, Form S (Boston: Houghton Mifflin, 1971–1972); E. F. Lindquist et al., *Iowa Tests of Educational Development*, Forms X5 and Y5 (Chicago: Science Research Associates 1942–1972); *Sequential Tests of Educational Progress*, Series II (Princeton, N.J.: Cooperative Tests and Services, Educational Testing Service, 1956–1972). Form T (copyright 1978) of the TAP has been retitled *Tests of Achievement and Proficiency*.

success in further academic work and out-of-school pursuits. Tests that measure the degree of mastery of these skills can be used to identify students in need of further instruction on them. TASK is also an example of a test for which the authors followed the conventional practice of surveying textbooks and curriculum guides and interviewing teachers and specialists to choose the objectives to be tested. The objectives chosen were restricted, however, to the basic skill areas of reading, English, and mathematics. There was no attempt to sample content objectives or the full range of application objectives of the schools.[14]

Level 4 of Form S of CTBS is also designed to survey basic skills prerequisite to studying and learning in high schools and colleges. The general features of this series have been described in the discussion of elementary batteries.

Earlier forms of the CTBS measured the skills of high-school students in the traditional areas of reading, language, arithmetic, and study skills. Form S (CTBS/S), which is now available, and Form T, in preparation at the time of this writing, add the measurement of inquiry skills in science—skills such as the ability to classify, measure, recognize trends, and analyze experimental data—and in social studies—skills such as map-reading, evaluating research studies, and using logic in problem solving. The items are classified by a taxonomy of intellectual skills as well as by content area to facilitate analysis of student performance.

A CONVENTIONAL BATTERY   The *Tests of Academic Progress* (TAP) for grades 9–12 are an example of a more conventional approach to measuring the outcomes of the secondary school. According to the authors, Form S of TAP is designed to provide efficient and comprehensive appraisal of students' progress toward widely accepted goals of secondary education. The battery is composed of tests for six areas of instruction: social studies, composition, science, reading, mathematics, and literature. The content of the tests in each area was based on a review of texts and curriculum guides. Items designed to measure common objectives for fundamental and complex skills in content areas are included, as well as items to measure knowledge. (For publication data see footnote 13.)

Standard scores and percentile norms for individual students and school averages are reported for the beginning, middle, and end of each grade. A student profile chart provides for a cumulative record of individual achievement on repeated administrations of the tests.

[14]Earlier *Stanford Achievement Test* series included a high school battery (1965–1966) that did have tests of science, social studies, arts and humanities, business, economics, and technical comprehension.

Individual items are keyed to content and skill outlines to permit the user to judge content validity and analyze student achievement by the classification of items on which students do well and poorly.

The TAP test booklet and manual are well designed, clear, and complete. A single booklet contains the tests for all areas and grades. All items for an area form a continuous series that may be as long as 100 items or more. The area test for each grade starts at a different place in the item series, includes 50–60 items, and takes 45 minutes. Thus, the six tests require about six class periods of testing time. The items for different grade levels overlap as they do in the companion series for the elementary grades, ITBS, and thus provide an appropriate range of difficulty for all students.

The standardization and statistical program for the control of test quality appears comparable to those of other major publishers. There is only one form of the test; hence, no alternative-form reliability is reported.

Because of the great variability in high-school courses and content, the results of a comprehensive survey test like TAP are based on a limited sample of performance. A science test of 45 minutes and 50–60 items cannot measure achievement in any particular area of science with great reliability. The user must be cautious in interpreting data that suggest student strengths and weaknesses when these are based on results for few items. Such data do offer clues for further study and more thorough evaluation, however.

FUNCTIONAL BATTERIES The *Iowa Tests of Educational Development* (ITED) and the *Sequential Tests of Educational Progress* (STEP), two popular batteries, are of special interest because they are well-known examples of the functional or generalizable skills approach to test development. The ITED has the longer history. It was first published in 1942. Forms X5 and Y5 of ITED were published in 1970, as the high-school battery of the *SRA Assessment Survey*, a coordinated series of tests for grades 1–12. STEP I was published in 1956, STEP II in 1969. (For further data see footnote 13.)

From the beginning the authors of ITED have sought to measure students' abilities to interpret and analyze new material and to apply broad concepts and skills to situations not generally encountered in the classroom. Their purpose was not so much to measure what students know as what they can do with what they know or with what is provided for them. The purpose of STEP is similar: "measurement of those skills and understandings that should be part of the repertoire of every well-informed citizen."[15]

[15]*Handbook for STEP Series II* (Princeton, N.J.: Educational Testing Service, 1971), p. 12.

The makers of ITED and STEP have not undertaken to sample all the content or objectives of secondary schools. Content for the ITED was based on "introspective analysis" of the skills used by educated people. Then, items were prepared by teachers all over the country. For STEP II, specifications and sample items were prepared by subject-matter experts and reviewed by other experts and by educators in relation to current curricula and teaching objectives.

The skills emphasized by STEP and ITED have been called prerequisites for further liberal arts education, and evidence of validity for predicting success in college is available for both batteries. Studies of the relationship of the scores of grade 12 seniors on one of these batteries to freshman grades in college typically show substantial correlation, comparable to that obtained for scholastic aptitude tests that also measure general abilities.

Despite their emphasis on a functional approach, the publishers of ITED and STEP have not ignored the concerns of those who wish to analyze test results by topic. Although the makers have not sampled achievement of content topics systematically or comprehensively, the separate tests of ITED and STEP cover much the same broad areas of the curriculum as do more conventional batteries. There are tests of reading, language arts, mathematics, social studies, and science. STEP substitutes Mechanics of Writing and English Expression for the ITED Language Arts tests in usage and spelling. ITED also has a test titled "Use of Sources." In addition, the manuals of both batteries classify the items of each area by course or topic. STEP classifies items by both topic and skill, but, except for the Reading test, ITED classifies items only by topic.

Examination of the items and item classifications of the batteries reveals that not all the items measure objectives unique to functional tests. The STEP handbook shows that about 60 percent of 75 science items for grades 10–12 require application and higher abilities, 20 percent require comprehension, and 20 percent require knowledge only. Of the 48 ITED science items, about two-thirds—the 18 reading-interpretation items and about 14 of 30 background items—appear to measure more general objectives.

The skills and abilities emphasized by functional batteries are not all unique to tests prepared by the functional approach. Tests such as TAP, based on comprehensive surveys of curriculum materials, also include items designed to measure more than knowledge. For example, 45 of 120 TAP items for science measure interpretation and reasoning.

The reading exercises of STEP amd ITED are somewhat different from those of most other test batteries. Reading selections are relatively long, at least several paragraphs, and they are based on science and social science materials as well as on literature. The science selections for ITED summarize actual experiments, and the accompanying questions require the student to demonstrate understanding of the approach and reasoning of experimental scientists, interpret the data presented, and draw conclusions from the findings. Student answers to the science reading questions are counted as part of the Reading score and also as part of the Science scores. Part of the Social Studies test of the ITED is also based on reading selections.

In choosing between conventional batteries and functional batteries, as well as when choosing among batteries of each kind, it is necessary to examine the actual contents of the test in relation to what one wishes to measure. The handbook for STEP II includes a recommendation that "each test user examine the actual test content in order to evaluate the content validity of STEP Series II with respect to his own instructional practices and educational objectives."[16]

Because earlier editions of ITED and STEP batteries were criticized for excessive length, the latest ITED revision requires less than half as much time as the previous edition, 3½ hours working time or about 4½ hours administration time. STEP II is longer than ITED, requiring 5 hours and 25 minutes working time, reduced from over 8 hours for the earlier STEP I. Each of the STEP II tests requires from 40 to 60 minutes. It is recommended that each be given in a separate session with 5–10 minutes recess between tests.

ITED and STEP are both good examples of the test-maker's art. Tests and user aids are attractive, complete, and easy to follow. Suggestions to assist the teacher, counselor, and administrator in reporting and using the test results meaningfully are included.

Technically, both batteries are of high quality. Extensive standardization programs based on representative national samples are reported. There are percentile norms for each test and subtest of each battery and for both individuals and groups. Both batteries are coordinated with elementary school tests and scholastic ability tests. Scaled scores provide a continuous measure of individual progress in each area throughout the elementary and secondary grades.

The STEP handbook has norms for both fall and spring administrations and percentile bands to aid in judging the significance of score differences. STEP shows the percentage of the norm group succeeding on each item. ITED will furnish this information for both norm and local groups. Like the elementary battery of the *SRA Assessment Survey*, ITED offers norms for a variety of significant subgroups of the national population.

[16]*Handbook for STEP Series II* (Princeton, N.J.: Educational Testing Service, 1971), p. 152.

5. Examine a specimen set for one level of the *Stanford Achievement Test,* the *Stanford Early School Achievement Test,* or the *Stanford Test of Academic Skills.* Compare the text's description of the test with the actual test.

6. Examine a specimen set of an achievement test battery not reviewed in the text or consult the *Mental Measurements Yearbooks* for a review of another test battery. Compare one level of this test with the text's review of the same level of the *Stanford Achievement Test.* What are the apparent strengths and weaknesses of the two batteries for different purposes?

7. Attempt your own "introspective analysis" of the abilities needed for success in one academic area with which you are familiar. Compare your analysis with that of the makers of ITED or STEP after studying the manual, if one is available, or by consulting the *Mental Measurements Yearbooks.* Prepare a one-page report summarizing your findings and conclusions.

TESTS FOR SINGLE AREAS OR SUBJECTS

One reason the tests of a battery have been reviewed in some detail is because separate tests for single areas, such as reading or mathematics, do not differ in principle from battery subtests for these same areas. Both single tests and battery subtests are concerned with assessing achievement, use similar items, yield scores of the same type, and offer similar aids to interpretation. There are some differences, however. Battery subtests tend to be briefer, so that a number of areas may be surveyed efficiently, and the content is more general, so that they are suitable for students with different course backgrounds. These characteristics of battery tests are advantages for some purposes but they are disadvantages when more thorough assessment of achievement is planned.

A battery test for science usually has very few items on any particular subject. Students' achievement in chemistry could not be measured reliably with so few items. Such a test would not be suitable as an end-of-course examination, for example. When a test to fit the objectives of a particular course, such as Chemistry I, American history, or Latin I is needed, a separate test is more apt to be found suitable. Separate tests cover many more topics and objectives than battery tests, and there are a very large number, literally hundreds, of separate tests available for different courses and subjects.

Of course, schools may sacrifice meaningful comparisons of student achievement from one subject area to another when they use separate tests exclusively. Separate tests are less likely to be standardized on the same population than are the different tests of a battery. For this reason, the best and most comprehensive testing programs use test batteries for general surveys of achievement and also give separate area or subject tests for more specific information about that achievement.

Separate tests are most commonly used in two areas: (1) basic skills, especially reading, because of the great importance of these skills in all educational efforts and (2) secondary school subjects, because the variety of such courses is too great to have any individual course well represented by the tests of a battery.

Examples of the major types of separate reading and subject tests will be described. The reader is urged to compare these examples with the descriptions of battery tests. Some consideration will be given also to the available tests in other skill areas, such as writing, arithmetic, spelling, and language arts.

Criterion-referenced tests have received more and more emphasis by publishers recently. New tests for skill and content areas are available; others will be made to the customer's order. Developments in criterion-referenced testing will be referred to when discussing other topics but will also be presented separately as the final topic of the chapter.

Reading tests have special significance because ours is a modern, print-oriented civilization. People who cannot read cannot progress far in our society, nor can they become effective citizens. It is not surprising, therefore, that schools everywhere place so much emphasis on reading achievement. Without the ability to read, a child cannot become educated according to our concepts of education. The person who has not learned to read well is constantly handicapped in progress through the schools. Evidence is accumulating, moreover, that many young people are not learning to read well. The Department of Health, Education and Welfare has reported that one million teenagers age 12–17 cannot read at the beginning fourth-grade level. Many cannot follow simple directions or the schedules of a TV guide.[17] Improvement in this area of education has become a national priority.[18]

[17]Simon S. Johnson, *Update on Education* (Denver: Educational Commission of the States, 1975), p. 75.
[18]"Reading Becomes Top National Priority," *NAEP Newsletter,* 6 (September, 1973), entire issue.

Because of the importance and the problems of reading, much research and study have been done on the nature of the reading process, on methods of teaching reading, on the causes and remedies for reading disabilities, and, together with all these, on the development of tests for measuring reading ability and skill. The literature in educational research contains a wealth of material on this subject. Much of this material is of interest and concern to every teacher from the kindergarten to the university level.

In order to acquaint the reader with measurement in reading, we shall describe tests in each of three areas of concern: (1) readiness for beginning reading, (2) achievement level, and (3) diagnosis of difficulties. Several of the tests reviewed or referred to are from a comprehensive testing program by Gates and MacGinitie. This program provides a continuous and related series of reading tests from kindergarten to grade 12. It includes tests of every type found in this area, with the possible exception of study skills. Although reading tests of any type are by no means all the same, the student who gains some familiarity and understanding of the tests used as examples will have a good orientation not only to the types of tests commonly used in reading but also to a variety of techniques of measurement of basic skills.

Reading Readiness Tests

A good deal of work has been done to develop tests that will give a fairly accurate measure of a child's readiness for reading instruction. The first standardized test a child takes is often a reading readiness test. Such tests do not include all the prerequisites for success in beginning reading, of course. A mental age of 6 years or more is usually required, and social and emotional adjustment is important. So, of course, is motivation.

THE GATES-MACGINITIE READING TESTS: READINESS SKILLS   We will describe the Gates-MacGinitie tests of readiness skills as an example of readiness tests.[19]

Purpose   The purpose of the tests is to determine which children are ready to begin reading, how rapid their progress is likely to be, and what specific abilities required in learning to read need development.

Content   Listening Comprehension measures the child's ability to understand the total thought of a simple story. The teacher reads a story aloud and asks a question, and the child marks one of three pictures that best answers it.

Auditory Discrimination measures skill in distinguishing two words of similar sound by marking one of two pictures.

[19]Arthur I. Gates and Walter H. MacGinitie, *Gates-MacGinitie Reading Tests: Readiness Skills* (New York: Teachers College, Columbia University, 1939–1969).

Visual Discrimination uses printed forms of four words, three alike and one different. The child marks the one that is different.

Following Directions measures the child's skill in following increasingly complex directions for marking panels of four pictures.

Letter Recognition uses items consisting of four letters of the alphabet. The child marks the letter named by the examiner in each set of four.

Visual-Motor Coordination measures ability to complete incomplete printed letters using the complete letter as a model.

Auditory Blending provides information about the child's ability to join parts of a word, presented orally, into a whole word.

Word Recognition measures ability to recognize whole words. The examiner pronounces one word in each set of three, and the child marks that word.

Measurement Qualities It seems evident that these tests measure what they are purported to measure—listening comprehension, auditory discrimination, and so on. Whether these have validity as measures of reading readiness skills is not as obvious. Essentially, their validity for this purpose is construct in nature, since they are the skills that fit the theory of the authors, two very highly respected authorities on reading, about what is necessary to succeed in learning to read. Total scores on the tests correlate about .60 with vocabulary and comprehension scores on grade 1 reading tests. About the same relationship between readiness scores and achievement in first grade reading is observed for other readiness tests.

No statistics are given on reliability of the total test, but internal-consistency reliability coefficients were computed for each of the subtests in each of the thirty-five schools in the norm sample. The median coefficients for the thirty-five schools varied from .63 for the Auditory Blending subtest to .87 for the Visual Discrimination subtest. The variation in the reliabilities of the subtests from school to school is not given. There are, however, a few cautions about the interpretation of scores on subtests, scores at the extremes of the distribution, and differences between scores on two subtests.

Administration The tests are easily and simply administered in four sittings requiring approximately one half-hour each.

Scores and Scoring All subtests are scored one point for each correct answer, except Visual-Motor Coordination, in which each exercise is scored 0–3 depending on the quality of the response of the child. The score on each subtest (except Word Recognition) is weighted by a factor of 1, 2, or 3 to obtain a total weighted score.[20] Scoring is by hand with printed keys.

---

[20]The score on Word Recognition is not included in the total weighted score since its purpose is said to be identification of children who already have acquired some reading ability.

Norms and Norming   Stanine, percentile, and standard-score norms are provided for students finishing kindergarten and beginning grade 1 separately. The stanine norms are provided for subtest scores; total weighted scores are used for percentile and normalized standard-score norms. The normative population is described as a nationwide sample of 4,500 students in representative schools in 35 communities carefully selected on the basis of size, geographic location, and socioeconomic level. The Lorge-Thorndike tests were administered in the same schools and used to adjust the readiness norms so that they would be more representative of a population that matched the national averages with respect to intelligence.

The Manual   The teacher's manual contains a description of the test; directions for administering, scoring, and interpreting scores; and tables of norms. There are suggestions for observing traits or characteristics that are not measured by the tests but that may have a bearing on reading readiness.

Test Format   The tests are printed on good quality paper in an 8½" × 11" booklet of eight pages. The teacher's manual is a twenty-page booklet of the same format as the test.

All reading readiness tests do not measure exactly the same things, and no one measures all the abilities needed to learn to read. Evidence of the predictive validity of any reading readiness test is not very strong. For these reasons there is a danger that teachers will be overly influenced by invalid test data. When interpreting test results, they should never be eager to conclude that a child cannot learn to read. Instead, the emphasis in test interpretation should be on what and how each child should be taught—that is, on adapting instruction to the child's level of development.

Reading Achievement Tests   The second area of measurement in reading concerns the student's general level of reading achievement. Survey tests of reading achievement are available for use at all levels from the first grade upward. They are directed toward the measurement of vocabulary, reading comprehension, and speed of reading. Many survey tests are designed to measure all three. The item types of different tests are also usually similar to those of the Gates-MacGinitie and the Stanford batteries. The content of the reading passages differs markedly from test to test, however. Some sample a variety of science and social science reading materials, particularly at higher levels; others are limited to selections from readers or literature.

The skills measured in the name of comprehension also differ significantly from test to test. Some tests measure little more than understanding of vocabulary, the identification of stated facts, and the ability to follow directions. Others place much more emphasis on abilities to interrelate information and draw conclusions. Reading tests prepared as criterion-referenced tests to measure mastery of specifically defined reading skills will be presented later under the topic of criterion-referenced tests.

THE GATES-MACGINITIE READING TESTS: PRIMARY A   The Primary A tests of the *Gates-MacGinitie Reading Tests* are an example of a test of reading achievement.[21]

Purpose   These tests are intended to measure level and range of ability in vocabulary and comprehension.

Level and Forms   The tests are for only grade 1, but there are two forms. There are both machine- and hand-scored editions available.

Content   The Vocabulary test consists of forty-eight exercises, each of which is made up of a picture followed by four words. The task is to select the one word in each exercise that "tells the most about the picture." For example:[22]

B.

bed   swim

milk   fly

The Comprehension test consists of thirty-four exercises, each containing four drawings followed by a sentence or a short paragraph directing the child to do something with the drawings. For example:

Where is the baby?

[21]Arthur I. Gates and Walter H. MacGinitie, *Gates-MacGinitie Reading Tests* (New York: Teachers College, Columbia University, 1964–1971).
[22]The sample items from the Vocabulary and Comprehension tests that follow are both from *Gates-MacGinitie Reading Tests.* (New York: Teachers College Press, copyright 1964 by Teachers College, Columbia University.) Reproduced by special permission of the publisher.

The items are in order of difficulty, and the hardest exercises contain paragraphs consisting of several sentences, usually describing the drawings or telling a little story. Following the directions requires an understanding of the sense of the paragraph.

Measurement Qualities   The validity of the Primary A tests appears to rest chiefly on the assumption of validity of their parent tests, the earlier Gates series, the validity of which was primarily construct in nature and dependent upon the author's theory of what is important in successful reading. The technical manual reminds the reader, however, that the user must judge how well the items of the test cover the objectives of a particular program. No relationships between tests at the various levels and other reading tests or other measures of achievement are provided. Extensive data on reliability are given, however. Alternate-form reliabilities are .86 and .83 for Vocabulary and Comprehension, respectively. Split-halves reliabilities are .91 and .94.

Administration   Directions are simple and easily followed. Mainly, the task is to make sure the pupils understand what they are to do and do their best. The teacher is encouraged to do anything that helps achieve this purpose, short of telling anyone the answer to any exercise. Also, no deviation from the established time limits, 15 minutes for the Vocabulary test and 25 minutes for the Comprehension test, should be permitted.

Scores and Scoring   The score is the number right, and the tests may be scored by hand with printed keys or by machine. Raw scores may be converted to grade equivalents, percentiles, or normalized standard scores. List reports of pupils' scores and reports of classroom, building, or system averages are available. Each is accompanied by explanations helpful in interpreting the scores.

Norms and Norming   Norms are based on a nationwide sample of approximately 40,000 pupils in 37 communities selected on the basis of size, geographical location, average educational level, and average family income. The standardization appears carefully done, although no details are provided on sample criteria nor on the numbers tested per grade or per form. Norms are given separately for October, February, and May administrations.

The Manual   The teacher's manual contains a description of the tests, directions for administering, scoring, and interpreting, and tables of norms. The technical manual includes descriptions of procedures for selecting items, establishing norms and reliability, interpreting differences between test scores, converting scores on earlier editions to comparable scores on this series, and averaging scores. The necessary statistical data for carrying out these procedures are presented in a series of tables.

THE GATES-MACGINITIE READING TESTS: PRIMARY B AND PRIMARY C   These are similar in organization to Primary A but at more advanced levels, being for grades 2 and 3, respectively. The grade 3 tests in Vocabulary and Comprehension require reading. Only the first twelve out of fifty-two items of the Vocabulary test for Primary C are pictorial; the rest are four-response multiple-choice items. The Comprehension test consists of twenty-four short stories, each followed by two questions, the answers to which are in four-response multiple-choice form. There are no pictorial items in this part. Measurement qualities and standardization are comparable to those for Primary A.

THE GATES-MACGINITIE READING TESTS: PRIMARY CS These tests measure objectively how rapidly grade 2 and grade 3 children read with understanding. The scores are for speed and accuracy.

THE GATES-MACGINITIE READING TESTS: SURVEYS D, E, AND F Surveys D, E, and F of the Gates-MacGinitie are tests of reading achievement for the higher grades.[23]

Nature and Purpose Three-part survey tests measure Speed and Accuracy, Vocabulary, and Comprehension.

Levels and Forms Survey D is for grades 4–6, Survey E for grades 7–9, and Survey F for grades 10–12. There are three hand- and three machine-scored forms for Surveys D and E, two for Survey F.

Content The Speed and Accuracy test consists of thirty-six paragraphs of relatively uniform difficulty. Each paragraph ends in a question or incomplete sentence followed by four choices. The Vocabulary test has fifty items in which a test word is followed by five other words, one of which is similar in meaning to the test word. The Comprehension test has twenty-one passages in which a total of fifty-two blank spaces have been introduced. For each blank space, five choices are provided.

Measurement Qualities Evidence of the validity of these tests is limited. The manual does not provide a description of the reading materials that the tests sample. Correlations between scores on the Vocabulary and Comprehension subtests and Lorge-Thorndike Verbal IQ scores show a high degree of relationship; correlations between Speed and Accuracy scores and Verbal IQ scores are lower. One reviewer notes that the Comprehension test seems to measure primarily vocabulary and "determining-meaning-from-context" skills.[24] Skills such as recognizing a writer's purpose, attitude, tone, and mood or drawing inferences from content are judged neglected.

---

[23]Arthur I. Gates and Walter H. MacGinitie, *Gates-MacGinitie Reading Tests: Survey D, Survey E, and Survey F* (New York: Teachers College, Columbia University, 1939–1972).
[24]Jason Millman, "Gates-MacGinitie Reading Tests: Survey F," review in *Seventh Mental Measurements Yearbook*, ed. by Oscar K. Buros (Highland Park, N. J.: Gryphon Press, 1972), p. 1,084.

Alternate-form and split-halves reliabilities range from .78 to .89 except for the Speed and Accuracy test, for which reliability figures are somewhat lower.

Administration   Directions are clear and complete. Tests are not difficult to administer, and there are sample exercises for each part. Speed and Accuracy, timed exactly, requires 5 minutes; Vocabulary, 15 minutes; Comprehension, 25 minutes.

Scores and Scoring   Hand scoring and machine scoring are both available. A total score is obtained by averaging the standard scores of the subtests. Grade equivalents are deemphasized for Surveys E and F because of their inaccuracy for high-school students.

Norms and Norming   The standardization of Survey D and Survey E occurred at the same time (1964–1965) and in the manner described for the Gates-MacGinitie Primary test. Survey F was standardized in 1969 on a new sample of 5,000 students in 35 communities. These communities, like those of the earlier sample, were selected to be representative of communities generally with respect to size, geographical location, average educational level, and average family income. As before, testing was carried out in schools judged by school officials to be representative of the whole community. Standard-score and percentile norms are provided for October, February, and May testing on Speed and Accuracy, Vocabulary, and Comprehension.

The Manual   The teacher's manual for each level and a technical manual for the entire series are quite complete, well organized, and easy to follow.

Format   All tests and manuals in the *Gates-MacGinitie Reading Tests* are alike in format.

Diagnostic Reading Tests

The third area of measurement in reading is diagnostic testing. This is most useful with the slow reader or the reader who has difficulties of one sort or another. Diagnostic tests are designed to require students to demonstrate many different aspects of reading skill in order that weaknesses and strengths may be pinpointed.

Study of a student's performance on a survey test of reading achievement will provide some clues to difficulties, but tests specifically constructed for that purpose do it better. Such tests have a larger number of subtests and part scores based on detailed analyses of reading errors that may occur. They also have a larger number of items on each particular skill or error so that the student's performance with respect to each may be evaluated reliably.

Not all diagnostic reading tests are equally reliable, of course; not all of them measure the same skills or errors, nor are they equally easy to use. It is important to study a test carefully before selecting it for use.

A fairly obvious difference among diagnostic tests is that some are individually administered whereas others are group tests. Individually administered tests tend to measure more aspects of the reading process than do group tests and so may be more revealing. They also require more training and experience to use effectively.

The *Gates-McKillop Reading Diagnostic Test* is an individual test that has twenty tests yielding twenty-eight different scores. It is obviously more thorough than a group test such as the *Stanford Diagnostic Reading Test* that has but seven or eight tests, depending on level.[25] The Stanford tests are Reading Comprehension, Vocabulary, Syllabication, Blending, Sound Discrimination, Auditory Discrimination, Beginning and Ending Sounds, and Reading Rate. The Gates-McKillop scores will be listed under the review of that test.

The typical classroom teacher will be better prepared to use the *Stanford Diagnostic Reading Test* than the Gates-McKillop. The latter, on the other hand, is favored by reading clinics and specialists. The Gates-McKillop is reviewed here because it is more complete and gives the reader a fuller understanding of what diagnostic testing in reading may involve. The *Prescriptive Reading Inventory*, reviewed under the section on criterion-referenced tests, is designed for the classroom teacher's use in diagnosing reading difficulties and planning remedial or individualized instruction.

THE GATES-MCKILLOP READING DIAGNOSTIC TESTS   The Gates-McKillop will now be described.

Nature and Purpose.   The Gates-McKillop is an individually administered test designed to identify strengths and weaknesses in a child's reading skills.

Level and Forms   It is described as being for all grades but it is expected to be most appropriate in the primary grades when reading skills are being developed. There are two forms.

Content   Seventeen tests yield twenty-eight scores: Omissions, Additions, Repetitions, Mispronunciations (eight scores: Reversals, Partial Reversals, Total Reversals, Wrong Beginnings, Wrong Middles, Wrong Endings, Wrong in Several Parts, Total Mispronunciations), Oral Reading Total, Words in Flash Presentation, Words in Untimed Presentation, Phrases in Flash Presentation, Recognizing and Blending Common Word Parts, Giving Letter Sounds, Naming Capital Letters, Naming Lowercase Letters, Recognizing the Visual Form of Sounds (four scores: Non-

[25]Arthur I. Gates and Anne S. McKillop, *Gates-McKillop Reading Diagnostic Tests* (New York: Teachers College, Columbia University, 1962). Bjorn Karlsen, Richard Madden, and Eric F. Gardner, *Stanford Diagnostic Reading Test* (New York: Harcourt Brace Jovanovich, 1966–1973).

sense Words, Initial Letters, Final Letters, Vowels), Auditory Blending, Spelling, Oral Vocabulary, Syllabication, Auditory Discrimination.

Measurement Qualities The question of validity in the usual sense is not easily answered for a diagnostic battery. The authors developed a series of measures in accordance with their constructs of the basic elements of reading ability. That these tests do differentiate between individual children with respect to the abilities measured seems evident. Whether the results of the tests agree with other criteria of reading ability (or disability) such as teachers' judgments, other tests, or grade progress is not stated. Use of the Gates-McKillop is well established among reading specialists.

No information is given on the reliability of the tests or scores of this test.

Administration Although the directions for administration of the Gates-McKillop are clear and complete, administration is necessarily complicated because the tests are so numerous and varied. The administration of this test resembles the administration of an individual intelligence examination in some ways. Anyone using the test will need careful study and preparation and some practice. The entire battery takes from one hour to several hours to administer.

Scores and Scoring The recording of a child's responses in the pupil record booklet is an important part of the use of the battery, essential to meaningful interpretation. The record is carefully studied to determine the types of errors made. In most tests the score is simply the number correct.

Norms and Norming For all tests, grade norms are provided. These are further classified as normal progress, low, and very low for most tests. The nature of the norm groups is not clear, however, and interpretation depends on the user's own experience.

The Manual The manual is a twenty-page booklet giving the rationale of the battery and providing detailed directions for administering the tests and for recording results. A strength of the manual is the suggestions for interpretation, but clinical judgment and experience are required to use them judiciously.

LEARNING EXERCISES

8. Does the Gates-MacGinitie-McKillop testing program provide an adequate set of measurements of all the outcomes of reading that

you think important? If not, which are inadequately provided for or omitted?

9. Examine a specimen set of a diagnostic reading test for high-school students, such as Level III of the *Stanford Diagnostic Reading Test* for grades 9–13. If a specimen set is not available, consult the *Mental Measurements Yearbook* for a review of such a test. Prepare a one-page report comparing the purpose, content, administration, and interpretation of the test for the high-school grades with those described for the *Gates-McKillop Reading Diagnostic Tests.*

Originally, the academic skills were the "three R's": reading, writing, and arithmetic. Now the concept of basic-tools subjects has been broadened to include, in addition to these three, spelling and language arts (capitalization, punctuation, grammar, and sentence structure) as well as oral communication. To be sure, instruction in most of these other areas was a related part of the three R's in earlier days, but spelling and the others were not generally regarded as separate subjects or areas of instruction. In this section consideration will be given to measurement practices and techniques in writing, arithmetic, spelling, and language arts—skills for which standardized tests have been developed, although not to the extent that they have for reading. *Other Skill-Area Tests*

HANDWRITING TESTS Writing and speech are sometimes referred to as the "expressive language arts," as contrasted with reading and listening, which are called the "receptive language arts." Of these, reading and writing are the ones considered here. Although tests measuring reading ability are extensive—as we have learned in the preceding section—few tests for the measurement of the other language arts, speech and listening, have been published.

There has been considerable change in emphasis in the teaching of writing in recent years. Attention and effort in teaching have shifted from mechanics to function. That is, in the teaching of handwriting a generation ago considerable attention was devoted to the pupil's development of a beautiful script. Much time was spent on practice from copy and on imitation of symmetrical handwriting. More recently, interest has shifted to the development of speed with legibility, and emphasis has been placed on handwriting as a means of communication and self-expression. Writing is regarded as a developmental process which presupposes the ability to think clearly. The objective is the ability to express ideas clearly and legibly; little attention is given now to the artistic qualities of handwriting. This is not to say that inartistic writing is encouraged or condoned; indeed, those who insist upon expressing their individuality through their handwriting—to the point where their writing is practically illegible—should be discouraged from this practice.

In measuring handwriting we find a number of attempts to produce what is sometimes referred to as a *product scale*. One of the earliest of these was the *Thorndike Scale for Handwriting of Children*. The scale reproduces samples of writing varying from Quality 4 (the worst writing of fourth-grade children) to Quality 18 (nearly the best writing of eighth-grade children). Each level of quality differs from the next higher or lower by one-tenth of the difference between the best and the worst of the formal writings of one thousand children in grades 5 to 8, as ranked by competent judges. A few samples follow:[26]

Quality 6

Quality 11

Quality 16

[26]Edward L. Thorndike, *Handwriting* (New York: Teachers College, Columbia University, 1910). Samples reproduced by permission of the publisher.

Standards are given in terms of the number of letters (of familiar material) written per minute without substantial loss of quality, for not more than three minutes; the quality of writing when the pupil is writing naturally; and the quality of writing when the instructions are to write as well as possible. The pupil's samples of handwriting are compared with the scale to find that level of quality in the scale that the writing most closely resembles.

Another scale similar to that of the Thorndike is the Ayres scale, often referred to as the *Gettysburg Edition*.[27] This was one of the most widely used scales ever devised, more than six hundred thousand copies having been printed between 1917 and 1935 alone, and it is still available. It derives its name from the fact that the opening lines of Lincoln's "Gettysburg Address" are used as the subject matter. The teacher writes on the board the first three sentences of this address and instructs pupils to read and copy until familiar with it. They then copy it, writing with ink on lined paper for exactly two minutes. The scale includes eight samples of levels of quality, graded from 20 to 90. The pupil's writing is compared with the samples for quality, and the total number of letters written in the two minutes is counted.

Norms are given for both speed and quality for grades 2 to 8. There are also distributions of quality and rate scores for each grade from 5 to 8, inclusive. The norms show a relatively constant and substantial relationship between speed and quality and steady progression in both from grade to grade.

Other scales for measuring handwriting are those introduced by Freeman and Hildreth.[28] The Freeman scale may be used for diagnostic purposes to identify handwriting faults in slantedness or straightness (too slanted or too straight), weight (too heavy or too light), regularity (too much variation in letter forms), and spacing (too much or too little space between letters or words). The Hildreth scale measures the quality of manuscript writing (printing) on a scale of 10 to 70. The quality of 50 is shown in the excerpt that follows:[29]

[27]Leonard P. Ayres, *Measuring Scale for Handwriting: Gettysburg Edition* (New York: Russell Sage Foundation, 1917), distributed by the Bureau of Educational Research and Service, University of Iowa.
[28]Frank N. Freeman, *Handwriting Measuring Scale* (Columbus, Ohio: Zaner-Bloser Co., 1930); the revisions are titled *Expressional Growth Through Handwriting Scale* (1958–1968); Gertrude Hildreth, *Metropolitan Primary Manuscript Handwriting Scale* (New York: Harcourt, Brace & World, 1933).
[29]*Metropolitan Primary Manuscript Handwriting Scale.* Reproduced by permission. Copyright 1933, renewed 1960 by Harcourt Brace Jovanovich, Inc., New York, NY. All rights reserved.

Come To my garden
In Spring Time and hear
Birds Sing

TESTS IN ARITHMETIC OR MATHEMATICS Except for reading, probably no subject in the elementary curriculum has been studied and investigated more than the teaching of arithmetic. Many books and articles have been written about it. Perhaps a few almost axiomatic observations about arithmetic will be useful before considering problems of measurement in this subject. In the first place, it is quite generally agreed that arithmetic is a comparatively difficult subject. It calls for thinking of a rigorously exact nature, understanding rather than memory, and the ability to apply principles in different though analogous situations. These objectives are not easily attained, and most pupils do not seem to come by them naturally.

In the second place, arithmetic is not a popular subject, partly because it is difficult. Some preparation in mathematics is required but students do not generally elect to take additional mathematics courses. Relatively few develop a special interest in mathematics or choose careers that require advanced mathematics.

The above statements might be interpreted to mean that arithmetic is inherently difficult and distasteful to many. This may be a safe assumption, yet it should be remembered that through improved teaching it may be possible to make arithmetic better liked and less difficult. Many students of the problem maintain that arithmetic has been poorly taught. It is said that the emphasis has been on memorizing and mechanical learning rather than on functional use and understanding. The problems and activities used in the teaching of arithmetic have often had little relationship to the lives and activities of people. It is believed that a reorientation and reorganization of the teaching of arithmetic to emphasize meaning, understanding, and applications would do much to make it more functional, less difficult, and consequently less distasteful. Many of the more recent textbooks and courses of study show evidences of thought and effort in this direction.

Much has happened in the teaching of arithmetic in the elementary grades during recent years. The curricular changes are such that it may be inappropriate to use the term *arithmetic. Mathematics* is often the preferred term in both elementary and secondary schools. As in other areas of instruction, recent years have been a time-of innovation and break with tradition. Concepts formerly introduced only at secondary school levels have been incorporated in the "new math" for elementary grades. Simpler phases of algebra and geometry are now often included in the subject matter of mathematics taught below the junior high school.

Challenging as these new developments have been to both pupil and teacher, they pose a problem to the maker of standardized tests. On the one hand, there is the continuing need for measures of the basic fundamentals, without mastery of which it is impossible to perform successfully at more advanced levels. On the other hand, there is a need for tests that adequately reflect the modern curriculum. To accomplish both objectives in one measuring instrument is, though perhaps not impossible, seemingly impractical. The test would have to be either too long for use in most situations or so thin in its treatment of many topics as to yield unreliable results.

These difficulties may partially explain why fewer new tests are being published in arithmetic than in reading, except as parts of batteries or for advanced courses. Except for criterion-referenced tests, there have been even fewer diagnostic tests than survey tests in this area. One example of a diagnostic test in arithmetic that has been used for a number of years is the *Diagnostic Tests and Self-Helps in Arithmetic* for grades 3–12.[30]

Four screening tests are used to measure pupil achievements in whole numbers, fractions, decimals, and general arithmetic knowledge and skills. Students who make more than one or two errors on one of the screening tests may then be given one or more of the twenty-three diagnostic tests, chosen in relation to the types of errors on the screening tests. The diagnostic tests are:

Addition Facts	Division by One-Place Numbers
Subtraction Facts	Division by Two-Place Numbers
Multiplication Facts	Percent
Division Facts	Operations with Measures
Uneven Division Facts	Regrouping Fractions
Addition of Whole Numbers	Addition of Like Fractions
Subtraction of Whole Numbers	Subtraction of Like Fractions
Multiplication of Whole Numbers	Addition of Unlike Fractions

[30]Leo J. Brueckner, *Diagnostic Tests and Self-Helps in Arithmetic* (Monterey, Calif.: California Test Bureau/McGraw-Hill, 1955). See also L. S. Beatty, R. Madden, E. F. Gardner, and B. Karlsen, *Stanford Diagnostic Mathematics Test* (New York: Psychological Corporation, 1978).

Subtraction of Unlike Fractions	Subtraction of Decimals
Multiplication of Fractions	Multiplication of Decimals
Division of Fractions	Division of Decimals
Addition of Decimals	

The causes of errors on the diagnostic tests may be further pinpointed by the administration of other related diagnostic tests that are suggested by the author's cross-referencing system. If a student makes mistakes in multiplying numbers such as 776 and 26, for example, additional tests would be given to reveal whether the errors were caused by one or more of the following possibilities: multiplication facts, addition facts, adding with carrying, or the placing of partial products.

The self-helps that accompany the tests provide practice exercises keyed to specific difficulties that may be revealed and designed to overcome them. The test manual provides the user with many helpful suggestions. The exercises show all the work required and how answers are obtained.

The usefulness of the tests and their validity for revealing student difficulties, like that of other diagnostic tests, depend primarily on the correctness of the author's analysis of the skills needed to perform particular tasks. Reliability is suggested by the provision of numerous items related to each step of operations tested. There is one form of the tests, and there are no norms or statistical data on reliability and validity.

SPELLING TESTS The process of spelling seems not to be fully understood from a psychological point of view. It involves memory, sensorimotor functions including vision, hearing, and muscular coordination, intelligence, phonics, and perhaps an indefinable (or at least a not-well-defined) sense of letter and word combinations, to name only the more obvious factors. It is intimately associated with reading and writing, both of which depend in part on the ability to spell and at the same time contribute to this ability. Individuals differ widely in spelling ability within the same grade, the same IQ group, and the same age level.

The measurement of spelling ability raises such questions as what words to test, how many, how to choose them, etc. Usually, words for this purpose are chosen from lists such as Thorndike's *The Teacher's Word Book*, a compilation from many sources of words found most frequently in running discourse, classified by frequency into the first, second, and third thousands and so on up to ten thousand.[31] Other lists of a

[31]E. L. Thorndike, *The Teacher's Word Book* (New York: Teachers College, Columbia University, 1921).

similar nature are also available. The assumption is that an educated person's needs in spelling are related to the frequency with which words are found in English usage and that the more difficult words are found, by and large, in the less frequently occurring groups.

In setting up tests of spelling, a random sample of words or even a dictionary will generally provide a list that covers a wide range of difficulty and frequency of use. The difficulty can be determined by trying out the words with pupils of varying ages and levels of development. After difficulty has been determined, the words are arranged in order of difficulty in what is usually called a *spelling scale.* In testing, the words are presented in this order, proceeding from easiest to hardest. The scale may be segmented so that a list of one hundred words is divided into a number of overlapping groups of perhaps twenty words each, the first twenty constituting the test for the lowest level, those from the eleventh to the thirtieth word, the next level, and so on to the highest level, the eighty-first to the hundredth.

Various methods are employed to make the testing of spelling ability more objective than simply having the person write the word as it is pronounced. One method is to present groups of four or five different words, one of which may be misspelled; another is to present several spellings of the same word, from which the correct one is chosen. A less objective though possibly more common practice is to pronounce the word, use it in a sentence, pronounce it again, and then have the pupils write it. For example:

crowd—There was a large *crowd* at the game.—crowd

Since a spelling test was described in the earlier part of this chapter in the discussion of test batteries, and since spelling tests do not occupy a particularly important place among standardized tests and are all essentially the same, no further detailed description of such tests will be given.

TESTS IN LANGUAGE ARTS   The concept of the language arts generally includes language skills other than reading, handwriting, and spelling, although the latter is often included in tests labeled "language arts." Broadly speaking, the concept may also include oral expression and listening comprehension as expressive and receptive language arts. Since tests measuring skills in spelling, punctuation, capitalization, phonics, syllabication, usage, dictionary skills, and sentence sense, as well as listening comprehension, have been described as part of the *Stanford Achievement Test,* none will be reviewed here.

10. What in your judgment is the correlation or relationship between mathematics ability and IQ? Can you find any reports of studies that throw light on this question?
11. Is it true that some people who seem otherwise competent, in and out of school, have difficulty with handwriting or spelling? If so, why? Can you find any evidence to support your opinion?
12. Should speech be included in the language arts? If so, what aspects of this subject could be measured with paper-and-pencil tests?

Survey Tests for Specific Subjects

While test batteries have been focusing more and more on basic skills and general abilities, the need for specific tests for use in content courses continues, particularly at the secondary school level. Although mathematics, science, and social studies battery tests may be purchased separately, these are but three of the many areas in which tests are needed. Also, as has been noted previously, a battery test for any area will not be very suitable for some purposes because of its limited coverage of parts of the area. It would not be suitable, for example, for use as a final examination in specific courses.

A hundred or more tests are published for use in separate courses of each of the three content areas for which battery tests are available. Other individual tests are published for commercial subjects, industrial arts, health and recreation, fine arts, and foreign languages, and this list is not exhaustive. Buros's *Tests in Print* and *Mental Measurements Yearbooks* provide an inventory of current tests under appropriate categories. Many other tests were formerly published but are now out of print. Like most things, tests become outdated.

Three well-known series of achievement tests are good examples of the variety of measuring instruments available for content areas: the *Evaluation and Adjustment Series* of Harcourt Brace Jovanovich, the *Content Evaluation Series* of Houghton Mifflin, and the *Cooperative Achievement Tests* of the Educational Testing Service, now published by Addison-Wesley.

The *Cooperative Achievement Tests* are listed by subject area and

Test title by subject   *Grade range*

Test title by subject	N-K	K-1	1-3	3-6	6-9	9-12	Coll.
English							
Cooperative English Tests (English, Reading)						■	
STEP Tests (English, Reading, Writing)				■	■	■	■
A Look At Literature				■			
Cooperative Literature Tests						■	
ANPA Foundation Newspaper Tests					■		
Mathematics							
Cooperative Mathematics Tests							
Algebra I					■		
Algebra II						■	
Algebra III						■	■
Analytic Geometry						■	■
Arithmetic					■		
Calculus						■	■
Geometry						■	
Structure of the Number System					■		
Trigonometry						■	
STEP Mathematics Tests (Basic Concepts, Computation)				■	■	■	■
Science							
Cooperative Science Tests							
General Science					■		
Advanced General Science					■		
Biology						■	
Chemistry						■	
Physics						■	
Physical Science Study Committee Tests						■	
STEP Science Test				■	■	■	■
Social Studies							
Cooperative Social Studies Tests							
American Government						■	
American History					■	■	
Civics					■		
Modern European History						■	
Problems of Democracy						■	
World History						■	
STEP Social Studies Tests				■	■	■	■
Topical Tests in American History						■	
Foreign Languages							
MLA Cooperative Foreign Language Tests							
French, German, Italian, Russian, Spanish						■	■
Cooperative French Listening Comprehension Test						■	■
Cooperative Latin Test						■	
Industrial Arts							
Cooperative Industrial Arts Tests					■		
Physical Education							
AAHPER Cooperative Physical Education Tests				■	■		
Health Education							
AAHPER Cooperative Health Education Tests				■	■		

grade range in Figure 8.2, which also includes the tests of the *Sequential Tests of Educational Progress* (STEP) that are available as separate tests. Except for the content coverage, individual tests are very similar to the subtests of a battery and need not be reviewed here.

13. Examine a specimen set of an achievement test in a high-school subject. Does it seem to you an adequate instrument for measuring important outcomes in the subject? Give your reasons. Consult one of the *Mental Measurements Yearbooks* to see how well you and the experts agree.

Criterion-Referenced Tests

In the last few years the public's desire for accountability in the schools has resulted in increased attention to tests that give more direct information about what students can and cannot do. Criterion- or objectives-referenced testing is planned from this point of view.[32] The pupil performance desired is defined in specifically stated objectives; then sets of items are prepared to assess whether students have mastered the performance.

Criterion-referenced tests (CRTs) are being recommended today for use in educational decisions about individuals, groups, and programs. When their use is primarily for decisions about what the individual student has or has not learned to do so that remedial efforts can be planned, they are diagnostic tests. CRTs may also be used for decisions about how the class group or the students of an entire school system have progressed with respect to the mastery of important objectives and perhaps to hold teachers and administrators accountable. Such uses of test results are more akin to the uses of survey tests. CRTs are being designed to serve either or both of these measurement functions.

THE PRI AND PMI   Several publishers offer criterion-referenced instructional systems designed to facilitate attention to the individual needs of students. Such a system may include diagnostic tests of objectives keyed to textbooks or other curricular materials, instructional prescriptions for remedying deficiencies, and additional tests to assess mastery of objectives following additional instruction. The *Prescriptive Reading Inventory* (PRI) and the *Prescriptive Reading Inventory Interim Evaluation*

---

[32]Some observers do not see the development of criterion-referenced tests as a new idea, however, and they trace the use of such appraisals to educational programs of the 1920s or even to China in 2200 B.C. or the Old Testament.

Tests are parts of one system for reading. The same publisher has a parallel system for mathematics, the *Prescriptive Mathematics Inventory* (PMI).[33] These two systems will be reviewed as examples.

Nature and Purpose Both the PRI and the PMI are criterion-referenced tests designed to measure students' mastery of commonly taught objectives and to provide specific diagnostic and prescriptive information from which an individualized instructional system for classroom use can be developed and implemented.

Levels and Forms The PRI has four levels for grades 1.5–2.5, 2.0–3.5, 3.0–4.5, and 4.0–6.5 and one form.

The PMI has four levels for grades 4–5, 5–6, 6–7, and 7–8 and one form.

Content The PRI gives scores on thirty-four to forty-two objectives per level, classified under seven process groups: Recognition of Sound and Symbol, Phonic Analysis, Structural Analysis, Translation, Literal Comprehension, Interpretive Comprehension, and Critical Comprehension. It consists of a total of 586 items with an average of three to four per objective.

In the PMI, objectives and items per level vary from 102 to 193 grouped in 16 to 20 categories; there is one item per objective. The level for grades 4–5 covers addition, subtraction, multiplication, and division of whole numbers; the properties of these operations; number theory; measurement; nonmetric geometry; place value; and problem-solving. The level for grades 5–6 adds problem-solving and basic operations with fractions and decimals. Grades 6–7 adds numeration systems, percentages, sets, and statistics. Grades 7–8 adds operations with negative numbers, functions, probability, trigonometry, and reasoning.

Measurement Qualities Content validity is stressed for both inventories. Classroom teachers and specialists culled common objectives from widely used text materials, classified these into broader classifications, and analyzed them with respect to content and interrelationships. Items were then developed to measure each objective. Reliability is suspect because of the small number of items per objective. No technical data on reliability or validity are provided, but a technical manual is in preparation.

Administration For the PRI, questions in the lower two levels are presented orally to groups of pupils; the upper two levels are read by pupils. Although the test is untimed, administration requires 2–3 hours and should be divided into sessions of 45 minutes or less. Directions are easy to follow.

---

[33]Elizabeth M. Layman, *Prescriptive Reading Inventory* (Monterey, Calif.: California Test Bureau/McGraw-Hill, 1972); John Gessel, *Prescriptive Mathematics Inventory* (Monterey, Calif.: California Test Bureau/McGraw-Hill, 1972).

The PMI is untimed but requires 4–5 hours divided into sessions not exceeding 1 hour. Directions are clear and easy to follow.

Scores and Scoring   For the PRI, machine-scorable answer sheets are scored by the publisher. One score (mastery, needs review, or nonmastery) is given for each objective. Mastery is interpreted as 66²/₃ and 75 percent correct on three- and four-item tests, respectively. Students who fail to master 60 percent of the objectives in each of the six objectives classifications are identified. See "Other Materials and Services" for a description of reporting services.

For the PMI, a mastery or nonmastery (pass-fail) score is given for each objective or item, and students who did not master 60 percent of the objectives (items) in each category are identified. Open-ended nonobjective questions are recorded by students on a special machine-scorable grid designed to eliminate guessing. Scoring is done by the publisher. See "Other Materials and Services."

Norms and Norming   Not reported.

Manuals and Format   The examiner's manual for each level of each inventory provides clear and comprehensive directions for administration. All test materials for each level are color coded. Interpretive handbooks for each inventory give a full description of item development and selection, list objectives tested, and suggest class activities to help remediate deficiencies.

Other Materials and Services   Complete scoring and reporting services that provide information on objectives mastered and not yet mastered are offered. A variety of excellent reports are available: (1) an individual diagnostic map that displays the student's score on each objective, (2) a class diagnostic map that reports average class scores on each objective, (3) an individual study guide that references pages in texts to study for objectives not yet mastered, (4) a class grouping report that lists students with deficiencies in each content category or classification.

Interim Evaluation Tests   These tests are an integral part of the same instructional systems as the inventories.[34] They are series of single-objective tests developed to help teachers determine whether remedial instruction has resulted in student mastery of the objectives measured by PRI or PMI. The tests of the series are organized in the same manner as the inventories, except that there is no *Interim Evaluation Test* series for PMI at grades 7–8. Guidelines for scoring tests for mastery, needs review, or nonmastery are presented in an examiner's manual. The manual also suggests a variety of activities that may be used to provide still more instruction on any objective not mastered. After this supplementary

---

[34]Elizabeth M. Layman, *Prescriptive Reading Inventory Interim Evaluation Tests* (Monterey, Calif.: California Test Bureau/McGraw-Hill, 1973); John Gessel, *Prescriptive Mathematics Inventory Interim Evaluation Tests* (Monterey, Calif.: California Test Bureau/McGraw-Hill, 1973).

instruction, the appropriate *Interim Evaluation Tests* are to be read-ministered to recheck mastery.

TAILORED TESTS Another recent development in criterion-referenced testing is the offer of publishers to tailor CRTs to the user's own objectives and specifications.[35] Catalogues of objectives are provided by the publisher and the user chooses the ones to be tested from the catalogues or prepares others independently. The user may also be able to specify the number of items per objective, the difficulty of the items, and their format. Then the publisher's authors prepare items or select them from item banks maintained for the purpose and assemble the desired tests. Scoring and reporting services are available as for other tests.

LEARNING EXERCISES

14. Make a point-by-point comparison of the reading and mathematics inventories described in this section with the text's descriptions of diagnostic tests for the same areas. Evaluate the similarities and differences in terms of the usefulness of each test in classroom situations with which you are familiar.
15. In the preparation of CRTs, the makers have chosen to measure a large number of competencies less precisely rather than a smaller number well. Explain this statement.
6. Locate a CRT in reading or arithmetic for the upper elementary grades. Administer the test to yourself, score the test, and use the interpretive aids provided to identify your deficiencies, if any.

SUGGESTED READING

ANASTASI, ANNE. *Psychological Testing.* 4th ed. New York: Macmillan, 1976. Chap. 14. Discusses uses and limitations of achievement tests and problems in construction. Achievement tests in special areas are described, and some of the items are illustrated.

BLANTON, WILLIAM E., ROGER FARR and J. JAAP TUINMAN, eds. *Reading Tests for the Secondary Grades: A Review and Evaluation.*

[35]Such services include: *School Curriculum Objective-Referenced Evaluation* (SCORE) by Westinghouse Learning Corporation; *Customized Objective Monitoring Service* (COMS) by Houghton Mifflin; *SRA Criterion-Referenced Measurement Program* by Science Research Associates; and *Instructional Objectives Exchange* (IOX), Box 24095, Los Angeles.

Newark, Dela.: International Reading Association, 1972. Reviews fourteen reading tests published for use with high-school students.

BUROS, OSCAR K., ed. *The Eighth Mental Measurements Yearbook.* Highland Park, N.J.: Gryphon Press, 1978. The most complete and useful review of measuring instruments and books on measurement in education and psychology. Reviews give factual information and reviewers' criticisms. Reviews in earlier editions are cited.

———. *Tests in Print II.* Highland Park, N.J.: Gryphon Press, 1974. Provides a comprehensive test bibliography and index of tests published in English-speaking countries. Titles, examinees and levels, publication dates, number of scores, authors, publishers, foreign adaptations, and pertinent special comments are given for each entry. In addition, cross-references within the volume and also to the *Mental Measurements Yearbooks* are included. The entries are classified by purpose of the test or subject matter tested.

GRONLUND, NORMAN E. *Measurement and Evaluation in Teaching.* 3d ed. New York: Macmillan, 1976. Chap. 12; App. D. A general discussion of standardized tests of achievement with some illustrations from tests is given in Chapter 12. Appendix D is a list of a few selected standardized tests.

JOINT COMMITTEE OF THE AMERICAN PSYCHOLOGICAL ASSOCIATION, AMERICAN EDUCATIONAL RESEARCH ASSOCIATION, AND THE NATIONAL COUNCIL ON MEASUREMENT IN EDUCATION. *Standards for Educational and Psychological Tests.* Washington, D.C.: American Psychological Association, 1974. Sets forth standards for published tests and devices for diagnosis, prognosis, and evaluation. Outlines in detail *essential, very desirable,* and *desirable* categories of criteria for authors and publishers as well as guidance for prospective users of published instruments. Reprinted in Buros's *Tests in Print.*

KNAPP, JOAN. *A Collection of Criterion-Referenced Tests.* ERIC Clearinghouse on Tests, Measurement and Evaluation, TM Report 31. Princeton, N.J.: Educational Testing Service, 1974. Describes the nature, uses, and limitations of criterion-referenced tests and provides information about the criterion-referenced tests available from publishers.

MEHRENS, WILLIAM A., and IRVIN J. LEHMANN. *Standardized Tests in Education.* 2d ed. New York: Holt, Rinehart and Winston, 1975. Chap. 4. Describes numerous diagnostic, readiness, criterion-referenced, and survey achievement tests for both elementary and secondary grades. The *Stanford Achievement Test* is reviewed in detail. Technical problems of testing are treated thoroughly.

THORNDIKE, R. L., and ELIZABETH HAGEN. *Measurement and Evaluation in Psychology and Education.* 4th ed. New York: John Wiley & Sons, 1977. Chapter 8 includes a comparison of the content coverage of widely used achievement batteries, a brief discussion of diagnostic tests, and descriptions of statewide testing programs.

Nine

THE MEASUREMENT OF CAPACITY:
GENERAL INTELLIGENCE

The term *capacity* as used here includes both intelligence and aptitude. This chapter is about the measurement of intelligence, and Chapter 10 is about the measurement of aptitude.

Numerous attempts have been made to define intelligence, yet educators and psychologists have never been able to come to complete agreement on the term or on the concepts it involves. Substantial progress has been made in the measurement of intelligence, however; such progress has resulted from attempts to find measures that would differentiate feeble-minded from normal children or pupils successful in school work from those who are less successful, as judged by their teachers. Actually, our definition of intelligence is circular, since we are in effect saying that intelligence is what intelligence tests measure and that it is what makes for success in academic work. This is true, at least insofar as the schools are concerned.

For a long time psychologists have been interested in the measurement of intelligence, and the history of the development of intelligence tests closely parallels the development of psychology as a science. Moreover, intelligence measurement is an area of study that is not without its controversial aspects. Also, it must be recognized that the use of intelligence tests requires in many instances a considerable amount of technical knowledge and training, and in no instance can one expect to use such tests properly without at least some preparation.

This chapter presents three aspects of the measurement of intelligence: (1) historical background and development, (2) basic concepts and principles of intelligence measurement, and (3) current procedures in measuring intelligence. Careful study of the chapter and Learning

Exercises should enable you to answer questions and to carry out assignments such as the following:

1. Summarize the theoretical and the practical contributions of Binet to the measurement of intelligence. Compare Binet's contributions with those of Terman.
2. Of the three theories of intelligence discussed in this chapter, which seems to you most sound and defensible? After careful consideration, give reasons for your choice.
3. Discuss in a paper of 500 words or less one of the major issues (constancy of IQ, heredity versus environment, testing the culturally disadvantaged), citing evidence to support your position. What contrary evidence could be advanced?
4. What are the major differences between verbal and nonverbal material in IQ tests? Give some illustrations of each.
5. Many group tests of intelligence yield two or even three scores—verbal, quantitative, and total. What is the rationale for this approach? Does it have a basis in any theory of intelligence? Explain.
6. What is meant by *culture-free?* by *culture-fair?* Is there a distinction? If so, describe it. What are the reasons behind efforts to devise tests that fit one or both classifications?

HISTORICAL BACKGROUND OF INTELLIGENCE MEASUREMENT

Present-day intelligence tests are based on the work of the French psychologist Alfred Binet (1857–1911). Associated with him were, first, V. Henri, and later, Théodore Simon. There can be no doubt that Binet was the shining light and genius of this most important contribution to modern psychological methods, even though many others contributed to the developments that culminated in and have grown out of his work.

For instance, the work of Francis Galton (1822–1911), an English scientist, did much to stimulate interest in individual differences and their measurement. He devised various tests of sensory discrimination involving weights, tones, and mental imagery and made important contributions to the advancement of statistical methods. He is generally regarded as having been the first to use standard scores and correlation.

In the United States a number of psychologists became interested in the possibility of measuring intelligence. At this point it must suffice to mention only one, James McKeen Cattell, who had more to do with early developments along these lines than anyone else in this country. Cattell studied psychology under the famous German, Wilhelm Wundt, who was not very favorably disposed toward the "new psychology"—that is, the measurement of mental abilities. However, Cattell became actively interested in the measurement of intelligence, and when he returned to this country he did much to stimulate interest in it. In 1896 he devised and administered to students at Columbia University a series of tests largely of the sensory-motor type. These tests measured such traits or abilities as keenness of vision and hearing, reaction time, mental imagery, and perception of differences in weights, colors, and tones. For the most part the tests were simple, objective, and easily administered. Almost without exception, however, the results showed little relation to teachers' estimates of their students' intelligence or to the students' success in school work as measured by marks or other means.

Binet also experimented with most such tests and dozens of others with similarly unsatisfactory results. He and his co-workers became convinced that the value of such tests for measuring intelligence was extremely limited. Gradually, however, he developed a new approach to the problem and began to make real progress. Binet based his theory on the assumption that success would depend on the measurement of complex mental processes rather than specific traits. In 1905, after years of research and experimentation, he published his first scale of intelligence, developed primarily for the purpose of identifying subnormal children in the schools of Paris. This scale represented a distinct departure from previous efforts. In the first place, Binet's tests were arranged in order of increasing difficulty, and thus they constituted a scale for measuring the individual's level of mental development. In the second place, although the tests were of considerable variety, they were intended to measure a complex, central factor in intelligence which Binet called *judgment*. Of course, Binet recognized that the thirty tests in the scale could not all be shown to measure this one factor; nevertheless, the originality and purpose of the tests were clearly evident. Some of the items required the student to execute simple orders such as "Close the door," to name objects designated in a picture, to cite from memory the differences between pairs of familiar objects or materials such as wood and glass, and to construct a sentence embodying three given words such as "Paris, gutter, fortune."[1]

This first scale was followed in 1908 by a revision in which the tests were grouped at ages or levels, a marked improvement over the serial order of the original scale. In 1911 a second revision was published. This was the culmination of Binet's work, since he died in the same year at

---

[1] See Joseph Peterson, *Early Conceptions and Tests of Intelligence* (New York: Harcourt Brace Jovanovich, 1925), pp. 172–174.

the age of 54. This third scale was more complete, more carefully standardized, and more systematically scored than either of its predecessors.

During Binet's lifetime several psychologists, most of whom were Americans, translated and used the first and second scales and criticized them, largely to Binet's benefit. However, the basic principles were established by Binet, and it was clearly demonstrated that the third scale in particular was an instrument superior in usefulness, accuracy, and scope to anything that had preceded it. The need now was for further translations and adaptations of the scale for use with children of different nationalities, cultures, and languages; this need was soon fulfilled, at least in the United States.

Three Americans are most closely associated with the development of the Binet tests. Henry Goddard translated both the 1905 and the 1908 scales into English and used them in his work at the Vineland, New Jersey, Training School for the Feeble-minded. In a similar way, Fred Kuhlmann used the early scales at an institution for the feeble-minded at Faribault, Minnesota. He published the first translation and thoroughgoing revision of Binet's scales for use with American children in 1912.

The major work in adapting the Binet scales for use with English-speaking subjects was done by Lewis M. Terman, who had carried on some experimentation with tests independently but had not gone very far when the Binet scales appeared. He set to work at once on these, and in 1916 he published what became the most widely used and accepted intelligence test, known as the *Stanford Revision of the Binet Scale.* This was a careful translation and revision, involving a complete standardization on American children and adults. There were tests at Years III, IV, V, VI, VII, VIII, IX, X, XII, XIV, and for levels called Average Adult and Superior Adult. Terman rearranged many of the tests from the positions established by Binet, added new tests, especially at the upper end of the scale, and eliminated others. This became and remained the standard instrument for the measurement of intelligence in the United States and other English-speaking countries for more than twenty years.

In time, certain shortcomings and weaknesses in Terman's scale became apparent, and in 1937 he and Maud A. Merrill published their revision of the Stanford-Binet scale, which remedied most, if not all, of these faults. The chief faults were a lack of equivalent forms; gaps in the scale, notably at Years XI and XIII; and incompleteness at both ends of the scale. The 1937 revision appeared in two equivalent forms; it provided tests for the missing years; it extended downward to age 2, with tests at half-year intervals from age 2 to age 6, thus providing a far more thorough testing at these levels; and it extended upward to a much higher level by adding three sets of tests, Superior Adult I, II, and III, giving the scale more "top" or "ceiling" for use with adults. Also, the normative population was more adequate and more carefully selected than in the earlier scale. A few samples from Form L of the *Revised Stanford-Binet Tests of Intelligence* will serve to show its nature.[2]

Year III–6 Drawing Designs: Cross

Procedure: Give the child a pencil and as you draw a cross making diagonal lines about two inches in length (X) say to him, "You make one just like this." Illustrate once only. Give one trial.

Score: The requirement for this test is that child shall make two lines which cross each other. We disregard the angle of crossing and the straightness and length of the lines.

Year VIII Comprehension IV

Procedure: Ask,

a. "What makes a sailboat move?"

b. "What should you say when you are in a strange city and someone asks you how to find a certain address?"

c. "What should you do if you found on the streets of a city a three-year-old baby that was lost from its parents?"

Score: 2 plus. [Sample answers are given. In *a*, for instance, "wind," "wind and water," "wind and sails," are acceptable; "water," "the motor," are not.]

Superior Adult III Repeating 9 Digits

Procedure: Say, "I am going to say some numbers and when I am through I want you to say them just the way I do. Listen carefully, and get them just right." Before each series repeat, "Listen carefully, and get them just right." Rate, one per second. Avoid accent and rhythm.

a. 3—7—1, etc.

b. 7—3—9, etc.

c. 8—5—2, etc.

Score: 1 plus. The series must be repeated in correct order without error after a single reading.

The administration of this scale requires training, practice, and skill.[3] No one should attempt it except as a learner under expert supervision without all three requisites. The examiner should be so thoroughly familiar with the procedure that he or she can give major attention to the presentation of the tasks, recording of responses, and legitimate encouragement of the subject. Assuming that the user has attained satisfactory skill and has established rapport with the subject, the procedure for administering the scale is as follows:

---

[2] Lewis M. Terman and Maud A. Merrill, *Measuring Intelligence* (Boston: Houghton Mifflin, 1937). Quoted by permission.

[3] Maud A. Merrill, *Training Students to Administer the Stanford-Binet Intelligence Scale Testing Today, No. 2* (Boston: Houghton Mifflin, n.d.).

1. Establish the basal mental age. This is the highest level on the scale at which the subject passes all the tests.
2. Proceed to give all the tests at successively higher levels, recording successes and failures at each level.
3. Stop at the level at which the subject fails all the tests.
4. Calculate the intelligence quotient.

   The procedure may be illustrated with the example of Mary, aged 8 years and 6 months. The examiner starts at the 7 year level, at which Mary passes all the tests; she does the same at 8; at the 9-year level, she passes five out of six; at 10, three out of six; at 11, two out of six; at 12, one out of six; and none at the 13-year level. To summarize:

Mary, Age 8-6

Basal MA, 8 years

9-year level passes $5 \times 2 = 10$ months[4]
10-year level passes $3 \times 2 = 6$ months
11-year level passes $2 \times 2 = 4$ months
12-year level passes $1 \times 2 = \underline{2 \text{ months}}$
22 months

Mental age: 8 years + 22 months = 9-10

$$IQ = \frac{MA}{CA} \times 100 = \frac{9\text{-}10}{8\text{-}6} \times 100 = \frac{118}{102} \times 100 = 116$$

   The tests are placed at age levels such that the standardization population yields an IQ very close to 100 at each level. Assuming the sample to be representative of the total population, this is as it should be. Earlier, Binet and others had placed tests at age levels where approximately three-fourths of the standardization population of a given age passed the test. This method was not entirely satisfactory and has been superseded by the method mentioned above. Under ideal circumstances, however, the two methods yield about the same results.

   After nearly a quarter-century of use of Forms L and M of the 1937 scale, still another revision was published in 1960.[5] It was made up of the items of Forms L and M that had proved to be most reliable and valid and whose content had not become out of date. Items that met these criteria were given a final tryout with several thousand cases and the best ones

---

[4] Since there are six tests at each year level at this part of the scale, each test is given a weight of 2 months—that is, $12 \div 6$. At earlier levels there are six tests every half-year. These count for 1 month each. At higher levels, tests have a weight of 3 or more months each.
[5] Lewis M. Terman and Maud A. Merrill, *Stanford-Binet Intelligence Scale*, 3d rev. ed. (Boston: Houghton Mifflin, 1960).

were combined into Form L-M. The 1937 Forms L and M are still available and widely used, but the best of them were put into the new form. Since this is so, Form L-M is superior in certain respects to its predecessors, although there is no equivalent form to go with it.

The new scale also provided tables of deviation IQs, which can be read directly without calculations when the chronological age is known and the mental age has been established, by administering either form of the 1937 scale or the 1960 L-M scale.

In 1972, Form L-M was restandardized on a national sample of 100 cases at each half-year age level from 2 to 5½ years and at each year level from 6 to 18, inclusive. The norms thus established are based on a more representative sample than those of the 1960 revision. However, the 1960 norms may still be used in particular situations where this is preferable, such as in comparisons with earlier data based on those norms.

Reliability coefficients of the 1937 revision are generally .90 or higher; at the lower age levels they approach .90; at upper age levels they range from .91 to .98 even though these coefficients are based on each age group separately, which greatly restricts the range.

Evidence of validity rests primarily on the test's power of age differentiation. However, vast amounts of data support validity of the Stanford-Binet as a measure of intelligence with a rather substantial weighting of a verbal factor. The scale has for many years been generally regarded as the criterion against which other intelligence tests, both individual and group, have been validated.

The Binet scales and their counterparts in other countries had one limitation, the significance of which was that only one person could be tested at a time by a trained examiner. This is a time-consuming procedure, although it has, nevertheless, certain desirable features, including the opportunity to establish rapport between subject and examiner and to observe the subject while being tested; also, when properly administered, it yields a very dependable appraisal. However, some American psychologists, notably Arthur S. Otis of The World Book Company, W. S. Miller of the University of Minnesota, Rudolf Pintner and E. L. Thorndike of Columbia University, and Terman himself, soon began experimenting with the adaptation of certain types of tests to group testing. In 1917, the entry of the United States into World War I gave this movement the impetus it required for success. Large numbers of men were being inducted into military service, and the need for and potential usefulness of some kind of rapid, accurate mental measurement of men soon became apparent. The government asked a number of psychologists to develop a test for this purpose. The result was Army Alpha, the first single, unified group test of intelligence. A counterpart test, Army Beta, was also constructed for use with illiterates and those who could not read well enough for Army Alpha, which presupposed about sixth-grade reading ability. Nearly two million men were tested by Alpha during the war, and in subsequent years it was widely used in schools and colleges.[6]

Soon after Army Alpha and Beta were produced, many group tests were published, some very closely patterned after the army tests, none differing materially from them. Army Alpha had been designed for use with adults; most of the new tests were adaptations for use with children and adolescents.

Although Army Alpha is rarely used today, it will be interesting and revealing to examine it a little more closely. It consisted of eight subtests or parts, each closely timed. The working time for the entire test was 40 minutes. Some samples from Form 6 of Army Alpha follow:

Test 3

This is a test of common sense. Below are sixteen questions. Three answers are given to each question. You are to look at the answers carefully; then make a cross in the square before the best answer to each question, as in the sample:
Sample:

Why do we use stoves? Because

☐ they look well

☒ they keep us warm

☐ they are black

Here the second answer is the best and is marked with a cross. Begin with No. 1 and keep on until time is called. Time: 1½ minutes.

Test 7

Sample:

sky—blue::grass—**table green warm big**
fish—swims::man—**paper time walks girl**
day—night::white—**red black clear pure**

In each of the lines above, the first two words are related to each other in some way. What you are to do in each line is to see what the relation is between the first two words, and underline the word in heavy type that is related in the same way to the third word. Begin with No. 1 and mark as many sets as you can before time is called. Time: 3 minutes (for 40 analogies).

---

[6] After the war the tests were released for civilian use. By 1920 and subsequently, a number of revisions have appeared, some of which are still available. Among the earlier ones were the Schrammell-Brannan Revision and the First Nebraska Edition. (See Buros's *Mental Measurements Yearbooks*, 4th, 5th, 6th, and 7th, for various revisions and reviews.)

The other tests in Army Alpha were Following Directions, Arithmetic, Opposites, Scrambled or Disarranged Sentences, Number Series Completion, and General Information. The items in each test were arranged in order of difficulty, closely timed, and speeded—that is, speed was strongly emphasized.

Army Beta was designed as a counterpart to Army Alpha, but it did not require the ability to read. It could be given without spoken or written directions, so it was strictly a nonverbal examination. It had the same number of parts as Alpha and was designed to parallel in purpose, but pictorially, most of the parts or subtests of Alpha. Army Beta was not nearly as extensively used as Alpha, either during the war or subsequently.

LEARNING EXERCISES

1. Besides the people mentioned in the brief historical sketch just given, others have been prominently identified with the early days of mental testing. Find five of these and give in a sentence or two the chief contribution of each. (Note: See references at the end of this chapter. Do not confine yourself to Americans.)
2. Binet died in 1911 at the age of 54. Look up his biography and make an outline of the main events of his professional life and his major contributions to psychology.
3. Examine a copy of Army Beta along with one of Army Alpha. See if you can pair the tests in the former with their counterparts in the latter. How would you set up an experiment to determine the extent to which Alpha and Beta were equivalent?

BASIC CONCEPTS
OF INTELLIGENCE MEASUREMENT

Before discussing current procedures in measuring intelligence, we should consider some of the fundamental ideas and associated problems. Most of these problems are theoretical and do not affect to any great extent the actual use of the tests. Nevertheless, it is important for users to understand this theory so that they can be more realistic in their approach and more aware of the strengths and limitations of the instruments they use. In instances where the topics discussed are controversial issues, we have tried to present some of the facts on both sides.

Binet, like many in his field, revised his thinking as he gained more experience and witnessed the results of his tests. It will be recalled that at the time of the publication of his first scale in 1905 he believed "sound judgment" to be the central factor. This was in sharp contrast to the views held by most of his predecessors and contemporaries, who believed that intelligence consists of a large number of specifics. The tests of reaction time, acuity of vision, hearing, and so on were consistent with this latter view, but they did not prove very useful in distinguishing between feeble-minded and normal children or in identifying those who were considered brighter by their teachers or those who did relatively poorly in school or college.

Binet's definition of intelligence included three capacities of ability in thinking: (1) to maintain a definite direction or to "stay on the track," (2) to choose appropriate means to ends or to adapt procedures to goals sought, and (3) to evaluate objectively one's own actions (autocriticism). In general, Binet held that the mind is unitary and possesses one overriding function: effective adjustment to environment.

More precisely defined theories of intelligence have been advanced by various people contemporary with and following Binet. The first of these is the *two-factor theory* developed by Charles Spearman, an English statistician. On the basis of correlation studies, he proposed a theory that intelligence consists of two factors—a general factor, g, and many specific factors, s_1, s_2, and so on. The g enters into all intellectual activities, while each particular activity is also subject to one or more specific factors.

In contrast with the *two-factor theory*, there is what has come to be known as the *multifactor theory*. Factor analytic research has resulted in the naming of a large number of factors, as many as one hundred or more having been identified by different investigators. Some students of the matter, notably J. P. Guilford, have attempted to develop a systematic theory based on the concept of many factors. Guilford calls his system a *structure of intellect model*. As shown in Figure 9.1, it consists of "three faces of intellect" designated *operation*, *product*, and *content*. There are five types of operations (of which memory is one); under product, there are six subdivisions (for example, relations); under content, there are four subdivisions (for example, symbolic). The model contains $5 \times 6 \times 4$ or 120 cells, in each of which the three major categories are represented. Each cell will presumably eventually be represented by a test.

A third theory, somewhat between these two, is called the *group-factor theory*, usually associated with L. L. Thurstone, an American psychologist and statistician. According to this theory, intelligence consists neither of g and s nor of many s's but of six to ten primary or group factors. Six named by Thurstone are number, verbal, space, word fluency, reasoning, and rote memory. While none of these factors is completely distinct from the others, statistical evidence has been presented to justify the assumption that they are not the same. The Thurstone theory is, in a sense, a middle ground or compromise between the other two.

Although all three of the theories are based on statistical foundations, they illustrate the fact that different individuals often interpret the same or similar data differently. It is clear that psychologists have not come to one mind on the structure of intelligence. Some lean strongly toward belief in the existence of a general factor, some espouse a theory based on the concept of group factors, and still others believe that intellect is comprised of many factors. No theory has yet found general acceptance, and it seems unlikely that one will in the foreseeable future.

Apparently Binet did not come to the concept of the IQ himself, but he clearly saw and expressed the mental-age concept at the time of the publication of his first scale, and the idea emerged clearly with the 1908 revision. A German psychologist, Wilhelm Stern, seems to have been the first to formulate the concept of the intelligence quotient, in 1912, a year after Binet's death. The intelligence quotient, or IQ as it is generally known, was quickly adopted by Terman and others, and today it is the *The Intelligence Quotient*

Guilford's "Three Faces of Intellect"   *Figure 9.1*

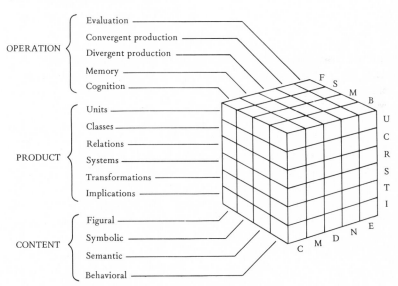

Reproduced by permission of McGraw-Hill Book Company from J. P. Guilford, *The Nature of Human Intelligence.* New York: McGraw-Hill Book Company, 1967.

generally accepted means of expressing intelligence, at least of persons below adulthood.

The ratio IQ, as has been shown already, is the ratio of mental age or level to chronological or life age. Thus, it is reasoned that a child developing normally should have a mental age equivalent to his or her chronological age and hence an IQ of 1, or, as it is commonly expressed, 100. The mental age or level for any given chronological age up to maturity is determined by testing a representative sample of children of that age. The mental age of 9, for example, is determined by giving a test to a representative sample of 9-year-old children. The average score in a group test made by these nine-year-olds is the mental-age norm for that life age. Subsequently, any child who makes that score is said to have a mental age of 9. On the other hand, this same score (and mental age) may be earned by children of varying life or chronological ages. Thus, Lynn, who is 12, may earn a score typical of nine-year-olds; therefore, Lynn's IQ is 9/12 × 100 = 75. Again, Jean may be 10, and if Jean's mental age is 9, her IQ is 90; still another child with a mental age of 9 may be only 7, in which case his IQ is about 130. Thus, the IQ represents the ratio of mental age to chronological age or the rate of mental development compared to age. In the first instance above, there is, on the average, three-quarters of a year of mental growth per year of life; in the second, nine-tenths of a year of mental growth; and in the third, some one and one-third years of mental gain for every year lived. The same facts may be shown in a different way by comparing children of the same age who have different mental ages.

The ratio IQ concept has been under fire from various quarters for a number of reasons. For example, it does not have the unqualified approval of educational statisticians because it does not have the same meaning at all levels or points on the scale. An IQ of 120 represents the ratio of 6/5 in a five-year-old and the ratio of 12/10 in a ten-year-old. Obviously, in the first case the difference between mental age and chronological age is 1 year; in the second, 2 years. However, this disadvantage is inherent in any ratio and applies to the IQ to no greater extent than it does to any other ratio.

Another criticism of the ratio IQ is that such IQs are not comparable from one test to another. This was early pointed out by W. S. Miller, who gave ten different intelligence tests to a group of fifty-seven ninth-grade pupils and found that there was a range of more than 3 years in the mean mental ages on the ten tests.[7] Thus a child might have an IQ of 116 on

---

[7]W. S. Miller, "Variation and Significance of Intelligence Quotients Obtained from Group Tests," *Journal of Educational Psychology*, 15 (September 1924), 359–366; "Variation of I.Q.'s Obtained from Group Tests," 24 (September 1933), 468–474.

one of the tests and 130 on another. Miller showed that this is largely due to differences in the tests themselves and differences in the standardization population. He suggested a method of equating such differences by converting the IQs to standard scores, as described in Chapter 3.

Another shortcoming of the ratio IQ resides in the assumption of a constant rate of mental development for a given individual. This assumption, although true (relatively speaking) for many, is not true for all. Research has shown that rate of mental development as measured by existing tests is not constant but fluctuates rather markedly in some instances.

One other aspect of the ratio IQ concept, also in the nature of a limitation, should be mentioned here. Experience has shown that the functions or capacities measured by existing intelligence tests reach their maximum about the same time as physical maturity is reached, which seems to be somewhere between the ages of 15 and 20, as reported in various studies. In some respects this would appear to be quite consistent, since we do not expect an individual to grow taller or to acquire more teeth or stronger eyesight when mature. On the other hand, most individuals like to think of themselves as gaining in wisdom and knowledge as long as they live, or at least until they grow quite old. Thus, as far as the ratio IQ goes, if we continue to use MA/CA and the individual's MA ceases to increase after a certain age, the IQ value declines. To illustrate, if MA/CA were 16/16, the IQ would be 100. If the MA was still 16 when the CA was 20, the ratio then would be .80, or IQ = 80. This, of course, is an obviously erroneous conclusion and certainly a demoralizing one. Consequently, it is customary with subjects past the age of 16 not to calculate IQs at all but to express the individual's position relative to others in the group, either by percentile ranks or by standard scores. This is the procedure followed almost entirely with adult groups such as college and university students, men and women in military service, and so on. In effect, this procedure results in an equivalent of the IQ, since we can assume that these persons have reached maturity. Therefore, the denominator of the MA/CA ratio is a constant factor and the score or percentile rank is really a measure comparable to the ratio IQ rather than simply a measure of rank or relative position. Many studies show that for adolescents the correlation between scores on a mental ability test and IQs based on the scores is .98 or higher.

To overcome the major weaknesses of the ratio IQ the so-called deviation IQ has come increasingly into use in recent years. As explained in Chapter 3, this is a standard score with an arbitrarily chosen mean and standard deviation. Although any values, such as a mean of 50 and standard deviation of 10 as used for the sigma scores in Chapter 3, could be employed, it has become quite general practice to use a mean of 100 and a standard deviation of 16. The reasons for using these values is that they are the mean and standard deviation, respectively, of Stanford-Binet IQs. IQs based on these constants are therefore numerically comparable to Binet IQs. Thus, a ratio IQ 1 standard deviation above the mean of a particular group test becomes a deviation IQ of 116; one that is 2 standard deviations above the mean on this test becomes a deviation IQ of 132; a ratio IQ 1 standard deviation below the mean of the test becomes a deviation IQ of 84, and so on.

The comparable values in terms of standard scores, deviation IQs, and percentile ranks can be seen clearly by reference to Figure 3.2.

LEARNING EXERCISES

4. Briefly discuss the major theories of intelligence, contrasting their differences. What implications for measuring intelligence can you draw from each?

5. Solve the following by using the formula IQ = MA/CA × 100:

MA = 7, CA = 10	IQ =
MA = 12, IQ = 125	CA =
CA = 10, IQ = 90	MA =
MA = 10-8, CA = 9-4	IQ =

6. Using $M = 100$ and $S = 16$, calculate the proportion of the total population with IQs above 116 and the proportion below 84. (Note: Refer to Chapter 3.)

7. Assume that group test A yields a mean IQ of 102 and a standard deviation of 18 for a representative sample of ten-year-olds. Convert the following ratio IQs into deviation IQs with a mean of 100 and a standard deviation of 16: (a) 120, (b) 84, (c) 75, (d) 138, (e) 93.

8. Plan an experiment with guinea pigs to show the effects of differences in heredity under the same environmental conditions. Plan another to measure the effects of changed environment with heredity constant. How would you measure the results?

---

*Constancy
of the IQ*

One of the continuing points of issue about the IQ concept is the question of constancy. Usually this means constancy from time to time in the development of the individual, though it may also mean constancy at dif-

THE MEASUREMENT OF CAPACITY: GENERAL INTELLIGENCE

ferent levels or points on the scale. The latter has been touched upon in the preceding section as a function of the ratio IQ and is a technical matter beyond the scope of this book. The question of constancy in an individual, however, is of direct concern to every user of intelligence tests. In essence, this question is: If I test a child today and obtain an IQ of 90, what is the result likely to be if I test again a year or more from now? This is probably what most persons have in mind when they discuss the constancy of the IQ.

Numerous longitudinal studies have been reported in which children have been tested annually or semiannually over a period of years. In one study[8] 61 children were tested at the preschool ages of 1 month to 5 years by the *California Pre-School Schedule* and from 6 to 12 years and at 14 and 17 years by the Stanford-Binet. At ages 13 and 15 they were tested by a group test, the Terman-McNemar, and at ages 16 and 18 by the Wechsler-Bellevue (an individual scale for adults). The study began with sixty-one infants. At the last testing at age 18, thirty-seven cases were tested. The results showed that (1) correlations between tests of children below age 6 ranged from −.13 to .73 (California with Binet) and (2) correlations between tests given between age 6 and 11 ranged from .73 to .93 (Binet at all levels).

In another study[9] 252 children were tested annually from age 21 months to 18 years by the *California Pre-School Schedule,* the Stanford-Binet, or the Wechsler-Bellevue. The results were similar to those reported above. In general they indicated that (1) the results of tests made after age 6 were much more stable than those of tests made before age 6; (2) individual children showed marked fluctuation in IQ over the sixteen-year period (the tested IQs of 58 percent of the children changed 15 points or more); (3) the longer the interval between tests, the greater the possibility of change; and (4) the maximum shift in average IQ for the group as a whole, between 21 months and 18 years, was from 118 to 123, or 5 points.

Another study[10] is of interest since it examines the question of whether deviation IQs are more stable than ratio IQs, as has been suggested by some authorities. Fifty boys and girls were tested by the 1937 Binet every six months from age 2½ to 5 and annually from 6 through 12 years of age. The results showed that (1) average IQs in the 140–169 range increased over the years by about 30 points; (2) averages

[8]Nancy Bayley, "Consistency and Variability in the Growth of Intelligence from Birth to Eighteen," *Journal of Genetic Psychology,* 75 (1949), 165–196.
[9]Marjorie P. Honzik, Jean MacFarlane, and L. Allen, "The Stability of Mental Test Performance Between Two and Eighteen Years," *Journal of Experimental Education,* 17 (December 1948), 309–324.
[10] Byron W. Lindholm, "Changes in Conventional and Deviation I.Q.'s," *Journal of Educational Psychology,* 55: (April 1964), 110–113.

below this range tended to be much more stable; (3) variability of IQs of the entire group decreased between ages 3 and 5, increased between 5 and 10, and declined again between 10 and 12; and (4) no difference was found in the relative variability of ratio and deviation IQs.

Taken altogether, the evidence on stability of measured IQs can be summed up as follows: (1) average IQs for groups remain remarkably stable over many years; (2) IQs of many individual children fluctuate by substantial amounts;[11] (3) tested IQs of children below age 6 are much less stable than those of the same children after age 6; and (4) the results of intelligence tests of many children show remarkable consistency over long periods of time.

Finally, it must be emphasized that a single test, either individual or group, constitutes only a very limited sampling of a child's behavior. Because of this fact, the results from a single testing should always be regarded as provisional and should be supplemented by additional testing whenever possible. It should be pointed out in this connection that many schools include in their testing programs at least two and often three to five testings of intelligence between grades 1 and 12.

Although it is currently fashionable to criticize all standardized tests, particularly intelligence tests, there should be no serious question of their overall value and usefulness. This point of view is epitomized in the words of a leading authority in the field, who says:

> The outstanding success of scientific measurement of individual differences has been that of the general mental test. Despite occasional overenthusiasm and misconceptions, and the fact that the established tests are rendered obsolescent by recent conceptual advances, the general mental test stands today as the most important technical contribution of psychology to the practical guidance of human affairs.[12]

The great majority of counselors and school psychologists know this, as do many teachers. To use these instruments wisely, with full recognition of their strengths and weaknesses, should be an objective of everyone involved in testing in the schools.

Distribution of Intelligence Quotients

Since there is no absolute standard of intelligence or of mental age, the basis for these must be relative. In other words, a mental age of 12 years is determined by what a sampling of children representative of the total population of twelve-year-olds can do on a given test. As has been

---

[11] In this connection it should be pointed out that in the Bayley and Honzik studies different tests were used at different age levels. Some of the changes found were almost certainly the result of differences between tests.

[12] Lee J. Cronbach, *Essentials of Psychological Testing*, 3d ed. (New York: Harper & Row, 1970), p. 197.

pointed out, this varies from one test to another because of differences in the tests themselves and differences in the population sample. Nevertheless, distributions of both raw scores and IQs obtained from adequate population samples quite generally show results closely approximating the normal curve. One such distribution for the revised Stanford-Binet is shown in Figure 9.2. This is based on a composite IQ on Forms L and M of the 1937 revision for 2,904 subjects, ages 2 to 18 inclusive.

The close approximation to the normal curve in the form of the distribution of IQs is of considerable importance. If IQs obtained from intelligence tests did not yield this kind of distribution from adequate population samples, there might be a basis for doubting the validity of such tests or, at least, the validity of the particular ones used. The basic assumption is that intelligence is normally distributed in the general population, and tests that do not yield results at least approximating the normal might be open to serious question. Also, this assumption provides a sound theoretical basis for interpreting the significance of any given IQ in comparison with the proportion of the general population having the same IQ.

When the normal distribution of IQs is broken down according to the areas under the curve, and a mean of 100 and a standard deviation of 16 are used as the constant values (based on Stanford-Binet IQ distributions), the proportions of various levels of IQ are as shown in Table 9.1.

Distribution of Composite L-M IQs of Standardization Group

Figure 9.2

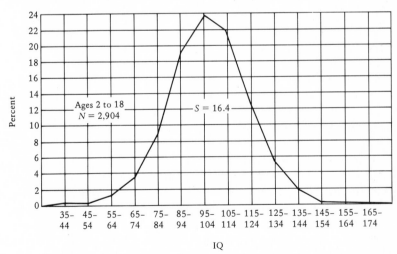

Table 9.1	Classification and Proportions of Various Levels of IQ in the General Population	
Classification	*IQ*	*Percentage in general population*
Very superior	140 and above	1.3
Superior	130–139	3.1
	120–129	8.2
High average	110–119	18.1
Normal average	100–109	23.5
	90–99	23.0
Low average	80–89	14.5
Borderline defective	70–79	5.6
Mentally defective	60–69	
	50–59	
	40–49	2.6
	30–39	

SOURCE: Lewis M. Terman and Maud A. Merrill, *Stanford-Binet Intelligence Scale* (Boston: Houghton Mifflin, 1973), p. 18. Reproduced by permission.

The classification of various IQ levels as shown in this table is generally accepted, though the limits are not to be regarded as exact. At the lower end of the distribution, the mentally defective have in the past been classed as morons, imbeciles, and idiots, in descending order; those whose IQs were below the lowest limit in the table were usually classed as idiots. However, today it is customary to use more functional designations, like *educable* or *trainable mentally retarded.* Another recommended set of designations is *mildly retarded, moderately retarded,* and *severely retarded.*

Heredity Versus Environment

Closely related to questions about the constancy of the IQ are others about the relative contributions of heredity and environment to its value. Questions such as "Are we born with it or is it learned?" "How much does heredity contribute to its value?" and "How much can it be changed?" have been debated for years. Psychologists have presented evidence to support one position or another with respect to the influence of heredity or environment. The general public is confused by the lack of agreement among scientists and swayed by their own biases.

We may understand the issue and the difficulties in reaching agreement if we remind ourselves that the scientist investigates differences in test scores or IQs. Although the general public tends to equate IQ with intelligence, it is merely one measure of differences in a person's abilities to perform the tasks of a test, not the underlying trait that is in some ways responsible for observed differences in the performance of the tasks. The tasks of IQ tests are like those most typical of schools; hence, the IQ is somewhat predictive of performance in school and some other situations for most persons.

The general public, on the other hand, usually thinks of intelligence as the combination of abilities needed for success in our society. Actually, although different tests do not all measure the same thing, they rarely if ever are intended to measure some abilities and characteristics important to success. Mechanical, musical, and artistic abilities and motivation are obvious examples of such variables. To further complicate the issue, the combination of abilities needed for success, what many mean by intelligence, would be expected to vary from culture to culture and from time to time within a particular culture. Even if psychologists were in complete agreement, which they are not, their answers to the question "How are differences in test scores (or IQs) related to differences in heredity or environment?" would not be a completely satisfactory answer to what lay people usually mean by "Why are some people more intelligent than others?"

The majority of psychologists and educators, and probably most lay people as well, appear to agree that heredity and environment interact to affect test scores and IQs. As one writer has put it, "The great mathematician, Sir Isaac Newton, if he had been brought up among African bushmen would probably have become a remarkable bushman but he would never have discovered the laws of motion."[13] Similar statements might be made about a Cassatt, an Einstein, or a Curie. In every instance, environmental opportunities were necessary to bring out a remarkable native endowment. On the other hand, it is improbable that any conceivable environment could make a Newton, a Cassatt, or a Curie of a child having no special talents or unusual endowments.

It is quite generally agreed that inadequacies and biases in tests or testing conditions may be a factor in the scores of some individuals and perhaps in the averages of some groups also. J. C. Loehlin and colleagues reviewed the currently available evidence on these factors and concluded that a rather wide range of different positions on their relative importance would all be reasonable. Furthermore, it would be reasonable to change one's position on their relative importance from one cultural or testing situation to another.[14] In other words, no generally acceptable formula relating these factors and test scores is expected.

Historically, arguments about factors that influence IQ were encouraged and intensified by the development and widespread application of tests of intelligence, first the individual tests, then the Army Alpha and its successors, the group tests. Individual tests, particularly the Binet

---

[13]Daniel Starch, *Educational Measurement* (New York: Macmillan, 1916), p. 87.
[14]J. C. Loehlin, G. Lindzey, and J. N. Spuhler, *Race Differences in Intelligence* (San Francisco: W. H. Freeman, 1975), p. 239.

tests, were used first. Later, immense amounts of data on individuals and groups of individuals were collected by the administration of group tests, which became readily available to investigators.

Many investigations and experiments have been made on this question from the time of Galton to the present. One method of investigation involves studies of persons who are obviously brilliant, feeble-minded, or degenerate to determine whether such traits tend to run in families. Results of such studies have generally been interpreted as showing the preponderant influence of heredity.

Another type of investigation involves the transplanting of children from a poor environment to a good one. The results of such studies are equivocal; some children show general and marked improvement in intelligence and other traits; others do not. One is almost forced to conclude that investigators tend to find the results they look for; much of the research showing marked changes has been severely criticized for poor control, careless procedures, or bad statistical treatment of data.

A third type of investigation uses twins as subjects. Identical twins are as nearly alike in heredity and environment as two humans can be. Starting with a large number of pairs of twins, the investigator studies many aspects of their resemblances—physical, mental, and affective. Most of these studies show remarkable and, in some instances, almost incredible similarities among pairs of identical twins. In the few cases where studies have been made of identical twins reared in different environments, the resemblances have been less close in mental and social traits than in physical traits.

Results of the earlier studies were more frequently interpreted as demonstrating the prepotency of heredity and the ineffectiveness of environmental factors in shaping behavior, although there was no universal agreement on this interpretation. More recently, on the other hand, there has been greater emphasis on the effects of the environment and environmental intervention. As we noted in the discussion of stability, changes in the IQ of individuals do occur even though group statistics, such as correlations, show considerable stability over time. Programs of planned intervention or compensatory education, such as Head Start, have been established to overcome environmental or cultural deficiencies that may be a factor in lower test scores and school difficulties.

Although evaluations of experimental compensatory education programs have tended to be disappointing,[15] attempts to produce significant and lasting modifications in human learning ability and behavior through environmental intervention have continued. Greater emphasis

[15]J. S. Coleman et al., *Equality of Educational Opportunity* (Washington, D.C.: U.S. Department of Health, Education and Welfare, Office of Education, 1966).

is now being placed on the development of specific skills that are considered prerequisites for effective learning rather than on evidence of changes in global measures such as the IQ.[16]

During the past few years, controversy about race, a particularly sensitive genetic characteristic, has become intense and sometimes emotional. Mental tests have fairly consistently shown somewhat lower average scores for members of some minority groups, and the question about the genetic or environmental origins of these average differences arises, just as it has for individual differences within each group.

The analyses and conclusions of Arthur Jensen have been the focal point of much recent debate over both individual differences in general and differences in the average scores of racial groups. Jensen estimated that 80 percent of the variation in IQ among Americans is contributed by genetic factors, thus bringing renewed attention to heredity as an explanation of individual differences. This is referred to as a *heritability ratio* of .80.[17]

Although Jensen's methods and his conclusions about heritability are frequently criticized, some of the criticism might be more appropriately directed toward interpreters who have overlooked the limitations he stated. Other authors have noted and clarified the limitations of heritability estimates also, showing what they are not as well as what they are.[18] When considering the practical implications of heritability estimates, it is especially important to note the following. (1) The estimates are for populations and do not represent the proportion of any individual's IQ that is due to heredity. (2) They are for a given group and may not hold for other groups. (3) They may not continue to hold for even one group if conditions for that group change. (4) They do not indicate how difficult it may be to change the scores of individuals or groups by changing the environment, perhaps by educational programs.

Jensen and his interpreters are criticized for placing so much emphasis on heredity in writing for educators. Cronbach has pointed out, for example, that educators must work with the environment. Emphasizing heredity may only remind educators how difficult it may be to change students. Cronbach does not see this as helpful.[19]

While not mentioning Jensen, Robert Ebel made somewhat the same point in his presidential address to the American Educational Research

[16]Irving E. Sigel, "Where Is Preschool Education Going: Or Are We en Route Without a Map?" *Proceedings, 1972 Invitational Conference on Testing Problems* (Princeton, N.J.: Educational Testing Service, 1973), pp. 99–116.
[17]Arthur R. Jensen, "How Much Can We Boost IQ and Scholastic Achievement?" *Harvard Educational Review*, 39 (1969), 1–123.
[18]Anne Anastasi, *Psychological Testing*, 4th ed. (New York: Macmillan, 1976), pp. 351–352.
[19]Lee J. Cronbach and Richard E. Snow, *Final Report: Individual Differences in Learning Ability as a Function of Instructional Variables* (Stanford, Calif.: Stanford University, School of Education, 1969), p. 197.

Association. He called it wrong educationally to assume "that a child who scores low on an intelligence test is biologically limited in learning ability" and wrong socially to assume "that a cultural group which scores lower on such tests than another is less well endowed biologically." He called these assumptions harmful, untestable at present, and not needed to explain the results of intelligence tests.[20]

Although the contributions of heredity and environmental factors to individual differences are a legitimate subject for further scientific study, those who use intelligence tests and the IQ for practical purposes should keep one or two facts about them clearly in mind, regardless of their views about the issues. One such fact is that the differences among individual IQs *within* racial, ethnic, or social groups are much greater than the differences among the averages of the groups. There are many individuals in the lower of two groups who score higher than some individuals in the group with a higher average. It is both unjust and incorrect to label individual members of one group inferior or those of another superior on the basis of group membership.

It is equally true that an IQ or other intelligence test score is but one important descriptive fact about an individual, not an explanation of one's present ability nor the sole determinant of one's future. We should guard against attributing too much importance to this one fact about an individual or to its origins.

Testing the Culturally Disadvantaged

It has been rather common in recent years to criticize all types of standardized tests, whether achievement, personality, or intelligence. Some of these criticisms have been reviewed and discussed in an earlier chapter. One of the more persistent objections to the use of intelligence tests maintains that they are loaded or saturated with middle-class culture and are therefore unfair to children from lower socioeconomic levels and especially to those who are considered to be culturally disadvantaged. It is maintained that existing group tests penalize children who come from poor homes and whose cultural patterns, parental attitudes, and group standards are not the middle-class ones said to dominate the school and testing situations. Some critics have gone so far as to suggest that the use of current mental ability tests be discontinued.[21] It has also been suggested that efforts be directed to the development of instruments on which the culturally disadvantaged will not be handicapped by previous experience or lack of it.[22]

---

[20]Robert L. Ebel, "The Future of the Measurement of Abilities II," *Educational Researcher*, 2 (March 1973), 5–12.
[21]The New York City school system discontinued the use of all mental ability tests in 1964.
[22]Kenneth W. Eells et al., *Intelligence and Cultural Differences* (Chicago: University of Chicago Press, 1951).

The question of the effects of cultural differences on performance on intelligence tests is not new. Numerous efforts have been made to develop "culture-free" or "culture-fair" tests of mental ability. The term *culture-free* has come to be regarded as meaningless if not positively misleading in this context. It is generally recognized that no test could be culture-free, since the only way to respond to it is in terms of what has been learned—that is, in terms of one's culture. Attempts to develop culture-fair tests have concentrated on finding or devising tasks, responses to which are minimally or not at all affected by cultural differences. One method for doing this is to construct items of pictorial or performance nature, not requiring ability to read or even understand spoken directions, these being given in pantomime or sign language. After tryout and item analysis, further refinements eliminate items that show consistent differences in response by groups having different cultural backgrounds. An example of a test developed by this procedure will be described in detail later in this chapter. Suffice it to say at this point that none of the tests produced as culture-fair up to the present has been widely used or widely substituted for the more conventional types of intelligence tests.

Concern with poverty, cultural deprivation, and related social problems in the United States has served to increase the tendency to question the use of intelligence tests in the schools and elsewhere, particularly with the disadvantaged. A publication of the Psychological Corporation outlines the common charges and attempts to answer the criticisms.[23] Though it deals with testing in industry, the matters discussed and points made are generally relevant to testing in schools. These will not be covered here, but it is suggested that the student will find the bulletin thought-provoking and well worth careful reading.

As has already been said in Chapter 1, much of the discussion and criticism ignores a basic issue—namely, the purpose intelligence tests are intended to serve. Some critics seem to be saying that the tests are bad because, in revealing individual differences, they make some people (for example, the disadvantaged) appear inferior to others. The fact is that the tests are *designed* to reveal individual differences. A test that did not reveal differences in probable competence to perform or learn would be useless. Furthermore, the tests are designed to predict success in academic work, job performance, or ability to learn how to perform well.[24]

[23]Jerome E. Doppelt and George K. Bennett, *Testing Job Applicants from Disadvantaged Groups*, Test Service Bulletin 57, (New York: Psychological Corp., 1967).
[24]On these points see Edgar Z. Friedenberg, "The Real Functions of Educational Testing," *Change* (January–February 1970), pp. 43–47; Irving Lorge, "Difference or Bias in Tests of Intelligence," *Testing Problems in Perspective* (Washington, D.C.: American Council on Education, 1966), Chap. 10; Anne Anastasi, "Some Implications of Cultural Factors for Test Construction," *ibid.*, Chap. 10.

Their purpose is to differentiate between individuals, some of whom do well, others less well. The value of a test as predictor is measured by criteria such as teachers' marks and performance on other tests or on the job. A test that does not reveal differences between individuals is quite useless for that purpose.

To date, no other measure or technique has been found or developed that equals the current best intelligence tests for the purposes for which they are intended. Some of the critics seem to be saying that we should kill the messenger who brings us bad news. Tests serve a useful purpose when they identify individuals' weaknesses and deficiencies as well as their strengths, whatever their cause or origin. The results of testing provide a basis for assisting individuals to remedy shortcomings, to guide them into appropriate lines of activity, and to help them realize their potential to the fullest.

LEARNING EXERCISES

9. What is meant by constancy of the IQ? Is the individual's IQ constant? If not, how much does it vary over time and why? How stable are average IQs of groups?
10. Discuss briefly some of the major problems and issues in testing intelligence of the culturally disadvantaged.

CURRENT PROCEDURES
IN MEASURING INTELLIGENCE

Verbal and Nonverbal Material

The content of intelligence tests is generally classified as verbal or nonverbal. Verbal material requires the ability to read or, at the very least, to understand material spoken or read aloud by the examiner. Therefore, a strictly nonverbal examination requires no use of language in its administration or in the pupils' answers. Such a test is Army Beta, the directions for which can be given in pantomime. Tests are rarely nonverbal to this extreme; indeed, we generally consider an intelligence test nonverbal as long as it does not require any reading ability. This type of test is useful and quite generally necessary in testing young children, illiterates, and the feeble-minded.

While nonverbal material may be pictorial, it may also be of the type known as *performance*. Formboards (which are a kind of jigsaw puzzle), building blocks, and tracing mazes are typical of the performance type of exercise found in individual intelligence tests. Samples are shown in Figure 9.3. In group tests the nonverbal material is generally pictorial, as will be illustrated later in this chapter.

Although the correlation between verbal and nonverbal types of tests of intelligence is far from perfect, it is generally high enough to justify the use of nonverbal material where verbal tests cannot be used. This is found most often in tests for young children. Nonverbal material of the performance type is also used extensively in tests of aptitude.

It should also be noted that many intelligence tests in current use include both verbal and nonverbal—that is, nonreading—material. This is

Typical Performance Tests: (A) Porteus Maze Test, (B) Knox-Kemp Feature Profile *Figure 9.3* Test: Pintner-Patterson Modification, (C) Minnesota Rate of Manipulation Test, (D) Seguin-Goddard Formboard

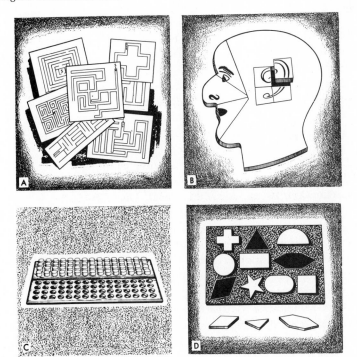

Reproduced by permission of Stoelting Company & American Guidance Service, Inc.

true of both individual scales like the Binet and of numerous group tests. In some instances the materials are arranged to yield both a verbal and a nonverbal IQ.

Individual Scales

A brief description has already been given of the nature of and the procedure for administering a Stanford-Binet examination. The method is essentially the same in other tests of the Binet type, such as the Kuhlmann, except that the latter takes both accuracy and speed of response into account. It will be recalled that one of the criticisms of the 1916 Stanford-Binet was lack of adequate "ceiling" or "top" for testing adults. Although this was remedied to a large extent in the 1937 revision, there was still some dissatisfaction on this point.

THE WECHSLER SCALES   Another frequently voiced criticism of the Binet scale and its revisions was that the scales were designed for use with children, and the adult materials added later were really not essentially different. Consequently, it was said that the scales were not appropriate for adults and not intrinsically interesting to them. To meet these criticisms, a scale for measuring adult intelligence was brought out by Wechsler in 1939.[25] This was an individual intelligence scale known as the *Wechsler-Bellevue Intelligence Scale.* It departs in certain important respects from the Binet-type scale. The tests are not grouped at age levels and the scale yields standard scores or deviation IQs. It was designed for and standardized largely on adults but attained some popularity in use with children as well. In 1949 Wechsler published another scale, the *Wechsler Intelligence Scale for Children* (WISC), along the same general pattern as the adult scale. Subsequently, he published a revised and improved *Wechsler Adult Intelligence Scale* (WAIS).[26]

The WAIS consists of eleven subtests divided into a Verbal scale and a Performance scale. The Verbal scale includes tests called Information, Comprehension, Arithmetic, Similarities, Digit Span, and Vocabulary. The Performance scale includes tests called Digit Symbol, Picture Completion, Block Design, Picture Arrangement, and Object Assembly. Each test is administered and scored separately; the scores of the Verbal scale are combined to yield a Verbal IQ, the tests of the Performance scale to yield a Performance IQ. All eleven tests combined yield a Full-scale IQ. Scores on each subtest are expressed in standard-score units with a mean of 10 and a standard deviation of 3. The IQs are expressed as deviation IQs with a mean of 100 and a standard deviation of 15. Five of the sub-

[25]David Wechsler, *The Measurement of Adult Intelligence* (Baltimore: Williams and Wilkins, 1939).
[26]David Wechsler, *Wechsler Intelligence Scale for Children* (New York: Psychological Corp., 1949), and *Wechsler Adult Intelligence Scale* (New York: Psychological Corp., 1955).

tests are scored in terms of both speed and accuracy; the other six are scored on the basis of the number right.

The WISC is very similar to the WAIS in its composition. It consists of twelve subtests also grouped into Verbal and Performance scales. Most of the subtests are of the same type as those in the WAIS, but they are easier. Procedures for scoring and calculating IQs on the two scales are almost identical.

More recently, Wechsler produced another scale for use with children from 4 to 6½ years. The scale, abbreviated WPPSI, is primarily a downward extension of the WISC. It consists of eleven tests, eight of which are downward adaptations of tests in the WISC; three are new. Five tests constitute the Verbal scale, five the Performance scale. One Verbal test is an alternate. Procedures for administering and scoring are essentially the same as in other Wechsler scales.

In 1974, Wechsler published still another scale, the *Wechsler Intelligence Scale for Children—Revised,* or WISC–R. There are twelve tests in this revision, but two are used primarily as alternates. In most respects, the WISC–R is like its predecessor. However, some items were changed to make their subject matter more like children's experience, and the standardization sample was more representative of the general population than that used with previous scales.[27]

These scales, together with the Stanford-Binet, are by far the most widely used individual intelligence tests and are regarded as standard in nearly all work where individual tests are used.

LEARNING EXERCISE

11. What are the basic differences between the current Binet scales and the Wechsler scales? What are the advantages and disadvantages of each?

OTHER INDIVIDUAL INTELLIGENCE TESTS Following is a listing of some other individual intelligence tests that merit the reader's inspection.

[27]David Wechsler, *Wechsler Preschool and Primary Scale of Intelligence* (New York: Psychological Corp., 1967); and *Wechsler Intelligence Scale for Children—Revised* (New York: Psychological Corp., 1974).

Arthur Point Scale of Performance Tests, revised. Form 11. Ages 5 to superior adults. Includes Knox Cube Test, Seguin Formboard (Arthur Revision), Arthur Stencil Design Test, Porteus Maze Test (Arthur Printing), Healy Picture Completion Test II (New York: Psychological Corp., 1947), 60–90 minutes.

Columbia Mental Maturity Scale, 3d ed. One form. Ages 3 to 10. One hundred cards each containing a series of drawings from which the examinee selects the one that does not belong. (New York: Psychological Corp., 1972), 15–20 minutes.

Leiter International Performance Scale, revised. One form. Ages 2 to adult. Fifty-four tests involving matching of colors and of objects, picture completion, spatial relations, footprint recognition, and so on. (Chicago: Stoelting Company, 1948–1952), 30–60 minutes.

Minnesota Preschool Scale. Form A. Ages 1½ to 6 inclusive. Twenty-six tests: Verbal includes pointing to and naming objects, comprehension, naming colors. Nonverbal includes copying figures, Knox Cube Test, paperfolding. (Circle Pines, Minn.: American Guidance Service, 1940), 10–30 minutes.

Group Tests

THE COGNITIVE ABILITIES TEST First published in 1954 as the *Lorge-Thorndike Intelligence Tests,* revised and published in 1964 as the *Lorge-Thorndike Intelligence Tests, Multilevel Edition,* and in 1971 as the *Cognitive Abilities Test, Multilevel Edition,* the *Cognitive Abilities Test* is said to be a measure of abstract intelligence, defined as the ability to work with ideas and relationships among ideas.[28]

Grade Levels and Forms The test series extends from kindergarten to grade 12 and college freshmen. Primary I is for use with kindergarten and grade 1. Primary II is for grades 2 and 3. The multilevel feature of the Cognitive Abilities is designed for grades 3 through 12 and is stated to be appropriate for college freshmen. There is one form.

The multilevel feature provides eight levels of tests, A to H, one for each grade in the elementary school (grades 3–8), one for grades 9–10, and one for grades 11–12. Each successive level overlaps with the preceding and succeeding levels, except, of course, Levels A and H, which overlap with only one level. This provides a continuous series of items and makes feasible the selection of testing level deemed appropriate for a given group, irrespective of actual school grade. This also contributes to the discriminatory power of the items.

Content Primary I and II consist of four subtests: Vocabulary, Relational Concepts (as in "Find the picture that shows the ball is under the

[28]Robert L. Thorndike and Elizabeth Hagen, *Cognitive Abilities Test, Multilevel Edition* (Boston: Houghton Mifflin, 1971).

chair"), Multi-Mental ("Mark the one that doesn't belong"—see the accompanying sample),[29] and Quantitative Concepts ("Find the picture of

the box that has only one stick in it"). All content of Primary I and II is pictorial, and all directions are given orally.

Multilevels A–H consist of three batteries, Verbal, Quantitative, and Nonverbal.[30] The Verbal battery includes four subtests:

1. Vocabulary

   Find the word that means the same or nearly the same as the word in dark type:

   wish   A. agree B. bone C. over D. want E. waste

2. Sentence Completion

   Pick the word that best fits the blank:

   _____ me my hat and coat.

   L. burn M. call N. see P. tell Q. bring

3. Classification

   All the words in dark type are alike in some way. Pick the word that belongs with them:

   Bob Jack Fred Bill

   F. Mary G. boy H. name J. Ed K. Jones

4. Analogies

   Pick the word that has the same relation to the third word as the second word has to the first word:

   drink – milk : eat – _____

   L. hungry M. bread N. fast P. alone Q. early

[29]From *Cognitive Abilities Test,* Primary level, by Irving Lorge, Robert L. Thorndike, and Elizabeth Hagen. Copyright © 1968 and 1974 Houghton Mifflin Company. Reprinted by permission.
[30]In the several sample items from these batteries that follow, the directions are abbreviated from those given in the test manual. From *Cognitive Abilities Test, Multilevel Edition,* Form 1, by Robert L. Thorndike and Elizabeth Hagen. Copyright © 1971 Houghton Mifflin Company. Reprinted by permission.

The Quantitative battery includes three subtests:

1. Quantitative Relations

    If the amount or quantity in Column I is more than in Column II, mark A; if
    it is less, mark B; if they are equal, mark C.

Column I	Column II	A B C
3 + 2	2 + 3	○ ○ ○

2. Number Series

    The numbers at the left are in a certain order. Find the number at the right
    that should come next.

    10 12 14 16 18 20 _____   L. 21 M. 22 N. 23 P. 24 Q. 25

3. Equation Building

    Arrange the numbers and signs below to make true equations and then
    choose the number at the right that gives you a correct answer.

    2 2 3 + ×   L. 6 M. 8 N. 9 P. 10 Q. 11

The Nonverbal battery includes three subtests:

1. Figure Analogies

    Decide how the first two figures are related to each other. Then find the one
    figure at the right that goes with the third figure in the same way that the
    second figure goes with the first.

2. Figure Classification

    The first three figures are alike in some way. Find the figure at the right that
    goes with the first three.

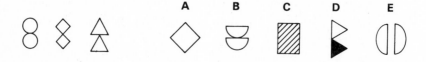

3. Figure Synthesis

For each shaded area, decide whether or not it can be completely covered by using all the given black pieces without overlapping any.

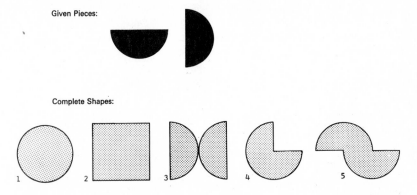

Given Pieces:

Complete Shapes:

1   2   3   4   5

Validity   Evidence for the validity of the CAT is of three types—content, criterion-related, and construct. Content validity is assumed on the basis that the tests measure abstract abilities expressed in verbal, quantitative, and pictorial and figural symbols requiring their interpretation and use.

Criterion-related validity is based on correlations between scores on CAT and (1) scores on achievement tests and (2) teachers' marks in reading and in arithmetic. Achievement tests were the *Iowa Tests of Basic Skills*, grades 3–8, and the *Tests of Academic Progress*, grades 9–12. Typical correlations with CAT Verbal are in the range of .80 to .85; with CAT Quantitative, they range from .70 to .80; with CAT Nonverbal, from .65 to .70. Correlations with teachers' marks in reading range from .40 to .70. In arithmetic the values vary between .45 to .65. As might be expected, the highest correlations with reading are with the Verbal battery; similarly, the highest correlations with marks in arithmetic are with the Quantitative battery, although the correlation of Verbal with arithmetic in grade 3 is equally high. Finally, correlations between CAT and grade-point average in grade 9 are .52 for Nonverbal, .55 for Verbal, and .59 for Quantitative. The correlation between total scores on CAT and grade-point average is .64. These correlations are based on 173 cases.

Three types of evidence for construct validity are suggested. The first is the substantial correlations between scores on CAT and school achievement. According to the manual, these correlations support the assumption that the tests "are relevant to the construct 'effective cognitive functioning'." The second type of evidence is correlation with generally accepted measures of intellect—in this case, the Stanford-Binet and several tests of the *Differential Aptitude Test Battery.* With the Binet, the Verbal test correlates in the .70s, the Quantitative in the higher .60s, and the Nonverbal in the .60s. Correlations between Verbal Reasoning, Numerical Ability, and Abstract Reasoning of the DAT and Verbal of the CAT are .74, .54, and .59, respectively; with Quantitative, they are .55, .70, and .59; with Nonverbal, they are .54, .65, and .65. A fourth test of the DAT, Space Relations, correlates .40, .45, and .61 with the three batteries of the CAT.

The third type of evidence for construct validity of the CAT results from factor analysis. In the case of the Primary batteries, the authors state that "of the total variance accounted for, some 83 percent is attributable to the general factor." With the multilevel battery, the manual states that the analysis showed evidence of a substantial loading on a general factor for each of the subtests.

It may also be mentioned in connection with the discussion of validity that items of the CAT were tried out in grades 4, 6, 8, 10, and 12 and were chosen on the basis of percent passing and amount of correlation of an item with the total score on the set of items in which that item appeared. Further item analysis was carried out to determine median difficulties and the semi-interquartile range of difficulties at each grade level for each subtest.

Reliability   Reliability estimates for the CAT are based on split-halves and Kuder-Richardson formulas. Coefficients were found for every subtest of each battery. They range from a low of .890 for Primary I in grade 1 to a high of .957 for the Verbal battery in grade 3. For the multilevel, all coefficients are above .90 with an average of about .93. When corrected for speeding, the average is about .02 lower. The lowest is .874 for the Quantitative in grade 3. Standard errors of measurement are based on raw scores converted to standard-score equivalents. For the Verbal battery, the values range from 3.16 to 3.50 standard age score units; for the Quantitative battery, from 4.55 to 4.82; for the Nonverbal battery, from 3.74 to 4.84.

Administration   As mentioned earlier, the overlapping feature of the multimental batteries makes it possible to administer the level of the scale deemed appropriate, regardless of grade level of the group being tested. The working time for the Verbal battery is 34 minutes; for the Quantitative battery, 32 minutes; for the Nonverbal battery, 32 minutes. The tests of the CAT are claimed, however, to be primarily power tests. All subtests are preceded by practice exercises. Directions for administering are clear and complete.

With the Primary tests it appears likely that almost as much time will be required for reading directions and for explanations as for actual work. The examiner will wish to allow ample time for testing and for rest periods between tests and even between parts of the tests, especially at kindergarten and grade-1 levels. In the multilevel there may be the possibility of confusion in the matter of starting and stopping at the proper points of the overlapping sets of items.

Scores and Scoring Types of scores provided on list reports include raw scores, grade percentile ranks, stanines, standard age scores, class averages, building averages, and system averages by grade. All tests may be scored by hand or electronically. MRC answer sheets may also be used.

Norms and Norming A base sample of approximately 20,000 cases (0.6 percent of the total school population) in each grade was drawn. Seven community sizes from one million or more to rural were included in this sample. Communities were chosen further on the basis of median educational level of adults over 25 and median family income. Scores were converted to a standard-score scale using level D as an anchor with a mean of 125 and a standard deviation of 20. These are called *universal scale scores* (USSs). The USSs are further converted to standard age scores with a mean of 100 and a standard deviation of 16. These may presumably be intended to yield values comparable to Stanford IQs, though not so designated. Norms for each grade are expressed in percentiles corresponding to USSs, which in turn are converted by use of tables to standard age scores.

Manuals There are four manuals for the CAT, one each for Primary I and Primary II, one for Levels A–H, and a technical manual for the series. The first three include the usual materials and instructions—directions for administering, scoring, and interpreting; norms; using test results; and the like. The technical manual describes in detail the construction of the tests; the establishing of norms; statistical data on validity, reliability, and correlations among batteries and subtests; and related matters. All manuals are clear and complete.

Summary The *Cognitive Abilities Test* is clearly one of the best measures of intelligence available for use in grades K through 12. The school administrator or other person in charge of a testing program may quite rightly wish that there were more than one form of this series of tests. There are many instances in which an alternate form would be useful. Nevertheless, the CAT ranks high among tests of its type with respect to item construction and selection, validity, reliability, norming, and other criteria of good test construction.

COOPERATIVE SCHOOL AND COLLEGE ABILITY TESTS, SERIES II The next group test to be described represents a quite different approach from that used in the *Cognitive Abilities Test*. Although designed basically for the same purposes, this next test uses fewer types of items. It is also simpler in organization and simpler to administer and score.

Nature and Purposes The *Cooperative School and College Ability Tests* (SCAT) are intended to be a measure of academic aptitude for the purpose of predicting success in school or college.[31] They purport to be measures of "developed abilities rather than abstract psychological traits." This would seem to imply a distinction between SCAT and other group tests of similar nature and purpose, but the difference is not obvious. The Series II tests are a revision of the original SCAT series published in 1955–1956.

Grade Levels and Forms   Grades 3 through 14; Level 1, 13–14; Level 2, 9–12; Level 3, 6–9; Level 4, 3–6. Forms A and B. Form C, one level only, for college and university.

Content   The content of all levels is of the same nature. There are two types of items.[32] Verbal Ability consists of fifty analogy items:

> Tinkle : bells : :
> A.   whistle : tunes
> B.   glide : snakes
> C.   rustle : leaves
> D.   wrinkle : fabrics

These items are unusual in form in that the task involves the choice of a pair of words rather than only one word. Quantitative Ability consists of fifty quantitative comparisons:

> A.   if the part in Column A is greater
> B.   if the part in Column B is greater
> C.   if the two parts are equal
> D.   if not enough information is given for you to decide

Column A	Column B
Value of 1 nickel	Value of 1 dime

The items at the various levels differ in difficulty. Items at the lowest level do not include the D option. The tests yield three scores—Verbal, Quantitative, and Total.

Validity   Evidence for validity is statistical in nature. Average correlations between SCAT Series II scores and teachers' grades in English, grades in mathematics, and grade-point average were determined in grades 5, 8, 11, and 12 in some 150 schools. In grade 5 these range from .54 to .69; in grade 8 they range from .52 to .61; in grade 11, from .50 to .65; and in grade 12, from .41 to .59, with most in the .40s.

Correlations of scores on SCAT Series II, Forms 1A and 1B (formerly the *Cooperative Academic Ability Test*) with rank in graduating class were .52 for Verbal, .51 for Quantitative, and .56 for Total scores. Corre-

[31]*Cooperative School and College Ability Tests, SCAT Series II* (Princeton, N.J.: Educational Testing Service, 1966, 1967).

[32]Two sample items are reproduced below. From *Cooperative School and College Ability Tests—Series II*© 1966, 1967 by Educational Testing Service. All rights reserved. Reproduced by permission.

lations between scores on the same forms of SCAT and on the *Scholastic Aptitude Test* of the College Entrance Examination Board were found to be .83 and .86 for Verbal and Quantitative sections, respectively.

Reliability   All reliability data are based upon Kuder-Richardson 20 and are therefore measures of internal consistency. Reliability coefficients are based on Form A only. For Verbal scores they range between .87 and .91; for Quantitative scores they lie between .90 and .92; for Total scores the coefficients are .94 for each of the four levels. Standard errors of measurement for Verbal and for Quantitative scores are typically in the range of 2.75–3.00 points of raw score. For total scores they average slightly more than 4 raw score points.

Administration   Each of the two subtests of SCAT is timed at 20 minutes. Total time for administering would be about 50 minutes. Directions for administering are clear and complete.

Scores and Scoring   All forms and levels require the use of separate answer sheets. These may be IBM 805, IBM 1230, Digitek, or SCRIBE (the ETS special scoring service). IBM and Digitek answer sheets may be scored by hand or machine. SCRIBE can be scored only by ETS. Since only one side of an answer sheet is used for any level or form, scoring is rapid and easy. Three scores—Verbal, Quantitative, and Total—are obtained for each student. Raw scores are changed to *converted scores,* a type of standard score. These in turn are converted to percentile ranks. Comparisons of a student's score with that of other students at the same level or adjacent levels may be made by use of the converted score scale. Percentile ranks are interpreted in terms of percentile bands, which represent confidence levels having a range of two standard errors, one on either side of a student's obtained score.

Norms and Norming   The normative population for these tests was chosen with great care. SCAT Series II was administered in October 1966 to groups of approximately thirty students in a minimum of 100 schools in each grade from 4 through 12. These schools were chosen by a rather involved process to yield a sample that would be representative of the total school population of the country in these grades. However, no school system, public or private, enrolling fewer than 300 pupils was included. A total of 950 schools, representing every state, participated in the testing.

The Manual   There is a comprehensive manual called the *Handbook* (1973), which contains a description of the test and directions for administering and scoring it and for interpreting scores. It also contains tables of norms, a brief discussion of the development of the test, and details of norming it. In addition, the handbook contains an abundance of technical data on equating the forms, scaling, validity, reliability, and other matters. There is also a separate, single sheet of directions for administering and a unique "student bulletin." The latter, a single page, tells prospective takers of the test what its purpose is and gives examples with answers of verbal and mathematical items similar to those in the test. This is obviously intended to allay anxiety and reduce tension.

Format In quality of materials, printing, and attractiveness of format, the SCAT series is of the highest order. The use of color on the covers of all booklets adds to their appeal.

Summary In quality of workmanship, attention to detail, simplicity of administration, and interpretation of scores, the SCAT Series II sets high standards. More recent norms, apparently not now available, would be very desirable.

DAVIS-EELLS TEST OF GENERAL INTELLIGENCE The *Davis-Eells Test of General Intelligence* is an example of an attempt to construct a test that is culture-fair. The procedure of trying out items and eliminating those that show consistent differences in response (in this case, less successful choices by children with lower socioeconomic and cultural backgrounds) was used in producing the final forms. Although acceptance and use of the test in schools was insufficient to keep it on the market, it is described here as a prototype of the culture-fair test and an interesting example of its kind.[33]

Nature and Purpose The test is said to consist of realistic problems in the experience of all urban children and is entirely pictorial except for directions read aloud by the administrator of the test.

Grade Levels and Forms Primary, grades 1 and 2; Elementary, grades 3 through 6. One form.

Content One part is called Best Ways problems. In each problem, three pictures are presented. Each picture shows a person or group of persons starting to solve a problem in a different way. The task is to find the picture that shows the best way of solving the problem. For example:

[33]Three sample test items appear in the description of the *Davis-Eells Test of General Intelligence* that follows. Reproduced by permission. Copyright 1953 by Harcourt Brace Jovanovich, Inc., New York, NY. All rights reserved.

Another type of problem is called Analogies. This consists of pictorial situations like the accompanying example. In each case the relationship between the first pair is made clear or suggested by the examiner before the child finds the answer.

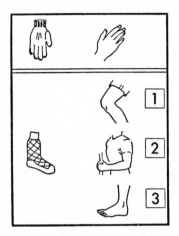

A third type of problem is called Probabilities. In each case a picture shows a situation, which is followed by three possible explanations. The task is to select the most likely explanation.

No. 1   The man *fell down* and hit his head.

No. 2   A ball *came through the window* and hit the man's head.

No. 3   The picture *does not show how* the man got the bump on his head. Nobody can tell because the picture doesn't show how the man got the bump.

Which number was true?

Validity   The content of the test is said to be independent of reading skill, in-school instruction, or speed of response. The test purports to be a measure of "over-all capacity to solve mental problems" and not a scholastic aptitude test. These problems are chosen as being of a kind encountered by most children. Correlations of the Davis-Eells test with the *Otis Quick-Scoring Mental Ability Tests* range from .39 to .66, with a median of .52. Correlations with scores on standardized achievement tests in reading, arithmetic, language, and spelling are in the neighborhood of .40.

Reliability   Split-halves reliability coefficients corrected by use of the Spearman-Brown Formula average about .83 in grades 2 through 6; for grade 1 this coefficient is .68. The standard error of measurement of a score ranges from 2.5 to 3.5. Test-retest coefficients with an interval of two weeks were approximately .70 in grade 2 and .90 in grade 4.

Administration   Directions for administering are very detailed and complete. Administration is comparatively complicated and time-consuming. Actual working time for grade 1 is two 30-minute periods; for grade 2, three 30-minute periods; for Elementary, two 60-minute periods.

Scores and Scoring   Scoring is quite simple. All items are of the three-response type, the pupil marking the number of the choice that seems best. No separate answer sheets are provided, though they could be used, at least at the upper grade levels. The score is the number right. Printed scoring keys are provided. The raw score is converted to an IPSA (Index of Problem Solving Ability) by use of tables. The IPSA is based on a normalized distribution with a mean of 100 and a standard deviation of 16. The authors state that this Index of Problem Solving Ability may also be called an IQ.

Norms and Norming   Means, medians, and standard deviations of raw scores are given for age groups by three-month intervals from 6-0 to 8-5 in grade 1; from 7-0 to 9-5 in grade 2; from 8-0 to 13-11 in grades 3 to 6.

The Manual   The tests are accompanied by directions for administering, which include directions for scoring, tables for converting raw score to an Index of Problem Solving Ability, and percentile equivalents. Information concerning development of the test, validity, reliability, and other statistical data is available in a separate manual.

Format   The tests are well arranged and well printed. Figures are large and spacing is generous.

Summary   The Davis-Eells test has been the subject of a substantial number of research studies correlating scores on it with scores on conventional intelligence tests and standardized achievement tests, with teachers' marks, and with various indexes of socioeconomic status. In general, it seems fair to state that results of such studies have failed to justify or recommend its use in place of more conventional group tests of intelligence.[34]

THE CULTURE FAIR INTELLIGENCE TESTS Cattell's *Culture Fair Intelligence Tests* represent another approach to the development of a measure free of cultural bias. Some sample items are shown below.[35]

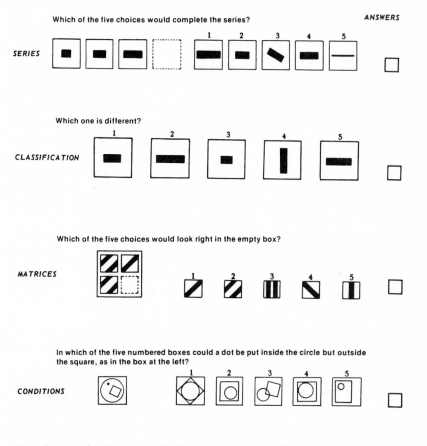

[34]See, for example, Victor H. Noll, "Relation of Scores on Davis-Eells Games to Socio-Economic Status, Intelligence Test Results, and School Achievement," *Educational and Psychological Measurement*, 20 (Spring 1960), 119–129.
[35]© 1949, 1957, Institute for Personality and Ability Testing, Champaign, Illinois. Reproduced by permission of the copyright owner.

Series items require selection of the choice that completes the series. Classification requires finding the choice that does not belong. In Matrices, the task is to find the choice that correctly completes the pattern. In Conditions, a dot must be placed in one of the choices that meets the same conditions as in the square.

Three levels of the CFIT are available for years 4–8, 8–13, and 10–16. These are stated to be appropriate also for mentally retarded, average adult, and superior adult, respectively. The tests are perceptual in requiring no reading and are claimed to be highly saturated with Spearman's g.

A number of studies have been reported showing that underprivileged children, both whites and blacks, make slightly higher scores on the CFIT than on the Binet and the *California Test of Mental Maturity*.[36] The differences between mean IQs were 1.9 and 2.5, respectively. These findings are interpreted as showing the superior culture fairness of the CFIT. The tests have been given in a number of foreign countries (Germany, Pakistan, Finland, Mexico, Canada, and the United Kingdom). On the whole, the results cannot be said to provide unequivocal evidence of the superiority of the CFIT over conventional tests of intelligence. The tests show substantial correlations with other intelligence tests: Correlations with Otis, Pintner, WISC, and Metropolitan and California achievement test scores are typically in the .50s and .60s. Correlations with teachers' marks are, on average, generally in the .40s. Most of the studies mentioned above used children in upper elementary grades as subjects and, presumably, Scale 2 of the CFIT.

As is generally true of similar tests, such as the Davis-Eells Games, the CFIT have not convinced specialists in measurement or those in charge of testing programs of their superiority over the more conventional tests of intelligence as predictive instruments or as being less culturally biased. On the basis of available evidence, they must still be regarded as essentially experimental in nature.

OTHER GROUP INTELLIGENCE TESTS Following is a listing of some other group intelligence tests that merit the reader's inspection.

Academic Promise Tests. Forms A and B. Grades 6–9. Verbal, numerical, abstract reasoning, language usage. (New York Psychological Corp., 1959), 90 minutes.

---

[36]See, for example, Keith Barton, *Recent Data on the Culture Fair Scales*, Information Bulletin 16 (Champaign, Ill.: Institute for Personality and Ability Testing, 1973).

Army General Classification Test. One form. Grades 9–12 and adults. Vocabulary, arithmetic, and block counting (spatial). (Chicago: Science Research Associates, 1948), 40 minutes.

Boehm Test of Basic Concepts. One form. K–2. Fifty concepts basic to understanding oral communications. (New York: Psychological Corp., 1971), 30 minutes.

California Test of Mental Maturity, revised. K–adult. Short form: opposites, similarities, analogies, numerical values, number problems, verbal comprehension, memory (delayed recall). Long form: rights and lefts, manipulation of areas, number series, inferences, and immediate recall added. (Monterey, Calif.: California Test Bureau/McGraw-Hill, 1963), short form about 50 minutes; long form about 1–1½ hours.

College Qualification Tests. Form A; Forms B and C restricted to colleges and universities. Grades 11–13. Verbal, numerical, information, total. (New York: Psychological Corp., 1955–1961), 80 minutes.

Henmon-Nelson Tests of Mental Ability, rev. ed. Forms A and B. Grades K–2, 3–6, 6–9, 9–12, college. Synonyms, analogies, number sequence, arithmetic. (Boston: Houghton Mifflin, 1931–1973), 30 minutes.

Kuhlmann-Anderson Measure of Academic Potential, 7th ed. One form (K–4, 4–12) K, grades 1, 2, 3–4, 4–5, 5–7, 7–9, 9–12. Verbal and quantitative. (Lexington, Mass.: Personnel Press, 1967), 50–60 minutes.

Kuhlmann-Finch Scholastic Aptitude Tests. One form. Grades 1, 2, 3, 4, 5, 6, 7–9, 10–12. Verbal and nonverbal materials. (Circle Pines, Minn.: American Guidance Service, 1956–1957), 45 minutes.

Ohio State University Psychological Test. Forms 21 and 23. Grades 9–12, 16 and adults. Vocabulary, word relationships, reading comprehension. (Ames, Iowa: Wilber L. Layton, 1968), 2 hours.

Otis-Lennon Mental Ability Test. Forms J and K. Grades K–12. Pictorial items, verbal material. Primary I, K; Primary II, grade 1; Elementary I, grades 1–3; Elementary II, grades 4–6; Intermediate, grades 7–9; Advanced, grades 10–12. (New York: Psychological Corp., 1967), 30–40 minutes.

Otis Quick-Scoring Mental Ability Tests, Forms A, B of Alpha; Em and Fm of Beta; Em and Fm of Gamma. Alpha, grades 1–4; Beta, grades 4–9; Gamma, high school and college. Alpha consists of pictorial items, Beta and Gamma of verbal material. Accessories at additional cost. (New York: Psychological Corp., 1954), Alpha, 40 minutes; Beta, Gamma, 30 minutes.

S.R.A. Tests of Educational Ability. One form. Grades K, 1, 2–3, 3–6, 6–9, 9–12. Language, reasoning, quantitative. (Chicago: Science Research Associates, 1966–1972), 26–42 minutes.

LEARNING EXERCISES

12. If you were responsible for choosing a group intelligence test for use with the fifth and sixth grades, how would you proceed? Decide the steps involved and justify each one.

13. Intelligence tests frequently include tests of vocabulary (same-opposites, word meaning, and the like) and numerical problems. How do you account for this?

14. Why is an individual examination like the Binet generally regarded as more accurate and dependable than a group test?

15. Compare two of the group tests of intelligence described above. What are their comparative merits?

SUGGESTED READING

ANASTASI, ANNE. *Psychological Testing.* 4th ed. New York: Macmillan, 1976. Chap. 9–12. Chapter 9 deals with the Stanford-Binet and the Wechsler scales. Chapter 10 discusses tests for special populations, infants and preschoolers, the physically handicapped, and the disadvantaged. Group testing is treated in Chapter 11, and psychological issues are examined in Chapter 12.

CRONBACH, LEE J. *Essentials of Psychological Testing.* 3d ed. New York: Harper & Row, 1970. Chap. 7–9. Chapter 7 describes commonly used methods of appraising general mental ability and gives some illustrations of them. Chapter 8 deals with problems of constancy of performance, interpretation of test results, and testing of infants and young children. Chapter 9 describes representative group tests and discusses validity of mental ability tests and the question of tests and cultural differences.

GRONLUND, NORMAN E. *Measurement and Evaluation of Teaching.* 3d ed. New York: Macmillan, 1976. Chap. 13. Group tests are described and illustrated. Treatment of individual tests includes the Stanford-Binet and the Wechsler scales. Discussion includes testing the culturally deprived, differential aptitude testing, and testing in special areas such as art and music.

MEHRENS, WILLIAM A. and IRVIN J. LEHMANN. *Measurement and Evaluation in Education and Psychology.* 2d ed. New York: Holt, Rinehart and Winston, 1978. Chap. 14. A general discussion of aptitude tests including consideration of theories of intelligence and issues in its measurement, individual and group tests, multifactor aptitude tests, and tests of special aptitudes.

MURPHY, GARDNER. *An Historical Introduction to Modern Psychology.* New York: Harcourt Brace Jovanovich, 1929. Chap. 21. A basic textbook on the history of modern psychology from the seventeenth century. Presents considerable background material on the development of modern intelligence tests and brief accounts of the work of Binet and other pioneers in this movement.

PETERSON, JOSEPH. *Early Conceptions and Tests of Intelligence.* New York: Harcourt Brace Jovanovich, 1925. The definitive book on the history of modern intelligence tests up to the end of World War I. Especially valuable reference on the development of Binet's scales and their successors.

TERMAN, LEWIS M., and MAUD A. MERRILL. *Stanford-Binet Intelligence Scale.* Boston: Houghton Mifflin, 1960. Describes in detail the work of developing the third revision, Form L-M. Also includes the complete scale with directions for administering and scoring and tables of deviation IQs.

THORNDIKE, ROBERT L., and ELIZABETH HAGEN. *Measurement and Evaluation in Psychology and Education.* 4th ed. New York: John Wiley & Sons, 1977. Chap. 10. Briefly describes the *Lorge-Thorndike Intelligence Test* as an example of current group tests, some individual tests, and some culture-fair tests. Discusses current issues and use of tests in schools.

WRIGHT, LOGAN. *Bibliography of Human Intelligence.* Washington, D.C.: U.S. Government Printing Office, 1968. The most extensive bibliography of studies and reports in the field. Lists nearly 7,000 titles classified by topical areas, historical antecedents and related concepts, theoretical works, the nature of intelligence, and group intelligence tests. An invaluable source for the serious student or researcher.

Ten

THE MEASUREMENT OF CAPACITY:

SPECIAL APTITUDES

In the preceding chapter we considered tests of general intelligence, which have shown their greatest usefulness as predictors of success in school and college, particularly in academic courses. There is another type of test, also used primarily for prediction, referred to as *aptitude tests*. These differ from general intelligence tests in that their usual purpose is to predict success in a more restricted area such as mechanical, clerical, or artistic pursuits. Aptitude tests differ from achievement tests also in that they are designed to measure potential or promise. They do not presuppose training in a particular field but purport to measure an individual's capacity to profit by instruction in that field.

After studying this chapter and working through the Learning Exercises, you should be able to answer questions and carry out assignments such as the following:

1. Distinguish between types of tests discussed in this chapter and those discussed in Chapter 9. What are the essential differences between them with respect to purposes, methods of construction and validation, and uses?
2. What criteria would you use in selecting an aptitude test for use as a measure of potential in a particular area?
3. How do multi-aptitude batteries differ from other types of aptitude tests? What are their advantages? their limitations?
4. Distinguish between *convergent thinking* and *divergent thinking*. In what area are these concepts considered to be relevant and valid? Explain.

5. Special aptitude tests have been developed in many areas of work. (See Buros's *Seventh Mental Measurements Yearbook.*) Why have they apparently not been used as much as other types of tests (for example, tests of general mental ability)?
6. Are there areas in which aptitude tests are very much needed today? Justify your answer.

THE TESTING OF POTENTIAL IN SPECIAL FIELDS

Specific aptitude tests are often designed to measure specific skills or knowledge essential to successful performance. Thus, a mechanical aptitude test may include such tasks as assembling a dismantled object like an electric bell, and a test of clerical aptitude may measure skill in locating numbers or alphabetizing. Tasks or skills of this nature are often referred to as *work samples.* Such skills may be based on job analyses that identify the specifics of successful performance in a given occupation or field. If a test is to screen applicants for a certain type of work, let us say that of an electrician, a detailed analysis of the job of an electrician may be made. On the basis of this analysis are determined the specific skills required of a successful electrician. Then a test is constructed to measure one or more of these abilities objectively and accurately. Job analysis is one widely used approach to planning and developing aptitude tests in special fields.

Another method used in constructing aptitude tests is based upon a theoretical, possibly more or less "armchair," attack. In this case an attempt is made to spell out basic qualities or abilities considered to underlie all successful, effective performance in a particular field. This approach is illustrated by aptitude tests in such fields as art and music. As we shall see when we examine prototypes of these tests, they purport to measure abilities of a fundamental nature—as, for example, tests of art aptitude attempt to measure a feeling for line, color, balance, and the like in a work of art or in producing the basis for a drawing, painting, or sculpture. Similarly, tests of musical aptitude commonly include measures of pitch discrimination, tonality, and rhythm. As we mentioned earlier, such tests do not presuppose previous training in the field, though it is generally agreed that scores on them are influenced by training.

One other approach is to test knowledge in a particular field. This assumes that interest in and aptitude for a particular type of work will cause the possessor of these qualities to read widely in the field of such work, to experiment and work with the "tools of the trade," and thus to accumulate a fund of information that can readily be tested. The amount, depth, and accuracy of knowledge possessed is believed to reflect interest and aptitude. Many illustrations can be cited. The child who likes to cook or sew and the child who enjoys tinkering with an old jalopy or an old radio will naturally accumulate information about these matters that indirectly reveals an interest and possibly an aptitude for cooking, sewing, auto mechanics, or radio, as the case may be. This point of view suggests the use of tests of knowledge in a particular field as elements of aptitude tests. And we often do find tests of knowledge included in aptitude tests, as we shall see shortly.

Finally, there are the aptitude test batteries or multi-aptitude tests, a number of which are now available. These tests are designed in some instances primarily to predict success in specific school subjects; others are for the purpose of predicting success in a number of different occupations. An example of the former will be described in detail later in this chapter. The *General Aptitude Test Battery* of the U.S. Employment Service is widely used to assist in fitting applicants for employment into types of training or work that they seem to have some aptitude for. This is, of course, a very large and difficult task, since there are so many different occupations to be considered.

The aptitude test batteries are based for the most part on factor analysis, the purpose being to construct a battery of a manageable number of subtests that will, in various combinations, be optimally predictive of success in many different occupations. This constitutes a continuing and never-ending task as new occupations are studied and as additional data accumulate from the use of the tests in the battery.

All the approaches to testing aptitude that have been briefly discussed will be found illustrated in one or another of the tests to be described. There are many aptitude tests in many different fields, but we shall confine our descriptions to a few areas in which the most work has been done and that, in general, are of greatest interest and value to teachers and counselors.

LEARNING EXERCISES

1. The terms *ability* and *aptitude* are sometimes used interchangeably. Defend or criticize this practice. (The article by Nelson in the *Encyclopedia of Educational Research* cited in the bibliography at the end of this chapter is pertinent.)

2. Compare and contrast tests of readiness, intelligence, and aptitude with respect to purposes, content, and methods of validation.

SPECIFIC TESTS
OF SPECIAL APTITUDES

One of the first specialized fields for which aptitude tests were developed is mechanical abilities. The reasons are not hard to find. Many occupations require mechanical ability, and they engage large numbers of persons in work with machines, mechanical toys, electrical equipment, and tools, including small, delicate work such as assembly of intricate parts of machinery. It is not surprising, therefore, to find some of the earliest work in the measurement of special aptitudes in this area. Some of the first tests developed, like the *Stenquist Mechanical Aptitude Test*, published in 1921, and the *MacQuarrie Test for Mechanical Ability*, published in 1925, are no longer available. However, work in this field has continued, although no new tests have appeared recently.

Mechanical Aptitude

THE MINNESOTA PAPER FORM BOARD Many of the older tests of mechanical aptitude included tasks of disassembling and assembling small pieces of equipment, such as an electric bell, as well as paper-and-pencil problems. The mechanical operations had the disadvantage of requiring individual testing. More recent tests have tended to concentrate largely on paper-and-pencil devices. The one described here, the *Minnesota Paper Form Board*,[1] is a paper-and-pencil test measuring spatial perception as indicated by the ability to visualize assembly of two-dimensional shapes into a whole design. (See the accompanying sample item, next page.)[2]

This test is part of a battery of mechanical ability tests developed at the University of Minnesota in the late 1920s. There has probably been more study and research of the Paper Form Board than of any other test ever developed in this field. Consisting of sixty-four items of the type illustrated, it is simple to administer and takes only 20 minutes of actual working time. Reliability of a single form is reported to be .85; of both forms together, .92.

[1] *Minnesota Paper Form Board, Revised;* Forms AA, BB (hand scored) or MA, MB (machine scored), grade 9–adult. (New York: Psychological Corp., 1930–1948).
[2] Reproduced by permission. Copyright 1941, renewed 1969, by The Psychological Corporation, New York, NY. All rights reserved.

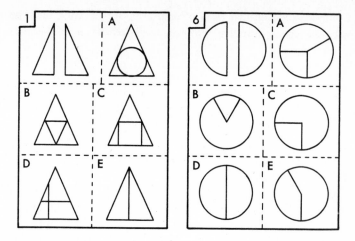

The test has been validated by correlating scores on it with ratings of performance in shop courses, mechanical drawing, descriptive geometry, and machine drafting. Scores of engineering students have been compared with scores of nonengineers. The test has also been given to students in dentistry and to workers in other mechanical pursuits.

Although the correlations between scores on the *Minnesota Paper Form Board* and ratings, grades in courses, production records of workers, and scores of criterion groups are not uniformly high or discriminatory, the mass of evidence accumulated about the test is generally quite favorable. It appears to be one of the best tests of a paper-and-pencil type yet devised for predicting success in a wide variety of fields of work that require more or less mechanical ability. It is, of course, particularly useful for counselors and guidance workers in helping students achieve a better appraisal of their fitness for certain occupations.

LEARNING EXERCISE

3. How do you account for the fact that paper-and-pencil tests of spatial relations seem to correlate at least as well with criteria of mechanical performance as do tests requiring the manipulation of objects or gadgets?

OTHER TESTS OF MECHANICAL APTITUDE Following is a listing of some additional tests of mechanical aptitude that merit the reader's inspection.

Bennett Hand-Tool Dexterity Test. One form. Adolescents and adults. Proficiency in use of wrenches and screwdrivers. (New York: Psychological Corp., 1946–1965), 4–12 minutes.

Bennett Mechanical Comprehension Test. Forms AA, BB, W1; Spanish forms available. Adolescents and adults. Mechanical relationships and physical laws in practical situations. Answer sheets and tape-recorded instructions at additional cost. (New York: Psychological Corp., 1940–1970), 30 minutes.

Crawford Small Parts Dexterity Test. One form. Adolescents and adults. Dexterity in use of tweezers and screwdrivers. (New York: Psychological Corp. 1946–1956), 9–25 minutes.

Detroit Mechanical Aptitudes Examination. One form. Grades 7–16. Tool recognition, motor speed, size discrimination, arithmetic fundamentals, disarranged pictures, tool information, direction and speed of pulley and belt movements, and digit-letter substitution. (Indianapolis: Bobbs-Merrill, 1939), 30 minutes.

MacQuarrie Test for Mechanical Ability. One form. Grades 7–adult. Tracing, tapping, dotting, copying, location, blocks, and pursuit. (Monterey, Calif.: California Test Bureau/McGraw-Hill, 1953), 20 minutes.

Mellenbruch Mechanical Motivation Test. Forms A and B. Grades 6–adult. Matching pairs of objects in pictures. (Munster, Ind.: Psychometric Affiliates, 1956–1957), 40 minutes.

Purdue Mechanical Performance Test. One form. Ages 15–adult. Transfer boards, spatial relations, hub assemblies. (Lafayette, Ind.: Lafayette Instrument Co., 1957), 20 minutes.

SRA Mechanical Aptitudes. One form. 1947. High school and adults. Tool identification, space visualization, and shop arithmetic. (Chicago: Science Research Associates, 1947–1950), 40 minutes.

Clerical Aptitude

When we talk of tests of clerical aptitude, we refer to tests in the commercial and business field. There are aptitude tests for general office work, typewriting, bookkeeping, and shorthand. Although extensive work has been done in the testing of these aptitudes, the tests so far developed have not been outstandingly successful as predictive measures, and they have not been widely used by teachers, employers, or counselors.

THE DETROIT CLERICAL APTITUDES EXAMINATION The *Detroit Clerical Aptitudes Examination* consists of eight parts.[3] Part 1 is a test of rate and quality of handwriting and involves the copying of a short selection. Part 2 consists of a comparison between two sets of numbers to determine whether they are the same or different (as, 2 7 3—2 7 5). Part 3 contains arithmetic problems. Part 4 is a test of manual dexterity and requires the student to perform such tasks as drawing crosses in circles as rapidly as possible without touching the circles. Part 5 tests miscellaneous knowledge related to office and business. Part 6 is a series of pictures, each presented in several sections or parts of the whole; the task is to indicate their proper order or sequence. Part 7 is a substitution test in which letters are numbered according to a key that is constantly changing. Part 8 is a test of alphabetization.

Each part of the *Detroit Clerical Aptitudes Examination* is timed separately. The test is designed for use with pupils at the intermediate and junior high school grade levels to identify those who will probably succeed in commercial courses in high school. The reliability, test-retest, is .85. The correlation between scores on the test and scholarship in bookkeeping is .563; between test scores and scholarship in shorthand, .366; between test scores and scholarship in typewriting, .317. The *Detroit Clerical Aptitudes Examination* is available in one form only. The handwriting scale used in Test 1 must be ordered separately.

OTHER TESTS OF COMMERCIAL AND BUSINESS APTITUDE Following is a listing of additional tests of commercial and business aptitude.

Bennett Stenographic Aptitude Test. One form. High school and college. Substitution of numbers for symbols and symbols for numbers and spelling. (New York: Psychological Corp., 1939), 25 minutes.

ERC Stenographic Aptitude Test. One form. Grades 9–10. Word discrimination, phonetic spelling, vocabulary, sentence dictation, and speed of writing. (Chicago: Science Research Associates, 1944), 33 minutes.

General Clerical Test. One form. High school and above. Clerical speed and accuracy, numerical ability, verbal facility. (New York: Psychological Corp., 1950), 43 minutes.

Minnesota Clerical Test. One form. Grades 8–12 and adults. Speed and accuracy in checking numbers and names. (New York: Psychological Corp., 1933–1959), 15 minutes.

---

[3] Harry J. Baker and Paul F. Voelker, *Detroit Clerical Aptitudes Examination, Revised* (Indianapolis: Bobbs-Merrill, 1944).

Personnel Research Institute Clerical Battery. Form A of 1–3; Forms A and B of 4–8. Adults. (1) classification, (2) number comparison, (3) name comparison, (4) tabulation, (5) filing, (6) alphabetizing, (7) arithmetic reasoning, (8) spelling. (Cleveland: Personnel Research Institute, 1945–1947), 100 minutes, including time for directions.

Purdue Clerical Adaptability Test. 1949–56. One form. Applicants for clerical positions. Spelling, computation, checking, word meaning, copying, reasoning. (Lafayette, Ind.: Purdue University Bookstore, 1949–1956), 60 minutes.

Short Employment Tests. Forms 1, 2, 3, 4 (1 is restricted). Adults. Vocabulary, arithmetic computation, clerical skill. (New York: Psychological Corp., 1951), 15 minutes.

Short Tests of Clerical Ability. One form. Applicants for office positions. Coding, checking, filing, directions—oral and written, arithmetic, business vocabulary, language. (Chicago: Science Research Associates, 1959–1960), 35–70 minutes.

THE SEASHORE MEASURES OF MUSICAL TALENTS Various tests of musical aptitude have been devised, though the total number of such tests is not large. Probably the best known is the Seashore,[4] which consists of tests of pitch, loudness, rhythm, time, timbre, and tonal memory, all on one phonograph record or tape. The tests are as follows: Pitch (the higher of two tones), Loudness (the louder of two tones), Rhythm (comparison of two rhythmic patterns), Time (the longer of two sounds), Timbre (comparison of tonal quality to decide whether two tones are the same or different), and Tonal Memory (comparison of two short musical figures differing in one note, to indicate by number which note is different). The tests are said to be applicable from the fourth grade up, but they seem to work best with older subjects. Reliabilities range from .62 to .88 with an average of about .80. The tests require about 1 hour to administer and may be given to individuals or groups. They show little relationship to differences in amount of musical training at advanced levels, but when administered in combination with an intelligence test, the Seashore shows a definite relationship to success in advanced musical study.

Many musical aptitude tests are largely paper-and-pencil tests that measure knowledge and understanding of musical terms and symbols, though a few include tests of some of the types of performance that are measured by the Seashore.

Musical Aptitude

---

[4] Carl E. Seashore, et al., *Seashore Measures of Musical Talents* (New York: Psychological Corp., 1919–1960). Available on one LP record or tape.

OTHER TESTS OF MUSICAL APTITUDE   Three additional tests of musical aptitude that merit inspection are the following:

Aliferis Music Achievement Test. One form. Grades 13–15. Matching
   melodies, harmonies, or rhythms with musical notations. Piano or tape
   recording necessary. (Minneapolis: University of Minnesota Press,
   1954).

Iowa Tests of Music Literacy. Form IA. Grades 4–12 and 7–12. (Iowa
   City: Bureau of Educational Research and Service, 1970–1971).

Musical Aptitude Profile. One form. Grades 4–12. Tonal imagery,
   rhythm imagery, musical sensitivity. (Boston: Houghton Mifflin, 1965),
   Test T, 29 minutes; Test R, 36 minutes; Test S, 45 minutes.

*Art
Aptitude*

Another area of aptitude testing in which considerable work has been
done is visual or graphic arts. A number of tests have been developed that
purport to get at artistic potential. As in other specialized areas, the distinction between achievement and aptitude in art is not easy to make or
maintain. In some instances so-called aptitude tests have measured
information or learned abilities on the theory that such outcomes are in-
dicative of interest and possibly aptitude as well. This is perhaps less
relevant in the measurement of art aptitude than in some other areas
since the most successful of the tests so far developed deal with abstractions. Some, however, are in the nature of work samples testing the ability of the subject to draw or to create.

THE MEIER ART JUDGMENT TEST   The *Meier Art Judgment Test* is
one of the best and most widely used tests of its type.[5] It consists of one
hundred pairs of pictures in which the task is to select the better in each
pair. One of the pair is a picture of a work of established merit. The other
is the same except that the picture has been altered in some way to im-
pair a fundamental and universal principle of art contained in the original
(see Figure 10.1).

   The material used was chosen from the works of old masters and contemporary artists. Three hundred pairs of pictures were tried out and
eventually reduced to one hundred. The pairs were submitted to
twenty-five art experts and were responded to by 1,081 persons ranging in
age from 11 years to past middle life. Final selection of item pairs was
based upon favorable critical reaction by the experts and a 60 to 90 percent preference by the 1,081 subjects. Scores on the final one-hundred-
item test differentiated consistently between various groups in expected

---

[5] *Meier Art Judgment Test,* one form, grades 7–12 and adults (Iowa City: Bureau of Educational Research and Service, 1928–1942).

Sample Pair of Figures from *Meier Art Judgment Test*   *Figure 10.1*

directions. Correlations between scores on the *Meier Art Judgment Test* and intelligence are generally low, averaging close to zero. Reliabilities (split-halves and Spearman-Brown) range from .70 to .84. Norms are based on students in junior and senior high school, primarily those interested in art.

More recently (1963) Meier produced a test of Aesthetic Perception designed to measure individual differences in perception of the aesthetic merit of different ways of constructing an art object.[6] The subject observes four versions of the same work of art and ranks them in order of aesthetic merit. There are fifty plates of such test items. The scores on the test show a wide range with means for different groups varying in keeping with expected directions according to artistic propensities and talent.

The usefulness of these tests as measures of art aptitude is based on the theory that aesthetic judgment is an important factor in the complex of factors that make up art aptitude. Aesthetic judgment, said to be the product of heredity and experience, is the unfailing response to a work of art embodying good principles of line, proportion, balance, and the like.

---

[6] *Meier Aesthetic Perception Test*, one form, grades, high school, and adult (Iowa City: Bureau of Educational Research and Service, 1963).

4. Against what criteria can tests of musical aptitude be validated?
5. Tests of musical aptitude and art aptitude do not usually have very high reliability coefficients. How could the reliability coefficients of these tests be raised?

OTHER TESTS OF ART APTITUDE   Three additional tests of art aptitude that merit inspection are the following:

Graves Design Judgment Test. One form. Grades 7–16 and adults. Ninety sets of two- and three-dimensional designs calling for discrimination on the basis of eight principles of art. (New York: Psychological Corp., 1963), 20–30 minutes.

Horn Art Aptitude Inventory. One form. Grades 12–16 and adults. Outline drawings of simple objects and creative composition. (Chicago: Stoelting Company, 1951), 50 minutes.

Tests in Fundamental Abilities of Visual Art. One form. Grade 3–adult. Proportion, line drawing, light and shade, vocabulary, visual memory of proportion, cylindrical, parallel, and angular perspective, color. (Monterey, Calif.: California Test Bureau/McGraw-Hill, 1957), 1 hour and 25 minutes.

Foreign Language Aptitude

In recent years interest in foreign languages has increased materially for reasons that are fairly obvious. The growing importance of international relations, improved means of travel, and the great increase in foreign travel have all affected foreign language instruction. The support of such instruction by the federal government through the National Defense Education Act has encouraged such developments. Instruction in foreign languages has been added to the curriculums of many elementary schools, and colleges and universities have greatly expanded their offerings in this field.

THE MODERN LANGUAGE APTITUDE TEST   As a result there is an awakened interest in the measurement of aptitude for learning a foreign language. A few tests of this nature have been developed over the years but they have not been widely used. Some new tests have been developed, one of which will be described. It is called the *Modern Language Aptitude Test*.[7] Although its title suggests that it is designed primarily as a measure of an individual's probable degree of success in learning a modern foreign language, it is claimed to be useful also in measuring potential success in Latin and Greek.

The test has five parts. Number Learning is intended to measure aural memory. Phonetic Script measures the ability to learn correspondences between speech sounds and orthographic symbols. Spelling Clues presents words spelled in disguised form ("luv" for *love*). The task is to select from a group of five words the one that means the same or nearly the same as the disguised word (for example, *affection*). Word in Sentences tests the ability to identify a word in a test sentence that has the same function as a designated word in another key sentence. For example:[8]

> LONDON is the capital of England.
> He liked to go fishing in Maine.
> A   B   C   D   E

Here, the word *he* has the same function in the second sentence as *London* has in the first. The last part is Paired Associates. It measures the ability to learn and recognize a short set of equivalents of English words in a foreign language.

All directions for the tests are given by tape recording. A short form consisting of Parts III, IV, and V may be given either by use of the tape or with oral instructions in about 30 minutes. The test may be scored by either hand or machine.

Validity of the *Modern Language Aptitude Test* was determined on the basis of correlations between scores on it and course grades in Latin, Spanish, French, German, Russian, Chinese, and Indo-European. These correlations range from .13 to .83, with the majority in the range of about .35 to .65. Included were classes in foreign languages in grades 9–11, college classes, and intensive courses for adults. The coefficients with scores on the total test and the short forms are generally almost identical, differing in most instances by less than .05.

Odd-even reliabilities for the total test are above .90; for the short form, they are slightly less, ranging from .83 to .93. Norms are based

---

[7] John B. Carroll and Stanley M. Sapon, *Modern Language Aptitude Test*. One form. Grade 9 to adult. Tape recording or reusable booklets. (New York: Psychological Corp., 1955–1958), 70 minutes. Also, *Modern Language Aptitude Test*, elementary grades 3–6. A downward extension of the preceding. (1960–1967).

[8] Sample item reproduced by permission from *The Modern Language Aptitude Test*. Copyright 1955, © 1958 by The Psychological Corporation, New York, N.Y. All rights reserved.

upon approximately 1,900 students beginning the study of a foreign language in grades 9–12 in fourteen high schools and approximately 1,300 students in ten colleges and universities. No students of current enrollment who had studied a language previously were included.

This test represents a praiseworthy attempt to develop a valid and reliable predictive instrument in foreign language study. It has many features that make it outstanding among those of its type.

ANOTHER TEST OF FOREIGN LANGUAGE APTITUDE   A second test of foreign language aptitude that merits inspection is the following:

Pimsleur Language Aptitude Battery. One form. Grades 6–12. Grade-point average, interest in studying a foreign language, verbal ability, and auditory ability. (New York: Psychological Corp., 1966), 50–60 minutes.

LEARNING EXERCISE

6. For what fields or subjects other than those discussed so far in this chapter have aptitude tests been developed? Consult Buros's *Mental Measurements Yearbooks* for examples.

Aptitude for Creative Thinking

During the past decade there has been much interest and activity in the field of "creative thinking." Perhaps it would be more appropriate to say renewed or increased interest, since such famous personalities as Galton and Terman have long been identified with studies of genius that have obvious bearing on creativity. More recently, work in this area has been directed chiefly along two lines—namely, the development of measures of creative thinking and their validation. New impetus was given to such endeavors by the work of Guilford, who theorized two different processes or types of thinking, which he called *convergent* and *divergent*.[9] In the former, the major emphasis is said to depend on use of known information in arriving at new information or principles. In the latter, new in-

---

[9] J. P. Guilford, "Creativity," *American Psychologist,* 5 (1950), 444–454; see also J. P. Guilford, *Psychological Bulletin* (1956), *Teachers College Record* (1962), *American Psychologist* (1966).

formation is held to be determined or derived with a minimum use of or reference to known information.

Guilford has also raised the question of the relation of creativity to intelligence as measured by conventional tests. His work has led to a great deal of activity in the development of tests purporting to be measures of creativity and in investigation of the relation of scores on such tests to performance on intelligence tests. Research on this question has produced conflicting results, although the preponderance of evidence seems to show that intelligence and creativity as measured by available instruments are not identical and that correlations between them tend to be low, in the range of .20 to .40.

On the development of valid and reliable tests of creativity, most work is still experimental. The tests that have been produced generally exemplify attempts to measure divergent thinking. Guilford himself has investigated a number of approaches to such measurement, including ideational fluency (quantity of ideas produced), associational fluency (synonyms for words), expressional fluency (making sentences using words beginning with a certain letter), alternate uses (uses of a common object like a brick), and consequences (possible results in a new situation).

The central problem in the development of tests of creative thinking is validity. From the standpoint of construct validity, the question becomes one of the relationship of divergent thinking to creativity. Assuming that it is possible to develop measures of unusual, unconventional, divergent thinking, is this characteristic of, and even a necessary element in, creativity? No one really knows, though some studies appear to suggest that it may be. Second, from the standpoint of criterion-related validity, the problem becomes one of validating the tests purporting to measure creativity by comparing scores on them made by individuals of recognized creative ability with scores on the same tests made by persons who have displayed little or no creative talents. Data of this nature are difficult to come by, though some attempts have been made.

THE TORRANCE TESTS OF CREATIVE THINKING   To give specificity to the discussion of this interesting subject, we present a brief description of one of the very few standardized tests of creative thinking.[10] Torrance's *Tests of Creative Thinking* appear in verbal and figural versions with Forms A and B of each. The verbal form tests are entitled Thinking Creatively with Words; the figural, Thinking Creatively with Pictures. In the former, a line drawing is the core element to which subjects respond by (1) asking all the questions they can think of about the picture,

[10] E. Paul Torrance, *Tests of Creative Thinking* (Princeton, N.J.: Personnel Press, 1966).

(2) listing as many possible causes as they can of the action shown in the picture, and (3) listing as many possible consequences of the action in the picture as they can. The next part of the test presents a picture of a stuffed toy animal to which subjects respond by listing as many ways as they can think of to change the toy to make it more fun to play with. The next activity is to list (1) as many unusual uses of cardboard boxes as possible and (2) as many questions about such boxes as possible, with emphasis on unusual aspects. The last activity asks subjects to list as many consequences of an improbable happening as they can—in one case, if clouds had strings attached to them hanging down to earth.

Thinking Creatively with Pictures consists of the following tasks: (1) constructing a picture around a curved shape and giving it a title, (2) adding lines to incomplete figures to produce interesting objects or pictures, and (3) making objects or pictures from a number of pairs of parallel lines or circles.

The actual working time on the verbal test is 45 minutes, and on the figural test it is 30 minutes. In each case about 15 minutes additional must be allowed for giving preliminary instructions, distributing papers, and so on. The separate parts of each test are timed exactly, and no deviations are permitted.

Scoring is rather complicated and subjective, although detailed instructions are given. It should not be attempted without careful study of instructions. Some supervised practice would also seem desirable. Four types of scores are determined. These are (1) Fluency (total number of relevant responses), (2) Flexibility (number of different categories used in responses), (3) Originality (number of more infrequent responses—that is, responses given by less than 2 percent of the subjects), and (4) Elaboration (number of details over and above what is necessary to communicate the basic idea).

A large amount of data on reliability and validity of the *Tests of Creative Thinking* is provided in the *Norms—Technical Manual.* Norms for grades 1 through 12 obtained in several school systems are also provided.

Interscorer reliabilities for verbal forms are quite high for Fluency, Flexibility, and Elaboration, being generally in the high .80s and .90s. The coefficients for Originality range from .66 to .94. For figural forms the reliability coefficients range from .86 to .99. Interform reliability coefficients range from .50 to .93, with a median in one situation for the seven subtests of .84; in another situation the median was .71 and in a third group, .73.

A large number of studies of the *Tests of Creative Thinking* that bear in one way or another on their validity have been reported in the literature. Many of these are reviewed in the *Norms—Technical Manual.* Under a category labeled "content validity," the author maintains that his tests sample a rather wide range of the abilities in a universe of creative thinking abilities. Under "construct validity," many studies are cited that purport to show that scores on the *Tests of Creative Thinking* support hypotheses regarding their relationship to such constructs as rigidity, originality, playfulness, nonconformity, and sense of humor. The validity of most of the criterion measures appears not to have been determined. At least it is not commonly reported in this review. Under "concurrent validity," scores on the tests are related to peer nominations and teacher nominations on creativity. Generally, these show significant differences between the mean scores of the high and low groups in the predicted direction. A number of studies of the relationship of scores on the tests to educational achievement as measured by standardized test batteries and tests of tool subjects in the grades are reviewed. The results are equivocal. Correlations reported range from near 0 to as high as .77. No correlations between IQ and scores on creative thinking are reported, although one investigator reported a correlation of .54 with scores in kindergarten on the *Metropolitan Readiness Test*, the *Tests of Creative Thinking* being taken in the sixth grade. The author attempts to explain these widely varying findings on the basis of differences in instructional methods and classroom climate. Some teachers encourage creativity; others, by their methods and attitudes, engender conformity.

The amount of work done with the Torrance tests is impressive. However, the basic questions of what they measure and their relationship to educational achievement, intelligence, and criteria of creative accomplishment need further and more definitive investigation.

Recognizing that knowledge and understanding about creative thinking are yet in a relatively underdeveloped state, the *Tests of Creative Thinking* are designated by author and publisher as a research edition. The tests constitute an example of a pioneering effort to develop and standardize tests in this field. Further studies are under way, and both author and publisher are conducting and supporting ongoing research.

OTHER TESTS OF CREATIVITY   Following is a listing of three additional tests of creative thinking that merit inspection.

Christensen-Guilford Fluency Tests. One form. Grades 7–16 and adults. Four tests: word, ideational, associational, and expressional fluency. (Orange, Calif.: Sheridan Psychological Services, 1957–1973).

J. P. Guilford et al., *Creativity Tests for Children.* One form. Grades 4–6. Ten tests of divergent production abilities. (Orange, Calif.: Sheridan Psychological Services, 1971).

Remote Associates Test. High-school level and college–adult level. Ability to think creatively. (Boston: Houghton Mifflin, 1959–1971).

A comparatively recent development in measuring aptitudes is the aptitude battery, or what is sometimes called the *differential* or *factored* aptitude battery. Such batteries have grown out of the development of factor analysis mentioned earlier in this chapter. The attempt to isolate and identify specific factors in general intelligence has carried over into the measurement of particular aptitudes. It was reasoned that test batteries could be devised to measure a number of important abilities or traits that enter into many types of work or activities. Then if the scores on the parts of the battery could be related to specific occupations or groups of occupations, these part scores could be differentially weighted according to their importance in such occupations.

In addition to the impact of factor analysis, the growing number of persons engaged in educational and vocational guidance or counseling has increased interest in and demand for such batteries. Obviously, no counselor could test a client with all aptitude tests to determine what advice to give. Therefore, a single battery or group of tests would be very useful.

Broadly speaking, one might include in the category of aptitude batteries the *Primary Mental Abilities Test* and any other tests that yield part scores that can be demonstrated to have *low intercorrelations*. Obviously, if the parts of a battery have high correlations with each other, they are measuring the same thing to a substantial degree and thus have little differential value. Not many test batteries meet this criterion very well. We are concerned here with batteries developed to meet the criteria outlined above and designed primarily for general counseling purposes. Several such batteries are now available, and a typical one will be described below.

THE DIFFERENTIAL APTITUDE TESTS   The *Differential Aptitude Tests* (DAT) are among the earliest of this type, the first edition appearing in 1947.[11] The most recent edition was published in 1972.

Nature   This battery consists of eight tests: Verbal Reasoning, Numerical Ability, Abstract Reasoning, Space Relations, Mechanical Reasoning, Clerical Speed and Accuracy, Spelling, and Language Usage. Item types in the most recent edition remain the same as before, but new items in Verbal Reasoning, Numerical Ability, Mechanical Reasoning, Spelling, and Language Usage replace some that had appeared in previous editions. The forms, S and T, are each published in one booklet, but Form T is also available in separate booklets for each of the eight tests.

---

[11] G. K. Bennett, H. G. Seashore, and A. G. Wesman, *Differential Aptitude Tests*, Forms S and T, grades 8–12 and adults (New York: Psychological Corp., 1972).

Purpose The DAT are intended for use in junior and senior high schools in vocational and educational guidance and counseling. The tests may, of course, also be used in counseling adults beyond high school. Originally the tests were designed with the idea of using them as predictors of success in vocations. However, experience has shown that their usefulness for this purpose is quite limited. Most of the voluminous data on validity cited below are in the form of correlations between scores on the DAT and achievement in junior and senior high-school subjects.

Content Typical items for each of the eight tests of the battery follow:[12]

1. Verbal Reasoning

_____ is to water as eat is to _____.
    A.   continue—drive
    B.   foot—enemy
    C.   drink—food
    D.   girl—industry
    E.   drink—enemy

2. Numerical Ability

Add: 13
          12

A. 14 B. 25 C. 16 D. 59 E. none of these

3. Spelling

		Right	Wrong
W.	man	W. ☐	☐
X.	gurl	X. ☐	☐
Y.	catt	Y. ☐	☐
Z.	dog	Z. ☐	☐

4. Language Usage

Ain't we / going to / the office / next week?   A B C D
   A   B   C   D   ☐ ☐ ☐ ☐

5. Abstract Reasoning assigns the task of selecting from among the answer figures the one that should come next in the series of problem figures.

Problem figures	Answer figures

6. Space Relations consists of items in which a pattern that can be folded into a figure is followed by five figures, one or more of which can be formed from the pattern. The task is to identify the figure that can be formed from the pattern at the left.

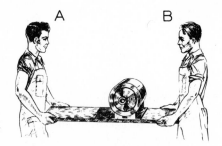

7. Mechanical Reasoning consists of a series of problems like the following:

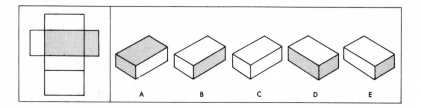

Which man has the heavier load? (If equal, mark C.)

8. Clerical Speed and Accuracy consists of sets of letter and number combinations in pairs. In the first set, one combination is underlined. The task is to find the same combination in the second set.

Test items	Sample of answer sheet

V.	<u>AB</u>	AC	AD	AE	AF
W.	aA	aB	BA	Ba	Bb
X.	A7	7A	B7	<u>7B</u>	AB
Y.	Aa	Ba	bA	BA	bB
Z.	3A	3B	<u>33</u>	B3	BB

V	AC :::::	AE :::::	AF :::::	AB ■	AD :::::
W	BA :::::	Ba :::::	Bb ■	aA :::::	aB :::::
X	7B ■	B7 :::::	AB :::::	7A :::::	A7 :::::
Y	Aa :::::	bA ■	bB :::::	Ba :::::	BA :::::
Z	BB :::::	3B :::::	B3 :::::	3A :::::	33 ■

Validity   The bulk of evidence for validity of the DAT consists of correlations between the scores on the tests and course grades—that is, teacher's marks. These include grades in English, literature, mathematics, science, social studies, history, and, to a lesser extent, business and business skills, vocational courses, and miscellaneous courses (career exploration, reading, driver education, and the like). The correlations with course grades vary widely among single tests and combinations of tests. On the whole, the best predictors of course grades in academic subjects are scores on Verbal Reasoning and Numerical Ability combined. Median r's range from −.11 between grades in music and scores on Verbal Reasoning to .56 between grades in business and business skills and scores on Verbal Reasoning and Numerical Ability combined and Numerical Ability alone. The highest correlations are found between scores on the DAT and scores on standardized tests of achievement and academic aptitude. Generally these are in the .70s and .80s.

Reliability   Interform reliability coefficients between Forms S and M (1963 edition) are generally in the .70s and .80s, as are those between Forms T and L (1963). These are based on testing with the two forms at an interval of approximately four weeks. The coefficients are given for each of the eight tests and the Verbal Reasoning and Numerical Ability combination. The only exception to the stated range occurs with the test of Clerical Speed and Accuracy, where the values are typically in the .50s and .60s. Split-half reliabilities were calculated by sex and form and grade level for Verbal Reasoning plus Numerical Ability and for each test separately except Clerical Speed and Accuracy. The values thus obtained are mostly above .90. Alternate-form reliability coefficients for Clerical Speed and Accuracy are also about .90. Standard errors of measurement average about 3 points of raw score for the separate tests.

Intercorrelation Between Individual Tests   As we stated earlier in this chapter, the usefulness of a multi-aptitude test depends to a considerable extent on the development of a set of tests that show substantial correlations with criteria such as course grades or success in particular types of work or activity and low intercorrelations. The higher the intercorrelations, the smaller the contributions of the individual tests to the diversity of the factors measured.

The intercorrelations of the tests of Form S (and T) range from .02 to .85. Generally the intercorrelations between every possible pair of tests, except for pairs with Clerical Speed and Accuracy, are in the .50s and .60s. However, correlations between Clerical Speed and Accuracy and each of the other tests of the battery range between .02 and .41, averaging about .20. Thus, except for Clerical Speed and Accuracy, the tests of the battery seem to be rather closely related. However, application of a formula to appraise the differentiating power of pairs of tests shows that every possible pair reaches or exceeds a minimum criterion for percentage (25 percent) of differences exceeding chance. The percentages range from 25 percent to 57 percent. Most are in the 30s and 40s.

Taking together the data on intercorrelations and differences between pairs of tests, one must conclude that the evidence for differentiating power of individual tests of the DAT is not too impressive, especially the data on test intercorrelations. The manual for the DAT avers that "It is evident that the Differential Aptitude Tests have, in general, sufficiently high reliability and sufficiently low intercorrelations to result in a test battery with good differentiating power." This statement is certainly acceptable with respect to reliability but may justifiably be questioned with respect to differentiating power.

Administration   Directions for administering the tests are clear and complete, including directions for use of different types of answer sheets. Each test is separately timed; time limits are from 3 minutes for Clerical Speed and Accuracy to 30 minutes each for several others. The total working time for the battery is 90 minutes. Altogether, the administration of the battery would require at least 2 hours, allowing for distributing booklets and answer sheets, reading directions, answering questions, and so on. The separate booklet edition of Form T would require somewhat longer.

Scoring   The tests may be scored by hand or by machine, using several different types of answer sheets—IBM, Digitek, and MRC.

Norms and Norming   Raw scores are converted into percentile ranks and stanines. Norms are based on more than 64,000 cases in grades 8 through 12. Included in the normative population were students in 76 parochial and public school systems in 33 states and the District of Columbia. There are separate norms for boys and girls, by grade level, and for fall and spring testing on each of the eight tests and combined Verbal Reasoning and Numerical Ability.

Manual   A manual supplies detailed information on the development and nature of the tests, directions for administering and scoring, norms and profiles, equivalence of forms, validity and reliability. The manual also contains many suggestions for using the results of the tests. There are also a counselor's manual for the career planning program and a questionnaire on which the student records preferences as to school subjects and fields of work. The questionnaire also includes an MRC answer sheet on which the student records responses to the test items and sex and grade. The latter provides the basis for a new feature of the DAT—namely, a computer printout of a counseling report.

Format   The format of this edition is excellent, including a judicious use of color.

Summary   The DAT have had wide acceptance and use for more than a quarter of a century. On the whole, their value as predictors of success as measured by teachers' marks and scores on standardized tests of achievement in academic subjects is substantial and well established. In this respect they compare favorably with other tests now available. As predictors of success in nonacademic courses, their value is less well proven. As a battery and as individual tests, they can be very useful, especially to counselors, teachers, and school administrators in appraising students' academic potential and, to some degree, their aptitude for specific fields of work and vocations.

LEARNING EXERCISES

7. Examine a specimen set of an aptitude battery other than the DAT. Compare it with the DAT with respect to purpose, content, and validity.
8. In what respects does the Lorge-Thorndike *Cognitive Abilities Test* resemble an aptitude battery? In what ways does it differ? Could the CAT and an aptitude battery be used for the same purposes?

OTHER APTITUDE BATTERIES   Following is a listing of three additional aptitude batteries that merit inspection.

Aptitude Tests for Occupations. One form. Grades 9–13. Personal-social, mechanical, general sales, clerical routine, computational, and scientific aptitudes. (Monterey, Calif.: California Test Bureau/McGraw-Hill, 1951), 107 minutes.

General Aptitude Test Battery. One form. Ages 16 and up. Intelligence, verbal, numerical, spatial, form perception, clerical perception, eye-hand coordination, motor speed, finger dexterity, manual dexterity. (Washington, D.C.: U.S. Employment Service, U.S. Dept. of Labor, 1947–1963), 145 minutes.

Multiple Aptitude Tests. One form. Grades 7–13. Word meaning, paragraph meaning, language usage, routine clerical facility, arithmetic reasoning, arithmetic computation, applied science and mechanics, spatial relations—two dimensions, and spatial relations—three dimensions. (Monterey, Calif.: California Test Bureau/McGraw-Hill, 1959), 177 minutes.

OTHER DIRECTIONS
IN APTITUDE TESTING

In addition to the aptitude tests described or listed in this chapter, a number of such tests have been developed in other fields. A perusal of Buros's *Seventh Mental Measurements Yearbook* shows listings of one or more tests or batteries in each of the following areas: medicine, nursing, dentistry, law, engineering, selling, accounting, dental hygiene, firefighting, driving and traffic safety, business management, law enforcement, carpentry, coach operation, and truck driving. This is not a complete list but it indicates the variety of purposes for which such tests have been devised.

The use of aptitude or prognostic tests was given considerable impetus during World War II. Large numbers of men and women were inducted into service with little or no training or experience that could be used in the armed forces. These people had to be screened and assigned either to training or to jobs, and this had to be done quickly. The need for reasonably accurate, objective, and rapid methods for appraising and assigning an individual was obvious. Consequently, a great deal of effort was expended on the development of aptitude tests, some of which have continued to be used in civilian life.

The development of aptitude tests or batteries is a challenging task. Research and development are likely to continue, particularly in business and industry. Perhaps the most promising development is the factored aptitude batteries, but these require great expenditures of talent and money as exemplified by the *General Aptitude Test Battery* of the U.S. Employment Service. They also demand continuing research and appraisal to meet changing requirements in occupations. However, valid and reliable aptitude tests are well worth what they cost if they save time, money, and energy and if they help avoid frustration and disappointment for millions of people faced with the necessity of making decisions about their life's work. Aptitude tests for specific occupations or types of work should also prove useful in guiding the so-called hard-core unemployed into types of training for productive work commensurate with their abilities.

SUGGESTED READING

ANASTASI, ANNE. *Psychological Testing.* 4th ed. New York: Macmillan, 1976. Chaps. 13, 15. Discusses the theoretical bases of multiple aptitude test batteries, including the application in their development of factor analysis. Several batteries are briefly described. Brief descriptions of tests of sensory capacities, motor functions, mechanical, clerical, artistic, and musical aptitudes and tests of creativity follow.

BUROS, OSCAR K. *Tests in Print.* Highland Park, N.J.: Gryphon Press, 1974. Lists multi-aptitude batteries and special aptitude tests with essential information and references to reviews in the *Mental Measurements Yearbooks.*

CRONBACH, LEE J. *Essentials of Psychological Testing.* 3d ed. New York: Harper & Row, 1970. Chaps. 11, 12. The first chapter deals in detail with the development and use of profiles based on multiple aptitude batteries in guidance. The following chapter treats of measurement of psycho-motor abilities and briefly of special aptitude tests including artistic aptitude and creativity.

MEHRENS, WILLIAM A., and IRVIN J. LEHMANN. *Standardized Tests in Education.* 2d ed. New York: Holt, Rinehart and Winston, 1975. Pp. 140–162. Several multifactor aptitude tests are briefly described; one is examined in detail. There is a brief discussion of special aptitude tests and some suggestions for use of the results of aptitude tests.

NELSON, MARTIN J. *"Intelligence and Special Aptitude Tests," Encylopedia of Educational Research.* 4th ed. New York: Macmillan, 1969. Pp. 667–677. The first half of the article deals with the historical background of individual and group intelligence tests and some of the controversial matters relating to them. The remainder is devoted to a discussion of the testing of special aptitudes with particular reference to tests of mechanical, clerical, art, and musical aptitudes. Extensive bibliography.

SUPER, DONALD E., and JOHN O. CRITES. *Appraising Vocational Fitness.* Rev. ed. New York: Harper & Row, 1962. Chap. 5, the nature of aptitudes and aptitude tests. Chap. 6, clerical aptitude, perceptual speed. Chap. 9, manual dexterities. Chap. 10, mechanical aptitude. Chap. 11, spatial-visual. Chap. 12, aesthetic judgment and artistic abilities. Chap. 13, musical talent. Chap. 14, standard batteries with norms for specific vocations. Chap. 15, custom-built batteries for specific occupations. The most complete survey and analysis of special aptitude tests available, though now somewhat dated.

THORNDIKE, R. L., and ELIZABETH HAGEN. *Measurement and Evaluation in Psychology and Education.* 4th ed. New York: John Wiley & Sons, 1977. Chap. 11. A discussion of the rationale of vocational aptitude is followed by descriptions of several multiple aptitude batteries and methods of establishing evidence of their validity. There are also brief discussions of measures of musical and artistic aptitudes and of creativity.

Eleven

THE MEASUREMENT
OF PERSONALITY AND AFFECT:
SELF-REPORT TECHNIQUES

Personality is often considered synonymous with popularity. The individual who knows a large number of people, who is the center of attention at social functions, and who is persuasive in dealings with others is said to have a "wonderful personality." While there is undoubtedly some basis for this point of view, it is quite inadequate as a definition of personality. In a deeper sense, personality is the most inclusive frame of reference in which an individual can be judged. It includes the sum of one's characteristics and behavior—intelligence, knowledge, attitudes, interests, and interactions with the environment. Personality thus broadly conceived is the total of all these qualities together with the effects of the combination of them on what one thinks, feels, says, and does.

Thus broadly defined, personality has two aspects: inner and outer. The inner phase refers to adjustment within the individual. Does one have a realistic and satisfying self-concept? Is one confident, sure of personal worth? Has one set suitable and challenging goals, keeping in mind personal limitations as well as strengths? Is one's occupation satisfying? Of course, many more factors importantly affect inner personality, but these are among the chief ones.

The outer or interpersonal phase of personality concerns a person's relationships with other people. Is the person a useful member of family and community groups? Does she or he have the respect and affection of associates? Such questions point up the social or interpersonal aspect of personality as it is conceived here.

The concept of adjustment is of central importance in this definition of personality. The person who is well adjusted is likely to be happy and to have a personality that makes a favorable impression on others. Conversely, the poorly adjusted person, almost by definition, is unhappy, and consequently finds that relationships with others tend to be strained and difficult. Thus, one's personality is not some superficial characteristic that may be briefly adopted; rather, it is a reflection of a person's innermost self, and it influences and becomes a part of everything one does.

Although the term *personality* is employed in a broad sense to encompass everything that helps determine what one is like as an individual, personality measurement emphasizes the assessment of characteristics in the affective domain—attitudes, values, interests, and motivation—rather than those in the cognitive domain—that is, abilities and achievement.

The psychologist's distinction between the cognitive and affective characteristics of individuals and the educator's classification of objectives as cognitive or affective are roughly equivalent to the age-old distinctions people have made between thinking and feeling. The classification of a particular trait or behavior in one or the other category occurs when one aspect is more obvious or of greater concern than the other. Actually, both cognition and affect are part of most activities and reactions. Taking a test in mathematics is classified as a cognitive task, but no one does it without feeling. How one feels about taking a mathematics test is, on the other hand, influenced by one's cognitive knowledge of the subject.

There are two fundamental approaches to the measurement of personality and affect. In the simplest terms, the first involves asking the individual what she or he thinks, feels, says, and does. The second involves observing the individual directly or asking others about her or him. The first is a *self-report* approach; the other is an *observational* approach. The examiner who uses the self-report technique asks questions or presents stimuli to which the individual being measured responds. From the replies, the examiner can formulate some idea of the person's personality or affective reactions. The examiner using the observational technique personally observes what a person does or asks people who know the person well to express opinions about that person. Both methods are widely used. Self-report techniques may be distinguished from observational ones by the fact that the former are more often tests or other devices that yield scores. Thus, personality inventories, tests of attitude, and tests of interests are typical self-report instruments, whereas rating scales, anecdotal records, and sociograms are examples of the observational report.

The nature and advantages and disadvantages of standardized and teacher-made self-report techniques will be discussed in this chapter; aspects of observational techniques will be discussed in Chapter 12. Study of the present chapter will enable you to answer questions and complete exercises such as the following:

1. How may information about personality and affective characteristics be used by individuals and their teachers and counselors?
2. Describe a self-report inventory that might be used to obtain each of the following types of information about students: adjustment problems, vocational interests, and study habits and attitudes.
3. What are the major shortcomings and limitations of self-report inventories?
4. Compare the nature and advantages and disadvantages of projective and nonprojective measures of personality.
5. Explain how forced-choice techniques have been used to prevent the faking of self-reports.
6. Compare the Likert, Thurstone, and Remmers approaches to attitude-scale development.
7. How may informal teacher-devised self-report procedures be used to evaluate the progress of a class group toward an affective objective such as motivation for learning?
8. Devise an attitude scale for classroom use to assess student attitudes toward a particular subject matter or learning activity.

PERSONALITY AND ADJUSTMENT MEASURES

An instrument published as a personality inventory is typically planned from some rationale conceived in terms of either areas of activity (such as at home, in school, and on the job) or a set of psychological constructs. In the latter case, an author's constructs might include such traits as sociability and confidence. Most inventories, past and present, represent one or the other of these two basic patterns of organization.

In the development of many early instruments, the selection of items for a test depended on the judgment of the test authors. This is sometimes called the *intuitive* approach. More recently, one of two empirical methods has usually been used. The first is based on the relationship between how subjects answer an item of a test and their scores on the total test. In this method, the criterion for item selection is internal—that is, of the test itself. Because this method results in the retention of a group of items that are highly related to each other, it has been called *homogeneous keying.*

The second method uses an external criterion and is called *criterion keying.* Items are selected that discriminate between external referent groups—for example, groups judged as adjusted and nonadjusted by psychologists, counselors, or teachers.

Methods that depend on the intuition of the authors rather than statistical evidence have long been suspect; Goldberg, however, who used all the methods in the same study, has shown that instruments constructed by intuitive methods are not as consistently inferior to those using empirical evidence as many have feared.[1]

Two other relatively recent developments in measurement theory have also been applied to the construction of self-report inventories. One of these is *factor analysis,* a statistical procedure for reducing the many different terms used to indicate similar differences in personality characteristics. The results of using factor analysis in test development have been promising in that a fairly small number of distinct factors or traits of personality have been identified.

The other development is the *forced-choice* technique. One of the nagging concerns of people who use any type of self-report device is the possibility of the examinee's faking or slanting the responses. By a judicious selection of responses, one may create an impression that is more favorable than the truth.[2] The forced-choice technique is designed to eliminate or at least reduce the possibility of such faking. A choice between pairs of equally complimentary or equally uncomplimentary alternatives is presented. One of each pair is a more significant response than the other with respect to some criterion such as emotional stability. The examinee is asked to choose one response most like and one response least like himself or herself. Since both of one pair sound equally complimentary and both of the other pair sound equally uncomplimentary, it is believed that the chances of faking are greatly reduced. An example of a forced-choice item is presented below in connection with the discussion of a typical personality inventory.

GORDON PERSONAL PROFILE AND PERSONAL INVENTORY The *Gordon Personal Profile* and *Gordon Personal Inventory* are companion pieces designed to measure eight factors of personality. In the Profile these include ascendancy, responsibility, emotional stability, and sociability. The Inventory covers cautiousness, original thinking, personal relations, and vigor. These eight traits or personality aspects were arrived at and identified by several successive factor analyses.

Typical Inventories or Questionnaires

Levels and Forms   One form is available in either hand- or machine-scored editions for use in grades 9–16 and with adults.

---

[1] L. R. Goldberg, "Parameters of Personality Inventory Construction and Utilization: A Comparison of Prediction Strategies and Tactics," *Multivariate Behavioral Research Monographs,* 7, No. 72-2 (1972), 58 pages.
[2] Biased responses may be given unintentionally, too, because of the tendency of some individuals to acquiesce (answer "Yes") to statements.

Content   Twenty forced-choice items are used in each instrument. Here is a sample item:[3]

1. Likes to work primarily with ideas.
2. Does things at a rather slow pace.
3. Very careful when making a decision.
4. Finds a number of people hard to get along with.

Here the first and third items are judged to be equally complimentary; the second and fourth are equally uncomplimentary. The person taking the test is to mark one that is *most* like and one that is *least* like herself or himself in each group of four. Each set of four consists of one item related to each of the four scales or traits. Thus, one item of a tetrad in the Profile pertains to cautiousness, one to original thinking, and so on; the Inventory is set up the same way.

Measurement Qualities   Extensive studies of the validity of both tests have been reported. They consist mainly of reports of scores of groups expected to differ—as, for example, males and females, clerks and stenographers, foremen and executives. Comparisons between students in various curriculums in high schools are also reported. Correlations between scores and personality ratings by peers, counselors, teachers, and supervisors and with scores on other personality measures are reported in a substantial number of investigations. The data on validity are more extensive than usual with instruments of this type and, on the whole, are quite encouraging, especially in the case of the Profile. Those for the Inventory are less extensive.

Data presented in the manuals for the two tests tend to support, at least in part, the claim that the tests measure significantly different aspects of personality. Intercorrelations among the four scales of the Profile range from −.18 (sociability with emotional stability) to .71 (ascendancy with sociability). The correlation between emotional stability and responsibility is about .50. Other intercorrelations for the Profile are low positive or low negative.

Intercorrelations among the four scales of the Inventory range from .42 (cautiousness with personal relations) to −.45 (cautiousness with vigor).

Intercorrelations among scales of the Profile and scales of the Inventory range between .47 (emotional stability with personal relations) and −.21 (sociability with cautiousness). Most of the coefficients are between 0 and .40.

Reliability of the two tests is reported in terms of split-halves coefficients. They are typically in the high .70s and .80s. In one study involv-

[3] From *Gordon Personal Inventory* by Leonard V. Gordon. Reproduced by permission. Copyright 1956 by Harcourt Brace Jovanovich, Inc., New York, N.Y. All rights reserved.

ing several hundred high school students, the separate reliabilities of the four parts of the Profile were found to be about .60.

Norms   Percentile norms are provided for high-school students, college students, and adult groups in various occupations. In each case separate norms are provided for each sex.

Administration and Scoring   The inventories are short, twenty items each, and easily administered and scored.

Summary   The *Gordon Personal Profile* and *Gordon Personal Inventory* were developed by sound procedures and have been extensively evaluated. They are useful to counselors and clinicians primarily for establishing rapport with clients, opening an interview, or exploring possible problems. Either of the pair may be used alone or both may be used together, seemingly without substantial overlap or duplication.

THE MOONEY PROBLEM CHECK LISTS   The *Mooney Problem Check Lists* are not tests in the usual sense.[4] They represent a different approach from that of the Gordon instruments. They are examples of inventories that give students the opportunity to report problems or difficulties in different areas of their life that may then be investigated more fully.[5]

Levels and Forms   Different forms are provided for the junior-high-school, high-school, college, and adult levels.

Content   The areas covered are essentially the same in each form, although there are differences in the items at the various maturity levels. The person responding is asked to read a list of several hundred items, underline those that are troublesome, and indicate the two or three that are of real concern. In the junior-high form, the areas are health and physical development; school; home and family; money, work, and the future; boy-girl relations; relations with people in general; and self-centered concerns. In the high-school and college forms, to these areas are added others such as morals and religion, and curriculum and teaching procedures. The following samples from the junior-high-school form show the nature of the arrangement:[6]

Health	1. Often have headaches
and	2. Don't get enough sleep
Physical	3. Have trouble with my teeth
Development	4. Not as healthy as I should be
	. . .

[4] Ross L. Mooney and Leonard V. Gordon, *The Mooney Problem Check Lists* (New York: Psychological Corp., 1950).
[5] Other examples are *STS Junior Inventory for Grades 4–8* and *STS Youth Inventory for Grades 7–12* (Bensenville, Ill.: Scholastic Testing Service, 1956–1972).
[6] From *Mooney Problem Check List*, Form J. Reproduced by permission. Copyright 1950 by The Psychological Corporation, New York, N.Y. All rights reserved.

School	6. Getting low grades in school
	7. Afraid of tests
	8. Being a grade behind in school
	. . .
Home	11. Being an only child
and	12. Not living with my parents
Family	13. Worried about someone in the family
	. . .

Measurement Qualities   Content validity was sought by selecting items identified by an analysis of statements of problems written by students and adults, other records of adjustment difficulties, and a survey of the literature. Statistical evidence of validity and reliability is not presented, but the number (20–30) of types of problems typically checked by students suggests good coverage of the problem areas students are willing to report.[7]

Norms   None are provided. The development and use of local norms are suggested.

Administration and Scoring   The person responding is asked to read the list of several hundred items, underline the items that are troublesome, and indicate the two or three that are of real concern. There are no time limits. The lists are not scored in the usual sense but are so arranged that a count can easily be made of the check marks in each of the different areas.

Interpretation   The manual states that this inventory is a simple communication between the respondent and the counselor. It is probably the type of personality instrument most used by teachers. The list of problems reported can provide useful leads for locating problem areas or conducting interviews. The data can also be used for planning guidance and orientation programs and as a foundation for increasing the teacher's understanding of students in the classroom.

Clinical and Research Instruments

Many other measures of personality are used extensively by psychologists in clinical and research settings. Any detailed or comprehensive consideration of these instruments is beyond the scope of this text, and they are not recommended to teachers. Nevertheless, several representative types will be briefly described to round out the reader's knowledge.

PAPER-AND-PENCIL TESTS   The *Minnesota Multiphasic Personality Inventory* (MMPI) is the most famous and widely studied example of personality inventories designed for use by clinical psychologists in the study of abnormal behavior. One form of the MMPI for use with groups

[7] Anne Anastasi, *Psychological Testing,* 4th ed. (New York: Macmillan, 1976), p. 495.

has 565 true-false statements about attitudes, feelings, psychosomatic symptoms, and behavior.[8]

The MMPI also exemplifies tests developed by selecting items by an external criterion—that is, differences in the response of normal subjects and subjects diagnosed as disturbed by psychiatrists. The items are scored to indicate psychological disorders suggested by scale names like Depression, Hysteria, Psychopathic Deviate, and Schizophrenia. Interpretations are based on a profile of the individual's scores on these and other diagnostic dimensions. A large number of unusually deviant scores is especially suggestive of maladjustment. Several subtests designed to detect faking or otherwise unreliable scores are of special interest. One score is based on the number of obviously desirable but highly improbable claims—for example, that one likes everyone one meets. Another score is based on the number of rare and unusual responses, and a high score here is an indication that the subject may not have followed the directions.

The MMPI is regarded as the forerunner of a large number of other tests that have used many of the same items and procedures with normal as well as abnormal subjects. The *California Psychological Inventory* is one example.[9] One-half of the 480 items of this test, which was designed to measure positive and normal categories of personality, are from the MMPI. Representative of the eighteen scores of the CPI are Dominance, Sociability, Responsibility, Tolerance, Intellectual Efficiency, and Flexibility. In contrast to the MMPI profile interpretation, CPI interpretation is more often based on statistical predictions of behavior such as delinquency, dropout, and educational or vocational success.

Personality instruments based on factor analysis of item pools to identify groups or clusters of items that measure the same thing have also had extensive use in psychological research. Examples include the ten-factor *Guilford-Zimmerman Temperament Survey* of such aspects of normal personality as general activity, sociability, friendliness, thoughtfulness, and masculinity (one form for men and women) for grades 9–12 and adults, and the *Eysenck Personality Inventory*, designed to measure neuroticism and extroversion-introversion in adults. The *New Junior Maudsley Inventory*, available from the same publisher, measures these traits in children aged 9–16. It is an American edition of a British inventory and recommended for research use only.[10]

[8] Starke R. Hathaway and J. Charnley McKinley, *Minnesota Multiphasic Personality Inventory* New Group Form R (New York: Psychological Corp., 1965–1967).

[9] *California Psychological Inventory* (Palo Alto, Calif.: Consulting Psychologists Press, 1956–1969).

[10] J. P. Guilford and Wayne S. Zimmerman, with Falsification Scales by Alfred Jacobs and Allan Schlaff, *Guilford-Zimmerman Temperament Survey* (Orange, Calif.: Sheridan Psychological Services, 1949–1955); H. J. Eysenck and B. G. Sybil, *Eysenck Personality Inventory*, (San Diego, Calif.: Educational and Industrial Testing Service, 1963–1969); W. D. Furneaux and H. B. Gibson, *New Junior Maudsley Inventory* (San Diego, Calif.; Educational and Industrial Testing Service, 1966–1967).

Factor analysis is a useful technique for developing "purer" tests of some personality characteristics; however, there is at present insufficient evidence of the usefulness of either these or other types of personality inventories for predicting educational, vocational, or general life adjustment.

PROJECTIVE TECHNIQUES   Another type of clinical instrument is the *projective test*, a self-report device to be used only by psychiatrists or clinical psychologists. It derives its name from the fact that in responding the subject "projects" feelings, emotions, conflicts, and problems. The projective tests are less structured than the personality inventories in that the questions, items, or stimuli are less specific and subjects are far freer to make responses in their own words.

The *Rorschach Ink-Blot Test* is a well-known example of a projective test. It consists of a series of what are purported to be inkblots, some black, some in color (see Figure 11.1 for an example of a kind similar to

Figure 11.1   Holtzman Inkblot (Similar to Inkblots in the *Rorschach Ink-Blot Test*)

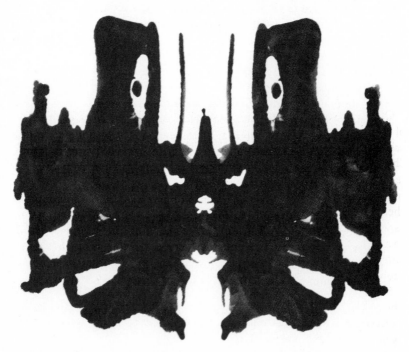

From Wayne H. Holtzman, *Holtzman Inkblot Technique.* Reproduced by permission. Copyright © 1958 by The Psychological Corporation, New York, N.Y. All rights reserved.

Rorschach inkblots). These are shown one at a time to a subject, who is asked to tell what each suggests or brings to mind. From the subjects' responses, the clinician can determine something of the presence and nature of deep-seated emotional conflicts and maladjustments that subjects may not understand or even be conscious of. Such a test obviously requires much training and experience to administer and interpret.

A simpler form of projective technique, probably antedating such instruments as the Rorschach, is the *word-association test*, in which the procedure is to present a list of words one at a time to the subject, who is asked to give the first word that comes to mind in each case. Some of the words carry emotional aspects for some individuals under certain circumstances. To be more specific, suppose a psychologist presented the words in the following list to children of a fifth-grade class and asked each child to tell or write the first word that came to mind in each instance. Let us assume that the list of words has been used in this way with many children and that certain conventional or nonemotional responses have been identified. The results might reveal that two pupils responded as follows:

Stimulus word	Pupil A	Pupil B
house	big	white
apple	eat	sour
paper	write	burn
teacher	lady	ugly
sky	blue	high

On the basis of the previous trials of these same words, the responses of pupil A might be regarded as quite conventional and normal. In the case of pupil B, however, certain responses are found to be different in character. To *apple,* pupil B responds "sour"; to *paper,* "burn"; and to *teacher,* "ugly." A psychiatrist might interpret these responses as reflecting some factors in pupil B's emotional makeup that would warrant further investigation. Not only the response itself, but other considerations as well, have significance. For example, long hesitation before responding to a given word may be a sign of emotional blocking. Such a word list is a simple projective device in that subjects often project their complexes or problems in the responses they make.

Some projective tests consist of pictures of people, and still others use objects such as toys or simple mechanical devices. There are many projective tests and devices, and they are especially popular with European psychologists and psychiatrists.

One rather well-known application of the association technique is the polygraph, or "lie detector." The person suspected of a crime is asked to submit to such a test. Usually suspects agree to do so. If they are inno-cent, they have nothing to fear or lose by taking it; if they are guilty, they are afraid that refusal will reflect on them adversely, so they generally agree to take it with the hope of "beating" it. The test depends on the known effect of strong emotion on blood pressure, pulse rate, and amount of palmar sweating, all of which are increased by heightened emotion. Normal rates of each are established for the subject under sim-ple and innocuous questioning; then loaded questions are introduced. If the pulse, blood pressure, and palmar sweating increase, it is judged that the subject is not telling the truth. This, of course, is not accepted as proof of guilt, but the results, when shown to a guilty suspect, often bring about a confession. In general, specialists in crime detection are of the opinion that the results of lie detector tests are quite reliable and that few persons are successful in beating the test. The harder the individual tries and the more determined to beat the test he or she is, the more pro-nounced are the telltale signs when a loaded question or some significant piece of evidence is suddenly introduced.

For students interested in further study of projective tests and proce-dures, the references in the bibliography at the end of this chapter should prove helpful.

Issues in the Use of Personality Inventories

Several questions are perennially raised concerning the self-report type of personality inventory. One has to do with its validity and reliability. A second, already mentioned, relates to the problem of the subject's faking or simulating responses. A third question concerns the usability of such inventories in schools. How much use should be made of them? By whom should they be used? Full discussions of these questions are be-yond the scope of this book, but a few statements will provide some in-formation on each point.

Concerning validity, a little reflection will make it clear that the usual methods of establishing validity cannot apply to personality inventories. It is not possible to establish validity of personality inventories by cor-relating the scores with age, grade, or IQ, except possibly in a negative way by showing a lack of relationship between such measures. One criterion often used is a comparison of scores with teachers' ratings of adjustment; another is a comparison of scores with case histories to see if people who make poor scores on the inventory show a history of malad-justment, problem behavior, and personality disorder. On the whole, such studies show the self-report inventory to have fairly satisfactory validity as a screening device. Although these instruments generally do not reveal minute adjustment differences, they serve to identify most of the serious cases of maladjustment.

As to reliability, data vary widely. Some inventories report reliability coefficients as high as .90. Some, as in the case of the Mooney, do not yield scores and thus do not lend themselves to statistical analysis. In general, the reliability of personality inventories is lower than that of good standardized tests of intelligence or achievement. The reliability coefficients range from the .60s to the .80s, with the average falling somewhere between .70 and .80. In this connection, it must be kept in mind that it is not the subject's response to one or even a few items that is meaningful but rather, the *trend* of the responses to a large number of items. For example, in the Gordon there are seventy-two items in each of the two tests; in the Mooney there are more than two hundred.

On the problem of faked or simulated responses there is considerable evidence from research.[11] The information obtained from a number of these studies may be summed up as follows:

1. It is possible to fake or slant answers on a self-report inventory.
2. It is not as easy to do this as might be supposed, especially to take a pose and maintain it consistently. Ability to slant answers is affected by, among other things, (a) the sophistication of the examinees, (b) the subtlety of the statements on the inventory, and (c) the number of items.
3. Some individuals cannot consistently fake answers in a desired direction even when told to do so.

It is obvious that a personality inventory differs from a test of achievement in this respect. In an achievement test there is little chance of faking or bluffing if it is a good test, while in a personality inventory the value of the responses depends on the respondents' willingness to be truthful and on their ability to give accurate representations of their behavior and feelings. Unless they are cooperative, the responses are of no value. The most promising tactic for combating dishonesty is to win the confidence of the respondents and convince them that it will be to their benefit to give truthful responses.

As to the question of whether personality inventories should be used in schools, it may be said, first of all, that they should be used very

---

[11]See, for example, Victor H. Noll, "Simulation by College Students of a Prescribed Pattern on a Personality Scale," *Educational and Psychological Measurement,* 11 (Spring 1951), 478–488; Bernard M. Bass, "Faking by Sales Applicants of a Forced-Choice Personality Inventory," *Journal of Applied Psychology,* 41 (December 1957), 403–404; and L. J. Stricker, "Test-wiseness on Personality Tests," *Journal of Applied Psychology Monographs,* 53, No. 3, Part 2 (June 1969), 1–18.

conservatively. Whereas the average classroom teacher can handle stan-dardized tests of achievement and intelligence with some help and guid-ance from the counselor or school psychologist, this is seldom true with personality tests. Using and interpreting these tests require more train-ing and experience than most teachers possess. As a rule, the personality test should be given individually rather than across a school. When a child asks the teacher or counselor for help or shows symptoms of malad-justment, the use of a personality inventory certainly may be indicated. It is important that the results be held in strictest confidence and used only with caution by persons qualified to interpret them. Even a tool like the *Mooney Problem Check Lists* should probably be used selectively rather than school-wide, and the results should be made available only to guidance workers or school psychologists. Every proposed use of personality tests should also be carefully scrutinized for the possibility of psychological hazards to the individual and of unfairness to cultural minorities, issues that were introduced in Chapter 1. When these princi-ples and precautions are not adhered to, the results often prove detrimen-tal to pupil morale as well as to the parents' confidence in the method used.

Although most of the words in the preceding paragraph were written for the first edition of this book, the principles expressed seem as sound today as they were originally. In fact, developments in the use of person-ality inventories during the past decade have intensified the need for care in their use.

LEARNING EXERCISES

1. Define *personality* and *adjustment.*
2. How might the results of personality tests be used by guidance work-ers and by school psychologists?
3. Is there any place for projective tests in the school? If so, describe the circumstances.
4. *Graphology,* the study of personality through handwriting, is much favored in some European countries. How might you find out whether differences in handwriting are related to differences in personality?
5. Write your own definitions of the traits measured by one of the in-ventories described in this chapter. Compare your definitions with those of other students in the class and discuss how differences in the definition of traits may affect the interpretation of inventory results.

6. Should self-report instruments be considered tests, or, as some texts suggest, should they be looked on as questionnaires?

INTEREST INVENTORIES

Interests reflect personality and are a part of personality; moreover, one's interests in relation to one's abilities, opportunities, and background may have a definite bearing on one's adjustment. The total number of inventories of people's interests is not large compared with the number of tests in other types of personality measurement. Yet if used appropriately, interest inventories can be important. They can help counselors and school psychologists assist individuals in making appropriate educational and occupational choices; and inappropriate or unsuitable choices often lead to maladjustment and serious loss of time and energy.

The interest inventory is based on the theory that a dependable picture of the pattern of a person's interests can be obtained by asking for expressions of likes and dislikes of a large number of diverse activities and things. It is assumed, furthermore, that people successful in the same occupation or field of work have similar patterns of interests. Thus, a successful motion picture actor usually has patterns of interests that are similar to the patterns of other successful actors. Finally, it is assumed that the patterns of interests of people successfully engaged in one occupation—teaching languages, for example—differ from those of people in another field—such as engineering or chemistry. These three assumptions are at the root of the development of interest inventories. Two typical inventories of this type will be briefly described.

Typical Interest Inventories

THE STRONG-CAMPBELL INTEREST INVENTORY One of the earliest and best-known interest inventories was developed by E. K. Strong in 1927 and 1928. Revised forms for men and women appeared from time to time until 1974, when the *Strong-Campbell Interest Inventory* (SCII) was published in a single form for both men and women.[12] SCII, like its predecessors, assesses individual differences in interests for use in counseling about career choices, particularly those that require college training.

[12]E. K. Strong and D. P. Campbell, *Strong-Campbell Interest Inventory* (Stanford, Calif.: Stanford University Press, 1974).

Content   SCII consists of 325 items grouped under seven topics: (1) occupations, (2) school subjects, (3) amusements, (4) activities, (5) types of people, (6) preferences between pairs of activities, and (7) agreement with statements about oneself. In each of the first five groups of items, the individual is asked to express a preference in terms of "like," "indifferent," or "dislike." For example, in the section on occupations, one is presented a list of occupations that includes actor, architect, artist, and so on and then is asked to circle "L," "I," or "D" for each. In the sixth part, each item requires the respondent to express a preference for one or the other of two activities presented as a pair. In the seventh part, the respondent is asked to rate agreement with each of a series of statements as self-descriptions by marking "Yes," "No," or "?"

An individual's responses to the inventory items are combined in several ways and compared with different norm groups to construct profiles of interests with respect to 6 General Occupational Themes (realistic, investigative, artistic, social, enterprising, and conventional), 23 Basic Interests (agriculture, mechanical activities, medical science, teaching, sales, and so on), and 124 Occupations (for example, artist, entertainer, farmer, dietician, police officer, psychologist, teacher). In addition, two nonoccupational scores, Academic Orientation and Introversion-Extroversion, are obtained and three administrative indexes are designed to reveal carelessness or other forms of inaccuracy in responding.

Levels and Forms   One form is used for age 14 and older.

Measurement Qualities   The Strong-Campbell scales are the result of a great deal of careful work from their beginnings in the several editions of the *Strong Vocational Interest Blanks* to the present. In each new edition, obsolete items were eliminated, some items were reworded, and a few new items were added. Some scales were dropped and new ones were added. Data on reliability and validity were collected continuously.

Although the bulk of the statistical evidence of reliability and validity was collected for earlier editions, it is expected to apply equally well to the *Strong-Campbell Interest Inventory*. Test-retest reliabilities of the several types of scales are consistently in the high .80s for periods of up to 30 days, and scores on the Basic Interests and Occupations scales have been shown to correlate between .60 and .70 with scores obtained 30 years earlier.[13]

Validity of the earlier Strong scales was judged by the fact that men and women entering a particular occupation made higher scores on the scale for that occupation than on any other, that men and women continuing

---

[13]David P. Campbell, *Manual, 1969 Supplement, Strong Vocational Interest Blanks* (Stanford, Calif.: Stanford University Press, 1969); *Handbook for the Strong Vocational Interest Blank* (Stanford, Calif.: Stanford University Press, 1971); *Manual for the Strong-Campbell Interest Inventory* (Stanford, Calif.: Stanford University Press, 1974).

in a suggested occupation made higher scores than those who changed from that occupation to another one, and that people changing ten years later from some occupation to some other occupation made higher scores as college seniors on the scale for the new occupation or one other occupation than they did on the scales for eighteen other occupations.[14] While such data do not show that scores predict success in an occupation, they do indicate that scores are related to occupational preference as judged by entrance into and persistence in an occupation.

More recently, evidence of validity has been presented in the now widely accepted forms of content, concurrent, and predictive validity. With respect to the first, it is said that item content is heavily oriented toward vocational activities; feelings toward such content constitute useful information for vocational planning.

Concurrent validity rests on generally acceptable evidence of the power of the scales to distinguish an individual's profile from the profiles of people in general, on the differences among occupational groups, and on differences among occupational groups and people in general. Every item on a particular occupational scale was chosen for that scale because people in that occupation answer the item in ways that are different from the answers of people in general.

Evidence of predictive validity from earlier studies has already been discussed. For college seniors and high-school seniors with definite interest patterns, it has been found additionally that the odds are about 3 to 1 that over ten to twenty years the individual will be found in an occupation consonant with an earlier profile. For the general population of college-bound high-school seniors, the odds are about 2 to 1. People found to be in an "inappropriate" occupation according to an earlier interest profile report dissatisfaction about four times as often as people in "appropriate" occupations.

Norms and Norming   All scores and norms for the SCII are for standard scores with a mean of 50 and a standard deviation of 10. Norms for scores on General Occupational Themes and Basic Interests scales are for a sample of 300 men and 300 women representative of all the occupations covered by the inventory. The norms used to interpret an individual's score for an occupation are for a sample of men or women in that occupation. Thus, each Occupations score has a different norm group. Norms for the Occupations scales are for men or women, not for men and women combined as they are for other scales. The 1974 form does not have norms for each sex on all Occupations scales, although both will be provided when available. The norm groups for different occupations typically include 100 to 500 people.

[14] Edward K. Strong, Jr., *Manual for Vocational Interest Blank for Women* (Stanford, Calif.: Stanford University Press, 1947), p. 14.

Administration The inventory may be administered to individuals or groups, or it may be self-administered. A copy may be obtained by mail. Instructions for taking the inventory are on the booklet and easy for individuals to follow. No time limit is set; most people complete it in 20 to 60 minutes.

Scoring Earlier editions could be scored by hand but SCII must be scored by computer through one of several agencies listed in the test manual. Scores on each type of scale are reported as standard scores in a two-page profile booklet.

Interpretive Aids The profiles of the booklet in which the scores are reported by the scoring services are excellent interpretive aids. One profile has the individual's standard score printed on each of the six General Occupational Themes scales. The score for each theme is labeled in relation to scores of other people of the same sex in the general sample with a descriptive phrase such as "very low," "moderately high," or "high." The individual's higher scores can be used to provide a global picture of occupational orientations and general preferences in environments and people.

A second profile has the individual's score printed on each of the 23 Basic Interests scales. This profile also shows the range between high and low points for people having the middle 50 percent and the middle 80 percent of the scores on each scale. Individuals can see whether their interests in different types of activities are average, exceptionally low, or exceptionally high compared to those of other people.

A third profile for the 124 Occupations scales shows the numerical value of the individual's score for each different occupation. In addition, it shows whether that score is "very dissimilar," "dissimilar," "average," "similar," or "very similar" to a sample of men or a sample of women now in that occupation. Scores are compared to both men and women if both were found in the norm groups for that occupation. Artist, musician, psychologist, and speech pathologist are occupations for which there are both male and female norms. There are only female norms for advertising executive and only male norms for farmer and forester.[15]

Scores on the Academic Orientation scale are typically interpreted as an indication of probable persistence in academic pursuits, and the Introversion-Extroversion score indicates whether one is likely to enjoy working in people-oriented occupations.

Finally, the three administrative indexes can be useful in discussing the confidence that one should place in the other scores as indicators of genuine interest.

[15]Campbell, *Manual for the Strong-Campbell Interest Inventory*, p. 18.

THE KUDER PREFERENCE RECORDS The *Kuder Preference Records* and the Strong inventories are the two best-known and most widely used series of interest measures. The Strong appeared first, in 1927 and 1928, and the first Kuder was not far behind it, in 1933 and 1934. The currently available Kuder inventories will be reviewed as a group.

Nature and Purpose These inventories were planned for use in vocational counseling and placement of students and employees. *Personal A* measures preferences for social relationships: participating in group activities, engaging in familiar and stable situations, working with ideas, avoiding conflict, and directing and influencing others. *Vocational C* and *General Interest Survey E* measure interest in ten broad areas: outdoor, mechanical, computational, scientific, persuasive, artistic, literary, musical, social service, and clerical. *Occupational Interest Survey DD* relates an individual's preferences to those of a large number of specific occupational groups and to those of persons pursuing various college majors. The occupations require some college training.[16]

Levels and Forms All inventories except DD and E are for grades 9–12, college, and adults. *Occupational Interest Survey DD* is for use with grades 11–12, college students, and adults—that is, with persons nearly ready to make specific career choices. The *General Interest Survey E* is a downward extension of Form C, suitable for students in grade 6 and above. Forms A and C have two forms each; DD and E have one form.

Content Each inventory calls for choices among a wide range of activities, but the choices are not grouped into categories as they are on the Strong-Campbell. The alternatives are presented in groups of three; in each group the respondent selects the most preferred alternative and the least preferred alternative. For example, Form DD has 300 items presented in 100 triads, like the following samples from the student's answer sheet:[17]

Examples	Activities	Answer
S1	Visit an art gallery	Ⓜ ●
	Browse in a library	Ⓜ Ⓛ
	Visit a museum	● Ⓛ

[16]G. Frederic Kuder, *Kuder Preference Record—Personal* (Chicago: Science Research Associates, 1948–1960); *Kuder Preference Record—Vocational* (Chicago: Science Research Associates, 1934–1970); *General Interest Survey* (Chicago: Science Research Associates, 1934–1970); *Occupational Interest Survey, Form DD* (Chicago: Science Research Associates, 1956–1964).

[17]From *Kuder Occupational Interest Survey*, Form DD, by G. Frederic Kuder. © 1956, 1964, G. Frederic Kuder. Reprinted by permission of the publisher, Science Research Associates, Inc.

S2	Collect autographs	
	Collect coins	
	Collect stones	

In the examples shown, the person answering S1 has indicated most preference for "Visit a museum" and least for "Visit an art gallery." The
other inventories have 168 triads each.

Measurement Qualities   Much research into the validity of the Kuder
inventories, particularly the occupationally oriented Forms C and DD,
has been published, although little is yet available for *General Interest
Survey E*. The general trend of the studies has shown marked differences
in scores on the separate scales for different occupational groups and for
different college majors. Definite relationships are also found between
scores on occupational and job-satisfaction measures for people in
specific occupations. The reliabilities of the various scales, determined
by the Kuder-Richardson formula, are typically between .85 and .90.

Administration   Instructions are simple, clear, and easily followed.
No time limits are set, but each inventory usually requires 30 to 60 minutes to complete.

Scoring and Interpretation   Kuder Forms A, C, and E use a pin-punch
answer pad that is practically self-scoring. Machine-scored answer sheets
are also available for these three forms. A major disadvantage of Form
DD is that it can be scored only by the publisher's scoring service.

For inventories A, C, and E, the raw scores on each scale are converted
to percentiles of representative samples of other people of the same age
and sex by simply plotting the scores on profile leaflets. The leaflets
direct students to vocational areas related to their score profiles, and
the manual provides other interpretive information of value to the counselor.

The *Occupational Interest Survey DD* scores are correlation coefficients between responses of the examinee and others of different occupational groups. No general reference group is used to interpret scores.
Instead, the individual's attention is directed to the specific occupational
groups that have interests most like his or hers, as indicated by the highest correlation coefficients. Scores (correlation coefficients) are reported
for seventy-seven occupations and twenty-nine college majors for men
and fifty-seven occupations and twenty-seven college majors for women.
A verification scale that indicates how carefully and seriously the examinee marked answers is also reported. The way the results and interpretive comments for one student might be presented is shown in Figure
11.2.

Figure 11.2 Sample Report of Scores for *Kuder Occupational Interest Survey,* Form DD

Report of Scores **Kuder Occupational Interest Survey** (Form DD)

NAME CULLEN LEONA   FEMALE   LOCATION   000-04291   DATE OF SURVEY 05-12-75

Left-margin annotations:

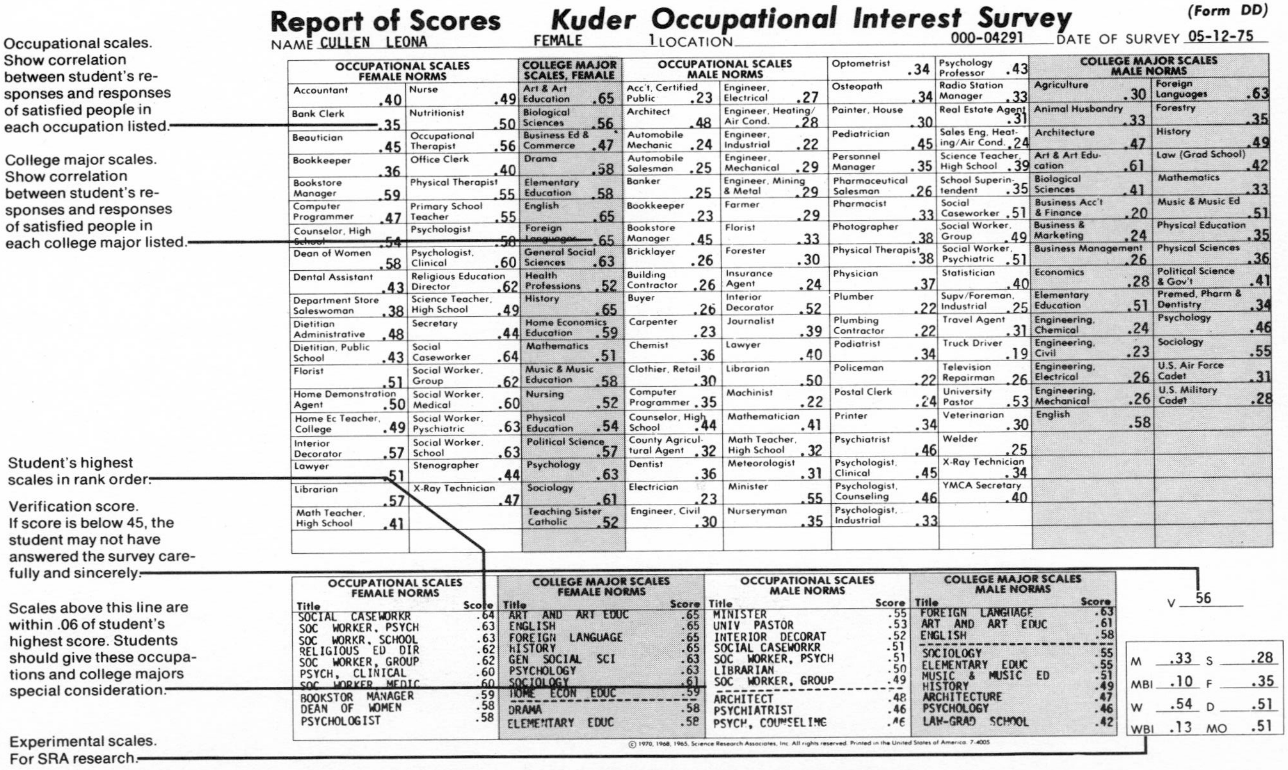

- Occupational scales. Show correlation between student's responses and responses of satisfied people in each occupation listed.
- College major scales. Show correlation between student's responses and responses of satisfied people in each college major listed.
- Student's highest scales in rank order.
- Verification score. If score is below 45, the student may not have answered the survey carefully and sincerely.
- Scales above this line are within .06 of student's highest score. Students should give these occupations and college majors special consideration.
- Experimental scales. For SRA research.

FEMALE — OCCUPATIONAL SCALES, FEMALE NORMS

Occupation	Score	Occupation	Score
Accountant	.40	Social Worker, Group	.51
Bank Clerk	.35	Social Worker, Medical	.50
Beautician	.45	Social Worker, Psychiatric	.49
Bookkeeper	.36	Stenographer	.57
Bookstore Manager	.59	X-Ray Technician	.51
Computer Programmer	.47	Teaching Sister, Catholic	.52
Counselor, High School	.54	Math Teacher, High School	.41
Dean of Women	.58	Nurse	.49
Dental Assistant	.43	Nutritionist	.50
Department Store Saleswoman	.38	Occupational Therapist	.56
Dietitian, Administrative	.48	Office Clerk	.40
Dietitian, Public School	.43	Physical Therapist	.55
Florist	.51	Primary School Teacher	.55
Home Demonstration Agent	.50	Psychologist	—
Home Ec. Teacher, College	.49	Psychologist, Clinical	.58
Interior Decorator	.57	Religious Education Director	.62
Lawyer	.51	Science Teacher, High School	.49
Librarian	.57	Secretary	.44
Math Teacher, High School	.41	Social Caseworker	.64

COLLEGE MAJOR SCALES, FEMALE NORMS

Major	Score	Major	Score
Art & Art Education	.49	History	.65
Biological Sciences	.56	Home Economics Education	.59
Business Ed & Commerce	.47	Mathematics	.51
Drama	.58	Music & Music Education	.62
Elementary Education	.58	Nursing	.52
English	.65	Physical Education	.54
Foreign Languages	.50	Political Science	.63
General Social Sciences	.63	Psychology	.63
Health Professions	.52	Sociology	.44

OCCUPATIONAL SCALES, MALE NORMS

Occupation	Score	Occupation	Score
Acct'g Certified Public	.23	Interior Decorator	.26
Architect	.48	Journalist	.23
Automobile Mechanic	.24	Lawyer	.40
Automobile Salesman	.25	Librarian	.36
Banker	.25	Machinist	.30
Bookkeeper	.23	Mathematician	.41
Bookstore Manager	.45	Math Teacher, High School	.32
Bricklayer	.26	Meteorologist	.31
Building Contractor	.26	Minister	.55
Buyer	.26	Nurseryman	.35
Carpenter	.23	Optometrist	.34
Chemist	.36	Osteopath	.34
Clothier, Retail	.30	Painter, House	.30
Computer Programmer	.35	Pediatrician	.45
Counselor, High School	.44	Personnel Manager	.29
County Agricultural Agent	.32	Pharmaceutical Salesman	.26
Dentist	.36	Pharmacist	.29
Electrician	.23	Photographer	.33
Engineer, Civil	.30	Physical Therapist	.38
Engineer, Electrical	.27	Physician	.24
Engineer, Heating & Air Cond.	.28	Plumber	.52
Engineer, Industrial	.22	Plumbing Contractor	.22
Engineer, Mechanical	.29	Podiatrist	.34
Farmer	.29	Policeman	.50
Florist	.33	Postal Clerk	.22
Forester	.30	Printer	.34
Insurance Agent	.24	Psychiatrist	.46
		Psychologist, Clinical	.45
		Psychologist, Counseling	.46
		Psychologist, Industrial	.33
		Radio Station Manager	.33
		Real Estate Agent	.31
		Sales Eng., Heating & Air Cond.	.24
		School Superintendent	.35
		Social Caseworker	.51
		Social Worker, Group	.49
		Social Worker, Psychiatric	.51
		Statistician	.25
		Supv. Foreman, Industrial	.31
		Travel Agent	.19
		Truck Driver	—
		Television Repairman	.26
		University Pastor	.53
		Veterinarian	.30
		Welder	.25
		X-Ray Technician	.34
		YMCA Secretary	.40

COLLEGE MAJOR SCALES, MALE NORMS

Major	Score	Major	Score
Agriculture	—	Foreign Languages	.63
Animal Husbandry	.30	Forestry	.35
Architecture	.49	History	.47
Art & Art Education	.61	Law (Grad School)	.42
Biological Sciences	.41	Mathematics	.33
Business Acct'g & Finance	.20	Music & Music Ed	.51
Business & Marketing	.24	Physical Education	.35
Business Management	.26	Physical Sciences	.36
Economics	.28	Political Science & Gov't	.41
Elementary Education	.51	Premed, Pharm & Dentistry	.34
Engineering, Chemical	.24	Psychology	.46
Engineering, Civil	.23	Sociology	.55
Engineering, Electrical	.26	U.S. Air Force Cadet	.31
Engineering, Mechanical	.26	U.S. Military Cadet	.28
English	.58		

Student's highest scales in rank order — FEMALE

Title	Score
SOCIAL CASEWORKER	.64
SOC. WORKER, PSYCH	.63
ENGLISH	.65
SOC. WORKR., SCHOOL	.63
RELIGIOUS ED DIR	.62
FOREIGN LANGUAGE	.63
SOC. WORKER GROUP	.60
HISTORY	.65
PSYCH. COUNSELING	.60
SOCIAL SCI	.63
PSYCHOLOGY	.63
SOCIOLOGY	—
TCHR. ECON. EDUC	.59
DEAN OF WOMEN	.58
DRAMA	.58
BOOKSTOR MANAGER	.59
ELEMENTARY EDUC	.58
PSYCHOLOGIST	.58

Student's highest scales in rank order — MALE NORMS

Title	Score
MINISTER	.55
UNIV. PASTOR	.53
INTERIOR DECORAT	.52
SOC. WORKR. PSYCH	.51
SOC. WORKER, PSYCH	.51
LIBRARIAN	.50
SOC. WORKER, GROUP	.49
ARCHITECT	.49
PSYCHIATRIST	.46
PSYCH., COUNSELING	.46
FOREIGN LANGUAGE	.63
ART AND ART EDUC	.61
ENGLISH	.58
SOCIOLOGY	.55
ELEMENTARY EDUC	.51
MUSIC & MUSIC ED	—
HISTORY	.47
ARCHITECTURE	.49
PSYCHOLOGY	.46
LAW-GRAD SCHOOL	.42

Verification score: V .56

Experimental scales:

M	.33	S	.28	
MBI	.10	F	.35	
W	.54	D	.51	
WBI	.13	MO	.51	

From *Report of Scores—Kuder Occupational Interest Survey*—Form DD by G. Frederic Kuder. © 1970, 1968, 1965, Science Research Associates, Inc. Reprinted by permission of the publisher.

Supplementary Materials All materials are attractive and well designed. Interpretive leaflets for students are well received by them, and manuals provide many useful suggestions for teachers and counselors.

*Other
Interest
Inventories*

Although the Kuder and Strong are probably the best developed and most widely used interest inventories, a number of others have been published. Some instruments still under development merit consideration for particular counseling needs.

The *Ohio Vocational Interest Survey* (OVIS) for grades 8–12 is unique in that it surveys interests in activities involving data, people, and things that are part of low-level or entry jobs listed in the U.S. Employment Service's *Dictionary of Occupational Titles.* [18] It appears thus directly relevant to the real world of work and is an excellent springboard for further career exploration. A student's scores are compared to percentile norms for other students, not to those for people already employed. Construct validity of the OVIS appears good, but there is limited evidence of predictive validity and reliability at present.

Other instruments may be useful for counseling students who are academically oriented because they focus on subjects or courses of study. For example, the scores of the *College Interest Inventory* for grades 11–16 are for agriculture, home economics, fine arts, social science, biological science, teaching, and other major areas of college study. [19]

One of the few inventories for the elementary schools, *What I Like to Do,* surveys interests of children in grades 4–7 in a wide range of topics and activities. [20] According to the manual, the results are useful in curriculum development, guidance, and instruction.

*Use of
Interest
Inventories
in Career
Education*

Interest measures are given a central role in career education programs, which are becoming a necessary and important part of the school curriculum. Two examples of programs developed by commercial publishers are the *Career Planning Program* of the American College Testing Program and the *Career Development Program* of Science Research Associates. [21] Both of these programs emphasize a comprehensive approach to career study and decision-making for all students, whether or not they plan to attend college.

The ACT *Career Planning Program* uses aptitude, achievement, and

---

[18]Ayres G. D'Costa et al., *Ohio Vocational Interest Survey* (New York: Harcourt Brace Jovanovich, 1969–1972).
[19]Robert W. Henderson, *College Interest Inventory* (Berea, Ohio: Personal Growth Press, 1967).
[20]Charles E. Meyers, Karen Drinkard, Elayne G. Zinner, *What I Like to Do* (Chicago: Science Research Associates, 1975).
[21]*ACT Career Planning Program* (Iowa City, Iowa: American College Testing Program, 1970–1973); *Career Development Program* (Chicago: Science Research Associates, 1974–1975).

interest tests, biographical data, and financial-need information to encourage and guide career exploration and planning. A *Student Booklet* includes a thorough discussion of a sample vocational interest profile and a variety of other useful information to aid students' interpretations of their own profiles. A *Counselor's Manual* answers questions frequently asked about the program, discusses problems in planning careers, and has suggestions for individual and group interpretations.

The SRA *Career Development Program* is planned for use in grade 9 in counseling or as a course of study. An individual *Career Planning Notebook* takes the student step-by-step through personal assessment, an introduction to the world of work, career investigation, and decision-making. The personal assessment section shows the student how to use information from a personal inventory of experiences, attitudes, plans, and achievements and an interest survey. The interest survey is an adaptation of the *Kuder Occupational Interest Survey DD*. A computerized interpretive report indicates possible career paths for each student. In addition, many suggestions for individual and group activities for career guidance are suggested in a *Program Guide*.

LEARNING EXERCISES

7. Would you expect the *Strong-Campbell Interest Inventory* to be more appropriate for persons above the age of 18 and the *Kuder Preference Records* to be more suitable for high-school ages? Give your reasons.

8. Does the fact that interests of adolescents are often not stabilized make the use of interest inventories inadvisable? What are some ways in which they can be used to advantage with high-school pupils?

9. Explain why the *Kuder Occupational Interest Survey* is an example of criterion-keying and the *Kuder General Interest Survey* is an example of homogeneous-keying.

10. Do you believe that students' ability to fake is a greater threat to the validity and usefulness of interest inventories or to that of personality tests? Give your reasons.

11. The Kuder inventories have been criticized because an individual who scores high on one interest scale must score lower on another scale. Explain why this is so. How serious do you believe this criticism to be?

MEASUREMENT
OF ATTITUDES AND VALUES

Attitudes may be considered another phase of personality. They are closely associated with feelings and emotions and are a large factor in determining our reactions and behavior. An attitude may be thought of as a response pattern or a tendency to think or act in a particular way under a given set of circumstances. Thus, a person has established attitudes toward certain activities, geographical regions, or political parties and toward particular individuals such as the principal of the school, the biology teacher, or classmates. When situations arise in which one or another of these is involved, one tends to react in each case in a certain way. One's attitude toward communists may be strongly antagonistic; toward the principal, neutral; and toward the football coach, strongly favorable. In the first instance the attitude may be generalized to include all communists; in the second and third, the attitude is specific with respect to a single individual. In every case there is likely to be some emotional reaction or component, however slight.

It has already been pointed out that attitudes condition behavior. An unfavorable attitude usually causes a reaction of either avoidance or aggression; a neutral attitude, indifference; and a favorable attitude, a seeking behavior. Of course, not all attitudes can be neatly classified as unfavorable, neutral, or favorable. Attitudes range by degrees from one extreme to the other, and the use of the three terms is merely for convenience.

Values are closely related to attitudes. A widely quoted *Taxonomy of Educational Objectives* finds the range of interpretations given these two terms to be much the same.[22] When distinctions are made, values are considered more general, more significant to self and society and more resistant to change.[23] Thus, an attitude may refer to a liking for a particular type of religious service, whereas the place or importance of religion in one's life may be considered a value. One's attitudes may change from time to time with little effect on personality, but significant changes in a person's value system may make that individual a quite different person indeed.

---

[22]D. R. Krathwohl, B. S. Bloom, and B. B. Masia, *Taxonomy of Educational Objectives, Handbook II: Affective Domain* (New York: David McKay, 1964), p. 37.
[23]W. L. Goodwin and H. J. Klausmeier, *Facilitating Student Learning: An Introduction to Educational Psychology* (New York: Harper & Row, 1975), pp. 304–305.

The measurement of attitudes is most often carried out by self-report methods. One method is to present to the subject a list of statements expressing attitudes varying widely from very favorable to neutral to very unfavorable; the subject is asked to check those with which he or she agrees. This method, known as the method of *equal-appearing intervals,* was devised some years ago by L. L. Thurstone and E. J. Chave.[24] A large number of statements of attitudes toward something (for example, the Republican party) are collected. These statements must vary by fine degrees in the attitudes they express, from extremely favorable to extremely unfavorable. A number of competent judges sort the statements into eleven groups according to the degree of opinion expressed. All statements in one group are those judged to be expressive of the same attitude. Each group differs from the adjoining ones above and below by apparently equal intervals or equal differences in attitude. Each judge sorts the statements independently.

The Method of Equal-Appearing Intervals (Thurstone)

   Next, the judges together select from each group the two or three statements that they regard as most typical of that group and that express most nearly the same degree of attitude. When these are assembled, there are generally twenty-five to thirty statements varying in expressed attitude from very favorable through neutral to extremely unfavorable. Each statement has a scale value according to its position or grouping. Thus, those at the most unfavorable end of the scale may each have a scale value of 11, the neutral ones, 6, and the more favorable ones, 5, 4, 3, 2, and 1, in that order. The statements are reproduced in random order and the person whose attitude toward the Republican party is to be measured is asked to check the statements with which he or she agrees. The score or attitude is based on the average scale values of the statements that were checked.

H. H. Remmers of Purdue University used Thurstone's method to develop a series of general scales to measure attitudes toward any school subject, vocation, institution, group, proposed social action, practice, or homemaking activity. The statements of each scale are general enough to apply to the object the user selects. Each scale has space for the names of five objects. For example, the scale for measuring attitude toward any school subject provides space for the names of the subjects about which attitudes are to be expressed and for evaluative statements such as:[25]

Remmers' Master Scales

---

[24]L. L. Thurstone and E. J. Chave, *The Measurement of Attitude* (Chicago: University of Chicago Press, 1929).
[25]From "A Scale for Measuring Attitude Toward Any School Subject," by Ella B. Silance. In H. H. Remmets, ed., *Purdue Master Scales.* Copyright © Purdue Research Foundation 1960, West Lafayette, Indiana 47907. Reprinted by permission.

(1) No matter what happens this subject always comes first. (10.3)
(2) I would rather study this subject than eat. (10.2)
(6) I really enjoy this subject. (9.4)
(17) This subject is O.K. (7.9)
(36) I have seen no value in this subject. (2.4)
(40) I detest this subject. (0.7)

The numbers in parentheses following the statements are the scale values to be added in scoring the scale. The attitude score is the sum of the scale values of statements with which the respondent agrees. The scale values do not appear on printed copies of the scale. The purpose of these general scales is to avoid the work required to build separate scales for each different subject.

The Likert Method

The Likert method of measuring attitudes is somewhat less time-consuming than that just described.[26] It, too, begins with a considerable number of statements of attitude toward something. However, in this case they are either decidedly favorable or decidedly unfavorable. Each statement usually has five possible responses: "SA" (strongly agree); "A" (agree); "U" (undecided); "D" (disagree); and "SD" (strongly disagree). The person taking the test reacts to every statement by marking one of the five possible responses. The responses have weights of 5, 4, 3, 2, and 1 for favorable statements, and 1, 2, 3, 4, and 5 for unfavorable ones. The subject's score is the sum of the weights of the responses checked. A high score indicates a highly favorable attitude, a low score the opposite.

The Likert method eliminates the sorting by judges, and therefore it requires less time to prepare a scale than the method of equal-appearing intervals. It also uses more statements as a rule, and the subject is required to check all of them, both of which factors tend to increase not only the reliability of scores but also the time required.

A sample set of statements set up by the Likert method might read as follows:

SA A U D SD Most parents today are too strict with their children.
SA A U D SD The old saying "Children should be seen and not heard" is more applicable today than ever before.

The Thurstone and Likert procedures are the traditional ways of measuring attitudes and are probably as good as any developed more recently. Other methods now in use require the subject to react to pictures

[26]Rensis Likert, "A Technique for the Measurement of Attitudes," *Archives of Psychology,* 22, No. 140 (June 1932), 40 pages.

or make forced choices from paired alternatives such as "salesman and mechanic," "professor and banker," "owner and operator." Factor analysis has also been used to select a relatively small number of statements highly related to basic attitudes from a much larger pool of statements previously used in Thurstone and Likert scales.

Scales are available for a wide variety of attitudes. One review of affective measures includes, for example, brief descriptions of scales to measure attitudes toward riding the school bus, punishment, handicapping conditions, progressivism and traditionalism, child-rearing practices, philosophies of human nature, and different subject areas of the school curriculum.[27] Most of these scales may be obtained from the authors; relatively few are sold by commercial publishers.

THE SURVEY OF STUDY HABITS AND ATTITUDES Among the published inventories of most interest to students and teachers are those that survey attitudes toward schools and school work. A good example of this type of instrument is the *Survey of Study Habits and Attitudes* (SSHA).[28]

A Sample Attitude Inventory

Nature and Purpose The SSHA is described as "a measure of study methods, motivation for studying and certain attitudes toward scholastic activities which are important in the classroom." The purposes are "(a) to identify students whose study habits and attitudes are different from those of students who earn high grades, (b) to aid in understanding students with academic difficulties, and (c) to provide a basis for helping such students improve their study habits and attitudes and thus more fully realize their best potentialities."[29]

Levels and Forms Form H is for grades 7–12; Form C is for college students.

Content and Scores Each of four basic scores—Delay Avoidance (DA), Work Methods (WM), Teacher Appraisal (TA), and Educational Acceptance (EA)—is based on the student's responses to 25 of the 100 statements about feelings, beliefs, and behaviors. The student responds to each statement by choosing one of the following answers: rarely (R), sometimes (S), frequently (F), generally (G), almost always (A). The following examples include one item of each of the four scales:[30]

---

[27]W. H. Beatty (ed.), *Improving Educational Assessment and an Inventory of Measures of Affective Behavior* (Washington, D.C.: Association for Supervision and Curriculum Development, National Education Association, 1969).

[28]William F. Brown and Wayne H. Holtzman, *Survey of Study Habits and Attitudes* (New York: Psychological Corp., 1953–1957).

[29]Brown and Holtzman, Manual for the *Survey of Study Habits and Attitudes* (New York: Psychological Corp., 1967), p. 5.

[30]From *Survey of Study Habits and Attitudes*, Form H. Reproduced by permission. Copyright 1953, © 1964, 1967 by The Psychological Corporation, New York, N.Y. All rights reserved.

Item	Circle Answer
If I have to be absent from class, I make up missed lessons without being reminded by the teacher. [Scale DA]	R S F G A
I have trouble saying what I want to say on tests, reports, and other work to be turned in. [Scale WM]	R S F G A
I believe that the easiest way to get good grades is to agree with everything the teachers say. [Scale TA]	R S F G A
I feel like skipping school whenever there is something I'd rather do. [Scale EA]	R S F G A

Scores on the four basic scales may be summed to obtain scores on Study Habits (SH = DA + WM), Study Attitudes (SA = TA + EA), and the total, Study Orientation (SO = SH + SA).

Measurement Qualities Reliability coefficients for the SSHA are quite satisfactory for this type of instrument. Test-retest reliabilities for the part and total scores over a 4- to 14-week period are .83 to .94.

In the development of the scales, a preliminary pool of items was developed by studying previous investigations and by interviewing and observing good and poor students. These items were administered to samples of students, and only those that were answered differently by honor students and students with scholastic difficulty were retained for the final instrument. Additional statistical data have been obtained to show that total scale scores (Study Orientation scores) have predictive validity for grades. Correlations of total scores with grades average about .40 at the high-school or college level. These scores are rather independent of academic objectives and may be used in combination with aptitude measures to improve scholastic prediction.

The separate subscale scores are not recommended for use as predictors of achievement. They are, however, useful in academic counseling and for increasing student awareness of academic problems. Of course, the SSHA, like other self-report measures, is subject to faking. Students must cooperate fully if the results are to be meaningful, and using the results for screening or selecting competing students is not advisable.

Norms and Norming Percentile scores are reported for each of the several scores of each form. The same norms are used for men and women. Norms for Form C were derived from scores of 3,054 freshmen at nine colleges; those for Form H were derived from scores for 11,218 students in sixteen different towns and metropolitan areas across the United States. In the norm sample for Form H, students from the Southwest appear to be somewhat overrepresented.

Scoring In scoring, extreme responses—"rarely" (0 to 15 percent of the time) and "almost always" (86 percent to 100 percent of the time)—are given twice the weight of "sometimes" (16 percent to 35 percent) or "generally" (66 percent to 85 percent). Answers of "frequently" are not scored. Hand- or machine-scoring is simple with an IBM 805 or 1230 answer sheet. A counseling key is also available for identifying academic behavior and scholastic motivations different from those of students who are "achievers." Students who have a large number of such responses may need counseling.

Administration Directions for administration are simple and straightforward. There is no time limit, but most students complete the inventory in 20–35 minutes. Every student should answer every question. Care is needed to ensure that the student understands that the answers are marked across the answer sheet, not down the sheet as they often are.

The Student Profile All materials are well designed. A diagnostic profile of percentile scores is easily plotted by the student. The profile provides a graphic display of scores that are above or below the 50th percentile or middle student of the norm group. The profile sheet includes an interpretation of each scale that students can use for help in understanding their strengths and weaknesses in comparison with students who get good grades and students who get poor grades. Discussion of items identified as weaknesses by use of the counseling key is suggested.

One of the chief problems in the construction and use of attitude scales is their validity. As with all self-report instruments, the value of the score depends on the cooperation of the person taking the test. It is very easy for anyone to simulate an extreme attitude, simply by checking all the strong statements one way or the other or by strongly agreeing or strongly disagreeing with all the statements of one type or another. Generally this is much easier to do in an attitude scale than in a personality inventory. In the latter the implications are not always obvious. Unless the subject is honestly trying to cooperate when checking the attitude scale, the results are of little or no value.

Validity and Reliability of Attitude Scales

In the second place, what a person agrees or disagrees with on paper is not necessarily a reflection of how he or she really feels or acts. There is no way of determining whether subjects are honestly expressing what they believe. Furthermore, what they endorse on the test is one thing, but actual behavior in the same or a similar situation may not be consistent with verbal responses. Some research has been done on this with widely varying findings. Some studies report substantial correlations between scores on an attitude scale and observed behavior; others report negligible correlations. Corey, for example, found practically no correlation in a college class between scores on a scale of attitude toward cheating and actual behavior in an examination.[31]

[31]Stephen M. Corey, "Professed Attitudes and Actual Behavior," *Journal of Educational Psychology,* 28 (April 1937), 271–280.

Much of the research suggests that there is a positive correlation in the neighborhood of .50–.60 between scores on attitudes scales and actual performance or behavior. This is not a close relationship, but it does indicate a substantial tendency. The ultimate validity of attitude scores depends on how well they correlate with action. It may be interesting and in some instances useful to know what an individual's verbalized attitudes are, but unless they can be used to predict how that person will act, such data are of limited value for practical purposes. In this respect there is still much to be accomplished in the area of attitude measurement.

CLASSROOM ASSESSMENT OF AFFECTIVE ATTRIBUTES

Attitudes, interests, and other personality outcomes may be important objectives of local schools. However, procedures for teachers to use in assessing attainment of objectives in the affective domain are not as well developed as those for testing the achievement of cognitive objectives. The procedures developed for the construction of attitude scales, for example, are more difficult and time-consuming than those for the construction of achievement tests. Also, locally constructed scales for the measurement of affective characteristics are usually less valid and reliable than conventional tests of scholastic achievement. Nevertheless, if care is exercised in constructing and interpreting self-report instruments, school faculties can devise inventories and scales that will contribute to the appraisal of attitudes of concern to their communities.

Another point of view is that it is important to begin somewhere and therefore even relatively crude informal measurement techniques should be used. There are, fortunately, several reasons why teachers may not always need to be as concerned about some of the limitations of procedures for measuring affective characteristics as they would be for measuring knowledge and understanding. First of all, the results may be needed to judge the success of the teacher's own efforts, not to grade students. Hence, information from self-report and observational procedures may be collected for the class as a whole; individual responses may be anonymous so that there is no reason for students to cheat. Moreover, teachers need not be preoccupied at this stage of their sophistication in measuring affect with matters of fine degree but simply with classifying responses as positive or negative, desirable or undesirable. Finally, the use of a variety of evidence instead of reliance on a single type of report or observation provides some safeguards against errors in judgment.

The measurement of attitudes toward learning and school subjects will be used to illustrate informal approaches, but similar considerations apply in the informal assessment of a wide range of affective objectives. Every teacher wants students to have favorable attitudes toward the subject taught, and a cherished goal of every teacher is to send students forth wanting to use what they have learned and eager to learn more. Although the ultimate concern is for how a student acts after leaving a class, this is difficult to assess. A teacher can, however, periodically check a student's approach and avoidance tendencies while in the class.

A useful statement of a measurable objective is as essential in evaluating the achievement of affective outcomes as it is in measuring knowledge gains. A practical place for a teacher to begin to assess the effect of the class on student attitudes is to state an objective in terms of an expected increase in the number and percentage of positive or approach responses recorded for students from the beginning to the end of the class. At the very least a teacher would wish to leave students with an attitude as positive as (or no more negative than) the attitude they held when they entered the class.

What evidence should we look for? R. F. Mager suggests doing three things: (1) Ask yourself what your friends do or say that reveals their likes or dislikes. (2) When others comment on the likes and dislikes of acquaintances, ask what these persons do or say that leads to this conclusion. (3) Jot down the things that lead you to believe a student is either favorably or unfavorably disposed toward a subject.[32] A variety of self-report responses (what students say) and observations of behavior (what one sees them do) will seem relevant. Several examples of self-reports will be given here. The use of observational evidence will be described in the next chapter, as well as summary records that are very useful in combining evidence from self-reports and observations.

Teachers may develop their own questionnaires to survey what students say about their class or teaching area. The following examples illustrate several types that may be used to suggest approach and avoidance tendencies. A variety of item types should be used and as many items as are needed to give one confidence in judgments.

Informal Questionnaires

1. If given a chance, would you take another course in ＿＿＿＿＿＿＿?
   a. yes
   b. no
   c. maybe
2. If you had it to do all over again, would you take this course?
   a. yes
   b. no
   c. maybe

---

[32] R. F. Mager, *Developing Attitudes Toward Learning*, (Palo Alto, Calif.: Fearon, 1968), p. 29.

3. Would you like to help others learn about _____?
   a. yes
   b. no
   c. maybe
4. Would you like to learn about _____?
   a. definitely
   b. probably
   c. probably not
   d. definitely not
5. How interested are you in some suggestions for further study in _____?
   a. very interested
   b. somewhat interested
   c. neither interested nor disinterested
   d. not too interested
   e. not at all interested
6. How important do you think it is for you to know _____?
   a. very important
   b. somewhat important
   c. neither important nor unimportant
   d. not too important
   e. not at all important
7. Check the following scale at the place on the line that indicates your opinion of _____.

(1)	(3)	(5)
Least-liked subject	Average subject	Best-liked subject

8. Which word in each of the following pairs best describes your opinion of _____? Circle one word of each pair.

pleasant	unpleasant
good	bad
boring	exciting
useful	useless
worthless	valuable

Corey's Method of Scale Construction

An example of a somewhat more sophisticated method of measuring attitudes that is also well suited to the needs of classroom teachers was used by one of the authors to measure student attitudes toward smoking. This was a project of the American Cancer Society in cooperation with the Milwaukee, Wisconsin, public schools. The method was an adaptation of the Thurstone method originally suggested by Stephen M. Corey.[33]

The first step in the method is to ask each member of the class or group of students to write three or four statements expressing different views about the attitude object. In this application of the method, the author

---

[33] Stephen M. Corey, "Measuring Attitudes in the Classroom," *Elementary School Journal,* 43, (April 1943), 457–461.

asked students for good and bad things that people might say about smoking, not what they themselves believed. The following statements are examples of statements given by fifth- and sixth-grade classes:

> Smoking helps you think better.
> It gives you a lift.
> Smoking shows you are grown up.
> It is fun.
> It helps make friends.
> Smoking makes you weak.
> It is dirty.

The second step is to edit the statements. Duplicates and statements of fact are eliminated. Usable statements must be debatable or matters of opinion. Thus: "Smoking is against school rules" was not used because it stated a fact. Double-barreled statements such as "Smoking is bad for you but everyone does it" were also rejected, as were all long, complex, or technical statements and statements that might be misread or misinterpreted.

Next, all the statements that survive editing are administered to the entire class or group. In this step students are asked to indicate whether each of the statements expresses a favorable or an unfavorable thing to say, not what they themselves think. In the smoking example, students did this by a show of hands when each statement was read aloud by the teacher. Students might have been given a printed list of statements and asked to mark favorable ones with a plus sign and unfavorable ones with a minus sign. When students do not agree that a statement is either favorable or unfavorable, that statement is eliminated from the list. As a general rule, statements are rejected unless 80 percent of the students agree that it is one or the other.

The final step of the method is to duplicate the selected items with appropriate directions for students. Corey recommended the following for general use:

> This is not a test in the sense that any particular statement is either right or wrong. All these sentences represent opinions that some people hold about _____. Indicate whether you agree or disagree with the statement by putting a plus sign before all the opinions with which you agree and a minus sign before those with which you disagree. If you are uncertain, use a question mark. After you have gone through the entire list, go back and draw a circle around the plus signs where you agree very strongly, and a circle around the minus signs where you disagree very strongly.[34]

[34]From Stephen M. Corey, "Measuring Attitudes in the Classroom," *Elementary School Journal*, 43 (April 1943), p. 460. Reproduced by permission of the publisher, the University of Chicago. Copyright 1943 by the University of Chicago.

In scoring responses to favorable statements, 5 points are given for a plus sign that is circled, 4 points for a plus sign, 3 points for a question mark, 2 points for a minus sign, and 1 point for a minus sign that is circled. Unfavorable statements are scored in the opposite direction, with a circled minus sign receiving 5 points and a circled plus sign 1 point. The author found it advisable to simplify the directions and the scoring for students below grade 7. In the elementary grades, a 3-point scale—agree, undecided, and disagree—worked better.

A student's attitude score on this type of scale is the sum of the points received on all items, and it may be interpreted as typical or atypical in reference to the scores of other students. The desirability of individual or group attitudes may be judged in reference to the objectives of the school or community for students.

LEARNING EXERCISES

12. List some matters such as school subjects, athletics, high marks, or senior trips toward which a high-school faculty might wish to test attitudes. Name some in which elementary teachers might be similarly interested.
13. Select one of the items from Exercise 12 and write out ten statements expressing different attitudes toward it that might become part of a scale, following either the Thurstone or the Likert plan.
14. What are some of the issues for which scales of attitudes have been devised? Find in the literature on educational measurement a report of one such project and prepare an abstract of it.
15. Consult another text or Buros's Yearbook for a description of an inventory to measure values, such as the *Allport-Vernon-Lindzey Study of Values.* Compare the nature and use of inventories of this type with those the text describes for attitude scales.

SUGGESTED READING

ANASTASI, ANNE. *Psychological Testing.* 4th ed. New York: Macmillan, 1976. Chapters 17–19 are about self-report inventories, measures of interests and attitudes, and projective techniques. Besides description and discussion of various instruments, there are evaluations of the various categories.

BEATTY, W. H., ed. *Improving Educational Assessment and an Inventory of Measures of Affective Behavior.* Washington, D.C.: Association for Supervision and Curriculum Development, National Education Association, 1968. Section 2 is a comprehensive, well-annotated resource list of devices for the measurement of attitudes, creativity, social interaction, motivation, self-concept, and other aspects of personality.

BLOOM, B. S., J. T. HASTINGS, and G. P. MADAUS. *Handbook on Formative and Summative Evaluation of Student Learning.* New York: McGraw-Hill, 1971. Chapter 10, "Evaluation Techniques for Affective Objectives," is an excellent source of ideas for questionnaires and interview schedules. The book also illustrates the contributions of historically important studies and offers brief comments on the use of projective techniques.

CRONBACH, LEE J. *Essentials of Psychological Testing.* 3d ed. New York: Harper & Row, 1970. Chapter 14 is about interest inventories and general problems of measuring interests. Chapter 15 is titled "General Problems in Studying Personality," which describes its content. Chapter 16 is concerned with self-report approaches to measuring personality. Chapter 17 is on ratings. Chapter 18 contains discussions of various "performance" tests of personality such as character, problem-solving, and projective techniques.

EDWARDS, ALLEN L. *Techniques of Attitude Scale Construction.* New York: Appleton-Century-Crofts, 1957. A scholarly discussion of the different methods of constructing scales for the measurement of attitudes. Also presents methods of evaluating scales derived by each method described.

GRONLUND, NORMAN E. *Measurement and Evaluation in Teaching.* 3d ed. New York: Macmillan, 1976. Chapter 16 discusses observational techniques: anecdotal records, rating scales, and check lists. In Chapter 17 are discussions of guess-who, sociometric, and self-report techniques. The latter include brief discussions of check lists of activities and problems, personality inventories, projective techniques, interest inventories, and attitude scales.

MEHRENS, WILLIAM A., and IRVIN J. LEHMANN. *Standardized Tests in Education.* 2d ed. New York: Holt, Rinehart and Winston, 1975. In Chapter 5 the authors discuss problems of measuring noncognitive characteristics and follow with description and analysis of interest inventories, self-report personality tests, and problem check lists. There are brief discussions of measures of attitudes and values, study habits, and projective tests.

PAYNE, D. A. *The Assessment of Learning, Cognitive and Affective.* Lexington, Mass.: D.C. Heath, 1974. Chapter 7 discusses general considerations in developing measures of affective learning outcomes, and Chapter 8 describes and illustrates the construction of a variety of items and scales.

SHAW, M. E., and J. M. WRIGHT. *Scales for the Measurement of Attitudes.* New York: McGraw-Hill, 1967. Describes, illustrates, and evaluates numerous unpublished scales developed by different authors. Good source of suggestions.

TEN BRINK, T. D. *Evaluation: A Practical Guide for Teachers.* New York: McGraw-Hill, 1974. Chapter 11, "Developing Questionnaires, Interview Schedules, and Sociometric Instruments," describes and illustrates the construction of self-report and peer-appraisal instruments.

THORNDIKE, ROBERT L., and ELIZABETH HAGEN. *Measurement and Evaluation in Psychology and Education.* 4th ed. New York: John Wiley & Sons, 1977. Chapter 11 includes brief descriptions and discussions of various methods of studying personality, including interviews, interest inventories, temperament and adjustment inventories, and measurement of attitudes.

TYLER, R. W. "Assessing Educational Achievement in the Affective Domain." *NCME Measurement in Education,* 4 (1973), 1–8. One of the country's leading educators, a pioneer in educational evaluation, identifies the cognitive and affective components in interests, attitudes, values and appreciations, discusses problems in selecting objectives in the affective domain, and offers suggestions for a variety of measurement techniques.

Twelve

THE MEASUREMENT
OF PERSONALITY AND AFFECT:
OBSERVATIONAL TECHNIQUES

In Chapter 11 various self-report approaches to the measurement of personality and affect were presented. This chapter continues and concludes the discussion of the measurement of personality and affect with a consideration of observational techniques. Observational techniques employ information from sources other than the individual being studied. The techniques discussed here are rating scales, systematic observation, anecdotal records, sociometry, other peer-appraisal methods, and classroom observation. In addition to describing and evaluating these techniques, we consider the use of observational data and procedures for efficiently combining evidence from self-reports, observations, and school records.

Study of this chapter will enable you to answer questions and complete tasks such as the following:

1. Describe good practice in the use of rating scales for the study of student traits.
2. Compare the advantages and disadvantages of different observational techniques.
3. Explain how time-sampling is used to improve classroom observation.
4. Explain how students' choices of companions may help in understanding the social structure of the classroom.
5. Describe the methods used to demonstrate that a teacher's response to a pupil's behavior can change that behavior.
6. How may one's observations of individual students be organized for more effective use?

7. How may observations of student behavior be related to one's success as a teacher?

RATING SCALES

The basic purpose of rating devices is to obtain systematically and objectively a sampling of opinion on certain characteristics of a given individual. Such judgments should be obtained from people who are well acquainted with the person being rated and who can express accurate and dependable opinions. In order to obtain satisfactory results, it is essential to follow certain well-established and tested procedures. Among other things, it is necessary to define the traits or characteristics on which the ratings will be based, to provide some kind of scale or range by which the rater can indicate a judgment of the amount or degree of a trait, and to have specific and carefully worked out instructions regarding the purpose and use of the instrument. It is highly desirable to meet with other raters in order to discuss the use of the device with them and, if possible, to give them some practice in using it. Instruction and information in addition to that printed on the scale *must* be given to persons untrained in using rating scales if the results are to be valid and reliable.

In constructing a rating scale, the first step is to divide the broad area to be analyzed into specific traits or characteristics. To ask for ratings in such wide areas as "personality" or "adjustment" would give almost meaningless results. Therefore, the concept of "personality" should be broken down into more specific and definable terms such as *persistence, cheerfulness, aggressive tendencies, generosity,* or *resourcefulness.*

When such an analysis has been made, the next step is to define each of these traits in terms that will be meaningful to the rater and will convey similar meanings to the various persons using the scale. This is difficult, and of course it is never possible to be sure that one has succeeded. However, if the traits are clearly defined in terms of behavior, rather than vague abstractions, it helps materially to ensure that those people using the scale will have a common understanding of the traits being rated.

Finally, the specific traits should be defined in such a way that the definitions provide descriptions of the varying degrees of each trait and lead the rater to make quantitative judgments rather than vague, meaningless generalizations.

Graphic Rating Scales

The most widely used form of rating device is generally referred to as the *graphic rating scale.* In this form each trait is represented not only by descriptions of varying degrees of the trait but also by a line divided into the same number of equal segments as there are trait descriptions. The rater expresses a judgment by placing a check mark on the line to indicate the estimate of the person being rated.

An excerpt from a graphic rating scale of personality is shown in Figure 12.1. It clearly illustrates the principles of construction and organization that we have just discussed.

This rating scale, or rating schedule, as it is called, provides opportunity for ratings on twenty-nine traits grouped in eight categories: mental alertness, initiative, dependability, cooperativeness, judgment, personal impression, courtesy, and health. A score may be obtained on each trait, and the scores may be averaged within each category or for all twenty-nine traits. A check mark placed as shown in the figure indicates the rater's appraisal of the person being rated—in this case, between average and somewhat above average. This rating could be given a numerical value of 3.5.

THE CHILD BEHAVIOR RATING SCALE   Another type of scale is the *Child Behavior Rating Scale*, which provides for numerical ratings in five adjustment areas: self, home, social, school, and physical. This is a standardized instrument for the assessment of personality adjustments of preschool, kindergarten, and first-, second-, and third-grade pupils and older children unable to complete conventional paper-and-pencil inventories. It may be completed by teachers, parents, or any adult who has observed the behavior of the child. The accompanying sample shows how this scale is arranged.[1] This is not a graphic scale in the usual sense

Numerical Rating Scales

The Child Behavior Rating Scale

Self Adjustment	Scale Values					
	1	2	3	4	5	6
1. Often prefers to be alone.	yes					no
2. Often seems unhappy or depressed.	yes					no
3. Often cries, and with little or no reason.	yes					no
4. Feelings are often easily hurt.	yes					no
5. Often appears to feel unwanted or disliked.	yes					no

of the term. The numbered boxes correspond to six levels for each behavior rated, and the rater simply checks the one that seems most appropriate. In-between ratings are not recorded. This type of scale, often

[1]From *Child Behavior Rating Scale* Manual. Copyright 1962 by Western Psychological Services. Reprinted by permission.

Figure 12.1   Excerpt from *BEC Personality Rating Schedule*

V. JUDGMENT

	5	4	3	2	1	0
1. *Sense of Values*	Is unfailingly keen of insight in distinguishing the important from the unimportant in classwork	Generally distinguishes the important from the unimportant in classwork even when confusion might be easy ✓	Distinguishes satisfactorily between the important and the unimportant in classwork	Occasionally confuses the important with the unimportant in classwork		Commonly neglects crucial issues in classwork through attention to the unimportant
2. *Deliberativeness*	Always considers carefully all aspects of problem situation before proposing solution	Usually considers all important aspects of problem situation before proposing solution	Seldom proposes solution to important problem situation without some preliminary analysis	Sometimes proposes solutions to problem situations without any preliminary analysis		Is constantly jumping at conclusions
3. *Tact*	Extremely gifted in discerning the best thing to do or say when dealing with others; never gives any offense	Usually says or does the suitable thing when dealing with others	Only rarely gives any offense through ill-considered speech or action	Sometimes says or does the wrong thing when dealing with others		Frequently gives offense through lack of discernment in speech or action

Reprinted by permission of the publishers from Philip J. Rulon and others, *BEC Personality Rating Schedule* (Cambridge, Mass.: Harvard University Press, 1936). Copyright, 1936, by The President and Fellows of Harvard College.

called a *numerical scale,* does not allow for ratings anywhere on the scale. In the opinion of some, this is a disadvantage in that it does not permit as much differentiation as the graphic scale.

A score is obtained for each adjustment area by adding the ratings for the behaviors of that area. Twenty kinds of behaviors are rated for self, home, and social adjustment. Twelve are rated for school adjustment; six are rated for physical adjustment. A Personality Total Adjustment score (PTAS) is obtained from three of the area adjustment scores by the following formula: (2 × Self-Adjustment) + (2 × Home Adjustment) + School Adjustment. The manual includes a table for converting the PTAS and the area adjustment scores to two types of standard scores, one for typical students and one for emotionally disturbed children. The two types of scores are used to construct two profiles for each child, one comparing the child's scores with those of a group of 2,000 typical children, the other with a group of 200 maladjusted children.

The authors state that the PTAS is most significant. If it is 60 or higher, the child would appear to have an excellent, better than typical, personality adjustment. If it is between 40 and 60, adjustment is typical in relation to the norm group. If the PTAS is below 40, the authors suggest that an emotional handicap is indicated. The area scores are used to identify areas of good or poor adjustment more specifically and provide suggestions for counseling or remedial work.

The items for the *Child Behavior Rating Scale* were obtained from case studies of over 1,000 school pupils referred for psychological or psychiatric services. Validity is suggested by evidence that typical children receive higher ratings than children referred to clinics because of behavioral adjustment problems. Scores on this scale are also related to school achievement test scores and to intelligence quotients and to measures of social development, although the correlation coefficients are not large, from .20 to .48. The reliability of the total score based on the correlation among the ratings of different raters is .656; that based on the correlation between ratings of teachers at two different times is .739; and split-halves reliability coefficients are .873 for typical children and .589 for maladjusted children. These reliability coefficients compare favorably with those obtained for personality inventories.

THE LEARNING DISABILITIES RATING SCALE   Another scale, somewhat more typical of numerical scales, is the *Pupil Rating Scale: Screening for Learning Disabilities.* One part of this scale, designed for use with children 7 through 10 years of age, provides for ratings on eight personal-social characteristics or traits: cooperation, attention, organization, reaction to new situations, social acceptance, responsibility, completion of assignments, and tactfulness. Four other areas of behavior related to learning deficiencies—auditory comprehension, spoken language, orientation, and motor coordination—are also rated. The areas and items were chosen from the author's long experience with learning-disabled children. The sample below shows how this scale is set up.[2]

Cooperation	Rating
Continually disrupts classroom; unable to inhibit responses	1
Frequently demands attention; often speaks out of turn	2
Waits his turn; average for age and grade	3
Above average; cooperates well	4
Excellent ability; cooperates without adult encouragement	5

There are five numbered levels for each trait, and the rater simply circles the number that seems most appropriate. A total score is obtained for personal-social behavior by adding numbers circled for the eight personal-social traits. The score for personal-social behavior may be added to the sums for the other areas of behavior to get a total score for learning disabilities.

This rating scale is suggested by its author for use as a screening device for identifying children who have deficiencies in learning. After pupils have been rated by their teachers and the scores have been calculated, study of the results for individuals or for groups can suggest what further evaluation, or what referrals to counselors or clinics, are necessary. Tables in the manual give the means and standard deviations of groups passing and failing a battery of screening tests and of typical pupils and pupils clinically diagnosed as learning-disabled. By comparing the scores of pupils being rated with the scores of these known groups, one can identify individuals with unusually low scores. The author suggests that every child with a low score be evaluated further.

Effective Use of Rating Scales

Rating scales and devices may, of course, be used for purposes other than rating personality and adjustment. For example, they may be used to rate performance on a job, the quality of a product such as a cake or a lampstand made by a pupil, or the quality of handwriting. The use of rating scales for such purposes has already been discussed in a previous chapter.

We mentioned earlier that it is not safe to assume that anyone can use a rating scale properly and effectively without instruction; indeed, it is generally recognized that some instruction is necessary if the results are to be of value. Some of the common errors in using rating scales may serve as a starting point in developing suggestions for effective use.

[2]From Helmer R. Myklebust, *The Pupil Rating Scale: Screening for Learning Disabilities* (New York: Grune and Stratton, 1971). Reproduced by permission of author and publisher.

A frequent cause of error is the *halo effect,* the tendency of the rater to let a general, overall impression of the person being rated influence the ratings on every trait. If a rater likes a person, there is a tendency to rate that person favorably on everything. A rater's dislike of a person also tends to color all ratings.

Another common error is the tendency to avoid the ends of the scale—that is, to avoid rating persons very high or very low. This is sometimes referred to as the *error of central tendency* and is likely to occur where raters are not well acquainted with the persons being rated. Similar is the *generosity error,* the practice of rating everyone average or above. When this happens no one gets a rating below the middle of the scale, a manifestly unrealistic situation, since there are usually as many below the average in a given group as there are above.

Still another common error is the *stereotype error,* in which some raters with preconceived ideas about members of certain groups—racial, religious, economic, or occupational—tend to rate them accordingly.

There are other types of errors in using rating scales, but these are among the most common and serious. The suggestions listed below should help counteract if not entirely overcome such tendencies toward error.

1. Rate each member of a group in comparison with all the others in the group. If only one person is being rated, compare that person mentally with others of the same level, class, occupation. Do not rate the person on the basis of some ideal that exists only in imagination or on the basis of unrealistic and unattainable standards.
2. Rate each person on one trait before going to the next. For example, if there are thirty-five pupils to be rated on ten traits, rate all thirty-five on trait 1, then all thirty-five on trait 2, and so on. This is believed to make ratings more accurate and dependable.
3. Wherever possible, use multiple ratings. That is, have several teachers or observers rate the same pupils without consulting each other. Ratings made independently by several raters and then considered collectively are much better than single ratings by one individual.
4. In making ratings, try to think of the individual's behavior in as many different situations as possible. Isolated incidents, although they may be very striking, are not always typical of behavior.
5. Do not rate individuals on traits or categories for which there is no specific evidence or behavior to support the rating. If you have no basis for making a judgment, do not rate. Leave the item unmarked and indicate for it that you have had no opportunity to observe it. A false or inaccurate rating is worse than none at all.

6. Instruct and assist the people who are to make ratings. A meeting or two could well be devoted to the development and discussion of such points as the five preceding.

LEARNING EXERCISES

1. Devise a short graphic rating scale for the five traits of industry, perseverance, courtesy, emotional stability, and sociability. Try to define degrees of each trait in terms of observable behavior.
2. Write out a set of instructions that will help fifth-grade teachers use the scale correctly.

THE BASIC OBSERVATION TECHNIQUE

Although each of the methods described in this chapter involves observation, there is an *observation technique* with several features that merit individual consideration. The observation technique has been developed primarily in connection with child study. Nursery schools and kindergartens, particularly where these are part of a laboratory or demonstration school, are commonly equipped with one-way-vision screens so that children may be observed without their seeing the observers or knowing that they are being observed. Some efficient and dependable procedures for making and recording such observations have been developed through experience and research, and these procedures will be considered briefly as a means of evaluating behavior, personality, and adjustment.

As in the case of rating scales, one basic principle in observation is to define the behavior to be observed. It has not been found very useful or satisfactory just to "observe" children. It is much more productive first to define what is going to be observed and then to concentrate on observation in terms of the definition established. For example, suppose one were interested in studying personality traits in a group of four- and five-year-olds. The first step would be to identify and define the traits to be observed—such traits, for example, as cooperative behavior. What constitutes cooperative behavior at this age? Probably a dozen or more kinds of behavior (sharing toys, helping the teacher, picking up) could be thought of as evidence of cooperation among five-year-olds.

When the particular characteristic in question has been analyzed and divided into specific acts or behavior patterns, these elements are listed on a schedule or check list that the observer uses as a means of recording observations. Each time a particular behavior is observed it is recorded on the check list. In addition, cooperative behaviors not listed can be added as they occur.

A second principle is that there should be frequent and distributed observations. This means that it is better to divide the total observation time per child into smaller amounts for frequent observation than to use it all in one or two observations. Assuming, for example, that the observer has 2 hours of observation time per child, what is the best way to use it? It can be used in one 2-hour block, two 1-hour periods, and so on, down to a hundred and twenty 1-minute observations. Although no arbitrary, hard-and-fast rule can be given, it is generally agreed that a total of 2 hours divided into twenty-four 5-minute periods is preferable to longer and less frequent observations. Some investigators would use shorter and more frequent periods than this. In general, expert opinion seems to favor frequent, short observations distributed over a period of several weeks and at different times of the day. The chief advantage of such a plan is that it is likely to yield a more adequate sample of a child's behavior and thus reduce the chance of getting erroneous impressions from a long observation on what might be a very nontypical day. Rotating the time of observation so that the same child is not observed at the same time of day in the several observation periods reduces the probability of getting consistently biased samples of behavior at a particular time of day, such as just before lunch.

It must be recognized, of course, that longer observation periods may be preferable under certain conditions or for certain purposes. This is particularly true where sequence of behavior is to be studied and where the development from beginning to end of certain behavior situations is to be observed. Instead of defining and concentrating the observation on a specific behavior, one may keep a running account of the total behavior of a given child over a period of several days. This procedure, often used by clinicians, has the advantage of giving a more complete picture of the child, though it usually lacks the objectivity of the other method and it does not yield data that can readily be expressed in quantitative terms, such as a count of the number of times the defined behavior occurred.

Much depends on the training and the skill of the observer. Observers must be able to observe and record objectively, keep personal bias out of the observations, and distinguish clearly between observation and interpretation. They should record only what happens and do so as promptly as possible to reduce the need to rely too long on memory for important data. It is generally best to concentrate on obtaining a complete and accurate record at the time of observation and to make interpretations of the record later when there is more time for careful study.

An illustration or two of the observation method should make it more definite and meaningful. One of the earliest applications of the *time-sampling* method of observing behavior in young children was a study reported by Willard C. Olson in 1929.[3] He observed nervous habits in elementary school children by using 5-minute observation periods for each child and recording the incidence of nervous habits (nose-picking, twitching, and the like). Later investigators have improved upon and refined his procedure, but Olson's was one of the first to yield quantitative data based on systematic time samples of children's observable behavior.

In the past few years observation techniques have been used extensively in studies of how behavior is modified by its consequences. Wesley C. Becker has reported, for example, a series of classroom experiments that show how teachers can evaluate student behavior by observation and change it by praise.[4]

Becker describes the experimental use of rules and ignoring and praising to decrease the incidence of inappropriate classroom behavior and to increase the frequency of appropriate behavior. In one study of elementary school classes, several categories of behavior that disrupted learning and violated school rules were observed. Examples of gross motor behavior included getting out of the chair, standing, running, skipping, and jumping. Other disruptive behavior included making noise with objects, being aggressive, blurting out, talking to peers, and engaging in other off-task behavior.

Children were observed for three 20-minute sessions each week. Each observation period was divided into intervals of 20 seconds each. If disruptive behavior occurred in a 20-second interval, that interval was checked as one containing an instance of deviant behavior.

The children were first observed for 5 weeks under typical classroom conditions. Then rules for classroom behavior were announced; teachers gave praise for appropriate behavior such as studying and paying attention, and disruptive behavior was ignored. The results for two children, Dan and Don, are shown in Figure 12.2.

During the baseline period, before the experimental treatment was started, Dan's behavior was deviant in 60 percent to 85 percent of the intervals during which he was observed. By the end of the experiment, his behavior was deviant only 10 percent to 40 percent of the time. The chart also suggests that his behavior improved only after reading tutoring began. A definite decrease in the percentage of deviant behavior intervals

[3]Willard C. Olson, *The Measurement of Nervous Habits in Normal Children,* Institute of Child Welfare Monographs 3 (Minneapolis, Minn.: University of Minnesota Press, 1929).
[4]Wesley C. Becker, "Applications of Behavior Principles in Typical Classrooms," in C. A. Thoreson (ed.), *Behavior Modification in Education,* Seventy-second Yearbook of the National Society for the Study of Education, Part 1 (Chicago: The Society, 1973), pp. 79–89.

PERSONALITY AND AFFECT MEASUREMENT: OBSERVATION

is also recorded for Don. The improvement noted for these two boys was all the more dramatic because earlier Don had been recommended for placement as an educable retarded boy and Dan had been considered a severely disturbed boy who was more than 2 years behind in reading. The reliability data below the chart give the percentage of agreement among different observers of each boy each week.

Mention of the percentage of agreement among observers—agreement is fairly high in the figure—brings up the importance of training and skill in observation. This can scarcely be overemphasized. People vary greatly in their ability to observe and report accurately what they have seen. It is well known, for example, that witnesses to an accident may give diametrically opposite accounts of what took place. Even under less strained conditions, observers in a laboratory or in a theater may differ in the accuracy of their observations, even though they have witnessed the same circumstances or events.

In research, the observers are usually carefully selected on the basis of tests, and they are thoroughly trained. Furthermore, their reports are checked against those of other observers for agreement and consistency. Data gathered under such conditions are likely to be acceptable in

Percentages of Deviant Behavior for Two Children in Class D   *Figure 12.2*

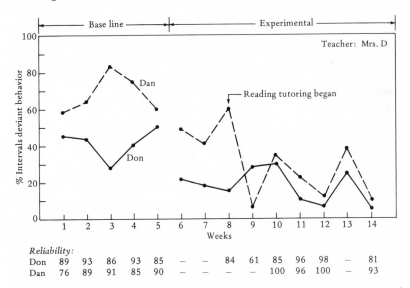

Reliability:

Don	89	93	86	93	85	—	—	84	61	85	96	98	—	81
Dan	76	89	91	85	90	—	—	—	—	100	96	100	—	93

From W. C. Becker, C. H. Madsen, Jr., Carole Arnold, and D. R. Thomas, "Attention and praise in reducing classroom behavior problems." *Journal of Special Education*, Vol. 1, No. 3 (Spring, 1967), p. 302. Reproduced by the permission of the publisher.

validity and reliability. However, there are many situations in which such precautions and safeguards are impractical, even though systematic observations are desirable. Observations must often be made by classroom teachers who are relatively untrained for this work. Not only where educational experiments are being conducted in the schools but also in the daily activities in the classroom, much of our information about pupils and activities is based on observation by teachers. Observation by classroom teachers is generally informal and unsystematic and is carried on without benefit of check lists or planned procedure. Anything that can be done to make teachers more reliable and accurate observers should add to our understanding of children, which in turn should contribute to better adjustment and more wholesome personalities. To become better observers, teachers must first of all have a genuine interest in improvement; they must be willing to accept instruction and assistance, and they must be willing to have their observations checked for accuracy and dependability. Perhaps above all, teachers must be able to put aside their personal preferences for and dislikes of individual students if their observations are to have any value.

LEARNING EXERCISES

3. Devise a record sheet in the form of a check list that might be used in observing and recording evidence of aggressive behavior in kindergarten children.
4. Devise a similar form for recording observations of changes in behavior as a result of instruction in a unit on personal hygiene in ninth-grade general science.

ANECDOTAL RECORDS

The method discussed in the preceding section is a systematic procedure for gathering observational data and is used more often in research than in everyday classroom situations. A method used more frequently and informally is the *anecdotal record*, which is the teacher's written record of an occurrence or incident involving a student. For example, the following might be typical:

Grade 5—Pat Jones

9/15   A new child, Jackie Long, came to school this morning. Jackie is large and strong for his age. I heard Jackie telling some of the other children during recess about his mother, who is a professional sportswoman. (Jackie didn't seem to be boasting—just proud.)

9/20   Jackie, the new pupil, got into an argument with Lynn about a percentage problem dealing with baseball batting averages. Later, Jackie hit Max with a ruler and Max cried. I made Jackie apologize. (Jackie may be inclined to bully. Time will tell.)

These are samples of what a teacher might record as significant anecdotes concerning a new pupil. They illustrate some of the generally accepted principles of making anecdotal records.

First, the record is in two parts—the incident itself and, in parentheses, the teacher's interpretation. This inclusion but separation of fact and interpretation is desirable and important if the records are to be maximally useful. When fact and interpretation are mingled, it makes the records less objective and more difficult to interpret. Also, different persons may interpret an anecdote differently.

Second, the examples suggest that the teacher will keep a continuing record on Jackie over a period of time and in a variety of situations. By this means the teacher will secure a more complete and accurate picture of Jackie's personality and will certainly be in a good position to give help if the pupil needs it.

Third, the samples indicate what the teacher considers to be significant aspects of the pupil's behavior. There are undoubtedly other occurrences that might have been recorded, but those reported seemed to give the most insight into the pupil's personality during the first few days of school.

It is not easy to know what is significant and worth recording. Teachers inevitably have preferences and dislikes among their pupils, often without being fully aware of them, and these biases tend to influence the choice of children about whom anecdotes are recorded, as well as the nature of the anecdotes. It is quite natural, also, to overlook the shy, quiet child and to record anecdotes only on the more aggressive children. The observation that "David sat in his seat and looked out the window while the other children came up to the desk to see the turtle" may be just as significant as the fact that "Lee brought a live turtle to school today, which attracted a great deal of attention to her as well as to the turtle."

A recurring question on the matter of anecdotal records concerns the number of children on whom to keep such records and the number of anecdotes to record. Some authorities advocate that anecdotes should be regularly recorded for all children. Ideally this is certainly desirable, but in most situations it would be impractical for busy teachers. A goal of only one anecdote per week per pupil would mean something like thirty-five or forty per year per pupil. Thus, a teacher with thirty-five pupils would have 35 × 35, or 1,275 anecdotes per year to record, which would be no small task in itself, to say nothing of the time required for interpreting and using the anecdotes. In this connection it should be noted that keeping anecdotal records presents quite different problems for elementary and high-school teachers. The former usually have about 25 to 30 pupils all day every day and thus have ample opportunity to observe significant happenings. High-school teachers, on the other hand, may see 150 pupils every day in groups of 30 for only one period each. Observing and recording significant anecdotes in this case is obviously more difficult.

In most situations it is probably best to begin by keeping records on a few pupils. After gaining some experience and confidence, one can undertake the recording of anecdotes on additional pupils. Even with a modest beginning, however, the teacher should take care to avoid the common mistake of keeping records on problem cases only. As we have already suggested, the shy, reticent child may be just as much in need of study and help as the one who is always causing trouble. In the beginning, when records are kept on only a few children, it would be well to select some of the less obvious cases as well as some who demand attention.

Records of anecdotes should be made as soon as possible after the incident has been observed, but never so that pupils are aware that this is being done. Many teachers find it best to make a few notes at the first opportunity and then to make a complete record during free time at noon or after school. Anecdotes should always be recorded on the day of their occurrence if at all possible, because the longer the time lapse between the occurrence and the recording of it, the less distinct and accurate one's memory of the incident becomes. Anecdotes are probably best recorded on cards. Each anecdote may be recorded on a single small card, or, as is sometimes preferred, several anecdotes may be recorded on one large card. The latter system makes the interpretation of trends or developments a little easier for some teachers. In any case, cards are the most convenient means of record-keeping since they are easy to file, sort, handle, and arrange.

To be most useful in the study of individuals, anecdotal records should be kept over an extended period of time. To obtain a reliable sample of a child's behavior and to make any useful assessment of changes that occur, it is essential that an adequate number of anecdotes or observations be made. These principles apply here no less than in the case of systematic observations discussed in the preceding section. It is of little value to record an anecdote or two about an individual and then neglect the individual for a month. By observing long enough to see how the pupil functions in a variety of situations from day to day, it is possible to gain much better insight into personality and whatever difficulties the pupil may have. The only exception to this might be in a school system in which anecdotal records are a part of the regular cumulative records kept on all pupils. In such a system it would probably be impossible to record anecdotes frequently and regularly on every child; occasional anecdotes would have to suffice. Nevertheless, the principle still holds that, other factors being equal, the more frequent and regular the anecdotes recorded for a given individual, the more dependable the results will be.

If anecdotal records are to be valuable they must be used, and if they are to be used they must first be interpreted. To interpret the records it is, of course, necessary to study and summarize them. Several anecdotes about a single pupil must be studied and compared. They tell a story, reveal characteristic behavior, show the individual in interactions with others in an accustomed setting. In these respects anecdotal records have certain advantages over other methods such as ratings or systematic observation. However, the task of summarizing and interpreting is not an easy one, and it invariably takes much thought and time. Ordinarily, summarizing should be done often enough to keep abreast of typical behavior and developments of the individual and yet not so frequently that the process will become a chore. Perhaps two or three times a year is often enough under ordinary circumstances. However, in individual cases it may be desirable to summarize and interpret more frequently.

Summarizing and interpreting are usually best done by the teacher who has written the anecdotal record, though they may also be done by a committee of two or three teachers, especially in a difficult case. The guidance specialist, counselor, or school psychologist may be consulted if need be.

The anecdotal record and summaries should be passed on to successive teachers as the pupil progresses so that each teacher will have the benefit of previous observations and can add to them. By this means a quite complete and valuable "behavior journal" of a pupil may be built up over a period of years.

Anecdotal records should always be related to all the other available information concerning a given child. Information on home conditions, health, ability, success in schoolwork, participation in extra class activities, and so on, should be considered along with the anecdotal records, and the whole should be taken into account in any interpretations that are made.

One factor that often causes difficulty in maintaining a system of anecdotal records is the clerical work involved. Reference was made earlier to the time involved in recording even one anecdote per pupil per week. Where a schoolwide program involving hundreds of children is maintained, the total amount of time and labor can grow to large proportions. Nevertheless, some programs of this nature have been tried and found feasible. In one school system six teachers in grades 4 to 7 recorded anecdotes for 3 months on every pupil.[5] During this time an extensive testing program was carried out with the same pupils. At the end of the 3 months the anecdotal records were compared with test results to determine how well the two sets of data agreed. Although the findings are too extensive to cite in detail here, it was found that teachers could keep such records without too much difficulty and that they were able to judge the social relations of their pupils accurately by comparing anecdotal records with test results. Among the most significant conclusions were: (1) The success of anecdotal records depends in large measure on the outlook of the teachers. Those having a formal, academic viewpoint will probably find little use for anecdotal records, and those they write will be of little value. (2) Unless the child has opportunity for many varied experiences it is probable that little useful information about that child will be found in anecdotal records. (3) Classes enrolling from seventeen to twenty-eight pupils show no appreciable difference in the number of anecdotes recorded.

The results of this study are encouraging. They suggest that keeping anecdotal records, at least in the elementary grades, is not an inhuman task, that teachers who are interested in studying problems of pupil adjustment can do it, and that the results seem to bear significant relationships to other measures of personality and adjustment.

LEARNING EXERCISES

5. Briefly describe a situation in which anecdotal records could be used to advantage.
6. What are the advantages and disadvantages of anecdotal records in comparison with other methods of personality appraisal?
7. Write out five or six imaginary anecdotes about a pupil who is shy and withdrawn. Do the same for one who is overly aggressive. Write your interpretations of each set.

---

[5]Arthur E. Hamalainen, *An Appraisal of Anecdotal Records,* Contributions to Education 891 (New York: Teachers College, Columbia University, 1943).

The last of the observational methods to be discussed are those known as *sociometric* or *peer nomination* or *interpersonal* methods. The instrument usually associated with these is called a *sociogram.* It is a pictorial or graphic representation of relationships of a specified nature among members of a group and is based on information gathered from members of the group. It differs from other observational methods discussed in this chapter in that the data are collected about individuals from their peers rather than from teachers or other observers.

The use of sociometric techniques probably stems from the work of Jacob L. Moreno, first published in 1934.[6] Much study has been made of the sociogram during the last 40 years, and it has been widely used in schools. The sociogram has proved valuable when properly used, but it has definite limitations and some dangers in the hands of people not adequately prepared in its use.

A sociogram is generally based on the written answers to a question put to members of a group. For example, a fifth-grade group might be told that they were about to begin work on a certain project and that they were to be grouped for this into committees of three. They might then be asked to list the names of two pupils with whom they would like to work as a committee. Or they might be asked to indicate a first choice and a second choice.

It may sometimes be desirable to ask for more than two choices, a third and perhaps even a fourth, depending on the purpose of the inquiry. If only a tabulation of the response is to be made, recording more than two choices presents no great problem. However, the construction of a sociogram involving three or four choices becomes quite complicated and its interpretation correspondingly difficult. Moreover, as the size of the group increases the complexities also increase. It is suggested, therefore, that unless the situation actually demands more than two choices, and especially with persons inexperienced in sociometric techniques, most purposes can be adequately achieved with two.

Members of a group may also be asked to name "rejects"—that is, one or more with whom they would rather not work, play, sit. There is some disagreement with respect to the desirability of this procedure and there are arguments on both sides of the question. We tend not to favor the use of the sociogram in this manner. For one thing, it seems to emphasize negative feelings, which would appear to have some undesirable aspects. Furthermore, rejection is surely implied in the case of individuals who

---

[6]Jacob L. Moreno, *Who Shall Survive?* (Washington, D.C.: Nervous and Mental Disease Publ. Co., 1934).

are not chosen at all or chosen by hardly anyone. The possibility of such interpretations seems sufficient in almost all situations, except possibly those in which it is necessary to identify an object of genuine hostility.

Once the data have been collected, the next step is to tabulate them in a form that is useful. Two forms are commonly employed, the table and the sociogram. Either or both may be used with a given set of data. Suppose a fifth-grade teacher has asked seventeen pupils to nominate their first and second choices of members of the class to work with on a certain project. The responses of the pupils might be tabulated as shown in Table 12.1.

These choices may be organized into a chart somewhat like the one shown in Figure 12.3. Here each pupil's first choice is indicated by a *1* under the name of the pupil chosen, and the second choice by a *2*. The number of times each pupil was chosen as a first choice and as a second choice is shown at the bottom. Those not chosen at all have no numbers in the columns under their names. Mutual choices are indicated by an asterisk. For example, Guy is Ken's first choice, and Ken is Guy's second choice.

A better way of showing the relationships in this group is by the sociogram shown in Figure 12.4. There are several methods of constructing such a chart, but to discuss these in detail is beyond the scope of this book. One of the easiest and most practical methods is described in a

Table 12.1   Tabulated Peer Nominations

Chooser	First Choice	Second Choice
Ken	Guy	Fran
Jack	Kevin	Len
Helen	Fran	Kathy
Ted	Mike	Kevin
Fred	Ken	Karl
Fran	Jane	Milly
Jean	Kathy	Kevin
Sally	Milly	Jane
Jessie	Helen	Fran
Karl	Fran	Ken
Mike	Jean	Kevin
Len	Fran	Ken
Guy	Karl	Ken
Milly	Fran	Jane
Kathy	Helen	Jean
Jane	Sally	Fran
Kevin	Ted	Jean

Chart Showing Peer Nominations

Figure 12.3

	Ken	Jack	Helen	Ted	Fred	Fran	Jean	Sally	Jessie	Karl	Mike	Len	Guy	Milly	Kathy	Jane	Kevin
Ken						2							1*				
Jack												2					1
Helen						1									2*		
Ted											1						2*
Fred	1									2							
Fran														2*		1*	
Jean														1*		2*	
Sally														1		2*	
Jessie		1				2											
Karl	2					1											
Mike						1											2
Len	2					1											
Guy	2*										1						
Milly						1*										2	
Kathy			1*			2*											
Jane						2*	1*										
Kevin				1*		2*											
First choice	1		2	1		4	1	1		1	1		1	1	1	1	1
Second choice	3				3	3	2			1		1		1	1	2	3

publication dealing explicitly with this matter, and any teacher or counselor can learn the method with a little study and practice.[7]

A conventional terminology has come to be used in interpreting a sociogram, which we may illustrate by reference to Figure 12.4. A *star* is an individual who is chosen by many. Fran is an example; so are Kevin and Ken. A *chain* is a sequence of choices in a line, none of whom is chosen by many; an example here is the Jessie-Helen-Kathy-Jean-Mike-Ted alignment. They are marginal and not actually members of a group. An *isolate* is one not chosen; examples are Jack, Jessie, and Fred. The term *island* refers to a small, more or less self-contained group or clique; an example is Milly, Sally, Fran, and Jane; another is Ken, Karl, Guy, and Fred. Such cliques are often the cause of concern to the teacher and may have an undesirable effect on the relations of the group as a whole.

[7]Horace Mann–Lincoln Institute of School Experimentation, *How to Construct a Sociogram* (New York: Teachers College, Columbia University 1950).

Figure 12.4   Sociogram Showing Peer Nominations

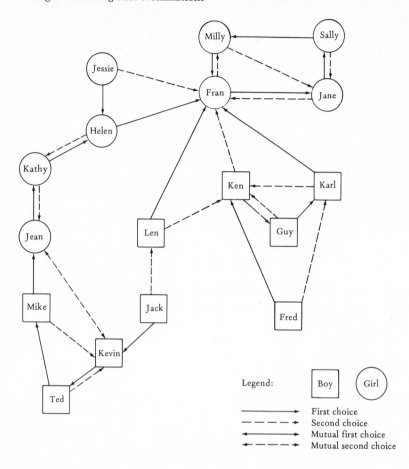

Legend:

Boy (in box)   Girl (in circle)

——————→   First choice
– – – – →   Second choice
←——————→   Mutual first choice
←– – – –→   Mutual second choice

In studying Figure 12.4 some other facts about the relationships become apparent. For one, there seems to be a distinct tendency for boys to choose boys and girls to choose girls. No boy is a girl's first choice, and only two girls are named as first choices by three boys. Perhaps at fifth-grade level this would not be unusual. However, one might expect the trend to be in the opposite direction—namely, more girls choosing boys than boys choosing girls, in view of the greater maturity of girls at this age. Again, the sociogram reveals what appears to be some tendency for the class to split into two parts. The link between the right-hand group and that on the left seems to be Fran, who apparently is extremely popular with most of the class; the only other link between the two is the choice of Ken (another star) by Len.

So far, we have dealt with methods of collecting sociometric data and ways of tabulating and summarizing them. Perhaps a more important question concerns the purposes for which the results may be used. A further question concerns the advantages and disadvantages of a sociogram.

It may be said that a sociogram is probably the best instrument yet devised to reveal the social structure of a group. It shows interrelationships among individuals and relationships of each individual to the entire group. It provides teachers or group leaders with information that will help in understanding the behavior of the group and in functioning more effectively in working with that group. Many relationships and subgroups within any class or group are not apparent on the surface.

It is important that appropriate action be taken soon after the sociogram has been completed and examined. If the teacher has asked pupils to tell with whom they would like to work, groupings should be formed on the basis of what the children have requested, as far as that is possible. The effect on pupils of carrying through is very wholesome. It goes without saying that not to do so has the opposite effect, and that pupils lose interest in sociograms if they come to believe that nothing happens as a result of their expressions of preference.

One publication[8] suggests the following uses of a sociogram:

1.   To identify mutual choices, stars, isolates, chains, islands, and triangles or circles.
2.   Studying race or nationality in relation to group structure. In this case racial groups may be coded by use of different-shaped figures [as was done for sex in Figure 12.4].
3.   Studying age or maturity in relation to group structure.
4.   Studying the relation of total group structure to out-of-school groupings, such as scouts, sororities, etc.
5.   Studying the effect of certain experiences. In this case there should be a sociogram "before and after." Thus it may be used to study the effect of various methods of choosing committees on the structure of the group.

In the same publication some limitations of sociograms are mentioned. First, it is pointed out that sociograms are only as valid as the rapport between teacher and pupils permits. Pupils must sign responses if the results are to be useful, and if there is resistance to doing this or to answering the questions the responses are not likely to be worth much.

[8]Horace Mann–Lincoln Institute, *How to Construct a Sociogram.*

Second, it is pointed out that since group structure, especially among younger children, is quite fluid, the reliability of a single sociogram may not be very high.

Third, the way in which the data are gathered may force misleading responses. For example, the sociogram does not reveal differences between strong and weak feelings, nor does it reveal hostility. The point is made that to require three choices may force the nomination of someone to whom there is really no feeling of attraction and for whom there is perhaps even a feeling of dislike.

Fourth, it is important to remember that a sociogram merely reveals conditions; it does not give answers or solutions. A teacher may decide that acceptance of an isolate by any other members of a group must be brought about by authority, if necessary. Measures taken to accomplish this, even though subtle, may result in stronger feelings of rejection instead of greater acceptance. The solution or amelioration of conditions revealed by a sociogram depends upon the use of other techniques such as anecdotal records, interviews with individual children, and further careful study of the total situation. Perhaps the role of sociograms is best summed up by this quotation from the same bulletin:

> Once a sociogram has been plotted, it is a beginning, not an end. It raises questions rather than answers them. Perhaps its greatest value is that it directs the attention to certain aspects of group structure which will lead to further observation of individual and group behavior. To date, we have few, if any, generalizations which can be applied in the interpretation of sociograms, although we are beginning to find certain tentative hypotheses. We are in great need of carefully reported anecdotes of group behavior recorded by teachers who are sensitive to problems of group behavior. If the making of sociograms encourages such observation and recording, they shall have fulfilled an important function.[9]

The use of sociometric tests by the teacher is criticized by some for the same reason that use of other assessment techniques is criticized—namely, that the information is not appropriate for teachers. Others believe, however, that a teacher who is professional in training and attitude should have the information and use it. Robeck predicts that even those teachers who think they know the interpersonal dynamics of a class are likely to learn some useful and surprising things from sociometric tests. As a primary teacher, she found them very helpful in individual guidance, parent conferences, and classroom organization.[10]

[9]Horace Mann–Lincoln Institute, p. 12.
[10]Mildred C. Robeck, *Infants and Children: Their Development and Learning* (New York: McGraw-Hill, 1978), p. 259.

8. Using the following data, construct a sociogram:

Chooser	First choice	Second choice
Gerry	Pat	Rae
Billie	Bobby	Jessie
Lee	Jackie	Gerry
Pat	Rae	Jessie
Jackie	Bobby	Jessie
Lynn	Jessie	Rae
Jessie	Billie	Terry
Rae	Pat	Lynn
Terry	Billie	Jessie
D.J.	Billie	Jackie
Bobby	Billie	Terry
Chris	D.J.	Bobby

Suggestions: Start with Jessie and Billie and place around them the pupils who chose them, and then work in the rest. Try to construct a graph that has straight, right-angle lines with no lines crossing each other. Use a solid line for first choices and a broken line for second choices.

9. Can you identify any stars, isolates, chains, or cliques in your chart?
10. If you were dividing this group into four subgroups or committees of three each, how would you proceed? Give reasons for your groupings.
11. What could you suggest to improve relationships in this group?

OTHER PEER-APPRAISAL METHODS

Peer-appraisal methods are not limited to sociometric techniques. Peer appraisals could be obtained by using any of the rating scale or observational methods previously discussed. Each student might, for example, fill out a rating form for every other student. A simpler method is the *guess-who* technique.

In the guess-who technique, each pupil is presented with a list of descriptions and asked to name the pupil who best fits each description.

The descriptions one uses depend on the characteristics to be measured. If one wishes to evaluate shyness, for example, the question might be "Who is the most bashful?" Or if one were interested in self-control, statements such as "This person never gets mad" and "This person wiggles a lot and can't sit still" might be used. The particular wording of the statements or questions is very important. It should always be appropriate to the age of the students.

To score guess-who items, simply tally the number of times each person is named for each description. Information on who named whom is seldom used as it is in sociometric approaches.

Guess-who techniques may also be built around specific school situations of interest to the students. In one example, reproduced as Figure 12.5, children were asked to help select personnel for class plays. Notice that each child must be assigned a number when this form is used.

LEARNING EXERCISE

12. Design a guess-who questionnaire that members of the class you are taking may use to check their agreement on certain behavior traits of their classmates.

CLASSROOM OBSERVATION OF AFFECTIVE CHANGES

The chapter on self-report techniques for the study of personality ended with a discussion of the assessment of group progress toward affective goals of instruction. The universal and noncontroversial goal of a more positive attitude toward the subject matter of a course was used to illustrate the usefulness of informal data-collection procedures readily available to the teacher. An increase in the number or percentage of positive responses or reactions from the beginning to the end of a course was suggested as the most direct evidence of a positive change in attitude.

There are a number of things that teachers observe students doing or failing to do that may be counted as evidence of their feelings or attitudes toward the subject matter of a class. A few of the many observations that might be made will be listed here. Because the teacher will be interested in changes in the incidence of these behaviors, these data should be

```
                    CASTING CHARACTERS FOR CLASS PLAYS

                                    School_____

   Name_____ Boy or Girl___ Class __

        Suppose your class was going to produce some plays for
   which twelve characters are needed. Twelve kinds of people
   are described below. Next to the description of each
   character, write the number of one classmate you think
   best suited for each part because he (or she) is just that
   way naturally. You may choose the same classmate for more
   than one part if you wish.

      1. Someone who is always in good humor; who        1.____
         smiles or laughs a good deal; who makes
         others happy

      2. Someone who is very shy about meeting peo-       2.____
         ple; who prefers to work alone rather than
         with others

      3. Someone who is snobbish and conceited; who       3.____
         feels superior to others in the class; who
         likes to order others around

      4. Someone who is always willing to co-operate;     4.____
         who is always ready to help others do a job

      5. Someone who is a "sore loser"; who can't         5.____
         take it when things go wrong; who grumbles
         or finds excuses easily

      6. Someone who is a "bookworm"; who prefers         6.____
         reading books to almost any other activity

      7. Someone who is usually a leader whenever         7.____
         something is started; who frequently sug-
         gests new things to do; who is respected by
         others

      8. Someone who always seems unhappy; who rarely     8.____
         smiles and never seems to have fun

      9. Someone who is always dependable and care-       9.____
         ful; who always completes a task when others
         want to drop it

     10. Someone who is very friendly; who likes peo-    10.____
         ple and is well liked by others

     11. Someone who likes to "show off" knowledge       11.____
         at every opportunity; who makes others
         feel they know less

     12. Someone who is always outstanding in every-     12.____
         thing; to whom all things come easily and
         naturally

   Which parts do you think you could play?
   Write the number of the character or characters here.____
   A. Put down the numbers of the three classmates you
      like best.   _____  _____  _____

   B. Put down the numbers of the three classmates you
      like least.  _____  _____  _____
```

Division of Tests and Measurements, Bureau of Education of the City of New York, 1948.

recorded periodically, at least once early in a course and once near the end. Some obvious examples are:

1. Number of assignments completed on time
2. Number of assignments shorter or longer than expected
3. Number of voluntary or optional assignments completed
4. Number of students seeking additional help
5. Number of volunteers for class-related project
6. Number of subject-related out-of-class experiences reported
7. Number of unassigned books checked out of the library
8. Number of students selecting an advanced course in the same area
9. Number of students paying attention (or working on assignments) during spot checks
10. Average number of absences and late arrivals each day

If the following notes were made for two students in a course, sport, or other school activity, an instructor should have little difficulty in identifying the student with the more positive attitude toward that activity.

Student A	Student B
Seldom late or tardy. Always asks what was missed.	Absent at least once a week; frequently tardy.
Completes every assignment and does more than necessary.	Failed to complete several assignments after accepting them.
Asked for additional help and further practice.	Asked to be excused from several planned activities.
Others report voluntary participation in related out-of-school activity.	Reported inability to find information on routine assignments.
Asked about points not yet covered. Volunteered information and suggestions.	During discussions, yawns; looks off into space. Seldom comments.
In interview asked about opportunities for future participation.	Questioned the value of practice during interview; asked permission to skip it.

The notes for the preceding example are intentionally general. Most such notes might be made during any instructional activity of the school—academic, athletic, cultural, or vocational, perhaps even for some voluntary club activities. It is important to emphasize, however, that such notes merely indicate student attitudes toward the activity for which they are made. They suggest nothing about general motivations, personality characteristics, or adjustment.

Some students may pretend an attitude they do not have in order to impress the teacher. It will be difficult for them to play this part convincingly and consistently, however, when they are not always aware that they are being observed. Furthermore, the motivation for deceiving the teacher is reduced if the teacher grades on performance only. We have suggested that attitudes be measured to assess group progress toward affective goals and the success of the teacher. For these purposes, individual students need not be identified.

When the purpose is to gauge the success of one's teaching efforts on students' progress toward affect objectives, it is not necessary to associate observed events with individuals. Record-keeping can be relatively efficient and easy. One may, for example, simply note the number of approach incidents and the number of avoidance incidents during the period of observation. A summary sheet may be prepared with columns labeled as follows: (1) "definitely avoidance," (2) "probably avoidance," (3) "probably approach," (4) "definitely approach." As incidents occur, they are classified by a check in the appropriate column. Counting the check marks reveals the type of attitude-related incidents that seem most characteristic of a class during the period of observation.

Summary Records of Affect

If the teacher desires to retain more information about each incident, incidents may be numbered consecutively as they occur, and, at the same time, a number, rather than a check mark, may be placed in the appropriate column. A brief description of each numbered incident can be recorded on a separate sheet.

When the teacher wishes to make a special study of certain individuals, their names are listed on the left of the sheet and checks or index numbers are placed in the appropriate column opposite their names. The record might appear like the one in Figure 12.6. As previously suggested,

Record Form for Attitude-Related Incidents

Figure 12.6

Record of Student Behavior Toward My Subject

Student	Definitely negative	Probably negative	Probably positive	Definitely positive
Craig	1			
Noll		2		
Scannell				3
H. Mifflin				4, 5, 6

a key to the numbered incidents may be kept on a separate sheet, as, for example:

1 Failed to turn in three of four assignments this week
2 Fell asleep in class today
3 Commented on unassigned reading
4 Library record shows related reading
5 Enrolled for independent study next semester
6 Joined school interest club

Still another modification in recording may be useful as one gains experience with the types of approach and avoidance that are usual in a subject or situation. A code may be used to replace the consecutive index numbers. One may, for example, have a short list of negative and positive events such as:

−1	Does less than expected	+1	Does more than expected
−2	Is tardy or absent	+2	Comes early or leaves late
−3	Expresses dissatisfaction or dislike	+3	Expresses interest
−4	Acts bored	+4	Acts excited
−5	. . .	+5	. . .

If the list is not very long, it is readily memorized. Replacing the check marks on the suggested record form with code numbers will provide more information for later study, and the procedure is easier and quicker than recording information on a separate sheet.

These are only a few examples of approaches and devices that may be used to accumulate evidence from a variety of sources. Other types of evidence and other methods of recording that are more useful or convenient in a particular setting or for a different affective goal will occur to the user. The advantages of such techniques lie in the validity that the systematic and comprehensive accumulation of different kinds of evidence can add to the judgments teachers are expected to make.

LEARNING EXERCISES

13. State an affective objective for a class you are taking or teaching. Make a list of positive and negative student behaviors related to that objective. Include behaviors that might be observed in class and behaviors that would be noted by the instructor, such as behavior relating to the completion of assignments.

14. Choose or devise a method of recording the occurrence of the behaviors identified in Exercise 13 for the class as a whole or for individuals.

SUGGESTED READING

AHMANN, J. S., and M. D. GLOCK. *Evaluating Pupil Growth; Principles of Tests and Measurements.* 5th ed. Boston: Allyn and Bacon, 1975. Chapter 13 discusses and illustrates anecdotal records, rating scales, check lists, interviewing, and sociometric and related techniques.

CARTWRIGHT, C. A. and G. P. CARTWRIGHT. *Developing Observation Skills.* New York: McGraw-Hill, 1974. General principles and guidelines are followed by examples of specific types of records for making tallies and charts of behavior, rating scales, participation charts, and anecdotal records.

GRONLUND, N. E. *Sociometry in the Classroom.* New York: Harper & Row, 1959. A how-to-do-it book on sociometric procedures that also interprets research and development in the field.

HAMMER, MAX. "A Teacher's Guide to the Detection of Emotional Disturbance in the Elementary School Child." *Journal of Learning Disabilities,* 3 (October 1970), 35–37. The author presents a checklist for teachers' use in detecting emotional disturbance.

MAGNUSON, H. W., C. A. LARSON, and T. A. SHELLHAMMER. *Evaluating Pupil Progress,* Bulletin of the California State Department of Education, 21, No. 6 (April 1952). 184 pages. Separate chapters direct attention to the uses of anecdotal records, check lists, time-sampling, autobiographies, rating scales, sociograms, and guess-who techniques. Includes many samples of evaluation devices used in the appraisal programs of school systems in California and other states.

SIMON, A., and E. G. BOYER, eds. *Mirrors for Behavior.* Philadelphia: Research for Better Schools, 1970. This anthology of observation instruments is an invaluable resource. Copies of seventy-nine observation instruments are included in the two volumes.

THORNDIKE, R. L., and ELIZABETH HAGEN. *Measurement and Evaluation in Psychology and Education.* 4th ed. New York: John Wiley & Sons, 1977. Chapter 12 includes an extended discussion of rating scales and a brief treatment of sociometric techniques. Chapter 13 includes discussions of systematic observational procedures and anecdotal records.

Thirteen

THE MEASUREMENT PROGRAM

Reference has already been made in Chapter 1 to large-scale or national testing programs. These are quite generally referred to as *external testing programs* because they are directed and administered by agencies outside the local school authorities. Among the most prominent of such programs are the College Entrance Examination Board, the National Merit Scholarship Qualifying Examinations, the American College Testing Program, Project Talent, the National Assessment of Educational Progress, and the statewide testing programs. The criticisms of testing cited in Chapter 1 have been directed mainly, though not exclusively, at such programs.

The type of measurement or testing program with which we are concerned in this chapter is the locally initiated and directed, systematic use of tests to meet local needs, solve local problems, and contribute to the attainment of local educational goals. If such a program serves wider purposes, so much the better, but its focus is basically on meeting the needs of a particular school or school system.

At the completion of this chapter you should be able to answer questions and solve problems such as the following:

1. Design a minimal testing program for a school district that has three elementary schools of grades K–4, three middle schools of grades 5–8, and two high schools of grades 9–12. The time of the year for test administration should be indicated.
2. Compare the advantages of various processes that can be used for test selection, including district-wide committees, building committees, and the assignment of the task to a test specialist.

3. What factors should be considered when decisions are made about the way in which tests will be scored and how the results will be disseminated within a school district?
4. What factors should be considered in deciding whether to use fall or spring testing for various types of instruments? What are the advantages and disadvantages of each?

COOPERATING FOR
A SUCCESSFUL PROGRAM

Without the support and cooperation of teachers and counselors, the results of a measurement program can scarcely be used to the fullest extent. When some action is to be taken as a result of the program, whether it is grouping, counseling, remedial work, or some other, teachers and counselors may defeat the very purposes for which the testing was done by not cooperating in the program. If the program has been "dictated" by authorities rather than carried out with their advice and cooperation, it is possible that the people involved will not respond wholeheartedly. Unfortunately, administrators, though fully aware of this fact, do not always take the trouble and time to secure the support of their staffs. The result is that the programs sometimes fall far short of attaining their maximum usefulness or fail entirely.

On the other hand, it must be recognized that it is not always easy to stimulate the active cooperation and interest of teachers in the systematic use of measuring instruments. Some teachers resent the interruption it may cause in their usual routine, some do not appreciate the extra demands on their time and energy, and a few are prejudiced against "outside" tests of any kind. They do not like the idea of having their pupils examined by any means other than those that they themselves have devised. Where such attitudes exist, they must be changed before a measurement program can be carried on with any reasonable assurance of cooperation and success. It may take some time to accomplish this, yet there are a number of ways of creating more favorable attitudes: selected teachers can be sent to summer school to take courses in measurement, professional libraries can be built up, and teachers can be urged to participate in workshops and institutes dealing with problems of measurement and evaluation. In-service training programs may also focus attention on measurement as a means of facilitating curriculum revision and improving instruction.

A measurement program of any consequence is always undertaken with the cooperation and responsibility of more than one person. The program may involve only classroom teachers and their supervisors or principals, or the work may be planned and carried out with the cooperation of the entire staff of a school or school system. In the latter case it is customary to entrust most of the actual direction to one qualified person or to a representative committee. As we have said, it is almost axiomatic that unless a measurement program has the active cooperation and support of all concerned it cannot achieve its maximum usefulness. When a measurement program is carried out to meet needs or to solve problems which the teachers themselves regard as important, and when those teachers participate actively in planning and carrying out the program, it will have a good chance of succeeding. It is also helpful to have parents understand the reasons for measurement so that they too will support the program. If parents can see that the results of measurement help to bring about better learning and adjustment on the part of their children, their confidence in the usefulness of measurement and their faith in the school will be increased.

PLANNING A MEASUREMENT PROGRAM

Purposes   A measurement program will be successful to the extent that it accomplishes the purposes for which it is designed and carried out. Therefore, it must be planned in accordance with those purposes. This is a matter for cooperative endeavor by all concerned. Although many teachers are not well acquainted with standardized tests and techniques of measurement and appraisal, most will know what the educational problems are, and they will know of many situations in which measurement may be helpful. School psychologists, counselors, directors of research, and other personnel with more specialized training can usually supply the leadership, the technical knowledge, and the skills needed for setting up a measurement program.

Whereas in a smaller school or community the planning of a measurement program may be undertaken by the entire staff, such a procedure will generally be too cumbersome or unwieldy in a larger system. In the latter case it is generally better to have a committee made up of representatives of various groups, grade levels, schools, or districts to assume responsibility for planning and carrying out the program. This is not to say that the entire staff loses contact with the program. On the contrary, general teachers' meetings from time to time may be devoted to overall planning, progress reports, discussions, and implementation of results. Furthermore, occasional reports to the community may be used as a means of improving relations between the schools and the parents.

Listed below are some of the major purposes for which a measurement program may be carried on. A more extensive discussion of each of these purposes, together with practical suggestions on using test results, will be found in the next chapter. The purposes of measurement programs include

1. Placement and promotion
2. Homogeneous grouping
3. Diagnosis and remedial work
4. Counseling and guidance
5. Marking
6. Curriculum evaluation
7. Motivation
8. Identification and study of exceptional children
9. Interpreting schools to the community
10. Improvement of school staff
11. Educational research

This list is based on various studies and reports of the use of measurement in schools, and, while not exhaustive, it probably includes most of the common purposes for which educational measurement is used.

When the purposes of the measurement program have been decided, several other considerations immediately come to the fore. One of these is the time of year for giving the tests. Often this matter resolves itself into a choice between giving the tests at the beginning of the school year or near the end. The decision on timing usually depends on the purposes for which the tests are intended. For example, diagnostic testing and testing for purposes of grouping or grade placement most profitably comes early in the school year, while testing for purposes of promotion, educational counseling, marking, and comparison of achievement with norms usually occurs near the end of the term or year. On the other hand, some of the purposes for which measurement programs are carried on are unrelated to the time of year. (See the list above.)

Time of Year for Testing

Questions that must be decided early are the frequency of the testing and the grade levels at which particular tests are to be given. In part, these are determined by the purposes for which the testing is intended. For example, if tests are to be given for counseling purposes, there is generally less emphasis on and less need for testing below the secondary level. On the other hand, diagnostic testing in arithmetic or reading almost certainly can be started in the earlier grades of the elementary school.

The frequency of testing also depends on the purposes, but it is further affected by such considerations as the kinds of measuring instruments being used and the amount of money and time available for the work required. Many a measurement program undertaken with enthusiasm and high hopes has failed because those responsible greatly underestimated

Frequency and Grade Levels of Testing

the expense, the time, and the effort necessary to carry it through. The initial cost of standardized tests is frequently the smallest item of expense; getting the tests properly administered, scored, and interpreted requires much time and effort. *It is far better to undertake a modest program and complete the work required to put the results to effective use than to try to carry on a more extensive and ambitious program, only to have it bog down.*

A Minimum Measurement Program No measurement program can be prescribed to fit every situation. Nevertheless, some general suggestions may help the prospective teacher, counselor, or administrator set up a priority list for the planning of a testing program.

If only one type of test is to be given, at least as a beginning, the first choice should almost certainly be a measure of academic aptitude such as is provided by a group intelligence test. If no standardized tests have been used before, it is desirable to give a group test to every pupil. Since the IQ based on one group test is not completely reliable, any students whose scores raise questions or present discrepancies with other known facts about the individual should be tested as soon as possible with another form of the same test. This point is important, because two forms of the same test give directly comparable results, whereas IQ's obtained through the use of two different tests must be equated by standard scores or similarly derived scores before they can be compared directly.

The recommendation of a test of intelligence as the essential minimum is based on several considerations. In the first place, the capability of a pupil cannot be determined accurately without such a test, whereas a teacher can determine a pupil's educational achievement with locally devised tests. In the second place, for educational purposes, a reliable measure of capability is probably the most useful and important information about a pupil that we can learn. The IQ gives more insight into a pupil's work, achievement, and general mental ability than any other single fact can provide.

If testing is to be done at regular intervals after the first year in which a measurement program is started, it is advisable to give intelligence tests in the second grade and again in the fourth grade; they should be given again in the sixth grade if there is a junior high school or in the eighth grade if the system is organized on the 8-4 plan, and again in the tenth grade. The results of these measurements should always be made a part of the cumulative record that accompanies the pupil through the elementary and secondary grades.

If more than one type of test can be given, and the results put to use, a reading readiness test should be administered at the end of the kindergarten year or early in the first grade; an achievement battery should be given in the third or fourth and sixth or seventh grades and once in high school; and an interest test or inventory should be given in the ninth and twelfth grades. These tests supplement the results of the intelligence tests at critical points in the pupil's school career in ways that are most useful and appropriate at those points.

The use of other types of tests such as diagnostic, personality, aptitude, and reading tests and tests in specific school subjects should be undertaken where necessary, with a view to the available resources of the school and to the other factors peculiar to each situation. In every case, the purposes of the measurement program should be dominant in determining its nature and extent.

A tabulation of a recommended minimum school- or community-wide annual testing program is given in Table 13.1. This program amounts to eleven separate tests given annually at various levels throughout the K–12 grades. The achievement battery recommended for grade 10 or 11 is desirable, if time and resources permit, for instructional planning and counseling, although separate subject-matter tests may be preferred for various reasons. Where two tests are recommended for use in either of two grades, it probably would be best, other factors being equal, to distribute the burden by giving one test in each grade instead of giving both tests at the same grade level. This is particularly desirable where the scoring is done by teachers, and it also requires less of the pupils' time for such testing in any given grade. However, there is one exception: the interest and aptitude tests in grades 8 or 9 should be given in the same grade to enhance the introduction of career planning, a process that should take into consideration both interests and aptitude.

A Recommended Minimum School-Wide or Community-Wide Annual Testing Program   *Table 13.1*

Grade	Test
K or 1	Readiness
2	Intelligence
3 or 4	Intelligence
3 or 4	Achievement battery, including reading
6 or 8[a]	Intelligence
6 or 7	Achievement battery, including reading
8 or 9[b]	Interests
8 or 9[b]	Aptitude
10	Intelligence
10 or 11	Achievement battery or separate subject-matter tests
12	Interests

[a]Depending on whether 6 or 8 is the last grade in the elementary school.
[b]Depending on when the district introduces pupils to career planning.

Such a program should not be undertaken lightly. It will require much time and work, although the results should be worth the effort many times over. The cost may safely be reckoned on an average of 40 cents per pupil annually, provided that scoring the tests and tabulating and interpreting the results will not necessitate additional expenditures, and provided that most test booklets can be used over and over again with separate answer sheets.

Larger school systems often carry on testing programs far more extensive than the one outlined. With a central staff organized for such work, and ample financial support, a great deal more can be done. However, the plan shown will provide a good foundation, and it represents the type of program that most schools with limited funds for measurement can afford.

It will take 3 or 4 years under this plan for every pupil to be reached unless a group intelligence test is given to every pupil the first year. If a school-wide test is given the first year of the program, there will be information available on every pupil as soon as the tests can be given and scored, and this will be a real advantage to teachers. The regular program may be launched the second year. Even if the school-wide intelligence test is not given the first year, there will still be test results available at four important levels of the child's progress through the school. This will be a useful beginning and will help introduce the program gradually so that the people responsible will more easily be able to absorb the load.

SELECTING AND OBTAINING THE TESTS

Selecting Tests

Chapter 4 contains a discussion of the important criteria for judging the quality of tests. Here we need only stress the point that in planning a measurement program one should use the best available instruments for it. The criteria of *validity, reliability, objectivity, ease of administration, ease of scoring, ease of interpretation, availability of equivalent forms, adequate norms,* and *economy* provide a sound basis for appraising any measuring instrument, although, as has been mentioned, all of these criteria do not necessarily apply to every type of instrument.

In addition to the criteria mentioned above, a number of less tangible considerations usually influence the selection of instruments. In the case of standardized tests, for example, the deciding factor may be simply a general impression of the whole test. If those responsible for the selection like an instrument, if it seems to measure objectives that are important, and if they think it is suitable for their situation, that test or instrument will often be chosen in preference to one that meets the technical criteria more adequately. Probably the best that can be hoped for is an objective choice based on careful consideration of all available information about the test and the situation in which it is to be used.

In a measurement program the task of selecting tests may be delegated to a committee. Sometimes the tests are selected by a member of the supervisory or administrative staff and occasionally by the director of research or by the counseling staff. However, if the program is to be of the type outlined above for all-around basic purposes, the tests should be selected by a committee on which teaching, counseling, research, supervisory, and administrative personnel all have representation.

This committee should have full responsibility and authority to obtain, examine, select, and purchase the tests in the quantities needed. It should also have the authority and the initiative to encourage local groups to develop measuring devices for local needs where commercially available instruments are not adequate. The committee should feel free to consult with experts and with any school personnel in making its choices, yet its decisions should be final and should be accepted as such by all concerned. That is, as long as all elements of the school staff have representation on the committee, and as long as the committee makes a thorough study of available instruments in relation to the purposes of the program, its choices should not be subject to veto by administrative authorities or other groups except in the most extraordinary circumstances. If the committee responsible for the overall program is a large one, smaller subcommittees may be appointed to look after various phases of the program. The selection of tests might well be done by such a subcommittee.

It is common practice for test publishers to put up tests in packages of *Obtaining* twenty-five or thirty-five. Each package contains the specified number of *Tests* copies of the test, a manual of directions, a scoring key, a class record sheet, and any other materials necessary for proper use of the tests, except answer sheets, which are sold separately. Test publishers, as a rule, will not break packages of tests; in ordering, therefore, it is advisable to request a number that can be shipped in unbroken packages. For example, if tests are needed for 170 pupils, one would ordinarily order 175 (seven packages of twenty-five each or five packages of thirty-five each). The same is true of answer sheets. Prices are usually quoted for quantities of twenty-five or more.

Of course, the above applies only to paper-and-pencil tests. If the program involves other types of materials such as sets of pictures, toys, nuts and bolts, or phonograph records, such equipment will usually have to be bought in single complete sets. Such material is not consumable, and the same instruments therefore may be used repeatedly.

The committee or person responsible should take charge of all measurement materials when they are received and keep them in a safe place until they are to be used. The assumption in the use of a standardized test is that everyone who takes it has an equal chance and that no one has an unfair advantage. Although classroom teachers are usually scrupulous in such matters, their enthusiasm and eagerness to see pupils do well sometimes lead them to give assistance they should not give.

The story is told about a high-school principal and the teacher of mathematics who had agreed that a certain test should be given in the plane geometry classes. The tests were ordered, received, and turned over to the teacher for safe-keeping until the time set for the testing. A few days before the tests were to be given, the principal dropped into the room to speak to the mathematics teacher and was surprised to find several problems from the test copied on the board and the teacher discussing these problems with the pupils. After the class had been dismissed, the principal asked the teacher to explain. The teacher replied, "I was so anxious to see what they would do with the problems that I couldn't wait. I just had to try them out on a few." While this teacher's enthusiasm and interest were highly commendable, it is clear that the teacher's understanding of the purposes and use of standardized tests left much to be desired.

Answer
Sheets
The use of printed answer media has developed greatly in recent years, as have techniques and services for scoring them. Several different types of answer sheets and answer cards are commercially available, and the organizations that produce them usually also offer a scoring service. The more advanced of these, using electronic equipment, not only score the answer sheets but also provide distributions of scores and part scores, intercorrelations between scores, percentile and standard score equivalents, and almost any type of analysis desired. For larger systems or large-scale testing programs such services are both efficient and economical. A sample of the electronically scored answer sheet is shown in Figure 13.1.

Some type of separate answer sheet is now available with nearly all standardized tests for grade 4 and higher. For testing in grades below this level it is still customary to have answers written or printed by the children in the test booklets. Research has shown that separate answer media may be used safely beginning at about the fourth- or fifth-grade level. Although marking answers in test booklets adds to the expense of testing since the booklets cannot be used again, this practice has certain advantages. First, of course, is the removal of the possibility of confusion on the part of the children taking the test if a separate answer sheet is used. Probably of equal importance is the value to the teacher who scores the papers of seeing which items each child answers correctly or misses. Teachers often feel that this type of information is the most valuable result achieved by testing.

Facsimile of a Portion of an Electronically Scored Answer Sheet *Figure 13.1*

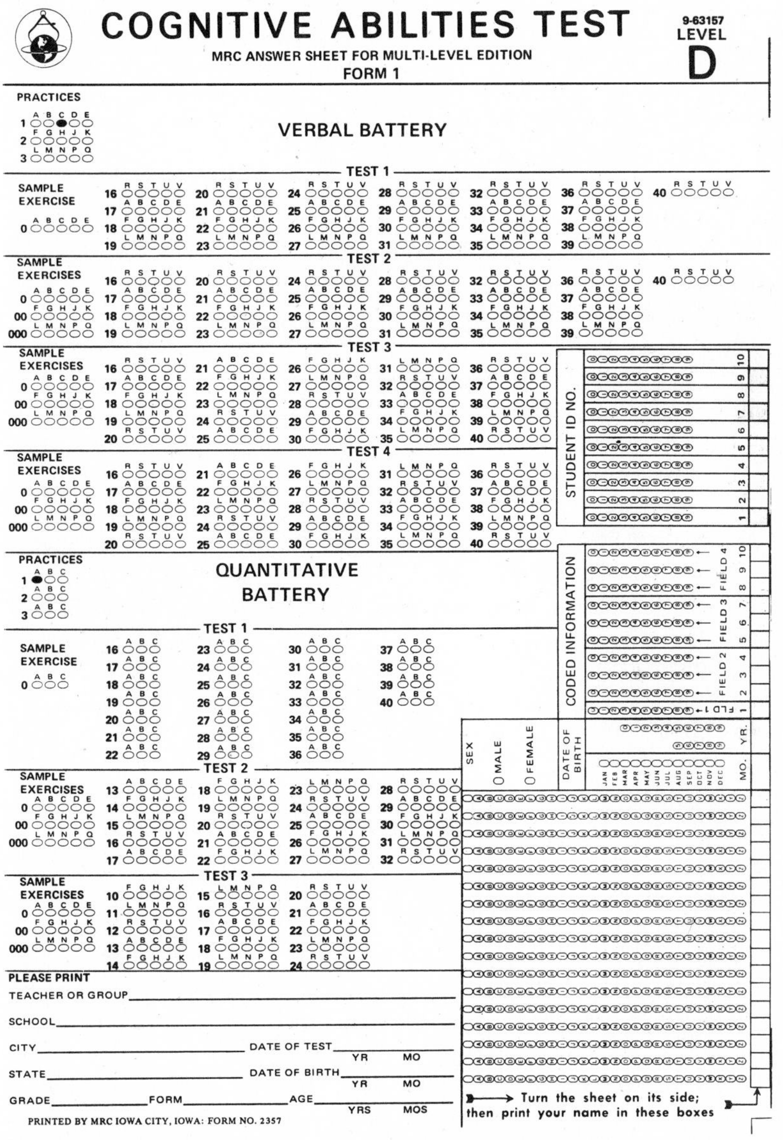
COGNITIVE ABILITIES TEST

9-63157 LEVEL D

MRC ANSWER SHEET FOR MULTI-LEVEL EDITION

FORM 1

PRACTICES

VERBAL BATTERY

TEST 1 — SAMPLE EXERCISE

TEST 2 — SAMPLE EXERCISES

TEST 3 — SAMPLE EXERCISES

TEST 4 — SAMPLE EXERCISES

STUDENT ID NO.

CODED INFORMATION — FIELD 1, FIELD 2, FIELD 3, FIELD 4

PRACTICES

QUANTITATIVE BATTERY

TEST 1 — SAMPLE EXERCISE

TEST 2 — SAMPLE EXERCISES

TEST 3 — SAMPLE EXERCISES

SEX — MALE — FEMALE

DATE OF BIRTH — YR. — MO.

PLEASE PRINT

TEACHER OR GROUP __________

SCHOOL __________

CITY __________ DATE OF TEST ____ YR ____ MO

STATE __________ DATE OF BIRTH ____ YR ____ MO

GRADE ____ FORM ____ AGE ____ YRS ____ MOS

Turn the sheet on its side; then print your name in these boxes

PRINTED BY MRC IOWA CITY, IOWA: FORM NO. 2357

MRC Answer Sheet for the *Cognitive Abilities Test,* Multilevel Edition, Level D. From *Cognitive Abilities Test* by Robert L. Thorndike & Elizabeth Hagen. Copyright © 1974 Houghton Mifflin Company. Reprinted with permission.

A facsimile of one of the most widely used types of answer sheets is shown in Figure 13.2. This form, known as IBM 1230, though designed primarily for use with multiple-choice items, may also be used with true-false items by using only the first two spaces—A for true and B for false. It may also be used for the 3 × 5 type of matching item described in

Figure 13.2 Portion of the IBM 1230 Answer Sheet

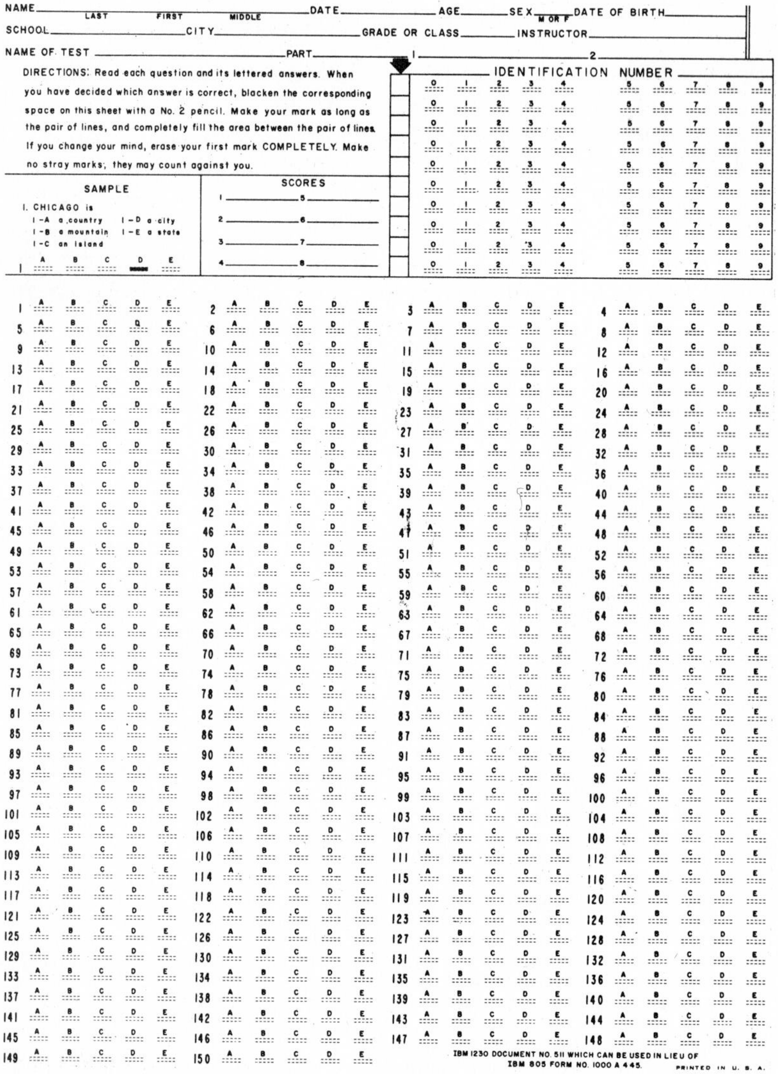
NAME ______ LAST FIRST MIDDLE DATE ______ AGE ______ SEX ______ M OR F DATE OF BIRTH ______
SCHOOL ______ CITY ______ GRADE OR CLASS ______ INSTRUCTOR ______
NAME OF TEST ______ PART ______ 1 ______ 2 ______

DIRECTIONS: Read each question and its lettered answers. When you have decided which answer is correct, blacken the corresponding space on this sheet with a No. 2 pencil. Make your mark as long as the pair of lines, and completely fill the area between the pair of lines. If you change your mind, erase your first mark COMPLETELY. Make no stray marks; they may count against you.

SAMPLE
I. CHICAGO is
I-A a country I-D a city
I-B a mountain I-E a state
I-C an island
I A B C D E

SCORES
1 ______ 5 ______
2 ______ 6 ______
3 ______ 7 ______
4 ______ 8 ______

IDENTIFICATION NUMBER
0 1 2 3 4 5 6 7 8 9

1 A B C D E 2 A B C D E 3 A B C D E 4 A B C D E
5 A B C D E 6 A B C D E 7 A B C D E 8 A B C D E
9 A B C D E 10 A B C D E 11 A B C D E 12 A B C D E
13 A B C D E 14 A B C D E 15 A B C D E 16 A B C D E
17 A B C D E 18 A B C D E 19 A B C D E 20 A B C D E
21 A B C D E 22 A B C D E 23 A B C D E 24 A B C D E
25 A B C D E 26 A B C D E 27 A B C D E 28 A B C D E
29 A B C D E 30 A B C D E 31 A B C D E 32 A B C D E
33 A B C D E 34 A B C D E 35 A B C D E 36 A B C D E
37 A B C D E 38 A B C D E 39 A B C D E 40 A B C D E
41 A B C D E 42 A B C D E 43 A B C D E 44 A B C D E
45 A B C D E 46 A B C D E 47 A B C D E 48 A B C D E
49 A B C D E 50 A B C D E 51 A B C D E 52 A B C D E
53 A B C D E 54 A B C D E 55 A B C D E 56 A B C D E
57 A B C D E 58 A B C D E 59 A B C D E 60 A B C D E
61 A B C D E 62 A B C D E 63 A B C D E 64 A B C D E
65 A B C D E 66 A B C D E 67 A B C D E 68 A B C D E
69 A B C D E 70 A B C D E 71 A B C D E 72 A B C D E
73 A B C D E 74 A B C D E 75 A B C D E 76 A B C D E
77 A B C D E 78 A B C D E 79 A B C D E 80 A B C D E
81 A B C D E 82 A B C D E 83 A B C D E 84 A B C D E
85 A B C D E 86 A B C D E 87 A B C D E 88 A B C D E
89 A B C D E 90 A B C D E 91 A B C D E 92 A B C D E
93 A B C D E 94 A B C D E 95 A B C D E 96 A B C D E
97 A B C D E 98 A B C D E 99 A B C D E 100 A B C D E
101 A B C D E 102 A B C D E 103 A B C D E 104 A B C D E
105 A B C D E 106 A B C D E 107 A B C D E 108 A B C D E
109 A B C D E 110 A B C D E 111 A B C D E 112 A B C D E
113 A B C D E 114 A B C D E 115 A B C D E 116 A B C D E
117 A B C D E 118 A B C D E 119 A B C D E 120 A B C D E
121 A B C D E 122 A B C D E 123 A B C D E 124 A B C D E
125 A B C D E 126 A B C D E 127 A B C D E 128 A B C D E
129 A B C D E 130 A B C D E 131 A B C D E 132 A B C D E
133 A B C D E 134 A B C D E 135 A B C D E 136 A B C D E
137 A B C D E 138 A B C D E 139 A B C D E 140 A B C D E
141 A B C D E 142 A B C D E 143 A B C D E 144 A B C D E
145 A B C D E 146 A B C D E 147 A B C D E 148 A B C D E
149 A B C D E 150 A B C D E

IBM 1230 DOCUMENT NO. 511 WHICH CAN BE USED IN LIEU OF IBM 805 FORM NO. 1000 A 445. PRINTED IN U. S. A.

Courtesy of IBM

Chapter 6. It may be scored by hand with a punched overlay stencil or by machine.

It must be realized that published standardized tests are copyrighted material. No part of such tests may be copied, duplicated, or reproduced in any form without written permission from the holder of the copyright. To do so is to violate copyright law. Aside from the legal aspects, there is a moral obligation that is equally great. Authors and publishers of standardized tests must spend large amounts of time, professional competence, and money in producing these tests. A single test may have involved the work of several persons for 3 to 5 years, as well as the cooperation of dozens of other people and the expenditure of thousands of dollars. Except for the professional recognition accorded the authors and, to some extent, the publishers, the only recompense they receive is a small profit from the sale of tests and answer sheets. Therefore, to reproduce such tests or accompanying materials or parts thereof without express permission is not only unlawful but also unethical, since it deprives those who have produced the tests of their rightful compensation.

Another aspect of the ethics of using standardized tests has already been touched on obliquely in the anecdote about the mathematics teacher and the principal, but it bears amplification here. The continued use of standardized tests of intelligence and achievement requires that their nature and content be kept confidential until the tests are administered. Obviously, if persons who are to be tested have prior knowledge of the contents of a test, standardized or otherwise, the results are invalidated. Such prior knowledge is even more undesirable if some individuals have it but not all. In either case, the results are meaningless and no comparison with norms is possible. The continued use of standardized tests with meaningful, dependable results requires that the contents must not be passed along from one person who has seen the test to another who has not. Consequently, it is axiomatic that tests should be safeguarded by their users as confidential material if their use as tests is to be continued.

The only possible exception is the standardized diagnostic test. With this type of instrument it may be permissible under certain circumstances to go over the test with the individual pupil to identify the types of errors, but even here it is usually possible to accomplish the same objective in other ways. The manual of directions for such tests contains specific instructions regarding how the results of a diagnostic test may be used most effectively in remedial work. The user who adheres to these directions and suggestions is usually successful *and* ethical.

If pupils are permitted to go over their diagnostic test papers for the purposes mentioned above, the teacher should always make sure beforehand that two or more equivalent forms of the test are available. Then, if retesting is to be done, a different form can be used, thus minimizing the effect of familiarity with specific details of the form first used. What we have said about achievement tests applies with even greater force to tests of intelligence and personality and to evaluative devices such as ratings, sociograms, and anecdotal records. The results of these as well as the original instruments are to be held in strict confidence and should be accessible only to authorized school personnel. These principles of usage may seem strict, especially to the inexperienced student and user of standardized tests, but they are not unduly so. Psychologists and educators involved in the production and proper use of measuring instruments are genuinely concerned with this problem and have published a code of ethics that includes recommendations for the proper use of psychological tests.[1]

Nothing said above should be interpreted to mean that teachers themselves should not analyze the results of standardized achievement tests to identify the strengths and weaknesses of pupils. On the contrary, this is one of the most important uses to which test results can be put. A teacher may thus determine which objectives or outcomes of instruction have been achieved to a satisfactory degree and by which pupils. Also, weaknesses can be identified for both individual pupils and the class as a whole and steps can be taken to remedy such weaknesses. More will be said about this matter in Chapter 14.

LEARNING EXERCISES

1. Assume that you have been asked by a district-wide committee to indicate the kinds of standardized test data that would be valuable to you in your teaching assignment. Indicate the tests you would request for the school program and how you would use the data.
2. If you were interested in selecting a test covering one subject you teach, solely for your own in-class use, what factors would you consider as you compared the available tests?

[1]Standards for the use of test results are included in *Standards for Educational and Psychological Tests,* prepared by a joint committee of the American Psychological Association, American Educational Research Association, and National Council on Measurement in Education (Washington, D.C.: American Psychological Association, 1974).

SCHEDULING THE TESTS

Considerations relating to the time of year for testing have already been mentioned. It is also necessary to decide when each test is to be given, particularly if a school-wide or community-wide program is planned. This involves a decision on the day of the week and the time of day for testing. It is usually best to have the tests administered to all pupils at the same time, for such a plan causes less disruption of the school program and has the added advantage that pupils' discussion of the tests will not work to the benefit of some and to the disadvantage of others. *Day of Week and Time of Day for Testing*

Pupils should be fully informed about the nature of tests they are to take and the way in which test results will be used. If pupils are convinced that results will be used constructively to improve instruction and that they individually will not be penalized for low scores, unnecessary fears will be reduced, if not eliminated. Pupils should also be advised that last-minute cramming is not needed and will not be helpful.

It is probably best to give the tests in the morning because pupils are likely to feel more alert then than later in the day. There is a psychological advantage, if not an actual, measurable difference in performance, in this. It is also desirable, generally speaking, to give tests near the middle of the week. Monday is often "blue Monday," and Fridays are likely to be crowded with activities of more compelling interest. While none of these factors may have a demonstrable effect on test performance, they may all have some effect on the state of mind of pupils, their attitudes toward the program, and their concentration. A favorable attitude toward the testing is advantageous to the teacher and to the pupil. Ideally, all pupils should feel that they have been able to do their best on the test.

Since absentees create additional testing problems, it is well to give the tests when absences are likely to be minimal. If the tests require more than one sitting, it may be necessary to spread the testing over several days. Some achievement batteries require several hours of testing time, which requires several sittings, especially for younger pupils. If there are large numbers to be tested it is probably best to arrange a schedule of sessions to which every class or group will adhere. If a small number of pupils are involved—perhaps one or two classes—the schedule can be arranged to suit the convenience of the people concerned.

Ordinarily, it is desirable to plan a schedule for administering tests in a testing program. This increases the efficiency of the program and helps to avoid the intrusion of personal preferences of the individual teachers. When the time for giving tests is left to the choice of the individual teacher, it is advantageous to require that the testing be completed within a specified number of days. Otherwise, delays and postponements may hold up the entire program.

The choice of the place for testing depends on circumstances. With younger pupils it is generally best to administer the tests to the pupils in their usual surroundings, if they provide the proper conditions for testing. It is also better, if possible, to test very young pupils in small groups of fifteen or less. With older pupils location is probably not as important. Testing pupils in their own homerooms eliminates the problem of working out a room-assignment schedule and considerably simplifies this aspect of the work. On the other hand, if large numbers are to be tested, it is more efficient to test as many pupils at one time as facilities permit. It is obviously more efficient to test two hundred pupils at once than to test five groups of forty separately. The number that can be tested properly at one time is limited by the facilities available and by the organizational ability of the people in charge. With the necessary facilities and assistance, one thousand pupils can be tested just as easily as one hundred or fewer.

The place of testing should provide conditions and facilities necessary to the correct and most satisfactory administration of the test. In part, the choice of location depends on accessibility and availability.

ADMINISTERING THE TESTS

It is essential that standardized tests be given exactly according to directions, which may be long and complicated. No one should expect to be able to pick up a manual just before the test is to begin, and, without previous experience and study, step into the job with complete assurance. Time and study are a necessary part of the preparation for giving a standardized test, even for the experienced examiner. The inexperienced examiner may profitably have a more experienced person help in reviewing instructions and procedures beforehand.[2]

If a considerable amount of testing is to be done, the best plan may be to have all of the administration handled by only a few people. They can be given fairly intensive training by the person best fitted to do it—the school psychologist, research director, counselor, or other qualified person. This small group of specially trained teachers can then administer all the tests. Such a plan is almost sure to increase accuracy, uniformity, and efficiency.

With very young pupils it is sometimes preferable to have the testing done by their own teacher, for children frequently will be more at ease

---

[2]Directions for administering a few standardized tests have been recorded on tape and phonograph records that are played back to the persons taking the test. This procedure eliminates all personal differences between administrators of the test. However, the great majority of tests are still administered in the usual way.

and will respond better with someone they know and like than with a stranger. However, when teachers administer tests to their own pupils, it is important that the testing be done objectively and that the instructions for administering the tests be followed precisely.

Most teachers and counselors can learn to administer standardized tests successfully, yet a few seem constitutionally unfitted for the task. A list of qualities the successful administrator of standardized group tests should possess would almost certainly include the following: *Qualities of a Good Examiner*

1. *Ability to understand and follow directions.* The person who is to give a standardized test must be able to follow directions exactly. Sometimes test directions require the performance of complicated activities by the pupil and accurate timing by the examiner. Not every person likes to undertake involved procedures of this nature, and not everyone is qualified to perform these tasks and supply students with the needed guidance and assistance. The examiner must be willing to read and study the directions until they are understood thoroughly. It is useful for the examiner to work through the entire test before attempting to administer it and to become familiar with every part of it.

Once in a discussion among teachers about the uses of tests in the classroom, one teacher raised a problem, stating that on a certain English test used for a number of years, pupils invariably made scores well above the norms for the grade. This puzzled the teacher, since the pupils were not otherwise unusual or exceptional, and their very high attainment on this test seemed unaccountable. No one in the group was able to explain it, and the matter was dropped for the time being. The conference proceeded to other matters, but sometime later the same teacher brought up the problem again, this time mentioning that when the English test was administered the teacher had ignored the time limits set in the directions and permitted pupils to work on the test as long as they wished! The teacher seemed quite innocent of any notion of error.

Thorough study of the test and directions for its use and careful adherence to instructions in every detail are the essentials for successful administration of a standardized test. Most teachers and school personnel can meet these requirements without difficulty. As teachers gain in experience and confidence, the administration of standardized tests becomes fairly easy, and often it is stimulating and enjoyable.

2. *Ability to maintain the attention and whole-hearted cooperation of a group.* The administrator of a standardized test must be able to command the attention of a group and draw the best effort from each member. If the test is a good one, the tasks it involves and the instructions to the pupils will help the examiner hold the pupils' attention.

Perhaps most important, the examiner must give an impression of serious attention and an attitude of regard for the importance of the task at hand. Many a well-meaning examiner, in an attempt to set pupils at ease, has spoiled the entire effort by such remarks as "Don't take this too seriously" or "It doesn't mean anything." Certainly, children should not suffer unnecessary emotional strain in taking a test, yet a test is a test and if the child is to do as well as possible, undivided attention and cooperation are required. The examiner must avoid instilling in pupils either an attitude of extreme emotional tension *or* an attitude of careless indifference, which will defeat the very purpose of the test.

3. *Ability to read directions aloud clearly and distinctly.* Administering a group test usually requires that the directions be read aloud clearly and distinctly. This requires a good voice and the ability to use it effectively. It is highly desirable for every examiner, even the experienced one, to practice reading the directions aloud before giving a test for the first time. By such rehearsal the proper inflections, pronunciations, and phrasing can be learned. Sometimes intonation can change the meaning of a sentence and cause confusion and misunderstanding.

By practicing reading the directions aloud, the examiner can also gain sufficient familiarity with them to make the reading more pleasant and meaningful to the audience. The examiner should be able to have periodic eye contact with the group being tested to make sure that the pupils are paying attention. It may be necessary for the examiner to interrupt the reading occasionally in order to explain an example in the directions or to make sure that all pupils understand what they are to do. A thorough mastery of the directions helps to smooth such breaks and avoid awkward pauses.

4. *Ability to be objective.* Teachers who administer standardized tests to their own classes may find it very difficult to be objective if the test results seem to conflict with their own judgment. The temptation to give help may be great. However, teachers should be careful not to give inappropriate help or even hints to the examinees. Even a frown, a smile, or other facial expression may provide a clue to a student, and care should be taken to avoid any actions that destroy the objectivity of a good testing situation.

Educational tests should be used as objectively and carefully as possible, with full realization of their limitations and with regard for the fact that using them carelessly or inaccurately may make the results quite valueless or misleading. Of course, the person administering standardized tests or other measuring instruments should demonstrate warmth, understanding, and every attitude calculated to encourage pupils to enjoy taking tests and to do their very best; yet the examiner in a desire to see pupils do well must do nothing that will invalidate the results of the testing.

The examiner should observe a few simple rules for the physical condi- *Physical* tions of testing. The room should be comfortable, well-lighted, well- *Conditions* ventilated, and well-heated. The seats should be comfortable and of *of Testing* appropriate height. It is not uncommon to enter a room where testing is going on to find it crowded, the temperature too high or too low for comfort, all windows tightly closed, and the air almost unbearable. Frequently, the occupants of the room are entirely unaware of these conditions. When pupils are shifted to a different room for testing, the desks in the new room may be too large or too small. Such discomforts can usually be avoided by calling conditions of the testing room to the attention of responsible persons before the testing begins.

It is also a good idea to place a sign on the door of a room being used for testing. This keeps out people whose business is not urgent and reduces interruptions.

The room should be large enough to permit the spacing of pupils in such a way that the temptation to copy is minimized. If the desks are movable they can usually be placed at a suitable distance from each other without much trouble. If there are too many pupils to be properly accommodated in a single room, the teacher or examiner should try to divide the pupils so that the test can be given in two or more rooms. If the desks are fixed, it is desirable to seat pupils at alternate desks and, if possible, in alternate rows. If tables and chairs are used pupils should be seated so that there is no temptation to compare papers. Such measures are taken to provide an equal opportunity for all examinees to show their level of achievement.

The person in charge of administering a standardized test is responsible *Duties* for the proper conduct of the examination. If the group is large, there *of the* should be one or more proctors or assistants, but the overall responsi- *Examiner* bility is the examiner's. Most standardized tests require timing, and this is always the examiner's responsibility. A good stopwatch or at least a watch with a sweep secondhand should be available. If a stopwatch is used, the examiner should know exactly how to operate it. Stopwatches of different makes and quality vary somewhat in technique of operation. After the testing has begun it may be impossible to correct an error in timing from the faulty manipulation of watch controls.

If the examiner has only a watch with a secondhand, the following procedure is recommended:

1. The examiner should synchronize the secondhand and the minute hand so that both are together—that is, end a minute at the same time.
2. When the directions for a timed test have been read and the examiner says "Begin" or "Go," the examiner should glance at the watch, look

at the secondhand first and then the minute hand, and immediately write down the time—for example, 9-42-21, which means that the pupils began work on that part of the test at 42 minutes and 21 seconds past 9 o'clock.

3. Next the time allowance for that part of the test should be added. If the time limit is 2 minutes and 30 seconds, this should be added to the starting time, thus:

$$9\text{-}42\text{-}21$$
$$\underline{2\text{-}30}$$
$$9\text{-}44\text{-}51$$

4. At 44 minutes and 51 seconds past 9, the examinees should be told to stop, to turn over the page, or to do whatever may be indicated.

No examiner should rely on memory for the time of beginning or attempt to figure out by mental arithmetic the time of stopping. It is impossible for most people to do this accurately. Furthermore, during the administration of a standardized group test there are many more useful and important things to do than trying to calculate and remember times of starting and stopping.

The examiner should be alert to everything that goes on in the room during testing. The examiner is responsible for seeing that the proper conditions for testing are maintained and for noting and recording any unusual happenings such as extreme nervousness, accidents, or illness. If the group is large, such responsibilities are discharged with the help of assistants or proctors, but the examiner is still the person ultimately responsible for the proper conduct of the test.

LEARNING EXERCISE

3. You are administering a group test of mental ability to seventy-five ninth-graders. You suddenly discover that you have allowed them 5 minutes too little on Part 1 and they are now working on Part 2. What do you do?

Proctors   Thirty or fewer pupils in a standardized testing situation can usually be handled by one person if the physical conditions are right. If the number being tested is between thirty and sixty, one proctor will be needed; two proctors will be needed for sixty to ninety students, and so on. The duties of proctors are to see that the pupils follow the directions given by the examiner; see that pupils have pencils and other necessary equipment; distribute and collect test blanks, answer sheets, and other necessary materials at the proper time; and help the examiner in every way to administer the test as effectively as possible.

The examiner should assign the proctors or assistants to definite sections of the room or to specific parts of the group being tested, and each proctor should be held responsible for that section or part throughout the test. The proctor should stay with that portion of the group and be available to its members at all times for any legitimate assistance. Inexperienced proctors occasionally make mistakes that can easily be avoided. For example, they sometimes line up at the front of the room while the examiner is reading directions. They should avoid this, remaining as much as possible at their stations or in the background. The examiner should be the sole focus of attention when instructions are given or directions are read. As far as possible, nothing should divert the attention of the pupils from the task at hand.

If the testing is not being done by the pupils' own teacher, the teacher should endeavor to be as inconspicuous as possible, either leaving the room or sitting quietly at the back while the testing is in progress. This may sometimes create a little awkwardness, but it can usually be handled by the principal of the school a day or two before the testing begins. The presence of the teacher in the formal testing situation may not be conducive to the best efforts of the pupils.

Finally, proctors should remain alert and interested in what is going on during the entire test. Sometimes they seem to feel that once the test has successfully gotten under way, no further attention on their part is needed. This may be just the time when they should be most alert; a pupil breaks a pencil, a pen runs dry, the student turns two pages at once, or something else happens that the alert proctor can remedy immediately. To be most useful, the good proctor should also be thoroughly familiar with the test and the details of its administration. Without this knowledge, active and proper assistance in carrying out the administration of the test is difficult.

How far may one go in giving help? A good rule to follow is to allow no assistance of any kind with the problems of the test proper. Also, it is generally considered good practice not to answer any questions regarding the test after work on it has actually begun. Though everyone is anxious for pupils to do their best, the ideal standardized test situation requires uniformity of conditions for everyone being tested. Any act that gives one pupil more help or explanation than is given to all is not permissible. In some tests, understanding and following directions are part of the test, and in such cases no explanation of directions other than what is provided by the manual is allowed. The manual of a well-standardized test is usually quite explicit as to what to say and read in giving the test, and it is not permissible to add to or depart from such instructions in any way.

SCORING THE TESTS

Who
Will Score
the
Tests?

After the tests have been given, the next task is to get the scoring done. If the tests can be scored by machine, there is usually no problem. In many situations, however, hand-scoring is still the common procedure. The labor in scoring by hand has been greatly reduced by the better arrangement of test items on the page, by the use of separate answer sheets with scoring stencils, and by the development of self-scoring techniques and other aids. However, we are still a long way from entirely relieving teachers of this job. If funds are available, some of the work may be done by clerks, but of course this adds to the cost of testing.

If teachers do the scoring, it is very desirable to make some adjustment in their regular duties to give them adequate time for the work. Some of their classes may be dismissed or assigned temporarily to other teachers or substitutes; or they may be excused from some of their nonteaching duties for the time. These adjustments will not only help get the scoring done quickly but will also help create favorable attitudes toward the testing program. Furthermore, there is the advantage that the scoring task will thus not become an extra burden for busy teachers.

Suggestions
for
Efficient
Scoring

In hand-scoring of standardized tests, certain methods and principles can contribute much to the speed and accuracy with which the work is accomplished. The suggestions that follow are particularly appropriate where large numbers of tests are to be scored, but most of them are applicable to every test-scoring situation.

In the first place, it is well to divide the task so that each person may develop speed and accuracy on a particular part of the scoring. For example, if there are eight pages or parts of a test, it is more efficient to have one individual score one page or part on all the tests than to have that person score each test in its entirety. If there are enough workers to assign one page or part to each, an assembly-line procedure can be set up to good advantage. If not, each scorer should concentrate on one page or part at a time and then go on to the next, as each is finished. This method sometimes enables scorers to memorize the scoring key quickly and soon dispense with it entirely. This contributes to both speed and accuracy, since scorers can concentrate on the scoring without having to manipulate scoring keys or compare the keys with answers written on the test papers. Moreover, with this system the scorers do not need to shift attention constantly from one part of the test to an entirely different part; they can concentrate on one part until it is finished.

The task of arriving at part scores and adding them to get the total score should also be done by one person. The transforming of raw scores into percentiles or standard scores should be the separate responsibility of another individual. If it seems convenient and efficient, the one who works out part scores and total scores can also do this, but, again, it is probably more efficient for each person to do one part of the job at a time.

The assembly-line procedure should be planned and carried out so that test blanks can move along the line smoothly without piling up at any one point. This requires that the work be assigned according to the difficulty of the separate tasks and the particular skill of each individual. A slow worker will necessarily be given a smaller or easier job to avoid delaying others. The person in charge of the scoring must experiment with helpers and the task at hand until an efficient and agreeable procedure is worked out.

Second, it is generally better to do the work of scoring in a group than to let individuals take tests away with them to score at their convenience. When the scoring is done in a group, it is possible to settle on the spot such problems as questions about procedure and allowable answers. Also, the scoring is more interesting and stimulating and delays are avoided. It is sometimes difficult to find the time or a suitable place for assembly-line scoring. However, it is often possible to find time when six or eight teachers can work together if, as has been suggested, the work is done during school hours.

The place for scoring of tests should be relatively quiet and free from interruptions, and the workers should be able to talk with each other freely without fear of disturbing others. If possible, there should be a large table or several smaller ones that can be put together so that all the scorers can work comfortably in a group.

Third, all hand-scoring—the entire operation, from beginning to end—should be carefully checked for accuracy. Every step should be systematically checked, and the person in charge should also check the accuracy of individual workers. Wide variations are nearly always found in the work of particular individuals; moreover, some perform their tasks with few errors, while others seem unable to score accurately no matter how much they practice.

Checking the scoring is best done by rescoring a sampling of papers. It may be desirable at the beginning to rescore entirely the first few papers, perhaps five or ten, to see what mistakes are being made by individual scorers and to help correct these mistakes. After this, a sampling of every fifth paper or perhaps every tenth paper should be completely rescored as a continuous check on the accuracy of the work. If it is found that errors are frequent in all parts of the tests, it will be necessary to rescore all papers. If errors are consistently found only in certain parts of the test or in certain phases of the work, it will suffice, as a rule, to rescore only those parts where error is found.

One basic fact often overlooked by users of standardized tests is that errors occur in all such work, and it is therefore absolutely essential that continuous and systematic checking take place.[3] The less experienced the workers are, the greater is the probability of error. But regardless of the experience of the scorers, the scoring should not be accepted as final and the results should not be recorded until every step of the process has been checked. To permit inaccurate scoring is to waste time and money and to allow grave injustice to be done to pupils.

Finally, it is important to train workers in the scoring process. One does not usually put scorers to work until they have had some instruction. It is usually desirable to have prospective scorers first read the manual, or at least the part dealing with scoring, so that they will understand what they are to do and how to do it. Then the person in charge should help score enough papers so that there is no doubt that the work is being done correctly.

RECORDING AND ANALYZING RESULTS

Recording
Test
Results

After the tests have been scored and checked, the results must be made a part of the permanent records of the pupil and the school. Most schools have some sort of permanent record for each pupil, usually a folder for recording information such as personal and home background data, schools attended, marks, honors, disciplinary or other special actions, and results of various tests. Many such record systems have been devised, some by national agencies, some on the state level, and some by larger city school systems. In Figure 13.3 one sample permanent record form is reproduced. Although the data in the sample record were gathered some time ago, they exemplify the full and complete use of the form and, except for one or two items,[4] are as appropriate for illustrative purposes as though they had been gathered yesterday.

Whatever the type of permanent record, it is important that there be one, that the test results be recorded as soon as possible after they are available, and that this record be readily accessible to people entitled to use it. Teachers may enter test data on the record form for their own

---

[3]See Beeman N. Phillips and Garrett Weathers, "Analysis of Errors Made in Scoring Standardized Tests," *Educational and Psychological Measurement*, 18 (Autumn 1958), 563–567.
[4]The identification of race, for one. This information is now given optionally.

pupils or clerks may do this if such help is available. Records are confidential and should not be available to unauthorized persons, however.

It is advantageous to keep the permanent cumulative records of pupils in some central place such as the principal's office. In some schools, records are distributed to teachers so that each will have custody of the records of his or her own pupils. It may also be desirable to have the records filed in the office of the counselor. There are arguments for and against centralized and distributed record systems, but they need not be reviewed here. The important thing is that the records be used—not just filed—and it should be determined in each situation what arrangement is best for all concerned.

LEARNING EXERCISE

4. Your testing program is proceeding nicely, with tests given as scheduled, scoring done promptly and accurately, and results tabulated and analyzed. However, you must see that the results are entered on the pupils' individual record forms. You have no money for clerical help. How will you get the records completed?

Before any follow-up of testing can be made, the results must be analyzed. The analysis may be very simple, as when a pupil's rank in the class is determined, or it may be more complicated, as in large-scale testing programs involving hundreds of schools and thousands of pupils in a large city system. Whatever is done, the basic procedures and techniques are usually statistical. A brief survey of statistical techniques, especially as they apply to educational and psychological test results, is given in Chapters 2 and 3. By the application of these techniques, a teacher or counselor can make all the usual types of analysis without going far into technicalities. For analysis of a more advanced nature, one of the standard textbooks in statistical methods should be consulted.

It is sometimes erroneously assumed that when we make a profile, a percentile curve, or some other graphic record of test results, we are making a further statistical analysis of test results. Users of tests and test results sometimes believe that profiles, distribution curves, and other graphic methods add something that statistical data do not yield. Profiles

Analyzing Test Results

Figure 13.3 Part of a Sample Permanent Record Form

Name __LESTER, WILLIAM LEE__
(Last) (First) (Middle)

Male ✓ No. of Other Boys _1_ Older _0_
Female ___ Children in Family _2_ Girls _1_ Younger _2_

Address (in Pencil) __Box 271, MORAVIA, NY__ Telephone No. (in Pencil) __315-497-0330__

Race (Optional) __Caucasian__
Church Preference (Optional) __Baptist__
Latest Date When Personal & Family Data Were Entered (in Pencil) __6-23-67__

Date of Birth __5/1/56__ Proof of Birth __Birth Certificate__ Source of Information __Mother__
Place of Birth __Auburn, NY__ Child Lives with __Parents__ Economic Status of Family (Optional) __Middle Class__

FAMILY DATA	FATHER[1]	MOTHER[2]
Name (First)	John	Mary
Home Address	951 Main St.	
Place of Birth	Ohio, N.Y.	Auburn, NY
Maiden Name		
Occupation 1	air condition mech.	
Occupation 2	director	
Employer (Pencil) 1	Singer Sew. Co.	
Employer (Pencil) 2	Carrier Machine Co.	
Language in Home	English	English
Education Level	Assoc. Deg.	Higher
Date Naturalized		
Cause of Death		
Step-Parent		
(Write Name in Correct Column)		
Guardian		
Marital Status		

CONSECUTIVE RECORD OF ALL SCHOOLS ATTENDED

School & Address	Date Ent.	Date Left	Reason Left*
Pt. Byron School, Pt. Byron, NY	9/61	6/74	G

*Code Reference for Column 3 Above:
TR - Transferred   G - Graduated
EP - Employment Permit   D - Deceased
PI - Permanent Illness   M - Married
OA - Over Required Age   X - Expelled
MFC - Moved from City

PROGRESS ESTIMATE

KINDERGARTEN

Check Appropriate Column:

	Outstanding	Satisfactory	Not yet
Forms Desirable Habits		✓	
School Adjustment		✓	
Social Adjustment		✓	
Works Independently		✓	
Creative Ability		✓	
Adaptability		✓	
Learning Attitude		✓	
Mental Development	✓		
Healthly Alert	✓		
Reading Readiness		✓	
Self-Expression		✓	

Date Entered __9/61__
Date Left __6/62__
Attendance:
Regular __✓__ Days Attended __175__
Irregular ___ Teacher __E. Barton__
Remarks:

STANDARD TEST RECORD

Date	Gr.	Name of Test	Form	Score	MA	CA	I.Q.	%ile	Rank in Group	Remarks
9/63	K	Metropolitan			9-2	8-7	110	75		
3/1/64	2	Kuhlmann Anderson								arithmetic 3-5
10/4/64	3	Kuhlmann Anderson	E							" 4 A-1
5/11/65	3	Stanford-Desnicke	E							" 5-8
11/65	4	Stanford Achievement	G			9-0		112		
1/67	5	Cleary Quick-Scoring	A							
4/67	6	Barli-Still	H			14-0	11-0	117		Gregory 9.5
4/69	7	Lorle Byst						115		
10/71	10	Kuhlmann Anderson	B							
1/73	11	Kuder Preference								High in artistic/natural/scientific
10/73	12	Career Planning	S						84	
10/17/73	12	Pt. Huron Comp.	AA							

LOW SCHOLARSHIP MARKS
In Each Column Indicate the Numbers in Which Low Marks Were Earned.

	Grade					
Reasons for Low Marks:	1	2	3	4	5	6
Excessive Absences						
Illness						
Carelessness					✓	
Below Average Ability				✓	✓	
Indifference						
Outside Work						
Poor Study Habits				✓	✓	✓
Subject Difficulty				✓	✓	✓
CAUSES OF ABSENCE						
Illness						
Parental Neglect						
Truancy						
CAUSES OF TARDINESS						
Parent's Responsibility					✓	✓
Child's Responsibility				✓	✓	✓

Guidance Cumulative Folder, Form 100CF, Copyright 1970
CHRONICLE GUIDANCE Publications, Inc., Moravia, N.Y. 13118
United States of America

426   THE MEASUREMENT PROGRAM

ELEMENTARY SCHOOL RECORD — Attendance and Scholarship

Year	19__		19__		19__		19__		19__		19__		19__		19__		Recommendations to Junior High School from Elementary School
Semester	1	2	Av	1	2	Av	1	2	Av	1	2	Av	1	2	Av	1	2	Av	
Reading	C	C	C	C	C	C	C	C	C	B	C	C							ACADEMIC
Writing	C	B		A	A		A	A		B	B	B							
Spelling	B	A	B	A	A	A	A	B	B	C	B	B							
Arithmetic	B	A	A	A	A	A	B	B	B	C	B	B							
Social Studies	C	C	C	B	B	B	B	B	B	B	B	B							
English	C	C	C	C	C	C	B	B	B	B	B	B							
Science	B	B	B	B	B	B	A	A	A	A	A	A							
Music	C	B	B	B	B	B	A	A	A	A	A	A							
Art	C	C	C	B	B	B	A	A	A	A	A	A							
Phys.Ed.	C	C	C	B	B	B	A	A	A	B	B	B							
Health	C	C	C	C	C	C	A	A	A	B	A	B							

Absences	3	8		5	3		11	2		10									
Tardiness	2	C		C	1		2	0		11									
Days Due																			
Date Entered	9/62		9/63		9/64		9/65		9/66		9/67								
Grade	ELEM		Elem		Elem		ELEM		5		6								
Building	H.Robinson		O.Adams		Whitham		Calvin		Signor		Elem. T.Brown								
Teacher																			
Progress Record (Show Promoted, Re-tained, Put Back, and Date)	Promoted 9/63		Promoted 9/64		Promoted 9/65		Promoted 9/66		Promoted 9/67		Promoted 9/68								

Code Reference Above Interpretation of Marks: A – Exceptional Work; B – Above Average; C – Average; D – Below Average; F – Failure; SS – Summer School Recommended but Not for Credit.

ACADEMIC

I consider it above average abilities, average abilities, should handle Jr. High without difficulty

SOCIAL RELATIONS

Inclined to shyness but gets along with peers satisfactorily

ATTENDANCE & DISCIPLINE

Regular in attendance Cooperative with no serious discipline problem

BEHAVIORAL OR PSYCHOLOGICAL

Normal behavior patterns

GENERAL RECOMMENDATIONS

Encourage to participate in extra curricular activities to overcome shyness. Fine student Well-mannered

INFORMATION FROM OTHER SCHOOL SYSTEMS ATTENDED

School System	Grade	Marks	Other Information

ADDITIONAL MISCELLANEOUS DATA

Permission to use sample copy of the Guidance Cumulative Folder #100CF has been granted by Chronicle Guidance Publications, Inc., Moravia, N.Y. 13118, ph: (315) 497-0330. Less than 100 blank folders are 15¢ each. Write or call for prices on larger quantities.

and other graphic methods are often very helpful, but principally because they express findings in a way more readily grasped than by mere statistics. It is possible that a graphic representation of data may clarify a statistical situation or even give new insight into its meaning, but a graph or chart simply expresses statistical data in another form. A profile is merely a graphic representation of data already known. By extending or extrapolating a curve, we may extend the data, but the results of such procedures are always hypothetical. Moreover, the same results may be determined statistically as well as graphically. But graphic records do not say anything that the numbers do not already say.

Before describing specific testing programs it seems pertinent to present some findings of a 1976 survey of such programs in Michigan schools.[5] This is the fourth survey of its nature conducted in Michigan, the three previous ones having been made in 1958–1959, 1963–1964, and 1969–1970. Much of what was revealed in all four is relevant to our discussion, but limitations of space prohibit a detailed review. However, a few of the many important findings of the 1976 survey interestingly and significantly indicate one state's present practices with regard to recommendations in the preceding section of this chapter.

The Michigan survey was based on the responses of 481 school districts enrolling pupils in grades K–12. This represents a 91 percent return. Some specific findings are as follows:

1. Organized testing programs that include standardized tests exist in 93 percent of the reporting districts. The figures for 1959 and 1970 are 90 percent and 88 percent.
2. The people most often involved in the testing program are, in order of frequency, counselors, chief school officers, and committees of teachers.
3. Testing committees function in slightly less than half the districts, and 84 percent of these function at the district level.
4. Testing is most often done near the close of the school year or in pretest and post-test situations in the fall and spring.
5. Test data are available in most schools to teachers, counselors, principals, and superintendents. Results compiled for the districts are available to school board members. In most districts results of an individual pupil are available to the parents and the pupil.
6. Greater emphasis is expected over the next 5 years on achievement testing, career guidance testing, and objective- or criterion-referenced testing.

[5]Evelyn J. Brzezinski, *Testing in Michigan, a Twenty-Year Perspective* (Ann Arbor, Mich.: Michigan School Testing Service, Bureau of School Services, University of Michigan,, n.d.).

7. In about half the districts, test scoring is done by the test publisher; in a third, it is done by other outside agencies.
8. More training is needed in the use of measurement for curriculum evaluation and change at both the individual pupil and the school levels.
9. Although testing is done in grades K–12 by at least some schools, the amount done after grade 6 declines markedly. The most common use of tests is in the lower elementary grades.

The Michigan Educational Assessment Program includes testing at grades 4 and 7. Some questions in the survey referred to the impact that a statewide program has on a local testing program and how the results of the statewide program are used. Generally the existence of a statewide program did have an influence on the grade levels selected for administration of other tests and on the types of tests used in local programs. The most common uses of MEAP results included reviewing teaching strategies, assessing success in accomplishing minimal objectives, and reporting to school boards.

ILLUSTRATIVE MEASUREMENT PROGRAMS

To complete this discussion of measurement programs, we offer two illustrations of actual practice in school systems of different sizes. Both programs have been developed through local leadership and experience. Therefore, they are practical, and their scope is such that they can be managed at the local level without undue expense or labor. The programs are for a city system comprising a large number of elementary schools plus junior and senior high schools and for a small community school with no secondary grades.

The city school program was developed by the public schools of Shawnee *A Program* Mission, Kansas, enrolling approximately 40,000 pupils in elementary, *for a* junior high, and senior high schools. Altogether, sixty-four schools are *City System* involved, of which forty-nine are elementary, grades K–6; ten are junior high schools, grades 7–9; and five are senior high schools, grades 10–12. The basic program throughout the district is shown as Figure 13.4.

The tests in the basic program are administered to all pupils at the levels and at the approximate times indicated. Tests are usually administered by counselors or by teachers, though sometimes in an elementary school they are administered by the principal. The only hand-scored test, the readiness test in kindergarten, is scored by teachers at the individual school sites; the machine-scorable answer sheets are sent to a central office and the scores are returned to the school with a tabulation of results. In addition, tabulations of all test results are sent to the office of the Director of Program Development and Evaluation, and the scored tests are returned to the schools. Test results are recorded in each pupil's cumulative record. Optional tests are available for pupils in grades 4, 5, 6,

Figure 13.4   The Testing Program for a City School System

SHAWNEE MISSION PUBLIC SCHOOLS
Department of Program Development and Evaluation

Adopted Schedule
Standardized Testing Program
1976-77

Grade	Test	Delivery of Testing Mtrl. to schools	Testing Dates	Answer Sheets Due for Scoring
K	Metropolitan Readiness	3-16	March 21 thru April 1	Hand-scored in school
1	Cognitive Abilities Primary II	1-24	January 31 thru February 11	February 16
3	Cognitive Abilities Level A	2-1	February 7-18	February 23
3	ITBS Form 5 Level 9	4-13	April 18-29	May 4
6	Cognitive Abilities Level D	2-1	February 7-18	February 23
6	ITBS Form 5 Level 12	4-13	April 18-29	May 4
8	DAT Form S	9-29-76	October 4 thru October 22	October 25
9	Cognitive Abilities Level F	1-10	January 17 thru January 21	January 26
9	ITBS Form 5 Level 14	3-23	March 28 thru April 1	April 13
10	OVIS	8-18	August 30 thru Sept. 24, 1976	Sept. 29
11	OVIS	8-18	August 30 thru Sept. 24	Sept. 29
12	Test of Academic Progress Form S	as per schedule	November 29 thru January 14	January 19

Optional Testing

4 and 5	Cognitive Abilities or Iowa Test of Basic Skills Make-ups		Scheduled During the 3rd and 6th Grade Testing Periods
6	Pimsleur Language Test		Scheduled as Per Recommendation of Foreign Lang. Department
9	Kuder E Interest		Scheduled by School for Instructional Purposes

Approved by the Executive Committee
May 7, 1976

Courtesy of the Shawnee Mission Public Schools

THE MEASUREMENT PROGRAM

	K	1	2	3	4	5	6	7	8	9	10	11	12
Readiness	X												
Intelligence		X		X			X			X			
Multiple aptitude									X				
Vocational interest											X	X	
Achievement batteries				X			X			X			X

and 9. Requests for optional testing are channeled through a building administrator to the Director of Program Development and Evaluation.

The Shawnee Mission Director of Program Development and Evaluation has developed a description of the standardized testing program that includes a brief analysis of each of the tests and the ways in which results can be used. In addition, descriptions of administrative procedures for the testing program, including suggestions as to how results can be discussed with parents, are distributed to all teachers in the district. Such carefully worked-out materials are essential in a large program such as this, where personal contact with all cooperating personnel is impossible. Table 13.2 summarizes the grade levels at which tests of various kinds are administered as part of the city's school-wide testing program.

The Shawnee Mission program is ambitious and requires cooperation among teachers, administrators, and counselors. The overall leadership is provided by the Office of Program Development and Evaluation, and the major share of the work is divided among the test coordinators throughout the school district.

The results of the Shawnee Mission testing program are used in various ways, including the following:

1. To assist the central office staff in identifying curricular fields of strength and weakness for the total district. If the district-wide test results in a given field are not satisfactory, special efforts are made to analyze the causes and then to correct conditions believed to be responsible for the weakness in pupil achievement.
2. To assist in identifying individual pupil needs and in diagnosing learning difficulties. Teachers are advised to regard test results as one source of information about their pupils and are encouraged to look for consistencies and inconsistencies in information about pupils.
3. To assist in evaluating individual progress and in identifying underachievers. If pupils are not achieving up to capability, special efforts

are made to identify the problem and to provide assistance to individual pupils.

4. To assist the counselor in educational and vocational counseling with students and parents. The district encourages teachers and counselors to discuss test results with parents, pulling together not only the test results but other information available through local tests and other evidence of accomplishment.

5. To assist the teacher in grouping for instruction and in planning appropriate instructional activities. The district strives to individualize instruction as much as needed and feasible, and the test results are used as one source of information in helping to plan instruction.

6. To provide baseline data so that changes in instruction can be assessed in terms of pupil achievement.

A Program for a Small School

Extensive programs like that in Shawnee Mission may be beyond the needs and resources of small schools. The program of a small elementary school enrolling fewer than three hundred pupils is outlined in Table 13.3. It follows closely the minimum program presented earlier in this chapter and can be managed easily.

This program is simple, and it is limited enough to be managed by the regular staff of the school without outside assistance. The results are used in various ways, including identifying exceptional children, both the slow-learning and gifted; counseling with parents; sectioning or grouping; diagnosing; and comparing test results with national norms.

The program gives information of several types, all useful in improving instruction. It reveals the stage of development or readiness of beginners for learning the fundamentals, it gives several appraisals of each child's general capacity for school work, and it provides a reasonably adequate survey of each pupil's progress in the common branches of the elementary school curriculum. The entire cost of the program, including test material and some clerical assistance for recording the results, can be kept to about 25 cents per pupil per year. This allows nothing, of course, for the time of the school staff or for any outside help. However, when teachers become educated to the value of the results of their work and feel that they have a real part in the program, they are usually glad to contribute a reasonable amount of time and energy to the work of carrying it through.

Other testing programs in similar-sized communities could be described, and these would differ in such details as grade placement of tests and areas tested. However, the two programs we have described have been found workable and useful in their respective communities. They are not extremely elaborate, and they are modest in cost. They serve to illustrate the principles discussed in the first part of this chapter and

Grade	Test	Time of year
K	Reading readiness	May
1 or 2	Intelligence	February
3 or 4	Achievement battery	October
5	Intelligence	February
6	Achievement battery	October

should suggest what can be done by other communities with similar needs and purposes.

In any measurement program the teacher or supervisor should anticipate the necessity for retesting in doubtful cases, and provision should be made for this on an individual basis. Accidents will happen to prevent pupils from finishing a test; there will be surprisingly low, or sometimes surprisingly high, scores; and of course there will always be absentees. When children miss the testing or when there is good reason to believe that they have not been adequately or accurately measured, a make-up test is in order. Whenever an alternate form of the same test is available, it should be used in such cases, especially when a child has started a test but has been unable to finish. It is usually more satisfactory to have the pupil take the entire test in another form than to continue at the point where the interruption occurred.

The discussion in this chapter has been concerned entirely with group tests. It is recognized that in some cases an individual examination like the Binet or the Wechsler or another individual test may be used. Such examinations must be administered by a person with special training, however, since most classroom teachers have not had the necessary instruction in the use of these instruments. Where such tests are needed and used, it is assumed that qualified persons are available to administer them and that the tests will be given as necessary.

LEARNING EXERCISES

5. Study the cumulative record form in Figure 13.3 in detail. What changes, including additions and deletions, would you suggest?
6. Give your judgment or rating of the Shawnee Mission program on the following factors: comprehensiveness; practicality; economy; usefulness; acceptability to teachers, counselors, and administrators.

7. Compare the small school program with the minimum program described on page 407. Do you consider the differences to be significant? If so, why?
8. If you were designing a testing program for a large school system, how would you alter the one presented on pages 430–431? Defend any additions or deletions you recommend.

SUGGESTED READING

DUROST, WALTER N. *What Constitutes a Minimal Testing Program for Elementary and Junior High School?* Test Service Notebook 1, Rev. New York: Harcourt Brace Jovanovich, 1956. Discusses the major phases of planning, conducting, and using the results of a testing program in a practical manner.

EBEL, ROBERT L. *Essentials of Educational Measurement.* 2d ed. Englewood Cliffs, N.J.: Prentice-Hall, 1972. Chapter 22 is a brief discussion of testing programs with emphasis on the use of results from standardized tests. Includes sections on judging teacher and pupil competence.

MEHRENS, WILLIAM A., and IRVIN J. LEHMANN. *Standardized Tests in Education.* 2d ed. New York: Holt, Rinehart and Winston, 1975. A general treatment of the nature and role of standardized tests. Includes test selection and the use of data from various types of standardized tests. Chapter 6 provides a broad overview of evaluation, including some controversial topics.

NATIONAL SOCIETY FOR THE STUDY OF EDUCATION. *The Impact and Improvement of School Testing Programs.* Sixty-second Yearbook of the Society, Part II. Chicago: University of Chicago Press, 1963. A comprehensive treatment of the subject by a committee of the Society. Considers different types of testing programs, their impact on the schools and on individuals, the function of programs in college preparation and guidance, and the selection and use of tests.

STANLEY, JULIAN C., and KENNETH D. HOPKINS. *Educational and Psychological Measurement and Evaluation.* Englewood Cliffs, N.J.: Prentice-Hall, 1972. Chapter 17 is a general description of planning and implementing a testing program. Includes the selection of tests, planning scoring services, and the use of results. A useful complement to the material included in this chapter.

THORNDIKE, ROBERT L., and ELIZABETH HAGEN. *Measurement and Evaluation in Psychology and Education.* 4th ed. New York: John Wiley & Sons, 1977. Chapter 14 is a detailed treatment of local testing programs, including discussions of desirable qualities and priorities in such programs, and planning, administering, and reporting results to the public. Contains tables and graphs illustrating how to depict and interpret results. Includes a brief discussion of external testing programs.

TRAXLER, ARTHUR E. "Fifteen Criteria of a Testing Program." *The Clearing House*, 25 (September 1950), 3–7. A brief and practical discussion containing a useful set of criteria for judging the efficiency and value of a testing program.

TUCKMAN, BRUCE W. *Measuring Educational Outcomes.* New York: Harcourt Brace Jovanovich, 1975. Chapter 15 is a general description of the development of a testing program and the ways in which results may be used. Includes sections on individual pupil and classroom applications of test data.

WOMER, FRANK B. "Testing Programs: Misconceptions, Misuse, Overuse." *Michigan Journal of Secondary Education,* 2 (Spring 1961), 153–161. A useful discussion of some of the more common mistakes made in carrying out school testing programs, with particular emphasis on errors in interpreting and implementing results.

Fourteen

USING THE RESULTS

OF MEASUREMENT

In preceding chapters many kinds of measuring instruments have been described and evaluated. We have suggested or discussed the uses of these instruments in many instances. In Chapter 13 we emphasized that measurement programs should be planned and carried out with definite purposes. In that chapter a number of broad objectives or purposes for a measurement program were also cited, and we stated that these would be discussed in some detail later. Listed below are the objectives mentioned there:

1. Placement and promotion
2. Homogeneous grouping
3. Diagnosis and remedial work
4. Counseling and guidance
5. Marking
6. Curriculum evaluation
7. Motivation
8. Identification and study of exceptional children
9. Interpreting schools to the community
10. Improvement of school staff
11. Educational research

These are probably the main purposes for which tests and other measuring instruments are used in schools today. Certainly, they seem important and worthy of careful consideration. It will be the aim of this chapter to discuss these purposes and to show how measurement can contribute to their attainment. At the completion of this chapter you should be able to answer questions such as the following:

1. How does the planned use of measurement data in a school or school system influence the nature of the measurement program?
2. For which of the objectives of a measurement program are standardized achievement tests particularly required and useful? tests of ability? interests? personality?
3. How does the planned use of measurement data influence the plan for storing and recording test data?
4. Are there traditional uses of measurement data that reduce the effectiveness with which the data can be used in meeting other objectives of a measurement program? If so, name or describe and define them.

INTERPRETATION OF TEST RESULTS

Basic to using the results of measurement is the interpretation of scores. As we pointed out in Chapter 3, a test score is merely a number, devoid of meaning in itself. Not until it is related to something does it become meaningful and useful. Much of Chapter 3 is concerned with the procedures by which test scores are given meaning. Before we discuss the various uses of test results, it would be well to take another look at a device that facilitates interpretation, to which reference has already been made. This is the *profile*, a graphic method of depicting the results of the testing of individuals and of groups. The profile typically shows the results of an achievement battery such as the Stanford, an aptitude battery such as the *Differential Aptitude Tests*, or scores on an interest inventory for various occupations such as the Strong. Although a profile actually adds nothing to the information given by scores, norms, and statistical interpretations, it does facilitate comparisons and interpretations by presenting results graphically and all in one package for a given individual or a group. Two examples of profiles are illustrated here.

Figure 14.1 shows a computer-prepared profile for an individual pupil on the *Stanford Achievement Tests.* Such reports can be obtained as part of the scoring service purchased by a school from the publisher, or, if tests are hand-scored locally, a similar form can be prepared by the classroom teacher. The individual record includes results expressed as number right, scaled scores, percentile rank, and grade equivalents, and the profile shows graphically the level of performance on each of the subtests in the battery. In this example, the scores are plotted as stanines; some publishers base profiles on grade or age equivalents, whereas others use percentile ranks. A pattern of strengths and weaknesses for a pupil can be discerned readily in a profile, and a teacher can plan instruction accordingly. Also, a profile report can be useful in parent-teacher conferences, which many schools schedule periodically.

Figure 14.2 depicts the test results for a total class. This report was prepared locally by a classroom teacher. Individual pupil results are indi-

Figure 14.1 Profile for Individual Pupil

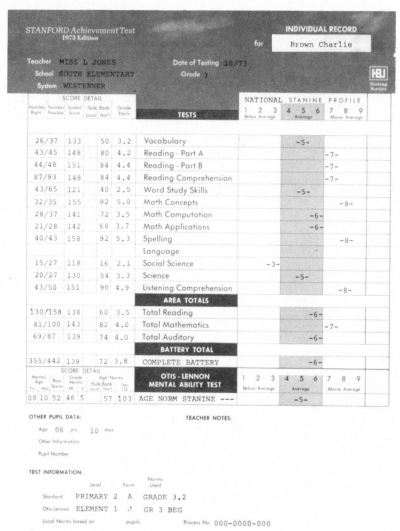

Reproduced from the *Stanford Achievement Test.* Copyright © 1972 by Harcourt Brace Jovanovich, Inc. Reproduced by special permission of the publisher.

Stanines based on Beginning ☐ Middle ☐ End ☐ of Grade   Form _____

Stanine Analysis of Pupils in Class

STANINE	Vocabulary	Reading (Parts A+B)	Word Study Skills	Mathematics Concepts	Mathematics Computation	Mathematics Applications	Spelling	Social Science	Science	Listening Comp.	STANINE	OLMAT* IQ
9	12				9 (10), 18	23	4	12, 22	23		9	23
8	12			9,(10), 18, 23	4, 6		18	11, 18, 21, 23		23	8	9, 10
7		23	18	2, 25	23	2, 4, 8, 15, 18	(10)	8, 20, 25	11, 12, 15	2, 9, 20	7	4
6	2, 4, 19	4, 18, 20, 22	4 (10), (10), 20, 22, 23	4, 6, 15, 20, 22	2, 20, 22	7/9, (10), 25	2, 9, 22	7, 9, (10), 19	2, 8, 22, 26	18, 22	6	2, 6, 11, 12, 18, 22
5	9 (10) 18, 22, 23	1, 6, 9 (10), (16), 24, 26	1, 6, 7, 9, 12, 19, 24		12, 15, (16)	5, 11, 20, 21	(3) 12, (10), 19, 20, 21, 23	2	1, 6, 8, 9, 14, 17, 19, 21, 25	7, 8, 15, 21, 26	5	1, 7, 8, 13, 15, 20, 21, 25
4	7, 20, 21	2 (3) 7, 19, 21, 25	25, 26	1, 7, 8, 12, (16)	1, 5, 8, 14, 25	6, 12, 14, 19, 22, 24	1, 5, 6, 7, 15, 24	1, 5, 14, 15, (16), 24	(3) 5, (10) 24	5, 6, (10), 11, 14, 19, 24, 25	4	5, 14, 16, 19, 24
3	1, 5, 6, 8, 24, 25, 26	5, 8	2, (3) 5, 8, 15, 21	5, 14, 17, 19, 21, 26	(3) 19	1, (16)	8, 17, 25, 26	17	(16), 20	4, (16), 17	3	17, 26
2	14, (16)	14, 15, 17	17		7, 17, 21, 26	(3) 17, 26	11, 14	(3) 6, 26	7	1	2	3
1	(3) 15, 17		14	(3)						(3)	1	

No. of Pupils in Stanine 7-9	1	2	1	6	6	6	3	9	4	No. of Pupils in Stanine 4	7-9	4
4-6	11	17	15	10	11	14	16	11	17	15	4-6	19
1-3	12	5	8	7	6	5	6	4	3	5	1-3	3

*Total Auditory, IQ's or other optional information may be distributed in the blank column.

Reproduced from the *Stanford Achievement Test*. Copyright © 1972 by Harcourt Brace Jovanovich, Inc. Reproduced by special permission of the publisher.

cated by numbers recorded in the appropriate stanine row, and at the bottom for each subtest are shown the numbers of pupils in the class who scored above average, average, and below average. Profiles for individual pupils could be prepared by connecting the number of each individual on the various subtests, as has been done for pupils 3, 10, and 16. Individuals who differ markedly from the other pupils in the class can be located readily, and the teacher would want to consider this information in planning instructional programs.

PLACEMENT AND PROMOTION

One of the widespread uses of test results is the placement of pupils at particular grade levels, including decisions about retention, promotion, or acceleration. Ideally, pupils should be placed at levels where they can learn without being unduly discouraged, overworked, or bored. A general school achievement battery is extremely useful in making such decisions. These batteries have grade norms for the separate subject tests, norms for the battery as a whole, and norms for converting the scores into age levels. With these three types of norms it is possible to determine fairly accurately a pupil's grade level with regard to achievement in school subjects.

When a pupil transfers from one school to another, particularly to a different school system or state, a standardized achievement battery is one of the most dependable tools for determining the pupil's level of achievement. It is probably more accurate to speak of *levels* of achievement, since these are not always the same in different subjects or parts of the test battery, and, as we have seen, the profile based on scores on the different subject tests is generally not a straight line.

A general intelligence test also provides useful information to parents and school officials as decisions with regard to placement are made; both educational and general mental development can be taken into account in placing the pupil. Knowing the grade level of achievement, chronological age, and IQ, it is possible to arrive at a decision based on objective data rather than guesswork. If the pupil's previous school record is available, this, too, should be considered, although for grade placement with regard to subject-matter achievement, the test battery is probably the more accurate measure.

In cases involving possible retention in grade or acceleration, the same types of information about the individual pupil will be useful. The research evidence is not clear regarding the efficacy of retaining a pupil at a grade level for a second year. In a review of forty-four research studies covering the educational literature up to 1973, little evidence could be found that retention in grade level leads to better achievement and better adjustment than promotion.[1] However, tests can be very useful in determining a slow learner's level of achievement and may be helpful in identifying possible reasons for the deficiency in educational development. The necessary preliminary information for the proper adjustment of a program to individual differences in ability and achievement is provided most quickly and efficiently by standardized tests.

The question of acceleration is related to that of nonpromotion. If it is undesirable to hold back slow pupils, the same argument applies for fast ones. When a very able pupil is kept at grade level, we are in effect not promoting the pupil just as surely as when we make a low-achieving pupil repeat a grade. S. L. Pressey has thoroughly reviewed the substantial evidence on this point, and, although the study was published in 1949, no contradictory evidence has been found.[2] The evidence shows clearly that students who are accelerated by extra promotions in school or who are permitted to finish college in less than the usual time seem to do well in their studies and are well adjusted socially; they seem not to suffer in health and not to be handicapped otherwise as a result of their acceleration. Nevertheless, many school authorities are reluctant to adopt such practices. Parents also often wish their children to remain with their group and are fearful of what acceleration might do to their children's social adjustment. It is unfortunate that high-school and college students who are both mentally and physically advanced for their age are generally required to sit through all the regular lessons and classes when they could proceed much faster in the environment of a more advanced grade or level. Acceleration would not only save much valuable time but it would also help avoid the boredom and the bad study habits that may be developed by a bright pupil who is required to wait while the slowest in the group catches up.

When achievement tests and mental tests reveal that a pupil is accelerated in achievement and mental development, and if that pupil has no physical and social handicaps, consideration should be given for extra promotions and adjustment of work to the pupil's level. Moreover, the pupil should be encouraged to progress through school and college as rapidly as possible, and at every level the tasks presented should be in keeping with the pupil's abilities and should require appropriately high standards of work. Able students are needed in today's world, perhaps

[1]Gregg B. Jackson, "The Research Evidence on the Effects of Grade Retention," *Review of Educational Research*, 45 (Fall 1975), 613–635.
[2]S. L. Pressey, *Educational Acceleration: Appraisals and Basic Problems*, Bureau of Educational Research Monograph 31 (Columbus, Ohio: Ohio State University, 1949).

more than ever before. To hold them back on the basis of fears that seem quite unsubstantiated by the available evidence is unjust to them and to society.

HOMOGENEOUS GROUPING

Various methods of grouping pupils according to ability are widely practiced, particularly in the elementary grades. Grouping may be done informally and more or less subjectively, as when a teacher of second grade forms thirty pupils into reading groups of ten to fifteen on the basis of reading ability. Or it may be done formally, as when a hundred pupils in the fifth grade are divided into three classes according to general mental ability.

Ability classification or homogeneous grouping is common in one form or another in the elementary schools where pupils read, recite, and do other academic work in groups whose members are usually judged by the teacher to be somewhat alike in ability. However, in the elementary school pupils are not sectioned and separated as high-school pupils usually are, and therefore the objection that grouping at the elementary level is undemocratic does not apply, or at least seems less important. There is ample opportunity in the elementary classroom for social intercourse among all pupils in a class, even if they are grouped for instruction according to ability in reading, arithmetic, and other academic work.

The assignment of pupils to groups has been based generally on measures of ability and achievement, but recently some different approaches have been tried. Herbert Thelen has suggested that pupils and teachers should be matched on preferred styles of teaching and learning. Other writers have suggested that pupils be grouped or taught individually in terms of their cognitive learning styles. These newer approaches may prove to be effective and, if so, will add new dimensions to the measurement needs of a school.[3]

Grouping is somewhat controversial. Its opponents have charged that pupils placed in fast groups are likely to become "conceited" while those in the slow group are stigmatized as "dumb-bells." They have also held that there is no such thing as a homogeneous group and that when pupils are grouped on the basis of one criterion, such as IQ, they are still heterogeneous with respect to other, perhaps equally important, criteria,

---

[3]Herbert A. Thelen, "Matching Teachers and Pupils," *Today's Education,* 56 (April 1967), 18–20. See also D. C. Berliner and L. S. Cahen, "Trait-Treatment Interaction and Learning," *Review of Research in Education,* 1 (1973), 58–94; and Rita Dunn, Kenneth Dunn, and Gary E. Price, "Diagnosing Learning Styles: A Prescription for Avoiding Malpractice Suits," *Phi Delta Kappan,* 58, No. 5 (January 1977), 418–420.

such as achievement. Furthermore, it is said that individual pupils vary widely in different skills or abilities. The profile charts in Figures 14.1 and 14.2 throw some light on this point. It is apparent that, while a given pupil does not perform at exactly the same level on each subtest of the achievement battery, there is much consistency of performance in many cases.

Recent years have seen a greatly increased emphasis on quality in education and greatly increased interest in providing stimulating and challenging opportunities for superior pupils. It is felt that we have permitted the most able pupils to go along at half speed with a resultant loss of interest and accomplishment. Advocates of homogeneous grouping believe that providing a more rewarding and challenging education for gifted·pupils can be done more easily and successfully if such pupils are grouped or sectioned so that they can have an enriched program and can also proceed at an accelerated pace. It is also maintained that homogeneous sections for slow learners are advantageous for them in that the instruction can proceed at a pace more suited to their abilities. Furthermore, it is felt that the slower learners in a class of similar capacity and interests avoid the discouragement and failure that are often their lot when they are instructed in classes with pupils who are much more able academically.

A great deal of research has been done on the question of homogeneous grouping. One of the earliest reports dealt largely with the question of reactions to the practice.[4] The conclusion on this point was that where such grouping was practiced, the majority of parents, pupils, and teachers were happy and satisfied with it. Similar reports seem to indicate that the slow learners, who are quite often the main concern of opponents of the practice, prefer homogeneous to heterogeneous classes. A study in point was conducted by Elizabeth Drews. This was a carefully designed, controlled experiment involving 432 ninth-grade pupils enrolled in English classes in four junior high schools.[5] The pupils were sectioned into superior, average, and slow groups on the basis of achievement in reading and language, IQ, school marks, and teacher judgment. The performance of homogeneous classes was compared with that of equivalent heterogeneous classes. Each of the heterogeneous classes included the full range of abilities represented in the three levels of homogeneous groups.

[4]*The Grouping of Pupils*, Thirty-Fifth Yearbook of the National Society for the Study of Education, Part I (Chicago: University of Chicago Press, 1936), pp. 302–303.
[5]Elizabeth M. Drews, "The Effectiveness of Homogeneous and Heterogeneous Ability Grouping in 9th Grade English Classes with Slow, Average, and Superior Students Including the Investigation of Attitudes, Self-Concept, and Critical Thinking" (manuscript, College of Education, Michigan State University, East Lansing, Michigan, 1961).

On a questionnaire of attitudes toward homogeneous and heterogeneous classes, 83 percent of the slow students in homogeneous classes gave positive reactions toward homogeneous classes, as against 60 percent positive reactions toward heterogeneous classes by slow students in such classes. On the same questionnaire, superior students in homogeneous classes gave 73 percent positive reactions toward such classes, as against 33 percent positive reactions of superior students in heterogeneous classes toward such classes.

Summaries of research studies of homogeneous grouping indicate that taken altogether the results are inconclusive. The findings in about half the studies are favorable to the practice, and in an equal number they are unfavorable.[6] In any case, wherever homogeneous grouping is used, several factors have a most important bearing on the success of the practice. First, it must be recognized that what teachers do in adapting content and method to different ability groups largely determines how effective the grouping will be in terms of increased learning and attaining of goals. To form different groups according to ability without making modifications in the methods and materials used with those groups is not likely to result in any advantage.

Second, any scheme of grouping should provide for shifting and adjusting the assignments of individual pupils. No pupil should feel that assignment to a particular group is final and permanent. The able pupil must demonstrate the right to stay in a faster group, while the slow pupil should always be made to feel that reassignment is possible if better work is done. Such flexibility, though perhaps difficult administratively, would go far toward meeting one of the most frequently voiced objections to ability grouping—namely, that it is not democratic. Moreover, it would provide excellent motivation for pupils at all levels and in every group.

Third, the profiles we presented clearly show that a pupil's achievement in different academic areas is often uneven. Consequently, it may be appropriate to place a pupil in a fast section in one subject, in an average section in another, and perhaps even in a slow section in a third subject. For example, the pupil whose profile is shown in Figure 14.1 is above the grade norm in many areas covered by the test but average in a number of areas and below average in social science. If ability grouping were practiced, the pupil would presumably be in fast, average, and slow sections in these respective areas. To be effective, any system of grouping should

---

[6]See Ruth B. Ekstrom, *Experimental Studies of Homogeneous Grouping: A Review of the Literature* (Princeton, N.J.: Educational Testing Service, 1961); Miriam L. Goldberg, A. Harry Passow, and Joseph Justman, *The Effects of Ability Grouping* (New York: Teachers College, Columbia University Press, 1966); Warren G. Findley and Marion Bryan, *Ability Grouping: 1970*, Center for Educational Improvement, University of Georgia, Athens (monograph).

take such differences into account. It seems reasonable to assume that flexibility would help eliminate or at least reduce any tendency to stigmatize pupils, since the same pupil would probably be in different groups for different subjects or activities.

In the past, the desire to individualize instruction as much as possible and the constraint imposed by pupil-teacher ratios have more or less required the use of homogeneous groups within classes that are heterogeneous. Recent legislation and court decisions assume that, regardless of ability or the nature of handicapping conditions, all children should be educated in the least restrictive environment commensurate with capabilities. The trend frequently referred to as *mainstreaming* places exceptional children in regular classrooms for at least part of their instruction. The resulting increase in the range of individual differences within most classrooms will undoubtedly require the continued and perhaps even expanded use of some form of homogeneous grouping. The usefulness of a sound measurement program will be emphasized by the new requirements imposed on classroom teachers.

LEARNING EXERCISES

1. What role should a teacher have in the decision concerning the promotion or retention of a pupil at the close of a school year? What information can a teacher provide that will supplement test data?
2. Summarize the arguments and the evidence for and against homogeneous and nonhomogeneous (or heterogeneous) grouping.
3. If three ability sections in ninth-grade general science were to be established for one hundred pupils who elected the course, what information should be considered in establishing the groups?

DIAGNOSIS AND REMEDIAL WORK

In contrast to the two areas of usefulness just discussed, the employment of tests for diagnosis is an instructional function rather than an administrative one. The purpose of a diagnostic test is to find the specific weaknesses and strengths of a pupil in a particular area of study or subject matter. In one survey of measurement practices and preferences of high-school teachers, it was found that diagnostic testing and remedial work are the most frequently mentioned uses of standardized test results.[7] Between 40 and 50 percent of the teachers using standardized tests reported these as their purposes in giving such tests. Similar findings were reported in the 1970 and 1976 surveys of testing practices in Michigan schools that we described in Chapter 13.

The process of diagnosis in education may be thought of as a progression from broad and general areas to narrower and more specific knowledges or skills. For example, one might begin by giving to a class of seventh-grade pupils a survey battery, including tests of language arts, social studies, mathematics, and science. After these tests are scored and the results analyzed, it might appear that the class as a whole is up to or above acceptable standards in all areas tested except language arts. Further testing in the language arts might show that vocabulary, reading, and spelling are acceptable but that there are serious weaknesses in fundamentals of grammar, sentence structure, punctuation, and capitalization. Knowing these weaknesses, one can then proceed to give diagnostic tests to determine which fundamentals have been inadequately mastered and require further study and drill. The real diagnosis is done only at this last level of measurement, although all that precedes it is basic to the last step. However, a teacher may begin at this point without going through the earlier steps. That is, a diagnostic test may be administered at any time to discover strengths and weaknesses in pupil learning so that additional attention may be given to points not mastered in previous teaching and study.

A truly diagnostic test should be planned and constructed with this function in mind. Many achievement tests may be used for diagnosis, but much time and energy are saved and a more systematic analysis is possible when a test is designed and built for diagnosis, if that is to be its function. Several important steps should be followed in the diagnostic testing procedure.

1. *There should be a careful analysis of the rules, principles, knowledges, or skills the test is intended to measure.* In the example cited above, this would mean analysis of the rules or principles of good usage with respect to grammar, sentence structure, punctuation, and capitalization in English. The Pressey *Diagnostic Tests in English Composition* are good examples of tests based on this kind of analysis.[8] Although the test was published originally in 1924, it is still published and used, and it remains one of the best diagnostic tests

---

[7]Victor H. Noll and Walter N. Durost, *Measurement Practices and Preferences of High School Teachers,* Test Service Notebook 8 (New York: Harcourt Brace Jovanovich, n.d.).
[8]S. L. Pressey, et al., *Diagnostic Tests in English Composition* (Indianapolis: Bobbs-Merrill, 1924).

available. The test in each of the four areas covers such rules as "Every declarative sentence should be followed by a period." The capitalization test covers such rules as "Begin every proper name with a capital letter," and similarly appropriate rules are covered in the tests of grammar and sentence structure.

2. *A good diagnostic test is planned and constructed so that every rule or principle is adequately and equally tested by objective items.* For example, in the Pressey test on capitalization each of seven basic rules is covered by four objective test items. By this method, no point of importance is slighted or overemphasized, and the user of the test can be sure of reasonably adequate and systematic coverage.

3. *The test items are generally arranged in groups to facilitate analysis and diagnosis.* That is, if there are four items on each rule, those dealing with the same rule will be placed together rather than scattered throughout the entire test. This makes it simpler, in analyzing the results, to determine specific areas of strength and weakness.

In addition to these matters, diagnostic tests are usually accompanied by a chart similar to the one reproduced in Figure 14.3. This permits the diagnosis of strengths and weaknesses of the class or group as a whole, as well as of individuals.

The diagnostic chart for the seventh-grade class reveals the standing of individuals and of the class. Reading across the page, it is possible to determine individual needs in capitalization. Jane Allen, for example, misses only five items out of twenty-eight, and these deal with rules 4, 5, 6, and 1, respectively. On the other hand, Mary Brady appears to be very weak on capitalization, for she has answered correctly only eight out of twenty-eight and has missed most of the items relating to every rule except rule 2.

Reading the chart vertically, by groups of items relating to each rule, we see that the class as a whole is strong on rules 2, 7, and 1 and is comparatively weak on rules 3, 4, 5, and 6—especially the latter two. This gives the teacher information useful in planning remedial work and drill for the whole class.

At the side of the chart the individual scores are tabulated and the median is determined. By comparison with seventh-grade norms it is evident that this class is quite deficient in knowledge and understanding of the rules of capitalization and will need thorough review and practice on fundamentals. Sometime later, another form of the test may be given to measure improvement. Since there are four forms of the test, the teacher may test and teach several times without giving the same test twice.

Equivalent forms are very advantageous for diagnostic tests, perhaps even more than for standardized tests in general. The most widely accepted method for using diagnostic tests calls for testing, remedial

Figure 14.3   Analysis Chart Showing the Results of a Seventh-Grade Class on the Pressey Diagnostic Test in Capitalization

Grade 7th   School Roosevelt   City Smithport   State Pa.   Date 11/15/55   Examiner Miss James.
Form of Test 1 (1, 2, 3 or 4)

Capitalization Test

Pupil's Name	Total
1. Allen, Jane	23
2. Belford, Jim	14
3. Brady, Mary	8
4. Clark, Mary Jane	15
5. Cole, Harvey	12
6. Drake, Alice	13
7. Ferguson, Charles	10
8. Probst, Marjorie	17
9. Grady, Bob	9
10. Linden, Elmer	10
11. Holt, John	12
12. James, Albert	12
13. Lane, Kenneth	10
14. Lang, Susan	13
15. Miller, Paul	21
16. Nelson, Jim	11
17. Reed, Henry	9
18. Ross, Bill	11
19. Scott, Bill	11
20. Watson, Carol	13
21. White, Frank	15

Total right—each sentence: 17 15 16 13 6 10 7 6 9 6 9 8 7 8 5 10 9 11 10 4 7 8 5 14 14 13 18

Rule illustrated (Forms 1 and 3): Rule 2, Rule 6, Rule 3, Rule 4, Rule 5, Rule 3, Rule 6, Rule 7, Rule 1
Rule illustrated (Forms 2 and 4): Rule 6, Rule 1, Rule 5, Rule 7

• Compare with rules in column to left.   • Notice what rules are most frequently violated.   • Teach each child what he does not know.

Norms (November testing)

Grade	Medians Forms 1 & 2	Forms 3 & 4
7	18.8	18.0
8	20.6	19.7
9	21.5	20.4
10	22.8	21.3
11	23.3	22.1
12	23.8	22.5
College	24.0	23.0

Class Record

Score	No. of Pupils
28	
27	
26	
25	
24	1
23	1
22	
21	1
20	
19	
18	
17	1
16	
15	1 1
14	1
13	1 1 1
12	1 1 1
11	1 1 1
10	1 1 1
9	1 1
8	1
7	
6	
5	
4	
3	
2	
1	
0	
Total	21
Median	12

CAPITALIZATION TEST
RULES COVERED BY TEST

1. Capitalize the first word of every sentence. Capitalize also the first word of every line of poetry, and the first word of a direct quotation. However, if the quotation is indirect do not use the capital.

2. Capitalize the names of persons, with their titles; however, do not capitalize titles when they are not part of a name.

3. Capitalize the names of countries, states, cities, streets, buildings, of mountains, rivers, oceans, or any word designating a particular location or part of the world; however, do not capitalize the points of the compass, or such terms as street, river, ocean, when not part of a name.

4. Capitalize the names of business firms, schools, societies, or other organizations; however, do not capitalize such words as company, school, society, when not part of a name.

5. Capitalize words derived from the names of countries, places, or organizations or persons.

6. Capitalize the days of the week, the months of the year, and holidays; however, do not capitalize the seasons.

7. Capitalize the first word, and all other important words, in titles (and sub-titles and headings) of themes, magazine articles, poems, books, of laws or governmental documents, and the trade names of commercial products.

Reproduced by permission of the publishers, The Bobbs-Merrill Company, Inc.

instruction, retesting, further remedial instruction, and so on, until adequate mastery is attained. For this process it is highly desirable to have available several equivalent forms of each test so that the second and subsequent testings may be done with different forms covering the same objectives. This avoids the repeated use of exactly the same questions and thus greatly reduces or practically eliminates gain in scores due to familiarity with the questions.

Chapter 8 describes other examples of diagnostic tests and discusses two criterion-referenced tests, the *Prescriptive Reading Inventory* and the *Prescriptive Mathematics Inventory*, in terms of how the results can be used in a diagnostic way.

Although the discussion so far has stressed the value and usefulness of diagnostic tests as such, it is quite possible for a teacher to make diagnoses by studying results of norm-referenced standardized achievement tests. Responses to individual items on a subtest of a battery can be tabulated to determine strengths and weaknesses of individuals and of classes or groups. Although this procedure is not likely to yield as systematic and thorough coverage as a planned diagnostic instrument, it nevertheless can provide the teacher much useful information on which to base remedial instruction. There can be no doubt that the diagnosis frequently mentioned by teachers as the most important use of results of standardized testing is often of this nature. Producers of standardized tests of achievement, particularly in basic tool subjects, would be well advised to facilitate and encourage such use of their tests by organizing them, insofar as practical, with that use in mind. It is also helpful to include tables of specifications and classification of items in manuals accompanying standardized achievement tests. Many publishers now provide this information.

Finally, it should be recognized that diagnostic testing does not necessarily reveal the causes of weaknesses. A diagnostic test in arithmetic may reveal certain specific deficiencies—let us say in the multiplication of two-place numbers by two-place numbers, such as 87×34. These weaknesses may be the result of a lack of correct knowledge of multiplication tables or of carrying or of adding or of some other process. But knowing that a pupil does not perform one or the other of these operations correctly is no guarantee that remedial work and drill on the specific processes will produce the desired improvement. Deficiencies in learning may have various causes coming from hearing or vision, home conditions, relations with classmates or the teacher, ability, and the like. In all diagnostic and remedial work, it is essential to attempt to identify the basic causes of deficiencies and to work on these. Otherwise, remediation is likely to be a waste of time and energy.

LEARNING EXERCISES

4. How does a diagnostic test differ from a conventional achievement test? Answer by comparing a standardized achievement test, perhaps in fundamentals of English, with one like Pressey's.
5. If you were selecting a test for diagnostic purposes in the fundamentals of multiplication in arithmetic, what would you look for?
6. Why are there more diagnostic tests available in elementary-school subjects than for high school or college?

COUNSELING AND GUIDANCE

Broadly stated, the function of the counselor or guidance worker is to help pupils achieve satisfactory and satisfying solutions to their problems. John Darley, as a result of a 1943 survey of high-school seniors in a large city, classified these problems, in a descending order of frequency, as follows: (1) vocational, (2) educational, (3) social or personal, (4) financial, (5) family adjustment, and (6) health.[9] The emphasis might be different at lower grade levels or in different communities, and it may differ slightly today, but the categories seem to encompass the major areas of concern to adolescents as well as to people in general.

The most common problems under these respective categories were (1) discrepancy between vocational goal and abilities, (2) discrepancy between educational goals and abilities, (3) feelings of inferiority, (4) too much outside work and inadequate finances, (5) family conflicts over educational and vocational plans, desire for independence, personality and age differences, and (6) poor health. To the educational problem of discrepancy between educational goals and abilities should probably be added problems related to the choice of subjects (such problems, for example, as whether to take algebra or homemaking) and those related to the choice of a curriculum or course of study.

Among the tools used by counselors, tests are often regarded as having central importance. This is recognized in the National Defense Education Act of 1958, which provides financial support for testing in programs

---

[9]John G. Darley, *Testing and Counseling in the High School Guidance Program* (Chicago: Science Research Associates, 1943), pp. 140–141.

of guidance and counseling. The extensive use and the value of tests in counseling and guidance is also attested by the requirement of courses in tests and measurements in training programs for counselors and by the publication of books specifically about the use of tests in the counseling process.[10]

It is difficult to imagine how a guidance program could function without the use of measures of intelligence, achievement, aptitudes, interests, and personality. Where discrepancies between goals and abilities exist, intelligence-test results tactfully and confidentially discussed with the pupil may help bring about a readjustment of plans more in line with talents. Marks and test scores representing a student's achievement in school work may bring that student to decide realistically that perhaps a career as an electrical engineer, in view of the advanced mathematics and physics required, is not desirable after all. Together with the results of measures of general academic ability, such data, when discussed sympathetically with pupil and parents, have great value in bringing about an acceptance of educational and vocational goals that are more consistent with abilities. Such counseling procedures often avoid frustration and unhappiness.

On the other hand, tests of academic ability may reveal a discrepancy of the opposite nature. This occurs when a pupil is not working up to capacity as shown by high performance on intelligence tests and poor marks in school subjects. Although much has been written about underachievers, not much is known about effective methods of motivating them to close the gap between achievement and ability. However, standardized tests of intelligence serve to identify such individuals and provide the counselor with facts and insights otherwise not available. At least they serve to identify the problem, though they do not provide a solution.

When a pupil seeks guidance in educational or vocational matters, tests of aptitudes and interests provide useful tools. The nature of such instruments has been discussed in Chapters 10 and 11, and the applications of these instruments in guidance and counseling are obvious, particularly with reference to educational and vocational decisions.

An aptitude test is a useful tool in counseling if the results are properly understood and used. A high score on a test of mechanical aptitude does not guarantee success in an occupation requiring mechanical ability, any more than a good score on a test of musical aptitude guarantees that the person who made the score will become a great musician. Many other

---

[10]See Leo Goldman, *Using Tests in Counseling*, 2d ed. (New York: Appleton-Century-Crofts, 1971); Ralph F. Berdie, et al., *Testing in Guidance and Counseling* (New York: McGraw-Hill, 1963).

factors besides aptitude enter into success: interest, effort, persistence, and opportunity, for example. Yet the counselor can encourage the person making a high score on an aptitude test to develop a talent and can help determine whether or not that person has other qualities needed for success in the field in question.

The counselor can also speak with more assurance in the case of a low score on a test. It is safe and pertinent in such instances to point out to the individual that statistics show that perhaps only one person in ten with an equivalent score is successful in some particular vocation.

In this connection the *expectancy table* is useful for estimating probabilities of success and for interpreting test scores to the student. An example is shown as Table 14.1. In this table, scores on *The General Clerical Test* are plotted against performance ratings. All making test scores of 200 or better are predicted to obtain ratings of average or better. Of those making scores of less than 100, only 55 percent are expected to be rated average or better. The percentages are also shown in the graph to the right.

With information of this nature, the counselor can say to a student whose test score falls in the 50–99 range, for example, that the probability of attaining average or better ratings is on the order of 1 in 2. The accuracy of such predictions depends, of course, on a number of factors including the size and representativeness of the sample and the reliability of the test and of the criterion (in this case, ratings). Furthermore, the counselor would want to consider other factors besides test scores, such as personal characteristics, plans, and attitudes. The limitations of expectancy tables are not to be overlooked, but they are useful to the counselor in helping students arrive at sound educational and vocational decisions.

The interest inventory provides a useful supplement to other kinds of tests. It should be emphasized perhaps even more strongly than in the case of aptitude tests that a particular pattern of interests or preferences is not in any sense a guarantee of success in a given field. All one can say is that the interest score or pattern of the individual tested resembles or does not resemble that of successful persons in a particular occupation or field of work.

Interest tests are widely used, especially in high school and junior college. The results of such tests, when carefully studied and discussed with the counselor, are considerably useful, particularly in giving students more insight into their own potentialities and causing them to think carefully about decisions and choices. Used in conjunction with the results of other tests and information about home background, financial status, scholastic record, and health, they help to round out the picture of the individual.

Expectancy Table and Graph Showing Percent Expected to Rate Average or Better in Office Clerical Tasks on the Basis of Scores on *The General Clerical Test* ($N = 65$, mean score = 136.1, $S = 39.1$, $r_{bis} = .31$)

Table 14.1

General Clerical Test scores	No. in score group	No. rated average or better	% rated average or better		
200–up	5	5	100		
150–199	18	15	83		
100–149	31	23	74		
50–99	11	6	55		
Total	65			0% 20% 40% 60% 80% 100%	

SOURCE: *Expectancy Tables—A Way of Interpreting Test Validity.* New York: The Psychological Corporation. Test Service Bulletin, No. 38 (December 1949).

Student problems also frequently occur in adjustment and personality. The survey reported by John Darley[11] revealed that feelings of inferiority, lack of confidence, and personality clashes in the home were among the most common problems of high-school seniors. The use of personality measures sometimes reveals the existence of such problems when interviews and other means have failed to bring them to light.

Personality measures of various types may be used with groups to identify more or less serious cases of maladjustment. In every hundred pupils there will be on the average from two to five who need help and who should be referred to a clinic or to someone trained in such cases. Tests can also be used by counselors to shed additional light on the cases of pupils who come for advice and help with personal, educational, or vocational problems. For the pupil who is having difficulties in school or at home, a personality test often gives helpful insight. The test may be supplemented by interviews, anecdotal records, ratings, and other information, all of which usually provide a basis for understanding and help.

Personality tests may be used to help a pupil make the most of talents by providing insight into problems of adjustment and getting along with other people. Knowing the nature of problems, a counselor may be able to help a student develop better emotional and social behavior. In short, such tests help an individual gain better self-understanding and learn reasons for behavior in certain situations.

Concerning financial problems and poor health, the counselor will obtain information about problems of this nature through means other than tests. These difficulties, particularly the health problems, usually require expert advice and treatment, and the responsibility of the counselor is

[11]Darley, *Testing and Counseling* (footnote 9).

mainly to identify such cases and refer them to people trained to help with them. There may be things a counselor can do to help a pupil earn money in after-school hours or to help those who are working too many hours outside, but these are not matters in which tests generally play a significant role. Yet a knowledge of a student's IQ may be useful in helping the counselor and the student decide how much work can be taken on to earn money without doing injustice to school work.

In recent years career education has been expanded in the curricula of many schools, and although this area is not the sole responsibility of counselors, there is a definite relationship between career education and the topics discussed in this section. The grade placement and sequence of curricular topics varies among schools, but a general model includes an awareness phase in the elementary grades, a more intensive study of career opportunities in the middle grades, and frequently observation or actual experiences during high school. The primary goal of career education is to help pupils make informed decisions about careers from careful study of the nature and requirements of various fields and from realistic self-assessment of talents, interests, capabilities, and personality characteristics. Career guidance test programs are described in Chapter 11. The use of tests and other assessment procedures, as described here and in Chapter 11, greatly enhances the effectiveness of a career education program by helping pupils learn more about themselves. And since most career education programs rely heavily on contributions from all teachers, the need is emphasized for teachers to be knowledgeable about various types of tests.

LEARNING EXERCISES

7. Make a list of the major types of problems of adolescents that a counselor is likely to encounter today in a city high school. Compare your list with that based on Darley's survey.
8. As a high-school counselor, what types of measuring instruments would you expect to find most useful? Give reasons for your choices.
9. Is there a place for counseling and guidance in the elementary grades? If so, what measuring instruments should prove useful?
10. What uses would a counselor have for achievement test results?

MARKING

It was stated early in this book that measurement and evaluation are a part of the job of teaching. Every teacher has the responsibility for making the best judgments possible about pupils' achievement and development in subject matter, maturity, citizenship, character, and other areas. These judgments may be expressed in various ways, but marks are the most common. As our schools and educational programs are constituted, marks are an integral part of the system. Pupils, parents, and administrators expect them. They are the terms in which appraisals of a pupil's accomplishments are communicated. It is therefore only sensible for the teacher to try to do the best possible job of evaluating and marking, to strive constantly to improve the marking system, and to keep abreast of improvements in marking practices.

That measurement has an important function in marking is self-evident. Teachers regularly use tests and examinations of their own devising as a basis for marking, especially when measuring achievement in subject matter. However, tests of capacity such as intelligence tests are also useful in marking, in that they provide a basis for judging whether a pupil is working up to capacity. It has been suggested that two marks be given, one expressing actual achievement (in terms such as A, B, C, D, or F) and the other expressing whether the pupil is doing satisfactory or unsatisfactory work in relation to ability (in terms of, say, S or U). Thus, one pupil of high academic aptitude might get a B and a U in algebra, while another pupil might receive a C and an S. In many schools some type of dual system is used to indicate quality of achievement and the extent to which potential is being realized.

A perennial question in arriving at marks has to do with the propriety of using standardized tests for this purpose. It may be said at once that the use of such tests as the sole basis for marks is seldom justified, since no standardized test is likely to provide adequate measures of all the outcomes of a course in a particular school or community. Few·teachers would be satisfied to base the evaluation of their pupils' accomplishments solely or even substantially on standardized test scores. Nevertheless, it is true that such tests may be useful in helping arrive at a semester's or a year's mark in a given course. That is, when a standardized test is judged by the teacher to be an adequate measure of one or more of the locally determined goals of instruction, there would seem to be no valid reason for not using it, together with other measures, for marking purposes. A standardized test can supplement or contribute to evaluation based on the teacher's own measurement procedures. A goal of every teacher should be the best possible evaluation of each pupil's accomplishments. It is only good sense to make use of every practical device that helps achieve this objective. It may even be that a carefully constructed standardized test will at times provide a better measure of certain outcomes of instruction than any the average teacher can make—as, for example, in the case of skills tests in elementary grades.

The school assumes some responsibility for the all-around development of each pupil to the extent of capacity and desire to achieve. This includes not only achievement in subject matter but also development of character and personality, physical development and health, maturity in selecting and planning for a future vocation, choosing a life partner, and so on. In any of these areas, the teacher may be called upon to express some judgment or evaluation of the pupil's status and development. Every measurement has something to contribute. Personality measures, interest inventories, measures of physical development, and records of health and physical examinations are all useful in making evaluations, whether they are expressed as a mark or in some other manner. Measurement can and should enter in some degree into every aspect of evaluating pupil accomplishment and growth.

How to define the categories of a marking system has been and remains a question about which widely differing and intense opinions continue to be expressed. Some argue that an A or comparable mark should be reserved to indicate only exceptional achievement reached usually by a small proportion of learners. At the other extreme are arguments that marks should be abolished entirely. There seems to be little doubt that the former view has been modified by many teachers. Numerous reports have documented what is called "grade inflation," a large increase in the average grade assigned in schools and colleges. Whereas a C is usually defined as average, the actual average in many schools has approached or in some cases even exceeded a B. The effect of inflated grades has been a concern to employers, college admissions officers, and parents who feel that their children have been passed through the grades without being required to attain the basic education required for effective adult citizenship.

Many factors have influenced the modification of traditional marking practices. The introduction of pass-fail options, contract grading, and mastery-learning instructional systems has had an effect on grade averages and entire marking systems. With the pass-fail option, pupils have been able to elect courses outside their area of expertise without earning low marks. Contract grading allows pupils to develop an individual plan with an instructor, identifying in advance the grade sought and the requirements to earn that grade. Mastery-learning approaches are based on the expectation that a test over a topic will be completed with no or only a few errors, and remediation followed by retesting is usually part of the system. In the contract and mastery approaches, a pupil's achievement is assessed against some predetermined standard of excellence, and no comparisons with other pupils are made.

While there may be good educational reasons for these modified systems, the fact remains that they have added to the problem of defining marks in such way that a given symbol will have the same or similar meaning within a school system and from community to community. One step that would help to reduce the problem would be the development of school-wide policies that teachers in a given system would be expected to follow. The process of developing the policies would be educational for a professional staff and would reduce the ambiguity of marks, at least within a given community.

Most schools still use an A, B, C system, and a vexing question is what proportion of the various marks to give. The conscientious instructor tries to do justice to all pupils and at the same time attempts to conform with good principles of marking. There is no simple method to satisfy both purposes. Recommendations on this point may be based on the concept of the normal curve. In any group or class, unless it is very small, numbering fewer than twenty, abilities and achievement are likely to be distributed in a fashion approximating the normal distribution. If this assumption is appropriate, then the distribution of marks should approximate the proportions of the normal curve, which means that the largest proportion should be average, which is usually C. Smaller proportions will be somewhat above and below the average, and these would be marked B and D, respectively. Approximately equal and quite small percentages would be found at the upper and lower extremes, and these would receive marks of A or F, as the case might be.

These principles can be embodied in a number of different systems or proportions, one of the most widely used being based on the standard deviation, illustrated in Figure 14.4. It can be seen that the middle group, or C, extends for one-half a standard deviation on either side of the mean, which area under the normal curve includes approximately 38 percent of

Distribution of Marks Based on Standard Deviation

Figure 14.4

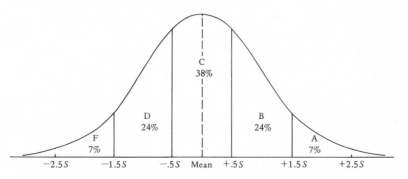

the total. One additional standard deviation beyond these limits on either side will include another 24 percent in each case; and another standard deviation beyond $+1.5S$ and $-1.5S$, extending to $+2.5S$ and $-2.5S$, will include approximately 7 percent more. The total is: $38 + 24 + 24 + 7 + 7 = 100$.[12]

Although the results of measurements of most classes will not be distributed in exactly these theoretical proportions, they will quite generally approximate them if (1) the classes are not highly selected, and (2) the measures used are adequate for all levels of ability represented in the group. No teacher will want to force a distribution of marks into these theoretical proportions, particularly if there is reason to believe that the nature of the group or the measuring instruments used do not justify it. Nevertheless, the concept of a normal distribution can be used as a guide and can help a teacher avoid giving marks that are clearly out of line with sound principles.

What has been said so far and the known facts about the distribution of human abilities and achievements provide a basis for some useful generalizations about marking and measurement in marking. A brief statement of these principles is given below. In reading and thinking about them, the student is cautioned to remember that no hard and fast rules can be laid down for every teacher to follow in giving marks. Each teacher will have to use personal judgment in each situation, since marking, generally speaking, is a responsibility that cannot be shared with anyone else. The unequivocal principle, if there is one, is that justice must be done to every pupil insofar as possible and that none be favored above any other.

1. *It is generally agreed that marks should be assigned on a comparative basis.* That is, the best pupils should receive the highest marks, the next best should receive B's, and so on. In most school situations, this practice is certainly preferable to setting some arbitrary and perhaps unrealistic standard and failing pupils who do not attain it. It should be pointed out that in classrooms where a mastery-learning model and criterion-referenced tests are used, a comparative grading system is probably not appropriate. In fact, some writers have suggested that grades and report cards be replaced by check lists of the skills and concepts that comprise a topic and that reports indicate which have been mastered by the pupil.[13] This approach is limited to subjects in which the objectives

---

[12]Theoretically, the curve touches the baseline only at infinity, so that within 2.5 standard deviations above and below the mean there will be only 98.76 percent of the total area under the curve. For all practical purposes, we may assume that 100 percent of the cases or scores will fall between these limits.

[13]For example, see Jason Millman, "Reporting Student Progress: A Case for a Criterion-Referenced Marking System," *Phi Delta Kappan*, 52 (1970), 226–230.

of instruction or the skills to be developed can be clearly and completely listed. Even so, the approach may gain in popularity and use as more complete lists of instructional objectives are developed for a wide variety of courses.

Various marking systems have been proposed for assigning letter grades that are criterion-referenced. None seems to have emerged as a recognized "best" approach. If tests are designed so that few, if any, errors are made, however, a definition of marks could be based on a percentage correct on the composite measure of performance. For example, this system could be used:

Grade	Percentage correct	Pupil's status
A	95 –100%	Mastery of major points and most minor ones
B	85 – 94%	Mastery of most major and minor points
C	75 – 84%	Mastery of most major and some minor points
D	65 – 74%	Remedial work recommended
F	Below 65%	Remedial activities and retesting required

We noted earlier that a criterion-referenced approach is most useful in subjects that can be analyzed into relatively small and homogeneous skills or processes. Thus, some other system such as comparative marking will undoubtedly be required in most subjects and at most grade levels.

2. *Practice now generally favors the use of a marking system employing a small number of categories such as letters, integers, or stanines.* Letter marks have several advantages: they are easy to use and easy to interpret. It is easier to mark a group with a five-point scale than with a scale having a hundred divisions. Letter marks are easier to understand for the same reason. It may be said with confidence that not many people can make the fine distinctions of judgment that percentage marks imply. It has been demonstrated that teachers can discriminate among five or six levels of quality or achievement but not one hundred.

3. *Marks should be based as much as possible on objective measurements.* Enough has been said in earlier discussions to show the unreliability of teachers' judgments of essay examinations. It may be assumed that what was demonstrated in those experiments applies with equal force to other subjective judgments or processes. It may not be possible to find or construct objective measures of all desirable outcomes, but the aim should be to move constantly in this direction and to increase the objectivity of our measurements as much as possible.

4. *As far as possible, marks should express accomplishments of specific goals rather than the results of global or omnibus appraisal.* A marking system that does not provide for precise differentiation—as, for example, between knowledge and skills—is less informative than one

that does. Also, one should not attempt to combine in one mark achievement in subject matter and such other traits as courtesy, punctuality, and effort. The measurement of these traits is important, but if the pupil is given a B in arithmetic the *mark should denote accomplishment in that subject.* If desired, grades may be given for courtesy, effort, and other important matters, but these should be expressed in *separate marks.* Otherwise, two pupils may receive B's in arithmetic, one of the marks representing achievement of A and effort of C, the other representing achievement of C and effort of A. To give them the same mark of B is an injustice to both pupils as well as to their next teacher, their parents, and any others who have no way of knowing what the marks really represent.

This principle applies also to the appraisal of growth or improvement. Such outcomes should not be combined in one mark with status or level of accomplishment. To illustrate, let us assume that marks are being given to two students learning how to type. X starts at 10 words per minute and progresses by the end of the year to 40 words per minute. Y starts at 30 words per minute and goes to 50 words per minute. X made a gain of 30 words while Y gained only 20. Yet Y is a more efficient typist than X. Would it be fair to give X a better mark than Y, because X had made a numerically greater gain? It would not seem so. Certainly, anyone seeking to employ a typist would be misled if both students received even the same mark. Here, as in cases already cited, it would be most accurate and fair to use two marks, one for status and another for improvement. Then the picture might be as follows:

Pupil	Status	Improvement
X	C	B
Y	B	C

In substance, we are saying that marks should mean and stand for what they are intended to mean and stand for. If a mark is given in English it should represent accomplishment in English and, if possible, should be differentiated to designate accomplishment in composition, American literature, English literature, or some other specific course or part of a course. If evaluations of other important qualities such as effort, citizenship, personal traits, and the like are desired, these should be reported separately with adequate labels so that they will not be confused or misunderstood. The use of objective measurements should contribute to the attainment of this principle in practice.

5. *Better marking can be attained by using a wide variety of measures.* The more measures of a pupil's achievement that are employed and the

more varied in approach and design they are, the better the sampling of accomplishment is likely to be. Even if the tests are quite similar in nature, the combined results of several of them should give a more accurate appraisal than any one of them alone. This is simply an application of the principle of sampling: the more samples taken the more accurate the measurement will be, always providing, of course, that there is no constant bias operating. Furthermore, by using a variety of measuring instruments we are likely to obtain a wider sampling than we otherwise would. In measuring the results of instruction in civics, for example, a teacher may find it desirable to use not only tests, but also rating scales, anecdotal records, and systematic observations of behavior—all contributing to the appraisal of achievement in civics.

The principles stated above should not be interpreted to suggest that the assignment of marks is a purely mechanical process. Even with the use of the most objective measurements, judgment by the teacher in translating them into marks is inescapable. This is particularly relevant with respect to decisions on failure or nonpromotion. Many factors besides test scores enter into such decisions, particularly in elementary grades, and it is right that they should. The most important consideration should be the best interests of the learner. At the same time, it should be remembered that soft-heartedness and emotionality are inimical to accurate measurement.

An example showing assignment of marks to a college class in tests and measurements will serve to illustrate the principles just enumerated. There were thirty-six students enrolled in the class, most of whom were juniors and seniors preparing to teach in elementary or secondary schools. The assignments and tests included a set of simple statistical problems; a blueprint or two-way chart showing content and objectives to be measured by an objective test; the test itself, constructed by the student; an objective midterm test of seventy-five items on the first half of the course; and an objective final examination of seventy-five items covering the second half. The assignments were marked by the instructor personally, either in points (in the case of the statistical problems) or in letter grades. The letter grades were converted to points on the basis of A = 50, B = 40, and so on. The midterm and final were scored on the basis of the number right. Thus, in the end, each student's marks or accomplishment were expressed in points. These points were added to obtain a total for each student.[14] The totals were then arranged in a frequency distribution and assigned marks as shown in Table 14.2.

[14]The writers have found by experience and empirical trial that considerations of variability in the separate point scores, where the number of possible points on each assignment or test is approximately the same, do not affect the comparative standing of students sufficiently to justify a system of differential weighting.

Table 14.2

Distribution of Total Points and Marks Earned by Thirty-Six Students in a Course in Educational Measurement

Totals	f*	Marks
200–204 ///	3	5 A's = 14 percent
195–199 //	2	
190–194 //	2	12 B's = 33 percent
185–189 ///	3	
180–184 //	2	
175–179 ////	5	
170–174 //	2	14 C's = 39 percent
165–169 ///	3	
160–164 /	1	
155–159 ////	5	
150–154 ///	3	
145–149	0	3 D's = 8 percent
140–144 /	1	
135–139 /	1	
130–134 /	1	
125–129	0	2 F's = 6 percent
120–124	0	
115–119 /	1	
110–114	0	
105–109	0	
100–104	0	
95–99	0	
90–94 /	1	
N = 36		

*Frequency

A number of aspects are at once apparent. First, the distribution is not normal in the sense of producing, if it were graphed, the bell-shaped curve. It is, in fact, bimodal because of the fact that some students did additional work on some assignments to obtain graduate credit.[15] Second, the assignments and tests did produce a spread or range. Some students did twice as well, in terms of total points earned, as others. Thus, there is a clear basis for differentiation. Third, it is óbvious that the proportions of the different marks assigned are not in accord with any theoretical distribution. There are more than twice as many A's as F's

[15]Many university classes enroll in the same section both upper-division undergraduates and graduate students. The latter must generally receive A's or B's to obtain credit. They are permitted by some instructors to do additional work for extra points or credits. The situation depicted in Table 14.2 was of this nature. The desirability of the practice is debatable.

and four times as many B's as D's. Here, the facts that the course is an upper-level elective for prospective teachers and that it enrolls graduate students as well as undergraduates have a bearing. This is clearly shown by the top-heavy nature of the distribution and is recognized in the proportions of the various marks given.

It should also be noted that the breaks between different marks are placed, insofar as possible, at points where there are gaps in the distribution. This is clearly the case between C and D and between D and F.

It must be admitted that no system of assigning marks is entirely objective. Even the teacher who adopts some arbitrary system such as 7 percent A's, 24 percent B's, 38 percent C's, and so on, is making a decision based on judgment or belief that that system is the right one. In the example above, the chief element of subjectivity comes at the choices of division points between marks. In this case, other factors as mentioned above also introduce elements of subjective judgment. Nevertheless, a review of the process illustrated will show that it adheres to and applies each of the principles of good marking we enumerated earlier. In larger classes, at lower levels with fewer selected and more heterogeneous students, and in required courses, it is possible by such a system of appraisal and marking to come much closer to theoretical proportions of marks based on the concept of a normal distribution. However, it must always be kept in mind that the fundamental purpose of marking is not to follow some theory but to communicate as accurate, unbiased, and true appraisal of a pupil's achievement as possible.

LEARNING EXERCISES

11. State your viewpoint on the place of marking in the schools. How would you differentiate between elementary, secondary, college? Why?

12. Name some situations in which the selection of persons (for example, airplane pilots) completing training on the basis of improvement alone, without reference to level of skill attained, would be dangerous. Name some in which the amount and nature of improvement would be more important than level of proficiency.

13. Consider the following forty-nine scores on a general science test: 71, 68, 67, 61, 60, 58, 58, 55, 54, 52, 50, 49, 47, 47, 46, 45, 44, 44, 44, 43, 43, 43, 42, 41, 41, 40, 40, 39, 38, 38, 38, 37, 36, 36, 36, 33, 33, 32, 28, 27, 25, 24, 22, 21, 18, 15, 13, 8, 3. Assign a mark to each score by

the method shown in this chapter. What proportions of A, B, C, D, and F does this yield? How closely does this conform to theoretical proportions? Explain the reasons for divergencies.

14. In what courses and at what grade levels might criterion-referenced marking be appropriate? Name some courses in which this type of marking would be less useful or even impossible.

CURRICULUM EVALUATION

Perhaps one of the most difficult areas in which to measure and evaluate is that of curriculum or program. Objectives and content are often broad and diverse (as, for example, in a year's course in biology or arithmetic); curriculum workers and evaluators often have difficulty in communicating with each other in a meaningful way; and valid methods of measuring and evaluating the outcomes of a course or program are not always easy to devise or readily available.

Probably no event or action has done more to bring about serious attempts at curriculum evaluation than the Elementary and Secondary School Acts of 1965 and subsequent years. These provide billions in federal funds for schools with high poverty populations, and they require school districts receiving such funds to evaluate the effectiveness of the programs or innovations supported by these funds. Although the quality of evaluative efforts thus instigated has sometimes left much to be desired, the effort is being made and the procedures and results seem to be improving.

In general, curriculum evaluators work in two major areas. First, they try to evaluate a course or program as it unfolds or proceeds. Thus, they may find by tests or other means that instruction in fractions is not producing the results desired and they therefore try to find better methods of instruction. Second, curriculum evaluation may focus on the end product to determine the effectiveness of the course of instruction as a whole. As an example, the evaluator may try to determine by various means how well the graduates of a course in psychology for nurses apply its principles in their relationships to patients. The two types of curriculum evaluation are known as *formative* and *summative evaluation*, respectively.

A pattern for summative curriculum evaluation has been evolving and is becoming standard practice, with local and generally minor variations. The first step is the identification and clear statement of objectives. All evaluation should begin with this. Objectives should be stated wherever possible in behavioral terms. They should indicate what changes in behavior are expected as a result of instruction. When objectives have been formulated, test items or other evaluative procedures are developed to measure them. This step is often the most difficult, since objectives may be quite broad and diverse and some may not lend themselves to testing by conventional methods. A variety of evaluative procedures including objective and other types of tests, ratings, interviews, observational and anecdotal records, and follow-up may be used as seems appropriate.

Closely related to this pattern of curriculum evaluation, and in a sense a part of it, is the formative assessment of pupil learning for the purpose of improving instruction. By formative assessment, a teacher collects information about pupil learning, primarily for deciding whether pupils need additional, perhaps different, learning opportunities. However, formative assessment data also reflect the effectiveness of instruction and may provide suggestions to the teacher for changes that could be made to improve instruction.

One of the most ambitious undertakings in evaluation of instructional programs is being carried on by the Center for the Study of Evaluation.[16] Objectives and related test items for sixteen subject areas (for example, mathematics, K–3; biology, 10–12) at elementary and secondary levels have been collected from school districts all over the country. In addition, the Center has participated in the development of additional collections of instructional objectives at the secondary level for nineteen subjects (including bookkeeping, woodworking, American history). To date, nearly 25,000 collections of objectives and test items have been distributed to educators in every state and beyond.

Statements of objectives are continuously refined by submission for reactions and criticism to groups of experienced teachers and by solicitation of comments from users of the collections in the field. A small group of ten pilot schools in different parts of the country has been formed to try out and criticize the collections of objectives and test items and to test the usefulness of the products of the Center to the schools. In both respects results have been positive.

The development of statements of objectives and test items to measure the objectives is important for all types of instructional programs and essential for individualized instructional programs based on mastery or criterion levels. A model for such a program is shown in Figure 14.5. It can be seen that assessment is involved at several points. First, the re-

---

[16]Center for the Study of Evaluation, *Products for Improving Education Evaluation,* Fifth Annual Report to the U.S. Office of Education, Evaluation Comment 2, No. 3 (Los Angeles: University of California, 1970).

Figure 14.5   An Individualized Mastery-Learning Sequence

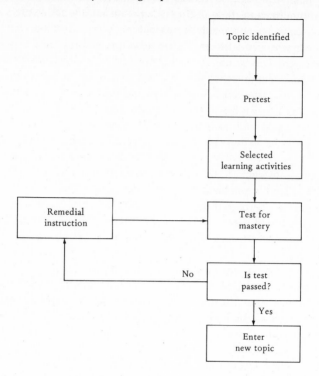

sults of the pretest will guide the teacher in selecting materials and learning activities for the pupil; second, measurements of progress are used to identify the need for remedial instruction and the achievement of sufficient mastery for the pupil to move to a new topic.

Evaluation can help at all stages of curricular development and instruction—planning, trial, revision, further trial, and further improvement. In fact, it is essential to the accomplishment of goals. There is evidence to suggest that attitudes toward curriculum and instructional evaluation are changing, and more systematic evaluation efforts may be characteristic of future program development in schools and colleges.

MOTIVATION

It is generally assumed that the prospect of taking a test motivates pupils to study. There is no doubt that most people make some preparation, if they can, when faced with the prospect of taking a final examination in a course. There are other aspects of the problem of motivation, however. For example, there is the question of whether pupils do better on a final examination if they have had occasional tests during the term or semester than they would without having had such periodic tests. The question is complicated by various factors such as the kinds of periodic tests used in relation to the kind of final examination given, whether students are simply told their scores on the tests or are permitted to go over them afterwards, and whether the tests are announced in advance or given without warning.

The question of motivation is not simple, and it is likely that many teachers and others assume the motivational value of tests without giving much thought to the various problems involved. It is a generally accepted principle of psychology that the practice of a skill with a knowledge of results—that is, of errors, successes, and overall improvement—produces much more progress than practice wherein such information is withheld from the learner. Indeed, there is evidence that the practice of a simple skill such as drawing a straight line just 2 inches long without knowledge of the accuracy of the preceding efforts or trials does not bring about any improvement in accuracy. In other words, practice under such conditions does not result in even slight improvement. It is a widely accepted fact that only when learners know their errors and know when they perform well does practice bring about noticeable improvement.

There is considerable experimental evidence on the effect of occasional testing on achievement as measured by success on final examinations. In most such experiments two groups, equal in ability and previous preparation, are formed. Both are taught by the same teacher using the same materials and methods. Both take the same final examination. The only difference is that one group, which may be called the experimental group, is given tests at intervals throughout the semester or term while the control group is not. Any difference in achievement as measured by the final examination can then be ascribed to the single variable of periodic tests. The results of numerous experiments of a similar nature may be summarized as follows.[17]

First, it appears that the effect obtained differs according to the way in which test results are used. If tests are used as a basis for specific remedial instruction, the results seem beneficial. When the tests are returned after being marked, with no indication that they were used for instructional purposes, there is little evidence that this procedure has any great

---

[17]Victor H. Noll, "The Effect of Written Tests upon Achievement in College Classes: An Experiment and a Summary of Evidence," *Journal of Educational Research* 32 (January 1939), 345–358.

value. Furthermore, most studies on the college level show no effect whatsoever on final achievement when measured by comprehensive objective examinations, even when the test results are discussed with the students or when they are invited to use them for study purposes.

Second, there is a suggestion in one or two reports that less able or below-average students are helped more by tests than those who are superior in accomplishment.

There is some indication, third, that younger and less responsible students, as those in secondary schools, are more likely to be motivated and helped by quizzes than older students, as in college, who are presumably more mature.

Another aspect of the question has to do with the reactions of students to frequent testing. One study is reported in which a college class in introductory psychology was given fourteen weekly objective quizzes in addition to unit tests and a final examination.[18] The quizzes were scored, returned to students, and discussed or commented upon by the instructor. At the end of the semester, students responded to a questionnaire asking for their reactions to the weekly quizzes and discussion of test results. Eighty percent of the students said that the quizzes helped them to learn more, and 20 percent said no more. Ninety-three percent reported that the quizzes motivated them to study more than usual. A third question asked students if weekly quizzes caused increased anxiety. Of those who answered in the affirmative, 87 percent said they still approved the use of weekly quizzes. On the matter of effect on grades, 31 percent said their grades would be better as a result of the quizzes, 55 percent said there would be no difference, and 14 percent said they would be poorer or lower. Also, 89 percent reported that frequent testing helped to check progress or learning and 11 percent that it made no difference.

With regard to the effect of class discussion of test results, 31 percent said it improved subsequent performance, 67 percent said it made no difference, and 2 percent said it resulted in poorer performance on succeeding tests. Fifty-three percent said discussions helped performance on the final examination, while 45 percent reported no difference.

In summary, the results of this study show student perceptions of frequent quizzes to be highly favorable. Discussions of test results were viewed as helpful by considerably fewer students, although 75 percent reported that they helped them avoid foolish or technical errors.

Teachers will probably go on using tests, particularly those of their own devising, at least partly to stimulate pupils to greater achievement, in the belief that the tests function in that way regardless of the findings of experimental studies. In this connection, it must always be remembered that situations and circumstances differ from one teacher and class

[18]John F. Feldhusen, "Student Perceptions of Frequent Quizzes and Post-Mortem Discussions of Results," *Journal of Educational Measurement*, 1 (June 1964), 51–54.

to another and that the use of tests for motivational purposes will depend on the individual teacher's judgment and experience of what is effective in that class.

The use of tests for motivation is confined largely and quite naturally to achievement tests. There is little that an individual can or should do beforehand in trying to improve scores on tests of intelligence, aptitude, interests, or personality. On those, we are interested in motivating the person tested to put forth a maximum effort at the time of testing, and we are interested also in eliminating any coaching, studying, or previous knowledge of the test that might give a pupil an unfair advantage and might result in an inaccurate and misleading measurement of that pupil's ability. Achievement tests have as their basic purpose the measurement of the results of teaching, and anything that can be done legitimately to improve such learning is desirable. Therefore, if periodic testing serves to stimulate interest and motivate the pupil to greater effort and accomplishment, there is justification for the use of tests for that purpose.

LEARNING EXERCISES

15. Would you expect the effect of tests announced in advance to be the same as that of unannounced tests? Give reasons for your answer.
16. Should a teacher discuss standardized tests of achievement, after they have been scored, with pupils in order to help them understand questions they have missed? If so, under what circumstances?

IDENTIFICATION AND STUDY OF EXCEPTIONAL CHILDREN

The majority of pupils in our schools fall within what may be thought of as the normal range. However, in nearly every class or group some are outside this range in some respect. They may be exceptionally bright or dull; they may have more or fewer than the usual number of adjustment problems, or their problems may be unusually severe or mild; some may be exceptional in physical qualities—either unusually gifted or perhaps handicapped in some way that interferes with normal participation and success in activities of various sorts. Such children are referred to in educational literature as *exceptional children.*

For those who are exceptional intellectually, tests have been found over many years to provide the best basis for screening and identifying both gifted and retarded.[19] The procedure that seems most effective is to use group tests of mental ability along with nominations by teachers as the initial basis for screening. Those thus located are then tested by a school psychologist or psychometrist with an individual examination such as the Stanford-Binet. In the study by Pegnato and Birch cited in footnote 19, seven different procedures for identifying gifted children were used and evaluated. The procedure found to be most efficient was initial screening by the use of group intelligence tests followed by individual testing for actual identification of the gifted.

In recent years much attention has been given to the study of creativity, and there have been attempts to devise tests of creativity. There is some difference of opinion among psychologists regarding the similarity between general mental ability and creativity. Some hold that these are essentially distinct and separate entities, others that they are very closely related if not the same thing. In Chapters 9 and 10 we have described and discussed tests designed to measure general intelligence and some designed to measure creativity. We need only add here that existing measures of intelligence have been found very useful in identifying intellectually gifted children and that tests of creativity may prove in time to have similar value for identification of giftedness.

Children with obvious physical handicaps such as those who are crippled, those having nervous disorders as a result of brain damage, and the like pose little problem as far as identification is concerned. The exact nature of the disability will be diagnosed and treatment prescribed by medical means. Less obvious but often equally serious handicaps, as far as school learning is concerned, are defects of vision and hearing. These often go unnoticed by teachers and even parents. Children are apt to try to hide such defects and in rare instances may themselves be unaware of them. They can be detected and measured quite accurately, however, by standard tests.

Visual acuity can be checked by devices such as the *Snellen Wall Chart;* color vision or color blindness can be measured by various tests designed for the purpose; and a thorough measurement of all visual functions can be made by such instruments as the Ortho-Rater, Sight Screener, and the Telebinocular.

[19]See, for example, Carl W. Pegnato and Jack W. Birch, "Locating Gifted Children in Junior High Schools: A Comparison of Methods," *Exceptional Children,* 25 (March 1959), 300–304; also Marion J. Erickson, "Current Trends and Practices in the Education of the Mentally Retarded," *Educational Administration and Supervision,* 44 (September 1958), 297–308; and Lloyd M. Dunn (ed.), *Exceptional Children in the Schools,* 2d ed. (New York: Holt, Rinehart and Winston, 1973).

Hearing acuity or hearing loss can be measured roughly by whisper or watch-tick. The examiner simply determines the greatest distance from which the child can hear a whisper or the tick of a watch. A more accurate and thus more reliable measurement of auditory acuity or defect is made with the *audiometer*. Such instruments as the *pure-tone audiometer* measure the hearing loss of an individual by determining how much louder the tone must be made for the individual to hear it than is required with normal hearing.

For use with physically handicapped children, the typical paper-and-pencil test of school achievement must often be modified in some way. Larger print for the visually handicapped, oral or Braille instructions for blind children, modification of directions for the deaf or hard-of-hearing, and various adaptations of test procedures for use with crippled children represent ways in which tests have been modified for the handicapped child. Individual tests such as the Stanford-Binet have also been modified for use with handicapped children.

Tests may also be very useful in measuring results of special programs. Usually after a handicapped child has been identified and diagnosed, there is an attempt to do something about the handicap and make adjustments for it. Special schools, special classes, remedial work, therapy of various kinds, and correction of defects by more radical means are used as each case may require. The amount of improvement—educational, psychological, or emotional—may be gauged by the use of suitable tests, either tests designed for the purpose or modifications of existing tests.

Another type of exceptional child, the gifted child, is often neglected and given even less attention than normal children. Teachers find it easy to ignore gifted children while energy and help are directed toward the others. The gifted child can usually be depended upon to "come through" without much help from anyone. Not to give gifted children special attention and encouragement is, however, a short-sighted policy. The development of standardized intelligence tests and, to a lesser degree, standardized achievement tests has made it possible to identify and measure more accurately than ever before these gifted children in our schools. Personality tests have made it possible to study their personal and social characteristics and have demonstrated that, contrary to belief among some persons, children who are gifted intellectually are usually normal and well adjusted, at least as much so as the general population. The use of tests with gifted children has opened a whole new field of study and research that should result in benefits of considerable importance to society.

The research on creativity referred to earlier, the National Merit Qualifying Examinations, the Advanced Placement Programs, the testing of high-school seniors by selective service, the many scholarships offered by public and private agencies, and loan funds for students are some of the ways in which individuals who have exceptional ability are being encouraged and assisted to obtain as much education as they can and to develop their talents to the fullest possible extent. Such provisions are advantageous not only to the person who is helped but also the community, state, and nation.

LEARNING EXERCISES

17. What kinds of measurements would you use to identify gifted children? How would you decide, on the basis of scores on each type, what your criteria for "gifted" would be?
18. Make a list of the various kinds of handicaps found among school children. Cite one or more types of measurement useful in each case.
19. What adaptations in a paper-and-pencil test must be made for the deaf? the blind? the feeble-minded? the spastic?

Reference has been made earlier to new laws and recent court decisions that will have the effect of increasing the range of individual differences in the classroom. Many children who are classified as learning disabled will be retained in their regular classrooms for a larger part of instruction. Teachers will need to be increasingly perceptive of the progress and needs of all children in the class, and tests and other instruments will be valuable in identifying pupils who could profit from additional testing and perhaps assignment to a resource room for additional instruction. Chapter 12 included several items from a rating scale that might be used to identify learning-disabled children.

INTERPRETING SCHOOLS
TO THE COMMUNITY

Recent developments in education have included a tremendous increase in the concern, interest, and participation of the public in school matters. These developments have affected the work of all school personnel, but their effects have been felt most strongly by principals, superintendents, and others in administrative and supervisory positions. They have usually been the ones to answer questions and criticisms, to explain and justify what schools were attempting to accomplish, and to present evidence that these objectives were, in fact, being achieved.

It is with respect to this last point that evaluation and measurement find particular usefulness. When citizens ask for evidence on what their children are learning, the results of testing programs are naturally among the first lines of evidence to be presented. Likewise, if the question has to do with how well the schools are achieving the objectives set up by and for them, test scores provide evidence on this matter. Evaluation and measurement thus provide one of the best means of interpreting schools to the community.

However, having said this, it is necessary to recognize that this use of test results embodies some problems. One of these is the tendency to react negatively to test results if they do not support or reinforce what the community or individuals want to believe. Reference has been made in an earlier chapter to the reaction to poor scores on a test by faulting the test. If an individual or one's child does badly on a test, the test is said to be biased or unfair. The ultimate result of this attitude would be tests that everyone did well on. This is plainly *reductio ad absurdum*. In some situations there has been a demand that tests such as the *Scholastic Aptitude Test,* an instrument of proven validity in predicting success in college, not be used with certain minority groups because members of these groups typically make poor showings. In some situations the results of such tests have been ignored or those who are well qualified to interpret them have not been called on or permitted to do so.[20]

One approach that seems to have some merit and acceptance is the development of unique prediction equations for different identifiable groups. While this approach has not eliminated all of the problems of selecting children most likely to succeed in a given school or program, it does eliminate the effect of some cross-cultural factors that cloud the effectiveness of one equation used with all people.

Another problem in using the results of measurement in interpreting the program and accomplishments of the schools is the development of understanding by the lay public and even by classroom teachers of the terms and concepts used in measurement and the meaning of the different types of tests scores. Unless there is adequate comprehension and understanding of these matters, the attempt to explain and interpet the results of measurement may mislead more than inform. In one community, a detailed outline of a program to explain test results to community groups was developed to provide information on the nature and scope of the testing program, the kinds of tests being given, the skills being tested,

[20]Donald T. Campbell, "Reforms as Experiments," *American Psychologist,* 24 (April 1969), 409–429.

and the types of norms and scores used.[21] When such an effort is made, parents and teachers have a much better understanding of the goals and accomplishments of their schools and a sounder basis for interpreting test scores of individual pupils. It seems reasonable to generalize that the results of standardized tests and other measures, when properly presented and understood, can be extremely useful in interpreting schools to the community.

LEARNING EXERCISES

20. Assume that you are responsible for public relations between the schools and the public in a community of 15,000 people. How would you use the results of measurement to interpret your program to the community?
21. If you had to meet with a parent who took the attitude that all tests are bad, how would you proceed to change that viewpoint?

IMPROVEMENT OF SCHOOL STAFF

The use of tests and other measuring techniques can contribute substantially to the professional development of teachers in several ways. In the first place, putting on a measurement program can result in professional growth through the cooperative planning, organizing, and conducting of such a project. In order to participate actively, teachers must learn something about available tests, the characteristics of good measuring instruments, methods of determining how good a test is, and sources of information that will provide a basis for making such a determination. Some teachers must also learn how to administer, score, and interpret tests and how to put the results to good use. All these experiences and skills can come out of participation by teachers in a measurement program.

Another way in which measurement contributes to staff improvement is through the construction of tests and other measures for local use. In this activity a teacher must identify objectives of instruction and try to

[21]Alden W. Badal and Edwin P. Larsen, *On Reporting Test Results to Community Groups*, National Council on Measurement in Education Special Reports 1 (East Lansing, Mich.: National Council on Measurement in Education, May 1970).

construct instruments that will measure progress toward them. This will direct attention not only to the objectives but also to methods and materials for attaining them. It will also bring the pupil into the picture, since in constructing tests the teacher will constantly be thinking of ways in which to measure pupil changes resulting from instruction.

After the results of measurement are known, these will promote professional growth in the teacher by revealing what has worked well in instruction and what has not. An appraisal of the apparent effectiveness of methods and materials will cause the teacher to examine these with new insight. Measurement programs may also help teachers learn from each other by revealing individual strengths and weaknesses and by encouraging them to exchange ideas much in the same manner as housewives improve their cooking by exchanging recipes.

Educational measurements may also contribute to the professional growth of a school staff by giving the teacher better insight into the individual pupil's capacities, interests, achievements, personality problems, and needs. Such improvement in understanding will almost certainly make the teacher more useful and effective as a teacher and as a friend and adviser.

Knowledge and use of measuring procedures may contribute to professional growth of the school staff through the development of a better understanding of the problems involved in accurate measurement of human traits and greater appreciation of the efforts of pioneers in this area. Also, such study and investigation by teachers should help to bring about improvement in their own tests and measuring instruments. The better the evaluative procedures used by teachers and counselors, the more effective will be their teaching and counseling.

Finally, the use of measuring instruments should be helpful to the administrator and supervisor in many ways. Tests may be used to help select personnel for teaching and other positions. Tests of pupil achievement, observations, and rating scales will be useful to the supervisor in the in-service education of teachers. Various measuring and evaluative devices such as check lists and score cards may also be useful in arriving at sounder judgments about physical facilities.

LEARNING EXERCISES

22. What are some ways other than those mentioned above in which a teacher may grow as a result of participation in planning and carrying out a measurement program?

23. Should scores on achievement tests of pupils be used by supervisors in assisting teachers to improve their effectiveness? If so, in what ways might this be done?
24. Of what benefit to teachers might self-rating be?

EDUCATIONAL RESEARCH

There is some evidence of a growing emphasis on educational research in the schools. In part this has been brought about through the various acts of Congress supporting elementary and secondary education that provide that programs benefiting from such grants be constantly subjected to evaluation. In part, increased amounts of educational research are the direct result of federal funding of both research projects and training of educational researchers. There can be little question also that the demand by the public for more evidence on the efficiency of the schools and on the degree of accomplishment of educational goals has stimulated research designed to provide such evidence. In most such activities, measurement plays an active and important role.

In school surveys, tests are useful tools for studying such problems as the grade placement of pupils, achievement in basic fundamentals, the relationship of the offerings of the school to the needs of the community, and the degree of success attained in realizing the educational goals of the school or community. Measuring instruments are not available yet for all the educational goals a school or community may set for itself, but existing ones are constantly being improved and new and better ones developed. This is true, for example, in the case of educational goals expressed in terms of subject matter and, to a lesser extent, of such goals as attitudes, desirable habits of work and study, and participation in school and community activities. In other areas such as social adjustment or citizenship, it may be necessary to devise original measures. This in itself is a worthwhile type of research activity for teachers, particularly if they have the advice and help of specialists.

Tests may also serve research purposes in the schools in conjunction with comparative studies of different methods of teaching. Most teachers are keenly interested in finding the most effective ways of doing things, not only because of the improved efficiency and consequent saving of time and energy but also because better methods result in better learning or achievement by the pupil. A common type of educational research is to form two equated or equivalent classes or sections and to compare the relative effectiveness of two methods of instruction, one class taught by one method, the other by a second method. If the two groups are equal at the beginning, then any difference at the end may be ascribed to the differences in method—provided, of course, that all other factors that might affect the results are held constant. In all such experiments measurement plays an important part. It is used to measure and equate the status of groups before the experiment has begun and to measure the results after it has been completed.

LEARNING EXERCISES

25. List three examples of educational research in which classroom teachers might engage and that would require the use of measurement.
26. Do research interests and problems of counselors differ from those of classroom teachers? If so, give some examples of possible interests and problems of each group and indicate what kinds of measurements they would use.
27. Larger school systems generally have a bureau of research. What measurement functions and activities would such an organization perform?

SUGGESTED READING

AMERICAN EDUCATIONAL RESEARCH ASSOCIATION. *Monograph Series on Curriculum Evaluation.* Chicago: Rand McNally, 1967–1970. A series of six monographs. Included are studies on perspectives of curriculum evaluation and instructional objectives. A good series covering many aspects of topics discussed in this chapter. Selective reference would complement the study of using measurement data in schools.

BERDIE, RALPH F., et al. *Testing in Guidance and Counseling.* New York: McGraw-Hill, 1963. Chapters 5–8 and 15. Covers the nature and uses of tests in counseling, the organization of a testing program, the administration of tests, and national testing programs. Chapter 15 consists of descriptions of a large number of tests used in counseling.

BLOCK, JAMES H. and LORIN W. ANDERSON. *Mastery Learning in Classroom Instruction.* New York: Macmillan, 1975. Describes how to develop and implement mastery learning in a classroom. Includes sections on constructing tables of specification, measuring achievement, and grading.

COTTLE, WILLIAM C. and N. M. DOWNIE. *Preparation for Counseling.* 2d ed. Englewood Cliffs, N.J.: Prentice-Hall, 1970. Chapters 6–11 cover a variety of topics related to assessment and interpretation of abilities, interests, and personal characteristics, and they include suggestions for choosing standardized tests and the approach to research by counselors. Although intended as an introductory text for counseling students, the topics are also important to teachers.

DUROST, WALTER N., and GEORGE A. PRESCOTT. *Essentials of Measurement for Teachers.* New York: Harcourt Brace Jovanovich, 1962. A capsule treatment of the major areas of educational measurement from the standpoint of the needs of the classroom teacher. Emphasizes the use of stanines in test interpretation.

FROELICH, CLIFFORD P., and JOHN G. DARLEY. *Studying Students: Guidance Methods of Individual Analysis.* Chicago: Science Research Associates, 1952. Chap. 9. Most of this book covers various techniques for gathering data about individuals and the use of such data. The major emphasis is on individual counseling, but there is much of value to teachers, school psychologists, and others concerned with measurement in the schools.

GOLDMAN, LEO. *Using Tests in Counseling.* 2d ed. New York: Appleton-Century-Crofts, 1971. The entire book is an excellent treatment of the use of tests in guidance for the test specialist and the counselor. Especially practical are Chapter 3 on selecting tests for counseling purposes and Chapter 11, describing the use of tests in ten case histories.

GRONLUND, NORMAN E. *Measurement and Evaluation in Teaching.* 3d ed. New York: Macmillan, 1975. Part 4 covers evaluation of learning; Part 5 covers measurement in improving instruction and marking practices.

HAVSEN, JAMES C., et al. *Counseling Theory and Process.* 2d ed. Boston: Allyn and Bacon, 1977. Chapter 16 reviews the use of tests in counseling, including selecting tests, administering and scoring, and test-score interpreting. Also includes a discussion on using tests for prediction, monitoring students, and evaluation.

LYMAN, HOWARD B. *Test Scores and What They Mean.* Englewood Cliffs, N.J.: Prentice-Hall, 1963. A brief treatment of educational measurement, including most of the topics usually discussed in more comprehensive books. The emphasis is on interpreting test scores. Useful as a supplement to the regular textbook in courses in measurement or guidance and as the basis for a refresher course.

THORNDIKE, ROBERT L., ed. *Educational Measurement.* 2d ed. Washington, D.C.: American Council on Education, 1971. Chap. 17–20. A somewhat advanced treatment of the role of measurement in learning and instruction, guidance, selection and placement, and program evaluation. Excellent presentations for students who want to be challenged on topics of great importance in educational theory and practice.

TRAXLER, ARTHUR E. *Techniques of Guidance.* Rev. ed. New York: Harper & Row, 1957. Chap. 10. A brief but excellent discussion of administrative and supervisory uses of tests. The main emphasis is on instructional and counseling uses of test results. The chapter also gives some of the limitations of tests in these areas and some suggestions on how to improve their usefulness. There is a good bibliography at the end of the chapter.

Appendix A

FURTHER STATISTICAL COMPUTATIONS

The problems in this appendix use as far as possible the data presented in Chapter 2. The chief purpose of this section is to supplement Chapter 2 by providing an opportunity for students to learn and practice the actual steps in computing the usual statistical measures and by giving them a deeper insight into the meaning and significance of these measures in interpreting the results of measurement.

FREQUENCY DISTRIBUTIONS

Ordinarily, a teacher works with classes or groups numbering between twenty-five and forty pupils. In most such cases the scores can be handled individually without special arrangement or grouping. However, it is often advantageous to arrange the scores in some systematic order; when the number of scores or cases is large, perhaps fifty or more, such grouping is practically a necessity. For a teacher who wishes to combine data for multiple-section courses, these steps are particularly useful.

A frequency distribution is merely a method of arranging scores into groups, or class intervals, as they are generally called, for ease in handling the figures. Since statistical data are frequently presented with scores arranged in such a frequency table or distribution, it is helpful to be able to construct and read one.

On the mathematics tests cited in Chapter 2 (Table 2.1) the scores of a class were as follows: 44, 21, 14, 18, 46, 45, 52, 30, 39, 36, 31, 22, 23, 38, 33, 33, 29, 38, 32, 29, 42, 28, 26, 33, 25. These were arranged in order from the highest to the lowest, producing this sequence: 52, 46, 45, 44, 42, 39, 38, 38, 36, 33, 33, 33, 32, 31, 30, 29, 29, 28, 26, 25, 23, 22, 21, 18, 14 (see Table 2.2).

J's score of 36, as we know, was ninth in the class; the arithmetic mean was 32.3; the median was 32. These results are easily obtained without further rearrangement of the scores. However, we can make a frequency table from these scores by the following steps:

1. Choose some convenient class interval, say 5. If the range of scores is small (the range is the difference between the highest and lowest scores), use a smaller class interval; if the range is large, use a larger interval, perhaps 10. In any case, use an interval large enough so that the table will be not too long for convenience and yet small enough to represent the scores with reasonable accuracy. Here we have used an interval of 5.
2. Make a table of class intervals that will serve to include all scores in the class or group. In general, the class interval should give a distribution containing not fewer than eight nor more than sixteen intervals. By using the interval of 5 in our mathematics-scores example, we establish nine such categories (see Table A.1).
3. Tally the scores one by one in the proper class intervals.
4. Add the tallies and write the sum opposite each interval. These sums are called *frequencies*. The total of all of the frequencies (N) gives the number of students tested.

Although we have gone through the essential steps in setting up a frequency table, we have not considered adequately some basic questions underlying this method. If we are to use the method correctly and intelligently, these questions must be considered and answers agreed upon. The first of these concerns the class interval.

Frequency Distribution   *Table A.1*

Class interval	Tally	Frequency
50–54	/	1
45–49	//	2
40–44	//	2
35–39	////	4
30–34	⅃⅃T /	6
25–29	⅃⅃T	5
20–24	///	3
15–19	/	1
10–14	/	1
		$N = 25$

*Limits
of Class
Intervals*

A score on a test is usually a whole number, such as 22. Generally, we do not use fractional scores in educational measurement. However, it is necessary to give some consideration to the actual value of a whole number. For example, we can consider the score of 22 as representing a range of all possible values from exactly 22.0 up to but not including 23.0. In this case the score of 22 should really be written 22.5, since that would be the most probable value, assuming the possibility of values ranging from 22.0 to 23.0.

On the other hand, we can consider the score of 22 as representing a range of all possible values from 21.5 up to but not including 22.5. In this case the score of 22 is taken to mean 22.0, which is the most probable value. This is most generally favored in statistical work.

The use of decimal places is arbitrary. *Exactly* 22 would mean 22 followed by an infinite number of zeros; *exactly* 22½ would mean 22.5 followed by an infinite number of zeros. When we write 22.0 we assume the rest of the zeros if we mean exactly 22. A similar assumption holds in the case of 22.5.

The same principles apply in interpreting the limits of class intervals. If we have a class interval of 5, we may indicate this in several different ways as shown in the three columns below:

1	2	3
25–30	25–29	24.5–29.49 . . .
20–25	20–24	19.5–24.49 . . .

The first, seldom used, is the least desirable, since the limit 25 appears in two successive intervals and may thus lead to errors in tabulation; the second has the advantage over the third of simplicity and does not have the obvious fault of the first; the third, although the most exact in statement, is cumbersome. The method in column 2 is therefore recommended, with the admonition that the value of a score be remembered as explained above. Then the interval 20–24 really means from 19.5 to 24.5. This constitutes an interval of 5 that contains all whole-number scores of 20, 21, 22, 23, and 24 or any score from 19.5 up to but not including 24.5.[1]

*Midpoint
of Intervals*

In statistical work with frequency distributions it is often necessary to use the midpoint of an interval. There are two steps in determining the midpoint:

---

[1] The whole numbers 20 and 24 are called *integral limits*. The numbers 19.5 and 24.5 are called *real limits*.

1. Find one-half of the size of the class interval.
2. Add this to the real lower limit or subtract it from the real upper limit of the interval whose midpoint is desired.

Let us take as an example the interval 20–24. The interval is, of course, 5, and so halfway through it would be 2.5. Then if we begin at the upper (24.5) or lower (19.5) real limit of the interval and subtract or add 2.5 steps or score points, we get $19.5 + 2.5 = 22.0$, or $24.5 - 2.5 = 22.0$. This must be the midpoint since it is equidistant from the upper limit and the lower limit of the class interval.

LEARNING EXERCISE

1. Find the midpoints of the following class intervals: (a) 50–59, (b) 27–29, (c) 30–35, (d) 13–14, (e) 96–101. (59 includes from 58.5 up to but not including 59.5; 29 includes from 28.5 up to but not including 29.5; and so on.)

One basic assumption is made in working with midpoints of class intervals. The interval 20–24 has a midpoint of 22; if nine cases fall in this interval, we assume that these nine scores are evenly distributed throughout the interval, or, in any event, that the average of these nine scores is equal to the midpoint of the interval.

What we have said concerning class intervals can be presented graphically as follows:

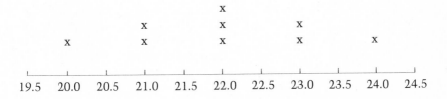

The actual or real limits of the interval are shown at the ends of the line; the midpoint 22 is shown at the center; the nine scores in the interval balance so that any average of them would give 22. Any distribution of the nine scores that gives an average equal to the midpoint of the interval will satisfy the assumption. In actual practice this assumption tends to be reasonably well met. This is particularly true when the number of cases is large and the class interval chosen is fairly small. The larger the class interval and the smaller the frequencies, the greater are the chances of introducing error. It is also likely that error introduced as a result of cases piling up at one end of a particular interval will be balanced by an opposite tendency in another interval, the two sources of error thus tending to balance or neutralize each other in computations involving the full set of scores.

Making a
Frequency
Distribution

A simple frequency distribution is given in Table A.1, with a brief statement of the steps involved in making it. Let us now take a series of scores and carefully work through the steps required to make a frequency distribution of them. The following scores represent actual scores of forty-nine pupils on a general science test: 33, 42, 47, 61, 43, 52, 71, 21, 43, 37, 60, 43, 54, 68, 13, 50, 38, 40, 67, 3, 45, 47, 49, 58, 38, 46, 58, 36, 44, 55, 15, 38, 44, 40, 28, 27, 44, 36, 41, 39, 22, 36, 18, 41, 24, 32, 8, 33, 25.

1. Choose a class interval of suitable size. This is usually done by first finding the range of scores (here it is $71 - 3 = 68$) and then dividing the range by a convenient class interval to see if it gives between eight and sixteen intervals. In this case:

$$68 \div 4 = 17$$
$$68 \div 5 = 13+$$
$$68 \div 6 = 11+$$
$$68 \div 7 = \ \ 9+$$

In practice, class intervals of 4, 6, or 7 are seldom used. The most commonly used intervals are 2, 3, 5, 10, or, if necessary, 20. Here we shall use 5 as our class interval since it is of a convenient size and, as we shall see, it actually gives fifteen class intervals.

2. Next, set up a frequency table designating the class intervals. Notice that we have chosen the lower limits of our intervals in such a way that they are multiples of the interval size—that is, of 5. We use these limits for the sake of convenience, but it would be just as satisfactory statistically to use limits that were not multiples of the interval. Some authorities recommend choosing the limits in such a way that the midpoints of the intervals are multiples of the interval, but this seems a less natural way of thinking about class intervals. The two methods are illustrated as follows:

Limits Are Multiples of the Interval		Midpoints Are Multiples of the Interval	
Limits	Midpoint	Limits	Midpoint
25–29	27	23–27	25
20–24	22	18–22	20
15–19	17	13–17	15

Since our scores range from 3 to 71, we will need a series of intervals that will include these extremes and all possible scores in between. Using the system at the left above, we arrive at the series of intervals given in Table A.2, showing intervals for the complete range of scores from 3 to 71 and all possible scores in between.

3. Tally the actual scores in the proper class intervals, adding the tallies in each class interval. The sums of the tallies give the frequencies. (See Table A.2.)

The sum of the frequencies (N) should be equal to the number of scores in the group. This is a rough check on the accuracy of the tabulation. However, the most common error in making a frequency distribution is the tabulation of a score in the wrong class interval. It is easy to make this mistake, and the only way to detect such errors is to tabulate the scores twice to see whether the frequencies in each class interval check. The second tabulation may be done alongside the first one or by placing a dot over each tally when going through the second time, thus:

$$35\text{–}39 \quad \overset{\cdots\ \cdots}{\cancel{||||}\ |\ |\ |}$$

A Table of Frequencies

Table A.2

Class interval (c.i.)	Tally	Frequency (f)
70–74	/	1
65–69	//	2
60–64	//	2
55–59	///	3
50–54	///	3
45–49	⊬⊬	5
40–44	⊬⊬ ⊬⊬ /	11
35–39	⊬⊬ ///	8
30–34	///	3
25–29	///	3
20–24	///	3
15–19	//	2
10–14	/	1
5–9	/	1
0–4	/	1
		N = 49

2. Make a new frequency table using the forty-nine scores on page 484 but with a class interval of 3.
3. Make a frequency table of the word-meaning test scores given in Learning Exercise 4 in Chapter 2.

MEASURES OF CENTRAL TENDENCY

The Mean   In Chapter 2 the mean and median were discussed and calculated with ungrouped scores. Let us now see how the mean and median are determined from a frequency distribution of the forty-nine scores on the general science test above.

The steps illustrated in Table A.3 are as follows:

1. Select an arbitrary origin. It is generally best to select a point near the center of the distribution, although any interval may be used without affecting the result. Here we chose the interval 40–44, whose midpoint, 42, we call the *assumed mean (A.M.)*.
2. In the *d* column, mark off steps by intervals above (+) and below (−)

Table A.3   Calculation of Mean Using Forty-Nine General Science Scores

c.i.	f	d	fd	
70–74	1	6	6	$M = A.M. + \left(\dfrac{\Sigma fd}{N} \times c.i.\right)$
65–69	2	5	10	
60–64	2	4	8	
55–59	3	3	9	M = mean
50–54	3	2	6	$A.M.$ = assumed mean
45–49	5	1	5	Σfd = algebraic sum of deviations
			44	about assumed mean
				N = number of scores
40–44	11	0	0	$c.i.$ = class interval
35–39	8	−1	−8	
30–34	3	−2	−6	$M = 42.0 + \left(\dfrac{44 - 66}{49} \times 5\right)$
25–29	3	−3	−9	
20–24	3	−4	−12	$= 42.0 + \left(\dfrac{-22}{49} \times 5\right)$
15–19	2	−5	−10	
10–14	1	−6	−6	$= 42.0 + \left(\dfrac{-110}{49}\right)$
5–9	1	−7	−7	
0–4	1	−8	−8	$= 42.0 - 2.2$
	$N = 49$		−66	$= 39.8$

the *A.M.* (*d* = deviations from the interval containing the assumed mean, in units of the class interval).

3. Multiply these steps by the frequencies in the respective intervals and enter these products in the *fd* column.
4. Add the positive *fd*'s (44) and the negative *fd*'s (−66) separately. Algebraically add the +*fd*'s and −*fd*'s to find Σ*fd*. The Σ*fd* divided by *N* gives the correction—that is, the amount expressed in units of the class interval by which our assumed mean differs from the actual value or mean.
5. The formula $M = A.M. + [(\Sigma fd / N) \times c.i.]$ simply converts the correction from units of the class interval to score units and applies this correction to the assumed mean, giving us the corrected value for the mean.

LEARNING EXERCISES

4. Check the value 39.8 (Table A.3) by adding the forty-nine scores and dividing by 49. Is there a difference? Why?
5. Check this value further by assuming the mean to be in some interval other than 40–44 and by recalculating the mean. Does it agree with the value already obtained?
6. Calculate the mean of the scores on the mathematics test by using the frequency distribution shown in Table A.1.

When data are grouped in a frequency distribution, calculating the median requires determining a point above and below which 50 percent of the scores or cases lie. This may be an actual score, but more often it is not. Table A.4 shows the steps in calculating the median from a frequency distribution:

The Median

1. Divide the total number of cases by 2. This gives the half-sum, or the number of cases above and below the middle of the distribution. In this example $N / 2 = 24.5$.
2. By inspection determine in which class interval this point will be. Since there are only twenty-two cases below the interval 40–44, and since the number of scores below the next interval, 45–49, is thirty-three, we know that the 24.5 point must be somewhere in the interval 40–44.
3. Subtract the number of cases below this interval, as shown in the cumulative frequency (cum. *f*) column, from 24.5. This gives us the

number of cases needed out of the interval in which the median falls. In this instance it is $24.5 - 22 = 2.5$ cases.

4. Divide this number by the total number of cases in the *interval*. Here, this is 11, and $2.5 \div 11 = .23$. Thus, we determine how far through the interval we must go to get the proportion of the cases needed. (Remember the assumption mentioned earlier that all scores in an interval are evenly distributed throughout the interval.)

5. Multiply this ratio by the size of the class interval to ascertain *score points* for this proportion of the interval. In our problem this gives 1.15 score points.

6. Add to this the lower limit of the interval containing the median. This gives the median: that point below and above which an equal number of cases or scores fall. As in the example, it is usually a theoretical point rather than an actual score, because of the method used in finding it.

Table A.4   Calculation of the Median from a Frequency Distribution of Forty-Nine General Science Scores

c.i.	f	cum. f	
70–74	1	49	
65–69	2	48	$\text{median} = l.l. + \left(\dfrac{\dfrac{N}{2} - F}{f_m} \right) \times c.i.$
60–64	2	46	
55–59	3	44	
50–54	3	41	
45–49	5	38	Median falls in this interval
40–44	11	33	$l.l.$ = lower limit of class interval within which median falls
35–39	8	22	
30–34	3	14	$N / 2$ = one-half of the scores
25–29	3	11	F = sum of all scores below $l.l.$
20–24	3	8	
15–19	2	5	f_m = number of scores within interval in which median falls
10–14	1	3	
5–9	1	2	
0–4	1	1	$c.i.$ = class interval
$N = 49$			

$$\text{median} = 39.5 + \left(\frac{\frac{49}{2} - 22}{11} \right) \times 5$$

$$= 39.5 + \left(\frac{24.5 - 22}{11} \right) \times 5$$

$$= 39.5 + 1.15$$

$$= 40.65$$

SOURCE: Adapted from *Statistics in Psychology and Education*, Sixth Edition, by Henry E. Garrett. Copyright © 1966 by Longman Inc. Reprinted by permission of Longman.

7. Using the frequency distribution of the scores shown in Table A.1 and that prepared in Exercise 3, calculate the median in each case.

The Mode

It was mentioned in Chapter 2 that there is one other measure of central tendency that is seldom used. It is a crude, imspectional average called the *mode*. This may be defined as the score occurring with greatest frequency; in a frequency table the mode is the midpoint of the interval having the largest frequency. In Table A.4 it is 42. The mode is of little importance, statistically speaking. Its chief use is to show the point of the greatest concentration of scores.

MEASURES OF VARIABILITY

The importance of measures of variability in describing a series of scores has already been discussed in Chapter 2. It will be the purpose here to supplement that discussion by showing how to calculate the two most commonly used measures of variability, or dispersion, using the frequency distribution of forty-nine science test scores already presented.

The Range

The range is a rough measure of variability. It is simply the difference between the highest and lowest scores in a distribution. We used it earlier in determining the size of class interval. Since the range is based on only two scores, it is not a very stable measure and is little used in statistical work.

The Semi-Interquartile Range

This measure is quite common in educational statistics. It is obtained by taking one-half the difference between the 75th percentile (Q_3) and the 25th percentile (Q_1). This can be expressed by the formula $Q = (Q_3 - Q_1) / 2$. We have already learned how to calculate the median in Table A.4. Using a comparable method, we can calculate Q_3 and Q_1, the 75th and 25th percentiles, respectively. This is illustrated in Table A.5.

One may ask why the formula for Q calls for one-half the range between Q_3 and Q_1. This is because many measures of variability are based on the deviations of scores from some measure of central tendency and

Calculation of the Semi-Interquartile Range from a Frequency Distribution of Forty-Nine General Science Scores

c.i.	f	cum. f		
70–74	1	49		
65–69	2	48		
60–64	2	46		
55–59	3	44		
50–54	3	41		
45–49	5	38}	Third quartile:	Q_3 = 75th percentile in this
40–44	11	33		interval
35–39	8	22		
30–34	3	14}	First quartile:	Q_1 = 25th percentile in this
25–29	3	11		interval
20–24	3	8		
15–19	2	5		
10–14	1	3		
5– 9	1	2		
0– 4	1	1		
	$N = 49$			

$$Q_3 = l.l. + \left(\frac{\frac{3N}{4} - F}{f_m}\right) \times c.i. \qquad Q_1 = l.l. + \left(\frac{\frac{N}{4} - F}{f_m}\right) \times c.i. \qquad Q = \frac{Q_3 - Q_1}{2}$$

$$= 44.5 + \frac{36.75 - 33}{5} \times 5 \qquad = 29.5 + \frac{12.25 - 11}{3} \times 5 \qquad = \frac{48.25 - 31.58}{2}$$

$$= 48.25 \qquad\qquad\qquad = 31.58 \qquad\qquad\qquad = 8.33$$

$l.l.$ = lower limit of class interval within which quartile point falls
F = sum of all scores below $l.l.$
f_m = number of scores within interval in which quartile point falls

are expressed as a distance on either side of that measure. To express the interquartile range in somewhat similar terms, it is halved. Although the semi-interquartile range is not based on deviations of individual scores from an average, it is roughly comparable to measures that are. In a symmetrical distribution, Q may be added to and subtracted from the average, and it will include the middle 50 percent of the cases. In an asymmetrical distribution, there is usually some variation from this proportion.

When a series of scores is quite homogeneous, Q will be smaller than when the differences between scores or individuals is greater. This principle is illustrated in Figure A.1. In distribution A the spread of scores is greater than it is in distribution B. As a consequence, Q_1 and Q_3 are farther apart and the Q is larger in A than in B. In other words, it is necessary to

Comparison of Q-Values of Two Distributions Differing in Spread   *Figure A.1*

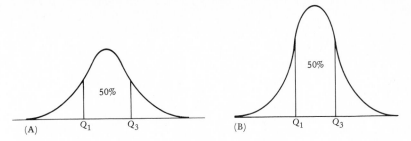

take in a wider range or variation of scores in A than in B to include the middle half (50 percent) of the cases in each distribution.

If we take each score in a class or series separately, find the difference between it and the mean, and add these differences without regard to sign, our result will be a number that gives some measure of the extent to which all the scores tend to vary from the mean. Obviously, if all the scores are the same, all of the differences between the scores and the mean will be zero, and the variability will also be zero. The larger the sum of these deviations from the mean, the greater the dispersion or variability. This is the principle upon which the calculation of most measures of variability or dispersion is based.

The Standard Deviation

In calculating the standard deviation (S), we square the deviation of each score from the mean. This has the effect of eliminating minus signs from the deviations of scores below the mean, and it gives the standard deviation more stability as a measure of variability than any similar measure. We further divide the sum of the squared deviations by the number of cases or scores, which gives us the mean of these squares. Finally, we extract the square root of this mean. (See Appendix B for square roots.) The quotient is called the standard deviation.

Table A.6 shows the steps by which the means and standard deviations of mathematics scores and reading scores may be calculated. Each step of the work is shown in Table A.6, which can be interpreted without further explanation.

Once the calculation of the standard deviation from ungrouped data is understood, we may proceed to Table A.7. This table demonstrates the method used for calculating S from grouped data—that is, from a frequency distribution. Fundamentally, the process is the same as for ungrouped data, but corrections must be made for the use of an assumed mean and for the use of class intervals. Careful study of this table and practice with the exercises following the explanation should make these differences in procedure meaningful.

FURTHER STATISTICAL COMPUTATIONS   491

Table A.6 Calculation of the Mean and Standard Deviation Using Ungrouped Data: Twenty-Five Mathematics Scores and Twenty-Five Reading Scores

Mathematics			Reading		
Score	Deviation from mean	d^2	Score	Deviation from mean	d^2
52	19.7	388.09	111	35.7	1274.49
46	13.7	187.69	102	26.7	712.89
45	12.7	161.29	94	18.7	349.69
44	11.7	136.89	92	16.7	278.89
42	9.7	94.09	91	15.7	246.49
39	6.7	44.89	87	11.7	136.89
38	5.7	32.49	86	10.7	114.49
38	5.7	32.49	81	5.7	32.49
36	3.7	13.69	80	4.7	22.09
33	.7	.49	77	1.7	2.89
33	.7	.49	77	1.7	2.89
33	.7	.49	76	.7	.49
32	−.3	.09	75	−.3	.09
31	−1.3	1.69	73	−2.3	5.29
30	−2.3	5.29	72	−3.3	10.89
29	−3.3	10.89	70	−5.3	28.09
29	−3.3	10.89	69	−6.3	39.69
28	−4.3	18.49	68	−7.3	53.29
26	−6.3	39.69	66	−9.3	86.49
25	−7.3	53.29	65	−10.3	106.09
23	−9.3	86.49	62	−13.3	176.89
22	−10.3	106.09	59	−16.3	265.69
21	−11.3	127.69	56	−19.3	372.49
18	−14.3	204.49	48	−27.3	745.29
14	−18.3	334.89	46	−29.3	858.49

$\Sigma m = 807$ $\Sigma d^2 = 2093.05$ $\Sigma m = 1883$ $\Sigma d^2 = 5923.45$

$N = 25$ $N = 25$

$$M = \frac{\Sigma m}{N} \qquad S = \sqrt{\frac{\Sigma d^2}{N}} \qquad M = \frac{\Sigma m}{N} \qquad S = \sqrt{\frac{\Sigma d^2}{N}}$$

$$= \frac{807}{25} \qquad = \sqrt{\frac{2093.05}{25}} \qquad = \frac{1883}{25} \qquad = \sqrt{\frac{5923.45}{25}}$$

$$= 32.3 \qquad = \sqrt{83.72} \qquad = 75.3 \qquad = \sqrt{236.94}$$

$$= 9.2 \qquad\qquad\qquad\qquad = 15.4$$

M = mean d = deviations from mean
Σ = sum N = number of scores or cases in group
m = scores or measures S = standard deviation

The steps in calculating the standard deviation are as follows: For steps 1, 2, 3 and 4, follow the first four steps described for calculating the mean (Table A.3). Then:

5. Multiply each entry in the *fd* column by its corresponding *d*. This gives the *fd²* values. Enter these in the *fd²* column.
6. Add all the *fd²* entries to get Σfd^2.
7. Substitute the proper values for each expression in the formula and solve for *S*, the standard deviation.

It should be noticed that $\Sigma fd/N$ is the correction used in calculating the mean from an assumed origin. Since we follow the same procedure here, it is necessary again to make the same correction, but since it is under the radical with the $\Sigma fd^2/N$, it too is squared.

The standard deviation is the distance that, laid off above and below the mean, includes the middle 68.26 percent of the cases or scores. This is exactly true in a so-called normal distribution only. In most situations where *approximately* normal distributions are the rule, one standard deviation on either side of the mean usually includes about two-thirds of the cases.

As we pointed out with *Q*, the more variable a group is, the larger will be the standard deviation or distance on either side of the mean required to include the middle of 68.26 percent of the scores. This is illustrated in Figure A.2. It will be noted that, in both A and B, one standard deviation (1 *S*) on either side the mean cuts off 34.13 percent of the cases but that the standard deviation is considerably larger in A than in B because of the greater spread or variability of the group represented by curve A. It should

Calculation of Standard Deviation from a Frequency Distribution of Forty-Nine General Science Scores
Table A.7

c.i.	f	d	fd	fd²	
70–74	1	6	6	36	
65–69	2	5	10	50	$S = \sqrt{\dfrac{\Sigma fd^2}{N} - \left(\dfrac{\Sigma fd}{N}\right)^2} \times c.i.$
60–64	2	4	8	32	
55–59	3	3	9	27	
50–54	3	2	6	12	*S* = standard deviation
45–49	5	1	5	5	Σfd^2 = sum of squared devia-
			44		tions of each score from mean
40–44	11	0	0	0	Σfd = algebraic sum of devia-
35–39	8	−1	−8	8	tions of each score from mean
30–34	3	−2	−6	12	
25–29	3	−3	−9	27	c.i. = class interval
20–24	3	−4	−12	48	
15–19	2	−5	−10	50	$S = \sqrt{\dfrac{456}{49} - \left(\dfrac{-22}{49}\right)^2} \times 5$
10–14	1	−6	−6	36	
5– 9	1	−7	−7	49	$= \sqrt{9.3061 - (.45)^2} \times 5$
0– 4	1	−8	−8	64	$= \sqrt{9.1036} \times 5$
	N = 49		−66	456	= 15.10

Comparison of Standard Deviations of Two Distributions Differing in Spread

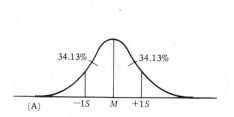
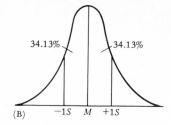

be emphasized, however, that such comparisons are valid only when the same test is administered to two groups or when the same group is tested twice.

The standard deviation is one of the most important and valuable statistical measures, though it is a little more difficult to calculate than some others. It has many uses, some of which have already been discussed; we shall learn about others shortly. Whenever the most stable and widely useful measure of variability is desired, the standard deviation is the one to employ. It is basic to, or enters into, the calculation of many other statistical measures.

LEARNING EXERCISE

8.   Draw a curve similar to the curves in Figure A.2 and show the approximate relationship of the standard deviation (S) and the semi-interquartile range (Q). Which is larger? Is this always so? Why?

PERCENTILE RANKS AND PERCENTILES

In Chapter 2 we discussed calculation and interpretation of *percentile ranks* (PRs) based on ungrouped data. Methods of calculating percentile ranks from grouped data or frequency distributions are somewhat more complicated. *Percentiles* are complementary to percentile ranks in a sense. A percentile is a score corresponding to a given percentile rank. Thus, the median is the 50th percentile, Q_3 is the 75th percentile, and so on.

Methods of calculating percentiles and percentile ranks based on the frequency distribution of the forty-nine general science test scores are shown in Table A.8.

GRAPHS OF FREQUENCY DISTRIBUTIONS

Two methods commonly used to depict frequency distributions—the *histogram* and the *frequency polygon*—are shown in Figure A.3. Both are based on the distribution of mathematics scores in Table A.1.

The Histogram and Frequency Polygon

Although both the histogram and the frequency polygon are based on the same data, the method of construction differs, as does the appearance of the two graphs. In both, frequencies are represented on the vertical axis, with class intervals on the horizontal axis. Thus, the height at any point represents the number of scores or cases in the interval directly below that point. In the histogram, points are located at the correct height at the beginning and end of each interval. These are connected by a horizontal line and by vertical lines to the adjacent points in the next higher and lower intervals. The graph ends on the base line at the lower limit of the lowest interval and at the upper limit of the highest interval of the distribution.

In the frequency polygon, points representing the frequencies of each class interval are located directly above the middle of the respective class intervals. These points are connected with straight lines. The graph ends at the base line, as in the histogram, but there is one difference. It is customary to end the frequency polygon at the midpoint of the interval *just below* the lowest one in the frequency distribution that contains any cases and at the midpoint of the next highest interval *above* the highest one in the frequency distribution.

Two Types of Graphs of Frequency Distribution of Twenty-Five Mathematics Scores: (A) Histogram, (B) Frequency Polygon

Figure A.3

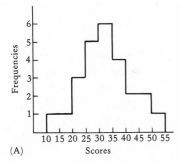

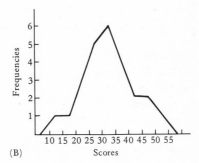

Table A.8   Methods of Calculating Percentiles and Percentile Ranks Based on a Frequency Distribution of Forty-Nine General Science Scores

c.i.	Percentile					Percentile rank	
	f	cum. f	% of N	n	Percentile	cum. f	PR
70–74	1	49	100	49	74.5	49	100.00
65–69	2	48	95	46.55	65.88	48	97.92
60–64	2	46	90	44.1	59.75	46	93.84
55–59	3	44				44	89.76
50–54	3	41	80	39.2	51.50	41	83.64
45–49	5	38	70	34.3	45.80	38	77.52
40–44	11	33	60 50	29.4 24.5	42.86 40.64	33	67.32
35–39	8	22	40 30	19.6 14.7	38.00 34.94	22	44.88
30–34	3	14				14	28.56
25–29	3	11	20	9.8	27.50	11	22.44
20–24	3	8				8	16.32
15–19	2	5	10	4.9	19.25	5	10.20
10–14	1	3	5	2.45	11.75	3	6.12
5–9	1	2				2	4.08
0–4	$\dfrac{1}{49}$	1	0	0	0	1	2.04

Sample Calculations

Percentile:

5th percentile $= l.l. + \left(\dfrac{\dfrac{N}{20} - F}{f_m} \right) \times c.i.\,^*$

$= 9.5 + \dfrac{2.45 - 2}{1} \times 5$

$= 11.75$

Percentile rank:
Percentile rank
of lower limit
of interval 5–9 $= \dfrac{1}{49} \times 100$

$= 2.04$

*.05N may be used in place of $N/20$ to find 5% of the scores.

These two graphs have certain important features in common that concern us in considering the normal curve. First, their form is basically humped or bell-shaped, because the frequencies are much smaller at the extremes than at the middle. That is, the number of cases increases more or less steadily as we go toward the middle or average from very high or very low scores. Second, the curves or graphs are continuous. There are no gaps, no class intervals with zero frequencies. These two features or characteristics are common to all so-called normal curves.[2]

The normal curve is a limiting curve that is approached by many distributions when a large number of measurements are made, or when there are many cases. It is necessary to assume that the measurements or cases are taken at random—that there is no bias or systematic error. For example, if it were desired to take an unbiased and representative sample of students on a given college or university campus, it would be necessary to plan the sampling procedure in such a way that *every* student would have an *equal chance* of being chosen. If these conditions were met, the sample would be unbiased and representative.

The Normal Curve

The graph of a normal curve is shown in Figure A.4. The base of the graph is divided into six units, and it can be seen that the curve ranges, for all practical purposes, 3σs above and 3σs below the mean.[3] The entries within the graph indicate the proportion of the total area (or the number of cases) that fall into each of the six segments. As we noticed earlier, in Figure A.2, 68.26 percent is in the two middle segments; 13.59 percent of the cases lie between points 1σ and 2σs from the mean; and 2.14 percent lie between points 2σs and 3σs from the mean. Adding these percentages for both halves of the distribution gives a total of 99.72 percent. In other words, all but .28 percent of the area under the normal curve (or the number of cases in a normal distribution of scores) will be found between the two points $+3\sigma$ and -3σ.

One situation in which the typical bell-shaped distribution curve occurs is in measurement of natural phenomena. Thousands of such measurements have been made of barometric and temperature readings at a given locality over a long period; of height, weight, and other bodily measurements of humans of the same sex and age; of the distribution of errors of measurement that are the result of chance; and of measures of ability and achievement, particularly when these are objective and based

---

[2]The term *normal* has a mathematical connotation that has no connection with *normal* and *abnormal* as used in psychology or education.
[3]As we noted in Chapter 2, the symbol S is used to represent the standard deviation of scores for a sample. However, when referring to a theoretical distribution, as we are here, it is customary to use the Greek letter σ to represent the standard deviation.

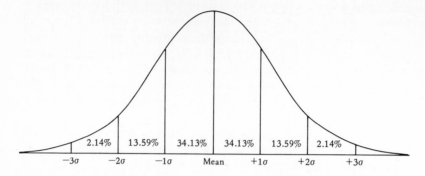

on large numbers of cases. Figure A.5 shows such a distribution curve for the stature of men; Figure A.6 shows the distribution of scores on an objective examination in educational measurement.

All these distribution curves approximate, more or less closely, the theoretical frequency curve. The larger the number of measurements and the more random the sample, the more symmetrical the curves become.

The significance of these results for educational and psychological measurement is great. In the first place, to the extent that human abilities tend to be distributed normally, we may expect to find relatively small proportions in the total population that are very gifted or extremely lacking in ability, and conversely we may expect the great majority to cluster around the average.

In the second place, we may expect to have few if any gaps or breaks in the distributions of such measurements. We find in nature not classes or types but all gradations from the lowest to the highest. This has particular significance in view of the widespread tendency to classify people into types—personality types or physical types or types based on some other feature. It is well to remember that human beings do not naturally fall into types or groups based on traits such as intelligence, personality, or achievement. When we do group them, it is generally for administrative reasons or reasons of convenience that, while important and often necessary, should not blind us to the fact of continuity in the distribution of human traits.

Finally, the concept of the normal distribution is very important to educational statistics and therefore to educational measurements. Many statistical measures are calculated by methods that assume a normal distribution. More particularly, techniques for estimating the accuracy of measurements rest on the concept of the normal probability curve. As we have emphasized, the usefulness of tests and evaluative techniques depends in part on their value for prediction. Such instruments as

Frequency Distribution of Stature for 8,585 Adult Males Born in the British Isles   *Figure A.5*

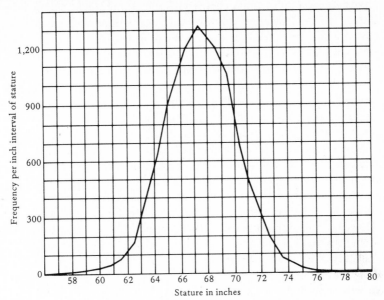

Reproduced by permission of the publishers, Charles Griffin & Co. Ltd. of London and High Wycombe, from Yule & Kendall, *Introduction to the Theory of Statistics*, 14th edition, 1950.

Frequency Distribution of Scores by 138 College Students on an Objective Final   *Figure A.6*
Examination in Educational Measurement

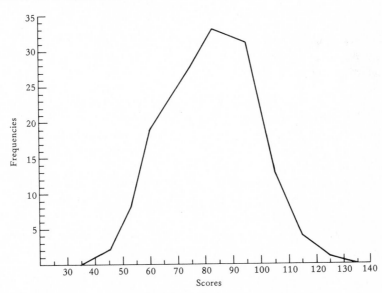

intelligence, aptitude, and prognostic tests are important tests for predictive purposes. Prediction is based squarely on the concept of probability. Given a certain score on a certain test, what will be the probable score if the test is given again? Or what is the probable score on another test of the same or similar abilities, traits, or potentialities? Or what are the probabilities that an individual who makes a certain score on a certain test will be successful in a chosen type of work? What are the chances (probabilities) that an individual's true score on an examination differs from the score actually made, and by how much? The answers to these and many similar questions depend on the normal probability concept.

It is erroneous to assume that unless the form of a distribution conforms almost exactly to that of the theoretical curve, the usual statistical tools discussed here are not applicable or that their use is highly questionable. It is true that a great many statistical procedures, particularly those relating to prediction, are based on the assumption of normality. However, the amount of error introduced by the usual departures from the theoretical is not great enough in most ordinary statistical work to invalidate the results. Furthermore, procedures are available that make possible certain corrections for various conditions resulting in departures from the normal distribution.

It has been emphasized and should always be remembered that the concept of the normal distribution has definite limitations as well as a definite usefulness in interpreting test scores. Yet on the whole, the concept of the normal distribution is very useful and even indispensable in educational and psychological measurement. Its usefulness, however, is not confined to measurement. It is basic to an understanding of individual differences in physical and mental qualities and characteristics that measurement serves to quantify. It has been and will undoubtedly continue to be an essential concept, both theoretically and practically.

LEARNING EXERCISES

9. What are some of the problems a teacher might encounter if student classifications (gifted, above average, and the like) were relied on to the neglect of the concept of continuity of abilities?
10. How would the likely distribution of test scores differ for a class representing a cross-section of students in a given grade? a class of mostly gifted students, the rest being average and below? a class of mostly slow learners, the rest being average and above?

MEASURES OF CORRELATION
OR RELATIONSHIP

In Chapter 2, illustrations of correlation were presented in the form of scatter diagrams and two-way tables. These provided pictorial or graphic representation of the extent of agreement between two variables and also showed whether the relationship was positive or negative. In each case a coefficient of correlation—a quantitative measure of the degree and direction of relationship existing between two or more variables—was given. This statistic is very important in that it forms the basis for gauging the efficiency of prediction.

Although there are several methods of calculating the coefficient of correlation, only two will be discussed here. The first and simplest is based on ranks. The theory underlying it is, briefly, that if two sets of scores are obtained on the same population, and if each individual is ranked on both, the size of the differences between the ranks gives a measure of the extent of agreement between the two tests. To illustrate, let us assume that four pupils have taken two tests, one in geography and one in intelligence. Their scores are as follows:

Rank-Difference Correlation

	Pat	*Lynn*	*Robin*	*Chris*
Geography	25	40	30	20
Intelligence	90	100	95	80

If we rank them, they take the following order:

	Pat	*Lynn*	*Robin*	*Chris*
Rank in geography test	3	1	2	4
Rank in intelligence test	3	1	2	4

The ranks on the two tests agree perfectly, as may be shown by taking the differences between the two sets of ranks, thus:

3	1	2	4
3	1	2	4
0	0	0	0

Since the agreement is perfect, the correlation will be perfect. Now let us suppose the scores, ranks, and differences are as follows:

	Pat	Lynn	Robin	Chris
Score in geography test	25	30	40	20
Score in intelligence test	90	110	100	80

If these are ranked they show the following order:

	Pat	Lynn	Robin	Chris
Rank in geography test	3	2	1	4
Rank in intelligence test	3	1	2	4
Differences between ranks	0	1	1	0

Here we have something less than perfect agreement, and the differences between ranks are greater than they were in the first case.

One more illustration will help to clarify this principle. Let us assume the following:

	Pat	Lynn	Robin	Chris
Score in geography test	40	30	20	15
Score in intelligence test	90	100	110	120
Rank in geography test	1	2	3	4
Rank in intelligence test	4	3	2	1
Differences between ranks	3	1	1	3

In this case we have a complete reversal of ranks between the two tests, and thus the differences are at a maximum total. This illustration, though greatly simplified, shows how agreement (or lack of it) between ranks gives a measure of the extent of correlation.

An eminent English statistician, Charles Spearman, worked out a method of determining the extent of correlation based on this principle. It is known as the *Spearman Rank-Difference Method*. As can be seen in Table A.9, we have determined the rank-difference correlation between scores in mathematics and reading for J's class. The results of these calculations, a correlation coefficient of .73, show that there is a substantial degree of relationship between scores on the mathematics test and scores on the reading test. We can say, therefore, that there is a marked tendency for pupils who do well on one to do well on the other, and vice versa. The correlation is not perfect by any means, and some individuals constitute important exceptions to the general trend—for example, R, T, and V and, to a lesser degree, D and O.

Product-
Moment
Correlation

One of the disadvantages of the Spearman Rank-Difference Method is that it is practical only with small groups. If there are large numbers of cases, the numbers denoting ranks and the possible rank differences be-

Calculation of Rank-Difference Correlation Coefficient (ρ): Scores of Twenty-Five
Pupils on Mathematics Test and Reading Test

Pupil	Score Mathematics	Score Reading	Rank Mathematics	Rank Reading	D	D²
A	44	86	4	7	3	9
B	21	68	23	18	5	25
C	14	48	25	24	1	1
D	18	70	24	16	8	64
E	46	94	2	3	1	1
F	45	102	3	2	1	1
G	52	92	1	4	3	9
H	30	72	15	15	0	0
I	39	91	6	5	1	1
J	36	80	9	9	0	0
K	31	69	14	17	3	9
L	22	62	22	21	1	1
M	23	56	21	23	2	4
N	38	73	7.5	14	6.5	42.25
O	33	66	11	19	8	64
P	33	77	11	10.5	.5	.25
Q	29	75	16.5	13	3.5	12.25
R	38	65	7.5	20	12.5	156.25
S	32	87	13	6	7	49
T	29	46	16.5	25	8.5	72.25
U	42	111	5	1	4	16
V	28	81	18	8	10	100
W	26	59	19	22	3	9
X	33	77	11	10.5	.5	.25
Y	25	76	20	12	8	64
						710.50

$$\rho = 1 - \frac{6\Sigma D^2}{N(N^2 - 1)}$$

ρ = rank-difference correlation
D = difference between ranks
N = number of cases

$$\rho = 1 - \frac{6 \times 710.50}{25(625 - 1)}$$

$$= 1 - \frac{4263}{15600}$$

$$= 1 - .27 = .73$$

come large, and when these are squared they become too cumbersome.
Aside from convenience, there are other reasons why statistical workers
generally prefer another method of correlation known as the *Pearson
Product-Moment Correlation*. Let us suppose we have measured the
heights and weights of some infants and we wish to determine whether
there is a correlation between these two variables. In order to simplify
the explanation, we use only five cases:

	Height X	Weight Y	Deviation from mean Height x	Weight y	x^2	y^2	xy
G	31	17	1	-2	1	4	-2
H	27	18	-3	-1	9	1	3
K	29	16	-1	-3	1	9	3
T	31	22	1	3	1	9	3
W	32	22	2	3	4	9	6
Mean	30	19			16	32	13

One formula (there are many variations) for the product-moment correlation is:

$$r = \frac{\Sigma xy}{\sqrt{\Sigma x^2 \times \Sigma y^2}}$$

Substituting the values obtained for cases G, H, K, T, and W gives us:

$$r = \frac{13}{\sqrt{16 \times 32}}$$
$$= \frac{13}{22.6}$$
$$= .57+$$

The product-moment coefficient of correlation shows the extent to which variations of individuals from the respective means of the distribution of two traits agree in direction and relative size. For example, T and W are both above the means in height and weight; H and K are below the means in both. Their xy products are all positive, yielding a positive value of r. However, G is above the mean in height but below the mean in weight. The xy product is negative, which reduces the Σxy and the size of r. If the sum of the negative xy's equals the sum of the positive xy's, the Σxy is zero and r is zero, showing that there is no consistent tendency for variations of individuals to agree. When the sum of the negative xy's exceeds the sum of the positive xy's, the correlation is negative, showing that variations of individuals on the two traits tend to go in opposite directions though similar in relative amount. Various types and degrees of relationships were shown graphically in Chapter 2.

LEARNING EXERCISES

11. Make a table similar to the text table above, using five cases that you think would give a negative correlation. Prove it.
12. Using the twenty-five scores in mathematics and reading (Table A.9), calculate the product-moment coefficient of correlation. (Suggestion: To reduce the labor of calculation, use 32 as the mean of the mathematics scores and 75 as the mean of the reading scores.) Compare your answer with that obtained by the rank-difference method.

A variation of the formula for r used above is:

$$r = \frac{\Sigma xy}{NS_x S_y}$$

This is useful if the standard deviation of each variable (in this case, mathematics and reading test scores) has already been calculated. All that needs to be done in addition is to calculate the xy products, substitute the different values in the formula, and solve for r.

The calculation of r from grouped data is more complicated than it is as shown here with actual scores. For further information on this procedure, textbooks in statistical methods may be consulted. A number of so-called correlation charts have been devised to make this task simpler and more mechanical. These can be obtained from publishers of standardized tests, and they are often very useful, especially if one has a large number of correlations to do. Of course, correlations as well as other statistics are most efficiently determined today by electronic computers.

USES OF CORRELATION

In Chapter 4 the criteria of a good measuring instrument were discussed. *Determining* It was stated that of all such criteria, *validity* is the most important, and *Test* different approaches to validating a test were described. One of these was *Validity* criterion-related validity, which may also be referred to as empirical or statistical validity. The extent to which a test (let us say of intelligence) correlates with a criterion—that is, with some accepted measure of intelligence—is a measure of its statistical validity. It is obvious that if the criterion is valid and the test under scrutiny does not correlate with the criterion to any noticeable extent, it cannot be regarded as having statistical validity. A test that is supposed to measure the intelligence of ten-year-old children, scores on which show the following correlations with other criteria of intelligence, would hardly be said to have statistical validity:

	With school marks over several years	*With Stanford-Binet mental ages*
Correlation of supposed test of intelligence	.17	.28

Such a test would be open to strong suspicion as a measure of intelligence, though it might conceivably prove to have validity as a measure of something else.

In situations in which statistical measures of validity are desired, the coefficient of correlation is the measure most frequently used. The correlation between scores on the measure or test whose validity is to be determined, and some established or generally accepted measure of the same quality or trait that the new test purports to measure, is a standard statistical measure of validity.

The criteria used for statistically determining the validity of a test purporting to measure mental ability would include teachers' marks, scores on standardized tests of achievement or of intelligence, chronological age (in the case of children), ratings of teachers, and possibly measures of socioeconomic status. Similar criteria would be used for validating achievement tests. The method of correlation is also used in establishing the validity of other types of tests such as aptitude, interest, and personality tests, though the criteria would necessarily be different. For example, aptitude tests and interest inventories might be validated by correlating scores on them with measures of success in the field of work they were intended to predict. Scores on personality inventories might be correlated with ratings or even clinical diagnoses.

As was discussed in Chapter 4, validity coefficients vary considerably with criteria used. The correlation of scores or IQs for a mental ability test will typically range from .40 or .50 with teachers' marks to .70 or .80 with standardized tests of achievement. As we mentioned in Chapter 4, the size of the coefficient and its interpretation depend on the situation.

Determining Test Reliability

Another important application of correlation techniques is in determining the reliability of tests. Reliability has been defined as the consistency with which a test measures whatever it does measure. There are three commonly used methods of determining reliability or consistency of measurement. The first is to give the same test twice to the same group and calculate the correlation between the two sets of scores. The second is to give two equivalent forms of a test to the same group. The third is to administer the test once only, score it by the split-halves method, correlate the half scores, and apply the Spearman-Brown formula. These methods have been explained and illustrated in Chapter 4 and are mentioned again here only as illustrations of the use of correlation techniques.

Reliability coefficients of standardized tests may be expected to reach or exceed .90; some published ones exceed .95. This presents a marked contrast with the size of the usual validity coefficients and illustrates the inadequacy of interpreting coefficients of correlation from magnitude alone. Whereas a validity coefficient of .50 may be quite acceptable, a reliability of .50 would be considered unsatisfactory for almost any test.

We may wish to know what the standard error of an obtained score is when we have given a test of known reliability. To put the problem in another way, what is the probability that a pupil's true score on a test does not differ significantly from the score actually obtained? This is another way of asking how reliable a single test score is. *Determining Reliability of a Single Test Score*

The formula for the standard error of measurement is based on the reliability coefficient. It is

$$S_{meas} = S\sqrt{1 - r}$$

where S_{meas} = the standard error of measurement
S = the standard deviation of the test
r = the reliability coefficient of the test

For example, if the reliability coefficient of a certain test is .84 and the standard deviation is 12, the equation becomes

$$\begin{aligned} S_{meas} &= 12\sqrt{1 - .84} \\ &= 12\sqrt{.16} \\ &= 12 \times .4 \\ &= 4.8 \end{aligned}$$

This tells us that the chances are approximately 2 in 3 that the true score on this test will not differ from any actual score on it by more than 4.8 points. Obviously, as the reliability of a test increases, the standard error of measurement decreases and approaches zero as a limit. This concept was explained and illustrated in Chapter 4.

Predicting Scores

When the correlation between two tests is known, it is possible to estimate a score for a pupil on one test knowing the score earned on the other test. For example, if it is known that in a given school the correlation between scores on an ability test and an achievement test in reading is .75, and if a pupil has already taken the ability test, the performance on the achievement test can be estimated before that test has been taken. Some prediction formulas are beyond the scope of this book, but one simple formula is based on z-scores:

$$z_y' = rz_x$$

where z_y' = the z-score predicted
r = the correlation between x and y
z_x = the score on the test that is known

Assume that a student has earned a z-score of +2 on the ability test and that we wish to predict the score on the reading test. Substituting in the equation, we get:

$$z_y' = (.75)2$$
$$= 1.5$$

The predicted score on reading is a z-score of +1.5, a score one and one-half standard deviations above the mean of the reading test. If this test has a mean of 50 and standard deviation of 10, the predicted score is 65.

There is nearly always error in making predictions such as the one illustrated above. The accuracy of a prediction can be estimated by finding a *standard error of estimate,* given by the formula

$$S_{est.y} = S_y\sqrt{1 - r^2}$$

where $S_{est.y}$ is the standard error of estimate. In the example of the preceding paragraph, if S_y is the standard deviation of reading scores and r is the correlation between ability and reading scores:

$$S_{est.y} = 10\sqrt{1 - (.75)^2}$$
$$= 10\sqrt{1 - .5625}$$
$$= 10\sqrt{.4375}$$
$$= 10 \times .66$$
$$= 6.6$$

This tells us that, knowing the score on the ability test, we can predict scores on the reading test with an estimated standard error of 6.6 points and that the chances are 68.26 in 100 that our prediction will not be in error by more than 6.6 points either way. In other words, if the most probable score on reading is 65, the chances are about 2 to 1 that the actual score in reading will be between 65 − 6.6, or 58.4, and 65 + 6.6, or 71.6.

We may go a step further. Adding and subtracting 2 standard errors to the estimated score of 65 gives upper and lower limits of 78.2 and 51.8, respectively, which tells us that the probability is approximately 95 to 5 that the actual reading score will be between 78.2 and 51.8. Similarly, we can predict with the probability of 99 chances in 100 that the actual reading score will be between 84.8 and 45.2, or within the limits of 3 standard errors of estimate.

LEARNING EXERCISES

13. Assume the following data: (1) correlation between IQ and marks in algebra = .64; (2) reliability of test of intelligence = .91; reliability of teacher's marks in algebra = .51; (3) standard deviation of scores on intelligence tests = 16; standard deviation of teacher's marks = 1.0 (on basis of 4 = A, 3 = B, 2 = C, 1 = D, and 0 = F). Using these data, calculate the standard error of measurement of the intelligence test and of the teacher's marks in algebra.

14. Calculate the standard error of estimate for scores on the intelligence test, knowing the pupil's mark; for the mark, knowing the score on the intelligence test.

Appendix B

EXTRACTING THE SQUARE ROOT

1. Point off from decimal by pairs in both directions. (Zeros have been added here in order to round off to one decimal at end.)

$$\sqrt{236.94} = \sqrt{2\ 36.94\ 00}$$

2. Take the nearest square root of the first number or pair—in this case, $\sqrt{2} = 1+$:

$$\frac{1}{\sqrt{2\ 36.94\ 00}}$$

3. Place this under the first digit or pair and subtract:

$$\frac{1}{\sqrt{2\ 36.94\ 00}}$$
$$\frac{1}{1}$$

4. Bring down the next pair of digits:

$$\frac{1}{\sqrt{2\ 36.94\ 00}}$$
$$\frac{1}{136}$$

5. Multiply the answer thus far obtained by 2, bring down the product, and add a zero:

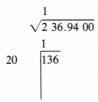

$$
\begin{array}{r}
1 \\
\sqrt{2\ 36.94\ 00} \\
1
\end{array}
$$

20 ⟌ 136

6. Use this number as a trial divisor. In this case the tentative quotient is 5.

$$
\begin{array}{r}
1\ 5 \\
\sqrt{2\ 36.94\ 00} \\
1
\end{array}
$$

20 | 136
5 |

7. Add the tentative quotient to the doubled figure with zero added, and multiply by the tentative quotient:[1]

$$
\begin{array}{r}
1\ 5 \\
\sqrt{2\ 36.94\ 00} \\
1
\end{array}
$$

20 | 136
5 |
25 | 125

(Step 8 follows.)

---

[1]Notice that although 20 goes more than six times into 136, adding 6 to 20 and multiplying by 6 would have given a product of 156, too large for our dividend of 136.

8. Subtract, bring down the next pair of numbers, and repeat the process:

$$
\begin{array}{r}
1\ 5\quad 3\quad 9 \\
\sqrt{2\ 36.94\ 00}
\end{array}
$$

$$
\begin{array}{r|l}
 & 1 \\ \hline
20 & 136 \\
\underline{5} & \\
25 & 125 \\
300 & \overline{1194} \\
\underline{3} & \\
303 & 909 \\
3060 & \overline{28500} \\
\underline{9} & \\
3069 & 27621
\end{array}
$$

9. Insert the decimal and round off: 15.39 or 15.4.

Appendix C

A SELECTIVE LIST

OF U.S. TEST PUBLISHERS

Addison-Wesley Testing Service
South Street
Reading, MA   01867
(Publisher of ETS Cooperative
Tests.)

American College Testing Program
P.O. Box 168
Iowa City, IA   52240

American Guidance Service, Inc.
Publishers Building
Circle Pines, MN 55014

Bobbs-Merrill Company, Inc.
4300 West 62nd St.
Indianapolis, IN   46206

Bureau of Educational Measurements
Kansas State Teachers College
Emporia, KS   66801

Bureau of Educational Research
and Service
University of Iowa
Iowa City, IA   52240

California Test Bureau/McGraw-Hill
Del Monte Research Park
Monterey, CA   93940

Consulting Psychologists Press
577 College Ave.
Palo Alto, CA   94306

Cooperative Tests and Services
Educational Testing Services
Princeton, NJ   08540
(See also Addison-Wesley)

Educational and Industrial Testing
Service
P.O. Box 7234
San Diego, CA   92107

Ginn and Company
P.O. Box 2649
1250 Fairwood Ave.
Columbus, Ohio   43216
(See also Personnel Press)

Harcourt Brace Jovanovich, Inc.
757 Third Ave.
New York, NY   10017
(See also Psychological Corporation.)

Houghton Mifflin Company
Test Editorial Offices
P.O. Box 1970
Iowa City, IA   52240

Institute for Personality and Ability Testing
1602 Coronado Drive
Champaign, IL   61820

Personnel Press, Inc.
P.O. Box 2649
1250 Fairwood Ave.
Columbus, Ohio   43216
(Testing division of Ginn and Company)

Psychological Corporation
757 Third Ave.
New York, NY   10017
(Testing subsidiary of Harcourt Brace Jovanovich.)

Psychometric Affiliates
1743 Monterey
Chicago, IL   60611

Scholastic Testing Service
480 Meyer Road
Bensonville, IL   60611

Science Research Associates, Inc.
259 East Erie St.
Chicago, IL   60611

Sheridan Psychological Services, Inc.
P.O. Box 6101
Orange, CA   92667

Stanford University Press
Stanford, CA   94305

C. H. Stoelting Company
1350 South Kostner Ave.
Chicago, IL   60623

Teachers College Press
1234 Amsterdam Ave.
New York, NY   10027

Western Psychological Services
12031 Wilshire Blvd.
Los Angeles, CA   90025

GLOSSARY OF MEASUREMENT TERMS

Achievement Test   A procedure or measuring instrument, usually a paper-and-pencil test, used to measure student progress toward curricular goals—that is, knowledge or skills usually acquired through classroom instruction.

Accountability   Ability to demonstrate the achievement of objectives. Also refers to the requirement that educators account for pupils' achievement and to a system for assigning responsibility for educational results.

Adjustment Inventory   An instrument designed to measure the reaction of an individual to aspects of environment. Either a self-report inventory used by an individual to describe reactions or perceptions or a device by which an observer records impressions of another person.

Affective Objective   A statement of a desired learning outcome that involves feelings and emotions more than knowledge or understanding. Examples include likes and dislikes, attitudes and interests, prejudices, morals, and values.

Age Norms   A table of average scores for different age groups. If the average test score for a group of children aged 8 years 6 months is 25, 8-6 would be the age norm for the score of 25. Also called *age equivalents.*

Alternate-Forms Reliability   Degree of correspondence as measured by a coefficient of correlation between equivalent or parallel forms of a test administered to the same subjects, usually at one sitting or with not more than a day or two intervening.

Anecdotal Record   A written description of an observed incident in the behavior of an individual.

Aptitude   Capacity or potential, whether innate or acquired, to learn from instruction or to develop proficiency in a particular area. A person of high aptitude in music has the characteristics basic to the acquisition of a superior degree of proficiency as a result of training. Academic aptitude refers to a pupil's ability to achieve in school.

Aptitude Test   A test designed to measure potential for success in a certain type of endeavor. Scores on aptitude tests are used to predict the success a student will have in a certain type of instructional program or in a particular line of work or vocation.

Arithmetic Mean   A common measure of the average of a set of numbers. Obtained by summing the scores and dividing by the number of scores. Frequently referred to simply as *mean*.

Attitude   A predisposition to approach or avoid or to favor or oppose a person, idea, group, or institution. Attitudes are related to biases, prejudices, and interests.

Average   One of several measures of central tendency. The most common measures are the median, the arithmetic mean, and the mode. The term *average* is often used as a synonym for *arithmetic mean*.

Battery   A set of different tests standardized on the same population. A battery of achievement tests would include separate tests covering several curricular areas.

Behavioral Objective   A statement of a desired outcome of instruction, put in terms of specific observable actions of the learner.

Ceiling   The upper limit of ability measured by a test. *Ceiling effect* refers to the inability of tests to differentiate between individuals with just enough ability to reach the ceiling and those with greater ability.

Central Tendency   A measure of average, the typical score, or the score around which the scores in a set tend to cluster.

Check List   A list of either-or characteristics or behaviors that are to be checked as present or not present in the individual, object, or institution being described or evaluated.

Class Analysis Chart   A table or profile that shows the relative performance of members of a class on a test or tests, usually the several parts of a test battery.

Class Interval   A category of a frequency distribution into which scores are grouped. In the computation of the arithmetic mean and standard deviation, the scores in a class interval are treated statistically as though their average were equal to the midpoint of the interval.

Classification Item   A form of matching item in which objects or terms are to be classified. For example, a test item could require the examinees to classify automobiles as foreign or domestic or to classify words as parts of speech.

Coefficient of Correlation (r)   A measure of the relationship between two sets of measurements for the same group. Usually a product-moment coefficient with a minimum of -1.00 showing perfect inverse relationship (that is, the largest score of one set associated with the smallest of the other set) and a maximum of $+1.00$ showing a perfect direct relationship.

Cognitive Objective   A statement of desired outcomes that emphasizes knowledge or understanding.

Completion Item   A test item requiring examinees to provide the missing word or phrase in a statement.

Concurrent Validity   A type of empirical (criterion related) validity in which a test is validated by correlating scores on it with some other measure taken simultaneously, such as teachers' marks.

Construct Validity   A form of logical validity established by showing the relationship between test scores and a construct, a logical criterion, established by analysis of relationships expected on logical grounds. If one or more factors, such as age, sex, or scholastic achievement, were logically related to the development of a skill, evidence of construct validity of a test might include data and reasoning about the relationship of these factors to the test scores.

Content Validity   The extent to which test items reflect and fully cover the curriculum the test was designed to measure. A form of logical validity determined by a careful analysis of a test in terms of the content, objectives, and instruction comprising the curriculum. Also called *curricular validity*.

Correction for Guessing   An adjustment of scores on choice-type tests to correct for the chance that some answers are correct because of successful guessing. The most common approach is to reduce the number of right answers by a fraction of the wrong answers. Seldom used in standardized tests today.

Correlation   *See* Coefficient of correlation.

Criterion   A standard against which items or, more commonly, test scores are compared. Used as the end result to be predicted by the item or score.

Criterion-Referenced Test   A test that is interpreted by comparing an individual's performance with an *a priori* criterion for passing or failing, such as a specified percent correct, rather than by comparing with the performance of other persons. The items of a criterion-referenced test are usually constructed to measure a specific behavioral objective. Individuals who achieve the criterion on the test may be said to have achieved the objective.

Criterion-Related Validity   The extent to which the scores of a test are related to standard measures or criteria of the same ability or characteristic. The relationship is usually measured by a correlation coefficient. Also called *empirical validity*.

Cumulative Frequency   The number of examinees earning a given score plus all those earning lower scores. Obtained in frequency distributions by adding the frequency in an interval to all those below the interval.

Decile   The score values that divide a score distribution into ten parts containing equal numbers of scores. The same as percentiles ending in 0 (for example, P_{10}, P_{20}, . . . , P_{90}).

Derived Score   Any score obtained by converting a raw score, such as the number correct, to another system of measurement. Examples include percentile ranks and standard scores.

Deviation   The difference between a score and some reference point, commonly the mean.

Deviation IQ   A standard score on an intelligence test based on the deviation between an individual's score and the average score for persons of that age. Deviation IQs have a normal distribution with a mean of 100 and usually a standard deviation of 16.

Diagnostic Test   A test designed to identify specific learning or achievement difficulties. Usually designed on the basis of a theory or research on the factors underlying successful achievement in a school subject.

Difficulty Index   The percentage of a defined group answering a test item correctly. Large indexes indicate easy items.

Discrimination Index   A measure of the extent to which a test item differentiates between high and low students as determined by some criterion. A commonly used index is based on the difference in success on an item for the top and bottom 27 percent of examinees according to total test score.

Dispersion   The extent to which scores in a set tend to be spread out or to vary about an average.

Distractor   An incorrect response to a choice-type item stem or question. Sometimes called *foil*.

Domain-Referenced Test   A test that contains a random sample of a well-defined set of tasks (a domain), interpreted with respect to the percentage of tasks performed correctly. If, for example, nine out of ten tasks from a much larger domain are performed correctly, the inference is that 90 percent of the tasks of the domain would have been performed correctly.

Educational Age   The age for which a given score on an achievement test is the average. If a pupil's composite achievement score is the same as the average earned by children 7 years and 5 months old, the educational age on the battery is said to be 7-5.

Empirical Validity   The extent to which a test measures other scores or values used as a criterion for the test. Usually reported as a correlation coefficient. (*See also* Criterion-related validity.)

Equivalent Forms   Two forms of a test with equal means and standard deviations, covering the same content and having items of the same difficulty and type.

Essay Test   A test that requires students to compose answers to questions. An examinee must recall and organize answers in written form. The scoring of such responses is subjective, calling for exercise of judgment by the scorer.

Evaluation   A judgmental process involving the comparison of data with a standard. Addresses questions of: How good? How adequate? How satisfactory? Evaluation may be based on only test scores, but more commonly it involves the use of many types of information, including subjective data.

Expectancy Table   A two-way table in which the relationship between measures of achievement (a criterion) and scores on a predictor measure is shown. Entries in the table show the relative frequency with which levels of achievement are reached by people at given levels on the predictor measure.

Face Validity   Apparent validity—that is, superficial appearances that suggest a test will measure what it is intended to measure.

Factor Analysis   A statistical procedure based on intercorrelations between tests. Its purpose is to identify a small number of hypothetical factors (fewer in number than the number of tests) that will account for the intercorrelations between the tests. Used to explore the nature and structure of intelligence and personality.

Forced-Choice Item   A multiple-choice item requiring a choice between responses that appear equally acceptable but that have been determined to have different discriminating value—for example, they are chosen more often (or less often) by people having leadership qualities than by people lacking them. Used almost exclusively in personality testing.

Formative Evaluation   The use of data to modify and improve an educational program while it is being developed, or student learning as it is taking place; in contrast to *summative evaluation*, used to determine effectiveness after a program has been completed.

Frequency Distribution   An orderly arrangement of scores in a series of intervals between highest and lowest scores showing the number of scores in each interval. Also referred to as a *distribution*.

Frequency Polygon   The graph of a frequency distribution. Usually the base line represents the score scale, and the heights of the vertical lines show the frequency or number of examinees earning the various scores. Dots placed at appropriate heights over the middle of intervals are connected by straight lines.

Grade Equivalent   The grade for which a given score is the average. If a pupil's score is equal to the average score for pupils in the seventh month of grade 5, the grade equivalent is 5.7.

Grade Norms   A set of scores showing the averages for pupils at different grade levels. (*See also* Grade Equivalent.)

Grade Point Average (GPA)   A measure of school achievement found by dividing honor points by credit hours. Most commonly, honor points are assigned A = 4, B = 3, C = 2, D = 1, F = 0. A person who carried five 3-hour courses and earned 2 A's, 2 B's, and a C would have 6 hours of A for 24 honor points, 6 hours of B for 18 points, and 3 hours of C for 6 points. The GPA would be (24 + 18 + 6) ÷ 15; 48 ÷ 15 = 3.2.

Graphic Rating Scale   *See* Rating scale.

Group Test   A test that can be administered by one person to more than one examinee at a time.

Guessing   Responding to a question in a random manner on a choice-type test or answering a question when not absolutely certain of the answer.

Guess-Who Technique   A method of peer appraisal in which the members of a group are asked to name other members who best fit a description—for example, best friend, most popular, best student.

Halo Effect   The tendency for a rater to allow a generally favorable impression to influence ratings assigned on a specific trait.

Histogram   A graph of a frequency distribution in which the base line represents the score scale, and rectangles of width equal to the size of the class interval have heights equal to the frequencies associated with intervals.

Individual Test   A test that can be administered by a person to only one examinee at a time.

Intelligence Quotient (IQ)   Originally the ratio of mental age to chronological age, multiplied by 100. The average IQ is 100. Developed as a means of expressing rate of mental development or brightness. (*See also* Deviation IQ.)

Intelligence Test   A test designed to measure general mental ability. Now frequently comprised of subtests of different types of materials (for example, verbal and nonverbal).

Interest Inventory   A test or test-like questionnaire designed to measure the areas or patterns of interest a person has. Usually norms are based on typical responses of different occupational groups. Used as part of educational and vocational guidance programs.

Interpretive Item   Test item, usually true-false or multiple-choice, based on a passage, graph, table, or other material presented to the examinee. Such items provide common factual material to all examinees so that emphasis may be placed on use of concepts or principles for interpreting the information.

Inventory   A questionnaire or check list designed, as the name suggests, to identify an individual's characteristics, usually characteristics associated with personality, interests, or attitudes. Not a test in the usual sense.

Irrelevant Clue   An element in a test item that calls attention to correct answers or tends to discredit incorrect responses or distractors.

Item   A single question or exercise on a test.

Item Analysis   The process of studying the characteristics of a test item, usually based on data obtained from examinees. Finding difficulty and discrimination indices is a common part of the process.

Kuder-Richardson Formulas   Formulas for estimating reliability from information about individual items, or the mean, standard deviation, and number of items in a test. Obtained from one administration of a test.

Likert Method   Employs a series of statements to which examinees respond by indicating the extent to which they agree or disagree. Used widely in attitude scales.

Marks   Measures of classroom achievement. Usually expressed as letters (A, B, C, D, F), although percentages and numbers are also used.

Mastery Test   A test covering material or skills in which perfect performance on an *a priori* criterion of mastery, such as 90 percent correct, is the goal when pupils have successfully completed an instructional unit—for example, a test over the addition of all one-digit numbers.

Matching Item   A test form in which items in one list are to be associated or matched with items in another list. Similar to classification tests.

Mean   *See* Arithmetic mean.

Measurement   Process of assigning numbers to quantity or quality of a trait or characteristic being measured.

Median   The point value above and below which 50 percent of a group of scores fall. The middle score of an odd-numbered group; midway between two middle scores of an even-numbered group.

Mental Age (MA)   A description of level of mental development based on the age of a reference group. A child whose score on a mental test is equal to the average score of children 9½ years old is said to have a mental age of 9½ years.

Mode   A measure of average. The score in a set earned by the largest number of people. In a frequency distribution, the mode is the midpoint of the interval with the largest number of cases or scores.

Multiple-Choice Item   A test item with a question or incomplete statement, called the stem, followed by a series of options, usually four or five. The examinees' task is to choose the best or the correct answer.

Norm   Typically, the average score on a test made by a defined group. A statistic that describes the performance of groups of examinees defined by age, grade, percentile, or other criterion.

Normal Distribution   A form of score distribution resembling a cross-section of a bell. A smooth curve with highest frequency at the middle, decreasing toward each extreme. Measurements of many traits, also random errors, tend to form a normal distribution.

Normalized Standard Scores   Scores expressed on a scale with known mean and standard deviation and a normal distribution. The process of obtaining such scores assures that the transformed distribution will be shaped as a normal distribution.

Norm-Referenced Test   A test that is interpreted by comparing an individual's score with the scores of other individuals in a group defined by some characteristic such as age or grade in school.

Objective Test   A test scored by a predetermined key or set of answers, often by test-scoring machine. A term used with multiple-choice, true-false, matching, or other similar types of items.

Objective   A statement of goals or desired outcome of instruction. Stated frequently as behavior or skill to be measured by tests or examinations.

Objectives-Referenced Test   A test interpreted with reference to the percentage of items for a particular objective that are answered correctly instead of with reference to the scores of others. If an *a priori* percentage is specified for passing the test, it may be referred to as a *criterion-referenced* test.

Ogive   A graph of a cumulative frequency distribution. With educational data, it frequently takes an S shape.

Percentile (P)   Point in a score distribution below which a certain proportion of the scores fall. The 65th percentile is the point below which 65 percent of the scores in the set fall.

Percentile Band   A range of percentiles within which the "true" percentile is expected to fall. Typically, the percentiles corresponding to a range of one standard error of measurement above and one below the observed score. Used to emphasize the fallibility of tests and to preclude the assumption that a single score is absolutely accurate.

Percentile Rank (PR)   A method of describing test performance based on the percentage of a reference group with lower scores than the one being described. A student who has earned a percentile rank of 42 has achieved a score that falls at the 42nd *percentile* of the reference group.

Performance Test   Usually a test requiring manipulatory or motor response, as in a test of manual dexterity. May also employ paper and pencil as in a test of shorthand, called a *work sample.*

Personality Test   A test used to assess some affective or nonintellectual characteristic of an individual.

Power Test   A test designed to measure level of knowledge or skill. The items usually range from easy to quite difficult, and the examinee does as much as ability permits, with generous time limits or no time limit.

Practice Effect   The influence on test performance of previous experience on the same or on a similar test or testing procedure.

Prediction   A method of forecasting, as predicting a student's college grades on the basis of high-school grades. Estimating performance of a person in one situation based on the experience of similar people for whom both measures are available.

Predictive Validity   A type of empirical validity determined by how well scores on a test correlate with some criterion in the future—such as success on the job or grade point average.

Product-Moment Correlation   *See* Coefficient of correlation.

Product Scale   A series of specimens of such things as handwriting, composition, or drawing that is arranged, and usually numbered in order, to represent different degrees of quality or merit. Another product that is to be evaluated is judged by comparing it with the specimens defining the scale. Also called a *quality scale.*

Profile   A graphic representation of scores on different tests, usually parts of a battery. A method for facilitating comparison on different tests for an individual or a group. Scores on the tests should be expressed in comparable units on the same scale.

Prognostic Test   A test on which scores are interpreted to show probability of future success or failure in a particular field of work or subject.

Projective Technique   A relatively unstructured measurement procedure that allows the examinee freedom to project thoughts, interests, motives, and values, which a psychologist then interprets. Usually consists of a set of stimuli to which the examinee responds without restrictions or inhibitions.

Quartile Deviation (Q)   *See* Semi-interquartile range.

Quartiles   The three score points dividing a frequency distribution into four equal parts, each containing one-fourth of the frequencies. The first quartile is P_{25}, the second P_{50}, the third P_{75}.

Random Sample   A sample drawn in such a way that every member of the population from which it is drawn has an equal and independent chance of being included, thus eliminating bias from methods of selection.

Range   A measure of dispersion of scores found by subtracting the smallest score in a set from the largest score.

Rank-Difference Correlation (ρ)   A measure of degree of association between two sets of measures based on difference between ranks of pairs of values for each individual. A conveniently found measure of relationship, especially for small groups.

Rating Scale   A method of obtaining a systematic sampling of opinion regarding specific characteristics of persons or things. Individuals or items being rated may be assigned to positions on a graphic scale that represents a continuum from little to much of the characteristic being rated, or they may be assigned one of a set of numbers representing different degrees of that characteristic.

Ratio IQ   *See* Intelligence Quotient.

Raw Score   The number or percent of items of a test answered correctly. May also be number right less some fraction of number wrong, or other first score not converted to another scale such as percentile ranks or standard scores.

Readiness Test   A measure of the basic skills or abilities needed for success in a given type of instruction. A reading readiness test, for example, measures the information, skills, and level of development requisite for success in learning to read.

Recall Item   A test question, either completion or free-response type, in which the solution requires recall from memory of previously learned material.

Recognition Item   A test item in which choices are presented and the examinee is required to identify or recognize the correct answer.

Regression Effect   The tendency for any predicted score to be closer to the mean of other predicted scores than the score from which it was predicted was to the mean of the scores used for prediction. This occurs whenever the correlation between the predictor and the predicted scores is less than perfect.

Reliability   The consistency of measurement. The accuracy with which a test measures whatever it measures. Expressed in the form of a coefficient of correlation or the standard error of measurement.

Representative Sample   A sample drawn in such a way as to ensure that the population is represented with regard to certain characteristics. Often, a sample stratified with respect to particular criteria such as geographic region or socioeconomic level.

Scaled Scores   A system of scores similar to standard scores that is developed to relate and give uniform meaning to the scores on different levels or forms of a test.

Scatter Diagram   A graph or chart showing classification of individuals on each of two measures at the same time. Frequently used as a method for showing the degree of association between two measures.

Self-Correlation   The correlation of two sets of measures obtained by using the same instrument on the same population at different times. Used to show stability of responses to a test over time. A form of test reliability called the *coefficient of stability*.

Semi-Interquartile Range (Q) A measure of the dispersion of scores found by taking half of the range between the 75th and 25th percentiles. $Q = (P_{75} - P_{25})$ 2.

Sigma The Greek letter sigma (σ) is used to indicate the standard deviation of the scores of a theoretical distribution or population when it is important to differentiate this value from the standard deviation (S), computed for a sample set of scores. The capital letter sigma (Σ) is used to indicate the mathematical procedure of summing.

Sigma Score A standard score with a mean of 50 and a standard deviation of 10. The distribution of sigma scores is not necessarily normal as is that of *T*-scores. Sigma scores are sometimes called *linear T-scores* or, more generally, *Z-scores*.

Skew The tendency of a distribution to have the concentration (greatest number) of scores near one extreme of the distribution—that is, to be nonsymmetrical. If the frequencies are concentrated at the low end of the distribution, it is said to be positively skewed; conversely for negative skew.

Sociometry A technique for measuring interpersonal relationships among members of a group. Generally, members are asked to answer questions revealing choice or rejection of other members. The results are often depicted in a chart or graph known as a *sociogram*.

Spearman-Brown Formula Given a test of some length and reliability, the formula shows the expected reliability for a test of similar quality but of different length. Commonly used to estimate reliability of a test for which correlation between split halves has been determined.

Spearman Rank-Difference Method See Rank-difference correlation.

Specific Determiner A characteristic of the statement of an objective test item that is an unintended clue to a correct or incorrect answer.

Split-Halves Correlation Correlation between scores on two halves of a test. Frequently based on scores on odd- and even-numbered items. This correlation, corrected by use of the Spearman-Brown formula, is one method of obtaining an estimate of reliability of a test.

Standard Deviation (S) A measure of the dispersion of scores around the average of the set. Based on the difference between each score and the mean. The greater the dispersion of scores, the larger the standard deviation, and vice versa.

Standard Error of Estimate (S$_{est.y}$) An estimate of the magnitude of the errors likely to be present when predicting individuals' scores on one measure from their scores on another measure. It is the standard deviation of the errors in such predictions and is estimated from the standard deviation of the predicted scores and the correlation coefficient between the predictor and the predicted scores. In approximately two-thirds of the cases, the observed score would not differ from the predicted score by more than one standard error of estimate.

*Standard Error of Measurement (S*meas*)* An estimate of the magnitude of errors likely to be present in scores obtained from a test. It can be estimated from the standard deviation of the test and its reliability coefficient. In approximately two-thirds of the cases, the obtained scores would not differ from the true scores by more than one standard error of measurement.

Standard Score A derived score expressed on a known scale. Standard scores are expressed in terms of the deviations of the raw scores from the mean in units of the standard deviation of the distribution; hence the name standard score. Examples are *z*-scores, sigma scores, and *T*-scores.

Standardized Tests A test carefully developed by experts according to accepted principles, administered according to standardized procedures. Used to obtain comparable measures in different classes or different schools. Usually interpreted in terms of norms or scales that have been predetermined.

Stanine A standard-score scale ranging from a low of 1 to a high of 9, with a mean of 5 and a standard deviation of 2. A prescribed percentage of a group are always within a given stanine—for example, the highest 4 percent receive 9s and the lowest 4 percent receive 1s.

Summative Evaluation Evaluation to determine the effectiveness of student learning or of an educational program after it has been completed. (*See also* Formative evaluation.)

Survey Test A test, frequently a battery, designed to measure achievement across a broad spectrum of areas or topics. Results may suggest areas for which more refined measures should be obtained.

Table of Specifications An outline of test content, specifying the number or proportion of items for each type of content. Often a two-way chart with content categories listed on one dimension and behavior or ability characteristics listed on another.

True-False Item A statement, usually declarative but sometimes in question form, that examinees are to judge as true or false. T-F, yes-no, right-wrong, or other similar responses are generally called for.

True Score A useful concept in test theory, it is the score one would obtain on a test under perfect conditions, free of all error. Also the average score of an individual on an infinite number of equivalent tests.

T-Score A normalized standard score with a mean of 50 and standard deviation of 10. Sometimes called *McCall T-score.*

Validity   The extent to which a test measures all of what it is intended to measure and nothing else. The value of a test for a specific purpose—selecting students who will succeed in a vocational program or the extent to which a test constitutes an adequate measure of the objectives and content of a course.

Variability   The dispersion of scores around the average of the set. The heterogeneity of a set of measures.

Variance   A measure of the dispersion of a set of scores about the mean of the set that is equal to the square of the standard deviation. A technical term not to be confused with *variability.*

z-Score   The simplest type of standard score, obtained by dividing the difference between a score and the mean of the score distribution by the standard deviation of the distribution.

Z-Score   *See* Sigma score.

INDEX OF NAMES

Hagen, Elizabeth, 298n
Hakstian, A. Ralph, 156
Harrow, Anita J., 126n
Hathaway, Starke R., 345n
Henderson, Robert W., 358n
Henri, V., 272
Hieronymus, A. N., 139n
Hildreth, Gertrude, 259n
Holtzman, Wayne H., 363n
Honzik, Marjorie P., 285n, 286n

Jacobs, Alfred, 345n
Jensen, Arthur, 291

Karlsen, Bjorn, 226n, 238n, 255n
Kirk, Samuel, 13
Kohn, Sherwood, D., 12n, 17
Krathwohl, David R., 126n
Kuder, G. Frederic, 106n, 217n, 355n
Kuhlmann, Fred, 274

Layman, Elizabeth M., 267n, 268n
Likert, Rensis, 362n
Lindholm, Byron W., 285n
Lindquist, E. F., 139n, 241n
Lindzey, G., 289n
Loehlin, J. C., 289
Lorge, Irving, 298n

McCall, William A., 63
McCune, George H., 140n
MacFarlane, Jean, 285n
MacGinitie, Walter H., 248, 251n, 253n
McKillop, Anne S., 255n
McKinley, J. Charnley, 345n
Madden, Richard, 226n, 238n, 255n
Mager, R. F., 367
Merrill, Maud A., 274, 275n, 276n
Merwin, Jack C., 226n, 238n
Meyers, Charles E., 358n
Miller, W. S., 277, 282–283
Mooney, Ross L., 343n
Moreno, Jacob L., 389
Morse, Horace T., 140n
Myklebust, Helmer R., 378n

Nelson, C. H., 137
Nelson, M. J., 86
Noll, Victor H., 153n, 175n

Odell, C. W., 5
Olson, Willard C., 382
Otis, Arthur S., 277

Pegnato, Carl W., 470
Pintner, Rudolf, 277
Pressey, S. L., 441, 446n

Remmers, H. H., 361
Richardson, M. W., 106n, 217n
Robeck, Mildred C., 394
Rudman, Herbert C., 226n, 238n

Sapon, Stanley M., 325n
Scannell, D. P., 241n
Schlaff, Allan, 345n
Schrammel, H. E., 278n
Seashore, Carl E., 321n
Seashore, H. G., 330n
Simon, Theodore, 96, 272
Spearman, Charles, 280
Spuhler, J. N., 289n
Starch, Daniel, 154
Stern, Wilhelm, 281
Stone, C. W., 5
Strong, E. K., 351, 353n
Sybil, B. G., 345n

Terman, Lewis M., 274, 275n, 276n,
    277, 281, 326
Thelen, Herbert A., 442
Thorndike, Edward L., 258n, 277
Thorndike, Robert L., 16n, 298n
Thurstone, L. L., 280, 361
Torrance, E. Paul, 327

Vallance, Theodore R., 156
Voelker, Paul F., 320n

Wechsler, David, 296–297
Wendel, Frederick C., 14
Wesman, A. G., 330n
Willingham, W., 12n
Wood, E. R., 278n
Wundt, Wilhelm, 272

Zimmerman, Wayne S., 345n
Zinner, Elayne G., 358n

INDEX OF SUBJECTS

Answer keys, *see* Scoring keys
Answer sheets, 113, 118–119, 202, 203 (fig.), 205, 410–412
Aptitude
  academic, *see* Achievement tests; Intelligence tests
  approaches to testing, 315–316
  for art, 322–324
  clerical, 319–321
  for creative thinking, 326–329
  for foreign languages, 324–326
  mechanical, 317–319
  musical, 321–322
Aptitude tests, 6, 14–15, 314–337
  batteries, 316, 330–336
  construction of, 315–316
  in counseling and guidance programs, 330, 451–452
Aptitude Tests for Occupations, 335
Area transformations, 63
Arithmetic mean, 36
Arithmetic, tests in, 260–262. *See also* Mathematics
Army Alpha test, 6, 112, 277–279
Army Beta test, 6, 278–279, 294
Army General Classification Test, 311
Art aptitude tests, 322–324
Arthur Point Scale of Performance Tests, 298
Arthur Stencil Design Test, 298
Assembly-line scoring, 423
Attitudes, measurement of, 135, 360–371, 396–399
Attitude scales, 361–370
Audiometer, 471
Averages, 35–38. *See also* Central tendency
Ayres scale, 259

Basal mental age, 276
Basic skills, tests of, 241–242, 257. *See also* Mathematics; Reading tests
Batteries
  aptitude, 316, 330–336
  basic skills, 241–242
  survey, 224–246, 264, 406–407, 439
BEC Personality Rating Schedule, 376
Behavior, 144, 365–366, 374
  modification of, 382–383
  observation of, 382–400
  rating of, 380–381

Behavioral objectives, 133–134
  list of verbs for, 133
Bennett Hand-Tool Dexterity Test, 319
Bennett Mechanical Comprehension Test, 319
Bennett Stenographic Aptitude Test, 320
Bias, in tests, 14, 240, 289. *See also* Culture-fair tests
Binet scales, 68, 273–277, 280, 284, 285, 287–289, 296, 302
Binet-Simon intelligence tests, 96
Boehm Test of Basic Concepts, 311
Business aptitude tests, *see* Clerical aptitude tests

California Achievement Tests, 239–241
California Pre-school Schedule, 285
California Psychological Inventory, 345
California Test of Mental Maturity, 310–311
Capacity, measurement of, 271–337
Career Development Program, 358–359
Career education, 358–359, 454
Career planning, 407. *See also* Occupational choice
Career Planning Program, 358–359
Center for the Study of Evaluation, 465
Central tendency
  error of, 379
  measures of, 35–38, 486–488
Chance, correction for, 167–168
Child Behavior Rating Scale, 375–377
Christensen-Guilford Fluency Tests, 329
Chronological age, 67–68, 276, 282–283
Civil Service examination, 15
Clapp-Young Self-Marking Tests, 113–114
Classification items, 171
Class intervals of distributions, 481–484
Class profile, 73, 115, 439–440
Clerical aptitude tests, 319–321
Clues, in test items, 173, 191, 202
Coefficient of correlation, 45, 49–52
  size of, and reliability, 108–110
Coefficient of reliability, 103–110

Coefficient of validity, 97–98
Cognitive Abilities Test, 298–303
Cognitive domain, educational objectives for, 126–127
College Entrance Examination Board, 6, 305, 402
College Interest Inventory, 358
College Qualification Tests, 311
Colleges and universities, 5, 88
Columbia Mental Maturity Scale, 298
Commercial aptitude tests, *see* Clerical aptitude tests
Completion test items, 153, 163–165
Comprehensive sampling approach, to test development, *see* Conventional approach
Comprehensive Tests of Basic Skills, 239–242
Concurrent validity, 94
Construct validity, 92, 95–97, 234
Content Evaluation Series, 264
Content validity, 92–95, 207, 233–234, 267
Conventional approach, to test development, 224, 241, 242–243
Convergent thinking, 326
Converted score, 73–74, 108. *See also* Standard scores
Cooperative Achievement Tests, 264–266
Cooperative English Tests, 74, 108
Cooperative Primary Test, 241
Cooperative School and College Ability Tests, Series II, 303–306
Correlation, 45, 49–50, 272, 501–509
  equivalent forms, 104–105
  interitem, *see* split-halves
  linear, 50
  measures of, 45–52, 501–505
  for prediction, 51–52
  product-moment (r), 46, 503–505
  rank-difference, 501–502
  and reliability, 103–107, 506–507
  self, 103–104
  size of coefficient of, 50–52
  split-halves, 105–106
  and validity, 94, 97–98, 505–506
Cost of testing, *see* Economy of testing
Counseling and guidance, 7, 330, 405, 436, 450–454
Course content, and objectives, 123, 136–144

Crawford Small Parts Dexterity Test, 319
Creativity tests, 326–329, 470
Creativity Tests for Children, 329
Criterion keying, 340
Criterion-referenced testing, 7, 22, 266–269
  analysis of results in, 215–217
  content validity in, 93
  development of, 82–83, 85, 247
  and marking, 459
  in mathematics, 268–269
  percent-correct scores for, 57–58
  purpose of, 80–81, 215
  in reading, 267–269
  reliability of, 218
  sensitivity to instruction, 83
  for single area or subject, 247
  and tailored tests, 269
Criterion-related validity, 92, 94–95
Culturally disadvantaged, testing of, 292–294. *See also* Minorities, issues in testing of
Culture Fair Intelligence Tests, 309–310
Culture-fair tests, 14, 293, 306, 309–310. *See also* Bias, in tests
Culture-free tests, 293
Cumulative record, *see* Record, permanent
Curricular validity, 93n. *See also* Content validity
Curriculum
  evaluation of, 405, 436, 464–466
  and standardized achievement tests, 222–223

Davis-Eells Test of General Intelligence, 306–309
Derived scores and norms, 54, 56–77
  relationships among, 68–69
Detroit Clerical Aptitudes Examination, 320
Detroit Mechanical Aptitudes Examination, 319
Developed abilities, test of, 224
Deviation IQ, 68, 277, 283–286. *See also* Intelligence quotient; Ratio IQ
Diagnosis, testing for, 405, 436, 445–450

Factor analysis
  and aptitude test batteries, 316, 330
  and attitude scales, 363
  and self-report inventories, 341,
    345–346
Faked responses, 341, 345, 349, 365
Forced-choice technique, 341
Foreign language aptitude tests, 324–
  326
Formboards, 295
Freeman scale, 259
Frequency distribution, 480–485. *See
  also* Graphs of frequency distributions
Functional approach, to test development, 224, 241, 243–245

Gates Basic Reading Test, 70
Gates-MacGinitie Reading Tests,
  251–254
*Gates-MacGinitie Reading Tests:
  Readiness Skills*, 248–250
*Gates-McKillop Reading Diagnostic
  Tests*, 255–256
General Aptitude Test Battery, 316,
  335, 336
General Clerical Test, 320, 452–453
General Education Provisions Act, 11
Generalizable skills approach, to test
  development, *see* Functional
  approach
Generosity error, 379
Gettysburg Edition, Ayres scale, 259
g factor, in intelligence theories, 280
Gifted children, 405, 436, 469–472
Goals, and objectives, 124–125
Gordon Personal Inventory, 341–343,
  349
Gordon Personal Profile, 341–343, 349
Grade equivalent, *see* Grade score
Grade placement, *see* Placement and
  promotion
Grade retention, 439, 441
Grade score, 70–71
Grading, *see* Marking
Graphic rating scales, 374–376
Graphs of frequency distributions,
  495–500
Graves Design Judgment Test, 324
Group-factor theory of intelligence,
  280–281

Grouping
  homogeneous, 405, 436, 442–445
  methods of, 442–443
Group testing, for intelligence, 277–
  279, 298–311
Guessing, at test answers, 166–168,
  169, 184
  correction for, 167–168
Guess-who technique, 395–396, 397
Guidance, *see* Counseling and
  guidance
*Guilford-Zimmerman Temperament
  Survey*, 345

Halo effect, 379
Handicapped children, 470–471
Handwriting tests, 257–260
Healy Picture Completion Test II, 298
Hearing tests, 471
*Henmon-Nelson Tests of Mental Abil-
  ity*, 311
Heredity, and IQ, 288–292
Heritability ratio, 291
High school, *see* Secondary school
Hildreth scale, 259
Holtzman Inkblot, 346
Home economics, rating device for, 143
Homogeneous grouping, 405, 436,
  442–445
Homogeneous keying, 340
Horn Art Aptitude Inventory, 324

Illiterates, intelligence tests for, 278,
  294
Individualized instruction, 134, 465–
  466
Individual testing, for intelligence,
  272–277, 296–298
Ink blot tests, 346–347
Instructional objectives, *see* Objectives
Intellect, *see* Intelligence
Intelligence
  basic concepts of measuring, 279–
    294
  and creativity, 329
  current procedures of measuring,
    294–311
  definition of, 271
  history of measurement of, 272–279
  measurement of, 271–313
  theories of, 271, 280–281

Normal distribution *(continued)*
  of IQs, 286–288
  and marking, 457–458
  of standard scores, 62–74
Norm group, 80
Norm-referenced testing, 22, 80–82, 449
  interpretation of, 115, 235–238, 240
Norms
  adequacy of, 90, 116–117, 408
  age score as, 70–71
  as basis for comparisons, 75–77
  establishment of, 84
  grade score as, 70–71
  for placement and promotion, 439
  for standardized achievement batteries, 236–237, 241
  for standardized tests, 66–67, 76, 90–91, 116–117
  tables of, 56, 115
  see also reports of norms in descriptions of individual tests
Numerical rating scales, 375–378

Objectives
  behavioral, 133–134
  categories of, 126–127
  and course content, 123, 136–144
  criterion-referenced, 134
  defining, 123–124
  function of, in good measurement, 135–144
  immediate, 124–125
  for language arts, 129–130
  mastery of, measuring, 80–81
  for psychomotor domain, 126–127
  samples of, 127–132
  for science, 128–129
  for social studies, 130
  statements of, 124–135, 465–466
  and test construction, 138–141, 151
  ultimate, 124–125
  see also Educational objectives
Objective-referenced measurement, 81
Objective tests, 151, 152–198
  arrangement of items in, 196–198
  ease of scoring of, 113
  item writing, 162–193
Objectivity
  of scoring, 111, 152–153, 159–161
  of tests, 90, 111–113, 408

Observation
  basic technique of, 381–384
  of behavior, 380–400
  in measurement of personality, 339, 373–401
  training in, 381, 383–384
Occupational choice, 316, 351, 358–359. *See also* Career education; Career planning; Counseling and guidance
Ohio State University Psychological Test, 311
Ohio Vocational Interest Survey, 358
Ortho-Rater, 470
Otis-Lennon Mental Ability Test, 236–237, 311
Otis Quick-Scoring Mental Ability Test, 308, 311
Otis Self-Administering Tests, 112

Paper-and-pencil tests, 125, 142, 144
Peer-appraisal methods, 389–401
Peer-nomination methods, *see* Sociometric methods
Percent-correct scores, 57–58
Percentile bands, 73–75, 108
Percentile ranks, 34–35, 56–57, 58–59, 494–497
Percentiles, 57, 494–497
Performance tests, 143–144, 295
Personality
  and adjustment, 338–339, 340–351
  definition of, 338
  interpersonal aspect of, 338
  measurement of, 6, 10–12, 338–401
  observational techniques in measuring, 339, 373–401
  projective techniques in measuring, 346–348
  self-report techniques in measuring, 339–372
Personality measures
  attitude inventories, 360–366
  clinical and research inventories, 344–348
  construction of, 340–341
  for counseling and guidance, 453
  interest inventories, 351–359
  issues in use of, 348–350
  reliability of, 109

typical inventories, 341–344
validity of, 94–95
Personnel Research Institute Clerical Battery, 321
Pimsleur Language Aptitude Battery, 326
Placement and promotion, 405, 436, 439–442
Polygraph, 347–348
Porteus Maze Test, 298
Practice effect, 103, 105, 467
Practice tests, 222
Prediction
 and aptitude tests, 316, 319, 452
 error in, 508–509
 and interest inventories, 351–353, 358
 as issue in educational measurement, 14–16
 and self-report techniques, 365–366
Predictive validity, 94
Prescriptive Mathematics Inventory, 267–269
Prescriptive Mathematics Inventory Interim Evaluation Tests, 268–269
Prescriptive Reading Inventory, 255, 266–269
Prescriptive Reading Inventory Interim Evaluation Tests, 266–269
Primary Mental Abilities Test, 330
Privacy, invasion of, 10–12
Probability and normal distribution, 498–500
Proctors, 419, 420–422
Product-moment correlation, 46
Product scale, 258–260
Profile analysis, 72–75, 115, 437–440
Profile charts, 72, 437–438, 440. *See also* Diagnostic chart
Projective tests, 346–348
Project Talent, 6, 402
Promotion, *see* Placement and promotion
Psychological hazards of testing, 12–14
Psychological tests, and invasion of privacy, 10
Psychomotor domain, educational objectives for, 126–127
Publishers of tests, 85–88
Pupil profile, 437–438
Pupil Rating Scale: Screening for Learning Disabilities, 377–378

Pupil record, *see* Record, permanent
Pupils, attitude toward testing, 12–14, 415, 418
Purdue Clerical Adaptability Test, 321
Purdue Master Scales, 361–362
Purdue Mechanical Performance Test, 319

Q, *see* Semi-interquartile range (Q)
Questionnaires, *see* Self-report
Quotient, *see* Intelligence quotient

Race, and IQ, 291–292
Range, of scores, 38–40, 489. *See also* Semi-interquartile range (Q)
Ranking, 33–35
Rating scales, 143–144, 374–380
 effective use of, 378–380
 graphic, 374–376
 numerical, 375–378
Ratio IQ, 282–284. *See also* Deviation IQ; Intelligence quotient
Raw score, 54, 62
Reading level
 in standardized achievement tests, 230–231
 in teacher-made tests, 193
Reading readiness tests, 248–250
 in minimum measurement program, 406
Reading tests
 achievement, 228, 229, 240, 247–254
 criterion-referenced, 267–269
 diagnostic, 255–256
Recall items, 153
Recognition items, 153
Record, permanent, 424–425, 426–427 (fig.)
Reference group, *see* Norm group
Relationship, measures of, *see* Correlation, measures of
Relative scores, 22
Reliability, 98–110, 217–218, 408, 506–509
 of achievement tests, 225
 conditions of testing and, 100–101
 and correlation of equivalent forms, 104–105
 of criterion-referenced tests, 218

Survey batteries *(continued)*
  reliability of, 225
  use of, 224–225
Survey of Study Habits and Attitudes,
    363–365
Survey tests for specific subjects, 264–
    265. *See also* Achievement tests;
    Subject matter tests

Table of specifications, 136–139
Tailored tests, 269
Taxonomy of Educational Objectives,
    360
Teacher-made tests, 4, 26, 129
  analyzing results of, 206–219
  assembly of, 196–206
  attitudes measured by, 366–370
  difficulty of, 212–213
  items in, 152–189, 196–198
  planning and construction of, 147–
    192
  professional development and, 474–
    475
  qualifications of maker of, 149–150
  reading level in, 193
  reliability of, 154–155, 159–161,
    217–218
  scoring, 154, 159–161, 180–181,
    204–206
  scoring key for, 204–206
  standardized tests versus, 116–117,
    148–149
  validity of, 207–217
Teachers
  attitude of, toward testing, 403–404
  interpretation of test scores by, 31
  measurement of attitudes by, 366–
    370
  observation of child behavior by, 382,
    383–400
  professional development of, 474–
    476
  scoring of standardized tests by,
    410–411, 422–424
  standardized tests administered by,
    416–417
  statement of objectives by, 123,
    130–132
  test construction by, 147–192
  test selection by, 81–82, 88

use of measuring instruments by, 4,
    26–27
Teaching
  comparative studies of, 476–477
  mastery model of, 134
  processes of, 122, 123
Telebinocular, 470
Test batteries, *see* Batteries
Testing, 24, 27
  conditions of, and reliability, 100–
    101
  counseling and guidance and, 450–
    454
  criticism of, 7–16
  of culturally disadvantaged, 292–294
  diagnosis and remediation and,
    445–450
  educational research and, 476–477
  external programs, 6–7, 402
  homogeneous grouping and, 442–445
  for identification and study of excep-
    tional children, 469–472
  interpretation of schools to commu-
    nity and, 472–474
  marking and, 455–464
  motivation and, 405, 436, 466–469
  National Defense Education Act and,
    7, 324, 450–451
  placement and promotion and, 405,
    436, 439–442
  process of, 148
  purposes of, 405, 436, 439–477
  psychological hazards of, 12–14
  scheduling of, 222, 223, 405–406,
    415–416
  staff improvement and, 474–476
  statewide, 6, 429
Test items
  arrangement of, 196–198
  completion, 163–165
  criterion-referenced, analysis of,
    215–217
  difficulty of, 83, 196–197, 212–217
  discrimination power of, 83, 207–217
  essay, 152–161
  file of, 152
  interpretive, 187–189
  key-list, 186–187
  matching, 152–153, 170–175
  multiple-choice, 152–153, 175–186,
    210–211, 230, 232–233
  numbering of, 202